THE ANNOTATED LUTHER

Volume 2
Word and Faith

Additional Praise for *Word and Faith*

"Luther's writings as contained in this fine collection are as helpful to read today as when he first wrote them to such a profound historical effect. They continue to be fertile for further theological reflection and biblical insight. Introductions and many marginal notes also explain items for better understanding—including those which criticize Luther, making this volume useful for instruction in church and classroom settings."

—**Peter Krey** | Pastor, Christ Lutheran Church,
El Cerrito, California

THE ANNOTATED LUTHER

Volume 2
Word and Faith

VOLUME EDITOR
Kirsi I. Stjerna

GENERAL EDITORS
Hans J. Hillerbrand
Kirsi I. Stjerna
Timothy J. Wengert

Fortress Press
Minneapolis

THE ANNOTATED LUTHER, Volume 2
Word and Faith

Fortress Press Publication Staff: Scott Tunseth, Project Editor; Marissa Wold Uhrina,
Production Manager; Laurie Ingram, Cover Design; Esther Diley, Permissions.

Copyeditor: David Lott
Series design and typesetting: Ann Delgehausen, Trio Bookworks
Proofreader: Laura Weller

Library of Congress Cataloging-in-Publication Data is available

Print ISBN: 978-1-4514-6270-8
eISBN: 978-1-4514-6511-2

Library of Congress

2017   303026

Contents

Series Introduction

Engaging the Essential Luther

Even after five hundred years Martin Luther continues to engage and challenge each new generation of scholars and believers alike. With 2017 marking the five-hundredth anniversary of Luther's *95 Theses*, Luther's theology and legacy are being explored around the world with new questions and methods and by diverse voices. His thought invites ongoing examination, his writings are a staple in classrooms and pulpits, and he speaks to an expanding assortment of conversation partners who use different languages and hale from different geographical and social contexts.

The six volumes of The Annotated Luther edition offer a flexible tool for the global reader of Luther, making many of his most important writings available in the *lingua franca* of our times as one way of facilitating interest in the Wittenberg reformer. They feature new introductions, annotations, revised translations, and textual notes, as well as visual enhancements (illustrations, art, photos, maps, and timelines). The Annotated Luther edition embodies Luther's own cherished principles of communication. Theological writing, like preaching, needs to reflect human beings' lived experience, benefits from up-to-date scholarship, and should be easily accessible to all. These volumes are designed to help teachers and students, pastors and laypersons, and other professionals in ministry understand the context in which the documents were written, recognize how the documents have shaped Protestant and Lutheran thinking, and interpret the meaning of these documents for faith and life today.

The Rationale for This Edition

For any reader of Luther, the sheer number of his works presents a challenge. Well over one hundred volumes comprise the scholarly edition of Luther's works, the so-called Weimar Ausgabe (WA), a publishing enterprise begun in 1883 and only completed in the twenty-first century. From 1955 to 1986, fifty-five volumes came to make up *Luther's Works* (American Edition) (LW), to which Concordia Publishing House, St. Louis, is adding still more. This English-language contribution to Luther studies, matched by similar translation projects for Erasmus of Rotterdam and John Calvin, provides a theological and historical gold mine for those interested in studying Luther's thought. But even these volumes are not always easy to use and are hardly portable. Electronic forms have increased availability, but preserving Luther in book form and providing readers with manageable selections are also important goals.

Moreover, since the publication of the WA and the first fifty-five volumes of the LW, research on the Reformation in general and on Martin Luther in particular has broken new ground and evolved, as has knowledge regarding the languages in which Luther wrote. Up-to-date information from a variety of sources is brought together in The Annotated Luther, building on the work done by previous generations of scholars. The language and phrasing of the translations have also been updated to reflect modern English usage. While the WA and, in a derivative way, LW remain the central source for Luther scholarship, the present critical and annotated English translation facilitates research internationally and invites a new generation of readers for whom Latin and German might prove an unsurpassable obstacle to accessing Luther. The WA provides the basic Luther texts (with some exceptions); the LW provides the basis for almost all translations.

Defining the "Essential Luther"

Deciding which works to include in this collection was not easy. Criteria included giving attention to Luther's initial key works; considering which publications had the most impact in his day and later; and taking account of Luther's own favorites, texts addressing specific issues of continued importance for today, and Luther's exegetical works. Taken as a whole, these works present the many sides of Luther, as reformer, pastor, biblical interpreter, and theologian. To serve today's readers and by using categories similar to those found in volumes 31–47 of Luther's works (published by Fortress Press), the volumes offer in the main a thematic rather than strictly chronological approach to Luther's writings. The volumes in the series include:

> Volume 1: *The Roots of Reform* (Timothy J. Wengert, editor)
> Volume 2: *Word and Faith* (Kirsi I. Stjerna, editor)
> Volume 3: *Church and Sacraments* (Paul W. Robinson, editor)
> Volume 4: *Pastoral Writings* (Mary Jane Haemig, editor)
> Volume 5: *Christian Life in the World* (Hans J. Hillerbrand, editor)
> Volume 6: *The Interpretation of Scripture* (Euan K. Cameron, editor)

The History of the Project

In 2011 Fortress Press convened an advisory board to explore the promise and parameters of a new English edition of Luther's essential works. Board members Denis Janz, Robert Kolb, Peter Matheson, Christine Helmer, and Kirsi Stjerna deliberated with

Fortress Press publisher Will Bergkamp to develop a concept and identify contributors. After a review with scholars in the field, college and seminary professors, and pastors, it was concluded that a single-language edition was more desirable than dual-language volumes.

In August 2012, Hans Hillerbrand, Kirsi Stjerna, and Timothy Wengert were appointed as general editors of the series with Scott Tunseth from Fortress Press as the project editor. The general editors were tasked with determining the contents of the volumes and developing the working principles of the series. They also helped with the identification and recruitment of additional volume editors, who in turn worked with the general editors to identify volume contributors. Mastery of the languages and unique knowledge of the subject matter were key factors in identifying contributors. Most contributors are North American scholars and native English speakers, but The Annotated Luther includes among its contributors a circle of international scholars. Likewise, the series is offered for a global network of teachers and students in seminary, university, and college classes, as well as pastors, lay teachers, and adult students in congregations seeking background and depth in Lutheran theology, biblical interpretation, and Reformation history.

Editorial Principles

The volume editors and contributors have, with few exceptions, used the translations of LW as the basis of their work, retranslating from the WA for the sake of clarity and contemporary usage. Where the LW translations have been substantively altered, explanatory notes have often been provided. More importantly, contributors have provided marginal notes to help readers understand theological and historical references. Introductions have been expanded and sharpened to reflect the very latest historical and theological research. In citing the Bible, care has been taken to reflect the German and Latin texts commonly used in the sixteenth century rather than modern editions, which often employ textual sources that were unavailable to Luther and his contemporaries.

Finally, all pieces in The Annotated Luther have been revised in the light of modern principles of inclusive language. This is not always an easy task with a historical author, but an intentional effort has been made to revise language throughout, with creativity and editorial liberties, to allow Luther's theology to speak free from unnecessary and unintended gender-exclusive language. This important principle provides an opportunity to translate accurately certain gender-neutral German and Latin expressions that Luther employed—for example, the Latin word *homo* and the German *Mensch* mean "human being," not simply "males." Using the words *man* and *men* to translate such terms would create an ambiguity not present in the original texts. The focus is on linguistic accuracy and Luther's intent. Regarding creedal formulations and trinitarian language, Luther's own expressions have been preserved, without entering the complex and important contemporary debates over language for God and the Trinity.

The 2017 anniversary of the publication of the *95 Theses* is providing an opportunity to assess the substance of Luther's role and influence in the Protestant Reformation. Revisiting Luther's essential writings not only allows reassessment of Luther's rationale and goals but also provides a new look at what Martin Luther was about and why new generations would still wish to engage him. We hope these six volumes offer a compelling invitation.

Hans J. Hillerbrand
Kirsi I. Stjerna
Timothy J. Wengert
General Editors

Abbreviations

ANF	*The Ante-Nicene Fathers: Translations of the Fathers down to A.D. 325.* 10 vols. Reprint, Grand Rapids: Eerdmans, 1978
Ap	*Apology of the Augsburg Confession*
BC	*The Book of Concord,* ed. Robert Kolb and Timothy J. Wengert (Minneapolis: Fortress Press, 2000).
BSLK	*Die Bekenntnichriften der evngelich-lutherichen Kirche.* 11th ed. (Gottingen: Vandenhoeck & Ruprecht, 1992).
CA	*Augsburg Confession (Confessio Augustana)*
CR	*Corpus Reformatorum: Philippi Melanthonis opera quae supersunt omnia,* ed. Karl Brettschneider and Heinrich Bindseil, 28 vols. (Braunschweig: Schwetchke, 1834-1860).
CSEL	*Corpus Scriptorum Ecclesiasticorum Latinorum (CSEL),* 99 vols. 1866–2011.
CWE	*Spirituality: Enchiridon/De contemptu mundi/Devidua christiana,* vol. 66 (University of Toronto Press, 1988), 39.
Ep	*Epitome of the Formula of Concord*
FC	*Formula of Concord*
LC	*Large Catechism*
LW	*Luther's Works* [American edition], ed. Helmut Lehmann and Jaroslav Pelikan, 55 vols. (Philadelphia: Fortress Press/St. Louis: Concordia Publishing House, 1955–1986).
MLStA	*Martin Luther: Studienausgabe,* ed. Hans-Ulrich Delius, 6 vols. (Berlin/Leipzig: Evangelische Verlagsanstalt, 1979–1999).
MPG	*Patrologiae Cursus Completus, Series Graeca,* ed. J. P. Migne, 61 vols., (Paris, 1857–1912).
MPL	*Patrologiae cursus completus, series Latina,* ed. Jacques-Paul Migne, 217 vols. (Paris, 1815–1875).
NPNF	*Nicene and Post-Nicene Fathers,* ed. Philip Schaaf and Henry Wace, series 1, 14 vols.; and series 2, 14 vols. (London/New York: T&T Clark, 1886–1900).
OHMLT	*The Oxford Handbook of Martin Luther's Theology,* eds. Robert Kolb, Irene Dingel, and L'ubomír Batka (New York: Oxford University Press, 2015)
SA	*Smalcald Articles*
SBOp	Sancti Bernardi Opera 3 (Rome: Editiones Cistercienses, 1963).
SD	*Solid Declaration of the Formula of Concord*
STh	*Summa Theologica*
TAL	*The Annotated Luther,* vols. 1–6 (Minneapolis: Fortress Press, 2015–2017).
Tr	*Treatise on the Power and Primacy of the Pope*

WA	Luther, Martin. *Luthers Werke: Kritische Gesamtausgabe* [*Schriften*], 73 vols. (Weimar: H. Böhlau, 1883–2009)
WA Br	Luther, Martin. *Luthers Werke: Kritische Gesamtausgabe: Briefwechsel*, 18 vols. (Weimar: H. Böhlau, 1930–1985).
WA DB	Luther, Martin. *Luthers Werke: Kritische Gesamtausgabe: Deutsche Bibel*, 12 vols. (Weimar: H. Böhlau, 1906–1961).
WA TR	Luther, Martin. *Luthers Werke: Kritische Gesamtausgabe: Tischreden*, 6 vols. (Weimar: H. Böhlau, 1912–1921).

ATLANTIC
OCEAN

NORWAY

SCOTLAND
• Edinburgh

SWEDEN

• Stockholm

ESTONIA
LIVONIA
KURLAND

IRELAND

North
Sea

DENMARK

Baltic
Sea

• Copenhagen

• Königsberg

PRUSSIA

York
•

ENGLAND

London
•

Ghent
•

POMERANIA

Hamburg
•

BRANDENBURG

POLAND

REFORMATION EUROPE
in the 16th century

ARTOIS
NETHERLANDS
FLANDERS

HESSE

COLOGNE

SILESIA

Holy Roman Empire
boundary
Provincial boundary

LUXEMBOURG

SAXONY

BOHEMIA

Paris
•

Mainz
•

UPPER
PALITANATE

MORAVIA

Nantes
•

LOWER
PALITANATE

BAVARIA

AUSTRIA

IMPERIAL HUNGARY

Orleans
•

Augsburg
•

Vienna
•

Budapest
•

FRANCE

FRENCH
COMTE

SWISS
CONFEDERATION

TYROL

CARINTHIA

HUNGARY

BOURBON
LANDS

SAVOY

Milan
•

Trent
•

CARNIOLA

Mohacs
•

Valladolid
•

Toulouse
•

Avignon
•

Pavia
•

Venice
•

VENETIAN REPUBLIC

PORTUGAL

SPAIN

Genoa
•

Florence
•

PAPAL
STATES

OTTOMAN
EMPIRE

Lisbon
•

Madrid
•

Barcelona
•

CORSICA
(TO GENOA)

ITALY

CASTILE

Toledo
•

ARAGON

BALERIC
ISLANDS

Rome
•

Seville
•

NAVARRE

Naples
•

NAPLES

Granada
•

SARDINIA
(TO SPAIN)

GRANADA

Tangier
•

Mediterranean Sea

SICILY
(TO SPAIN)

Algiers
•

Bizerte
•

Tunis
•

Lucidity Information Design, LLC

0   300 Miles

LUTHER'S GERMANY

---- Major political subdivisions

N

Baltic Sea

DENMARK

Hamburg
Wolgast
POMERANIA
Stettin
Elbe

Bremen

Amsterdam
NETHERLANDS

Magdeburg
Wittenberg
POLAND

Brussels
Cologne
Eisenach
Eisleben
Torgau
Breslau
Oder

Marburg
Erfurt
Leipzig

LUXEMBURG
Schmalkalden
Prague

Mansfeld

Worms
Nuremberg

Metz
Rhine
Regansburg

Strasbourg
Danube
Augsburg

FRANCE
AUSTRIA
Vienna

Zürich
Salzburg

*SWISS
CONFEDERATION*
HUNGARY

Milan
Venice

0   200 Miles

*VENETIAN
DOMINION*

*Adriatic
Sea*

Introduction
to Volume 2

KIRSI I. STJERNA

Martin Luther was an angst-driven theologian of the Bible with a pastoral heart and expansive horizons. He was immersed in the affairs of the world and cared deeply for the health of his church and the spiritual well-being of his fellow Christians. He was fundamentally enthralled with the Scriptures, the proper interpretation of which he sought and defended throughout his tumultuous career. He was shaped by deeply disturbing personal spiritual struggles that led to his understanding of the power of the word and justification by faith. His nearly obsessive sense of responsibility and his combative will, combined with his tireless engagement in a seemingly endless stream of ecclesial and theological issues, made the originally lonely religious rebel an international leader beyond Wittenberg where he lived and taught.[a]

---

a   On Luther's emergence and evolution as a reformer, see *The Annotated Luther,* vol. 1: *Roots of Reform,* ed. Timothy J. Wengert (Minneapolis: Fortress Press, 2015). For a thorough treatment of Luther as a theologian and a reformer, see Martin Brecht's three-volume biography, *Martin Luther: His Road to Reformation 1483–1521* (Philadelphia: Fortress Press, 1985); *Martin Luther: Shaping and Defining the Reformation 1521–1532* (Minneapolis: Fortress Press, 1994); and *Martin Luther: The Preservation of the Church 1532–1546* (Minneapolis: Fortress Press, 1999), all translated from German by James L. Schaaf.

Luther sought to define a particular "Christian" way of living. The young monk's relentless pursuit of the gracious God transformed him into a talented university teacher enthused with the uninhibited study of the Scriptures. With the help of St. Paul and his letters to the Romans and Galatians, and a reexamination of the book of Psalms, Luther found his ground of being in the gospel about Jesus Christ and the meaning of his life and death for humanity. Luther's approach to life and theology became uncompromisingly Christocentric. He found himself challenging the central teachings and practices of his church and spearheading sweeping reforms throughout Europe.[b] Early on he lost control of the actions others had taken in response to his broadly published theology and ongoing proclamation from the pulpit.[c] Regardless of the many issues that required Luther's attention, the persistent interest for him remained in the existential questions and theological convictions about God's grace for the sinner.

Luther's vast list of publications demonstrates the depth and breadth of his involvement in the affairs of the church and society in his day. The reformer's works are peculiarly situational or audience-specific as his theological expositions were often prompted by a request or demanded by a situation. In the turmoil of an extraordinarily busy life, Luther made some efforts to offer his confession of faith in a single document. None of these succeeded in becoming an obvious *summa* of Luther's theology fitting for all constituencies, even if some works have arisen as clear favorites.

[b] For an in-depth look, see, e.g., Heiko A. Obermann, *Martin Luther: Man between God and Devil*, trans. Eileen Walliser-Schwarzbart (New Haven: Yale University Press, 2006); and Hans-Martin Barth, *The Theology of Martin Luther: A Critical Assessment*, trans. Linda M. Maloney (Minneapolis: Fortress Press, 2013).

[c] For contextualizing Luther in the larger picture of the Reformations, helpful resources in English include: Hans J. Hillerbrand, ed., *The Protestant Reformation* (New York: Perennial, 2009); Carter Lindberg, *The European Reformations*, 2d ed. (Malden, MA: Wiley Blackwell, 2012); Denis Janz, *A Reformation Reader: Primary Texts with Introductions*, 2d ed. (Minneapolis: Fortress Press, 2008); and Kirsi Stjerna, *Women and the Reformation* (Malden, MA: Wiley Blackwell, 2008).

WORD-CENTERED THEOLOGY OF FAITH

This volume presents works featuring some of Luther's most original and consistent theological assertions. The texts representing different genres are from different stages of Luther's career, spanning the period 1519–1538. Both his theological orientation and his modus of theological argumentation are visible. Studied together, the distinct pillars and idiosyncratic "system" of Luther's theology can be detected and appreciated.[1] That is, the works illustrate several clearly defined pieces in Luther's theology and also prove that his "formula" remains persistent: his starting and ending point is always how he understands the word about Christ, and his lens in interpreting his main source, the Scriptures, is always the meaning of Christ.

The title of the volume, *Word and Faith*, indicates the central nerves in Luther's theology: his radical faith perspective, and his absolute reliance on the word. This volume is explicitly devoted to Luther's theological voice and vision around the arguments he makes with his fundamental understanding of the saving word and justifying faith. It is through the working of the word that Luther explains the active presence of God in human life. His word-centered theology points to faith as the connector between divine and human realities. It is faith that makes one right with God, and the mechanisms of this relationship are revealed by the word. On the foundation of how and what the word works, one's most proper approach in life is that of faith that holds God at the center. With his wide-ranging interpretation of the Scriptures, as the *solus* source, Luther targets the manifold presence and action of God's word—in the world, in the church and its sacraments, and, most importantly, in all of human life's aspects. These discoveries are, he readily admits, a matter of faith.

When explaining the effect of the word, Luther makes the persistent argument about the saving faith, offered as the new orientation in spiritual life. Luther extrapolates the meaning of faith that connects one with God and brings about forgiveness. Far from a theoretical matter of a right "belief," Luther strives to communicate the transformative impact of the word-induced renewal of the God–human relationship that hangs on faith "gifted" by Christ and sustained by God's own Spirit. Not only

1. For a theology that developed through controversy and that entails academic work, debate, and proclamation, the word *systematic* hardly does justice. That said, Luther's theological method is systematically biblically oriented, always centering on the meaning of the word. He does systematically and exhaustively elaborate on the key concepts of faith and grace, and, related, the working of the law and gospel in the life of a sinner-saint. In a way, Luther's whole theological work could be characterized as his effort of systematizing his view of justification, and from a paradoxical premise.

forgiven but transformed, and as if born again (or regenerated) with Christ, Christians so redeemed are called to a life of repentance and renewed love for one's neighbor.

Justification, the key word for Luther, unfolds from two standpoints, both of which are essential. On the one side, the gift is received passively as an alien righteousness in the immediate God relationship (*coram Deo*); on the other, it is the way of life expressed externally as a human being's "own" proper righteousness in relation to other creatures (*coram hominibus*). For Luther these are not theoretical but reality-altering matters, for both individual and communal life. His challenge was, then, to translate this experience and vision through preaching, teaching, and writing in order to illumine and invite all to encounter the word for themselves.

LUTHER'S TEXTS IN THIS VOLUME

The works in this volume are introduced and annotated by an international group of scholars and feature Luther's central theological principles and his unique theological arguments. One can embrace them as a teaching or a preaching tool, as a source for spiritual formation, and as a guide for ongoing scholarship.

Two Kinds of Righteousness[d] from 1519 is a short early sermon that offers one of the most succinct explications of Luther's doctrine of justification. Luther distinguishes between the two dimensions of righteousness: the alien righteousness as a gift from Christ and complete in the *coram Deo* reality, and proper righteousness as one's own growing in the following of Christ *coram hominibus*. Using bridal imagery, Luther explains the nature and fruits of the intimate faith union between the justified sinner and the gracious God.

Another text that originated as a sermon, *A Brief Instruction on What to Look for in the Gospels*[e] from 1522, illustrates Luther's major discovery about the ongoing paradox between law and

---

d　LW 31:297–306.

gospel: Christ the crucified annihilates the condemning law. At the heart of the mystery of justification, says Luther, is the "happy exchange" wherein Christ assumes human sin, while humans receive all that is Christ's. Luther identifies the gospel message as the key to the interpretation of the entire Scriptures, including the Old Testament's law.

A sermon from just a few years later returns to the topic that would continue to require Luther's extended attention: law in the life of a Christian. In his *How Christians Should Regard Moses*[f] from 1525, Luther delineates the distinction between law and gospel, making a case about Moses being dead for Christians whose hope rests in Christ only. At the same time, he defends the place of the Old Testament and its faith examples for Christians, whose reinterpretation of the texts takes place in light of the gospel, in order to stay clear from "works righteousness" (Catholic tradition) or law-based religiosity—all of which Christ has made futile.

From the same period (1525) comes the feisty *Against the Heavenly Prophets in the Matter of Images and Sacraments*.[g] Andreas Bodenstein von Karlstadt and his followers, whom Luther dubbed the "heavenly prophets," had opposed Luther on the question of the actual implementation of reform and the meaning of the sacraments. Luther felt obligated to attack the "spiritualists," who were, in his opinion, a threat to the unity of the growing reform movement. Here Luther addresses the challenge in two parts: the first section deals with the topic of images, and the second with the sacrament of the altar. Offering also an incisive explanation of the relation of law and freedom, Luther accuses Karlstadt of having lapsed into works righteousness and argues vigorously for Christian freedom.

The title page of *Instructions for the Visitors of Parish Pastors in Electoral Saxony*. Luther urged Elector John Frederick I to institute a systematic church visitation of Saxony (see the introduction to the *Large Catechism*, p. 279). Melanchthon wrote most of the document, but Luther contributed some passages, including the preface.

---

e   LW 35:[115–16] 117–24.

f   LW 35:161–74.

One of the most famous works of Luther, and one he was not displeased with himself, is the *Bondage of the Will*[h] from 1525. The main argument in this verbose, milestone document is simple yet radical: human beings are not free to make right choices in relation to God. Even more so, human beings in their condition of bondage to sin are actually born enemies of God. Thus the depravity with sin is so deep that only God can rescue human beings from the abyss of self-induced damnation. Luther never compromised on this point, the reason being a christological argument: if human beings were able to save themselves, Christ would have died in vain, and that would be a terrible tragedy.

Luther's "Confession of Faith"[i] is part of a larger *Confession Concerning Christ's Supper* from 1528, a text deemed and intended as a *summa* of Luther's theology. Embracing the Apostles' Creed, Luther gives a prototype for a "good confession" at the time of death, along with an evangelical statement of central faith articles. Underscoring salvation out of God's grace alone, Luther's focal point is the working of the word that creates life and enables salvation.

The *Large Catechism*[2] from 1529 uses a pedagogical format to explicate the basics of faith. Luther proceeds in the *Large Catechism* with a deliberate and distinct theological rationale: the Ten Commandments express God's expectations, the Creed proclaims God's promise, the Lord's Prayer translates law and gospel into a personal discourse with God, and the sacraments offer tangible expressions of God's grace and signs to lean on in faith. Through all these pieces, Luther follows the tracks of the Holy Spirit as the overarching enabler.

The Smalcald Articles[3] was deliberately written as a confession to unite. Its spirited tone makes it a battle call and a poignant reminder of Luther's original reformation urgencies. The text gives an animated rationale for needed reforms in religious practice, from the Mass to calling on the saints, and offers a step-by-step summation of the central arguments in evangelical theology. A shift in theological orientation is argued on the basis of Luther's discovery of the chief doctrine on which everything stands: Christ's redeeming work. A matter of faith, one

2. *The Book of Concord: The Confessions of the Evangelical Lutheran Church*, Timothy Wengert and Robert Kolb, eds. (Minneapolis: Fortress Press, 2000), 379–480.

3. Ibid., 297–328.

g   LW 40:79–223.
h   LW 33:15–295.

relies on the manifold work of the gospel that reaches people through preaching, sacraments, community, and mutual consolation of Christians.

This volume is offered as an invitation and a tool for a critical and compassionate study of Luther's theology in new contexts, with diverse frameworks and languages, and with global conversation partners. While the historical-theological prospects for further study with each text are endless, equally manifold are the existential and spiritual questions at stake.[j]

---

i   LW 37:360–72.

j   See, e.g., Christine Helmer, ed., *The Global Luther: A Theologian for Modern Times* (Minneapolis: Fortress Press, 2009).

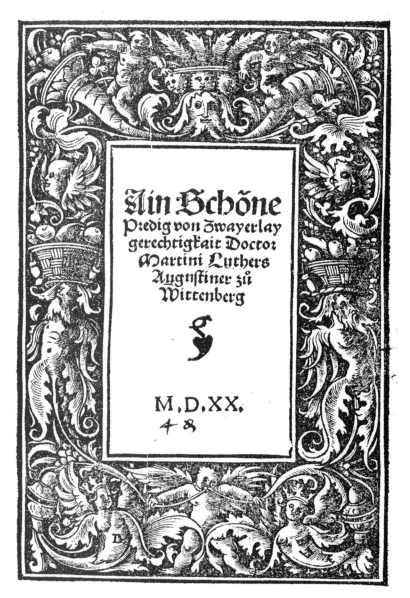

This title-page woodcut for the German version of Luther's sermon (in 1520 German: *Predig*) on the two kinds of righteousness features the title of the sermon within a richly ornamented frame. However, the adjective *beautiful* (in German: *schön*) has been added to the title of the sermon, and it states that its author, Martin Luther, is an Augustinian friar attached to (the University of) Wittenberg.

Sermon on Two Kinds of Righteousness

1519

ELSE MARIE WIBERG PEDERSEN

INTRODUCTION

Martin Luther wrote two Latin sermons on righteousness,[a] the *Sermon on Two Kinds of Righteousness* (*Sermo de duplici iustitia*), which he composed first, and the *Sermon on Three Kinds of Righteousness* (*Sermo de triplici iustitia*), which he published first.[b] It has been a matter of discussion whether Luther wrote the first text in late 1518 or early 1519, but it is most likely that the *Sermon on Two Kinds of Righteousness* was originally preached on Palm Sunday, 28 March 1518, and then published in both an unauthorized and an authorized version in 1519. Luther wrote about the sermon, along with another sermon on matrimony, in a letter to Johannes Lang (c. 1487–1548) on 13 April 1519; since it is based on Philippians 2:5-11, the pericope for Palm Sunday, it is assumed that it was preached in 1518. There is no doubt that the text is one of Luther's early reformatory works composed in the aftermath of his *95 Theses* in 1517 when he was forced to

---

a   Except where noted, the Latin words *iustus* and *iustitia* will be translated "righteous" and "righteousness," not "justice," which in current English usage denotes legal conformity to a legal principle.

b   Martin Brecht, *Martin Luther, Volume 1: His Road to Reformation 1483–1521* (Philadelphia: Fortress Press, 1985), 229-31.

explain and justify his views, particularly in the disputations with Cardinal Cajetan[1] in 1518 and with Johann Eck[2] in 1519. The sermon was translated into German by Georg Spalatin[3] in 1520, the year of some of Luther's epoch-making publications,

1. Cardinal Thomas de Vio Cajetan (1469-1534) was an Italian Dominican, general of the Dominican Order, and a Scholastic who specialized in the philosophy of Thomas Aquinas (1225-1274). Cajetan was a leading spokesperson of the papal opposition to Luther and the pope's legate at the Diet of Augsburg in October 1518. He remained a zealous opponent of the Reformation till his death. For further details, see Martin Brecht, *Martin Luther, Volume 1: His Road to Reformation, 1483–1521* (Philadelphia: Fortress Press), 246-62.

2. Johann Eck (1486-1543) was a German Scholastic and a strong opponent of Luther. He attempted to persuade Elector Frederick III of Saxony (1463–1525) to have Luther's work burned in public and also induced the authorities at the universities of Cologne and Leuven to condemn Luther's work. In July 1520, he returned from Rome to Germany as Pope Leo X's spokesperson, with the pope's bull *Exsurge Domine* ("Arise, O Lord"), which condemned forty-one propositions of Luther as either heretical or erroneous. Luther refused to recant and burned a copy of the bull on 10 December 1520 after having composed his appeal, *The Freedom of a Christian*, dedicated to the pope.

Cardinal Cajetan, baptized Giacomo de Vio, is best known for his interview of Luther at Augsburg in 1518, but he was also a prolific theologian in his own right who authored more than 150 works and would produce an influential—and controversial—interpretation of Thomas Aquinas.

Portrait of Johann Eck (1486–1543), a theologian and defender of the Catholic faith who opposed Luther.

Portrait of Georg Spalatin
by Lucas Cranach the Elder
(1472–1553).

3. Georg Spalatin (1484–1545), captivated with Luther's reform cause, read all of Luther's writings to the elector, Frederick III of Saxony, and translated the Latin texts into German. Spalatin accompanied the elector both to the Diet of Augsburg in 1518 and to the Diet of Worms in 1521. Even though advising Luther not to publish books in opposition to the papacy, he nevertheless translated them once they were published. For further details on Spalatin's role, see Brecht, *Martin Luther*, 240–43.

4. A timeline of key Luther writings and events during the period.
   1517   *95 Theses*
   1518/1519   *Sermon on Two Kinds of Righteousness* and its printing
   1518   *Diet of Augsburg* (Cajetan)
   1519   *The Leipzig Debate* (Eck)
   1520   *Address to the Christian Nobility, The Babylonian Captivity of the Church, The Freedom of a Christian*
   1520   The papal bull *Exsurge Domine*
   1520   Translation of the sermon into German

such as *Address to the Christian Nobility, The Babylonian Captivity of the Church*, and *The Freedom of a Christian*, where he unfolds many of the ideas developed in this sermon.[4]

The sermon, admonishing in character, is theologically far more complicated than its brevity might suggest. It can be divided into two main parts, each representing one of the themes that became vital first in Luther's reformation and later in the reception of Luther: the theme of righteousness and the theme of the two regimes. While the sermon as such takes its point of departure in Philippians 2:5f.: "have this mind among yourselves, which you have in Christ Jesus,"[c] it is only in the first part that Luther deals with the two kinds of righteousness of a Christian: the primary, alien righteousness (*iustitia aliena*) and the secondary, proper righteousness (*iustitia propria*), based on the servant Christology of the Philippian hymn.[5] In order to

5. In his letter to the community in Philippi, Paul has placed the famous hymn, which in the first part, Phil. 2:6-8, depicts Christ's self-debasement by emptying himself, taking on the form of a servant and becoming like a human being, humiliating himself even to the death on a cross. The second part, Phil. 2:8-11, states that due to this total emptying of the form of God and taking on the form of servant, he is ultimately exalted.

c   All Bible quotations follow Luther's original wording. Since Luther employed the Vulgate in 1518, it would make no sense to refer to the NRSV or any other modern Bible version when translating his biblical citations.

Mein geliebter ist mein, vnd ich bin sein, der vnder den Rosen gewendet wird, bisses tag werd, vnd die schatten weichen. Cantic: 2.

£ del.   33.   *Melch: Küsell sc.*

"My beloved is mine" (Song of Solomon 2:16).

explain the operation of this double righteousness, Luther uses the famous bridal imagery that he further employs in *The Freedom of a Christian*: Christ as bridegroom and the church as bride are one flesh (Gen. 2:24) and one spirit (Eph. 5:29-32). As the bridegroom's alien righteousness is given to the bride against her alien original sin, it prompts the bride's proper righteousness to sanctify her through faith. Hence, the marriage is consummated as the righteousness that seeks the welfare of the others in the exclamatory exchange of bridegroom and bride: "I am yours" (Song of Sol. 2:16).

The second part of the sermon demonstrates the earliest example of Luther's idea of the two regimes. While differentiating between how justice works in the public and the private spheres (*vel publici vel privati*), Luther contrasts justice with injustice. On the basis of Romans 13:4, he states that in the public sphere, justice must be exercised through a worldly regime in the service of God and for the sake of order. Hence, his words on Christian righteousness and its servant form (*forma servi*) in the first part of the sermon do not apply to the public sphere or to those who act according to the law for the sake of themselves. They only apply to the private sphere and those who act according to the gospel for the sake of the other. The sermon's message of benevolent righteousness and warning against mingling the justice of the two regimes thus stands in stark contrast to the double ban Luther received from both regimes when he was excommunicated by Pope Leo X (1475–1521) on 3 January 1521 and subsequently condemned as an outlaw by Emperor Karl V (1500–1558) on 25 May 1521.

SERMON ON TWO KINDS OF RIGHTEOUSNESS[6]

"BROTHERS AND SISTERS,[7] have the same understanding between you as that of Christ Jesus, who, though in the form of God, did not regard it a robbery to be equal to God" [Phil. 2:5-6].

Christians have two kinds of righteousness,[8] just as there are two kinds of sins in humans.

The first is alien and infused from outside of oneself.[9] This is the righteousness by which Christ is righteous and by which he justifies others through faith,[10] as it is written in 1 Cor. 1[:30]: "Whom God made our wisdom, our righteousness and sanctification and redemption." In John 11[:25-26], Christ himself states: "I am the resurrection and the life; whoever believes in me . . . shall never die." Later he adds in John 14[:6], "I am the way, and the truth, and the life." This righteousness, then, is given to human beings[d] in baptism and whenever they are truly repentant. Therefore a human being can with confidence boast in Christ and say: "Mine are Christ's living, doing, and speaking, his suffering and dying, mine as much as if I had lived, done, spoken, suffered, and died as he did."[11] Just as a bridegroom possesses all that is the bride's and the bride all that is the bridegroom's. For the two have everything in common. For they are one flesh [Gen. 2:24], just as Christ and the church are one spirit

---

d   Throughout the sermon Luther uses the inclusive term *homo*, which means "human being," and will sometimes also be translated into "person" or, when in plural, "people." The English translation in LW 31:297–306 inserted many male nouns and pronouns that are not found in Luther's Latin text. Luther's text is far more gender inclusive than the LW translation. In the same vein, Luther is unconventional in his—to use a contemporary term—*queering* use of biblical images, such as the nuptial imagery in the tradition of Origen (c. 185–c. 254) and Bernard of Clairvaux (1090–1153; see below, n. 23). Luther considered any Christian soul, irrespective of sex, could perform as the bride of Christ. This English version of Luther's sermon is thus a corrective to the LW's interpretative version by staying loyal to Luther's Latin text and language.

---

6. The following translation of *Sermo de duplici iustitia* is based on WA 2:145–52 and is a revision of *Luther's Works*, vol. 31: *Career of the Reformer I*, trans. Lowell J. Satre, ed. Jaroslav J. Pelikan, Hilton C. Oswald, and Helmut T. Lehmann (Philadelphia: Fortress Press, 1957), 297–306. All notes and annotations are new.

7. Luther is quoting Paul verbatim. The Latin *fratres*, in plural, does not bear the meaning "brothers" only. It may also mean "siblings," or "brothers and sisters" as it is rendered here, and as it was doubtless the case that Paul, who wrote the letter to the Philippians while in prison, was denoting dear and intimate friends and allies.

8. *Duplex est iusticia Christianorum.* Luther is here addressing a Christian righteousness, different from justice in a juridical sense.

9. Christ's righteousness is infused into the Christian: *Prima est aliena et ab extra infusa.* Luther throughout the sermon uses this terminology of infusion. Cf. his terminology of intimate union, a consummated marriage, between Christ and the believer.

10. The very essence of Luther's doctrine of justification is expressed in this formula: *Haec est qua Christus iustus est et iustificans per fidem*; "This is the righteousness by which Christ is righteous and by which he justifies others through faith."

11. Luther employs Paul's teaching on how the drama of Christ's justifying suffering and crucifixion works in the human being who is baptized into the life, death, and resurrection of Christ in Romans 6.

12. Luther combines the nuptial imagery of Gen. 2:24 where Adam and Eve are one flesh, *"sunt enim una caro,"* with that of Eph. 5:29-32 where Christ and the church are one spirit, *"sunt unus spiritus."* As in *The Freedom of a Christian*, Luther draws here on the biblical nuptial imagery typically utilized to explain the intimate union of God/Christ with human beings, namely: Genesis 2, Hosea 2, Jer. 7:34, Song of Songs, and Ephesians 5. Marriage is described as both a physical and a spiritual union, based on the biblical imagery of Gen. 2:24 and Eph. 5:29-32. In relation to the alien righteousness of Christ, the marriage of Christ and the human being can be said to have begun, but it is not yet consummated. Cf. below, n. 24.

13. As Luther continuously emphasizes the abundance of divine mercy, God is not only the Father of mercy but the Father of mercies, *pater misericordiarum.*

14. Luther, in fact, combines two different Bible quotes from Paul's letters. The first section of the citation is quite correctly from 2 Corinthians as indicated by Luther, whereas the second section, "who has blessed us in Christ . . . ," is taken from Eph. 1:3.

15. Luther understood the promise to Abraham that through his seed all nations would be blessed as a promise that was repeated, enhanced as part of his seed until the coming of Christ. Cf. *A Sermon on the New Testament*, where Luther drills on this promise with the "First Gospel," God's words to Eve in Gen. 3:15: a promise that was kept with the coming of Christ as a pact with all those who like Abraham believed the promise. They are Abraham's children, from "Abraham's bosom" (Luke 16:22f.; WA 6:356–58). Cf. also Luther's

[Eph. 5:29-32].[12] Thus the blessed God and Father of mercies, according to Peter, has given us the greatest and most precious in Christ [2 Pet. 1:4]. Paul writes in 2 Cor. 1[:3]: "Blessed be the God and Father of our Lord Jesus Christ, the Father of mercies[13] and God of all comfort, who has blessed us in Christ with every spiritual blessing in the heavenly places."[14]

This grace and inexpressible blessing was once promised to Abraham in Gen. 12[:3]: "And in your seed (that is, in Christ) shall all the nations of the earth be blessed."[15, e] Isaiah 9[:6] says: "For to us a child is born, to us a son is given." "To us," it says, because he is entirely ours with all his benefits if we believe in him, as Rom. 8[:32] says: "He who did not spare his own Son but gave him up for us all, will he not also give us all things with him?" Therefore everything which Christ has is ours, given us unworthy for free out of God's sheer mercy, although we have rather deserved wrath and condemnation, and hell also. Even Christ himself, therefore, who says he came to do the most sacred will of his Father [John 6:38], became obedient to him; and whatever he did, he did it for us and desired it to be ours, saying, "I am among you as one who serves"[f] [Luke 22:27]. And furthermore: "This is my body, which is given for you" [Luke 22:19].[g] Isaiah 43[:24] says, "You have burdened me with your sins, you have wearied me with your iniquities."

Thus, through faith in Christ, Christ's righteousness becomes our righteousness and all that he has, rather, he himself, becomes ours. Therefore the Apostle calls it "the righteousness of God" in Rom. 1[:17]: For in the gospel "the righteousness of God is revealed . . .; as it is written, 'The righteous lives from

---

e   Gen. 12:3 reads "in you," not "in your seed." Luther actually cites Gen. 22:18. Cf. also Gal. 3:8. The Latin *semen* can be translated either "seed" or "child" and is here rendered "seed" though "child" would correspond with Luther's parenthesis.

f   Luther uses the Latin verb *ministro*, not *servo*. Cf. his understanding of ecclesial ministry as that of being a servant of the word, *ministerium verbi.*

g   Cf. 1 Cor. 11:24.

faith.'"[16] Finally, in the same epistle, chapter 3[:28], such a faith is called "the righteousness of God": "We hold that a human being is justified through faith." This is an infinite righteousness,[17] and one that swallows up all sins in a moment, for it is impossible that sin should exist in Christ. On the contrary, who trusts in Christ is attached to Christ, is one with Christ, having the same righteousness as he. Thus, it is impossible that sin should remain in that person. This righteousness is primary; it is the basis, the cause, the source of any own actual righteousness.[18] For this is the righteousness given in place of the original righteousness lost in Adam. It accomplishes the same as that original righteousness would have accomplished; rather, it accomplishes more.

It is in this sense that we are to understand the prayer in Psalm 30:2 [Ps. 31:1]: "In you, O LORD, do I seek refuge; let me never be put to shame; in your righteousness liberate me." It does not say "in my" but "in your righteousness," that is, in the righteousness of Christ my God which becomes ours through faith and by the grace and mercy of God. In many passages of the Psalter, faith is called "the work of the LORD," "confession," "power of God," "mercy," "truth," "righteousness." All these are names for faith in Christ, rather, for the righteousness which is in Christ. The Apostle therefore dares to say in Gal. 2[:20], "I live, though not I, but truly Christ lives in me"; and in Eph. 3[:17]: "that Christ may reside[h] in your hearts through faith."

Therefore this alien righteousness, infused in us without our works by grace alone—while the Father, to be sure, inwardly draws us to Christ—is set opposite original sin, likewise alien without our works, inherited and caused by birth alone.[19] Christ daily drives out the old Adam more and more in accordance with the extent to which faith and knowledge of Christ grow. For alien

---

Commentary on the Magnificat on Jesus Christ's Jewish origins by his mother (LW 21:295-358).

16. According to Luther, it was exactly Rom. 1:17 that led him to his Reformation theology. Late in life (1545), Luther explained "how I hated the righteous God who punishes sinners" until he suddenly understood with Paul that the gospel of the righteousness of God is revealed through faith: "He who through faith is righteous shall live'" (LW 34:336-37). Luther's discovery thus was that the term "to be justified" does not mean judgment of the sinner but, rather, that God considers the sinner righteous (LW 34:167). Cf. Luther's *Lectures on Romans* (LW 25:136). See, e.g., Heiko Oberman, *Martin Luther: Man between God and the Devil* (New Haven: Yale University Press, 2006), 164-66.

17. Luther further states that God's righteousness is infinite, *iustitia infinita,* thereby emphasizing the abundant mercy of God, recurrently titling God the Father of mercies. Cf. n. 13 above.

18. Luther is explaining how the alien righteousness, *iustitia aliena,* becomes the proper righteousness, *iustitia propria,* of any Christian.

19. Luther is referring to the Augustinian idea of original sin, according to which sin came into the world through Adam's pride and desire (Genesis 3). This understanding of sin, already with the church fathers, developed from Paul's Adam-Christ typology in Rom. 5:12-21, contrasts fallen Adam with Christ, the second Adam, who, due to his lack of sin, saved fallen creation. While Luther builds on this typology in his deliberations on human sin and Adam as the type of

---

h Luther uses the Latin verb *habitare*, which could also be rendered to "live in," to "inhabit," or to "dwell."

sinful humanity, in contrast to Christ's redeeming righteousness, he does not seem to employ the parallel Eve-Mary typology developed by Justin Martyr (c. 100–165) and popular among the church fathers as a parallel to the Adam–Christ typology.

20. Luther employs the traditional tripartite sequel of beginning, progressing, and becoming perfect (*incipit, proficit et perficit*), in death, about the life of the Christian believer. Righteousness is not a state obtained in this life, but a process, a justification, from outside (Christ's alien righteousness) and from inside (through faith) that continues through life.

21. This brief passage holds the essence of Luther's reformation theology: humans are made righteous through Christ's alien righteousness, which is infused (*iustitia infusa*) gradually and works by grace alone (*sola gratia*), while it daily drives out their alien original sin (*alienum peccatum originalis*)—instilled by birth alone—and through faith in Christ as it grows in the human being. Luther developed this thought in 1521 in his treatise *Against Latomus* (LW 32:137–260). Jacobus Latomus (c. 1475–1544) was a distinguished member of the Faculty of Theology at the University of Leuven and an adviser to the Inquisition. With his colleagues, in 1520 he burned Luther's books and condemned a number of isolated sentences. Having published their condemnations and asked for the basis of their actions, Latomus's refutation against him prompted Luther to expound his doctrine of justification in June 1521 while at Wartburg.

22. Luther here presents us with the idea of cooperation between Christ's alien righteousness and humans' good

righteousness is not infused all at once, but it begins, makes progress, and is finally perfected[20] at the end through death.[21]

The second kind of righteousness is our proper righteousness, not because we alone work it, but because we work with that first and alien righteousness.[22] This is that manner of life spent profitably in good works, in the first place, in mortifying the flesh and crucifying the self-centered desires, of which we read in Gal. 5[:24]: "And those who belong to Christ Jesus have crucified the flesh with its passions and desires." In the second place, this righteousness consists in love of our neighbors, and in the third place, in humility and fear toward God. The Apostle

Jacobus Latomus (c. 1475–1544) was a distinguished member of the Faculty of Theology at the University of Leuven and an adviser to the Inquisition.

is full of references to these, as is all the rest of Scripture. He briefly summarizes everything, however, in Titus 2[:12]: "In this world let us live soberly (pertaining to crucifying our own flesh), righteously (pertaining to our neighbor), and piously (pertaining to God)."

This righteousness is the product of the righteousness of the first type, actually its fruit and consequence, for we read in Gal. 5[:22]: "But the fruit of the spirit [i.e., of a spiritual person, whose very existence depends on faith in Christ] is love, joy, peace, patience, kindness, goodness, faithfulness, gentleness, self-control." For because the works mentioned are human works, it is obvious that in this passage a spiritual person is called "spirit." In John 3[:6] we read: "That which is born of the flesh is flesh, and that which is born of the Spirit is spirit." This righteousness goes on to complete the first, for it persistently strives to extinguish the old Adam and to destroy the body of sin. Therefore it hates itself and loves its neighbor; it does not seek its own good, but that of another, and in this its whole way of living consists. For in that it hates itself and does not seek its own, it crucifies the flesh. Because it seeks the good of another, it works love. Thus in each sphere it does God's will, living soberly with self, justly with neighbor, devoutly toward God.[23]

This righteousness follows the example of Christ in this respect [1 Pet. 2:21] and is made to conform to his image (2 Cor. 3:18).[24] It is precisely this that Christ requires. Just as Christ in person did all things for us, not seeking his own good but ours only—and in this he was most obedient to God the Father—he desires that we would likewise set the same example for our neighbors.

We read in Rom. 6[:19] that this righteousness is set opposite our own actual sin: "For just as you once yielded your members to impurity and to greater and greater iniquity, so now yield your members to righteousness for sanctification." Therefore through the first righteousness arises the voice of the bridegroom who says to the soul, "I am yours," but through the second comes the voice of the bride who answers, "I am yours." Then the marriage is consummated;[25] it becomes strong and complete in accordance with the Song of Solomon [2:16]: "My beloved is mine and I am his," which means that my beloved is mine and I am his.[26] Then the soul no longer seeks to be righteous in and for itself, but it has Christ as its righteousness and therefore seeks only the welfare of others. Therefore the Lord of the Synagogue threatens through the Prophet, "And I will make to cease from the cities of Judah and from the streets of Jerusalem the voice of mirth and the voice of gladness, the voice of the bridegroom and the voice of the bride" [Jer. 7:34].

This is what the theme proposed says: Have the same understanding between you, etc.; that is, have such a mind and affection towards each other such as you see that Christ is affected towards you. How? Though he was in the form of God, he did not regard it a robbery to be equal to God, but he emptied himself,

works (*opera bona*): the second kind of righteousness, the proper, comes about through human cooperation with Christ's alien righteousness and Christ as example, in three manners: crucifixion of the self, love of neighbor, and humility toward or fear of God.

23. Luther may be inspired by Bernard of Clairvaux's idea that God's grace sets charity in order (Song of Sol. 2:4, Vulgate) in humans, the bride in three manners: how to will the good, how to fear God, and how to love God; see *On Grace and Free Choice* (*De gratia et libero arbitrio*) 6:17, *Sancti Bernardi Opera 3* (Rome: Editiones Cistercienses, 1963), 165–203.

24. Luther is quoting in part from the Vulgate, stating that humans will be conformed (*conformis*) to Christ's image (*imago*) by following Christ's example. However, his deliberations on Christ being in the "form of God" and humans becoming "conformed to God" are most likely inspired by Bernard's *On Grace and Free Choice* 10:33–34, where Bernard explicates how Christ, the form of God, reforms the sin-deformed humans who will thus be conformed to the will of God.

25. According to canon law, *Decretals of Pope Gregory IX* (lib. 3, tit. 32, cap. 7), marriage is fully consummated and hence indissoluble only through carnal copulation (*copula carnis*). This rule is founded on Gen. 2:24 (adduced by Luther together with Eph. 5:29-32 at the opening of this text); Matt. 19:5; and 1 Cor. 6:16.

26. Luther combines justification and sanctification, employing the famous words of conjugal love from Song of Sol. 2:16 in tandem with Jer. 7:34 to depict the happy exchange between

Christ and the soul—different from above where he combined Genesis 2 and Ephesians 5 to depict the union of Christ and the church. Luther later employs the same nuptial imagery in *The Freedom of a Christian*, taken from Eph. 5:26-32 as above (adding a physical dimension); Hos. 2:19ff. (adding a grace-economical dimension), and finally, in the Latin version of the treatise only, from Song of Sol. 2:16 (adding a social dimension): *Dilectus meus mihi et ego illi, q. d. dilectus meus est meus et ego sum sua*—"My beloved is mine and I am his, which means that my beloved is mine and I am his"—to stress the intimate relationship of bride and bridegroom as a way to explain what happens when sinful humanity is united with the justifying Christ. Cf. above, n. 12.

27. Luther briefly returns to Phil. 2:6-8, while quite obviously working intertextually through the sermon.

28. Luther contrasts the divine substance of Christ, *substantia Dei*, with human substance, *substantia humana*, accentuating that these should not be confused with Christ in the form of God, *forma Dei*, and in the form of a servant, *forma servi*.

29. The idea of Christ being God formed and becoming servant formed (*forma servi*) in the likeness of humans (*similitudo hominis*), an idea that reflects the kenotic Christology of Phil. 2:5-8, is fundamental in Luther's treatise *The Freedom of a Christian* from two years later.

accepting the form of a servant [Phil. 2:5-7].[27] The form of God here does not mean the substance of God because Christ never emptied himself of this. Neither can form of a servant be said to mean human substance.[28] But the form of God is wisdom, power, righteousness, goodness, and, furthermore, freedom. Thus, though Christ was a free, powerful, wise human being,[i] subject to none of the vices or sins to which all other human beings are subject[29]—preeminent in such attributes that are particularly proper to the form of God—he was not arrogant in that form; he did not please himself (Rom. 15:3); nor did he disdain and despise those who were enslaved and subjected to various evils. He was not like the Pharisee who said, "I thank you, God, that I am not like other people" [Luke 18:11], and who was delighted that others were wretched; at any rate he was unwilling that they should be like him. This is the type of robbery by which people[j] are arrogant about themselves—rather, they keep and do not give back what clearly is God's (as they should), nor do they serve others with it that they may become like others. People of this kind wish to be like God, sufficient in themselves, pleasing themselves, glorifying in themselves, under obligation to no one, and so on.

Christ, however, did not understand it that way; he did not think this way, but relinquished that form to God the Father and emptied himself, unwilling to use his status against us, unwilling to be different from us. Rather, for our sakes he became as one of us and took the form of a servant, that is, he subjected himself to all evils. And although he was free, as the Apostle says of himself also [1 Cor. 9:19], he made himself the servant of all [Mark 9:35], acting in no other way than as if all the evils which were ours were his own. Accordingly, he took upon himself our sins and our punishments, and although it was for us that he

---

i   Luther's Latin text reads *Christus homo*, Luther's point always being that Christ became human, not that he became male. The traditional English translation of *homo* into "man," also meaning "human," tends to be misread by the modern reader as meaning "male." The latter possibility, however, would presuppose that the Latin text read *vir*, which means "man" in the sense of "male," and that Luther should have found Christ's maleness rather than his humanity the decisive factor.

j   The Latin text reads *homo*, in the singular. But since Luther shortly after shifts to plural, the whole sentence here is rendered in the plural for the sake of coherence.

was conquering those things, he acted as though he were conquering them for himself. Although he with respect to us could be our God and Lord, he did not want it so, but rather wanted to become our servant, as it is written in Rom. 15[:1, 3]: "We ought not to please ourselves, as Christ did not please himself"; but, as it is written: "the accusations of those who accused you fell on me'" [Ps. 69:9]. The quotation from the Psalmist has the same meaning as the citation from Paul.

It follows that this passage, which many have understood positively, ought thus to be understood negatively: That Christ did not understand himself as equal to God means that he did not want to be equal to God as those do who through pride rob it and (as St. Bernard says) say to God: "If you will not give me your glory,[30] I shall seize it for myself." The passage is not to be under-

Bernard of Clairvoux, monastic innovator
and doctor of the Church.

30. Luther "cites" Bernard without adducing any exact reference to Bernard's vast opus, which he knew quite well. Luther is most likely referring to Bernard's *De diligendo deo* 2:4–6, SBOp 3, 122f. Instead of distancing himself from Bernard, Luther is echoing Bernard, with reference to Ps. 113:9, when admonishing those who give themselves the glory that belongs to God solely.

Bernard of Clairvaux, a contemplative monk and a busy abbot of the Cistercian monastery in Clairvaux from 1115 until his death in 1153 was one of the most influential theologians as well as a counselor of leading political and ecclesial figures of his century. Like Luther later, Bernard wanted to reform the papal church toward an apostolic church following the pattern laid out by Paul, with a focus on the gospel more than the canon law. Checkmated by Pope Eugenius III (c. 1080 –1153) and the French king Louis VII (c.1120–1180), who made him responsible for the failed Second Crusade (1146–48), Bernard wrote a letter treatise, *On Consideration*, to call the pope to discern between the two swords that were part of God's order—the spiritual word, which the church should concentrate on using to serve, and the material sword, which should only be used by secular power; see *On Consideration* (*De consideratione*) 2,11 and 4,7, SBOp 3, 393–493. The popular treatise inspired many reformers, including Luther, who refers to it, e.g., in his letter sent to Pope Leo X along with *The Freedom of a Christian* (WA 7:10, 29).

Oil painting by Lucas Cranach the Elder, 1525. Mary Magdalene was often portrayed with an oil jar as here. According to Mark 16 and Luke 24, Mary Magdalene was one of the women who brought spices to anoint Jesus' dead body, and according to all the four gospels, she was the first witness to his resurrection. It was the medieval tradition of western Christianity since Pope Gregory I to conflate Mary Magdalene with the unnamed sinner anointing Jesus' feet in Luke 7:36-50 and with Mary of Bethany who anoints Jesus' feet in John 11:1-2.

stood affirmatively as follows: he did not think himself equal to God, that is, the fact that he is equal to God, this he did not consider robbery. For this sentence cannot be properly understood since it speaks of Christ the human being. The Apostle means that the individual Christians shall become the servants of one another in accordance with the example of Christ. If they have wisdom, righteousness, or power, as if in the form of God, with which they can boast and excel others, they should not keep all this to themselves. They should surrender it to God and become altogether as if they did not possess it [2 Cor. 6:10], and become as one of those who have nothing.[k] As a result, any one person[l] who forgets and empties herself of God's gifts, acts with her neighbor as if the neighbor's weakness, sin, and foolishness were her very own in order that one does not boast or get puffed up, nor despise or triumph over one's neighbor as if being God to one's neighbor or equal to God. Since God's prerogatives ought to be left to God alone, such a stupid pride becomes robbery.

It is in this way, then, that one takes the form of a servant, and that the command of the Apostle in Gal. 5[:13] is fulfilled: "Through love be servants of one another." And in Rom. 12[:4-5] and 1 Cor. 12[:12-27] he teaches, through the analogy of the members of the body, how the strong, honorable, healthy members do not triumph over those that are weak, less honorable, and sick as if they were their masters and gods; on the contrary, they serve them the more, forgetting their own honor, health, and power. For thus no member of the body serves itself; nor does it seek its own welfare but that of the other. And the weaker, the sicker, the less honorable a member is, the more the other members serve it. To use Paul's words [1 Cor. 12:25]: "that there may be no discord in the body, but that the members may have the same care for one another." From this it is now evident how one must conduct oneself with one's neighbor in each situation.

---

k   This translation follows the Latin text, which has the subject in the third person plural.

l   The Latin text shifts to third person singular.

If we do not freely desire to put off that form of God and take on the form of a servant, let us be compelled to do so against our will. In this regard, consider the story in Luke 7[:36-50], where Simon the leper, pretending to be in the form of God and perching on his own righteousness, arrogantly judged and despised Mary Magdalene, seeing in her the form of a servant. But see what happens to this judge, how Christ immediately stripped him of that form of righteousness and then clothed him with the form of sin by saying: "You gave me no kiss; you did not anoint my head." See, how many the sins that Simon did not see were! Nor did he think himself deformed by such a loathsome form that he had. His good works are not at all remembered. Christ ignores the form of God in which Simon was arrogantly pleasing himself; he does not recount that he was invited, dined, and honored by him. Simon the leper is now nothing but a sinner; he who seemed to himself so righteous sits deprived of the glory of the form of God, confused in the form of a servant, whether he wants it or not. On the other hand, Christ honors Mary with the form of God and, adding it to her, elevates her above Simon, saying: "She has anointed my feet and kissed them. She has wet my feet with her tears and wiped them with her hair." See how many were the merits which neither she nor Simon saw. Her faults are remembered no more. Christ ignored the form of servitude in her whom he has exalted with the form of sovereignty. Mary is nothing but righteous, elevated into the glory of the form of God, etc.[31]

In like manner, he will treat all of us whenever we, on the ground of our righteousness, wisdom, or power, are arrogant or angry with those who are unrighteous, foolish, or less powerful than we. For when we act thus—and this is the greatest perversion—righteousness works against righteousness, wisdom against wisdom, power against power. For you are powerful, not that you may make the weak weaker by oppression, but that you may make them powerful by raising them up and defending them. You are wise, not in order to laugh at the foolish and thereby make them more foolish, but that you may undertake to teach them as you yourself would wish to be taught. You are righteous so that you may vindicate and pardon the unrighteous,[32] not that you may only condemn, disparage, judge, and punish. For this is Christ's example for us, as he says: "For the child of humanity did not come to condemn the world, but that

31. Luther delivers a unique interpretation of Luke 7:36-50. He highlights Mary Magdalene as a prominent disciple of Jesus Christ, and also as a person being exalted in the form of God, *forma Dei*, and thus conformed to Christ. While deliberately following the medieval tradition of conflating Mary Magdalene (Matthew 27 and 28 with parallels, and John 20) with the anonymous woman who according to Luke 7 anointed Jesus' feet (and with Mary of Bethany who, according to John 11, also anointed Jesus' feet), Luther departs from the traditional portrayals of her as a sinful "woman of the city" and accentuates her as nothing but righteous. Both here and in his *Commentary on the Magnificat*, Luther notably highlights female figures as those who by way of their self-humiliation conform to Christ's kenotic self-debasement (Phil. 2:6-8) and are exalted as true disciples who conform to Christ (Phil. 2:9-11).

32. Luther again emphasizes the merciful character of Christian righteousness and the justification in Christ, to make the point that righteousness is a redeeming process, not condemning in any way: "*Sic iustus es, ut iustifices et excuses iniustum.*"

33. Cf. John 12:47. Although the term *Filius hominis* came to bear the meaning "Son of man," as the church fathers considered it a title and function of Jesus, it is here rendered "child of humanity," the plain meaning also of the Greek *o uios anthropou*, to correspond with Luther's point that Christ became human for the sake of saving the world. Cf. Luther's *Sermon on Galatians 4:1-7*, in which he expounds on Paul's wording that Christ was born by a woman and therefore became a true human being. Luther accentuates Christ's human status with the terms "natural human" (Ger.: *natürlicher mensch*) and "child of humanity" (Ger.: *menschen kind*), and firmly states that what comes from a woman is a true natural human, whereas Christ, in order to stay free from sin, is not from a man, that is, not from a male, like other children (WA 10/1/1, 355–56). Cf. also Luther's *Commentary on the Magnificat* (Luke 1:46-55), where his point is that Mary was chosen as the mother of Christ due to her low status as a poor and plain Jewish girl, for Christ "is born of the despised stump, of the poor and lowly maiden" (LW 21:357).

34. Lat.: *vel publici vel privati*. Here opens the second part of the sermon, on the public and the private spheres. The differentiation between the two, *vel publici vel privati*, is central to Luther's—and Lutheran—teaching and is reflected in the way the *Augsburg Confession* is structured. Neither order in the church (CA XIV) nor civil government (CA XVI) are to be tolerated unless they are conducted correctly in public, namely, for the sake of others and for the sake of order.

the world might be saved through him" (John 3:17).[33] He further says in Luke 9[:55-56]: "You do not know what manner of spirit you are of; for the child of humanity came not to destroy souls but to save them."[m] But nature[n] violently rebels, greatly delighting in punishment, glorying in its own righteousness and in the shame of its neighbors' unrighteousness. Therefore it pleads its own case, and it rejoices that this is better than its neighbor's. But it opposes the case of its neighbor and wants it to appear mean. This perversity is wholly evil, contrary to love, which does not seek its own good, but that of another [1 Cor. 13:5; Phil. 2:4]. It ought to feel pain that the condition of its neighbor is not better than its own and wish that its neighbor's condition were better than its own; and if its neighbor's condition is the better, it ought to rejoice no less than it rejoices when its own is the better. "For this is the law and the prophets" [Matt. 7:12].

But you say, "Is it not permissible to chasten the evil? Is it not proper to punish sin? Who is not obliged to defend righteousness? To do otherwise would give occasion for lawlessness."

I answer: A single solution to this problem cannot be given. Therefore one must distinguish between humans. For people are either public or private individuals.[34]

The things which have been said do not pertain at all to public individuals, that is, to those who have been placed in a responsible office by God. It is their necessary function to punish and judge the evil, to vindicate and defend the oppressed, because it is not they but God who does this. They are his servants in this very matter, as the Apostle shows at some length in Rom. 13[:4]: "He does not bear the sword in vain, etc." But this must be understood as pertaining to the cases of others, not to one's own. For no person acts in God's place for the sake of herself and her own things, but for the sake of others. If, however, someone has a case

---

m   This quote of Luke 9:55-56 is from the Vulgate in older editions and can also be found in the King James Version. It cannot be found in new editions of the Vulgate or in the NSRV, and it is adduced in the Nestle-Aland Greek New Testament in the note apparatus only. Luther's Latin text plainly follows the Vulgate and reads "souls" (*animas*), not "men's lives" as it is rendered in LW 31:304. As in his employment of the nuptial imagery, Luther here speaks about the relationship between Christ and the individual human beings by using the term *soul*.

n   The Latin text plainly reads "nature" (*natura*) without defining this as "carnal" or as being "of man" as it is rendered in LW 31:304.

of her own, let her ask for someone else to be God's representative, for in that case one is not a judge, but one of the parties. But on these matters others speak in other places, for it is too broad a subject to cover here.

Private individuals with their own cases are of three kinds. First, there are those who seek vengeance and judgment from the representatives of God, and there are quite a few of these nowadays. Paul tolerates that, but he does not approve of it when he says in 1 Cor. 6[:12], "All things are lawful for me, but not all things are helpful." Rather, he says in the same chapter, "To have lawsuits at all with one another is a defeat for you" [1 Cor. 6:7]. But yet to avoid a greater evil he [Paul] tolerates this lesser one lest they should vindicate themselves and one should use force on the other, returning evil for evil, demanding their own advantages. Nevertheless, such persons will not enter the kingdom of heaven unless they have changed for the better by forsaking things that are merely lawful and pursuing those that are helpful. For that passion for one's own advantage must be destroyed.

The second kind is those who do not desire vengeance. On the other hand, in accordance with the Gospel [Matt. 5:40], to those who would take their coats, they are prepared to give their capes as well, and they do not resist any evil. These are children of God, brothers and sisters of Christ, heirs of future good things [Rom. 8:16; Gal. 4:7].[o] In Scripture, therefore, they are called "orphans," "minors," "widows," and "poor" because they do not avenge themselves. God wishes to be called their "Father" and "Judge" [Ps. 68:6]. Far from avenging themselves, if those in authority should wish to seek revenge in their behalf, they either do not desire it or seek it, or they only permit it. Or, if they are among the most advanced, they forbid and prevent it, prepared rather to lose their other possessions also.

Suppose you say: "Such people are most rare, and who would be able to remain in this world if acting like this?" I answer: This is not a discovery of today, that few are saved and that the gate is narrow that leads to life and those who find it are few [Matt. 7:14]. But if none were doing this, how would Scripture, which proclaims the poor, the orphans, and the widows the people of

---

o   Luther is again employing Paul's terminology, and again *fratres* should be understood inclusively as "brothers and sisters" (or "friends") along with the terms "children" (*filii*) and "heirs" (*haeredes*) of God.

35. Cf. Luke 6:27-28.

36. The zealots, *zelosi*, form a diverse group in Scripture, but mostly the term denotes a group of overanxious Jews with ultra-nationalist affinities in opposition to Rome (e.g., Acts 5:37). Luther here utilizes the term to designate those who overeagerly pursue a legal justice in order to improve an offender at the expense of a Christian righteousness, the purpose of which is forgiveness of one's neighbor. Luther regards such zealous righteousness a result of a mistake, if not a perversion so subtle that it can only be discerned by the most "spiritual."

Christ, stand? Thus, those of this second type feel more pain over the sin of their offenders than over the loss or offense to themselves. And they do this that they may recall those offenders from their sin rather than avenge the wrongs they themselves have suffered. Therefore they put off the form of their own righteousness and put on the form of those others, praying for their persecutors, blessing those who curse, doing good to evildoers, prepared to pay the penalty and make satisfaction for their very enemies that they may be saved [Matt. 5:44].[35] This is the gospel and the example of Christ [cf. Luke 23:34].

The third kind is those who in affect are like the second type just mentioned, but in effect are different. They are the ones who demand back their own property or seek vengeance to be meted out, not because they seek their own advantage, but through this vengeance and restoration of their own things they seek the betterment of the one who has been stealing from or offending them. They discern that the offender cannot be improved without punishment. These are called "zealots"[36] and the Scriptures praise them. But no one ought to attempt this unless one is perfect and highly experienced in the second manner just mentioned; otherwise they could mistake wrath for zeal and be convicted of doing from anger and impatience what they assume is done from love of justice. For anger is like zeal, and impatience is like love of justice, thus they cannot be sufficiently distinguished except by the most spiritual. Christ exhibited such zeal (as narrated in John 2[:14-17] when he made a whip [1 Cor. 4:21] and cast out the sellers and buyers from the temple; and similarly Paul, when he said, "Should I come to you with a twig," etc. [1 Cor. 4:21].   FINIS

A Brief Instruction on

What to Look for and Expect in the Gospels

1522

WANDA DEIFELT

INTRODUCTION

While in exile at the Wartburg Castle, from 1521 to 1522, Luther began writing a series of sermons that became known as the *Church Postil* (*Kirchenpostille*) or *Wartburg Postil*.[1] The turbulence over the indulgence controversy and ecclesiastical excommunication had come to an end, leaving Luther's Wittenberg supporters in uncertainty and unrest. It was time to focus on the solidification of the movement, and Luther busied himself.[a] Besides the sermons of the *Church Postil*, Luther also translated the New Testament into German during his hiding at Wartburg. These two enterprises go together: the accessibility of the New Testament in the vernacular enabled common people to read the Scriptures, while the homiletic material of the *Postil*[b] enabled preachers to announce the good news of the gospel from the pulpit.[2]

[a] A comprehensive analysis of Luther's activities while at the Wartburg, in Eisenach, can be found in, e.g., Ernest G. Schwiebert, *Luther and His Times: The Reformation from a New Perspective* (St. Louis: Concordia, 1950), 519–31.

[b] A detailed historical and technical exposition of the *Postil* is presented by Gottfried G. Krodel in LW 48:237–45.

1. The term *postil* derives from the Latin term *postilla*, meaning "exposition." It comes from the phrase *post illa verba sacrae scripturae*, "according to these words of Sacred Scripture." The practice of beginning expository preaching with this sentence came into usage in the early part of the sixteenth century. The purpose of the *postil* was to expound on the meaning of particular biblical passages and offer detailed analysis of its content.

2. Timeline:

- 1521 January: Luther excommunicated
- 1521 April: Diet of Worms, Luther outlawed
- 1521 May–March 1522: Luther in Wartburg
- 1521 NT translation and sermon writing
- 1521 May: letter to Melanchthon about sermons

1521 June: *Wartburg Postil* part 1 ready

1521 Summer: *On the Abrogation of the Private Mass, On Confession, Whether the Pope Has the Power to Require It*

1521 November: *The Judgment of Martin Luther on Monastic Vows*

1521 November: letter and sermons dedicated to Albrecht of Mansfeld

1521 December: *A Sincere Admonition by Martin Luther to All Christians to Guard against Insurrection and Rebellion*

1522 February: *Wartburg Postil* part 2 ready

1522 March: Christmas sermons to print

1522 April: Advent sermons to print

---

3. These sermons were not preached by Luther but were to serve as homiletic expositions, that is, as sermon guides to be used by other ministers. Of course, giving Luther's popularity, it is possible that many of these sermons were used (verbatim or not) by sympathizers of the Reformation.

4. The Greek word εὐαγγέλιον means "good news." Each one of the New Testament Gospels begins with the title "The Gospel According to . . ." (εὐαγγέλιον κατα . . .), denoting that each author presents the liberating message of Christ in accordance with their records.

The *Postil* marks the beginning of Luther's effort to have sermon guides for all the Gospel and Epistle lessons for the church year. The text *A Brief Instruction* functions both as an introduction to these sermons but also as a separate commentary on the nature of the gospel.[3] In it Luther stresses the power of the word and its proper interpretation. Although there are many different books to be found in the Bible, there is only one gospel, which Luther summarizes as "a story about Christ, God's and David's Son, who dies and was raised and is established as Lord."

Having just returned from the Diet of Worms in 1521, where he had been declared an outlaw, Luther had a renewed sense of urgency in proclaiming that the church needed to hear God's message. In his assessment of his church's teaching at the time, Christ had been made into a new Moses or, at best, as an example to be followed. It was necessary, therefore, to clarify that the gospel is not a literary genre but the *evangelion*, the message of good news proclaimed in Christ.[4] The paradox of law and gospel is at the center of the argument Luther wishes to make.[5] Christ is not a law-giving Moses, but a gift comprehensible solely through the lens of the cross. The overwhelming goodness of God can only be understood and experienced by preaching Christ as the one who is crucified. This happy exchange is the true and central argument of the gospel, "the message on which the church is founded and in which Christians put their hope."[c]

Before setting off for the Diet of Worms, Luther had written and sent to the printer a short explanation, in Latin, on the Epistles and Gospels for the four Sundays of Advent. In a letter to his Wittenberg colleague Philip Melanchthon (1497–1560), on 26 May 1521, Luther announced that he would publish a *Postil* in German.[6] He asked his friends in Wittenberg to send him a copy of the Latin *Advent Postil*—perhaps with the intention of translating it from Latin into German—but they could not find his

---

c Timothy F. Lull, ed., *Martin Luther's Basic Theological Writings* (Minneapolis: Fortress Press, 1989), 71.

personal copy.*d* Apparently Luther had entrusted it to somebody and it got misplaced. While waiting for his Latin *Advent Postil*—and without his library—Luther began working on the homilies for the Christmas season. He decided that the *Postil* should be divided into four parts, one for each quarter of the church calendar.*e* The first sermon of the *Wartburg Postil* was completed in June of 1521 and the last one in February of the following year.

In a letter from 19 November 1521, Luther dedicates the sermons to his territorial ruler, Albert VII [Albrecht], Count of Mansfeld (1480–1560). By this time, Luther had finished twelve of the sermons (those from Christmas Day through Epiphany) and was planning to prepare four more for Advent. The dedicatory letter and the introduction were supposed to cover both parts.[7] However, the portion about Advent was not concluded and the *Christmas Postil* ended up published first, even if Luther had planned that the homilies for the four Advent Sundays were to come first (following the church year).

The Christmas sermons, along with *A Brief Instruction*, were sent off in secret and published in March 1522, by Johann Grünenberg (d. c. 1525), in time for the Easter fair at Frankfurt-am-Main. By 15 April 1522, the Advent sermons were also sent to the press.*f* Only in 1525 were the two parts published together, as originally intended. The *Wartburg Postil* encompasses these two sets of publications covering the Sundays of Advent and Christmas, known as *Christmas Postil* and *Advent Postil*.

5. Luther often writes and thinks in a paradoxical manner. The law and gospel tension is one of these paradoxes. Although we are justified by faith, the process of being renewed by the Holy Spirit is not fulfilled in our lives as we fail to follow the commandment to love God wholeheartedly and our neighbor as ourselves. Thus, with respect to the law, we remain sinners; with respect to the gospel, we are justified and made righteous according to the gospel's promise. Therefore, a Christian is at the same time justified and yet a sinner (*simul iustus et peccator*).

6. Luther writes: "I had decided to put the expositions of the Epistles and Gospels into German, but you have not yet sent me a copy of the *Postil*. I am sending the Psalm that was sung on these days. If you wish, and the presses are idle, you may have it printed, and dedicated to whomever you wish. I have worked on this in my leisure, since I have no books here" (LW 48:229).

7. E. Theodore Bachmann points out that Luther had already completed the text of *A Brief Instruction* by the time he sent the letter of dedication to Albert, the count of Mansfeld, by 19 November 1521. See LW 35:115.

---

d Luther was waiting for a copy of his Latin *Advent Postil*, titled *Enarrationes Epistolarum et Evangeliorum, Quas Postillas Vocant*, published in Wittenberg by Johann Grünenberg in March 1521 (WA 7:458ff., 152 n. 2). This is referred to in Luther's 26 May 1521 letter to Philip Melanchthon (LW 48:229).

e LW 48:238.

f Gottfried G. Krodel in LW 48:238–39.

8. The German word is *Unterricht*. While the English term here is *instruction*, it should not be downplayed as a mere set of directions in how something should be done. *Unterricht* signifies a shorter lesson or class, but it also conveys a broader notion of education. Thus, for instance, a confirmation program (where the principles of the Christian faith are taught in church) is called *Unterricht*.

9. Jerome, born Eusebius Sophronius Hieronymus (b. c. 347 in Stridon, Dalmatia—d. 420 in Bethlehem, Palestine), translated the Bible from the original Hebrew and Greek into Latin, in a translation known as the Vulgate. He was a renowned biblical scholar of the ancient church.

10. In the prologue to his commentary on the Gospel of Matthew, Jerome writes, "By all of these things it is plainly shown that only the four Gospels ought to be received, and all the lamentations of the Apocrypha should be sung by heretics, who, in fact, are dead, rather than by living members of the Church" (Jerome, *Commentary on Matthew*, trans. Thomas P. Scheck, Fathers of the Church 117 [Washington, D.C.: Catholic University of America Press, 2008], 56).

11. Luther's Christocentric argument is that the gospel is not a literary genre but the message of good news proclaimed in Christ. This good news

A BRIEF INSTRUCTION[8] ON WHAT TO LOOK FOR AND EXPECT IN THE GOSPELS[g]

IT IS A COMMON PRACTICE to number the gospels and to name them by books and say that there are four gospels. From this practice stems the fact that no one knows what St. Paul and St. Peter are saying in their epistles, and their teaching is regarded as an addition to the teaching of the gospels, in a vein similar to that of Jerome's[9] introduction.[10] There is, besides, the still worse practice of regarding the gospels and epistles as law books that teach us what we are to do, and the works of Christ are pictured as nothing but examples to us.[h] Where these two erroneous notions remain in people's hearts,[i] neither the gospels nor the epistles may be read in a profitable or Christian manner; they remain as pagan as ever.

One should thus realize that there is only one gospel,[11] but that it is described by many apostles. Every single epistle of Paul and of Peter, as well as the Acts of the Apostles by Luke, is a gospel, even though they do not record all the works and words of Christ, but one is shorter and includes less than another. There is not one of the four major gospels anyway that includes all the words and works of Christ; nor is this necessary. *Gospel* is and should be nothing else than a discourse or story about Christ,[j]

g　The following version comes from the original German, *Eyn kleyn unterricht, was man ynn den Evangelijs suchen und gewarten soll*, reprinted, with annotations, WA 10/1/1, 8–18. *Luther's Works*, the American edition, presents this text with two different translations: vol. 35 (from 1960) with translation and introduction by E. Theodore Bachmann and vol. 75, *Church Postils 1* (St. Louis: Concordia, 2013), ed. Benjamin T. G. Mayes and James L. Langebartels.

h　Bachmann's original translation reads "law books in which is supposed to be taught what we are to do and in which the works of Christ are pictured to us as nothing but examples."

i　Luther's original text reads *"im Hertzen"* ("in the heart"), but for the sake of better understanding the form, "people's heart" has been employed.

just as happens among us when one writes a book about a king or a prince, telling what he did, said, and suffered in his day. Such a story can be told in various ways; one spins it out, and the other is brief. Thus the gospel is and should be nothing else than a chronicle, a story, a narrative about Christ, telling who he is, what he did, said, and suffered—a subject which one describes briefly, another more fully, one this way, another that way.

For at its briefest, the gospel is a discourse about Christ, that he is the Son of God and became a human being*k* for us, that he died and was raised, that he has been established as a Lord over all things. This much St. Paul takes in hand and spins out in his epistles. He bypasses all the miracles and incidents [in Christ's ministry] which are set forth in the four gospels, yet he includes the whole gospel adequately and abundantly. This may be seen clearly and well in his greeting to the Romans [1:1–4], where he says what the gospel is, and declares, "Paul, a servant of Jesus Christ, called to be an apostle, set apart for the gospel of God which he promised beforehand through his prophets in the holy scriptures, the gospel concerning his Son, who was descended from David according to the flesh and designated Son of God in power according to the Spirit of holiness by his resurrection from the dead, Jesus Christ our Lord." There you have it. The gospel is a story about Christ, God's and David's Son, who died and was raised and is established as Lord. This is the gospel in a nutshell. Just as there is no more than one Christ, so there is and may be no more than one gospel. Since Paul and Peter too teach nothing but Christ, in the way we have just described, so their epistles can be nothing but the gospel.[12]

Yes, even the teaching of the prophets, in those places where they speak of Christ, is nothing but the true, pure, and proper gospel—just as if Luke or Matthew had described it. For the prophets have proclaimed the gospel and spoken of Christ, as St. Paul here [Rom. 1:2] reports and as everyone indeed knows. Thus, when Isaiah in chapter fifty-three[13] says how Christ should

is found not only in the Gospels of Matthew, Mark, Luke, and John, but at any place in Scripture (Old and New Testaments alike) where the liberating power of the Word is found. This, of course, differs from the Jewish reading of the Old Testament. Luther reads the Hebrew Bible though the lens of Christ, and this hermeneutical key lets him see a continuity between the two testaments.

12. In his letter of dedication to Albert VII, Count of Mansfeld, Luther articulates the centrality of the gospel by paraphrasing Paul: "[The gospel] turns everything upside down and is contrary to reason. What they call shame is honor; what they call honor is shame. . . . Because they act contrary to reason and judge unjustly, He will act the same and, contrary to reason, judge them justly" (LW 75:6). The themes of the gospel, the good news, appear throughout the entire Scripture, and Luther does not tire to repeat it.

13. This offers an illustration of Luther's Christocentric hermeneutic. Isaiah 53:4-6 reads: "Surely he took up our pain and bore our suffering, yet we considered him punished by God, stricken by him, and afflicted. But he was pierced for our transgressions, he was crushed for our iniquities; the punishment that brought us peace was on him, and by his wounds we are healed. We all, like sheep, have gone astray, each of us has turned to our own way; and the LORD has laid on him the iniquity of us all." Isaiah's last of the four Songs of the Suffering Servant is interpreted by Luther as a prophecy of Christ's salvific role for humanity.

---

j   LW 75 translates the German original, *"ein rede oder historia von Christo,"* as "The gospel is and should be nothing else than a report and history about Christ."

k   *Mensch*, in the original German, had previously been translated as "man."

14. Actually 1 Pet. 2:21; cf. 4:1.

15. The crucifixion scene painted by Lucas Cranach the Elder offers an artistic depiction of Luther's words. See image.

16. The original term is *Tzwellff botten*. Luther points out the intrinsic connection between the "messenger" (*Bote*) and the "message" (*Botschaft*). He relates the Greek word ἀπόστολος (*apóstolos*), meaning "one who is sent," with the actual content of the message delivered. The apostles are both messengers and preachers of the gospel. As messengers, they speak of the life, ministry, death, and resurrection of Jesus Christ to those they encounter. As preachers, they are living testaments of this joyful, good, and comforting message.

17. The theme of justification by faith pulsates in Luther's words. By grace, God's initiative establishes a saving relation to humanity. The gift of grace can only be received: it is a gift mediated by a divine promise. It cannot be received except by faith, without human merit or work. Salvation takes place by grace alone and, as a consequence of justification, human beings bear good works.

18. Luther describes this logic in his *Sermon on Two Kinds of Righteousness* (see pp. 8–24 in this volume) in which he elaborates how the righteousness in Christ is received and relates to Christian life. The first is alien righteousness, the righteousness that is of another, instilled from without. This is the righteousness of Christ, which justifies us through faith. The second type of righteousness is our proper righteousness, not because we alone work it, but because it is the product

die for us and bear our sins, he has written the pure gospel. And I assure you, if a person fails to grasp this understanding of the gospel, he will never be able to be illuminated in the Scripture nor will he receive the right foundation.

Be sure, moreover, that you do not make Christ into a Moses, as if Christ did nothing more than teach and provide examples as the other saints do, as if the gospel were simply a textbook of teachings or laws. Therefore you should grasp Christ, his words, works, and sufferings, in a twofold manner. First as an example that is presented to you, which you should follow and imitate. As St. Peter says in 1 Peter 4,[14] "Christ suffered for us, thereby leaving us an example." Thus when you see how he prays, fasts, helps people, and shows them love, so also you should do, both for yourself and for your neighbor. However, this is the smallest part of the gospel, on the basis of which it cannot yet even be called gospel. For on this level Christ is of no more help to you than some other saint. His life remains his own and does not as yet contribute anything to you. In short this mode [of understanding Christ as simply an example] does not make Christians but only hypocrites. You must grasp Christ at a much higher level. Even though this higher level has for a long time been the very best, the preaching of it has been something rare. The chief article and foundation of the gospel is that before you take Christ as an example, you accept and recognize him as a gift, as a present that God has given you and that is your own.[15] This means that when you see or hear of Christ doing or suffering something, you do not doubt that Christ himself, with his deeds and suffering, belongs to you. On this you may depend as surely as if you had done it yourself; indeed as if you were Christ himself. See, this is what it means to have a proper grasp of the gospel, that is, of the overwhelming goodness of God, which neither prophet, nor apostle, nor angel was ever able fully to express, and which no heart could adequately fathom or marvel at. This is the great fire of the love of God for us, whereby the heart and conscience become happy, secure, and content. This is what preaching the Christian faith means. This is why such preaching is called gospel, which in German means a joyful, good, and comforting "message"; and this is why the apostles are called the "twelve messengers."[16]

Concerning this, Isaiah 9[:6] says, "To us a child is born, to us a son is given." If he is given to us, then he must be ours; and so we must also receive him as belonging to us. And Romans 8[:32], "How should [God] not give us all things with God's own[1] Son?" See, when you lay hold of Christ as a gift which is given you for your very own and have no doubt about it, you are a Christian. Faith redeems you from sin, death, and hell and enables you to overcome all things. No one can speak enough about this. It is a pity that this kind of preaching has been silenced in the world, and yet boast is made daily of the gospel.[17]

Now when you have Christ as the foundation and chief blessing of your salvation, then the other part follows: that you take him as your example, giving yourself in service to your neighbor just as you see that Christ has given himself for you. See, there faith and love move forward, God's commandment is fulfilled, and a person is happy and fearless to do and to suffer all things. Therefore make note of this, that Christ as a gift nourishes your faith and makes you a Christian. But Christ as an example exercises your works. These do not make you a Christian. Actually they come forth from you because you have already been made a Christian.[18] As widely as a gift differs from an example, so widely does faith differ from works, for faith possesses nothing of its own, only the deeds and life of Christ. Works have something of your own in them, yet they should not belong to you but to your neighbor.[19]

So you see that the gospel is really not a book of laws and commandments which requires deeds of us, but a book of divine promises in which God promises, offers, and gives us all

An oil painting titled *Crucifixion by Lucas Cranach the Elder (1472–1553)*, painted in 1532.

of the first type of righteousness, done through Christ (LW 31:297–306).

19. Justification by faith is never the end of the story. It frees us to love the neighbor and serve the world in need. We love others because we are loved by God—and this creates a nurturing environment that affirms the vocation of the Christians in the world. On

1   Here "his" is replaced with "God's."

groundbreaking work on faith and love in justification, see Tuomo Mannermaa, *Christ Present in Faith: Luther's View of Justification* (Minneapolis: Fortress Press, 2005); and idem, *Two Kinds of Love: Martin Luther's Religious World* (Minneapolis: Fortress Press, 2010).

20. Luther's views on the law are further developed in his 1523 treatise *Temporal Authority: To What Extent It Should Be Obeyed* (LW 45:[77–90] 81–129. While the fulfillment of the law does not assure salvation, the law is still necessary. The law teaches us to recognize sin, it prevents chaos, and it ensures that human beings live peacefully. Furthermore, the law is a benefit. Because Christians do not live and labor on earth for themselves, but for the well-being of the neighbor, they will ensure that laws are created and enforced to constrain evil, keep the peace, and do what is good.

his possessions and benefits in Christ.*ᵐ* The fact that Christ and the apostles provide much good teaching and explain the law is to be counted a benefit just like any other work of Christ.[20] For to teach correctly*ⁿ* is not the least sort of benefit. We see too that unlike Moses in his book, and contrary to the nature of a commandment, Christ does not horribly force and drive us. Rather, he teaches us in a loving and friendly way. He simply tells us what we are to do and what to avoid, what will happen to those who do evil and to those who do well. Christ drives and compels no one. Indeed he teaches so gently that he entices rather than commands. He begins by saying, "Blessed are the poor, Blessed are the meek," and so on [Matt. 5:3, 5]. And the apostles commonly use the expression, "I admonish, I request, I beseech," and so on. But Moses says, "I command, I forbid," threatening and frightening everyone with horrible punishments and penalties. With this sort of instruction you can now read and hear the gospels profitably.

When you open the book containing the gospels and read or hear how Christ comes here or there, or how someone is brought to him, you should therein perceive the sermon or the gospel through which he is coming to you, or you are being brought to him. For the preaching of the gospel is nothing else than Christ coming to us, or we being brought to him. When you see how he works, however, and how he helps everyone to whom he comes or who is brought to him, then rest assured that faith is accomplishing this in you and that he is offering your soul exactly the same sort of help and favor through the gospel. If you pause here

m   This ecumenically fruitful teaching of Luther is summarized in The Report of the Lutheran-Roman Catholic Commission on Unity in its document *From Conflict to Communion: Lutheran–Catholic Common Commemoration of the Reformation in 2017* (Leipzig: Evangelische Verlagsanstalt, 2013), 45: "The image [of the happy exchange] shows that something external, namely Christ's righteousness, becomes something internal. It becomes the property of the soul, but only in union with Christ through trust in his promises, not in separation from him. Luther insists that our righteousness is totally external because it is Christ's righteousness, but it has to become totally internal by faith in Christ. Only if both sides are equally emphasized is the reality of salvation properly understood. Luther states, 'It is precisely in faith that Christ is present.' Christ is 'for us' (*pro nobis*) and 'in us' (*in nobis*), and we are 'in Christ' (*in Christo*)."

n   The original German *recht leren* was previously translated as "teach aright."

This altarpiece painting in Wittenberg Church
by Cranach shows Luther preaching and illustrates
how Christ is to be at the center of a sermon, wherein
Christ comes to us and we are brought to Christ.

and let him do you good, that is, if you believe that he benefits
and helps you, then you really have it. Then Christ is yours, presented to you as a gift.

After that it is necessary that you turn this into an example
and deal with your neighbor in the very same way, be given also
to him as a gift and an example.[21] Isaiah 40[:1, 2] speaks of that,
"Be comforted, be comforted my dear people, says your LORD
God. Say to the heart of Jerusalem, and cry to her, that her sin is
forgiven, that her iniquity is ended, that she has received from
the hand of God a double kindness for all her sin," and so forth.
This double kindness is the twofold aspect of Christ: gift and
example. These two are also signified by the double portion of
the inheritance which the law of Moses [Deut. 21:17] assigns to
the eldest son and by many other figures.

What a sin and shame it is that we Christians have come to
be so neglectful of the gospel that we not only fail to understand
it, but even have to be shown by other books and commentaries
what to look for and what to expect in it. Now the gospels and
epistles of the apostles were written for this very purpose. They
want themselves to be our guides, to direct us to the writings

21. Love of neighbor is how one could
summarize Luther's ethics: "I will
therefore give myself as a Christ to
my neighbor, just as Christ offered
himself to me; I will do nothing in
this life except what I see is necessary,
profitable, and salutary to my neighbor,
since through faith I have an abundance
of all good things in Christ" (LW
31:367).

of the prophets and of Moses in the Old Testament so that we might there read and see for ourselves how Christ is wrapped in swaddling cloths and laid in the manger [Luke 2:7], that is, how he is comprehended*o* in the writings of the prophets. It is there that people like us should read and study, drill ourselves, and see what Christ is, for what purpose he has been given, how he was promised, and how all Scripture tends toward him. For he himself says in John 5[:46], "If you believed Moses, you would also believe me, for he wrote of me." Again [John 5:39], "Search and look up the Scriptures, for it is they that bear witness to me."

This is what St. Paul means in Romans 1[:1, 2], where in the beginning of his greeting he says, "The gospel was promised by God through the prophets in the Holy Scriptures." This is why the evangelists and apostles always direct us to the Scriptures and say, "Thus it is written," and again, "This has taken place in order that the writing of the prophets might be fulfilled," and so forth. In Acts 17[:11], when the Thessalonians heard the gospel with all eagerness, Luke says that they studied and examined the Scriptures day and night in order to see if these things were so. Thus when St. Peter wrote his epistle, right at the beginning [1 Pet. 1:10-12] he says, "The prophets who prophesied of the grace that was to be yours searched and inquired about this salvation; they inquired what person or time was indicated by the Spirit of Christ within them; and he bore witness through them to the sufferings that were to come upon Christ and the ensuing glory. It was revealed to them that they were serving not themselves but us, in the things which have now been preached among you through the Holy Spirit sent from heaven, things which also the angels long to behold." What else does St. Peter want here than to lead us into the Scriptures? It is as if he should be saying, "We preach and open the Scriptures to you through the Holy Spirit, so that you yourselves may read and see what is in them and know of the time about which the prophets were writing." For he says as much in Acts 4 [3:24], "All the prophets who ever prophesied, from Samuel on, have spoken concerning these days."[22] Therefore also Luke, in his last chapter [24:45],

22. While at the Wartburg, Luther translated the New Testament from its original Greek into German within eleven weeks. The work was edited by Philip Melanchthon and printed in 1522. It became known as the "September Testament."

---

o The original German reads *Vorfassett*, which is translated as "contained" in LW 75.

says that Christ opened the minds of the apostles to understand the Scriptures.

And Christ, in John 10[:9, 3], declares that he is the door by which one must enter, and whoever enters by him, to him the gatekeeper (the Holy Spirit) opens in order that he might find

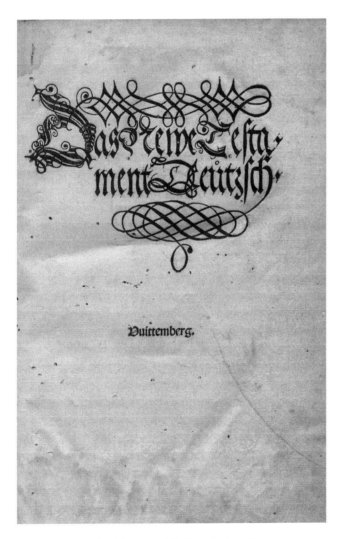

The title page of the first edition of
Luther's New Testament, September 1522.

23. Luther's concern with the proper comprehension of the gospel is evident here. While his translation of the New Testament into German made the text more accessible for common people to read the Bible for themselves, the sermons would enable preachers to better proclaim the good news from the pulpits.

24. The gospel is not "dead writing," put into books, but is a living voice. It is the living word of God. Luther here makes an implicit connection between the life and words of Jesus Christ, recorded in oral and later written tradition, and the presence of the same Christ in the word and sacrament. The *Smalcald Articles* (BC, 319) states: "We now want to return to the gospel, which gives guidance and help against sin in more than one way, because God is extravagantly rich in God's grace: first through the spoken word, in which the forgiveness of sins is preached to the whole world (which is the proper function of the gospel)."

pasture and blessedness. Thus it is ultimately true that the gospel itself is our guide and instructor in the Scriptures, just as with this foreword I would gladly give instruction and point you to the gospel.[23]

But what a fine lot of tender and pious children we are! In order that we might not have to study in the Scriptures and learn Christ there, we simply regard the entire Old Testament as of no account, as done for and no longer valid. Yet it alone bears the name of Holy Scripture. And the gospel should really not be something written, but a spoken word which brought forth the Scriptures, as Christ and the apostles have done. This is why Christ himself did not write anything but only spoke. He called his teaching not Scripture but gospel, meaning good news or a proclamation that is spread not by pen but by word of mouth.[24] So we go on and make the gospel into a law book, a teaching of commandments, changing Christ into a Moses, the One who would help us into simply an instructor.

What punishment ought God to inflict upon such stupid and perverse people! Since we abandoned his Scriptures, it is not surprising that he has abandoned us to the teaching of the pope and to human lies. Instead of Holy Scripture, we have had to learn the *Decretales*[25] of a deceitful fool and an evil rogue. Would to God that among Christians the pure gospel were known and that most speedily there would be neither use nor need for this work of mine. Then there would surely be hope that the Holy Scriptures too would come forth again in their worthiness. Let this suffice as a very brief foreword and instruction. In the exposition[p] we will say more about this matter.[q]

25. The basic elements of canon law were the *Decretum* (c. 1140) and the *Decretales* (1234). The *Decretum*, compiled by a monk named Gratian (359–383) brought together materials related to the law and the administration of the church. The *Decretales* were organized by St. Raymond of Peñafort (Pennafort) [c. 1175–1275], a Dominican, by order of Pope Gregory IX (c. 1145–1241). The *Decretales* consisted of approximately two thousand decretal letters and judicial decisions, issued by various popes between the mid-twelfth and the early thirteenth centuries. Eventually several smaller collections were added as well: the *Liber sextus* ("The Sixth Book of Decretals"; 1298); the *Constitutiones Clementinae* ("The Clementine Constitutions"; 1317), and the *Extravagantes a Johanne Papa XXII* ("Decretal Letters of Pope John XXII"; 1325). The last brief collection was the *Extravagantes communes* compiled at the end of the fifteenth century.

p   The reference is to Luther's commentary on the various texts of the *Wartburg Postil*, to which the text *A Brief Instruction* was intended as a foreword.

q   The 1522, 1528, 1532 editions add "Amen."

Widder die hyme-
lischen propheten /
von den bildern
ynd Sacrament zc

Martinus Luther.

M **L**

Yhre torheyt wird yderman offin
bar werden .2. Timoth .3.

Gedruckt Zu Wittenberg
1525,

Title page of *Widder die hymelischen propheten, von den bildern und Sacrament ec.*
Martinus Luther. Wittenberg: Cranach & Döring, 1525
(*Against the Heavenly Prophets in the Matter of Images and Sacraments*).

Against the Heavenly Prophets in the Matter of Images and Sacraments

1525

HANS J. HILLERBRAND

INTRODUCTION

This treatise is one of several important theological statements Luther published in 1525 to lay out his understanding of key issues of the Christian faith.[1] In terms of its theological content, the two-part treatise stands between Luther's *Invocavit Sermons* of March 1522,[2] which it is constantly engaging, and the fierce controversy over the Lord's Supper that agitated the reformers after 1525 and presented the spectacle of internal dissent among their ranks. The treatise must be understood as Luther's vigorous and somewhat abusive pushback to what he perceived as a growing influence of a group of reformers whom he labeled the "heavenly prophets."[3] With this somewhat denigrating label, he meant to argue that these reformers, like the prophets of old, proclaim a message they received in dreams and visions. Luther saw this coterie of reformers, beginning with Andreas Bodenstein von Karlstadt (1486–1541), and including Thomas Müntzer (c.1489–1525), Nikolaus Storch (d. 1525), Markus Huebner (dates unknown), and others, as detrimental to the true gospel.[4]

Luther used the treatise to place his own understanding of the great themes of "word" and "spirit" into the context of a

1. Of relevance are his treatise on the bound will, written against Erasmus; his three treatises on the German Peasants' War; and his first treatise on the Lord's Supper.

2. Invocavit Sunday is, according to the liturgical calendar, the first Sunday in Lent. Its name (Lat.: "called") derives from Matt. 4:1ff.

3. The full original title was *wider die himlischen Propheten von den bildern und Sacrament* (Augsburg, Ulhart, 1525). with the title page also reproducing ij Timothy iil "*jre thorhait wird yederman offenbar werden.*"

4. Brief biographical sketches of these partisans of the Reformation are found in Hans J. Hillerbrand, ed., *The Oxford Encyclopedia of the Reformation*, 4 vols.

(New York: Oxford University Press, 1996).

5. The most detailed study of Karlstadt continues to be Hermann Barge, *Andreas Bodenstein von Karlstadt. Teil 1 Karlstadt und die Anfänge der Reformation. Teil 2 Karlstadt als Vorkämpfer des laienchristlichen Puritanismus* (Leipzig: Fredrich Brandstetter, 1905–1906).

A portrait of Andreas Bodenstein
von Karlstadt, c. 1541.

6. A rich discussion of aspects of the life and thought of Karlstadt is in Ulrich Bubenheimer, ed., *Querdenker der Reformation: Andreas Bodenstein von Karlstadt und seine frühe Wirkung* (Würzburg: Religion und Kultur Verlag, 2001).

relentless analysis (and rejection) of the theological notions of Karlstadt, his erstwhile colleague on the Wittenberg faculty.[5] Andreas Bodenstein was a native of the small town of Karlstadt on the Main River, and accordingly he came to be known, in the custom of the time, as Karlstadt and hardly ever by his real name.[6] After studying at the universities of Erfurt and Cologne, Karlstadt received his doctorate at the recently founded University of Wittenberg in 1510. His academic career flourished; he became archdeacon, professor, and eventually dean of the theological faculty. As dean, Karlstadt presided over Martin Luther's promotion to the doctorate in theology in 1512. In 1515-16, he studied canon and civil law (*utriusque juris*) in Italy, a venture that led to some ill will among his colleagues at the university, since he had not received a formal leave of absence but had simply disappeared to Italy one day. The sentiment among his colleagues was that Karlstadt's legal interests were less due to the subject matter than to better advancement with a legal degree. Understandably, there was little excitement and congratulatory spirit when he, adorned with new doctoral titles, returned to Wittenberg.

A student of Thomas Aquinas (1225-1274), Karlstadt had at first opposed Luther's Augustinian theology, but was converted to Luther's understanding once the indulgences controversy[7] had erupted. By the famous Leipzig debate (1519),[8] Karlstadt was by all odds the more assertive protagonist of the new Wittenberg theology. While Luther was in hiding at the Wartburg Castle, Karlstadt became an ardent advocate of and a leader in implementing the practical consequences of the new theological insights, which, while quickly associated with Martin Luther, owed a great deal to Karlstadt's consistent drawing out of the consequences of Luther's thought. (Accordingly, when the papal bull *Exsurge Domine*[9] was issued in the summer of 1520, to settle the controversy by threatening Luther and his supporters with excommunication, Karlstadt's name was prominently included.) For instance, if marriage was seen as an honorable estate even for priests, then they should feel free to marry. Monastic vows should be abolished. The gap between laity and clergy could be eliminated; that is, clergy needed no special robes to distinguish them from laity who also should receive communion in both kinds. Publicizing his theological notions in one pamphlet after the other, Brother Andreas turned into a public antagonist of Luther, demonstrating that recourse to the Bible, rather than the church, as final authority was problematic.

Karlstadt and Wittenberg Reforms

While Luther was at the Wartburg Castle and the theological call for reform increasingly raised the question of practical action and change, Karlstadt emerged as leader of the majority activist faction in Wittenberg. At issue were the practical implications of the many theological points Luther had made, such as that all Christians were priests or that neither the monastic commitment nor clerical celibacy had biblical mandates. Karlstadt, always striving to be utterly consistent in his theological views, proceeded to marry. His bride, Anna von Mochau (c. 1507), was fifteen years of age.[10] That Karlstadt himself was around forty seemed no problem. Disorderly conduct occurred in Wittenberg: for example, a priest celebrating Mass was pushed from the altar. For most Wittenberg burghers, life undoubtedly continued as heretofore, seeing things as triggered by rambunctious undergraduates with too much time on their hands. Continuing to face the practical consequences of the new theological insights, being a university professor suddenly seemed incompatible with a true Christian profession; Karlstadt left his professorship without notifying the university authorities.

These developments occurred in late 1521 and early 1522, when the excommunicated and outlawed Luther was in hiding in the Wartburg. He was far removed from the developments in Wittenberg, and Karlstadt assumed the leadership role in this challenge to reform life and thought. On Christmas Day 1521, he presided over a communion service that was meant to embody the new theological emphasis. Karlstadt did not elevate the elements, he wore secular clothing—according to an account from a participant, he was "in his shirt sleeves"—and offered the communion cup to laity. All references to sacrifice that are found in the Roman Mass were eliminated from the service. To make things even clearer, Karlstadt shouted rather than whispered the words of institution—"This is my body. . . ," and so forth—and did so in German instead of Latin. He also

7. The term universally used to describe the theological and political controversy triggered by Luther's *95 Theses* and the concomitant response of the Roman curia.

8. Formally, the debate was to be between Johann Eck (1486–1543) and Karlstadt, but as matters turned out, the overpowering presence was Luther, especially after his statements that church councils had been in error. Karlstadt did not present such a splendid figure since he insisted that references to previous authors had to be read from the source rather than cited from memory. The proceedings of the debate are found in *Der authentische Text der Leipziger Disputation, 1519: Aus bisher unbenutzten Quellen* (Berlin: C. A. Schwetschke, 1903).

9. The papal bull that threatened Luther with excommunication unless he recanted the theological positions found in his publications. In accord with Roman Catholic practice, papal bulls are known by their opening words, here "Rise, O Lord."

10. The marriage between Karlstadt and Anna von Mochau took place 19 January 1522. Karlstadt became thus the first of the reformers to reject practically the vow of celibacy. Luther did not get married until the summer of 1525.

11. In his 1520 treatise, *On the Babylonian Captivity of the Church,* Luther had rejected the Roman Catholic understanding of Holy Communion being best understood as "transubstantiation," an understanding that appropriated the Aristotelian distinction between a "substance" and the "accident" of everything. Thus, "table" was as substance a table, but as accident a use of wood. Likewise, in medieval practice, the priest celebrated Mass in Latin and spoke the words of institution ("Take, eat, this is my body . . .") in a whispered tone. The laity generally did not receive the wine, though efforts were made to engage in practical alternatives, such as giving the laity unconsecrated wine. Of course, the fifteenth-century Bohemian movement, declared heretical by the church, had under the leadership of Jan Hus (c. 1369–1415) made the reception of both bread and wine a hallmark by which it became known ("Utraquists").

allowed the communicants to take both bread and cup in their own hands when receiving the elements.[11]

Karlstadt pushed for other changes as well, notably the removal of "images," paintings, and sculptures from the Wittenberg churches. In fact, in early January 1522, the Wittenberg city council authorized the removal of the images and also affirmed the changes in the communion service Karlstadt introduced on Christmas Day, a rather revolutionary step since now a local political body claimed authority for liturgical and theological change.

On 20 January 1522, however, the political environment of ecclesiastical reform and change was drastically altered, when the so-called *Reichsregiment*, the committee of representatives of the estates, which was to act on the absent emperor's behalf, ordered Elector Frederick III of Saxony (1463–1525) to rescind the Wittenberg changes in the Mass. Practical reform in Wittenberg had become politicized. Promptly, the city council reconsidered its earlier endorsement, while Karlstadt, still the nominal head of the reform faction, remained adamant and responded by insisting that once a biblical insight had been gained, its practical ramifications had to be carried out. To make things more complicated, the back and forth of practical change triggered public demonstrations in Wittenberg, mainly by eager but restive students, who even then seemed to have time on their hands. Luther, who depended on sporadic and incomplete news from Wittenberg, decided, without the elector's permission, to return to Wittenberg to make sure that things did not get out of hand. He was convinced that ecclesiastical reform and renewal were impossible if accompanied by civil unrest. Moreover, his theological approach allowed him to be more patient, making haste slowly in matters of reform in comparison to Karlstadt.

As soon as he was back in Wittenberg, Luther preached a series of no fewer than eight *Invocavit* (Lenten) sermons in March 1522, so called after the liturgical calendar.[a] These sermons not only laid out his understanding of reform and change, but also gave public expression to his disagreement with his colleague Karlstadt.

---

a　See Invocavit sermons (March 1522) in LW 51:67–100; also TAL, vol. 5 (forthcoming).

Luther and Karlstadt Pursue Reform

Karlstadt's notion to implement reform had thus been rejected. In the months that followed Luther's return to Wittenberg, the differences between Karlstadt's impatient moving ahead, and Luther's concern to be patient, became ever more obvious. Rather than follow Luther's lead of patience, Karlstadt turned into a biblical literalist[12] who renounced his academic degrees and ceased lecturing at the university, again much to the chagrin of his colleagues and university officials. He donned peasant garb and insisted that he was to be called "Brother Andreas." Theologically, he increasingly emphasized mystical themes that were alien to Luther.

Eventually, Karlstadt decided to move to the small town of Orlamünde, some one hundred miles south of Wittenberg, where he legally held an appointment (and received a stipend) as the senior priest; this arrangement—widely practiced—allowed him to derive the income from that position, while the actual priestly responsibilities were carried out by a vicar. Karlstadt's arrival in Orlamünde meant that the substitute vicar had to leave, which created a problem, a point subsequently belabored by Luther.[13] In Orlamünde, far from Wittenberg, Karlstadt undertook to institute the vision of the reform he considered crucial to authentic Christianity; for a short while, Orlamünde was a model of a comprehensive congregational reform. The problem (in light of subsequent developments) was that Karlstadt began to publish relentlessly on his understanding of authentic Christian faith, making it perfectly clear that Luther and he disagreed widely. And so Karlstadt got increasingly under Luther's skin. One suspects that alongside the real theological differences, there must have been operative, on Karlstadt's side, the conviction that the broader course of reform could yet be directed along the lines of his, rather than Luther's, understanding, while for Luther, theological or biblical disagreement among the advocates of reform called into question the viability of the Bible as final source of authority. Clearly, Luther became determined to silence his former colleague. In 1524 Luther sought to have Karlstadt's publications prohibited.[14] The situation was made complicated by a another dissenting reformer: Thomas Müntzer had settled in as clergy in the village of Allstedt where he sought to do the same as Karlstadt was doing in

12. This designation should be understood as referring to someone who interprets biblical incidents, stories, and comments to be literally fulfilled.

13. Luther comments that, in his opinion, Karlstadt had no legal right unilaterally to assume the Orlamünde post.

14. Karlstadt attempted in vain to persuade Luther that nothing insurrectionist was attempted at Orlamünde; an open letter on the topic was published in Wittenberg toward the end of July, *Der von Orlemund schrifft an die zu Alstedt, wie man Christlich fechten soll*, which rejected reform by force. Cf. the word of Jesus to Peter not to use his sword and Paul's emphasis on spiritual warfare (Ephesians 6).

Orlamünde and undertake the reform the way he understood it. Both Müntzer and Karlstadt publicly and explicitly attacked Luther's vision of the gospel. Whereas other reformers thought it best to minimize any theological differences with Luther, Müntzer and Karlstadt were determined to confront Luther theologically and move reform in their direction.

The War of Words

In July, Luther published the *Brief an die Fuersten zu Sachsen von dem aufruehrerischen Geist* ("Letter to the Saxon Princes Concerning the Insurrectionist Spirit"),[15] in which he argued that Müntzer and Karlstadt were not only ignorant theologians but also dangerous sectarians with revolutionary tendencies. Luther had been concerned, ever since his return to Wittenberg in March 1522, that reform and renewal not lead to insurrection, which the restlessness among the southwest German peasants seemed to herald. Luther's public charge in his letter of such dangers was bound to introduce fear in light of the incipient uprisings in southwest Germany that later turned into the German Peasants' War.[16] Luther, in short, faced two fellow reformers who publicly, and aggressively, opposed him.

In the late summer of 1524, Karlstadt was formally expelled from Saxony, after some controversy over the legitimacy of his appointment in Orlamünde. A peripatetic life ensued, where it is not altogether clear whether Karlstadt succeeded in staying clear of the centers of increasingly violent peasant unrest. In the fall of 1524, Karlstadt clearly decided to take Luther and his challenge at his word, and turned out in rapid succession no fewer than eight treatises, seven of which were at a Basel printer's office before the year had passed.[17] Subsequently, Karlstadt claimed that he had had no intention of actually publishing them, a strange explanation that raises the question why, then, he wrote them. No fewer than five of the eight treatises dealt with various aspects of Karlstadt's understanding of the Lord's Supper, particularly the meaning of the words of institution. Three treatises addressed other topics of disagreement, such as *Ob Man gemach fahren* ("Whether One Should Move Slowly"), which was written against Luther's compromising policy of enacting change and the meaning he gave on faith. A final tract, on the baptism of

15. The string of economic and political grievances that led to an uprising in late summer 1524 of peasants and townspeople in southwestern and central Germany was undoubtedly aided by various pronouncements of Martin Luther, who distanced himself the moment the revolutionary character of the uprising became evident. Thomas Muentzer became the public ideologue of the uprising in that he concluded that the same rulers who had suppressed his preaching were also the suppressors of the peasants.

16. The uprising in German called the Peasant's War was waged during 1524–1525. Peasants in southern Germany who were inspired by Luther's Reformation attacks on authority began to demand agrarian rights and freedom from a feudal system in which they were oppressed by nobles and landlords. Luther's condemnation of Müntzer, a supporter of the uprising, likely contributed to the revolt's downfall, in which thousands of peasants were killed.

17. The haunting question is why Karlstadt focused so much in the proper understanding of the Lord's Supper, which, other than through Luther's reinterpretation of the nature of a sacrament, had not been a central issue. Alongside this reinterpretation one sees the central influence of Luther in determining the course and scope of renewal.

infants, is lost; it stands to reason, however, that it most likely rejected the universal practice of infant baptism. Even though the city council of Basel confiscated the manuscript, it is more than probable that its essential argument must have been known to the circle of future Anabaptists in Zurich.[18]

Karlstadt's tracts triggered a discussion among the reformers about the proper biblical understanding of the Lord's Supper. This discussion or debate dominated, inconclusively, the remainder of the decade—and beyond. Early on, the Strasburg reformers were particularly undecided, and in November 1524 they contacted Luther (providing him with several of Karlstadt's treatises) and asked for his opinion. Luther was made aware thereby of Karlstadt's extensive support in south Germany. Luther's *Brief an die Christen zu Strasburg von dem Schwärmergeist* ("Letter to the Christians at Strasburg against the Fanatic Spirit") of December 1524 constituted his initial reaction.[19]

It took Luther about three weeks to complete a comprehensive rebuttal of Karlstadt's notions. Given the formidable array of topics, he decided to publish his retort in two parts, of which the first dealt with faith, together with the use of the word *sacrifice* in conjunction with the Mass; the second part focused exclusively on Karlstadt's understanding of the Lord's Supper and in particular his interpretation of the words of institution.

Luther wrote against Karlstadt in his treatise titled *The Sacrament of the Body and Blood of Christ—Against the Fanatics.*[20] For one, Luther uses the word *Geist* (here translated as "spirit") to refer to Karlstadt, to whom he also as a rule refers as "Doctor," clearly a sarcastic notion that a doctor of theology is so wrong in understanding Scripture properly. But Karlstadt is also *Geist.* What Luther wants to express here is that Karlstadt is not down to earth; as a spirit he hovers over the waters, so to speak. Luther personalized the spirit to describe and also denigrate Karlstadt.

Karlstadt publicly expounded the Christian faith in ways different from Luther who, perhaps with a whiff of overstatement, saw the whole edifice of theological and ecclesiastical reform in danger of collapsing. In the summer of 1524 Luther paid a brief visit to Orlamünde, but it did not go so well. When Luther caused a commotion by insisting that Karlstadt leave the room because he had no business being there, simple peasants sought to instruct him on exegetical issues. Karlstadt and Luther met again to iron out their differences in the Black Bear Inn in Jena,

18. Struebind's study (*Eifriger als Zwingli. Die frühe Täuferbewegung in der Schweiz.* Berlin, 2003) pays considerably more attention to theological forces leading to the affirmation of believer's baptism than was the case in Anabaptist scholarship of the last generation.

19. From 1523 on, when his differences with Luther became blatantly evident, Karlstadt sought to influence the momentum of reform and renewal; the Strasburg clergy were an important factor.

20. LW 36:329–61.

in August 1524,[21] arguably the most dramatic of all Reformation encounters, but that occasion did not go too well, either. Eventually, Luther hurled a gold coin across the table, the symbolic gesture of encouraging Karlstadt to be Luther's public antagonist.[b] One suspects that Luther must have been a bit nonplussed when Karlstadt sallied forth with no fewer than eight treatises (see above).

The Issue of the Words of Institution in the Lord's Supper

In focusing on the meaning of the words of institution, Karlstadt triggered the most fateful intra-Protestant controversy in the sixteenth century—and beyond—over the real presence of Christ in bread and wine. In his 1520 treatise on the *Babylonian Captivity of the Church*, Luther had rejected the Roman Catholic dogma of transubstantiation, the understanding that the pronouncement of the words of institution by the priest turns the substance of the bread into the body of Christ and the substance of the wine into the blood of Christ. This rejection raised the issue of a viable alternate understanding of the words of institution. Rejecting any real presence of body and blood of Christ in the elements of bread and wine, Karlstadt came up with the intriguing notion that the sentence in the Gospel account, "Jesus took bread and blessed and broke it," ended with "Take, eat." Furthermore, he claimed, the next words, "This is my body," were the beginning of a new sentence, thereby grammatically severing the connection between the eating and the body. Interestingly, Karlstadt argued that when speaking the words "this is my body . . . ," Jesus had pointed at himself. This prompted a facetious Lutheran to say that, while it worked for the bread, for the wine it presumed that Jesus had a nosebleed.

---

b See here the contemporary account *Wes sich Doctor Andreas Bodenstein von Karlstadt mit Doctor Martino Luther beredet zu Jena, und wie sie wider einander zu schreiben sich entschlossen haben.* Idem. *die Handlung Doctor Martini Luthers mit dem Rath und Gemeine der Stadt Orlamünd, am Tag Bartholomäi daselbst geschehen.* [*Acta Ienensia.*] 1524. WA 15:327.

Karlstadt, who been expelled from Saxony as a troublemaker, perhaps even a political one, was making a considerable impact in his peripatetic travels in south Germany, including the crew of Strasburg reformers, who in their perplexity had written Luther (23 November 1524), asking for his views. There clearly was sympathy for Karlstadt's interpretation of the sacrament. Luther answered with his *Letter to the Christians at Strasburg* of December 1524.[22] When Karlstadt's eight tracts came to Luther's attention, he seemed apprehensive of their impact and decided to write a comprehensive repudiation. In his letter to the Strasburg clergy he had briefly enumerated (in a somewhat self-conscious pastoral tone) his main issues with Karlstadt and mentioned that a comprehensive assessment of Karlstadt's theology was called for. This assessment took the form of the treatise *Against the Heavenly Prophets Concerning Images and the Sacrament* (*Wider die himmlischen Propheten, von den Bildern und Sakrament*).

22. *Ein brieff an die Christen zů Straßburg/ wider den schwermer geyst.* Martini Luther. Straßburg, 1525. VD16 L 4156. LW 40:61–71.

Luther's Response

Several aspects of Luther's treatise merit attention. One is that the number of reprints of both sections, roughly a dozen, clearly indicates the interest and involvement of other reformers in south Germany and Switzerland. The treatise shows Luther at both his best and worst. It is Luther at his best, because he succeeds in relating the specific issues at hand to the grander themes of the Christian faith. Once again there is the theme of Christian freedom that permeates most prominently Luther's reflections.[23] Related is Luther's emphasis on the "inwardness" of the faith, causing him to accuse Karlstadt of focusing too much on externals. Luther also outlines once more the proper sequence of how one comes to the Christian faith: from recognition of sin to trust in divine forgiveness, and a new walk of life. Luther argues this to be the proper sequence and accuses Karlstadt of reversing this sequence by focusing on the externals of the walk of life. As regard to the words of institution in communion, Luther enunciates their interpretation in the way his view has entered the history of theology: the words mean literally what they say.

At the same time, the treatise also shows Luther at his worst. His language is frequently abusive. Perhaps even more striking is the fierceness and intensity with which he attacks Karlstadt. He

23. E.g., see *On the Freedom of a Christian*, LW 31:[329–31] 333–77; also TAL, vol. 1.

did so by invoking a wide diapason of literary styles—sarcasm, irony, attacks on the opponents' integrity. It was forgotten for a decade that the two had been colleagues and (one presumes) friends. Here was no minor disagreement on related theological issues. On the contrary, the issue at stake was enough to agitate, by 1524, the entire camp of reformers of whatever stripe. It must not be forgotten that Luther himself had contributed to the beginnings of the discussion with his declaration, in his treatise *On the Babylonian Captivity of the Church*, that a sacrament is only effective through the faith of the recipient.

Despite the divergence of their respective understanding of the Christian faith, the two men also misunderstood each other. Luther appeared convinced that Karlstadt had revolutionary tendencies, despite the fact that Karlstadt had all along rejected violence in the name of the Christian faith, and had rejected Thomas Müntzer's invitation to join the Allstedt League of the Elect.[24] At issue was the pursuit of religious goals (for which, in fact, even the mainstream reformers needed the support of the political authorities) or of political objectives as were pursued by townspeople and peasants in 1524.

Karlstadt's response to Luther's allegation was published in 1524 in Wittenberg. This response showed that Karlstadt was steadfast in his rejection of the violence that led to the German Peasants' War. Another charge was Luther's accusation that Karlstadt was not authorized to preach at the city church in Wittenberg during Luther's stay at Wartburg. In September 1524 Karlstadt was exiled from Saxony by the order of Elector Frederick the Wise (1465–1525) and Duke George of Saxony (1471–1539). The tenor of Luther's treatise alternated between sadness that he and Karlstadt no longer saw eye to eye, and scathing satire and sarcasm, arguably the worst in any of Luther's writings. His vile remarks made it clear that Karlstadt had gotten under his theological skin, with only an occasional glimpse of the former friendship between the two colleagues remaining. Karlstadt had also been a bit on the prickly side in his eight tracts, while Luther increasingly saw himself as the very center of the new theology and wanted to make sure that there be no dissent in the reformers' ranks.

24. It has been generally accepted in scholarship that after his expulsion from Allstedt, Thomas Müntzer became a major leader and ideologue of the peasants. See n. 16, p. 44. It seems more realistic to see him as chaplain of the peasants, who offered a salvation-history kind of reading of the uprising and demands from the biblical text. See *Thomas Müntzer - Zeitgenossen - Nachwelt. Sigfried Bräuer zum 80. Geburtstag.* Muehlhausen, 2010. Harmut Kuhne, Hans-Jurgen Goertz, Thomas T. Muller and Gunter Voglers, eds. (Muhlhasen: Verroffentlichungen der Thomas-Muntzer-Gesellschaft, 2010).

The Text

Thus it was largely on the question of the actual implementation of reform and the meaning of the sacraments that Karlstadt opposed and challenged Luther. Luther became convinced of the seriousness of Karlstadt's challenge and began his *Against the Heavenly Prophets*. The work expanded, and Luther decided to divide it into two parts. The first was ready by the end of December 1524, the second a month later in January 1525. The first section dealt with the topic of images, the second with the sacrament of the altar. But Luther also offered throughout the treatise an incisive delineation of the relation of law and freedom, accusing Karlstadt of having lapsed into works righteousness and arguing vigorously for Christian freedom. This is where the famous sentence from Luther occurs that the law of Moses is for the Jews what the Saxon Mirror, *Sachsenspiegel*,[25] is for Germans.

Finally, the full meaning of Luther's title for the text must not be ignored. The enemy explicitly was the "heavenly prophets," and Luther clearly wanted to demonstrate that it was not only Karlstadt who misinterpreted the authentic faith, but also a whole coterie of "spirits" or "prophets" who were doing the same. Chief among them was Thomas Müntzer,[26] who according to Luther not only perverted the true faith but was also a revolutionary (in conjunction with the uprising of the peasants). Luther must have seen a conspiracy of sorts at work, a dangerous enemy, a phalanx out to demolish and destroy what the recovery of the gospel had brought.

Thus it was on the question of the sacraments that the two erstwhile colleagues clashed. Karlstadt's tracts with their delineation of the new view of the Lord's Supper helped trigger, together with an open letter by a Dutch physician by the name of Cornelisz Hoen (1460–1524),[27] the first communion controversy in the ranks of the reformers.

Whatever the theological insights of the tract, the most salient characteristic is its abusive, even violent style. Thus, while Karlstadt's name is frequently mentioned, even more frequent are the references to the *Geist* (here translated as "spirit"). What Luther meant to denote thereby was that instead of relying on the word, Karlstadt relied on the inspiration of some sort of spirit. As is not surprising in view of the intensity of polemic, Luther offered a distorted view of Karlstadt's views. Luther

25. At the same time, Luther argues in the text that the Ten Commandments also include universally valid natural law.

26. The sources allow us to see Müntzer as a kind of spiritual guide or leader of the insurrectionist peasants.

27. See here Bart Jan Spruyt, *Cornelius Henrici Hoen (Honius) and His Epistle on the Eucharist (1525): Medieval Heresy, Erasmian Humanism, and Reform in the Early Sixteenth-Century Low Countries* (Leiden: Brill, 2003).

accused Karlstadt of putting the law ahead of the gospel, but that is exactly what Karlstadt did not do. Even the interpretation of the words of institution in the Lord's Supper was a disagreement over grammar, not one of word against spirit. Luther was profoundly upset by Karlstadt's notions because they suggested that Scripture, the new locus of authority, could be interpreted differently. And while Luther derided the Orlamünde peasant who offered a rather bizarre biblical justification for the removal of images, the peasant can surely be said to have taken Luther's appeal to take the Word seriously. The primacy of the word of God as a basis for all doctrines caused Luther to repel the mysticism that underlay Karlstadt's notions.[28]

28. See also Karlstadt's *Missiue vonn der allerhochste tugent gelassenheyt*, published first in Wittenberg in 1529.

AGAINST THE HEAVENLY PROPHETS CONCERNING IMAGES AND SACRAMENTS[29]

29. The translation follows a German text as printed in Wittenberg in 1525. See WA 18:62–125, 134–214. This English rendition is based on the translation by Bernard Erling and Conrad Bergendoff in LW 40:79–223. There were no fewer than nine reprints in 1525, from important presses in Strasburg, Augsburg, and Nuremberg.

Part I

IN THE NAME OF GOD and our dear Lord Jesus Christ. There has been a change in the weather. I had almost relaxed and thought the issue was dead; but then it suddenly arose again and it is as the wise man says: "When you are finished, you must begin again" [Sir. 18:6].

Doctor Andreas Karlstadt has deserted us and has become our worst enemy. May Christ grant that we are not alarmed and give us his mind and courage, that we will not err and despair before Satan who pretends to vindicate the sacrament, but has much else in mind. Since he has not thus far succeeded to suppress the teaching of the gospel through force, he seeks to destroy it with a cunning interpretation of Scripture.

I have anticipated, and my prophecy will become true (I fear), that God will visit our ingratitude and permit the truth to be cast down, as Daniel says (Dan. 8:[12]). Because we persecute and reject the truth, we must again deal with vain error, false spirits, and prophets. These have been with us to some extent for three years, though thus far hindered by his grace.[30] Otherwise they would long ago have wrought havoc in our ranks. Whether God will keep this disturbance in check any longer, I do not know, since no one cares, no one prays for it, and all are without fear, as though the devil were sleeping who, however, goes about as a furious lion [I Pet. 5:8]. Although I hope that there will be no restraint as long as I live. Therefore, as long as I live, I will resist as God gives me strength, and be of help whomever it will help. And this is my earnest, sincere warning and admonition:

First, that everyone with complete earnestness pray to God for a proper understanding and for God's holy, pure Word. In view of the fact that with such a mighty ruler and God of this world—the devil—it is not within our power to preserve either faith or God's Word, there must be divine power which protects it, as Psalm 12 well prays and says [Ps. 12:6-8], "The promises of the LORD are promises that are pure, purified seven times. Do thou, O LORD, protect us, guard us ever from this generation. On every side the wicked prowl, as vileness is exalted among the sons of humanity." If we boast that we have God's Word and do not take care as to how we are to keep it, it is soon lost.

Second, we, too, ought to do our part and not close our eyes, but be on guard. For God always holds his grace firmly over the world, so that he allows no false prophets to attempt anything except external matters, such as works and subtle minute findings about external matters. No one is concerned with faith and a good conscience before God, only with what glitters and shines before reason and the world. Just as the Arians apparently put up a good case in the court of reason, when they alleged that God was only one person, the Father, while the Son and the Holy Spirit were not true God.[31]

Likewise, it was easy and pleasant for the Jews[32] and Pelagius to believe that works without grace made one pious; and under the papacy it was said attractively that the free will of humans also contributes something toward grace.[33] So, since it is in accord with reason, it sounds altogether agreeable to say that there is simply bread and wine in the sacrament. Who cannot

30. Luther, writing in 1525, is referring to the disturbances that occurred in Wittenberg under the aegis of Karlstadt in the spring of 1522. Strikingly, Luther acknowledges with his reference to "his grace" that the Saxon authorities had lined up behind Luther's strategy of slow reform.

31. The Arians, a theological movement declared heretical by the Latin church, derived their name from Arius (c. 250–336), of Alexandria, who proposed early in the fourth century the notion that there had been a time when Jesus was not in existence and therefore he is not God in the full sense. The consequence of this view is, of course, that Jesus cannot be understood as fully God. Arius's teaching was declared heretical by the first Council of Nicaea in 325. The so-called Nicene Creed is the creedal manifestation of the conciliar decision. On Arianism, see Carlos R. Galvão-Sobrinho, *Doctrine and Power: Theological Controversy and Christian Leadership in the Later Roman Empire* (Berkeley: University of California, 2013).

32. Luther frequently refers to Judaism as an example for a religion "of works."

33. The name derived from the English monk Pelagius (c. 354–c. 420) who argued the essential good of humans who would be able to fulfill the divine commandments if only properly taught. Pelagius's great adversary, Augustine (354–430), bishop of Hippo, saw to it that Western theology asserted the depravity of all human beings. On

Pelagius, see John Ferguson, *Pelagius: A Historical and Theological Study* (Ann Arbor, MI: AMS, 1977); B. R. Rees, *Pelagius: A Reluctant Heretic* (Suffolk: Boydell, 1991); and Robert F. Evans, *Pelagius: Inquiries and Reappraisals* (London: A. & C. Black, 1968).

34. Refers to the iconoclastic reactions in Wittenberg in the spring of 1522.

35. This reference to Christians wearing such simple gray garb occurs repeatedly in answer to Luther's polemic against Karlstadt as an indication of a form of works righteousness.

36. Luther's dismay over any form of works righteousness is evident here.

believe that? If anyone today would grant to the Jews that Christ was simply human, I think it would be easy to convert them.

So our concern here should now be that we keep these two teachings far apart from each other: the one that teaches the main articles of the faith, to govern conscience in the spirit before God; the other, which teaches external matters or works. For more hinges on the teaching of faith and a good conscience than on the teaching of good works. When works are lacking, help and counsel are at hand so that one can produce them if the teaching of faith remains firm and pure. But if the teaching of faith is pushed into the background and works are put forward, then nothing can be good and there is neither counsel nor help. Then works lead to vain glory and seem to people to be something great, while God's glory disappears.

So it is with these honor-seeking "prophets" who do nothing but break images, destroy churches, abuse and manhandle the sacrament, and seek a new kind of mortification, that is, a self-chosen putting the flesh to death.[34] Thus far they have not set aright the conscience, which is nonetheless most important and most necessary in the Christian teaching, as has been said.

And if they had completely succeeded so that there were no images, no churches, no one in all the whole world held that the flesh and blood of Christ were in the sacrament and all went about in gray peasant garb, what would be accomplished thereby?[35] What did they expect to achieve by pressing, straining, and pursuing this course of action? Would they thereby have become Christian? Where would faith and love be? Should they come later? Why should they not have precedence? Fame, vain glory, and a new monkery[36] would well thereby be achieved, as happens in all works, but the conscience would not be helped in any way. Thus such false spirits do not care where faith or love are to be found, just as the pope does not care, but presses on if only he can make sure of the works belonging to his obedience and laws. And when they do occur, still nothing has occurred.

Since Dr. Karlstadt pursues the same route and despite his many books does not even teach what faith and love are (yes, they speak derisively and disdainfully of us on this account, as though it were an unimportant good teaching), but emphasizes external works, let everyone be warned of him. Everyone should know that he has a perverted spirit that thinks only of murdering the conscience with laws, sin, and good works, so that thereby nothing is set aright, even if everything happened that he professes in all his books, and with mouth and heart. Even rascals are able to do and teach all that he urges. Therefore, something higher must be present to absolve and comfort the conscience. This is the Holy Spirit, who is not acquired through the destruction of images or any other good works, but only through the gospel and faith.

Now in order that we do not open our mouths too wide and marvel at the skill of these false spirits, and thereby abandon the main articles of the faith, and thus deceitfully be led off the track (for thereby the devil succeeds through these prophets), I will here briefly recount these articles of the Christian faith to which everyone is above all things to hold fast and pay attention.

The first is the law of God, which is to be preached so that one thereby reveals and teaches how to recognize sin (Rom. 3[:20] and 7[:7]), as we have often shown in our writings. However, these prophets do not understand this correctly, for this means a truly spiritual preaching of the Law, as Paul says in Rom. 7[:14], and a right use of the Law, as he says in 1 Tim. 1[:8].[37]

Secondly, when sin is recognized and the law is so preached that conscience is alarmed and humbled before God's wrath, we are then to preach the comforting word of the gospel and the forgiveness of sins, so that the conscience again may be comforted and established in the grace of God, etc.

Christ himself teaches these two articles in such order (Luke 24[:47]). One must preach repentance and the forgiveness of sins in his name. "And the Spirit (he says in John [16:8]) will convince the world of sin and of righteousness and of judgment." You do not find either of these two articles in these false prophets. They do not understand them, and yet these are the most important and necessary articles.

The third is judgment, the work of putting to death the old person, as in Romans 5, 6, and 7. This involves works, and suffering and affliction, as we through discipline and fasting, watching, working, etc., or through persecution and disgrace put to death our flesh. This putting to death is also not handled correctly by these false prophets. For they do not accept what God gives them, but what they themselves choose. They wear gray garb, as if they were and would be as peasants, and carry on with such foolish nonsense.[38]

37. Luther here summarizes what has been called the "three uses of the law."

38. Luther here comments sarcastically on Karlstadt's demeanor while at Orlamünde. Karlstadt's response was simple: "of what harm is my common attire, since I do not give occasion with my gray garb to suspect a false kind of holiness as Doctor Luther does with his monk's cowl" (WA 18:64).

In the fourth place, such works of love toward the neighbor should flow forth in meekness, patience, kindness, teaching, support, and counsel, spiritually and physically, free and for nothing, as Christ has dealt with us.

In the fifth and final place, we ought to proclaim the law and its works, not for the Christians, but for the crude and unbelieving people. For among Christians, we must use the law spiritually, as was said above, to reveal sin. But among the crude masses, on Mr. Everyman and Mrs. Everywoman,[39] we must use it bodily and roughly, so that they know what works of the law they are to do and what works ought to be left undone. Thus they are compelled by sword and law to be outwardly pious, much in the manner in which we control wild animals with chains and pens, so that external peace will exist among the people. To this end temporal authority is ordained, which God would have us honor and fear (Rom. 13[:1]; 1 Pet. 3) [1 Pet. 2:13, 17].

However, we must see to it that we retain Christian freedom and do not force laws and works on the Christian conscience, as if through them one were upright or a sinner. Here questions are in order concerning the place of foods, clothing, places, persons, and all external things, etc. Whoever does not teach according to this order certainly does not teach correctly. From which you now see that Dr. Karlstadt and his spirits replace the highest with the lowest, the best with the worst, the first with the last. Yet he would be considered the greatest spirit of all, he who has devoured the Holy Spirit feathers and all.[40]

Therefore I beg every Christian who observes how we bicker in this matter to remember that we are not dealing with important issues, but with the most trivial ones. Bear in mind that the devil is eager to spruce up such minor matters, thereby drawing the attention of the people away so that the truly important matters are neglected, as long as they go in his direction. From this everyone should recognize Dr. Karlstadt's false and evil spirit. He is not content to be silent about and ignore the great and significant articles; he inflates the least significant ones as if the salvation of the world depended more on them than on Christ. Also, he compels us to turn from the important articles to minor ones, so that we lose time and are in danger of forgetting the main articles of the faith. Let this be the first fruit by which one is able to know this tree [Matt. 7:16–20]. [. . .]

39. The original German word here is *Herr Omnes*, meaning "everybody." The word is undoubtedly a German rendering of the title figure of the late fifteenth-century English morality play *The Summoning of Everyman*.

40. A reference to the standard iconographic portrayal of the Holy Spirit as a dove.

On the Destruction of Images

I approached the task of destroying images by first tearing them out of the heart through God's Word and making them worthless and despised. This indeed took place before Dr. Karlstadt ever dreamed of destroying images. For when they are no longer in the heart, they can do no harm when seen with the eyes. But Dr. Karlstadt, who pays no attention to matters of the heart, has reversed the order by removing them from sight and leaving them in the heart. For he does not preach faith, nor is he able to preach it; unfortunately, only now do I see that. Which of these two forms of destroying images is best, I will let all people judge for themselves.

For where the heart is instructed that we please God alone through faith, and that in the matter of images nothing that is pleasing to God takes place, but is a fruitless service and effort, people themselves willingly drop it, despise images, and have none made. But where one neglects such instruction and forces the issue, it follows that those blaspheme who do not understand and who act only because of the coercion of the law and not with a free conscience. Their idea that they can please God with works becomes a real idol and a false assurance in the heart. Such legalism results in putting away outward images while filling the heart with idols.

I say this so that everyone may see the kind of a spirit that is lodged in Karlstadt. He blames me for protecting images contrary to God's Word, though he knows that I seek to tear them out of the hearts of all and want them despised and destroyed. It is only that I do not approve of his wanton violence and impetuosity. If the Holy Spirit were here, the Holy Spirit would not lie as knowingly and unashamedly as that, but would say, "Yes, dear Luther, I am well pleased that you so utterly destroy images in the heart. Thereby it will be all the easier for me to destroy them before the eyes, and I accept your help as necessary to this end." Now I am supposed to be acting contrary to God's Word, and protect images, I who do destroy images outwardly and inwardly. And I am not to say that those act contrary to God's Word, who only smashes them in pieces outwardly, while he permits idols to remain in the heart and sets up others alongside them, namely, false confidence and pride in works.

41. Luther is thinking about governmental authority of the two swords and order, etc. Unlike medieval theology, which saw church and state as immediately tied together, making the state the servant of the church and vice versa, Luther argued for their clear separation.

42. Karlstadt had taunted Luther for proceeding too slowly with the implementation of practical reform measures. He did so particularly in his tract *Ob man gemach faren/und des ergernüssen der schwachen verschonen soll/ in sachen so gottis willen angehn. Andres Carolstadt. M.D.XXIIII* (Basel: Thomas, 1524) ("If one should move slowly").

43. Luther is here referring throughout to the First Commandment, making it the core consideration for the discussion of images.

Furthermore, I have allowed and not forbidden the outward removal of images, so long as it takes place without rioting and tumult and is done by the proper authorities.[41] In the world it is considered foolish to conceal the true reason for a good venture out of fear that it may fail.[42] However, when Karlstadt disregards my spiritual and orderly removal of images and makes me out to be only a "protector of images," it is an example of his holy and prophetic art, though I only resisted his factious, violent, and fanatical spirit. Now since the evil spirit sits so firmly in his mind, I am less than ever inclined to yield to obstinacy and wrong. I will first discuss images according to the Law of Moses, and then according to the gospel. And I say at the outset that according to the Law of Moses, no other images are forbidden than an image of God that is worshiped. A crucifix, on the other hand, or any other holy image is not forbidden. Wait a minute! You breakers of images, I defy you to prove the opposite!

In proof of this, I cite the first commandment (Exod. 20[:3]): "You shall have no other gods before me." Immediately, following this text, the meaning of having other gods is made plain in the words: "You shall not make yourself a graven image, or any likeness . . ." [Exod. 20:4]. This is said of the same gods, etc. And although these spirits cling to the little word "make" and stubbornly insist, "Make, make is something else than to worship," yet they must admit that this commandment basically speaks of nothing else than of the glory of God. It must certainly be "molded" if it is to be worshiped, and unmade if it is not to be worshiped. It is not valid, however, to single out one word and keep repeating it. One must consider the meaning of the entire text in its context. Then one sees that it speaks of images of God which are not to be worshiped. No one will be able to prove anything else. From subsequent words in the same chapter [Exod. 20:23], "You shall not make gods of silver to be with me, nor shall you make for yourselves gods of gold," it follows that "make" certainly refers to such gods.

For this saying, "You shall have no other gods," is the central thought, the standard, and the end in accordance with which all the words that follow are to be interpreted, connected, and judged.[43] For this passage points out and expresses the meaning of this commandment, namely, that there are to be no other gods. Therefore the words "make," "images," "serve," etc., and whatever else follows, are to be understood in no other sense than that neither gods nor idolatry are to develop therefrom. Even as the words "I am your God" [Exod. 20:2] are the standard and end for all that may be said about the worship and service of God. And it would be foolish if I sought to conclude from this something that had nothing to do with the divine or the service of God, such as building houses, plowing, etc. No conclusion can be drawn from the words, "You shall have no other gods," other than that which refers to idolatry. Where, however, images or statues are made without idolatry, then such is not forbidden, for the central saying, "You shall have no other gods," remains intact.

If they do not want to apply "make" to images of God, as the text requires, then I will also say that worship is not forbidden (since we are clinging so strictly to the letter). For in the first commandment nothing is said about worship. I might say, "Don't make images yourself. Let others make them. But you are not forbidden to worship them." If they, however, from other passages connect "make" with "worship," which is not done in this text, then in all fairness I may connect in the same text "make" with the gods, as the text clearly states. Thus we have no example of punishment being inflicted on account of images and altars, but it has followed on account of worship. We read thus that Moses' brazen serpent remained [Num. 21:8] until Hezekiah destroyed it solely because it had been worshiped [2 Kings 18:4].

Concerning this I have a powerful passage in Lev. 26[:1], "I am the LORD your God. You shall make for yourselves no idols and erect no graven image or pillar, and you shall not set up a figured stone in your land, to bow down to them." How is this? Here I think the interpretation is sufficiently clear. It is because of worship that idols and figured stones are forbidden. It is without doubt so that they will not be worshiped, and where they are not worshiped they might well be set up and made. What would be the need otherwise of referring to bowing down? Therefore the "making" in the first commandment must refer to worshiping and to no more. So also in Deut. 4[:15f.], where it is forbidden to make images, the passage speaks clearly of worship. [. . .]

Now I wonder what these Jewish saints, who hold so strictly to the Law of Moses and rage against images, do about the images on coins and jewelry. For I hear they have much money

44. Luther, by using the phrase "Jewish saints," both symbolically and literally calls attention to medieval anti-Jewish stereotypes that Jews through usury became rich. At the same time, he has again Karlstadt and his followers in mind.

45. Joachimsthal was a town in the northwest region of Bohemia, known for the silver mines in the vicinity.

46. The silver coins minted were in the sixteenth century known as *thaler*, from the "thal" of Joachimsthal, leading to the word *dollar* and similar terms in other languages. According to tradition, Joachim was the husband of St. Anne, therefore the father of Jesus' mother.

47. Luther here wants to show that Karlstadt and his followers gorge in medieval mysticism with its special vocabulary.

and jewelry.[44] In Joachimsthal[45] St. Joachim is minted on coins.[46] It would be my advice that one should rescue these great saints from sin, taking from them the guilders and the silver coins and goblets. For though they may be opposed to images, it is to be feared that they have not "put away all selfish desire" nor advanced in their "concentration," "adoration," and "sprinkling" to the point where they are of themselves able to cast away these treasures.[47] Human nature is probably still so weak that even the living voice from heaven is not strong enough for the task.[c] To accomplish it, good strong apprentices are needed, who otherwise wouldn't have much to fritter away.

This breaking of images has also another weakness in that they themselves do it in a disorderly way, and do not proceed with proper authority. As when their prophets stand, crying and arousing the common people, saying: hey, hew, rip, rend, smash, dash, stab, strike, run, throw, hit the idols in the mouth! If you see a crucifix, spit on its face, etc. This is to do away with images in a Karlstadtian manner, to make the common people furious and foolish, and secretly to accustom them to insurrection. Those who rush into this thing think they are now great saints, and become proud and impudent beyond all measure. When one looks at the matter more closely, one finds it is a work of the law that has taken place without the spirit and faith. Yet it makes for pride of heart, as though they by such works had gained a special status before God. Actually this means teaching works and the free will all over again.

We read however in Moses (Exod. 18[:20ff.]) that he appointed chiefs, magistrates, and temporal authority before he gave the law, and in many places he teaches: One is to try, judge, and punish in all cases with justice, witnesses, and in an orderly way. Otherwise, why have judges and sovereigns in the land? Karlstadt always skips over this matter altogether too easily. What Moses commands, Karlstadt applies to the disorderly common people and teaches them to break into this field in disorder like pigs. This certainly is and must be called a seditious and rebellious spirit, which despises authority and itself behaves wantonly as

c   See Karlstadt's important tract *Missiue von der aller hochsten tugent gelassenhait. Andree Bodenstayn von Carolstat Doctor* (Augsburg, 1520 VD16 B 6170). Karlstadt spoke much of "*Gelassenheit*," the willingness and ability to "let go" earthly notions and desires.

though it were lord in the land and above the law. Where one permits the common people to break images without having proper authority, one must also permit anyone to proceed to kill adulterers, murderers, the disobedient, etc. For God commanded the people of Israel to kill these just as much as to put away images. Oh, what sort of business and government that would turn out to be! Therefore, though I have not said that Dr. Karlstadt is a murderous prophet, yet he has a rebellious, murderous, seditious spirit in him, which, if given an opportunity, would assert itself.[48]

For this reason we always read in the Old Testament, where images or idols were removed, that this was done not by the common people, but by the authorities, just as Jacob buried the idols of his household [Gen. 35:4]. Thus Gideon pulled down the altar of Baal when he was called by God to be a chief [Judg. 6:27]. Thus Jehu the king (not the crowd) demolished Ahab's Baal [2 Kings 10:26ff.]. So did Hezekiah also with the bronze serpent [2 Kings 18:4]. Josiah did the same with the altars at Bethel [2 Kings 23:15]. From this one sees clearly that where God tells the community to do something and speaks to the people, God does not want it done by the common people without the proper authorities, but through the proper authorities in conjunction with the people. Moreover, he requires this so that the dog does not learn to eat leather on the leash, that is, lest accustomed to insurrection in connection with images, the people also rebel against the authorities. Talk of the devil and his imps.

Now that we are under our princes, lords, and emperors, we must outwardly obey their laws instead of the laws of Moses. We should therefore be calm and humbly petition them to put away such images. Where they will not do so, we nonetheless have God's word meanwhile, whereby they may be put out of the heart, until they are forcibly put away outwardly by those properly authorized. However, when these prophets hear this, they call it papistic and fawning before princes.[49] That they, on the other hand, arouse the disorderly common people and make them rebellious, that is not to fawn. Thus we will not be cleared of fawning until we teach the common people to kill the princes and the lords. However, if I am a papist or one who fawns before princes, of that the pope and the princes themselves should be more honest witnesses than this lying spirit, who here speaks. For he well knows that the contrary is known to the whole world.

48. In the famous encounter and conversation with Luther in the Black Bear Inn in Jena, Karlstadt complained that Luther misrepresented him in the matter of obedience to governmental authority. See WA 15:335ff. and the detailed discussion in WA 4:366ff.

49. Luther must have Thomas Müntzer in mind, whose attacks on Luther were more severe. Müntzer, whose eloquence rivaled that of Luther, had a long list of taunting terms for Luther, such as *Doctor Luegner* ("Doctor Liar") and *"sanftlebige Fleisch zu Wittenberg"* ("a soft-living flesh in Wittenberg"); see Thomas Müntzer, *Von dem getichten glawben auff nechst Protestation außgang Tome Muentzers Selwerters zu Alstet* (Eilenburg, 1524). The best study in English is Abraham Friesen, *Thomas Müntzer, a Destroyer of the Godless: The Making of a Sixteenth-Century Religious Revolutionary* (Berkeley: University of California Press, 1990).

Let this be said about images strictly according to the Law of Moses. The meaning is not that I wish to defend images, as has been sufficiently indicated. Rather, murderous spirits are not to be permitted to create sinful behavior and problems of conscience where none exist, and murder souls without necessity. For although the matter of images is a minor, external thing, when one seeks to burden the conscience with sin through it, as through the law of God, it becomes the most important of all. For it destroys faith, profanes the blood of Christ, blasphemes the gospel, and puts all that Christ has won for us at naught, so that this Karlstadtian abomination is no less effective in destroying the kingdom of Christ and a good conscience than the papacy has become with its prohibitions regarding food and marriage, and all else that was free and without sin. For eating and drinking are also minor, external things. Yet to ensnare the conscience with laws in these matters is death for the soul.

From this let every person note which of us two is the more Christian. I would release and free consciences and the souls from sin, which is a truly spiritual and evangelical pastoral function, while Karlstadt seeks to capture them with laws and burden them with sin without good cause. And yet he does this not with the law of God, but with his own conceit and mischief, so that he is not only far from the gospel, but also not even a Mosaic teacher. And yet he continually praises the "Word of God, the Word of God," just as if it were therefore to become God's Word as soon as one could say the Word of God. Usually those who make great ado about praising God's Word do not have much to back them up, as unfortunately we have previously experienced under our papistic tyrants.[50]

However, to speak evangelically[51] of images, I say and declare that no one is obligated to break violently images even of God, but everything is free, and one does not sin if one does not break them with violence. One is obligated, however, to destroy them with the Word of God, that is, not with the law in a Karlstadtian manner, but with the gospel. This means to instruct and enlighten the conscience that it is idolatry to worship them, or to trust in them, since one is to trust alone in Christ. Beyond this let the external matters take their course. God grant that they may be destroyed, become dilapidated, or that they remain. It is all the same and makes no difference, just as when the poison has been removed from a snake.

50. Here, as throughout his treatise, Luther again uses the derogatory word *papistisch* instead of the common place *paepstlich*.

51. E.g., on the basis of the gospel.

Now I say this to keep the conscience free from mischievous laws and fictitious sins, and not because I would defend images. Nor would I condemn those who have destroyed them, especially those who destroy divine and idolatrous images. But images for memorial and witness, such as crucifixes and images of saints, are to be tolerated. This is shown above to be the case even in the Mosaic Law. And they are not only to be tolerated, but for the sake of the memorial and the witness they are praiseworthy and honorable, as the witness stones of Joshua [Josh. 24:26] and of Samuel (1 Sam. 7[:12]).

The destruction and demolishing of images at Eichen, Grimmenthal, and Birnbaum,[52] or places to which pilgrimages are made for the adoration of images (for such are truly idolatrous images and the devil's hospices), is praiseworthy and good. However, to teach that those who do not demolish them are therefore sinners is to go too far and to require more than is necessary of Christians who do enough when they fight and struggle against images with God's Word.

If you say, however, "Yes, but while they remain, some will be offended by them and attracted to them," I answer: What can I do about that, I who as a Christian have no power on earth? Appoint a preacher who will instruct the people against them, or arrange to have them removed in an orderly way, not with tumult and riots.

Now then, let us get to the bottom of it all and say that these teachers of sin and of Mosaic prophets are not to confuse us with Moses. We do not want to see or hear Moses. How do you like that, my dear rebels?[53] We say further, that all these Mosaic teachers deny the gospel, banish Christ, and annul the whole New Testament. I now speak as a Christian to Christians. For Moses is given to the Jewish people alone, and does not concern us Gentiles and Christians. We have our gospel and New Testament. If they can prove from them that images must be put away, we will gladly follow them. If they, however, through Moses would make us Jews, we will not endure it.

What do you think? What will become of this? It will become evident that these factious spirits understand nothing in the Scriptures, neither Moses nor Christ, and neither seek nor find anything therein but their own dreams. And our basis for this assertion is from St. Paul (1 Tim. 1[:9]), "The law is not laid down for the just" (which a Christian is). And Peter (Acts 15[:10-11]),

52. Three village communities in Thuringia and Saxony that were traditional pilgrimage centers.

53. Another derogatory term: Luther means to chide Karlstadt for "rebelling" against the clear meaning of the text.

"Now therefore why do you try God by putting a yoke upon the neck of the disciples which neither our fathers nor we have been able to bear? But we believe that we shall be saved through the grace of the Lord Jesus, just as they will." With this saying (as Paul with his) Peter abrogates for the Christian the whole of Moses with all his laws.

Yes, you say, that is perhaps true with respect to the ceremonial and the judicial law, that is, what Moses teaches about the external order of worship or of government. But the Decalogue, that is, the Ten Commandments, are not abrogated. There is nothing of ceremonial and judicial law in them. I answer: I know very well that this is an old and common distinction, but it is not an intelligent one. For out of the Ten Commandments flow and depend all the other commandments and the whole of Moses.

Because God would be the only God and have no other gods, etc., God instituted many different ceremonies or forms of worship. Through these God interpreted the first commandment and taught how it is to be kept. To promote obedience to parents, and unwilling to tolerate adultery, murder, stealing, or false witness, God gave the judicial law or external government so that such commandments will be understood and observed.

Thus it is not true that there is no ceremonial or judicial law in the Ten Commandments. Such laws are in the Decalogue, depend on it, and belong there. And to indicate this, God expressly introduced two ceremonial laws, namely, concerning images and the sabbath. We can show that these two are ceremonial laws which are, each in its way, abrogated in the New Testament, so that one may see how Dr. Karlstadt deals about as wisely with the sabbath as with images in his book. For St. Paul (Col. 2[:16-17]) speaks frankly and clearly: "Therefore let no one pass judgment on you in questions of food and drink or with regard to a festival or a new moon or a sabbath. These are only a shadow of what is to come." Here Paul expressly abrogates the sabbath and calls it a shadow now past, since the body, which is Christ himself, has come.

Also, Galatians 4[:10-11], "You observe days, and months, and seasons, and years! I am afraid I have labored over you in vain." Here Paul calls it lost labor to observe days and seasons, among which is also the sabbath. Isaiah has also prophesied this (Isa. 66[:23]), "From new moon to new moon, and from Sabbath to Sabbath," that is, there shall be a daily sabbath in the New Testament, with no difference as to time.[54]

We must be grateful to Paul and Isaiah, that they so long ago freed us from these factious spirits. Otherwise we should have to sit through the sabbath day with "head in hand" awaiting the heavenly voice, as these spirits would delude us. Yes, if Karlstadt were to write more about the sabbath, even Sunday would have to give way, and the sabbath, that is, Saturday, would be observed. He would truly make us Jews in all things, so that we also would have to be circumcised, etc.

For it is true, and no one can deny it, that whoever keeps the Law of Moses as a law of Moses, or deems it necessary to keep it, must regard the keeping of all laws as necessary, as St. Paul (Gal. 5[:3]) concludes and says, "Every man who receives circumcision—he is bound to keep the whole law." Therefore also, whoever destroys images, or observes the Sabbath (that is, whoever teaches that it must be kept), that person also must surrender to let himself be circumcised and keep the whole Mosaic Law. In time (where one leaves room for these spirits) they would surely be compelled to do, teach, and observe this. However, by God's grace they now do even as St. Paul says (Gal. 6[:13]), "For even those who receive circumcision do not themselves keep the law, but they desire to have you circumcised that they may glory in your flesh." Thus the image breakers themselves do not keep the law. For just as they fail to keep all the other laws, so also they destroy images unspiritually, as a work, so that they lose Christ, the fulfillment of the law, and seek only that they may attain a glory in us, as if they had taught something excellent and masterful. [...]

[Paul] especially points out that "an idol is nothing in the world" [1 Cor. 8:4] in relation to external matters. In relation to God, idols are no joke. Such idols in the heart are a false righteousness; are glory in works, unbelief, and anything else that takes the place of Christ in the heart in the form of unbelief. As if he were to say, the Jews avoid the external idols in the world, but before God their hearts are full of idols. He also says of them (Rom. 2[:22]), "You who abhor idols, do you rob temples?" With these words he interprets the first commandment in fine fashion, which states: "You shall have no other gods before me" [Exod.

54. Luther's basic concern here is to offer a proper understanding of "keeping the sabbath" for Christians.

20:3], as if saying, "In relation to yourself or the world idols are nothing, but in relation to me, that is, in the heart, you may not worship or trust in them."

Since St. Paul declares that in all these three points the Corinthians have freedom, and would have these regarded as nothing, namely, idols, idol's temples, and food offered to idols, all three of which are strictly prohibited in the first commandment and those following from it, it is indeed clear and proven forcefully enough that the reference to images in the first commandment is to a temporal ceremony, which has been abrogated in the New Testament. For just as I may with good conscience eat and drink that which has been offered to idols, and sit and dwell in an idol's temple [1 Cor. 8:7-10], as St. Paul teaches, so I may also put up with idols and let them be, as things which neither make any difference nor hinder my conscience and faith. [. . .]

If, however, these destroyers of images will not show any mercy, we beg them at least to be merciful to our Lord Jesus Christ and not to spit on him and say, as they do to us, "Phooey on you, you servant of idols!" For the three evangelists, Matthew [22:19ff.], Mark [12:15ff.], and Luke [20:24ff.] write that Jesus took a coin from the Pharisees upon which was minted a likeness of Caesar, and asked whose likeness it was and said it should be given to Caesar. If all kinds of images had been forbidden, the Jews should not have given any to him, nor possessed any, much less should Christ have accepted it and allowed this to be unrebuked, especially since it was the image of a pagan." He must also have sinned when, according to Matt. 17[:27], he asked Peter to take a tax shekel out of a fish's mouth and pay the tax for him. Jesus must have created the image and shekel in that very place and placed it in the fish's mouth. I presume also that the gold which the three holy kings offered to Christ [Matt. 2:11] was also coined with images, as is the custom in all lands.[55] The same thing is true of the two hundred denarii (John 6[:17]) with which the disciples wanted to buy bread. Yes, accordingly, all the fathers and saints are guilty insofar as they have used money. [. . .]

Would you here say, "You don't mean that the first commandment has been abrogated, for, after all, one ought to have a single God? Furthermore, one ought not to commit adultery,

55. A reference to the wise men who came to adore the newborn infant Jesus as the "King of the Jews."

kill, steal?" Answer: I have spoken of the Mosaic Law as laws of Moses. For to have a single God is not alone a Mosaic Law, but also a natural law, as St. Paul says (Rom. 1[:20]), that the heathen know of the deity, that there is a God. This is also evidenced by the fact that they have established gods and arranged forms of divine service, which would have been impossible if they had neither known nor thought about God. For God has shown it to them in the things that have been made, etc. (Rom. 1[:19-20]). Is it therefore surprising to find that the heathen[d] have missed the true God and worshiped idols in the place of God? The Jews also erred and worshiped idols instead of God, even though they had the law of Moses. And they who have the gospel of Christ still misapprehend the Lord Christ.

Thus, "Thou shalt not kill, commit adultery, steal, etc.," are not Mosaic laws only, but also the natural law written in each person's heart, as St. Paul teaches (Rom. 2[:15]). Also Christ himself (Matt. 7[:12]) includes all of the law and the prophets in this natural law, "So whatever you wish that people would do to you, do so to them; for this is the law and the prophets." Paul does the same thing in Rom. 13[:9], where he sums up all the commandments of Moses in the love which also the natural law teaches in the words, "Love your neighbor as yourself." Otherwise, were it not naturally written in the heart, one would have to teach and preach the law for a long time before it became the concern of conscience. The heart must also find and feel the law in itself. Otherwise it would become a matter of conscience for no one. However, the devil so blinds and possesses hearts, that they do not always feel this law. Therefore one must preach the law and impress it on the minds of people till God assists and enlightens them, so that they feel in their hearts what the Word says.

Where then the Mosaic Law and the natural law are one, there the law remains and is not abrogated externally, but only through faith spiritually, which is nothing else than the fulfillment of the law (Rom. 3[:31]). This is not the place to speak about that, and elsewhere enough has been said about it.[56] Therefore Moses' legislation about images and the sabbath, and what else goes beyond the natural law, since it is not supported

56. The reference is to Luther's treatise on monastic vows *De votis monasticis* (*On the Monastic Vows*) in LW 44:223–400; also WA 8:573ff.

---

d   Original Ger.: *Heiden*; there is no good German equivalent for *Gentile*.

by the natural law, is free, null and void, and is specifically given to the Jewish people alone. It is as when an emperor or a king makes special laws and ordinances in his territory, as the *Sachsenspiegel* in Saxony, and yet common natural laws such as to honor parents, not to kill, not to commit adultery, to serve God, etc., prevail and remain in all lands. Therefore one is to let Moses be the *Sachsenspiegel* of the Jews and not to confuse us Gentiles with it, just as the *Sachsenspiegel* is not observed in France, though the natural law there is in agreement with it.[57]

Why does one then keep and teach the Ten Commandments? Answer: Because the natural laws were never so orderly and well written as by Moses. Therefore it is reasonable to follow the example of Moses. And I wish that we would accept even more of Moses in worldly matters, such as the laws about the bill of divorce [Deut. 24:1], the Sabbath year [Lev. 25:2-7], the year of jubilee, tithes, and the like. Through such laws the world would be better governed than now with its practices in usury, trade, and marriage. This occurs whenever a country follows examples from laws of other lands, as the Romans appropriated the Twelve Tables from the Greeks.[58]

It is not necessary to observe the sabbath or Sunday because of Moses' commandment. Nature also shows and teaches that one must now and then rest a day, so that both the people and the beasts may be refreshed. This natural reason Moses also recognized in his sabbath law, for he places the sabbath under man, as also Christ does (Matt. 12[:1ff.] and Mark 3[:2ff.]). For where it is kept for the sake of rest alone, it is clear that someone who does not need rest may break the sabbath and rest on some other day, as nature allows. The sabbath is also to be kept for the purpose of preaching and hearing the Word of God.

There are, besides this, much better matters in Moses, namely, the prophecy and promise of the coming of Christ, as St. Paul says (Rom. 3[:21]).[59] Also, Moses tells us about the creation of the world, the origin of marriage, and many precious examples of faith, love, and all virtues. In the writings of Moses, we also find examples of unbelief and vice, from which one can learn to know God's grace and wrath. All are written not only for the sake of the Jews, but for the Gentiles as well. Much in these writings speaks of unbelievers and Gentiles, so that all such parts serve as examples to teach the whole world. However, the law of

57. The *Sachsenspiegel*, a legal compendium, was written by Eycke von Reptow and attempted to summarize economic and social laws and statutes pertaining to Magdeburg and Halberstadt; it was published between 1220 and 1230. In addition to being the first German legal compendium, the *Sachsenspiegel* is also the first prose work written in Middle-Low German. Heiner Lück, *Über den Sachsenspiegel: Entstehung, Inhalt und Wirkung des Rechtsbuches*, 2d ed. (Frauenkirchen, Austria/Dossel [Saalkreis], Germany: Stekovics, 2005).

58. According to Livy III:31, three representatives were sent to Athens to learn about Athenian and Greek law before the Law of the Twelve Tables (Lat.: *Leges Duodecim Tabularum* or *Duodecim Tabulae*), the first codification of Roman law, was delineated. Cf. WA 18:81.

59. Luther has in mind all five books of Moses (Genesis–Deuteronomy), which in German were custom labeled the First, Second, Third, etc., book of Moses.

Moses concerns only the Jews, and such Gentiles as have willingly submitted to it and accepted it. They are called proselytes. So St. Paul says in Rom. 9[:4] that the Jews have been given the law, the covenant, and the promise. Psalm 147[:19-20] says, "God declares his word to Jacob, his statutes and ordinances to Israel. God has not dealt thus with any other nation; they do not know his ordinances," etc.

I have myself seen and heard the iconoclasts read from my German Bible. I know that they have it and read it, as one can easily determine from the words they use. Now there are a great many pictures in those books, both of God, the angels, people and animals, especially in the Revelation of John and in Moses and Joshua. So now we would kindly beg them to permit us to do what they themselves do. Pictures contained in these books we would paint on walls for the sake of remembrance and better understanding, since they do no more harm on walls than in books. It is to be sure better to paint pictures on walls of how God created the world, how Noah built the ark, and whatever other good stories there may be, than to paint shameless worldly things. Yes, would to God that I could persuade the rich and the mighty that they would permit the whole Bible to be painted on houses, on the inside and outside, so that all can see it. That would be a Christian work. [. . .]

However, I must end lest I hereby give occasion to the image-breakers never to read the Bible, or to burn it, and after that to tear the heart out of the body, because they are so opposed to images. I only referred to the use of the Bible to show what happens when reason wants to be wise and gain the upper hand in understanding God's Word and works. Also I wanted to show what lies behind Dr. Karlstadt's brash boast that he has God's Word and must suffer so much on that account. Indeed, the devil, too, must suffer on account of it—not that he uses it rightly, but rather perverts it and thereby increases his wickedness and lies, as Dr. Karlstadt also does because of the same vexation.

And if I had time, I would like to satisfy my desire against Satan and before the whole world again stuff down his throat the saying that he wrings out of Scripture in such nonsensical fashion in Karlstadt's little book, so that he would have to be ashamed. For I have really caught Karlstadt at a vulnerable point; it seems like a divine miracle to me that he can make a fool of the devil. However, I have other things to do. Whoever will not be instructed by this argument, let him go and break images his whole life long! I cannot be blamed.

In conclusion I must give an example of what I am saying in order to see whether Dr. Karlstadt might learn a bit himself and be ashamed that he teaches his disciples so well. When I was in Orlamünde and discussed images with the good people there, and showed from the text that all the sayings from Moses that were brought forward dealt with idolatrous images which one worshiped, a man stepped forward who wanted to be the most wise among them and said to me, "Do you hear? I would like to address you in the informal 'you.'[60] Are you a Christian?" I said, "Address me as you will." He would just as soon have struck me. He was so full of Karlstadt's spirit that the others could not make him keep silent. So he continued and said, "If you will not follow Moses, you must nevertheless endure the gospel. You have shoved the gospel under the bench. No, no! It must come forth and not remain under the bench."

I said, "What then does the gospel say?" He said, "Jesus says in the gospel (I don't know where, though my brethren know it) that the bride must take off her nightgown and be naked if she is to sleep with the bridegroom.[e] Therefore one must break all the images, so that we are free and cleansed of what is created." So far the words of our conversation.

What was I to do? I had come among Karlstadt's followers and then I learned that breaking images meant that a bride should take off her nightgown, and that this was to be found in the gospel. Such words, and words about shoving the gospel under the bench, he had heard from his master. Perhaps Karlstadt had blamed me with hiding the gospel under the bench, while he was the man who was to draw it forth. Such idle pride had brought the man into all misfortune, and had pushed him out of the light into such darkness, that he gave as a reason for breaking images, that a bride should take off her nightgown. Just as if they thereby were rid of created things in the heart, in that they madly destroy images. What though, if the bride and

60. This sentence refers to the fact that the German language makes a distinction between a formal you (*Sie*) and an informal you (*du*), the latter nowadays employed in the family, with friends. In the sixteenth century the use of the formal *Sie* was also a matter of social standing.

e   The origins of this intriguing exegesis are not clear; the whole encounter is recorded in the *Acta Jenesis*, WA 15:346.

bridegroom were so chaste that they kept nightgown and robe on? It would certainly not hinder them much if they otherwise had desire for each other.

But so it goes, when one brings the disorderly people into the picture. Due to great fullness of the spirit they forget civil discipline and manners, and no longer fear and respect anyone but only themselves.[61] This appeals to Dr. Karlstadt. These are all pretty preliminaries to riot and rebellion, so that one fears neither order nor authority. Let this be enough about images. I think it has been adequately proven that Dr. Karlstadt does not understand Moses at all. He peddles his own dreams as the Word of God and thinks less of orderly authority than he does of the disorderly common people.[62] Whether this be conducive to obedience or to rebellion, I leave to all to determine for themselves.

About the Complaint of Dr. Karlstadt, That He Was Expelled from Saxony.

Thus far we have seen what kind of a Word of God Dr. Karlstadt has, for the sake of which he exalts himself and makes himself a holy martyr. Now let us see the work of God, for the sake of which, as he boasts, he suffers such great persecution. Although I would rather that he had kept silent and not compelled me to deal with his aversion. However, since he has also attacked the princes of Saxony, in that he has not even refrained from inveighing against the motto[63] which they in all honor wear upon their sleeves (so meanly does the bitter resentment in his heart seek occasion to bring infamy on people), I must, insofar as I have knowledge of the matter, defend the honor of my gracious lords.*f* For the princes of Saxony have certainly deserved better of Dr. Karlstadt than that he should leave with such thanks, as he well knows. Well now, on with it and we shall see.

First, may I say this, that I have had no dealings with the elector of Saxony about Karlstadt.[64] For that matter I have in my whole life never spoken one word with this prince, nor heard him speak, nor have I even seen his face, except once in Worms before the emperor [18 April 1521] when I was being examined for the second time. It is to be sure true that I have often communicated

61. This is one of several instances in the treatise where Luther draws a close causal connection between theological position and civil disobedience. It shows both that Luther was convinced that this was indeed a proper appraisal of Karlstadt and also a most serious danger for the movement of renewal and reform.

62. Here Luther's fundamental opposition against Karlstadt comes to the fore: Karlstadt substitutes his own "dreams" for Scripture.

63. The details of the motto remain enigmatic. Later, at the diet at Speyer in 1529, the evangelical rulers wore the acronym VDMA (*Verbum Deo Manet in Aeternum*) on their garments. Karlstadt comments on this in his account of his expulsion: *Ursachen, derhalben Andres Karlstadt aus den Landen zu Sachsen vertrieben* (Strasburg 1524).

64. Luther, in short, asserts that, having had no contact with Elector Frederick in the matter, he had nothing to do with Karlstadt's expulsion. At the same time, Luther concedes his steady contact with the elector's secretary, Spalatin.

f   In his treatise *Von dem Alten und Neuen Testament.*

65. Georg Burkhardt was born in the Franconian town of Spalt in 1484 (d. 1545), and thus became known as Spalatin. He pursued humanistic studies in both Erfurt and Wittenberg, was tutor first (1508) to the Saxon Duke John Frederick (1503–1554), and then oversaw the ducal library in Wittenberg. In 1516 he served as Elector Frederick's private secretary and in 1522 as his court preacher. Spalatin and Luther were good friends and shared the vision of a renewed Christian faith.

66. Luther clearly has in mind here Thomas Müntzer, who wrote a biting attack on Luther, *Hochverursachte Schutzrede gegen das sanftlebende Fleisch zu Wittenberg*, in which he accused Luther of not understanding that the Christian life is one of spiritual and actual suffering.

67. John Frederick became the duke of Ernestine Saxony in 1532 and served till 1547 when the emperor removed him from office.

68. The reference is to Müntzer who, much like Karlstadt, is labeled a "spirit" and all his followers with the same spirit.

69. In the original *Schwaermer*.

with him in writing through Master Spalatin[65] and especially insisted that the Allstedtian spirit be suppressed. However, I accomplished nothing, so that I was also much annoyed with the elector, until this spirit voluntarily fled, unexpelled. For this reason Karlstadt ought to have spared the princes and become better acquainted with the matter before he cried out to the world in his slanderous booklet.[g] Also it is not right, much less Christian, even if it were true that he was driven out by the elector, to gain revenge in this way with libel. One should first humbly have asked the reason and set forth what was right, and thereafter suffered in silence. It could not be expected of me, who is made out to be simply flesh, which unfortunately I also am.[66] But the high spirit of Karlstadt cannot do wrong or err. He is the right itself.

I have spoken about the matter with my young lord, Duke John Frederick (this I admit) and pointed out Dr. Karlstadt's wantonness and arrogance.[67] However, since "the spirit" burns with such blinding intensity, I will here recount the reasons, some of which, indeed, are not known to the princes of Saxony, why I am happy that Dr. Karlstadt is out of the country. And insofar as my entreaties are effectual, he shall not again return, and he would again have to leave were he to be found here, unless he would become another Andreas, which God may grant. If God wills, I will fawn before no princes. But much less will I suffer that the rebellious and the disobedient among the common people are to be led to despise temporal authority.

And my humble admonition and request to all princes, lords, and authorities is first, as I previously have also written against the Allstedt spirit,[68] that they will assiduously see to it that preachers who do not teach peacefully, but attract to themselves the mobs and on their own responsibility wantonly break images and destroy churches behind the backs of the authorities, forthwith be exiled. Or they should so be dealt with that they refrain from such action. Not that I thereby would hinder God's Word, but I would put a limit and bounds to the wantonness of mischievous enthusiasts[69] and factious spirits, which the temporal authority is obligated to do. Above all, however,

---

g   A reference to Karlstadt's pamphlet about his expulsion from Electoral Saxony: *Ursachen der halben Andres Carolstatt auß den landen Zu Sachsen vertryben / Andres Carolstatt* (Straßburg: Johann Prüss, 1524).

Portrait of Duke
John Frederick
by Lucas Cranach
the Elder, 1531.

Thomas Müntzer from a copper
engraving by C. van Sichem, 1608.

Dr. Karlstadt with his gang must be stopped, for he is obdurate and will not be instructed, but goes on justifying and defending his factiousness.

And this is my ground and reason: We have noted above how Dr. Karlstadt and the image breakers of his kind do not interpret Moses' commandment as referring to the constituted authority, as is proper, but to the common people who are disorderly. That is certainly not the proper spirit and attitude. For, as I have said, were the common people to have the right and power to carry out a divine commandment, then one must thereafter give in and permit them to carry out all the commandments. Consequently, whoever arrives on the scene first must put to death murderers, adulterers, and thieves, and punish rogues. And thereby justice, law, rules, and all authority would fall apart. Matters would take their course in accordance with the proverb "Give a rogue an inch and he takes a mile." For why do we have rulers? Why do they carry the sword, if the common people are to rush in blindly and straighten things out themselves?

After that, such disorder will gain in momentum, and the common people will have to kill all the wicked. For Moses, when he commands the people to destroy images (Deut. 7[:16]), also commands them to destroy without mercy those who had such images in the land of Canaan. For this killing is just as strictly commanded as the destruction of images, which commandment these factious spirits so obstinately introduce and emphasize. Moses, however, commanded this of a people that had Joshua as chief and many magistrates and, besides, was a law-abiding people. Moreover the commandment did not apply to all of the wicked, but only to the heathen Canaanites, who through God's judgment were given over to death because of their wickedness, as the text clearly indicates. For he exempted the Edomites, Moabites, and Ammonites though they also were wicked.[70] Thus this work of God took place through regular governmental authority and affected those whom God, not humans, publicly tried and condemned to death.

Since our murderous spirits apply Moses' commandment to the people, and do not have God's judgment over the wicked, but themselves judge that those who have images are wicked and worthy of death, they will be compelled by such a commandment to engage in rebellion, murdering and killing, as works which God has commanded them to do. Let the Allstedtian spirit be an example, who already had progressed from images to people, and who publicly called for rebellion and murder contrary to all authority. How could he act otherwise? For so he must teach. Since he had invited the devil to be his sponsor up to this point so that the common people without due process were to destroy images, as enjoined by God's commandment, then he had to continue and press the auxiliary commandment, which follows from it, and commands the people to murder. If I were to destroy images in the same sense as they, I, too, would be compelled to follow through and command people to be murdered. For the commandment is there pressing its claim. Dear lords, the devil does not care about image breaking. He only wants to get his foot in the door so that he can cause shedding of blood and murder in the world.

But, you say, Dr. Karlstadt does not want to kill. That one can see from the letters which those of Orlamünde wrote to the people of Allstedt.[71] Answer: I also believed it! But I believe it no longer. I no longer ask what Dr. Karlstadt says or does. He has not hid the truth for the first time. Of the spirit which they have and which impels them, I say that it is not good and is bent on murder and rebellion. Although he bows and scrapes because he sees that he is in a tight spot, I shall clearly show that what I have said is so. God forbid, but suppose Dr. Karlstadt won a large following, which he thought he could assemble on the Saale,[72] and the German Bible alone was read, and Mr. Everybody[h] began to hold this commandment (about killing the wicked) under his own nose, in what direction would Dr. Karlstadt go? How would he control the situation? Even if he had never intended to consent to something like that, he would have to follow through. The crowds would mutiny and cry and shout as obstinately, "God's Word, God's Word, God's Word is there. We must do it!" As he now cries against images, "God's Word, God's Word!" My dear lords, Mr. Everybody is not to be toyed with. Therefore God would have authorities so that there might be order in the world.[73]

If it were really true, and I could believe, that Dr. Karlstadt does not intend murder or rebellion, I would still have to say that he has a rebellious and murderous spirit, like the one at Allstedt, as long as he continues with wanton image breaking and draws the unruly rabble to himself. I well see that he neither strikes nor stabs, but since he carries the murderous weapon and does not put it aside, I do not trust him. He could be waiting for time and place, and then do what I fear. By the "murderous weapon" I mean the false interpretation and understanding of the Law of Moses. Through it the devil comes and the common people are aroused to boldness and arrogance. [. . .]

This I am recounting in order to show that Dr. Karlstadt's offer to be instructed is pure falsehood. Thereby he would only use forbearance and a good appearance as a smoke screen for his obdurate mind, and so dishonor both the rulers and princes and me. Also it is not proper to preach and teach divine things and then immediately thereafter ask whether preaching and teaching were correct. Then either the teaching must be wrong or the question is hypocritical. But if he is really in earnest, well then, let him desist from his fanaticism. I have previously dealt quite extensively with the matter of images, so that he may understand how he is in error. Let him be instructed and separate himself

72. The Saale River flows through Orlamunde.

73. Luther here not only affirms the divine function of governmental authority to provide for law and order in a community; he makes the subtle distinction between having a "rebellious spirit" and acting on it.

---

h   Again, *Herr Omnes*, that is, "the common people."

74. Luther seems to assume that of his two major antagonists, Karlstadt is the more open and more persuadable.

75. Clearly Luther assumes that Karlstadt had not been fully open with him, notably, his erratic behavior of appearing in Wittenberg from Orlamünde to resume his professorship and abruptly leaving Wittenberg.

from the heavenly prophets.[74] All will simply be forgotten and I will do for him and grant him all that I am able. I will gladly have him as friend if he will. If he will not, then I must leave it in God's hands.[75] [. . .]

If I were a ruler, and paid a salary to a professor to lecture and to preach in a city or in a territory of mine, and this professor without my knowledge and consent went elsewhere and wantonly took possession of what was rightfully due me and I meanwhile ordered him officially and through the university to resume his duties, but he, nevertheless, did what he pleased on my salary and my livings, and later wrote me a letter and asked for safe conduct so that he might take part in a disputation in my city, to which whereto I had already ordered him and he was obligated to come, what should I answer, since he so completely took me for a fool? And if I now did not answer, and he subsequently circulated an insulting letter against me, as though I had not been willing to permit him to dispute or be heard, what should I think? I would secretly think: He is a rascal. Not that I thereby call Dr. Karlstadt a rascal. But I indicate what in such a case might occur to a ruling, reigning prince as an individual.

However, this individual lacked nothing except that his ruling authorities were too indulgent. One could well have found rulers who, had he performed such tricks in their territories with such mischief and arrogance, would have put him and his gang to the sword, and probably that would not have been just. Therefore I would advise Dr. Karlstadt not to insult the rulers and to thank them that they have so graciously let him off, so that they be not compelled at last to deal with him more severely according to what he deserves on his merits.

Nor is this the least of all reasons why he trails along with the heavenly prophets from whom, as is known, comes the Allstedtian spirit. From them he learns, to them he cleaves. They secretly smuggle error into the land and gather stealthily on the Saale River, where they plan to nest.[76] The feeble devil will go nowhere but to our place, where already through the gospel we have created opportunity and security, and seeks only to defile and destroy our nest, as the cuckoo does with the hedge sparrow. These same prophets claim that they speak with God, and God with them, and are called to preach, and yet none of them dares come forth and appear openly, but they lay their eggs secretly and pour their poison into Dr. Karlstadt. He then promotes it with tongue and pen. But when he could not do this at Wittenberg, he began to do it on the Saale.[77]

These prophets teach and hold also that they are going to reform Christendom and establish it anew in this manner. They must slaughter all princes and the wicked, so that they become lords on earth and live only among saints. Such and much else I myself have heard from them.[78] Dr. Karlstadt knows also that these are fanatics and murderous spirits and that such calamity has originated with them, which should be warning enough. Yet he does not avoid them. And I am to believe that he would not bring about murder and rebellion? Also when I reproached him about this in Jena,[79] he himself admitted it and moreover defended it, saying, why should he not side with them in what they teach correctly rightly? Why then does he not also hold to us or to the papists, where we are in the right. Or is nothing right with us, or with the papists? No, against these prophets he can neither preach nor write, but against us there must be preaching, writing, and raging. [. . .]

Is it not annoying that the common people now and again are made so arrogant and restless by these spirits, before it becomes known to the princes, so that as soon as they hear a preacher who teaches them to be peaceful and obedient to the authorities, they immediately call him a toad eater and a fawner before princes and point their fingers at him? Who, however, says: "Strike them dead, give no one anything, and be free Christians, you are the true people of God, etc.," he is a true evangelical preacher. They take the nightgown off the bride at Orlamünde and the trousers off the bridegroom at Naschhausen.[80] They do not hide the gospel under the bench, and yet they teach not at all who Christ is, or what should be known about him.

If then a ruler found Dr. Karlstadt of such a kind that he held to with the factious and murderous spirits, thereby making the subjects arrogant and restless, and if he furthermore sought to justify and defend himself, would it not be time that the prince said to him: "If you are the troublemaker, get out of here before I have to speak to you in some other way?" For what good can be expected when such prophets remain in the land, in which the seed already shows itself so powerfully? He dare not object

77. This is Luther's verdict on the changes undertaken in Wittenberg during his absence, while at Wartburg Castle.

78. Luther here sees the insurrection of the peasants and townspeople not so much as an attempted redress of new grievances as the effort to radically alter societal structures.

79. At the often-cited encounter of Karlstadt and Luther in Jena. See the introduction, p. 45–46.

80. A village adjacent to Orlamünde.

that he has not been admonished before this, and that he has not known that there has been no love for him. Who could admonish, when they move so secretly, until they have spread the poison all around so that no one could know what they were doing? Have they not been admonished sufficiently and publicly through my writing against the Allstedt spirit? How graciously have they allowed themselves to be instructed? Also, have they not known that I have judged the spirit of these prophets as the devil's spirit? How has that helped, other than that they are more hardened than ever and have planned to resist me, with secret cunning have planned to resist me?

Yes, why have they themselves shown so little love, and so busily worked against us behind our backs in their hiding place, written against us in several territories and in the pulpit pulled no one to pieces but the Wittenbergers, and yet they have thus far not shown us our error? Wittenberg has done it, on that the spirit feasts. Otherwise all is well in the world. And this is done under the protection of our rulers, indeed, under our name and sponsorship. But take care, you evil and wrathful spirits. It is still true that Wittenberg is too big a bite for you, and God may ordain that in swallowing you may choke to death on it.[81] We know Satan, and if sometimes we doze off being human, it will do you no good, for the one who protects and watches over us does neither slumber nor sleep, and protects and watches over us [Ps. 121:4]. We commit ourselves to this one.

Dr. Karlstadt has brought this trouble and misfortune upon himself, in my opinion, inasmuch as he carries on his enterprise without call while willfully forsaking his own calling.[82] For he has forced himself upon Orlamünde as a wolf. For this reason it was impossible for him to do any good there. He was appointed to Wittenberg on a royally endowed income, as an archdeacon, to preach God's Word, lecture, and participate in the formal disputations in the university.[83] God had sent him there, and he agreed to discharge his responsibilities. He did serve for a time, usefully and with honor, and was liked and cherished. He cannot say it was otherwise. He received more advancement from the elector than many others, until the murderous prophets came and made the man wild and restless, so that he wanted to learn something better and more unusual than God teaches in the Bible.

Then he wantonly left and went to Orlamünde, without the knowledge and consent of either the prince or the university. He

81. Probably a reference to Korah's rebellion [Num. 16:32-33].

82. Luther chides Karlstadt for having acted on his own without having received proper authorization. Again, that is not completely correct, for in January 1522 the Wittenberg city council endorsed the various reforms that had been undertaken under Karlstadt's aegis.

83. Karlstadt's responsibilities in Wittenberg were to preach, to teach, and to participate in the life of the university. His income derived mainly, however, from the benefice in Orlamünde.

drove out the pastor who by order of the prince and university privilege was placed there, and personally took over the parish.[84] What do you think of a stunt like that? Does it contribute to quiet obedience to authority, or to insolent rebellion among the masses? The spirit of which I speak peered forth, for the very same spirit which swallows such a little strap would also very likely venture to devour a whole harness, when opportunity presented itself. He who is so venturesome that he dares in full view of a reigning prince greedily and wantonly to abrogate his property, jurisdiction, and statutes, what would he do behind the back of a prince, if he found occasion? This is the way to honor and fear the authorities and to teach the common people both with word and example that the priest is like the people, as Isaiah says [Isa. 24:2].

Even if the devil bursts, he will be unable to deny that the rulers of Saxony rule it as governing authorities ordained by God. The land and the people are subject to them. What kind of a spirit then is this that despises such a divine ordination, proceeds with headstrong violence, treats princely possessions, prerogatives, and rights as though they were his own, and does not even once recognize the prince or confer with him about it, as though he were a blockhead, and he himself were ruler in the land? Should not a good spirit fear God's order a little more, and since the estate, the pastorate, and the land belong to the prince, first humbly beg permission to leave and resign one position, and beg the favor of being installed in another?

Now, however, Dr. Karlstadt forsakes his duties at Wittenberg behind the prince's back, robs the university of his preaching and teaching and what else he is obligated to do by reason of the prince's endowment, and retains nevertheless the salary or revenue income for himself, and puts no one else in his place. At Orlamünde he also takes over the pastoral position belonging to the university, drives out him whom he had not appointed, nor had the power to appoint, much less to dismiss. Dear friends, why all this? Some suppose in order that he might draw that much more income, and because he believed the elector would be lenient and not quick to penalize. But I believe that a secondary reason was that the "Prophets" sought a hideout on the Saale, where they could spread their spirit and poison, creeping around in the darkness like mice—something they would not be able to do for long in Wittenberg.

84. The reference is to the complicated legal arrangement of the income accruing from Orlamünde. The parish essentially supported a faculty member at the university, with the actual pastoral responsibilities carried out by a substitute.

He cannot pretend that he could not remain in Wittenberg on account of heresy, for, thank God, the gospel itself is there, pure and fine. And if it were not, he would not for that reason be driven to godless behavior. Even if the devil and his members are around us in the world, we dare not on that account be devils or members of the devil. Dr. Karlstadt was unusually free to devote himself alone to God's Word, letting the other priests do what they would.[85] And even if there had been nothing but devils in Wittenberg, he should nevertheless not therefore, behind the prince's back, move without leave or permission, meanwhile retaining his living, and shamelessly appropriating the prince's possessions at another place.

Nor can he say that he moved out of pity for Orlamünde, to teach the erring sheep. For this pastorate was served through the university by a Christian pastor, namely, Master Konrad Glitzsch who correctly understood and taught the gospel.[86] And even if it had been so, he should nevertheless have petitioned the authorities about it. For one is not to do evil for the sake of the good (Rom. 3[:8]). It has been done only to give room and place for the evil spirit to circulate its poison, as I have said, so that we might be pictured as remarkable masters, with no one equal to us.

If he did not seek to gain wealth or to concentrate his poison, but sought only the glory of God, why did he not request to preach God's Word in other cities, where he would not have received such income, however? Yet the preaching might well have been needed and the cities could have been closer. Indeed it was because it was not convenient for the spirit and the belly. However, if such mischief was to occur "from an inner call of God," then it is necessary that it be proved with miraculous signs. For God does not change God's old order for a new one unless the change is accompanied by great signs. Therefore one can believe no one who relies on his own spirit and inner feelings for authority and who outwardly storms against God's accustomed order, unless one therewith performs miraculous signs, as Moses indicates in Deut. 18[:22].

When, however, he alleges, together with the people of Orlamünde, that he has been elected by them as their minister, and thus externally called, I answer: To me it does not matter that they afterward elected him. I speak about his first coming. Let him produce letters to show that the people of Orlamünde sum-

85. Karlstadt clearly was troubled by this cumbersome arrangement and sought to deal with it by actually occupying the position that in theory, so to speak, was his.

86. Part of the subsequent complication was Glitzsch's unwillingness to vacate the position for Karlstadt and complained to the elector.

moned him from Wittenberg and that he did not himself run over there. Dear friends, if being called means that I, out of a sense of duty and obedience, move to another city, and thereafter place myself in so favorable a light and persuade the people to choose me and oust my predecessor, then I say that no principality is so great, but that I would be prince therein and drive out the incumbent. How easy is it not to persuade the common people? That is not the way to extend a call. It is to promote faction and rebellion and to despise authority.

Nor did the Orlamünders have a right to elect a pastor on another's salary, for it belonged to the prince and his jurisdiction. Nor is the prince or the university un-Christian, burdening them with wicked pastors. And even if the prince had appointed a godless pastor to Orlamünde, which he had not done, they should nevertheless not deprive their sovereign of his right, possession, and authority, and behind his back elect a pastor and give away revenues (which were not their own) to whomever they wanted. Much less should he [Karlstadt] have accepted it without petitioning the ruler. Rather, as is becoming of subjects, they should humbly have submitted a complaint to the prince and the university, and requested that a Christian pastor be assigned to them. If then he had not been willing, they could thereafter have planned as best they could.

Now, however, they plot without the knowledge of the prince, elect pastors, and appoint them as they themselves please. They appear to regard their natural liege lord and reigning prince as so much dirt, whose possessions and prerogatives they wantonly wrest from him and take into their own hands. Indeed both Karlstadt and the Orlamünders have deserved a good strong jolt, as an example to other such people, so that they would know that they have a sovereign and are not themselves lords in the land. However, I would pardon and excuse the good people of Orlamünde on the ground that they were too feeble in the face of Dr. Karlstadt's overbearing spirit. Overcome by his humble bearing and high-sounding words (as is his custom), they were unable to see how they acted against their own lord. Possessed of a factious spirit, Dr. Karlstadt has my answer on the basis of what is apparent from the manner in which he has carried on in this situation, for he will not rest until he has tied the pitiable people to his person and ignored political authority. [. . .]

When no end to this game was in sight, but only rash action with total disregard of both the prince and the university, I nevertheless came to the Saale region by order of the prince, and preached against such fanaticism as well as I could. Then the devil also welcomed me, in a way which I have no doubt long deserved. How he panted, rushed, and writhed, just as if Christ had come to drive him out. Dr. Karlstadt even caught me off guard at the table with such a mild manner and gentle words that I instantly felt the "spirit" speak from him. Thereupon I pointed out to my gracious young lord, Duke John Frederick,[i] that his grace should not put up with this, for what was being done rather than said was apparent. He would be factious and reject the authorities. This is how much I know about the matter, and no more.

And what should I say? There is no earnestness nor truth in what this spirit and his followers propose. They do not even themselves believe what they say, nor keep what they promise, except this that the devil seeks only to cause trouble in the world. For when Dr. Karlstadt was last in Wittenberg he willingly agreed to leave the pastorate in Orlamünde, since he saw that nothing else would do, and promised then that he would return to Wittenberg.[87] Had he then been certain that he had been called to be pastor, he should not have given it up, but rather have given up his life, as until then he had struggled and defended himself? For one ought not to renounce a divine call when they [with whom one is associated] boast of having pure fellowship with God. [. . .]

I have had to make this extended explanation, although very unwillingly, because the spiteful spirit is so prone to embellish himself to the shame of the princes of Saxony, by whose favor he received honor and goods. I think also if he had not fled in such misery and despondency, but had had the moral courage at the time to request reasons[88] from the princes of Saxony, these and others, of which I am perhaps unaware, might have been indicated to him. Though more could be said about that, I am of the opinion that the land belongs to the princes of Saxony and not to Dr. Karlstadt, who is a guest therein and possesses noth-

87. 15 April 1524.

88. I.e., for his banishment.

i   See n. 67, p. 70.

ing. When they take from someone what belongs to him and at the same time, for reasons of their own, no longer want someone in their land, I do not believe they are obligated to say to each and every one what has influenced them, nor to take the matter to court. For princes must conceal many things and keep them secret. If a landlord did not have the right and the power to ask a guest or a servant to move out, without first giving a reason and settling the matter in court, he would be but a poor landlord imprisoned in his own estate, and the guest would himself be landlord.

This spirit does not consider this, but presses on and attacks the princes with public abuse, as though he were their equal lord in the land of Saxony and defies them with the law in their own possessions. How shall one answer such an arrogant and venturesome head other than as the householder in the gospel says: "Friend, I am doing you no wrong. . . . Take what belongs to you and go. . . . Shall I not do what I choose with what belongs to me?" [Matt. 20:13-14]. This evil-eyed rogue also wanted to know the reason and justification for the householder's dealing with his possessions as he chose. Oh you fine spirit, to what extent are you able to conceal what you have in mind? You would be lord, and that which you affirm and do is to be considered right. That is the sum of it.

What think you now? Is it not a fine new spiritual humility? Wearing a felt hat and a gray garb, not wanting to be called doctor, but Brother Andreas and dear neighbor, as another peasant, subject to the magistrate of Orlamünde and obedient as an ordinary citizen. Thus with self-chosen humility and servility, which God does not command, he wants to be seen and praised as a remarkable Christian, as though Christian living consisted in such external hocus-pocus. At the same time, he strives and runs counter to duty, honor, obedience, and the power and right of the reigning, ruling prince and the governing authority, which God has instituted. This is God's new sublime art, taught by the heavenly voice, which we at Wittenberg, who teach faith and love, do not understand and cannot know. This is the nice "turning from the material," the "concentration," the "adoration," the "self-abstraction," and similar devil's nonsense.

Concerning the Mass

Herewith an answer has been given to several of Dr. Karlstadt's books.[89] We shall now pay our attention to the book which has to do with the Mass, so that we may deal specifically with the sacrament. For I do not know why he makes so many books, all of which deal with the same subject. He could well put on one page what he wastes on ten. Perhaps he likes to hear himself talk, as the stork its own clattering. For his writing is neither clear nor intelligible, and one would just as soon make one's way through brambles and bushes as to read through his books. This is a sign of the spirit. The Holy Spirit speaks well, clearly, in an orderly and distinct fashion. Satan mumbles and chews the words in his mouth and makes a hundred into a thousand. It is an effort to ascertain what he means.

Dr. Karlstadt has observed that we at Wittenberg opposed the Mass as a sacrifice and a good work with great earnestness, both in writings and in action.[90] Moreover, we were the first to do so. He was probably concerned that we receive honor therefrom and thus through vainglory be led to sin. He reasoned with himself how he might help us in the following way: What shall I do to bring the Wittenbergers into such disrepute that all their writings and deeds concerning the Mass will mean nothing, and that they be defamed in their holding the Mass as a sacrifice and a good work, and I alone will be the hero who has brought into the world the awareness that the Mass is not a sacrifice? I will do this. I will not pay attention to what they write, confess, or do. Then I could be no knight, for all this is too evident. I will inveigh against them because they call it Mass, which means sacrifice, and because they elevate the sacrament as though they offered it. Then I can say: The Wittenbergers all grievously err, and with them the "poor bishop at Zwickau."[91]

Well then, we must in turn be thankful for the good deed and see to it that the high honor also does not deceive the rich vagabond and "uncalled" preacher Karlstadt. In matters relating to the name of the Mass and the elevation of the sacrament, we shall make reply in such manner that more shame than honor will come to him. Not that it is necessary to refute such childish tomfoolery other than to show that no good spark of true right understanding is left in Dr. Karlstadt. Therefore, let everyone

89. Luther must be referring to Karlstadt's *Ob man gemach faren soll: Von dem Sabbat und geboten Feiertagen.*

90. The relevant writing from Luther's pen is his sermon *Von dem Neuen Testament (Essay on the New Testament),* in WA 6:353.

91. Luther is quoting Karlstadt here and his reference to Nikolaus Hausmann (c. 1478–1538) who was a priest in Zwickau.

be on guard against this mad spirit, and not trust his splendid words. Lurking behind them are false, murderous snares, confusing the conscience with utterly unnecessary trickery.

First of all, he takes us to task for calling the sacrament a Mass, and accuses us of being Christ's hangmen and murderers, using other horrible words even worse than those used by the papists, because Mass is supposed to mean sacrifice in Hebrew.[j] Having taken the risk of contending with such earnestness that the Mass is not a sacrifice is of no help to us. Even in the eyes of the world it is disgraceful, childish, and effeminate to be in agreement in substance and yet to quarrel about words. In forbidding this, Paul calls such people *logomaxous*, "word warriors," and wranglers, etc. [1 Tim. 6:4; 2 Tim. 2:14]. However it is the devil, as I have said, who would like to use Karlstadt's head, to burden conscience grievously with sin and horrible danger in things which are in themselves free and without sin. Therefore he has no peace unless he destroys good consciences and kills souls, which should live, as Ezekiel [18:19] says.

In the second place, if it really were true that Mass means sacrifice, and there were a fragment of good in Dr. Karlstadt, he should have first informed and admonished us before publicly attributing to us such great vices before the whole world. Since we in fact deny and struggle against the Mass as a sacrifice, it might have been expected that we would very gladly also drop the name, were we instructed that by using the name we make the Mass a sacrifice. What has happened to brotherly love in the high spirit? Is it no sin for these saints so grievously and shamefully to make accusations against the neighbor without any cause? Plagued with blindness, Dr. Karlstadt pays no attention to nor does he recognize such truly great sins, as is apparent from his desire to burden the whole world with erroneous, imagined, and great sins. Acting in this manner is, in my opinion, to have the log in one's own eye and to want to take the speck out of another's eye [Matt. 7:5; Luke 6:42].

I have never known, also do not know now, that Mass means sacrifice. Dr. Karlstadt must excuse me. Although I do not know

j   Cf. *Treatise on the New Testament That Is the Holy Mass*, WA 6:353ff. See also Luther's *On the Babylonian Captivity of the Church* (1520), which includes references in WA 6:484ff.

much Hebrew, yet I am more competent to speak and to judge than he is. I have by now also translated almost the entire Bible into German, and I have not yet found that Mass means sacrifice. I think he must have found it written in the vent of a chimney, or recently invented his own Hebrew language, as he can invent sins and laws and a bad conscience, or probably the heavenly voice speaks in this way. It would be in order, when one does not understand a language, not to make claims for oneself in the field, and to give honor to those who are competent in it, so that no one might say: See, what a presumptuous ass he is! And especially when one would establish an article of faith, as Karlstadt here does, and hence raves: "I have dreamt that Mass in Hebrew means sacrifice. Therefore the Wittenbergers seize, hang, murder, scourge Christ and are worse than Caiaphas, Judas, and Herod, because they call it Mass." Take it easy, factious spirit. If it were a carnival play, buffoonery would be in place. [. . .]

Where are you now, dear factious spirits and sin drovers, with your Hebrew language? Tell me why I should not call the Christian office a collect or Mass, as the apostles and first Christians did? Yes, tell me, where have you gotten the lie to blame us for calling the consecrated bread and wine a Mass, even if Mass means sacrifice? One calls the whole service a Mass and says, "during the Mass," or "in the Mass," one consecrates the bread and wine. Also, in the Mass one receives the sacrament. Who has ever heard it said, "I will receive the Mass," or "I have received the Mass" when one has received the sacrament? I do not know if I have even once written or said it. Be that as it may, I know for sure that we do not teach or speak so at Wittenberg, although there would be no danger if the sacrament were or were not called a Mass. The lying spirit has certainly invented this about us, just as he, as the result of his own dream, calls Mass a sacrifice, to demonstrate his wantonness.

What, however, if the apostles had also called the sacrament itself a Mass? I think they would defend themselves quite well before the factious spirit and say: The Jews had to bring their Mass, that is, their first fruits, to the priests, by which they gave nothing to God, but rather thereby confessed and thanked God, that they received these and the whole land from his grace. We observe the sacrament or our Mass in a similar way. We do not celebrate it in order to give or offer something to God, but only that we may thereby confess and thank God, who has given us the same, together with all the riches of the kingdom of heaven, as also the words of Christ state: We should do this in his remembrance [1 Cor. 11:24, 25]. With this I think they would have quite well stopped the mouth of the spirit and instructed him, so that he might better learn the Hebrew language and Moses, before he slanders and condemns that which he neither knows nor understands.

This I say as though it were proven that *Mass* is a Hebrew word, which I would not depend on. Whether it is Hebrew or not makes no difference, although it is much like the Hebrew. However, what one would make into an article of faith by which to rule conscience must be something that is known much more definitely than one knows that Mass is from the Hebrew. There is nothing of this in Scripture. Besides, whatever occurs to or strikes the fancy of the scatterbrained, factious spirit must be a definite article of faith. After that speedily force it with fury and raging upon poor consciences, create sin where none exists, as is the nature of all his teaching and spirit. If a good spirit were moving him, he would first be sure of the matter and prove that "Mass" is Hebrew before he interprets it in a Hebrew manner. Then he should also prove that it means sacrifice. Finally, he should also demonstrate that one must not call it Mass. He does none of this. He only slavers his drivel about, and this we are all to accept as an article of faith. [...]

Yes, I will say further, that if we publicly confess with hearts, tongues, pens, and actions that it is no sacrifice, and besides that imprudently were to call it the Mass, as do those who do not know that a Mass is a sacrifice, would God not judge us more according to the heart and all other outward evidence rather than so on account of giving the appearance and using the name Mass condemn us as the devil does through Dr. Karlstadt? For God says that he sees and judges according to the heart, not according to appearance (Isa. 11[:3]). Dr. Karlstadt, however, because of the external appearance of a name of whose meaning we are not sure, slanders us so shamefully, and will neither judge according to the heart, nor take into account all of its fruits, which we show forth with deeds. [...]

So senseless and possessed have envy and vain ambition made this man, that he no longer sees how the heart gives the name to the deed, and not the deed the name to the heart. If the heart is right and good, no matter what the name, it can do no harm. How can there be a good and proper understanding of dealing with the Scripture or divine things in the head of one whose mind is so perverted that he has lost even the common understanding of the function of human reason? Does he not know that one must judge everything according to the belief and the fruits of the heart, not according to the name or appearance, as also all natural law teaches? Let those who will believe that such a teacher who, seeing all things through a colored glass and judging according to his embittered and false heart, writes correctly and in a Christian way about the sacrament. If he knows this and writes wantonly nevertheless, it's all the worse, as thereby one clearly perceives that he must be possessed. For a person who is in his right mind does not act so wantonly.

Now, what if in these days we continued and called the sacrament not Mass, but in plain German a sacrifice, just to spite the factious spirit? Do you think we would be equal to the task? According to our way of thinking, all we have done at Wittenberg, and yet intend to do, will be so fashioned by God's grace that the devil with all gates of hell and factious spirits may assault, but will gain nothing, as is borne out by the past. Come now, I shall call the sacrament a sacrifice anew, not because I consider it a sacrifice but because the god of this factious spirit, the devil, would prevent me from calling it thus. I shall therefore do what he does not want me to do, and not do what he wants me to do. Moreover, I shall set forth the reason and basis for the action I propose.

I will call St. Peter a sinful fisherman, as he calls himself in the gospel [Luke 5:8], and say: "St. Peter, the poor sinner, has converted the world with his gospel" [Acts 2:41-42]. St. Paul, the persecutor of Christendom, is teacher of the Gentiles [Acts 9:4; 1 Cor. 15:9]. St. Mary Magdalene, the sinner, has been saved [Luke 7:48], and the like. This I write in order to give Karlstadt's spirit occasion to write still more books (although nothing is commanded of him) and thunder at me, saying: "The Wittenberg 'high-minded preacher' defames the grace of God, the blood of Christ and the Holy Spirit, since he calls the saints sinners. With the heart he regards them as holy, but he "shrieks" (according to his German manner of speech) otherwise with the pen. Since he calls them sinners, he also regards them as such and turns them into sinners, murders and hangs Christ, and sheds his blood, etc." In this manner the "depth-minded" vagabond preacher is accustomed to carrying on.

Yes, I will even make it worse. I will call Jesus Christ, the Son of God, the crucified and one who died. Let the factious spirit demonstrate his skill and say: "Christ now sits in heaven and is no longer crucified. Since you, however, still call him thus, well then, to that extent you crucify him, and are worse than the Jews by whom he was crucified, even though you say otherwise with the heart and pen." How does that strike you? This spirit would eventually prevent us from using any names from prior history. For if I may not say of the Mass, that it has been a sacrifice, and this is an abominable thing, in case I say: "Here is a sacrifice of the papists, or we receive the sacrifice" (note, that formerly was a sacrifice), then we can no longer in the gospel call Simon the leper, Peter a sinner, nor Paul a persecutor, nor Christ the crucified. For all this is past and due to the devil and now is no more. [...]

Therefore I ask the factious spirit and stuff his own words down his throat: "Say, why do you call the bread and wine a 'martyred, crucified, murdered sacrament'? Are you not also executioners and murderers of Christ, even if you no doubt shriek otherwise with the pen?" If you say, however, that you do not thereby intend this, but only point out what others are doing—ah, dear squire, why can I not then also call it a sacrifice, with the meaning others have developed, rendered, and given? Do you not see, what all the world and even children see, that one is not to judge according to names and appearance, but according to the heart and the deed? I have said all this at greater length than necessary (as though there were some among us who call it a sacrifice), in order to show how unable the spirit is to accomplish anything. For even if his dreams were true, he would still achieve nothing. It stands to reason that a spirit who has lost the fundamental truth and deals only with externals should have a theology of semblance and shadows.

To be sure, it is a sin and a shame, as has been said, to waste so many words and so much time and paper over these trifles. However, it has been fruitful in that the mask has been pulled from this spirit and he has been brought into the light. Being aware of where Dr. Karlstadt has taken up his position, and what he has in mind, everyone will beware of him as of the devil. For that could be granted him as a person, if he taught something about names and semblance, but left alone and did not touch the fundamental truth in the heart and the deed. No one but the devil would stage such a useless show and with high-sounding words pretend as though everything depended on its contention. In addition, he outrageously condemns and slanders the true internal basis,[92] which he himself admits we have and would eagerly have destroyed. For no upright, pious person behaves this way. Were he able to bring it about, he would do everything in his power to destroy utterly the good light of truth and the grace of God that has been given us at Wittenberg, and to persuade the people that through him the true sun had arisen at Orlamünde. [. . .]

The other matter about the elevation of the sacrament is of the same kind.[k] This must also be anti-Christian and papistic. Oh if someone could advise this man to leave both preaching and writing alone and do some other work! He is unfortunately not suited for it. He wants to make new laws and sins and set up new articles of faith. Whether it pleases God or not, he can do nothing else.

Already, early on we have taught Christian liberty from the writings of St. Paul.[93] There is to be freedom of choice in everything that God has not clearly taught in the New Testament, for example, in matters pertaining to various foods, beverages, attire, places, persons, and various forms of conduct [Rom. 14:2-6; 1 Cor. 8:8-10]. We are obligated to do nothing at all for God, except believe and love. Now tell me, where has Christ forbidden us to elevate the sacrament or commanded us to elevate it? Show me one little word, and I will yield. Yet Dr. Karlstadt ventures to burst out and say that it is forbidden by Christ, and considers it a sin as great as the denial of God. He is unable to prove this. Nor is it true. Is it not a woeful, pitiable blindness, so to burden souls with sin and murder them, and make laws where none exist?

92. I.e., of our position.

93. The classic statement is Luther's 1520 treatise *Von der Freiheit eines Christenmenschen* (*Concerning Christian Freedom*), which was reprinted more often than any of Luther's other writings.

---

k   Cf. Karlstadt, *Wider die alten und neuen papistischen Messen*; see Luther's commentary in WA 18:110.

Tell me, my brother, what do you think of the spirit who dares command and direct the Christian to do what Christ does not do, yes to do that of which Christ does the opposite? For Christ does not forbid elevation, but leaves it to free choice. This spirit forbids it, and ensnares the conscience due to his own wanton ambition. Is not this to slander Christ? Is not this to deny Christ? Is not this to set oneself in Christ's place and in Christ's name to murder souls, bind consciences, burden with sins, make laws, and, in short, so to deal with souls as if one were their God? All this, and what more there is to be added, he does who makes law and sin where Christ would have freedom and no sin. For this same reason, we have shown the pope to be the Antichrist, in that he infringes on such freedom with laws, where Christ would have freedom. And my factious spirit blunders upon the same way. He would make captive what Christ would have free.

However, in this respect the profile of the factious spirit differs from that of the pope. They both destroy Christian freedom, and they are both anti-Christian. But the pope does it through commandments, Dr. Karlstadt through prohibitions. The pope commands what is to be done, Dr. Karlstadt what is not to be done. Thus through them Christian freedom is destroyed in two ways: on the one hand, when one commands, constrains, and compels what is to be done, which is nevertheless not commanded or required by God; on the other hand, when one forbids, prevents, and hinders one from doing that which is neither prohibited nor forbidden by God. For my conscience is ensnared and misled just as much when it must refrain from doing something, which it is not necessary to refrain from doing, as when it must do something which it is not necessary to do. When people must refrain from doing that from which they need not refrain and are compelled to do what they need not do, Christian freedom perishes in either case.

The pope destroys freedom in commanding outright that the sacrament is to be elevated, and would have it a statute and a law. Individuals who do not keep his law commit a sin. The factious spirit destroys freedom by forbidding outright that the sacrament be elevated, and would have it a prohibition, a statute, and a law. One who does not act in accordance with this law commits a sin. Here Christ is driven away by both parties. One pushes him out of the front [door], the other drives him out the rear [door]. One errs on the left side, the other on the right, and neither remains on the path of true freedom. I am very much surprised, however, and had I not read it myself in Dr. Karlstadt's books, the whole world could not have convinced me that he should not know this, for I have, you know, instructed him in this and considered him sensible. Oh, Lord God, what are we when you let us fall? What can we do when your hand is removed? What can we achieve when you no longer enlighten us? Is this free will and its power that so quickly makes out of the learned person a child, out of the intelligent a fool, out of the wise person a madman? How terrible are you in all your works and judgments [Ps. 66:3]. [...]

A priest with tonsure and wearing a chasuble raises the host in the Sacrament of the Altar; from 1516 publication.

Teaching and doing are two different matters. I say, furthermore, that one should separate teaching and doing as far from each other as heaven from earth. Teaching belongs only to God. God has the right and the power to command, forbid, and be master over the conscience. However, to do and refrain from doing belongs to us so that we may keep God's commandment and teaching. Where doing or to refrain from doing is in question, and concerning which God has taught, commanded, and forbidden nothing, there we should permit free choice as God himself has done. Whoever though goes beyond this by way of commandments or prohibition invades God's own sphere of action, burdens the conscience, creates sin and misery, and destroys all that God has left free and certain. In addition, he expels the Holy Spirit with all his kingdom, work, and word, so that nothing but devils remain.

Now the elevation of the sacrament, wearing the tonsure, putting on the chasuble and alb, etc., are matters concerning which God has given neither commandments nor prohibitions.

Therefore, everyone is to have freedom of choice to observe these things or refrain from observing them. God wants us to have such freedom, etc. Since the pope does not allow such freedom of action, but curbs it with his teaching and commandment, he usurps the divine office and sets himself arrogantly in God's place, as St. Paul has forewarned concerning him [2 Thess. 2:4]. He makes sin where God would have no sin, and thereby kills souls and binds consciences. Since Dr. Karlstadt does not allow for freedom to refrain from doing what need not be done, but compels with prohibitions and teaching, saying one must not elevate the host, etc., he also usurps the office of God and sets himself in God's place. He makes sin where there neither can nor should be any sin. Thus he kills souls on this side, as does the pope on the other side, and both of them, like murderers of souls, destroy Christian freedom.

We, however, take the middle course and say: There is to be neither commanding nor forbidding, neither to the right nor to the left. We are neither papistic nor Karlstadtian, but free and Christian, in that we elevate or do not elevate the sacrament, how, where, when, as long as it pleases us, as God has given us the liberty to do. Just as we are free to remain outside of marriage or to enter into marriage, to eat meat or not, to wear the chasuble or not, to have the cowl and tonsure or not. In this respect we are lords and will put up with no commandment, teaching, or prohibition. We have also done both here in Wittenberg. For in the monastery we observed Mass without chasuble, without elevation, in the plainest and simplest way, which Karlstadt extols as following Christ's example. On the other hand, in the parish church we still have the chasuble, alb, and altar, and elevate the host as long as we are comfortable.

Therefore my factious spirit ought not fight against us Wittenbergers in this manner: "They elevate the sacrament. Therefore they sin against God." But this might be said: "They teach and command that one must elevate the sacrament lest there be mortal sin. Therefore they sin against God." For so the papists do and teach. We, however, do not so teach, and yet permit freedom to do this as long as it pleases us. The doing does no harm; the teaching, however, is the very devil. On the other hand, in the monastery we refrain from it, but we do not so teach as Dr. Karlstadt does. The refraining does no harm; the teaching, however, is the very devil. From this you may gather, who are "the cousins of the Antichrist," we or Dr. Karlstadt. We do as the papists, but we do not tolerate their teaching, commandment, and constraint. We refrain from doing like the Karlstadtians, but we do not tolerate the prohibition. Thus the pope and Dr. Karlstadt are true cousins in teaching, for they both teach, one the doing, the other the refraining. We, however, teach neither and do both.

Now, my dear sirs, we are speaking of minor matters, insofar as the observation is concerned. For what does it mean to elevate the sacrament? But when the teaching is taken into account we are dealing with most important matters. The factious spirit is too frivolous and meddles all too impudently in this matter. He has such a low regard for teaching and such a high regard for the doing that he does not see the beam in his own eye, and is too much concerned with the splinter in our eye [Matt. 7:5]. For with teaching he manhandles conscience, which Christ has won with his own blood, and kills souls, which God has dearly purchased, with commandments and sins. For thereby the kingdom of Christ will be destroyed and everything that the gospel has brought us will be done away with. For Christ cannot remain in the conscience that goes whoring after outlandish teaching and human commandments. There faith must perish. Therefore let everyone know that Dr. Karlstadt has a spirit which is hostile to faith and to the whole kingdom of God, which he in turn would destroy with his conceit and human nonsense, as you may well understand from this part of the discussion and concerning which you will hear more later.

However, we thank him kindly for teaching us that Christ did not elevate the sacrament in the Last Supper, although we also already knew this, and almost as well as he. We are talking here about teaching, not doing, and we beg him to show us where Christ teaches or forbids elevation. We already know where he refrains from doing it or does not do it. But we are of the opinion that it is not necessary to do or refrain from doing all that Christ has done or refrained from doing. Otherwise we would also have to walk on water and do all the miracles that he did. Furthermore, we would have to refrain from marriage, reject temporal authority, forsake field and plow and all that Jesus has refrained from doing. For that which he would have us do or not do, he has not only done or not done himself, but in addition he has explained in words that command and forbid what we are to do and refrain from doing. For when he says, "I have given you an example, that you also should do as I have done to you" [John 13:15], he applies this, not to Lazarus, whom he had raised from the dead, but to the act of foot washing.

Therefore, we will admit no example, not even from Christ himself, much less from other saints, for it must also be accompanied by God's Word, which explains to us in what sense we are to follow or not to follow it. We do not consider works and examples adequate; indeed we do not want to follow any example: we want the Word, for the sake of which all works, examples, and miracles occur. For certainly he is sufficiently wise and articulate, and able to anticipate the future so as to indicate in words everything which is commanded or forbidden. Well now, hey, you factious spirits, rave on as best you can and show us, where has Christ with one tittle forbidden the elevation of the sacrament? Since you still boast and bluster that Christ prohibits it, where is the prohibition? I imagine it is to be found in the nightgown of the bride in Orlamünde or in the trousers of the bridegroom in Naschhausen.

If the rule is to be that one is so strictly to follow the example of Christ and not the word alone, then it will follow that we should observe the Last Supper nowhere but in Jerusalem, in the upper room [Luke 22:12]. For if incidental circumstances are to be strictly binding, the external places and persons must also strictly be adhered to. And it will come to this, that this Last Supper was only to be observed by the disciples, who were the only ones who were addressed at that time and commanded to observe it. And what St. Paul says (1 Cor. 11[:17ff.]) will become utter foolishness. Also, since we do not know and the text does not state whether red or white wine was used, whether wheat rolls or barley bread were used, we must by reason of doubt at this point refrain from observing the Last Supper until we become certain about it so that we do not make any external detail differ a hairsbreadth from what Christ's example sets forth. Yes, we must also previously in a Jewish manner have eaten the paschal lamb. Also, since the text does not state whether Christ took it in his hands and himself distributed it to each one, we must also wait until it is ascertained so that we do not elevate and administer it differently than Christ did. For where we overlook this, the factious spirit appears and cries: We hang, murder, and crucify Christ. This matter is so very important, and salvation is buried here much more than in Christ's wounds, blood, word, and spirit. [. . .]

And although I had intended also to abolish the elevation, now I will not do it, to defy for a while the fanatic spirit, since he would forbid it and consider it a sin and make us depart from our liberty.[94] For before I would yield a hairsbreadth or for a moment to this soul-murdering spirit and abandon our freedom (as Paul teaches) [Gal. 5:1], I would much rather tomorrow become a strict monk and observe all the monastic rules as stringently as I ever did. This matter of Christian liberty is nothing to joke about. We want to keep it as pure and inviolate as our faith, even if an angel from heaven were to say otherwise [Gal. 1:8]. It has cost our dear, faithful Savior and Lord Jesus Christ too much. It is also altogether too necessary for us. We may not dispense with it without the loss of our salvation.

At this point you should carefully examine Dr. Karlstadt's spirit, noting the way he proceeds, how he would tear us from the Word and lead us toward works. To achieve this all the better, and to make a good impression, he holds before you the works of Christ himself, so that you might thereby be alarmed and think: *Oh, really, who should not follow Christ?* And yet all the while he conceals the Word. For he has none to which he can point. For after he has seen how we will pay no attention to human words and works, be they ever so holy or ancient, etc., and would have Christ alone as our Master, the rogue divides Christ into two parts. Namely, how Christ, on the one hand, without words does and refrains from doing certain works, and, on the other hand, how with words he does and refrains from doing works. Dr. Karlstadt is so knavish that he presents Christ alone as he does and refrains from doing without words, wherein he is not to be followed by us, and is silent where Christ does and refrains from doing with words, wherein we are to follow him. [. . .]

So it is in the world, as the saying goes: He who cannot sing always wants to sing, whoever cannot preach or write, he wants to preach and write. But whoever can, hesitates and does so reluctantly. Dr. Karlstadt, who hereby proves that he does not understand Christ at all, just as above he does not understand Moses, must preach and write when no one has commanded or requested him to do so, and when he is requested to do so, he does not do it. He interprets Moses in such a way that the disorderly populace is incited to punish public misdeed. However, Dr. Karlstadt does not and cannot teach Moses spiritually, as he reveals sin and physically drives rough and rude people to works. He constructs his own Moses. Thus here he also constructs his own Christ, so that we are to follow his works without the Word. But he does not understand how Christ is first of all our salvation, and thereafter his works with the Word are our example. He knows no more about the New Testament than he does about the Old, and yet he would write about the sacrament and such matters, as though there were great need for his absurd and blind art, and, indeed, his folly.

For how is a true understanding of Moses or the law possible, so that the knowledge of sin is taught (Rom. 3[:20], and coarse people are driven to works (Lev. 18[:4-5]), when one so interprets it that the disorderly common people are to revolt and usurp the office of the temporal authority and thereby overturn the whole order and meaning of the law? Furthermore, how is it possible for anyone to understand Christ correctly, as he is given to us in faith unto life, and his words and works are given in love as an example, who goes off in another direction and only emphasizes how we, bidden and unforbidden, are to regard Christ's works as a necessary example and are to follow them? There faith and love together with the whole gospel must perish. And that is why they speak so scornfully of the doctrine of faith and love, as even Dr. Karlstadt himself threw it in my face in Jena, just as if they knew something much higher and better. Yet they do not speak out plainly, nor do they want to bring it out into the open. Even when taken by itself this behavior shows that the devil speaks through them, since they ridicule the doctrine of faith and love, that is, Christ himself with his gospel.

Thereafter the fellow comes again with his Hebrew language and contends thus against us: "The Wittenbergers elevate the sacrament. Therefore they regard it as an offering. For they do precisely what the Law of Moses prescribes, in which there were two offerings, the heave offering and the wave offering[95] [Exod. 35:5; 22; Num. 18:8; 11]. One who elevates makes a heave offering, etc." This is a bit too much! If this is not blindness, what then is blindness? This spirit calls everything that one elevates an offering and argues from the particular to the universal.

95. These types of sacrificial offerings are described in detail in *The Anchor Bible Dictionary*, vol. 5 (New York: Doubleday, 1992), 870–91.

96. In two writings of 1523, Karlstadt had pointedly referred to himself as a "new layperson." He must have meant this as an antipode to Luther's declaration that all Christians were priests.

97. In the Karlstadt–Luther encounter in Jena, Karlstadt had said that he would earn his living with a plow and thus know what a plow can do. See WA 15:338ff.

98. The elevation was thus understood as an invitation to adore the host and the cup.

Thus, there is one elevation in the law that is an offering; therefore all elevation is offering. This would be as if I were to say: One finds an elevation that is an offering; therefore elevation of all kinds is an offering. Or thus, a cow in Orlamünde is black; therefore all cows in the world are black. I must speak in a lay and rustic manner with the new layman and peasant.[96] Here we see what the plowman from Naschhausen is able to do, of whom Dr. Karlstadt boasted at Jena, that he would put all the doctors in the world to shame.[97] When the maid lifts the mirror to look at herself, she offers it. When the farmer lifts the ax or the flail, to chop or to thresh, he offers it. When the mother raises the child and dandles it, she offers it. Therefore she trespasses against Christ's prohibition, hangs, murders, slays, crucifies Christ and does all the evil that those do who offer Christ. How the fanatic spirit raves! For the plowman at Naschhausen has said it: He who elevates, offers.

Tell me, has not this peasant amply deserved that one should set his plow right? In this manner God ought to cast down those who rise and set themselves against the knowledge of God and decide to act on a knowledge of their own. The Egyptians were not to be stricken with a common darkness, but with one that could be felt [Exod. 10:21]. In my opinion an attitude of this kind implies the loss of reason, sense, and understanding. The papists themselves have never been so foolhardy nor of the opinion that they offered the sacrament by elevating it, although they otherwise regard it as a sacrifice. But they elevate it in order to show it to the people, to remind them of the passion of Christ, etc.[98] For this reason the priest does not say a word, either about sacrifice or anything else, when he elevates it. How should we then offer it through the elevation, we who insist so strongly that it is no sacrifice?

But it is the same fiddle upon which he always fiddles, namely, that the external appearance is the main thing, according to which everything that the heart, mouth, pen, and hand confesses is to be regarded and judged. Therefore it does not help that we believe with the heart, confess with the mouth, testify with the pen, and demonstrate with deeds that we do not regard the sacrament as a sacrifice, though we still elevate it. The elevation is so important and by itself counts for so much that it outweighs and condemns everything else. Is this not a vexatious spirit, who so juggles with external appearance against the truth in the spirit? If only the elevation were permitted to remain an external matter, the brides would be truly undressed and naked regardless of how one felt about it in his heart. [. . .]

This, however, I have said as though it were true and conceded that possibly an elevation could take place which would be an offering, as this spirit pretends. But no one on earth calls elevation an offering, except this spirit, who has invented this and sought to burden us with it, since he did not know anything else to write about. Nor will he ever be able to show where elevation means a sacrifice. He himself has forgotten his own words, where he says: Sacrifice is equivalent to slaying, killing, hanging, murdering, burning, etc. Who, however, would be so mad as to say that elevating was the same as slaying, killing, murdering, burning? Only this spirit, who perhaps also learns a new German from his heavenly voice. Thereupon he raves and fights against himself, in that whoever elevates, sacrifices.

To demonstrate his excellent command of the Hebrew language, he produces from the Hebrew the two words *thnupa* and *thruma*, which I have translated as "wave offering" and "heave" offering, or heave and wave. The world is to marvel at the plowman of Naschhausen's understanding of the Hebrew language. Yet it is not the common Hebrew, which everyone speaks, but that which the Spirit teaches daily anew and daily, with the aid of the heavenly voice. For my Hebrew language[99] teaches me that before one offers something according to the law, one must heave and wave it. And it must be heaved and waved so as to acknowledge God and give thanks to him as for a gift, which is not offered or given to God, but received from him. Just as I have said above about the term *Mass*. Only after it had been heaved and waved was it offered and kindled, so that even in the law heave and wave cannot by any means be sacrifice.

Behold, what expert knowledge this spirit has of the law of Moses and the Hebrew tongue, and yet he is so arrogant and wanton that he builds articles of faith on such dreams of his, and would have the consciences so completely ensnared thereby, that they become Christ's murderers, hangmen, and executioners, if they elevate the sacrament. Thus the devil must always have his mouth full of slander in order to destroy Christ.

Dr. Karlstadt has fallen from the kingdom of Christ and has suffered shipwreck with respect to faith. Therefore he wants to

99. Of course, Luther means to say here that there is a normative language, which is his.

get us out of the kingdom right into works and simply make Galatians of us also. For take note, dear reader, what gross blindness it is to fight as he does. "If anyone be circumcised, should he not in all fairness be called a Jew? Thus, whoever elevates is rightly called one who brings a sacrifice, etc." You poor, miserable spirit, where on earth have you read that he is rightly called a Jew who is circumcised? Did not Paul circumcise Timothy when he was already baptized and a Christian (Acts 16[:3])? Does not Paul declare circumcision a matter of free choice (1 Cor. 7[:19]): "Neither circumcision counts for anything nor non-uncircumcision," that is, one may be circumcised himself or not, have a foreskin or not? And this spirit pits his judgment blithely and boldly against that of Paul, saying it is not a matter of free choice, but makes one a Jew. He ought rather say that whoever is circumcised himself as though he were compelled to do so by law and for conscience's sake, he is rightly a Jew. For circumcision does not make a Jew, since one does find those who due to illness or on account of an infection must be circumcised. Should they therefore be called Jews?

He, however, is a Jew who, compelled by his conscience, by law, feels he must be circumcised. This Jewish disposition and conscience makes one a Jew, even if he never was physically circumcised or could circumcise himself. The foreskin thus makes no one a Jew. But if he thinks in his conscience, he must have a foreskin, he is a Gentile, even if he permitted himself to be externally circumcised a thousand times. Similarly, since he thinks it necessary to have the foreskin and to condemn circumcision without leaving it a free choice as Christ would have it, Dr. Karlstadt actually is a Gentile and has lost Christ. Here one sees clearly how this man is completely swallowed up in works and drowned in external appearance, so that he is not able to give one single right proper judgment in spiritual matters of conscience. For it is impossible that a spark of Christian understanding should still be found in him, since he holds that an external work makes a Jew or Christian, Gentile or Turk, and does not judge according to the conscience, but according to semblance and appearance, which even reasonable people do not do.

In this instance, too, he should have said, "Whoever elevates the sacrament out of necessity of conscience, as if he had to elevate it, would also be a Jew." But we do not do so, as he well knows. Therefore he feared that he would be put to shame, as one who publicly lies against us. But he did not see that he hereby acquires much greater shame, in that he lies against God and forbids an action, as condemned by God's prohibition, which God, however, has not forbidden. On the other hand, whoever insists that the sacrament may not be elevated, as a matter of necessity is a Gentile. In doing this Dr. Karlstadt sets up a law compelling the conscience, which only God has a right to do. But whoever elevates the sacrament with such a conscience and the intention of making it an offering, is one who sacrifices, and a papist. For where such a conscience exists, there one sacrifices, even if one never elevated the sacrament or even sank it into a deep well. Where, however, such a conscience does not exist, there one does not sacrifice, even if one raised it above the heavens and the whole world shouted: Sacrifice, sacrifice! For everything depends on the conscience. Of this the fanatic spirit knows nothing, or does not want to know anything.

I imagine the reading of this treatise will annoy many, since it deals with such charlatanry. But how can I avoid it? This mad spirit drives me to it. Yet, as I said above, we have some fruit from it in that we defend and understand more clearly our Christian freedom. We also recognize this false spirit for what he is and see how he is blind and stupid in all things. Everyone may therefore govern himself accordingly. For since he does not understand such trifling external things, but so magnifies them as to usurp the office of God, making laws, sin, and matters of conscience, where none exist, destroying Christian liberty, and enticing consciences away from an understanding of grace to external works and appearance, so that Christ is denied, his kingdom destroyed, and the gospel reviled—who then can hope that he will ever be able to write or teach anything that is good? For certainly one can prove from this matter that the spirit of Christ is lacking. It must be the devil that is there, and so he is. Let each one govern himself accordingly.

I am pleased the Mass now is held in German among the Germans. But to make a necessity of this, as if it had to be so, is again too much. This spirit cannot do anything else than continually create laws, necessity, problems of conscience and sin. To be sure, I have read in 1 Cor. 14[:27-28] that he who speaks with tongues is to be silent in the congregation when no one understands anything of what he says. One tends, however, to skip over the other words: "Unless there is someone to interpret." That is, St. Paul permits speaking in tongues, "if at the same time it is interpreted," so that one understands it. Therefore, he also commands that they are not to prevent those who speak in tongues, etc. Now we administer the sacrament to no one unless he understands the words in the sacrament, as is well known. So in this matter we do not act contrary to St. Paul, since we satisfy his intention.[1] If we do not satisfy this spirit, who only looks at external works and has no regard for either conscience or intentions, it is of no importance. We attach no importance to his new articles of faith.

I would gladly have a German Mass today. I am in fact occupied with it.[100] But I would very much like it to have a true German character. For to translate the Latin text and retain the Latin tone or notes has my sanction, though it doesn't sound polished or well done. Both the text and notes, accent, melody, and manner of rendering ought to grow out of the true mother tongue and its inflection, otherwise all of it becomes an imitation, in the manner of the apes. Now since the enthusiastic spirit presses that it must be, and will again burden the conscience with laws, works, and sins, I will take my time and hurry less in this direction than before, only to spite the sin-master and soul-murderer, who presses upon us works, as if they were commanded by God, though they are not.

For whoever goes to the sacrament understanding these words in German or having them clearly in his heart: "Take, eat; this is my body," etc. [Matt. 26:26], which he has learned and borne in mind from a sermon just heard, and thereupon and therewith receives the sacrament, receives it rightly and does not merely hear speaking in tongues, but something that has real meaning. On the other hand those who do not comprehend or understand these words in their hearts, nor thereupon receive the sacrament, would not be helped if a thousand preachers stood around their ears and shouted themselves into a frenzy with such words. However, for the mad spirit everything depends on external works and appearance, which out of his own head he would continually set up as necessary and as an article of faith, without God's commandment.

100. Luther's *The German Mass* (*Deutsche Messe und Ordnung des Gottesdiensts*) was published in January 1526. See LW 53:51–90; also in TAL, vol. 3, forthcoming.

1 A reference to 1 Cor. 12:29.

Also the fool does not understand St. Paul's words correctly when he writes of speaking in tongues (1 Cor. 14[:2-29]). For St. Paul writes of the office of preaching in the congregation, to which it is to listen and to learn from it, when he says: Whoever comes forward, and wants to read, teach, or preach, and yet speaks in tongues, that is, speaks Latin instead of German, or some unknown language, he is to be silent and preach to himself alone. For no one can hear it or understand it, and no one can get any benefit from it. Or if he should speak in tongues, he ought, in addition, put what he says into German, or interpret it in one way or another, so that the congregation may understand him. Thus St. Paul is not as stubborn in forbidding speaking in tongues as this sin-spirit is, but says it is not to be forbidden when along with it interpretation takes place.

Hence has come the custom in all lands, to read the gospel immediately before the sermon in Latin, which St. Paul calls speaking in tongues in the congregation. However, since the sermon comes soon thereafter and translates and interprets the tongue, St. Paul does not reject or forbid it. Why should I then, or anyone condemn it? Yes, would to God, that only this order of St. Paul were everywhere in effect so that after the Latin gospel nothing else was preached than its exposition. Now this enthusiastic spirit would condemn everything that St. Paul permits and forbids one not to condemn. In addition he will allow no singing or Latin words, and applies the teaching of St. Paul about speaking in tongues not to the office of preaching alone, but to all external forms. This is always his method, though these forms are not essential.

Not that I would oppose using nothing but German in the Mass, but I will not endure that someone without God's Word and out of arrogance and wantonness forbids the reading of the Latin gospel and makes sin where none exists, lest we get the factious spirit with his fanaticism as master in the place of God. For we cannot establish or strengthen our cause against the papists with such charlatanry. Otherwise we would stand before them in disgrace. Our whole ground must be certain and the words of God pure upon which we build and do combat against the papists, so that they are unable honestly to oppose our arguments. For even if we now get the Mass in German, it will still not be enough to speak the words of the sacrament in German. For they must be spoken earlier and beforehand, before we receive the sacrament, so that they who go to receive it might have the words in the heart and not in the ears. What difference does it make if they do not hear in the sacrament, if, immediately preceding the reception they have heard the words in the sermon and have comprehended them, and then make their confession, unless one would yell the same words in the ears of everyone who goes to receive the sacrament, and consecrate the sacrament as many times as there are individuals to receive it. [...]

Part II

Our controversy has no doubt given great joy to the papists and inspired among them the hope that our cause would thereby suffer defeat. So be it, let them boast and exalt over us. Often and repeatedly I have said that if our cause is of God no one will be able to suppress it. If it is not of God, I will not be able to support it whatever someone else does. I can lose nothing by it, for I have won nothing. But this I know, that no one but God alone can take it from me. However much I regret this vexation, I am glad that the devil now reveals himself and his shamefulness through these heavenly prophets. They have long grumbled to themselves and would not even have come out into the open unless I had lured them out through a gulden.[101] This I believe, by God's grace, to be a good investment that I do not regret.

I am not worried as long as God is with me. I know and am sure who is master of the situation. He has not hitherto failed me in the face of many a hard blow. He will not fail me now. Those who have the gospel can be calm and confident. We trust joyfully and are of good courage. Our adversaries are dejected, dumb, despairing, and anxious spirits who tremble at the rustling of a leaf [Lev. 26:36], but, as always with the godless (Ps. 36[:2]), know no fear of God but do violence to God's Word and work. God is concealed and cannot be seen or felt. Were he a present, visible person, he could drive them out of the land with a stem of straw.

For this spirit has wrought thus: At first he sneaked around and came out boldly upsetting things and seeking followers.[102] Then, when he thought he had a following, he emerged boldly, thinking all was won. But his trust is not in God, though his followers claim that God speaks to them. Rather, he depends on

101. Luther refers to a gold coin of the time, perhaps of the Holy Roman Empire.

102. Luther seems to be saying here that even early on Karlstadt had notions different than those of Luther, only waiting for the opportune moment to come out into the open.

the favor of the common people and builds on flesh and blood. For when God compels anyone to speak, a public proclamation is made, even if he is alone and no one follows him, as in the case of Jeremiah [Jer. 2:2ff.]. I too can claim that this was my way. It is the way of the devil to glide around in secrecy and in conspiracy, afterward making the excuse that at first his spirit was not strong enough. No, Sir Devil, the spirit that is of God makes no such excuse. I know you well.

The true nature of the devil is not yet apparent. For he has still other ideas that I have smelled for a long time. They too will be revealed, if God wills. It has come to the point, God be praised, when this is not particularly my affair. There are plenty of others who can answer such a spirit, without my having to be involved with him during my lifetime. I am well aware that Dr. Karlstadt has been cooking this brew for a long time without being able to get anything under way. I have also known that he could not do it any better than he has done no matter how long he chewed on his clever notions. For no art or wit or imagination is of avail before God. With one word he can bring all to shame. He knows that human thoughts are vain [Prov. 21:30].

If anyone is so weak that he has fallen before this onslaught and now has doubts about the sacrament, let him follow that advice and get along for a while without the sacrament. Let him busy himself with the Word of God, in faith and love, and let those who are secure in their conscience concern themselves with the sacrament. You are not condemned if you are without the sacrament. But let the papists who rejoice over this controversy beware lest they harden their hearts. For it is not the first time God has ordered things so as to appear foolish and weak and God's Word and purpose seem on the point of extinction, in order that the godless should thereby be hardened and blinded. At such times God's purpose has emerged the more strongly, and they who were hardened and blinded by God's seeming foolishness and weakness have been the more terribly destroyed. Such was the case of the Jews when Christ was crucified and such the case when the martyrs were made to suffer [1 Cor. 1:18ff.].

Just as the devil is disorderly and jumbles things together, so Dr. Karlstadt's treatise and head are equally disordered and confused, so that it is exceedingly annoying to read (and difficult to remember) what he writes. Yet I will try to create some order in view of his passion and poison and to consider his argument part by part. I would first present in broad outline the fundamental idea from which all his raving emanates, so that the reader may be clearer in observing and judging this spirit. This is the argument.

Out of his great mercy God has again given us the pure gospel, the noble and precious treasure of our salvation. This gift evokes faith and a good conscience in the inner man, as is promised in Isa. 55[:1], that his Word will not go forth in vain, and Rom. 10[:17], and that "faith comes through preaching." The devil hates this gospel and will not tolerate it. Since he has not succeeded hitherto in opposing it with the power of the sword, he now, as indeed always, seeks victory by deceit and with false prophets. I ask you, Christian reader, to note this carefully. If God wills, I will help you to discern the devil in these prophets so that you can yourself deal with him. It is for your good, not mine, that I write. Follow me thus:

Now when God sends forth the holy gospel, God deals with us in a twofold manner, first outwardly, then inwardly. Outwardly God deals with us through the oral word of the gospel and through material signs, that is, baptism and the sacrament of the altar. Inwardly God deals with us through the Holy Spirit, faith, and other gifts. But whatever their measure or order, the external factors should and must precede. The inward experience follows and is effected by the external. God has determined to give the inward to no one except through the outward. For God wants to give no one the spirit or faith outside of the outward Word and sign instituted by him, as Luke 16[:29] says, "Let them hear Moses and the prophets." Accordingly Paul can call baptism a "washing of regeneration" wherein God "richly pours out the Holy Spirit" [Titus 3:5]. And the oral gospel "is the power of God for salvation to everyone who has faith" (Rom. 1[:16]).

Observe carefully, my brother and my sister, this order, for everything depends on it. However cleverly this factious spirit makes believe that he regards highly the Word and Spirit of God and declaims passionately about love and zeal for the truth and righteousness of God, he nevertheless has as his purpose to reverse this order. His insolence leads him to set up a contrary order and, as we have said, seeks to subordinate God's outward order to an inner spiritual one. Casting this order to the wind with ridicule and scorn, he wants to get to the Spirit first. Will a handful of water, he says, make me clean from sin? The Spirit, the Spirit, the Spirit, must do this inwardly. Can bread and wine profit me? Will breathing over the bread bring Christ in the sacrament? No, no, one must eat the flesh of Christ spiritually. The Wittenbergers are ignorant of this. They make faith depend on the letter. Whoever does not know the devil might be misled by these many splendid words to think that five holy spirits were in the possession of Karlstadt and his followers.

But should you ask how one gains access to this same lofty spirit, they do not refer you to the outward gospel but to some imaginary realm, saying: Remain in "self-abstraction"[103] where I now am and you will have the same experience. A heavenly voice will come, and God himself will speak to you. If you inquire further as to the nature of this "self-abstraction," you will find that they know as much about it as Dr. Karlstadt knows of Greek and Hebrew. Do you not see here the devil, the enemy of God's order? With all his mouthing of the words, "Spirit, Spirit, Spirit," he tears down the bridge, the path, the way, the ladder, and all the means by which the Spirit might come to you. Instead of the external order of God in the material sign of baptism and the oral proclamation of the Word of God he wants to teach you, not how the Spirit comes to you but how you come to the Spirit. They would have you learn how to journey on the clouds and ride on the wind. They do not tell you how or when, whither or what, but you are to experience what they do. [. . .]

They pay no attention to God's design of inward things, such as faith. They approach and force all external words and Scriptures belonging to the inward life of faith into new forms of putting to death the old Adam. They invent such things as "turning from the material," "concentration," "adoration," "self-abstraction," and other such foolishness that has not an inkling of foundation in Scripture.[104] My Karlstadt plunges in like a sow to devour pearls, and like a dog tearing holy things to pieces [Matt. 7:6]. What Christ has said and referred to the inner life of faith, this man applies to outward, self-contrived works, even to the point of making the Lord's Supper and the recognition and remembrance of Christ a human work, whereby we in like manner, in "passionate ardor" and (as they stupidly put it) with "outstretched desire," put ourselves to death. By throwing up a smoke screen, he obscures the clear words of Christ, "My

103. Ger.: *Langweile.* One of the seven stages of the mystic apprehension of God.

104. In the German original *Entgroebung; Studierung; Sonderung; Langweile,* all terms taken from the medieval mystical vocabulary.

blood poured out for you for the forgiveness of sins," etc. [Matt. 26:28; Mark 14:24; Luke 22:20]. Their meaning undoubtedly is grasped, received, and retained only by faith, and by no kind of work. This will become clearer as we proceed. [. . .]

So, my brother, cling firmly to God's order. According to it the putting to death of the old Adam, wherein we follow the example of Christ, as Peter says [1 Pet. 2:21], does not come first, as this devil urges, but comes last. None can mortify the flesh, bear the cross, and follow the example of Christ before they are Christians and have Christ through faith in their hearts as an eternal treasure. You do not put the old nature to death, as these prophets do, through works, but through the hearing of the gospel. Before all other works and acts you hear the Word of God, through which the Spirit convinces the world of its sin (John 16[:8]). When we acknowledge our sin, we hear of the grace of Christ. In this Word the Spirit comes and gives faith where and to whom he wills. Then you proceed to the mortification and the cross and the works of love. Whoever wants to propose to you another order, you can be sure, is of the devil. Such is the spirit of Karlstadt, as you will more clearly see presently.

So to our task, by the power of God.

First, what a fuss this spirit makes over the word and name, "sacrament." He makes a mountain out of a molehill. I regret to have to answer him. But it is necessary in view of his overbearing attitude. Christ and the apostles, he says, never used the word. He wants a biblical word. God has given names to what he has created. We humans should not give names to divine things. At last he becomes a Jew and calls it a *"sekerment,"* as the Jews ridicule us Christians, deriving the word from *seker theminith,* that is, a false image. So Hebrew is taught at Naschhausen, *seker* meaning false, and *ment,* an image. Why this parading of words? In order to impress the mad mob who with open mouth and nostrils exclaim, "Believe me, that is something. Here is a learned man. Here is a spirit."

This illustrates what I have said above. Outward names and signs that God has neither commanded nor forbidden become the main subject on which all emphasis is laid, just as in the matter of the names of Mass and elevation. If you don't speak of sacrament, you are supposed to be spiritual and holy. But whoever uses the word *sacrament*, he makes black white, and deceives the people about God and perpetrates similar horrible vices. In short, he denies Christ. But is it not a terrible thing for this frivolous spirit to make so much of nothing? Listen, murderer of souls and sinful spirit! We admit that God has not called it a sacrament, nor commanded us to call it a sacrament. But tell me, on your part, where has he forbidden it? Suppose it is only a name. What then? Who has given you the power to forbid what God has not forbidden? What reason is there for your sacrilege in framing up great sins where God has not considered them such? Are you not indeed a murderer of souls who sets himself above us in God's place and takes away our Christian liberty and subordinates consciences to himself?

Indeed you do not use the name employed by Christ and the apostles. Why do you lie so grossly? We also call it the Lord's Supper, or the bread and cup of the Lord, as we read it in the words of the Apostle in 1 Cor. 11[:25]. Yet, stupid spirit, you ought to accuse us, saying, "They forbid us to call it a sacrament and forbid us to speak of it as the Lord's Supper." If you were to pin something like that on us, your bitter poisonous hatred would have something on us. Since we neither command nor forbid anything in this respect, but, in free conscience call it a sacrament, you are the one who denies and blasphemes Christ when entirely on your own, without God's command, you forbid, condemn, and slander a freedom which we have from God, as a gift, and when you make so great and necessary and spiritual a thing out of your external names and signs.

May I not call my Lord Jesus Christ by a name not in Scripture? How about such names as crown of my heart, joy of my heart, my ruby—if I do not make it a matter of conscience, claiming that thus and in no other way is he to be designated? But where do you find these names in Scripture? If we want to speak of baptism and the Lord's Supper collectively, what are we to do? We find no word in Scripture that comprehends all the sacraments or signs. So we must be silent or not speak of them collectively, else these prophets judge us as deniers of Christ. Similarly in regard to the several articles of faith, the various points of Christian doctrine, the various chapters in the Bible. How are we to treat them? These names, articles, points, chapters are not in the Bible. So we are no longer to say anything about articles of the faith, points of doctrine, chapters of the Bible. What will even these heavenly prophets do, since they refer by name to chapters of the Scriptures? Are not also they murderers of Christ, by their own judgment, since they give names that are not in the Bible to divine things?

We might let it pass if we were dealing with clowns at carnival time. But surely we are not dealing with a good spirit when we find these lofty minds, these heavenly prophets, clowning so childishly in such serious matters and on top of it wanting us to look on these trifles as chief articles of the Christian faith. What light can there be in heads that hold such tangible darkness? I say this in order to expose for you this devil and prove what I have said above. Observe therefore how this rogue institutes ordinances that God has not commanded, and calls spiritual what he has himself contrived. Also, he slanders and deprives us of the Christian freedom that is ours in spirit and conscience. Dear friend, do not lightly regard this prohibition of what God has not forbidden, or the violation of Christian freedom that Christ purchased for us with his blood, or the burdening of conscience with sins that do not exist. Whoever does and dares do this, dares also do any evil. Indeed he denies thereby all that God is, teaches, and does, as well as his Christ. So it is no wonder that in the sacrament he wants nothing else than bread and wine, and is the cause of still other disasters. What good can the devil do?

Therefore, my brother, listen to me. You know that for the sake of every article of the Christian faith including that of Christian freedom we ought to be willing to risk body and soul. Therefore do what is prohibited and allow what is commanded by those opposing freedom. Even so St. Paul taught the Galatians [Gal. 5:1ff.]. Since this same Christian freedom is in danger in regard to this word and name, sacrament, you are henceforth obligated to call the Lord's Supper a sacrament, in defiance of these prophets of the devil. And if you are among them or come upon them, you must call it a sacrament, not on account of your own conscience, but in order to confess and maintain Christian freedom. Do not allow the devil to make a commandment, prohibition, sin, or matter of conscience where God wants none. If you allow them to make this a sin, Christ is no more; they take him away. For with that kind of a conscience we deny the true Christ, who takes away all sin. So you see that though it may seem a small thing, there is no small peril when you make these issues a matter of conscience.

It is the same as in regard to the prohibition of meat on a fish day. Eat meat on that day. Do not eat it on a day you are commanded to do so. If you are forbidden to marry, get married, or declare your willingness to do so. So also in other matters. When human beings want to make commandments, prohibitions, designations of sin, good works, scruples, and perils where God gives freedom and neither commands nor forbids, you must hold firmly to such freedom and always do the contrary until you gain this freedom. Paul would not consent to the circumcision of Titus (Gal. 2[:3]) when others sought to compel him and said it was necessary. Yet he had Timothy circumcised (Acts 16[:3]) when he was under no compulsion. So in this instance you may or may not call it a sacrament. But when these prophets try to force you and forbid you, then you should and must call it a sacrament.

Furthermore, when he goes on to prove that the body and blood of Christ are not in the sacrament, he himself confesses to having been influenced by the traditional statement that the natural body of Christ is as large, broad, thick, and long in the sacrament as it was on the cross. This he says, he cannot believe. This he (as Caiaphas) was compelled by God to say of himself, so that everyone can see that he did not derive his interpretation from but outside of Scripture, and that he wants to bring this kind of notion to Scripture, bending, forcing, and torturing it according to his own conceit instead of letting his stupid mind be changed and directed by the Word and Scripture of God.

But it happens that the common people and reason easily fall for such talk and conceit, and there is really no cause to boast of heavenly voices and lofty exalted minds. Even the most mediocre intellect is inclined thus and would rather believe that only bread and wine were present than that the body and blood of Christ are here concealed. One needs no unusual spirit for that which anyone easily believes. All that the stupid common populace needs is that someone with a bit of reputation is smart enough to preach this and he has pupils enough. It would not be hard for me to believe and preach such a doctrine, so Dr. Karlstadt need not in this respect boast of much knowledge or skill.

But if we are so disposed to treat our faith that we bring our pet ideas into Scripture and deal with Scripture according to our understanding, attending only to what is common to the crowd and generally accepted notions, then no article of the faith will remain. For there is no article in Scripture that God has not placed beyond the reach of reason. On this account, Dr. Karlstadt's error reveals itself in his attitude toward faith and the Word of God, namely, that reason readily and willingly accepts it, while in reality reason balks at the Word of God and the articles of faith. And he dares to make this the chief foundation of an article of his own. I too could say that I cannot believe that the Son of God has become human and comprehended in the narrow womb of a woman a majesty that heaven and earth could not contain and then allowed himself to be crucified. And I could then twist and interpret all Scripture and the word of God according to my opinion, as Mani did.[105] So at the very beginning it is sufficiently known that he has brought his pet ideas into Scripture and not drawn them thence, as indeed he cannot derive them thence. He could have kept this method to himself, but God has so ordered it that the cuckoo should call out his own name.

Then he proceeds to Scripture, before which he fears for his life, and seeks to bewitch it so that it will not fell him, saying, "This verse," etc. But while he is mumbling in the dark out of fear, let me set forth his meaning a bit more clearly. He interprets the words in which the Evangelists describe the Lord's Supper in this manner, "Jesus took the bread, gave thanks and broke it and gave to his disciples, saying, take, eat, this is my body which is given for you, do this in remembrance of me."

He says that the words "this is my body given for you" form an independent sentence and do not belong to the preceding ones, "Take, eat." Their meaning and message is isolated from the rest so that, although they have been added, the passage would be complete without the preceding words.

In short Dr. Karlstadt's contention is that Christ might as well have omitted the words "This is my body given for you" in the Lord's Supper, and that it would be sufficient to say, "Jesus took the bread, gave thanks and broke it, and gave it to his disciples saying, Take, eat, do this in remembrance of me" [1 Cor. 11:24; Matt. 26:26].

105. Luther refers to the Persian Mani (b. 242, martyred in 277) founder of a religion named after him (Manicheism). Mani not only interpreted Scripture in a broad way, but also posited the eternal tension between spirit and matter.

That he has given his body, that is, his body [life] for us, he holds, is mentioned in many other places in Scripture. Here it is introduced superfluously, but to remind the disciples why they should hold him in remembrance. You might almost think that Christ was a drunkard who had indulged so much that night that he became loquacious with his disciples.

How think you? Is not his an irresponsible spirit who so shamelessly deals with God in his Word and twists it as he pleases? While these spirits boast that they dare not use a word unless it is enforced by clear passages of Scripture, and that this must be the procedure, as he constantly urges Gemser[106] in his treatises, saying, show the basis for your argument, cite Scripture, compel, force, pin down, and insist on your interpretation so no one may escape you. But we are willing to accept his own rule and say, dear spirit, you claim two things, first, that the passage "This is my body given for you" is an independent assertion and does not depend on its context. We ask you, do not heed what we see but show us the basis for your argument, cite Scripture, forcing and compelling us to acknowledge your position. How about it? Can you do it? For God's sake, show us at least one syllable that clearly declares or compels us to believe that this passage is an isolated one, and we will believe it. Won't you? Where is your spirit? Where is your God? Asleep? [1 Kings 18:27]. Or is God vanquished? Alas, dear children, how silent and speechless the spirit is now who has written so many books and yet cannot adduce one word to prove that this passage stands by itself. [...]

For if it were an additional statement it ought not to be in the midst of other words nor involved with such as refer to eating. Instead, if the other sentence is complete, the words should follow, and according to Karlstadt the text would read thus: "Take and eat. Do this in remembrance of me. For I say to you that here sits the body which will be given for you."

So Christ would have spoken if it were an additional sentence and if Christ had followed Dr. Karlstadt's opinion. But he is not so loquacious or confused in the head as Dr. Karlstadt, though Dr. Karlstadt thinks that because he himself mixes everything and brews without any order, Christ does the same. But this he should first prove. That he himself has such a mind and method needs no further proof.

106. Luther refers here sarcastically to Jerome [or Hieronymus] Emser (1477–1527). Emser studied at Tübingen and Basel and was, in fact, one of the first professorial appointments at Wittenberg. In the indulgences controversy, Emser increasingly took positions supportive of the "old" church and became Luther's foremost antagonist. His major contribution was a German translation of the New Testament from the Vulgate.

A title page of Hieronymous Emser's translation of the New Testament into German, published 1527 in Dresden, Saxony.

In the second place this spirit must prove his statement that "This is my body" is added here in order to teach and remind the disciples why they are to remember Christ. Well, the spirit has said so, and so it is it is out in the open, because the spirit has said so. But where are the grounds and proof that Christ for this reason added these words? Oh, Peter of Naschhausen,[107] show your poor companion one little syllable so as to press, force, and compel him so to confess. For he hears well enough what you say, but it is a great shame that you have forgotten that you must prove it. Where is it written? What passage in Scripture says that these words were added to give instructions about remembrance? I know that we are to remember the death of Christ. But that these words, found in the biblical account, were added for this purpose I do not know, namely, that the Supper is complete without this sentence, and plenty of other passages indicate why we should remember Christ. Had I been with you, Peter, I would have introduced you to another kind of Gemser who would have set the ruffian straight. [. . .]

This tearing and torturing of God's Word reminds me of an author whose book I read as a young Master of Arts. He twisted and tortured the Lord's Prayer thus: Our Father, hallowed be Thou in heaven, Thy name come, Thy kingdom be done, etc. The subdivisions were strange and rare, and reasons for doing so were not lacking. It also reminds me of the way some Jews have treated Gen. 2 [1:27]: "God created man in his own image; male and female he created them." This they interpret to mean that God created Adam in such a way as to include both a male and female image. If such cutting and dividing were valid, especially in passages of importance, and such as are the basis of articles of faith, what a fine Bible we would have. In other passages it may not be so important.

This then is our ground. Where Holy Scripture is the ground of faith, we are not to deviate from the words as they stand nor from the order in which they stand, unless an express article of faith compels a different interpretation or order. For else what would happen to the Bible? For instance, when the Psalmist says, "God is my rock" [Ps. 18:3], he uses a word which otherwise refers to a natural stone. But inasmuch as my faith teaches me that God is not a natural stone, I am compelled to give the word "stone," in this place, another meaning than the natural one. So also in Matt. 16[:18], "On this rock I will build my church." In the passage we now are treating, no article of faith compels us to sever it and remove it from its place, or to hold that the bread is not the body of Christ. Therefore we must take the words just as they stand, making no change and letting the bread be the body of Christ.

But, says Peter Rültz, it is a special sentence, because the phrase "This is my body" begins with a capital letter, and it is preceded by a period, which usually indicates the beginning of a new passage. What do I hear? I demanded a reason and basis in Scripture, and you give me a period and capital letter. Is a period and a capital letter Holy Scripture in the mind of the Naschhausen plowman? Indeed I hear you give me your peculiar notion in place of divine Scripture and return dirt for gold. Because you have the opinion that a period and capital letter indicate something different and new, you want to talk me into thinking the same without scriptural authority. Peculiar notions and crying Scripture, Scripture, Scripture, compel, urge, force me by a word of God, will not prove that a period and a capital letter introduce something new. Where in Scripture do you find a clear assertion that a period and a capital letter mark the beginning of an independent statement? Don't you hear, Peter? Peter, do you hear?

Is it not a sin and shame that this spirit seeks to base so important a matter on such idle prattle yet makes so terrible a racket if we do not give a scriptural basis? Suppose my book had no periods or capitals and yours had both. Our faith might come to depend on ink and pen, and even on the disposition of writer and printer. That would be a fine foundation! To put it briefly, we must have sober, lucid words and texts, which by reason of their clarity are convincing, regardless of whether they are written with capital or small letters, with or without punctuation. For even if it were true (which it is not) that a period and capital indicated something new, should it follow in regard to Holy Scripture that my faith should rest not on expressions and words alone but on frail periods and capitals which really say or sing nothing. That would indeed be a false foundation.

How about the use in some books (not all are alike) of capital letters and punctuation marks to indicate the importance of what is said, so that the reader will the better observe and remember it, rather than that something new is signified? On what doubts my faith would then be founded if it were claimed that a period and a capital letter introduced something new? How often do we consistently spell the name Christ with a capital letter? How often do we underline or draw a hand or some figure alongside the text, though it is not a question of something new. Punctuation marks and letters are a human invention and tool, and individuals have full freedom to put them wherever they wish. My Dr. Karlstadt wants to base a godly faith and word on such shifting human conventions.

Alas, what can I say? The spirit can truly not be serious.[108] It is clear that he is concerned only about self-contrived matters and not much about faith and God's Word. Woe to a faith that, compelled to seek support and aid from such scraps, is not grounded on any word from the great and wide Scriptures, where all articles generally have a substantial and solid base. Even if Dr. Karlstadt's opinion were correct and true, I might and could not believe it, because of his tomfoolery with dots and capitals. He produces nothing from the Word and does nothing more than deny our clear, forthright, ordered text. I cannot but think, "O my, this is foolishness without any foundation."

With this, I address myself to all who accept the opinion of Dr. Karlstadt. I say that Dr. Karlstadt's sole and best argument rests on the passage, "This is my body," as a separate text, as the beginning of a new and additional sentence, as we heard. If he cannot prove or explain this, his entire case collapses. He has nothing more than his *touto*,[109] and such like, and everything depends on its being a new and separate sentence. If this falls and our contention stands, that this passage is connected to the other, Karlstadt is helped by neither *touto* nor *tatta*,[110] and we carry the day. The context forcibly urges and compels us to accept the meaning that the bread is the body of Christ. Since the words read, "Take, eat, this is my body," and are dependent on each other, they forcefully compel us to hold that what he asks them to eat is his body. Dr. Karlstadt himself recognized this and therefore was so anxious to tear and divide the words from each other. But he found only a period and a capital letter, and even those are not found in all books. Even if they were, it would be uncertain whether they were there as an introduction of a new thought or for the sake of the reader's devotion; the latter is more likely.

---

108. The "spirit" here is meant to be Karlstadt.

109. Greek word for "this."

110. *Tatta* is sarcastic mimicry or a corruption of the Greek *tauta,* plural of *touto.*

But faith should and must rest on certainty, not on punctuation marks and capitals. It must have clear, distinct passages and altogether plain words from Scripture as its foundation. There now, you Karlstadtians, you all lie in one heap as many as there may be of you. Your faith rests on frail, uncertain dots and letters. Satan[111] may wager his conscience and salvation on such, but not I. Dear Karlstadtians, dear gentlemen, you write many books, but for God's sake give attention to the point where you are in trouble and consider how you may prove the passage "This is my body" to be the beginning of a new thought. Everything depends on this; this is the focal point, dear brother, whether you sever, divide, or separate. Even if you write as many books as there is sand on the seashore, if you cannot prove this point, you have lost. As I have said and repeat once more, the text combines, "Take, eat, this is my body." If you let the word "eat" remain with "body of Christ," you must meet the argument that the bread is the body, and it is the body that is to be eaten. This you cannot escape. I dare you and I dare you twice over. [. . .]

Yet I am willing to answer further, in order to strengthen my position. To begin with, if he were to demand that I should also prove my faith that this sentence, "This is my body," belongs to the preceding words, while he denies this and cannot prove that the one passage is separable from the other, I would reply thus: I let the one stand with the other as I find them in the text because in speaking, hearing, and reading, the one naturally follows the other, and I know no reason why I may or should separate the natural order and sequence of the words. Since I find them connected, the burden of proof lies on him who would separate them. This is sufficient confirmation for me. Just as I take the words of The Lord's Prayer as they stand, "Our Father who art in heaven," I need no further confirmation than that this is the order of the words. I know no reason why I should divide thus "Our Father who art, in heaven hallowed be," etc. If you so divide the words, I want to know the reason and offer objections. So here the natural manner of speaking is, "Take, eat, this is my body." One word follows the other, and I know no reason for separating them. For Karlstadt's dots and capital letters mean nothing, and neither he nor anyone else has another reason. For good measure, we shall go on to show from the clear message and meaning of Scripture, not from punctuation or capital letters, that the one

111. Belial, the biblical name for Satan.

word should and must follow the other. For the present, let this be answer enough to the objection of the devil.

In the third place, he comes with his Greek language and chokes on the *touto*. For in Greek the sentence reads, "*Touto esti to soma mou.*" Originally and still today, these Greek words mean in translation, "This is my body." In Latin the words, "*Hoc est corpus meum.*" They are a complete and correct rendering of the Greek phrase, without missing the point by one whit, as all those who know Greek would have need to affirm. Peter Rültz[112] of Orlamünde alone has discovered something new. Pretending that one cannot adequately translate the whole phrase, he thinks it would be well to let *touto* remain untranslated, and we read "*touto* is my body." What can I say? I would laugh at this monkey business if it did not concern matters of such great importance. The ass's head wants to master Greek and knows neither German nor Latin, let alone Greek and Hebrew. He presents himself unashamedly before the whole world as if there were only Peter Rültz of Naschhausen here who does know the Greek language.

Now this rebel spirit only intends to rouse the malicious mob and gather it around him, for always it desires the unusual and what is new. They will smack their lips and exclaim, "What a wonderful man is this Dr. Karlstadt. He discovers what is concealed from all the world, yet in his humility wears the gray coat and felt hat of a peasant and does not want to be called Doctor but neighbor Andreas." Here God dwells and the Holy Spirit with all his feathers and eggs.[113] Karlstadt certainly does not appeal to the crowd because they understand his reasoning. This they cannot do, for he mumbles, strains himself to the breaking point, and chokes on his words and can hardly express what he wants to say. Perhaps God resists him, or he simply lacks the ability to speak German. I know that none of them can tell what his reasoning is, even though one had consumed all his books. On the other hand, they fall for him because of his great cleverness and big words and because he calmly blasphemes in suggesting how contrary to reason it is to believe that the body of Christ is in the sacrament. In this way he can arouse the crowd and make a fool of it. That he knows nothing about the foundation of faith does not much matter much. But this will not last.

I have two tasks in hand. First, I must more clearly expose Dr. Karlstadt's point of departure and reasoning; secondly, I must

112. See n. 107, p. 112.

113. Luther is again using the imagery of the dove for the Holy Spirit, an allusion to the descent of the Spirit at Pentecost.

offer my own explanation. Now with regard to Dr. Karlstadt's dream about his *touto*, this needs to be said. The German, Latin, and Greek languages employ three genders in their pronouns: masculine, where we in German use *der, dieser, jener*; feminine, where we use *die, diese, jene*; and neuter where we use *das, dies, jenes*. So we say *der Himmel* (the heaven), *der Mond* (the moon), *der Stern* (the star), *der Mann* (the man), *der Knabe* (the boy), *der Hund* (the dog). So also *die Sonne* (the sun), *die Erde* (the earth), *die Luft* (the air), *die Stadt* (the city), *die Frau* (the woman), *die Magd* (the maid), *die Kuh* (the cow). Also, *das Wasser* (the water), *das Holz* (the wood), *das Feuer* (the fire), *das Licht* (the light), *das Pferd* (the horse), *das Schwein* (the pig). But the Hebrew language does not have these genders, only the masculine and feminine *der* and *die*.

Now Karlstadt contends this. In the Greek and Latin languages, *bread* is preceded by *der*, not *das*. For they say *der artos, der panis*. We Germans, however, say *das Brot*. Body, however, is *das* in Greek and Latin. For they say, *das soma, das corpus*. We Germans say, *der Leib*. Since Christ here says, *"Touto esti to soma mou," "Das ist mein Leib,"* and does not say, *"Der ist mein Leib,"* he cannot be referring to bread, which would be *der* in Greek, but to his body, which is *das* in Greek. Do you now understand what Dr. Karlstadt is after? It is his Greek *touto*, which in German is *das*. As a modern Greek, he wants to contend from the Greek language that the body of Christ is not in the sacrament, for Christ does not say, *"Der ist mein Leib,"* but *"Das ist mein Leib."* To speak of bread as *"Das ist mein Leib"* is not in keeping with Greek grammar.

Such skill no Greeks ever witnessed, from Christ's time to ours, even if they were native speakers of the language. But now they have discovered this skill at Orlamünde, perhaps in an ancient image when they destroyed the images, or they received it from some heavenly voice. And the man who has hardly seen the alphabet in Greek gives no credit to those born and bred in the language, or to those who now in Germany and other lands have competent knowledge of Greek. Since nothing is easier than to sense and observe a discrepancy of this kind, surely they would have done so all this time. For there is no child reared in the German language who would not laugh if someone said to him about a woman, *"Der Frau ist schön"* (the woman—masculine—is beautiful), *"Das Mann ist fromm"* (the man—neuter—is devout), and would say that you are a Tartar[114] or a gypsy. Would not all Greece and the whole world have sensed the same if Christ

114. Refers to members of several Turkic-speaking peoples that first appeared as nomadic tribes living in northeastern Mongolia. Unlike the Mongols, these peoples spoke a Turkic language. After various groups of these Turkic nomads became part of the armies of the Mongol conqueror Genghis Khan in the early thirteenth century, a fusion of Mongol and Turkic elements took place, and the Mongol invaders of Russia and Hungary became known to Europeans as Tatars (or Tartars).

had said, "*Touto* is my body," though the entire world knows that *touto* has been and still is understood as referring to "bread"! If a Greek child heard someone say, *das artos* (the—neuter—bread) he too would soon laugh. Yet no one has laughed when all the world has said of the bread, "*Das ist mein Leib*" (this is my body).

Yet this dumb spirit presumes now to instruct the Greeks. But as I have said, the man has lost head, eyes, brain, and heart, since he knows neither shame nor fear, and dares wager all according to his whims. He knows well enough that he is ignorant of Greek and proves it fully by translating the Greek, "*Touto esti to soma mou*," into Latin "*Istud panis est hoc corpus meum*," and into German, "*Touto ist der Leib mein*," making the article into a pronoun and inserting *panis*, etc. What German speaks thus: "*This is the body, mine?*" Yet on such ignorance he consciously ventures to build a faith for himself and all the world. If someone dares build articles of faith on conscious and admitted ignorance and so to teach the world, how much more would he dare do it on a vague illusion or doubt? Indeed, what would such an impudent spirit not dare? I am terror stricken at the boldness and outrage of men in divine things, while in their attitudes to men on earth they are weak, unstable, and despairing.

Let me now explain why Christ said *touto* or *das* of the bread instead of *der*. In the German language, we have a way of speaking that allows us when we point to something before us to designate and call it *das*, whether in itself it be *der* or *die*. So I say, "*Das ist der Mann* (that is the man) of whom I speak," "*Das ist die Jungfrau* (that is the young lady) whom I mean," "*Das ist die Magd* (that is the maiden) who sang there," "*Das ist der Geselle* (that is the fellow) who told me," "*Das ist die Stadt* (that is the city) that did it," "*Das ist der Thurm* (that is the tower) that lies there," "*Das ist der Fisch* (that is the fish) which I brought." Here I call to witness all Germans, if I am speaking German. After all, this is our mother tongue, and we commonly speak so in German lands.

The Greeks do the same in their language in regard to *touto* and the bread when they point to it and say, "That is my body, given for you." I call to witness all those who know Greek. But the Latin language is different—it has no [definite and indefinite] articles as do the Greek and German languages. Especially is it so among my Saxons who "*tutten*" and "*tatten*"[115] just like the Greeks, with whom they are in complete agreement in saying, "*Touto esti to soma mou*," this is your body, this is the woman,

115. The phrase is a play on the Greek words *touto* (neuter, singular) and *tauta* (neuter, plural), which in their onomatopoeic effect bear a resemblance to *taten,* the past tense of the German verb *tun* (LW 40:164 n. 127).

this is my body. Were Dr. Karlstadt's dream to prevail, one would have to claim that it would not be German to say, "*Das ist mein Leib*" (this is my body) given for you, since *Leib* (body) requires "*der*" in German. Though we say, "*der Leib* (the body) is large," yet we say, "*Das ist der Leib*" (this is the body) that pleases me. So also, "*Das ist der Leib*" (this is the body) given for you. But Dr. Karlstadt thus reveals that he knows no more German than he does Greek.

In the sacrament, then, when I speak German and have a wafer or host before me in my hand, though both would require "*die*," I say, "*Das ist die Speise*" (this is the food), and not, "*Die ist die Speise*." So also Christ said of the same wafer or host, "This is my body," etc. You ask, why I cannot say "*das Mann*" and yet say *Das ist der Mann*. I cannot say: *das Frau, das Magd, das Stadt, das Geselle*, and yet I have to say: "*Das ist die Frau*," "*Das ist die Magd*," "*Das ist die Stadt*," "*Das ist der Geselle*." I know no other reason than that this is the genius of languages as God has created them. Thus no Greek will say "*das artos*" and yet he will say "*Das ist der artos*." So also he says, "This is my body, given for you."

Again, my dear Peter Rültz, Gemser[116] wants to try to open your ears. You say *touto* refers to the body of Christ and not to the bread, when Christ says *touto*, or, this is my body. Tell me, dear Peter, to what then does the other *touto* that follows refer? Luke 22[:20] and Paul in 1 Cor. 11[:22] speak thus of the second part of the sacrament: "In the same way he took the cup, after supper, and said, *touto*, or this cup is the new testament in my blood," etc. Here the word *touto* is clearly expressed in the text and refers to the cup, which he offered, and not to the blood of Christ contained therein. For in Greek it reads, "*Touto to poterion he kaine diatheke estin en to haimati mou*" (this cup is the new testament in my blood). Tell me, if the *touto* must refer to Christ and yet here in the text it expressly refers to the cup, do you believe and call the blood of Christ or Christ himself, the cup? Would it not be better if you made all your ideas completely new and did not call his blood a cup, but a dinner basket or a spoonbowl?

Do you hear, Peter? Why do you sweat? It is winter and freezing weather. Do you want a handkerchief? Won't a capital letter or a period help here? Or will not the *touto* become a *das* and the cup a *der*, so that grammar might come to your aid when the spirit fails! For "cup" in Greek is also a *das* and not a *der*, *touto poterion*. Are you not the man who loves the straight truth? And

116. See n. 106, p. 111.

who boasts that he is bold in the face of lies but yielding before the truth? Well, yield now and listen. Acknowledge the truth and confess that you have been mistaken about the *touto*, and that the one who came and told you was not your heavenly Father, as you lied and blasphemed, but the harassing devil or his mother, who pointed you to the *touto* referring to the bread but said nothing about the one referring to the cup. [. . .]

Even if, in spite of everything, Dr. Karlstadt remained unshaken and stayed with his *touto*, I have already shown that it would not help him, since he has not achieved and cannot achieve that the phrase "This is my body" is something new and separated from the rest of the passage. When my poor factious spirit finds himself in straits, he wants to get out. For if it is not an independent passage, but dependent on the other part, everything is swept away which Dr. Karlstadt "*toutos* or *tautas*, clucks or cackles.". . . So Dr. Karlstadt fares ridiculously not only in his knowledge of Greek but in that he tries to ground articles of faith on grammar. If my faith had to rest on Donatus or Primers,[117] I would be in a bad way.

How many new articles we would have to establish, if we were to master the Bible in all passages according to grammatical rules? How often it speaks contrary to custom in regard to number, gender, person, etc. Indeed, what language does not do so? We Germans use *die* before *Nacht* (night) and say *die Nacht*. Yet at times we change the *die* to *das* and speak of *des Nachts*. "*Es ist des Nachts still und gut schlafen*" ("It is still at night and good to sleep"). So Dr. Karlstadt had better have stayed at home with his grammar. He could have produced words and text more fittingly from Scripture so as to win us over to his *touto* as a reference to the person of Christ instead of the bread. He asks us to produce passages from Scripture. So we require him to do the same. All right, tackle the task briskly, Peter. Show us one syllable from Scripture that *touto* applies to the person of Christ and not to the bread. Why not? We don't believe your grammar, for its foundation is sand and uncertain.

So you see, my dear reader, how this *touto* matter stands. Dr. Karlstadt obstinately denies that it refers to the bread, saying it is not clearly and certainly proven. So he holds to his position, which shows a purely malicious objection to the natural meaning and order of language. He has to be convinced that it refers to

117. Donatus was a fourth-century Roman grammarian whose book was used in the teaching of basic Latin. The German word used by Luther for what is here translated as "ABC Books" ("Primers") is *Fibeln*.

the bread. Though the nature of speech supports us, yet we have for good measure and overwhelmingly proved from the text that it must refer to bread since in the following part it refers to the cup. Consequently, Karlstadt's mouth has been stopped.

So we, on our side, hold to our "no" and demand that he prove how the *touto* refers to the body of Christ, as Karlstadt says and affirms. For whoever affirms must prove his assertion against the denier. Despite objections let him produce a text in support of his assertions, as we have done for ours. That he says "no" to what we affirm, despite the nature of language, and affirms what we deny, means nothing. He must refute our "no" with a clear biblical text and prove his assertions, just as we have refuted with a clear text what he denies and have established our position. If he overcomes our objection, he will have won. We pray, however, for his mercy and ask that he doesn't burn the marsh. [. . .]

Let us now take the text and see how nice it would turn out if this passage, "This is my body," were a separate phrase and referred to the person of Christ, and not to the bread. For as Christ took the bread in his hands, gave thanks, and broke it, gave it to his disciples, saying, "Take and eat," and immediately continued without a transition, "This is my body," the meaning and natural order of the words compel us to conclude that he spoke of the bread which he took in his hands and gave it to them and told them to eat of it. Otherwise the disciples could not have understood him nor could anyone else who heard him speak. For their eyes must have turned to his hand as he took the bread, broke it, gave and distributed it, and their ears must have heard the words which he spoke while he offered and gave it to them. For in giving the bread he only spoke the words "This is my body."

Were it not his body which he offered and told them to eat, as he said, "Eat, this is my body," he would have deceived them and mocked them with words. How would it sound if I gave someone a gray coat, saying, "Here, put this on, this is my velvet cape trimmed with martin," etc., and applied the words to the garment I am wearing? Would that not be deceit and mockery if after I had said, "Here, put this on," I immediately continued without a break to say, "This is my velvet cape trimmed with martin"? Of course, there must be words of transition that would turn his attention from the gray coat I offer him and tell him to put on my cape. Otherwise he would not be able to understand. And how would it sound if I gave someone a piece of bread and said, "Take and eat," and as I offered and asked him to eat it, I immediately went on to say, "This is a pound of gold in my pocket"?

Truly it must not be a *touto* or *tauta* or period or capital that comes between, to indicate the beginning of a different and new meaning, for the words follow each other too closely. Clearly expressed words must be interposed to separate the parts, as, "Take, eat, for I have, or there is still, a pound of gold in my pocket." Or, "Here, put this on. I still have, or there is still, another white cape with martin trim." So here Christ would have had to say, "Take, eat, for I tell you here my body is seated, which will be given for you." Otherwise it would be mocking and ridiculous. As if one were to hand a drink to another and would say, "Take, drink, here I sit, Hans in the red pants," or "Here, drink, the Turks have slain the Sultan," or otherwise bring in an alien notion that has nothing to do with drinking. So it would be if Christ said, "Take, eat, this is my body, given for you," and were introducing a new thought.

If Jesus had not said these words just in the same moment as he offered the bread, but a little before or after, there might have seemed to be some argument. But now that he said, "This is my body," just as he gave and offered to them the bread and bade them eat, no one can draw any other conclusion from the meaning of words than that it was his body that he offered and asked them to eat. Or else it must be admitted that no one can be sure about what one says to another. If anyone so tears apart these clear and distinct words, let no one hereafter speak with me without knowing I may interpret his words differently, or I must be concerned that he will misinterpret my words. Why should Christ have to say such a word the moment that he offered them bread and bade them eat, when he had plenty of other occasions to say it and well knew that they would not apply it except to the bread which he gave them and asked them to eat.

It is not true, therefore, as Dr. Karlstadt claims, that he spoke so as to teach them what the remembrance should be. This he said boldly in his own imagination and is unable to prove it by Scripture or otherwise. One does not teach by abruptly, suddenly, and deceivingly breaking off a thought and, without warning and notice go on to another matter, while offering something of which he is not speaking. In so doing one obscures, deceives, and deludes. In teaching one must proceed with simplicity, plainness, and clarity, even showing what one teaches, and not giving or showing one thing while teaching or referring to something else. It is not good teaching to show you white while teaching you about black, or to show you the devil while teaching you about God. Clowns and deceivers or scoffers and jesters do so either to mislead or to ridicule. A devout man who is in earnest does not do so.

Or why was it necessary for Christ to point twice to himself—once toward his body, once toward his blood? Had it not been enough if he had said, "I am he," or, "This is my body, of which the prophets have said that it will be given for you," as Dr. Karlstadt wants it? Now, however, everything points toward eating and drinking, and both are expressly mentioned. He takes something hard, similar to the bread, namely, his body, and something liquid, similar to what they drink, namely, his blood. Why did he have to do that? He could just as well have taken something else, not as similar to bread and wine. As we said, he could simply have asserted, "I am the one who is given for you," and there would have been no reference to anything that could be eaten or drunk.

Now that he gives both, the one in the bread in the form it is eaten, and the other in the wine in a form that is drunk, and he only does it when they are at the table eating, and from the moment he offers it and asks them to eat and drink, no conscience can be certain if this is denied. And I am sure that even Dr. Karlstadt's conscience is uneasy and uncertain so as to render it unable to digest such blows, however hardened and blinded he may be. For Christ could have taught this at some other time and not saved it up until they ate and drank, and until he offered it to them and told them to eat and drink.

What does it mean? When he had given the bread and said, "This is my body," etc., he begins anew with the cup and this time gives the wine and says, "This is my blood." If he begins something new when he says, "This is my body," wanting thereby to teach on what the remembrance was based, he would not have separated and divided the one part from the other, but would have combined body and blood closely with one another and said, "This is my body and blood, which is given for you and shed for you," and then the teaching could be considered clear and complete. But now that he separates, and says one word about eating and another about drinking, and inserts other words between the two, namely, "Likewise he took the cup, gave thanks, and gave it to them, saying drink ye all of this," one certainly can conclude that the eating and drinking is of concern to the Lord, as he says, "This is my body, this is my blood."

See, indeed, how neatly this spirit soils himself with his cleverness. He pretends that the passage, "This is my body given for you," does not belong to what immediately precedes, namely, "Take, eat," but is to be considered a new, independent sentence. Yet he admits, and must admit, that this last passage, "This do in remembrance of me," belongs to the first words, "Take, eat." Is it not obstinate mischief, when in a passage three parts follow each other and are related to each other, some one dares claim that the first and last belong together, but that the second and middle part is independent and belongs to neither, and does this on his own initiative without any basis in Scripture? How can a mind tolerate that the third or last should belong to the first, and the second or middle part between the two belong to neither of them? [. . .][118]

118. At this point, several pages of the treatise are cut prior to Luther's final comments.

Herewith I will be content for this time. To Dr. Karlstadt's contention as to our authority to bring the body and blood of Christ into the sacrament, we have given sufficient proof, and he will have to let us keep our belief that the bread that "we" break is the body of Christ. This "we" has truly its authority from the words of Christ himself at his supper. What he imagines concerning the righteousness of mortification, and its coming before the inner righteousness of the spirit, is his own fancy and is without any foundation. For above you have heard of the right order: At the beginning and first of all is the faith in the heart, the righteousness of the spirit, then follows the mortification and death of the old nature (Rom. 8[:13]), "For if by the Spirit you put to death the deeds of the body you will live." By the Spirit, he says, which thus must be there.

This is my answer to all the books of Dr. Karlstadt on the sacrament which he has written and contrived over the past three years. I have answered him in three weeks, and will give him another three years, and three more, or six in all, to make a decent reply to me. I warn them once more to see to it that they meet the issue, for they need it. For my part I courteously give them thanks from my whole heart and ask for none in return, because they have so greatly confirmed me in regard to this article of faith. For now I see that it is not possible to produce anything in opposition to this article. I have gone to such lengths and written so much in order to show clearly how obscurely and disorderly Dr. Karlstadt writes. I hope that from this book Dr. Karlstadt first of all may better understand himself. For I do not doubt that up to now he has not himself understood what he has been doing or whither his teaching may lead. He cannot rightly grasp or understand anything, much less develop his ideas or write.

In closing, I want to warn everyone truly and fraternally to beware of Dr. Karlstadt and his prophets, for two reasons. First, because they run about and teach without a call. This God condemns through Jeremiah [23:21], who says, "I did not send them, yet they ran. I did not speak to them, yet they prophesied." For this reason they are judged by Christ (John 10[:1]), as thieves and murderers who do not enter by the door, but climb in by another way. They boast of possessing the Spirit, more than the apostles, and yet for more than three years now have secretly prowled about and flung around their dung. Were he a true spirit he would at once have come forward and given proof of his call by signs and words. But he is a treacherous, secret devil who sneaks around in corners until he has done his damage and spread his poison.

The second reason is that these prophets avoid, run away from, and are silent about the main points of Christian doctrine. For in no place do they teach how we are to become free from our sins, obtain a good conscience, and win a peaceful and joyful heart before God. This is what really counts. This is a true sign that their spirit is of the devil, who can use unusual new words to excite, terrify, and mislead consciences. But their spirit cannot give quietness or peace, but goes on and teaches special works in which they are to exercise and discipline themselves. They have no idea how a good conscience can be gained or ought to be constituted. For they have not felt or ever recognized it. How can they know or feel it, when they come and teach of themselves without a call. No good can come in this way.

The grace of God be with us all. Amen.

How Christians Should Regard Moses

1525

BROOKS SCHRAMM

INTRODUCTION

Luther completed his translation of the Pentateuch into German in the late winter or early spring of 1523.[1] Immediately thereafter he began preaching a weekly sermon series[a] on each of these books on Thursdays in the Wittenberg town church.[2] The sermons on Genesis were completed by September 1524, and then he turned directly to Exodus. This sermon series would last from 2 October 1524 through 2 February 1527. On 27 August 1525, Luther had reached Exodus 19, that point in the pentateuchal narrative where Moses and the Israelites arrive at Mount Sinai and prepare to receive the divine law. The sermon preached on that day, which would come to be known as *How Christians Should Regard Moses*, functioned as Luther's programmatic introduction to Exodus 19–20 and thus to the Ten Commandments as well. This is an essential Luther text for numerous reasons, not least because he here takes up the ancient and perennial theological problem of which Mosaic commandments or laws are to be regarded as binding on Gentile Christians. His answer to this question, which is also the central point of the sermon, is: "Moses is dead.... Not one little dot in Moses pertains to us."

1. Although the translation was primarily the work of Luther, he was aided by his colleagues Philip Melanchthon (1497–1560) and Matthäus Aurogallus (1490–1543; professor of Hebrew at Wittenberg since 1521). Published by Melchior Lotter the Younger in Wittenberg under the title *Das Alte Testament Deutsch*.

2. St. Marienkirche.

a   *Reihenpredigten.*

3. Andreas Bodenstein von Karlstadt (1486–1541), professor at the University of Wittenberg since 1505, pastor at Orlamünde, and supporter of Luther in the first years of the Reformation. As a leader of the iconoclastic movement and a wandering reformer, he would become a bitter opponent of Luther.

4. Timeline
  1523 German translation of the Pentateuch
  1523–1527 Weekly sermon series on the books
  1525 January: *Against the Heavenly Prophets in the Matter of Images and Sacraments*
  1525 February: Deuteronomy commentary
  1525 March: the Peasants' Wars
  1525 May: *Against the Robbing and Murdering Hordes of Peasants*
  1525 May: the Battle of Frankenhausen; Thomas Müntzer beheaded at Mühlhausen
  1525 June: Luther and Katharina married
  1525 August 27: sermon on Exodus 19: *How Christians Should Regard Moses*
  1525 *The Bondage of the Will*
  1525 Sermons on Exodus, lectures on the Twelve Prophets
  1526 May: *How Christians Should Regard Moses*; a sermon pamphlet published
  1528 The sermon included in *Explanation of the Ten Commandments*

Context

The sermon, however, did not take place in a vacuum, for the year 1525 was a tumultuous one for the forty-one-year-old Luther. In January, he finished the major treatise against Andreas Bodenstein von Karlstadt,[3] *Against the Heavenly Prophets in the Matter of Images and Sacraments*,[b] and in February, he completed his commentary on Deuteronomy.[4] In March, the Peasants' War,[c] which had been ebbing and flowing since the summer of 1524, finally exploded. In April, Luther began a series of treatises against the

The Cranach pulpit in Marienkirche (St. Mary's Church) in Wittenberg.

b   See pp. 38–125 in this volume and LW 40:79–223.

peasants and their supporters.[d] On 5 May, the elector of Saxony, Frederick III [the Wise] (1463–1525), his protector, died. Shortly thereafter Luther wrote the notorious treatise *Against the Robbing and Murdering Hordes of Peasants*.[5] On 15 May, the peasants were crushed at the Battle of Frankenhausen, and on 27 May, Thomas Müntzer[6] was beheaded at Mühlhausen.[7] (See image of Müntzer on p. 71.) On 13 June, less than a month after the war had ended, Luther and Katharina von Bora (1499–1552) were married in Wittenberg. In July, he issued a mild apology for the notorious treatise against the peasants.[e] In the fall, he would go on to write the seminal treatise, *The Bondage of the Will*,[f] against Erasmus of Rotterdam (1466–1536). And throughout this entire time, in addition to the sermons on Exodus, he was lecturing on the Twelve Prophets at the University of Wittenberg.

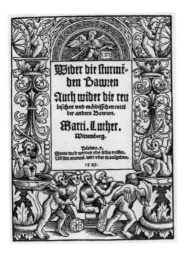

Title page for *Against the Murderous, Thieving Hordes of Peasants*, by Martin Luther in response to the German Peasants' War, published in Wittenberg, 1525.

5. LW 46:49–55. Luther composed the document as an addition to *Admonition to Peace*, but it would soon be issued as a freestanding text. See also *Temporal Authority: To What Extent It Should be Obeyed* [1523] (LW 45:80–130); *Letter to the Princes of Saxony Concerning the Rebellious Spirit* [July 1524] (LW 40:49–59); *A Dreadful Story and a Judgment of God against Thomas Müntzer* [pre–27 May 1525] (*Eine schreckliche Geschichte und ein Gericht Gottes über Thomas Münzer*, WA 18:367–74); *Dr. Martin Luther's Defense of the Booklet against the Robbing and Murdering Peasants*, delivered on Pentecost [4 June 1525] (*Verantwortung D. M. Luthers auf das Büchlein wider die räuberischen und mörderischen Bauern getan am Pfingstag*, WA 17/1:264–68).

6. Pastor in Zwickau and then Allstedt, Thomas Müntzer (1488–1525) was initially a staunch supporter of Luther. His alienation from Luther derived from his conviction that Luther's theology short-circuited the full revolutionary implications of the gospel. In a July 1524 sermon in Allstedt, in which he stated that "the godless have no right to live," he referred to Luther as "Brother Fattened-Hog and Brother Soft-Life"; later that year he referred to Luther in print as "the Soft-Living Flesh of Wittenberg." (See the discussion in Martin Brecht, *Martin Luther*, vol. 2: *Shaping and Defining the Reformation 1521–1532*, trans. James L. Schaaf [Minneapolis: Fortress Press, 1994], 153, 155). He became a leading figure in the Peasants' War, and his role in that war cost him his life.

7. Although estimates widely vary, it is conceivable that as many as one hundred thousand peasants were killed over the course of the long war.

c   See Hans J. Hillerbrand, "The German Reformation and the Peasants' War," in *The Social History of the Reformation*, ed. Lawrence P. Buck and Jonathan W. Zophy (Columbus: Ohio State University Press, 1972), 106–36; Tom Scott and Bob Scribner, *The German Peasants' War: A History in Documents* (Atlantic Highlands, NJ: Humanities Press, 1990).

d   *Admonition to Peace: A Reply to the Twelve Articles of the Peasants in Swabia* [April 1525] (LW 46:17–43; WA 18:291–334).

e   *An Open Letter on the Harsh Book against the Peasants* (LW 46:63–85).

f   See pp. 152–257 in this volume and LW 33:15–295.

8. In terms of these principles of biblical interpretation, the crucial companion document is Luther's August 1543 treatise, *On the Last Words of David* (LW 15:267–352). On this see Heinrich Bornkamm, *Luther and the Old Testament*, ed. Victor I. Gruhn, trans. Eric W. and Ruth C. Gritsch (Mifflintown, PA: Sigler Press, 1997), 149–64.

9. Immediately after the war ended, a number of Catholic polemicists began charging Luther with being the root cause of the revolt.

10. Melanchthon.

11. Nicholas von Amsdorf (1483–1565).

In *How Christians Should Regard Moses*, Luther concisely formulates his essential principles for distinguishing antithetically between law and gospel, Moses and Christ, the secular, external kingdom and the spiritual, internal kingdom, the Old Covenant and the New Covenant, as well as the related question of the relationship between the Testaments—in other words, those fundamental principles of biblical interpretation that would drive his theology for the remainder of his career.[8] All of this, it must be emphasized, was worked out in the midst of major real-life events, with the Peasants' War being the most serious.

Luther viewed Karlstadt and Müntzer as cut from the same cloth, and thus his arguments against the former regarding images and against the latter regarding the cause of the peasants are strikingly similar. For him, both share the error of attempting to impose Mosaic law on contemporary German church and society, and both, through their failure to understand Moses correctly, threaten the peace and well-being of the land. To be sure, Luther himself was often the target of similar accusations regarding the fomenting of rebellion,[9] and he clearly realized the incendiary potential of the Reformation movement. But, as the following passage from a 1522 Lenten sermon demonstrates, Luther regarded his rebellion as one of the pen and the pulpit, not of the sword. For him, there could be no equation of reformation and political revolution.

> In short, I will preach the word, teach it, write it, but I will constrain no one by force, for faith must come freely without compulsion. Take myself as an example. I opposed indulgences and all the papists, but never with force. I simply taught, preached, and wrote God's word; otherwise I did nothing. And while I slept, or drank Wittenberg beer with my friends Philip[10] and Amsdorf,[11] the word so greatly weakened the papacy that no prince or emperor ever inflicted such losses upon it. I did nothing; the word did everything. *Had I desired to foment trouble, I could have brought great bloodshed upon Germany; indeed, I could have started such a game that even the emperor would not have been safe.*[g]

g LW 51:77. Emphasis added.

Text and Translation

The sermon was first published as a pamphlet in May of 1526 under the title *How Christians Should Regard Moses*. This earliest form of the sermon is known as Text U in WA 16:363–93. In 1527 the sermon was included as a preface to Luther's 1523–24 sermons on Genesis, WA 24:1–16. For this occasion, Luther also composed a brief introduction in which he states that his sermons on Moses were directed against the "Müntzer-like spirit" which threatened to make Christians into Jews via a false estimate and wrong understanding of the Old Testament.[h] Then again in 1528, the sermon was included as a preface to a volume entitled *Explanation of the Ten Commandments*, which simply contained Luther's sermons on Exodus 19–20 from the Exodus series. This form of the sermon is known as Text A and is printed beneath Text U in WA 16:363–93.

The following translation is a revision of LW 35:161–74, which was based on Text U. Insofar as possible, the revision attempts to render the same German words and phrases consistently throughout the document. WA 24:1–16 and Text A are somewhat more expansive texts than Text U, and these have been incorporated selectively for the sake of clarity. The revision is also informed by Aland's rendering of the sermon into modern German.[12]

This image of peasants carrying weapons is from the cover of the 1525 publication of *The Twelve Articles of the Christian Union of Upper Swabia*, a document that demanded far-reaching rights that would signal an end to feudalism.

12. Kurt Aland, ed., *Luther Deutsch: Die Werke Martin Luthers in neuer Auswahl für die Gegenwart*, vol. 5: *Die Schriftauslegung*, 2d ed. (Stuttgart: Ehrenfried Klotz Verlag; Göttingen: Vandenhoeck & Ruprecht, 1963), 93–109. Hereafter Aland.

h   WA 24:1, 19–27.

INSTRUCTION ON HOW CHRISTIANS SHOULD REGARD MOSES, PREACHED BY MARTIN LUTHER[13]

13. *Eyn unterrichtung, wie sich die Christen yn Mosen sollen schicken gepredigt durch Mar. Luth.* See also the final paragraph of the introduction above.

DEAR FRIENDS, you have often heard that there has never been a public sermon from heaven except twice. Apart from these two, God has spoken many times through and with human beings on earth, as in the case of the holy patriarchs Adam, Noah, Abraham, Isaac, Jacob, and others, on down to Moses. But in none of those cases did God speak with such glorious splendor and external existence, or with such a public cry and proclamation, as on these two occasions. Rather, God illuminated their heart internally and spoke through their mouth, as Luke indicates in the first chapter of his Gospel, where he says, "As God spoke of old through the mouth of the holy prophets" [Luke 1:70].

Now the first sermon is in the nineteenth and twentieth chapters of the Second Book of Moses,[i] where God was heard from heaven with great splendor and might. For the people of Israel heard the trumpets and the very voice of God. On the second occasion, God delivered a public sermon through the Holy Spirit on Pentecost [Acts 2:2-4]. On that occasion the Holy Spirit itself came with great splendor and external impressiveness, such that there came from heaven the sudden rushing of a mighty wind, and it filled the entire house where the apostles were sitting. And there appeared to them tongues as of fire, distributed and resting on each of them. And they were all filled with the Holy Spirit and began to preach and speak in other tongues. This happened with great spendor and glorious power, so that thereafter the apostles

Michelangelo's sculpture of the horned Moses holding the commandments dates to c. 1515.

---

i Luther's own biblical citation formulas have been preserved throughout the revised translation. His normal practice was to refer to the books of the Pentateuch as "The First Book of Moses," "The Second Book of Moses," etc.

preached so powerfully that the sermons which we hear in the world today are hardly a shadow compared to their sermons, in so far as external splendor and existence is concerned. For they spoke in all sorts of tongues and performed great miraculous signs, etc. Yet through our preachers today, God is neither heard nor seen, since nothing comes down publically from heaven. This is why I have said that there are only two such special and public sermons which have been seen and heard from heaven.

To be sure, God spoke also to Christ from heaven, when he was baptized in the Jordan [Matt. 3:17], and [at the Transfiguration] on Mount Tabor [Matt. 17:5]. However, none of this took place in the presence of the community. God wanted to send that second sermon into the world, which had earlier been announced through the mouth and in the books of the holy prophets. God will no longer speak that way publicly through sermons. Instead, on the third occasion, God will come in person with divine glory, so that all creatures will tremble and quake before the divine presence [Luke 21:25-27]. God will no longer preach to them; instead, God will be seen and touched by them [Luke 24:39].

The first sermon and doctrine is the law^j of God; the second is the gospel. The two do not agree. Therefore one must have a good understanding of them, such that one knows how to distinguish between the two and knows what the law is and what the gospel is.[14] The law commands and demands of us what we are to do. The law is thus directed solely to our conduct and consists in

This woodcut (c. 1529) by Lucas Cranach the Elder is titled *Law and Grace*, also known as *Fall and Redemption*.

14. Luther's distinction between law and gospel and his doctrine of justification are inextricably related; indeed, one can even say that the latter is dependent on the former. Already in his 1521 *Expositions of the Epistles and Gospels* (*Enarrationes epistolarum et euangeliorum*, WA 7:463–537), he states, "Almost all Scripture and the understanding of all theology hangs on the proper understanding of law and gospel." (Quoted in Bernhard Lohse, *Martin Luther's Theology*, trans. Roy A. Harrisville [Minneapolis: Fortress Press, 1999], 267.)

j   In modern German writing, all nouns are capitalized, but in the original Luther texts, the use of capital letters is highly irregular. Throughout this translation, we are staying with the publisher's standard style for lowercasing the word *law*, as well as the word *gospel*, except when it refers to a biblical book or genre.

15. The distinction between law and gospel corresponds to that between two kinds of righteousness (active and passive). There can be no middle or common ground here, for law and gospel are antithetical and are neither to be confused nor combined. The ability to distinguish between them properly is the mark of good theology. (See Luther's programmatic statement in his preface to the *Lectures on Galatians* [1535], LW 26:4–12.) See also *Sermon on Two Kinds of Righteousness* in this volume, p. 8–24.

16. The great biblical interpreters, both Jewish and Christian, have always known that the common biblical phrase "God said" cannot simply be taken literally.

demanding, for God speaks through the law, saying, "Do this, avoid that, this is what I want from you." The gospel, however, does not preach what we are to do or to avoid. It demands nothing of us, but instead reverses the matter, does the opposite, and says, "This is what God has done for you: God's son came in the flesh for you, and God let him be killed on account of you." So, then, there are two kinds of doctrine and two kinds of works: those of God and those of human beings. Just as we and God are separated from one another, so also these two doctrines are widely separated from one another.[15] For the gospel teaches solely what has been given to us by God, and not—as in the case of the law—what we are to do and give to God.

Now we want to see how this first sermon sounded forth and with what splendor God gave the law on Mount Sinai. God chose the place where God wanted to be seen and heard. Not that God actually spoke, for God has no mouth, tongue, teeth, or lips as we do.[16] But the one who created and made the mouth of all human beings [Exod. 4:11] can also make language and voice. For no one would be able to speak a single word unless God first gave it, as the prophet says, "It would be impossible to speak except God first put it in our mouth."[k] Language, speech, and voice are thus gifts of God like any other gifts, such as the fruit on the trees. The one who created the mouth and put language in it can also make and use language even though there is no mouth present. Now the words which are written here were spoken through an angel. This is not to say that only one angel was there; rather, there was a great multitude which served God there and preached before the people of Israel at Mount Sinai. The angel, however, who spoke and did the talking, spoke just as if it were actually God speaking and saying, "I am your God, who brought you out of the land of Egypt," etc. [Exod. 20:1], as if Peter or Paul were speaking in God's stead and saying, "I am your God," etc. Paul says to the Galatians [3:19] that the law was

---

k   It is unclear exactly what passage Luther is alluding to here. LW 35:163 n. 2 suggests Num. 22:38. If so, then "the prophet" would be Balaam (see also Num. 23:5, 12, 16). But these Balaam texts refer only to a specific situation and do not support the general rule that Luther is attempting to establish. Though his command of biblical texts was immense, when Luther quotes from memory he often paraphrases and even mixes or blends discrete texts in order to make his point.

decreed*l* through the angels.[17] That is, it was decreed that the angels were to give the law of God in God's stead, and Moses, as a mediator, received it from the angels.[18] I say this so that you might know who gave the law. God did this to them, however, because God wanted thereby to compel, seize, and corner*m* the Jews.

You might well wonder what kind of a voice that was. It was a voice like a human voice, such that one actually heard it. The syllables and letters thus made sounds which the physical ear was able to grasp. But it was a bold, glorious, and great voice, as stated in the fourth chapter of the Fifth Book of Moses [Deut 4:12], where he says that they heard the voice but saw no one. Rather, they heard a strong voice; for he spoke in a strong voice, as if in the dark we should hear a voice from a high tower or rooftop, and could see no one but only hear the strong voice of a man. And this is why it is called a voice of God, because it was beyond a human voice.

Now you will hear how God used this voice in order to stir and arouse the people. For God's intention was to institute the [external, spiritual]*n* government.*o,p* It was previously stated how, on the advice of Jethro, his father-in-law, Moses had established the secular*q* government and appointed rulers and judges

l Reading with Aland, *verordnen* rather than *ordnen*.

m Reading with Aland, *in die Enge treyben* rather than *eintreyben*.

n Reading with WA 16:370, 30–31 and 24:5, 27–28. Text U reads "external and spiritual."

o The term *Regiment* has been translated "government" throughout and the related term *Reich* as "kingdom." Luther's concepts of "government" and "kingdom" are closely related but not identical. The precise distinction is captured by Heinrich Bornkamm, who argues that "*kingdom* denotes a sphere of rule, whereas *government* denotes a type of rule." (Quoted in Lohse, *Martin Luther's Theology*, 318.)

p At first glance, this rare formulation ("external, spiritual government") appears to be a contradiction in terms. See below for further clarification.

q Luther's term *weltlich* has been translated as "secular" throughout. English translations of Luther often render this term as "worldly" or as "temporal." But the latter has its own German equivalent, *zeitlich*, and the former, though accurate, does not quite capture the specific valence of *weltlich*, which for Luther is the counterpart to *geistlich* ("spiritual"). Luther uses *weltlich* for both the Latin *saecularis* and *mundanus*.

17. During the late Second Temple period and on into the rabbinic period, there was a debate within Judaism regarding which laws were given directly by God and which came through Moses. The most common view was that God spoke only the Ten Commandments directly to the people, while the remainder were spoken by God to Moses, who then delivered the divine words to the people. Thus, the model for the Ten Commandments is: God → People. The model for the remainder of the commandments is: God → Moses → People. Paul in Gal. 3:19-20 represents a strain of Second Temple Judaism that entertained the notion that angels had a hand in arranging, formulating, and delivering the laws of Sinai. The problem inherent in this notion is, of course, that angels can be either good or bad, and Gnostic writers would soon expand this belief into the claim that the angels who gave the Torah were the very same evil demons who created the world. Paul certainly does not move in that direction, but, by giving the angels such a prominent role, he does sever the intimate connection between God and the Torah.

18. Luther accepts Paul's model of God → Angels → Moses → People, but he only wants to establish the point that God spoke nothing directly; rather, everything came via the angels who spoke on God's behalf. He does this, however, without implying the speculative polemic that can be derived from Paul's claim. For Luther, as for Paul, the law is good. (See Luther's extended treatment of this matter in LW 26:318–23.) See also the *Large Catechism*, "Ten Commandments," pp. 300–351 in this volume.

19. A reference to Luther's two recent sermons on Exodus 18 (WA 16:338–63).

20. The distinction between two kingdoms/governments—one secular, the other spiritual—is one of Luther's central and most controversial teachings and closely corresponds to that between law and gospel. The essential idea is that God engages the world in a twofold manner, and human existence in the world has a twofold character as a result; the human being lives simultaneously "before God" (*coram Deo*) and "before the world" (*coram mundo*). (See Lohse, *Martin Luther's Theology*, 151–59, 314–24; Hans-Martin Barth, *The Theology of Martin Luther* [Minneapolis: Fortress Press, 2013], 313–48.) Luther's hostility toward Müntzer is anchored in the conviction that the latter has confused the distinction between the kingdoms/governments.

21. This rather odd formulation is derived in part from Luther's interpretation of Exod. 19:6, "You will be to me a priestly kingdom" (see WA 16:404–7). For Luther, biblical Israel was completely unique among all the nations of the world, in that it and it alone was chosen to be the bearer of the promise of the Messiah and of the kingdom of God. Thus, in the nation of Israel, the two kingdoms came together in a peculiar fashion; biblical Israel was both a secular and a spiritual phenomenon. With Israel's rejection of the Messiah and the subsequent destruction of Jerusalem, that unique status was forever lost.

[Exod. 18:13-26].[19] Beyond that there is yet a spiritual kingdom[r] in which Christ[s] rules in the hearts of human beings; one cannot see this kingdom, for it consists only in faith and will continue until the last day.

There are two kingdoms:[20] the secular, which governs with the sword and is visible; the spiritual governs solely with grace and the forgiveness of sins. [This kingdom cannot be seen with physical eyes; it can only be ascertained with faith.][t] Between these two kingdoms there is yet another kingdom, placed in the middle, half spiritual and half secular.[21] This kingdom encompasses[u] the Jews with commandments and external ceremonies, which prescribe how they are to conduct themselves toward God and toward other human beings.

The law of Moses does not bind Gentiles[v] but only Jews

The law of Moses [pertains to the Jews].[w] It is in no way binding on us, because the law was given only to the people of Israel.[22] Israel accepted it for itself and its descendants, but the Gentiles were excluded. To be sure, the Gentiles have certain laws in common with the Jews, such as these: that there is one God, that no one is to abuse another, that no one is to commit adultery, murder, steal, etc. These are written naturally on their hearts;[23] they did not hear them straight from heaven as the Jews did. This is why this entire text[24] does not pertain to the Gentiles. I say this

---

r WA 16:370, 33 and 24:5, 30 read *Regiment* ("government").

s WA 16:371, 17 and 24:5, 31 read *Gott* ("God").

t Supplemented from WA 16:371, 21–22 and 24:6, 3–4.

u Reading with Aland, *umfasst* for *fassen*.

v *Heiden* is literally "heathen" or "pagans." In Luther's German Bible, *Heiden* is one of his translations for Hebrew *goyim* ("nations"), while at other times he uses *Völker* ("nations" or "peoples"). Our English word *Gentiles* comes from the Latin *gentes*, "nations." Throughout this document, *Heiden* is translated "Gentiles," which carries the basic sense of non-Jews.

w Reading with WA 16:371, 27 and WA 24:6, 9.

Jewish family celebrating Passover by reading sacred texts, from Agada Pascatis, a fifteenth-century Hebrew manuscript

on account of the fanatic spirits.ˣ For you see and hear how they read Moses, cite him frequently,ʸ and bring up the way Moses governed the people with commandments. They try to be clever and think they know something more than is included^z in the gospel; they regard faith as something small, introduce something new, and boastfully claim that it comes from the Old Testament.[25] They want to govern the people according to the letter of the law of Moses, as if no one had ever read it before.

x The terms *Schwärmer* and *Schwärmergeister* have no exact English equivalents. In his Latin writings, Luther uses the terms *fanatici* and *fanatici spiritus*, from which the English translations "enthusiasts," "fanatics," and "fanatic spirits" are derived. The German terms are more colorful, deriving as they do from the world of bees and other swarming insects, and they imply that the persons so described are fanciful, daydreaming, confused, unclear thinkers. Luther used these terms to refer to a host of people associated with the "left wing" of the Reformation, e.g., the "Zwickau prophets" (see n. 44, p. 145), Karlstadt, Müntzer, etc. The terms do not occur in Luther's Bible translation. In this translation, *Schwärmergeister* is consistently rendered as "fanatic spirits." See also pp. 39–50 in this volume.

y Reading with Aland, *sie zitieren ihn vielfach* for *sie ziehen hoch an*.

z Reading with Aland, *inbegriffen* for *begriffen*.

22. Ironically, Luther is here in agreement with the entirety of rabbinic Judaism. For the rabbis, Mosaic law is the exclusive prerogative of the Jewish people; Gentiles, on the other hand, are subject only to the "Noahide laws." According to t. AbodZar 9:4 and b. Sanh 56a, there are seven of these laws—the first six of which are prohibitions against idolatry, murder, theft, sexual immorality, blasphemy, and the eating of flesh taken from a living animal. The seventh is prescriptive, requiring the maintenance of courts of law, apparently for the purpose of enforcing the first six. The reference in Acts 15:19-20 is thought to be an early reflection of this developing idea.

23. Luther's thinking on nature and natural law is consistently based on Rom. 2:14-15, "When the Gentiles, who do not have the law, nevertheless do the work of the law by nature, these, though not having the law, are a law to themselves. They show that the work of the law is written on their hearts, to which their own conscience also bears witness."

24. Luther is most likely referring here to the entire Mosaic legislation and not merely the Ten Commandments.

25. The Old Testament was the central focus of Luther's career as a university professor, and the quest to articulate a proper Christian interpretation of it was a driving force in his overall intellectual output.

26. For Luther, the heart is the seat of faith, and, therefore, it can only have one master. This is a classic statement of Luther's regarding the antithetical relationship of Christ (here a cypher for gospel) and Moses (here a cypher for law) in the life of a Christian. A related, common refrain in his writings is the warning not to turn Christ into a Moses. These types of antithetical statements are obviously subject to differing interpretations, and, as a result, Luther would have to clarify exactly what he understands the role of the law to be in Christian life. See esp. his explanation of the Ten Commandments in *The Large Catechism*; *Against the Antinomians* [1539] (LW 47:107–19); and esp. the *Antinomian Disputations*, now available in English: Holger Sonntag, ed., *Only the Decalogue Is Eternal: Martin Luther's Complete Antinomian Theses and Disputations*, trans. Holger Sonntag (Minneapolis: Lutheran Press, 2008).

27. As will become explicit further below, Luther is here dependent on Gal. 5:3 (cf. James 2:10): "I testify again that every circumcised man is obligated to keep the entire law." Luther is in agreement with rabbinic tradition, for which it is axiomatic that the entire Torah is binding; one cannot pick and choose. According to rabbinic calculation, the Torah contains 613 commandments, 248 of which are prescriptions and 365 of which are prohibitions.

28. In a letter to Chancellor Brück of Saxony dated 13 January 1524, Luther wrote that the people of Orlamünde, Karlstadt's parish, would probably circumcise themselves and be wholly Mosaic (LW 35:165 n. 4). See WA Br 3:231.

Moses holds tablets of the
Ten Commandments in Hebrew script.

a Ger.: *Maul* ("mouth"), used for the mouths of animals. When used in reference to a person, it is highly pejorative.

b The terms *Rotten* and *Rottengeister* admit different translations. In his Latin writings, Luther uses the terms *sectarii* and *sectarii spiritus*, from which our English translations "sectarians," "sectarian spirits," and "factious spirits" are derived. The German terms imply "gangs," "hordes," and "mobs," and specifically activity that is illegal and forceful (see Brecht, *Martin Luther*, 2:37–138), as is also the case with *Bildstürmer* ("iconoclasts"), the term that Luther uses so often in *Against the Heavenly Prophets*. All of this comes out clearly in the title of the treatise *Against the Robbing and Murdering Hordes of Peasants*, where "hordes" represents *Rotten*. In this translation, *Rottengeister* is consistently rendered as "factious spirits."

But we will not allow this. We would rather not preach again for the rest of our lives than to let Moses in and allow Christ to be torn out of our hearts.[26] We will not have Moses as ruler or lawgiver anymore. Indeed God will not allow it either. Moses was a mediator for the Jewish people alone; it was to them that he gave the law. Therefore one must shut the yaps[a] of the factious spirits[b] who say, "Thus says Moses," etc. Here you simply reply: "Moses does not pertain to us." If I were to accept Moses in one commandment, I would have to accept the entire Moses.[27] Thus the consequence would be that if I accept Moses as master, then I would have to be circumcised,[28] wash my clothes in the Jewish manner, eat and drink and dress thus and so, and observe all that stuff. So, then, we will neither observe nor accept Moses. Moses is dead.[29] His government ended when Christ came.[c] He is of no further use.

That Moses does not bind the Gentiles can be demonstrated from the text in the twentieth chapter of the Second Book of Moses [v.2], where God speaks as follows: "I am the LORD your God, who brought you out of the land of Egypt, out of the house of servitude." This text makes it clear that even the Ten Commandments do not pertain to us. For God never led us out of Egypt, but only the Jews.[30] The factious spirits want to hang Moses and all the commandments around our necks, but we will just leave that be. We will regard Moses as a teacher, but we will not regard him as our lawgiver—unless he agrees with the New Testament and natural law.[31] Therefore it is clear enough that

29. This precise formulation occurs only here and in Luther's 1542 *Treatise against Bigamy* (*Lutheri Schrift wider die Bygamie*, WA 53:190–201; [196, 25]). The same idea, however, is expressed in his 1535 *Lectures on Galatians*, LW 27:15. See also LW 26:151.

30. In Luther's 1538 treatise *Against the Sabbatarians*, he further expands on this point in colorful fashion. "For if I [a Gentile] were to approach God and say, 'O Lord God, who brought me out of Egypt, out of misery,' etc., I would be just like a sow entering a synagogue, for God never performed such a work for me. God would [even] punish me as a liar, because I would be making God into a false god" (WA 50:331, 24–29; LW 47:90 [translation revised]).

31. That is, what is binding on Christians is not Mosaic law but, rather, natural law, the same law that is binding on all people. For Luther, the Ten Commandments represent the clearest and most concise written statement of natural law; they are binding not because Moses gave them but because they cohere with natural law and are, therefore, timeless. Even within the Ten Commandments, however, there is material that was intended only for the Jews and is not included in natural law, e.g., the prohibition against images, the sabbath command, etc. Luther calls this special material "temporal adornment" (*zeitlicher Schmuck*); it was intended only for the Jews. Thus, "law of God" ≠ "law of Moses"; rather, "law of God" = "natural law" = "Ten Commandments" minus their temporal adornments.

c   The biblical text that stands behind this formulation is Rom. 10:4, one of the most debated passages in the Pauline corpus. Luther's translation of the passage in his German New Testament is: "For Christ is the end of the law; whoever believes in him is righteous." By this he understands that the law of Moses terminated at a specific time in history, the time of the coming of Jesus the Messiah. Of equal importance is Gal. 3:24, which Luther interprets as follows: "For the law had its limits until Christ, as Paul says below (Gal. 3:24): 'The law, until Christ.' When he came, Moses and the law ceased. So did circumcision, sacrifices, and the Sabbath. So did all the prophets" (1535 *Lectures on Galatians*, LW 26:7). In Luther's view, just as the Mosaic law terminates with the coming of Christ, so Judaism does as well. It is a consistent assumption of his that postbiblical Judaism is a dead religion. Thus, "Moses is dead" also means "Judaism is dead."

Moses is the lawgiver of the Jews and not of the Gentiles. Moses gave the Jews a sign whereby they should lay hold of God, when they call upon God as the one who brought them out of Egypt.[d] The Christians have a different sign, whereby they conceive of God as the one who gave them his Son, etc.[e]

Similarly, one can prove from the third commandment that Moses does not pertain to Gentiles and Christians. For Paul [Col. 2:16] and the New Testament [Matt. 12:1-12; John 5:16; 7:22-23; 9:14-16] abolish the sabbath, to show us that the sabbath was given to the Jews alone, for whom it was[f] a strict commandment.[32] The prophets also referred to the fact that the Jewish sabbath would be abolished. For Isaiah says in the last chapter [66:23], "When [the Savior][g] comes, it will be like this:[h] one sabbath after the other, one month after the other," etc., as if he were trying to say, "Every day will be the sabbath, and the people will be such that they make no distinction between days." For in the New Testament the sabbath is disregarded with respect to its crude, external mode, for every day is a holy day," etc. Now if anyone confronts you with Moses and his commandments, and wants to urge you to observe them, simply answer,

---

32. That the sabbath is not binding on Gentiles is another agreement between Luther and rabbinic Judaism. Note the traditional line from the Amidah prayer for sabbath mornings: "The LORD our God did not give the Sabbath to the nations of the world, nor did our king bequeath it to the worshipers of idols, nor will the uncircumcised dwell in its rest. Rather You gave it to Israel, Your people, in love; to the seed of Jacob, whom You chose."

---

d　In Luther's 17 September 1525 sermon on Exod. 20:2, he explains that this "sign" was actually an instruction to the Jews that they were to address and know God as follows: "I call upon you, my God and LORD, who brought us out of the land of Egypt, out of the house of servitude. You brought us wonderfully through the Red Sea, through the wilderness, fed us with bread from heaven, gave us to drink from a hard rock, and brought us through the Jordan into the promised land, etc." (WA 16:425, 12–16).

e　Christians, conversely, are to address and know God in this manner: "O God, creator of heaven and earth, who sent your son Jesus Christ into the world for me. He was crucified for me, died, and rose again on the third day; he went to heaven, that he might sit at your right hand, have everything in his power, and send his spirit. We await his coming, when he will rule over the living and the dead, and thus with him we will obtain the eternal kingdom, our inheritance, which you will give us through him. Thereunto, O Lord God, you have established and given us baptism and the sacrament of the body and blood of your son, etc." (WA 16:425, 22–29).

f　LW 35:165 inexplicably translates this as present tense.

g　Reading with WA 16:375, 23 and 24:7, 27.

h　The phrase "When the Savior comes, it will be like this" is not in Isaiah; it is added by Luther to bring out his specific messianic interpretation.

"Go to the Jews with your Moses; I'm not a Jew. Don't bother me with Moses." If I accept Moses in one respect (says Paul to the Galatians in chapter 5[:3]), then I am obligated to observe the entire law. For not one little dot[i] in Moses pertains to us.

Question:
Why then do you preach Moses if he does not pertain to us?
Answer to the Question:
Three things are to be noted in Moses.

I want to keep Moses and not sweep him under the rug,[j] because I find three things in Moses [that can be useful for us].[k] In the first place, I dismiss the commandments given to the people of Israel [that is, those that concern external matters].[l] They neither compel nor urge me. Those laws are dead and gone, except insofar as I gladly and willingly accept something from Moses, as if I said, "This is how Moses governed, and it seems fine to me, so I will follow him in this or that particular."

I would even be glad if today's lords ruled according to the example of Moses. If I were emperor, I would take from Moses a model for my statutes; not that Moses should compel me, but that I should be free to emulate him in governing as he did. For example, tithing is a very fine commandment, because with the giving of the tenth all other taxes would be abolished.

For the common person it would also be easier to give a tenth than to pay the rents and fees now required. Suppose I had ten cows; I would then give one. If I had only five, I would give nothing. If my fields yielded only a little, I would give little; if much, I would give much. All of this would be under God's control. But as things are now, I must pay the Gentile tax[33] even if the hail should ruin my entire crop. If I owe a hundred gulden in taxes, I must pay it even though there may be nothing growing in the field. This is also the way the pope decrees and governs. But

33. "Luther criticized above all other kinds of credit transactions the *Zinskauf*, a form designed to avoid the canonical prohibition of interest. This loan was disguised as a sale. In exchange for money from his possession of property the lender received a part of the produce which the lender gained from his work on the property—the so-called *Zins*. In the form of a 'sale of interest for repurchase' the debtor took on the obligation of paying a certain amount beyond the money lent, which the lender 'bought'" (Ricardo Rieth, "Luther's Treatment of Economic Life," in Robert Kolb, Irene Dingel, and L'ubomâir Batka, eds., *The Oxford Handbook of Martin Luther's Theology* [New York: Oxford University Press, 2014], 383–96, at 391). See Luther's 1524 *Trade and Usury*, LW 45:245–310 and esp. the introductory material (233–43).

---

i   This is a possible wordplay on the Hebrew vowel points.

j   *Unter den banck stecken* (literally, "put under the bench") is a proverbial expression meaning to put aside, hide, or forget some despicable thing [taken from LW 35:166 n. 7].

k   Supplemented from WA 16:376, 21–22 and 24:8, 5–6.

l   Supplemented from WA 16:376, 8 and 24:8, 6–7.

34. See the jubilee year legislation in Leviticus 25.

35. Written by Eike von Repgow (c. 1180–c.1235), knight and juryman, the *Sachsenspiegel* ("Saxon code of law"; early thirteenth century) contains economic and social laws obtaining in and around Magdeburg and Halberstadt. Although fourteen of its articles were condemned by Pope Gregory XI (1331–1378) in 1374. The book remained influential in the codification of German law until the middle of the nineteenth century. (LW 40:98 n. 20).

36. See the virtually identical discussion in *Against the Heavenly Prophets*, LW 40:97–98.

it would be better if things were so arranged that when I raise much, I give much; and when little, I give little, etc.

Similarly, in Moses it is also stipulated that no one should sell their field as a perpetual estate, but only up to the Jubilee year.[34] When that year came, each one returned to the field or possessions which they had sold. In this way the possessions remained in the family relationship. There are also other extraordinarily lovely commandments in Moses which one should like to accept, use, and put into effect. Not that one should compel or be compelled by them; rather, (as I said earlier) the emperor could here take an example for setting up a good government on the basis of Moses, just as the Romans conducted a fine government, and just like the *Sachsenspiegel*[35] by which affairs are ordered in our land. The Gentiles are not obligated to obey Moses. Moses is the *Sachsenspiegel* for the Jews.[36] But if a fine example for governing were to be taken from Moses, one could adhere to it without compulsion as long as one pleased, etc.

Similarly, Moses says, "If one dies without children, then his brother or closest relative should take the widow into his home as his wife, and thus raise up seed*m* for the deceased brother or relative. The first child thus born was credited to the deceased brother or relative" [Deut. 25:5-6]. So it came about that one person had many wives. This is also a fine commandment.

But when these factious spirits come and say, "Moses commanded it," then let Moses go and say, "I'm not asking about what Moses commanded." "Yes" (they say), "he commanded that we should have one God, that we should trust and believe in God, that we should not swear by God's name; that we should honor father and mother; not kill, steal, commit adultery; not bear false witness, and not covet [Exod. 20:3-17]. Should we not therefore observe these commandments?" You reply: nature also has these laws. Nature teaches that we should call upon God. The Gentiles also attest to this, for there have never been Gentiles who did not call upon their idols, even though they neglected the true God. This was the case among the Jews as well, for the Jews also practiced idolatry as did the Gentiles; except that the Jews

m   "Seed" is a Hebrew idiom for "offspring" or "descendant." The idiom is taken over literally in the Greek and Latin Bibles as *sperma* and *semen* respectively. Luther always renders the term with *Samen*, "seed." See below for the christological significance of the term.

had received the law. The Gentiles on the other hand have it written on their heart, and there is no distinction [Rom. 3:22], as St. Paul also shows in the second chapter of Romans [:14-15]: the Gentiles, who have no law, have the law written on their hearts.

But just as the Jews err, so also do the Gentiles. Therefore it is natural to honor God, not steal, not commit adultery, not bear false witness, not kill. What Moses commands is not new. For what God gave the Jews from heaven through Moses, God has also written on the hearts of all human beings [, Jew and Gentile alike, except that God had it written and proclaimed abundantly with a bodily voice and writing to the Jews as his own chosen people]." Thus I observe the commandments which Moses has given, not because Moses commanded it, but because they have been implanted in me by nature, and Moses agrees exactly with nature,[37] etc.

The other commandments in Moses, which are not [implanted] by nature, the Gentiles do not observe. Nor do these pertain to them, such as the tithe and others equally lovely, which I wish we had too. Now this is the first thing that I ought to see in Moses, namely, the commandments to which I am not bound, except insofar as they are [impressed by nature in each one and written on one's heart].°

The second thing to notice in Moses

In the second place, I find something in Moses that I do not have from nature, namely, the promises and pledges of God about Christ.[38] This is the best thing. It is not something that is written naturally on the heart, but rather comes from heaven.[39] God promised, for example, that God's Son would be born in the flesh. This is what the gospel proclaims. It is not a commandment. [It demands nothing of us, that we should do or not do something; rather, these are comforting, joyful promises of God, which we are to accept and boldly depend upon against every temptation of sin, of death, of the devil, and of hell].^p And it is

37. For Luther, the Ten Commandments are technically not Mosaic. "If the Ten Commandments are to be regarded as Moses' law, then Moses came far too late, and he also addressed himself to far too few people, because the Ten Commandments had spread over the whole world not only before Moses but even before Abraham and all the patriarchs. For even if Moses had never appeared and Abraham had never been born, the Ten Commandments would have had to rule in all people from the very beginning, as they indeed did and still do" (*Against the Sabbatarians*, LW 47:89). To be sure, however, this natural law inscribed on the heart is well-nigh illegible, due to the sinful character of the human condition. For that reason, the written form of the Ten Commandments is indispensable.

38. Whenever Luther speaks of the gospel in the Old Testament, he does so on the basis of these promises referred to here. Because the Old Testament contains gospel (and, therefore, Christ), the phrase "Old Testament and New Testament" is not interchangeable with the phrase "law and gospel."

39. A fundamental claim about the nature of the gospel, and, thus a crucial element in the law/gospel distinction. Unlike the law, which is part of creation itself, the gospel comes only via divine revelation. In addition, the gospel is eternal while the law is not.

---

n   Supplemented from WA 16:380, 20–23 and WA 24:9, 31–10, 3.
o   Supplemented from WA 16:380, 30–31 and 24:10–11.
p   Supplemented from WA 16:381, 22–27 and WA 24:10, 18–22.

40. This is the single most important christological proof text in the Old Testament for Luther. Throughout his career, he interpreted "the seed of the woman" as "The Seed," i.e., Christ, and the woman as "The Blessed Virgin Mary." The roots of this interpretation go back at least to Justin Martyr (c. 100–165) in the second century. In Lutheran theology, this passage would come to be known as the *Protevangelium* ("First Gospel").

41. The second most important christological proof text in the Old Testament for Luther. As a rule, the LW series used the RSV (here, "descendants") for biblical quotes rather than translating Luther's own biblical citations (here, *Samen*, "seed"). As a result, many crucial intertextual connections in the biblical text are lost; in this instance, e.g., the linkage that Luther is making between Gen. 3:15 and 22:18.

42. The third most important christological proof text in the Old Testament for Luther. He interprets the "prophet like Moses" as a reference to the coming Christ. Once he has come, Moses ceases to have any claim. Thus, Luther could say in his 17 September 1525 sermon on Exod. 20:2: "It is all over for Moses, for his office lasts only until the time of Christ" (WA 16:429, 26–27).

43. Now begins an extended digression on the misuse of the Old Testament by Luther's opponents, in terms of what is and what is not applicable to a contemporary Christian.

the most important thing in Moses which has to do with us. The first thing, namely, the commandments, do not have to do with us. I read Moses because such excellent and comforting pledges are there recorded, by which I can strengthen my weak faith. For things happen in the kingdom of Christ just as I read in Moses; therein I also find the sure foundation.

In this manner, therefore, I should accept Moses, and not sweep him under the rug. First, because he provides lovely examples of laws, from which excerpts may be taken. Second, in Moses there are the pledges of God by which faith is sustained. As it is written of Eve in Genesis 3[:15], "I will put enmity between you and the woman, and between your seed and her seed;[40] he shall trample on your head, [and you will bite him on the heel]."[q] [This was said about Christ.][r] Similarly, Abraham was given the pledge by God, speaking thus in the First Book of Moses [22:18]: "In your seed[41] all the Gentiles will be blessed"; [that is, through Christ the gospel is to arise].[s] Similarly, in the Fifth Book of Moses in the 18th chapter [:15-16], Moses says, "A prophet like me the Lord your God will raise up from among you and your brothers—him you shall obey; just as you asked from the Lord your God at Horeb on the day of the assembly," etc.[42] There are many such sayings in the Old Testament, which the holy apostles quoted and drew upon.[43]

But our factious spirits come and say of everything they find in Moses, "No one can deny that it is God who is speaking here; therefore we must observe it." So then the mob goes to it. Whew! If God has said it, who can say anything against it? Then they're pressed hard like pigs at a trough. Our dear prophets[44] have blabbered thus to the people, "Dear people, God told his people

---

q   Supplemented from WA 16:382, 22 and 24:11, 5.

r   WA 16:382, 22–26 and WA 24:11, 5–9 insert in place of this line the following, which is also identical to the Luther Bible gloss at Gen. 3:15: "This is the first gospel and promise about Christ which took place on earth, that he would overcome sin, death, and hell, and save us from the power of the serpent. In this Adam believed together with all his descendants, and by this he became a Christian and was saved from his fall."

s   WA 16:382, 29–30 and WA 24:11, 12–13 replace this last phrase with: "This was the second gospel about Christ, that through him all people would be blessed and saved, as St. Paul interprets this passage to the Galatians [in 3:8ff.]."

Caravagio's painting of the Madonna
and St. Anne depicts the child Jesus
trampling on the head of a snake.

44. Luther initially used the term
prophets pejoratively against
the preachers Nicholas Storch
(d. 1525), Thomas Drechsel (dates
unknown), and Marcus Thomae (dates
unknown), who were part of Müntzer's
circle in Zwickau in the early 1520s. He
labeled them "prophets" because of
their claims to direct divine revelation.
He went on to use it directly against
Karlstadt in *Against the Heavenly Prophets*
(see pp. 38–125 in this volume). Here
he is referring to Müntzer. See Brecht,
Martin Luther, 2:146.

to kill Amalek"[45] [Exod. 17:8-16; Deut. 25:17-19]. This has led
to nothing but sorrow and misery. Thus the peasants arose, not
knowing any difference, and were led into this delusion by those
mad factious spirits.

If there been had educated preachers around, they could have
confronted the false prophets and opposed them, and said this to
them: "Dear factious spirits, it is true that God commanded this
of Moses and spoke thus to the people, but we are not the people
[to whom God said it].*t* Dear ones, God also spoke to Adam, but

45. Müntzer, in a sermon of July 1524
at Allstedt, demanded that the princes
wipe out all the godless, including
godless rulers, priests, and monks
(taken from LW 35:169 n. 11). See also
the discussion in Brecht, *Martin Luther*,
2:153–55.

t Supplemented from WA 16:384, 23 and 24:12, 4.

that does not make me Adam. God commanded Abraham to kill his son [Gen. 22:2], but that does not make me Abraham such that I should kill my son. God also spoke to David. [That all of it is God's word is in fact true].*u* But whether it's God's word here or God's word there,*v* I must know and pay attention to whom God's word is addressed. You are still a long way from being the people with whom God spoke." The false prophets say, "You are the people, God is speaking to you." Prove it to me! In this way they could have been refuted, but they wanted to be beaten, and so the whole mob went to the devil.

One must deal and proceed cleanly with the Scriptures. From the beginning the word has come to pass in various ways. It is not enough simply to consider whether something is God's word, whether God has said it; rather, much more must one consider to whom it has been spoken, whether it concerns you [or somebody else].[46],*w* The difference is like that between night and day. That God said to David, "Out of you shall come the king," etc. [2 Sam. 7:13], does not pertain to me, it was not spoken to me. God can indeed speak to me if God wants to. But you must be attentive to the word that concerns you, that is spoken to you, [and not what concerns somebody else].*x*

The word in Scripture is of two kinds: the first does not pertain or apply to me, the second does apply to me. And I can boldly trust in that word which does pertain to me and rely upon it, as upon a strong rock. But if it does not concern me, then I should just be still. The false prophets come along and say, "Dear people, this is the word of God." That is true; we cannot deny it. But we are not the people. God did not tell *us* to do that. The factious spirits came along and wanted to stir up something new, saying, "We must also observe the Old Testament." So they got the peasants all heated up and ruined them in wife and child. These mad people imagined that [the word of God]*y* had been withheld from them, such that no one had told them that they were

46. This is a fundamental principle of biblical interpretation for Luther: just because something is in the Bible, and is thus God's word, does not make it automatically applicable to or binding on Christians. In a sense, this entire sermon is an attempt to explicate just this point.

u   Reading with WA 16:384, 27 and 24:12, 8.

v   A more dynamic translation would be: "But let God's word be what it may."

w   Supplemented from WA 16:348, 16 and 24:12, 17.

x   Supplemented from WA 16:385, 25 and 24:12, 21.

y   Reading with WA 16:386, 24 and 24:34.

supposed to kill [the godless].*z* It serves them right. They didn't want to follow or listen to anybody. I have seen and experienced it myself, how mad, raving, and senseless they were.[47]

Therefore say this to [those same factious spirits]:*a* Leave Moses and his people together; they have had their day and do not pertain to me. I listen to the word which applies to me. We have the gospel. Christ says, "Go and preach the gospel," not only to the Jews, as Moses did, but to "all the Gentiles," to "all creatures" [Mark 16:15]. To me it is said, "Whoever believes and is baptized will be saved" [Mark 16:16]. Similarly, "Go and do to your neighbor as has been done to you."*b* These words concern me too, for I am one of the "all creatures." If Christ had not added, "preach to all creatures," then I would pay no heed to it and would not be baptized, just as I now pay no heed to Moses, because he is not given to me but only to the Jews. [But because Christ says that the gospel ("whoever believes and is baptized will be saved") should be preached not only to one people, nor in only this or that place in the world, but to all creatures],*c* therefore no one is excluded. Rather, all are thereby included, and no one should doubt that the gospel is to be preached to them too. And so I believe this word; it pertains to me too. I too belong under the gospel, [and]*d* in the New Testament. Therefore I put my trust in that word, even if it should cost a hundred thousand lives.[48],*e*

The preachers who would teach other people, and indeed all Christians, should note well, grasp, and take to heart this distinction,[49] because absolutely everything depends on it. If the peasants had understood it this way, much could have been salvaged for them, and they would not have been so pitifully seduced and ruined. And where we understand it differently, there we make sects and factions, when we—without making any

47. In April and May 1525 Luther had preached personally against the insurrection, both in Mansfield and in Thuringia (taken from LW 35:171 n. 1). We know that these sermons were not well received. In Nordhausen, for example, the people rang bells while he preached as a sign of protest against him. During this exceedingly tense period of time, Luther's sermons likely placed his life in danger. See Brecht, *Martin Luther*, 2:178–85.

48. One hundred thousand is a common estimate of lives lost in the Peasants' War.

49. That is, the distinction between that which is spoken to all and that which is spoken to one or only a few. The gospel, by definition, is addressed to all, while Moses was addressed only to a few.

---

z   Supplemented from WA 16:386, 24 and 24:12, 35.

a   Reading with WA 16:386, 28 and WA 24:13, 3.

b   An apparent allusion to Luke 10:36-37: "'Which of these three, do you think, was a neighbor to the man who fell into the hands of the robbers?' He said, 'The one who showed him mercy.' Jesus said to him, 'Go and do likewise.'"

c   Reading with WA 16:387, 24–27 and 24:13, 14–16.

d   Reading with WA 16:387, 30 and WA 24:13, 20.

e   *Helss*, literally "necks."

distinction—spew [and slobber]*f* among the mob and the mad, uncomprehending people, saying, "God's word, God's word."*g* But, dear fellow, it depends on whether [or not]*h* it is said to *you*. God indeed speaks also to angels, wood, fish, birds, animals, and all creatures, but that does not make it pertain to me. I should pay attention to that which applies to me, that which is said to me, [whereby God admonishes me, urges me, and demands something of me].*i*

Consider this illustration. Suppose a housefather had a wife, a daughter, a son, a maid, and a hired man. Now he speaks to the hired man and tells him to hitch up the horses and bring in a load of wood, [plow]*j* the field, and do some other job. Then he tells the maid to milk the cows, churn some butter, and so on. Then he tells his wife to take care of the kitchen and his daughter to do some spinning and make the beds. All of this would be the words of one master, one housefather. But imagine if the maid decided to handle the horses and bring in the wood, the hired man sat down and milked the cows, the daughter drove the wagon or plowed the field, the wife made the beds or spun and neglected the kitchen; and then they all said, "The master told us to do this; these are the housefather's orders!" Then what? The housefather would come and grab a club, throw them all together,*k* and say, "Although it was my order, I did not order *you* to do it; I gave each of you your instructions, and you should have stuck to them."

It is the same way with the word of God. Suppose I were to take up something that God had ordered someone else to do, and then I declared, "But you said it." God would answer, "Let the devil thank you; I did not say it to *you*." You must make a clear distinction between that which concerns only one person and that which concerns everyone. If, for example, the housefather should say, "On Friday we are going to eat meat," that

---

f Supplemented from WA 16:388, 24 and 24:13, 28.

g See the identical expression and usage in *Against the Heavenly Prophets*, LW 40:91, 105.

h Supplemented from WA 16:388, 25–26 and 24:13, 29.

i Reading with WA 16:388, 27–28 and 24:13, 31–32.

j Reading with WA 16:388, 31 and 24:14, 2.

k Reading with Aland, *allzumal zusammenwerfen* for *alle zumal auff eyn hauffen schmeissen*.

would be a word addressed to everybody in the house. Thus the commandments spoken to Moses by God concern the Jews alone. But the gospel goes throughout the whole world in its entirety; no one is excluded, for it is proclaimed to all creatures. Therefore the whole world should accept it, and accept it as if it had been proclaimed to each person individually. The word "We should love one another" [John 15:12] pertains to me, for it pertains to all who belong to the gospel. Thus we read Moses not because he applies to us, that we must observe what he says, but because he agrees with natural law and is better composed*l* than the Gentiles would ever have been able to do.[50] Thus the Ten Commandments are a mirror of our life,[51] in which we see wherein we are lacking, etc. The factious spirits have also misunderstood [Moses]*m* with respect to the question of images; for that too pertains only to the Jews, etc.[52]

With regard to this second part, as is now said, we read Moses because of the promises that speak about Christ, who belongs not only to the Jews but also to the Gentiles. For through Christ all the Gentiles should have the blessing, as was promised to Abraham [Gen. 12:3].

The third thing to see in Moses

In the third place, we read Moses for the lovely examples of faith, love, and the cross, [as shown] in the fathers, Adam, Abel, Noah, Abraham, Isaac, Jacob, Moses, and all the rest. From these examples we should learn to trust and love God. Conversely there are also examples [of the unbelief] of the godless [and of the wrath of God],*n* namely, how God does not pardon the unbelief of the unbelievers; how God punished Cain, Ishmael, Esau, the whole world with the flood, and Sodom and Gomorrah, etc. Such examples are necessary, for although I am not Cain, yet if I should act like Cain did, I will receive the same punishment as Cain received. Nowhere else do we find such lovely examples of both faith and unbelief. Therefore we should not sweep Moses

50. See the similar passage in *Against the Heavenly Prophets*, LW 40:98: "Why does one then keep and teach the Ten Commandments? Answer: Because the natural laws were never so orderly and well written as by Moses. Therefore it is reasonable to follow the example of Moses."

51. This metaphor of the law as that which shows us what we really are is common in Luther. It coheres with what he will later call the "theological use of the law" (*usus theologicus legis*), which is to be distinguished from the "political/civic use of the law" (*usus politicus/civilis legis*). The biblical text that has so influenced Luther's thinking on the law as mirror is Rom. 3:20, "No flesh will be justified in God's sight by works of the law, for through the law comes the knowledge of sin."

52. For Luther's arguments on the place of images in the church, see *Against the Heavenly Prophets* (part 1), LW 40:79–143; and his 24 September 1525 *Sermon on Exod 20:3-4* (WA 16:436, 29–445, 5).

---

l   Reading with Aland, *abgefasst* for *gefasset*.

m   Reading with WA 16:390, 31 and 24:14, 30.

n   Supplemented from WA 16:391, 23 and 24:15, 6.

under the rug. Moreover the Old Testament is properly understood when we retain from the prophets the lovely sayings about Christ, when we grasp well and take note of the lovely examples, and when we use the laws as we please to our benefit.[53]

53. This single sentence concisely summarizes the entire sermon.

Cain murders his brother Abel. This scene illustrates the commandment against murder on a page of a German catechism printed in 1530.

Conclusion and Summary

I have stated that all Christians, and especially those who deal with the word of God and teach other people, should take special care to learn Moses correctly. Thus when he gives a commandment, we are not to accept him except insofar as he rhymes[54] with natural law. Moses is a master and doctor of the Jews. We have our own master, Christ, who has set before us what we are to know, observe, do, and not do. However, it is true that Moses sets down, in addition to the laws, lovely examples of faith and unbelief—punishment of the godless, exaltation of the pious and faithful—and also the sweet and comforting pledges concerning Christ which we should accept. The same is true also in the Gospel writers. For example, in the account of the ten lepers, that Christ tells them go to the priest and make their sacrifice [Luke 17:14] does not pertain to me. The example of their faith, however, does pertain to me; I should believe Christ, just as they did.

Enough has now been said about this, and it is to be noted well because it is really crucial. Many great and outstanding people have gotten it wrong, and even today many great preachers still stumble over it. They do not know how to preach Moses, nor how to regard him properly. They are insane as they rant and rage and riot, blabbering to the people, "God's word, God's word!" All the while they seduce the poor people and drive them to the grave. Many learned people have not known to what extent Moses ought to be taught. Origen,[55] Jerome,[56] and others like them have not shown clearly to what extent Moses can serve us. This is what I have attempted to say by way of introduction to Moses, namely, how Moses is to be regarded, how he is to be understood and accepted and not swept under the rug. For such a lovely order [and external government]*o* is contained in him, that it is a pleasure, etc. [Not to mention that he describes many outstanding, lovely things, as you have heard, which are not only not to be thrown away but are to be highly esteemed and accepted with an earnest heart, so as to encourage and strengthen our Christian faith, through which we as well as the dear holy ancestors are saved.]*p*

God be praised.

o   Supplemented from WA 16:393, 26 and 24:16, 13.

p   Supplemented from WA 16:393, 27–31 and 24:16, 13–18.

54. The concept of "rhyming" will be used at length in Luther's 1543 treatise, *On the Last Words of David* (LW 15:267–352), where he takes up the question of the extent to which the Old Testament "rhymes" with the New. Heinrich Borkamm has referred to this treatise as "the indissoluble counterpart to *How Christians Should Regard Moses*" (idem, *Luther and the Old Testament*, 149).

55. Origen of Alexandria (c. 185–c. 254). Though one of the greatest minds in Christian history, Luther rarely if ever has anything good to say about him due to his allegorical method of exegesis.

56. St. Jerome (c. 342–420). His translation of the Bible into Latin in 400 CE, known as the Vulgate, displaced all previous Latin translations and became the standard Bible of the Western church. His translation of the Old Testament was the first in Latin to be made directly from the Hebrew text as opposed to the Greek text. The exclusive status of the Vulgate within the Roman Church was reaffirmed by the Council of Trent in 1546.

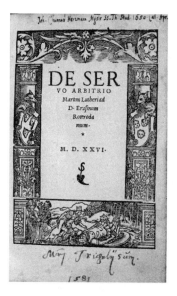

The title page of Luther's
On the Bondage of the Will.

The Bondage of the Will

1525

VOLKER LEPPIN

INTRODUCTION

There would have been no Reformation without humanism: going back to the sources—*ad fontes!*—was the key motto of many of the humanists, and Luther's program of *sola scriptura* fitted best to it. Also, it was the *Novum Instrumentum*, Erasmus's new edition of the New Testament, that helped Luther develop his ideas while reading Paul's letter to the Romans.[1] Even more, when Melanchthon came to Wittenberg in 1518, and when Luther was admired by the humanists at the Heidelberg disputation[2] the same year, the alliance between humanism and reformation seemed to be perfect.[3]

This is true, although in Heidelberg, among other positions, Luther maintained this radical conclusion: the free will after the fall is nothing more than a name. Later on, this issue would become the point of serious contention between Erasmus of Rotterdam (1466–1536), the leader of the humanists in the north of the Alps, and Luther. Erasmus did not come into the struggle on his own, but he was strongly encouraged by others to write against Luther on the question of the free will. Concerning his planned tract, he was in contact with King Henry VIII of England (1491–1547) as well as with Pope Clement VII (1478–1534). Finally, in the beginning of September 1524, Erasmus's *De libero*

1. In his 1545 *Preface to the Complete Edition of Luther's Latin Writings* (LW 34:327–38), Luther recalls his reformation discovery with Romans 1:17: "Here I felt that I was altogether born again and had entered paradise itself through open gates. There a totally other face of the entire Scripture showed itself to me" (337).

2. Luther's "friendly" hearing with his Augustinian monks. The twenty-eight theses Luther defended at the disputation were published as the *Heidelberg Disputation* in 1518 (LW 31).

3. Timeline

    1524 September Erasmus's *On the Free Will*

    1525 January *Against the Heavenly Prophets in the Matter of Images and Sacraments*

arbitrio diatribe sive collation (*On the Free Will. Discourses or Comparisons*), was published.

The title indicates the two parts of his treatise: the first part was a comparison of biblical sentences relevant to the question of the free will. With this, Erasmus accepted Luther's methodological demand to discuss on biblical grounds only. But at the same time, he argued that the biblical view on this matter was not absolutely evident or decisive. He showed that different passages of the Bible argued for one or the other side of the question and thus led to possibly different answers. This observation gave Luther the justification for the discourse that ensued in the second part where he argued philosophically in a balanced manner.

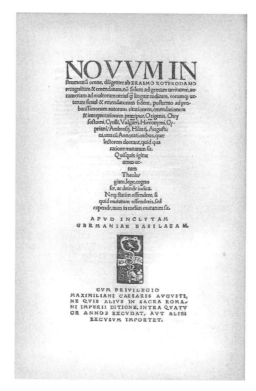

The title page of Erasmus' text of the New Testament, 1516.

Portrait of Desiderius Erasmus of Rotterdam by Pilaster Hans Holbein the Younger (1498–1543).

Holding with Luther that human salvation depended fully on God, nevertheless, Erasmus stated that the human free will had survived the fall, but in a weakened mode.

When Luther read this treatise, he was horrified. It was not a surprise to him that the former collaborator did not share all his convictions. But now he was faced with something he could not accept or ignore, even if his first reaction had been to not even bother responding in public, as he wrote to Georg Spalatin[4] on 1 November 1524.[a] Just sixteen days later, Luther announced: "I will answer to Erasmus, not just because of himself, but because of those who misuse his authority for their own glory against Christ."[b] He was not the only one to distance himself from Erasmus: also the Strasburg reformers Wolfgang Capito (1478–1541), Caspar Hedio (1494–1542), and Martin Bucer (1491–1551) supported Luther in his opposition of the man they saw opening the way for the Antichrist—even if, they confessed, they had learned a lot from Erasmus.[c]

Actually, Luther had no time to answer quickly. Other problems were coming into the foreground, mainly the Peasants' Wars. Asked for his statement, Luther suddenly became engaged in a severe debate about the legitimacy of this uproar of peasants demanding their rights. Luther felt his popularity failing and feared that the war could destroy all his efforts for reforms. In addition, he got married in 1525 to Katharina von Bora (1499–1552)—an important step in his development as a man and a reformer—but also one that only further fueled his critics who jeered about the monk becoming a spouse. Luther took the whole spring of 1525 to stew on his answer against Erasmus, as his letters reveal, with several allusions to this issue,[d] but he had no time. As late as 27 September 1525, Luther wrote to Nicholaus Hausmann (c. 1478–1538):[5] "I am now fully engaged in confuting Erasmus."[e] Not long after, in December, the *De servo arbitrio* (*The Bondage of the Will*) was published.

4. Georg Spalatin (1484–1545) was Luther's friend and a counselor/diplomat of the Elector of Saxony.

5. A Lutheran preacher in Anhalt-Dessau, superintendent, and teacher—from Bavaria but with the call in Bohemia—Hausmann was interested in the worship reforms and actively corresponded with Luther.

a   WA Br 3:368, 30–31 (No. 789).
b   WA Br 3:373, 6–8 (No. 793).
c   WA Br 3:386, 207–15 (No. 797).
d   See for example WA Br 3:462, 6 (No. 847): "I must [write] against the Free will." WA Br 3:462, 6 (No. 789).
e   WA Br 3:582, 5 (No. 926).

The treatise is important on four accounts: (1) as a witness of the serious intellectual debates in the Reformation time; (2) as a contribution to the developing Lutheran teaching on the Holy Scripture; (3) on free will; and (4) on God. Concerning the culture of debate in which Luther operated, one sees Luther acting as someone who wanted to show his own humanist education. No text of his is as full of allusions to antic traditions as *De servo arbitrio* is. Luther wanted to show Erasmus and, even more, the public that he was not intellectually inferior, even if he, in a figure of humility, confessed his own limitations. And he did not hide the main difference: while Erasmus tried to open the discussion and left it to his readers to decide which position would be right, Luther impressed upon his readers that the struggle was about the truth and that it was urgent to come to the conclusion that Luther himself clearly suggested.

Luther's absolute conviction about what was right lay in his doctrine of Scripture. Against Erasmus, who had maintained that the question of free will could not be decided just on the basis of the Bible, Luther stressed the clarity imbedded in Scripture: if human beings did not understand Scripture satisfactorily, this was not the failure of Scripture but of the human reason, which was not able to understand the depth of God's truth. With these passages, Luther laid the grounds for the fundamental Lutheran understanding of the infallibility of Scripture and its centrality in Lutheran theology, especially prominent in the so-called Lutheran orthodoxy.[6]

Luther's position on the main question seems easy to summarize—and yet it is not. There is no question at all that he upheld his early conviction that human beings do not have free will. But he tried to reconcile this with the human experience, which calls on individuals to be able to decide on many things in everyday life. Luther thus stressed that his denial of the free will pertained to the issue of salvation, while in other areas of life, not relevant for this fundamental existential matter, free will could be acknowledged. Luther's conclusions have continued to stir reflection and debate among Lutherans over the centuries and continue even today. Luther's argument on the matter of bound/free will poses a challenge and an invitation for constructive contemporary theology.

The same can be said about the fourth question: Luther's doctrine of God. He introduces the distinction of the revealed

6. Lutheran orthodoxy refers to a period from the compilation of the 1580 *Book of Concord* to the Age of Enlightenment.

and the hidden God to make clear that a Christian must focus on God as shown in Jesus Christ rather than speculating about God's potency in general. Depending on one's own convictions, one can see this as one of Luther's deepest spiritual insights, or as a speculative idea, leading to a destruction of a consistent image of God. However, the idea is rooted in Luther's early conversations with his confessor Johann von Staupitz (c. 1460–1524),[7] who was instrumental in directing Luther's mind and attention to move from the fear of predestination[8] to trust in the Redeemer, Jesus Christ.

These basic ideas are part of a long and sometimes confusing text that Luther completed hastily. The original Latin text was addressed to the learned scholars, but soon Luther's colleague and the Wittenberg city pastor, Justus Jonas (1493–1555), provided a German translation to make it known also for the broader public. Erasmus himself was mainly disturbed with Luther's style. He criticized Luther's ferocity, idiosyncrasy, and even malice[f] and wrote his answer, *A Defense of the Diatribe* (*Hyperaspistes diatribae*), which was published in two volumes in 1526 and 1527. Again, external challenges and his inner reluctance prevented Luther from returning the favor with his new answer. Thus the debate eventually petered out between the two, while the issue did not die.

The consequences of this relatively brief public debate were immense: many humanists retreated from Luther because of his intransigent manner of debating. The coinciding Peasants' Wars made things even worse. Luther's glory failed; the former hero became a representative of intellectual headiness. Nevertheless, the text of *De servo arbitrio*, read independently from its immediate context, provides an abundance of theological insights for new generations of theologians to address the fundamental concerns about human freedom, God's omnipotence, and the premise of the God–human relationship—and thus, naturally, the question about salvation.

In the text of *The Bondage of the Will* that follows, several cuts have been made in order to provide a representative portion of the whole. The following symbol [. . .] is used to indicate where content has been edited out.

7. Staupitz was a university preacher, the Vicar-General of the Augustinians in Germany, and Luther's abbot and spiritual father who had a significant influence on his theology of grace. See Franz Posset, *The Front-Runner of the Catholic Reformation: The Life and Works of Johann von Staupitz* (Farnham, UK: Ashgate, 2003).

8. The concept of predestination, rooted in Romans 9–11, was shaped by Augustine. To him, all human beings formed a mass of perdition after the fall. But with divine incomprehensible volition, God decided to save some of them by no reason than God's good will alone, which on the other hand meant there was no other reason why the other human beings should not be preserved.

f WA 18:583.

9. This translation is based on the translation provided by Philip S. Watson, in collaboration with Benjamin Drewery, in *Luther's Works,* vol. 33: *Career of the Reformer III,* ed. Jaroslav J. Pelikan, Hilton C. Oswald, and Helmut T. Lehmann (Philadelphia: Fortress Press, 1972), 3–295. Revised by Volker Leppin according to the principles of *The Annotated Luther,* with a new introduction and enhanced annotations. The Latin text of *De servo arbitrio* used is from WA 18:600–787 and MLStA 3:177–356. The latter provided important support for annotation.

10. Luther here does not call Erasmus a "master" in the technical sense of an academic graduate.

11. Being concerned with the Peasants' Wars (1525), it took Luther about one year to answer Erasmus's *Diatribe,* which was published in September 1524. Luther's *De servo arbitrio* was published in December 1525.

12. The Maccabees were the leaders of Jewish revolt against the Hellenist ruler Antiochus Epiphanes IV in the second century before Christ.

THE BONDAGE OF THE WILL[9]

TO THE VENERABLE MASTER[10] ERASMUS of Rotterdam, Martin Luther sends grace and peace in Christ.

[Introduction]

[Luther Explains His Delay in Replying and Admits Erasmus's Superior Talent]

That I have taken so long[11] to reply to your *Diatribe Concerning Free Choice,* venerable Erasmus, has been contrary to everyone's expectation and to my own custom; for until now I have seemed not only willing to accept, but eager to seek out, opportunities of this kind for writing. There will perhaps be some surprise at this new and unwonted forbearance—or fear!—in Luther, who has not been roused even by all the speeches and letters his adversaries have flung about, congratulating Erasmus on his victory and chanting in triumph, "Ho, ho! Has that Maccabee,[12] that most obstinate Assertor,[13] at last met his match, and dares not open his mouth against him?" Yet not only do I not blame them, but of myself I yield you a palm such as I have never yielded to anyone before; for I confess not only that you are far superior to me in powers of eloquence and native genius (which we all must admit, all the more as I am a barbarian who has always lived among barbarians[14]), but that you have quite damped my spirit and eagerness, and left me exhausted before I could strike a blow.

There are two reasons for this: first, your virtuosity in treating the subject with such remarkable and consistent moderation as to make it impossible for me to be angry with you; and second, the luck or chance or fate by which you say nothing on this important subject that has not been said before.[15] Indeed, you say so much less, and attribute so much more to free choice than the Sophists[16] have hitherto done (a point on which I shall have more to say later) that it really seemed superfluous to answer the arguments you use. They have been refuted already so often by me, and beaten down and completely pulverized in Philip Melanchthon's *Loci Communes* [*Commonplaces*][17]—an unanswerable little book, which in my judgment deserves not only to be honored with immortality but also with ecclesiastical authority.

LOCI

COMMVNES RERVM.
THEOLOGICARVM
SEV HYPOTY·
POSES THEO·
LOGICAE.

VVITTEMBERGAE.
AN. M. D. XXI.

The title page of Philip Melanchthon's *Loci communes rerum theologicarum, seu, Hypotyposes theologicae,* a volume that later proved to be the first Protestant attempt at systematic theology.

13. In his *Assertio omnium articulorum Martini Lutheri per bullam Leonis X novissimam Damnatorum,* Luther had asserted his articles that had been damned in the bull *Exsurge Domine* by Pope Leo X (1475–1521).

14. Actually, Luther had enjoyed a good humanist education in Erfurt, but his Latin was far worse than Erasmus's was, even if he tried to show his good abilities in this tract. This may be a possible allusion to Erasmus's book *Against the Barbarians* (1520). For Erasmus the "barbarians" were those who opposed *bonae literae* or "good letters" (LW 33:15).

15. Allusion to the Prologue in Terence's comedy *Eunuchus*: "Nothing is said now, that was not said before."

16. Sophists were the counterparts of Socrates in Plato's dialogues, always blamed to twist everybody's words. In Luther's use, the word *sophists* was an overall invective against the Scholastics.

17. Melanchthon's *Loci communes,* written in 1521, was the first systematic dogmatic treatise in the Wittenberg Reformation. In *Loci,* most important concepts of the Bible, as structural elements of the dogmatics, meant a change from the Scholastic kind of systematic dialectical structuring.

18. Obviously, Luther, as a humanistically trained teacher, uses here the argument of distinguishing the fine humanist form from unimportant matters.

19. This, indeed, was Luther's impression of Erasmus's *Diatribe* from his first view on, as revealed in his letter to Spalatin from the 1 November 1524, where he argues against the *Diatribe* as an "unlearned book of such a learned man" (WA Br 3:368, 30–31 [No. 789]).

20. Luther was convinced, in light of Rom. 1:18-21, that every person's conscience was confronted with God and able to hear God's will.

21. Passages like this, later on, could give rise to the hermeneutics that made a sharp distinction between the letters of Scripture and a spiritual interpretation of it. Luther himself was convinced that the Spirit was connected with the Scripture and its letters.

Compared with it, your book struck me as so cheap and trivial that I felt profoundly sorry for you, defiling as you were your very elegant and ingenious style with such trash,[18] and quite disgusted at the utterly unworthy matter that was being conveyed in such rich ornaments of eloquence, like refuse or ordure being carried in gold and silver vases.[19]

You seem to have felt this yourself, from the reluctance with which you undertook this piece of writing. No doubt your conscience warned you that[20] no matter what powers of eloquence you brought to the task, you would be unable so to gloss it over as to prevent me from stripping away the seductive charm of your words and discovering the dregs beneath, since although I am unskilled in speech, I am not unskilled in knowledge, by the grace of God. For, in full faith, I venture thus with Paul [1 Cor. 11:6] to claim knowledge for myself that I deny to you, though I grant you eloquence and native genius such as I willingly and very properly disclaim for myself.

What I thought, then, was this. If there are those who have imbibed so little of our teaching or taken so insecure a hold of it, strongly supported by Scripture though it is, that they can be moved by these trivial and worthless though highly decorative arguments of Erasmus, then they do not deserve that I should come to their rescue with an answer. Nothing could be said or written that would be sufficient for such people, even though it were by recourse to thousands of books a thousand times over, and you might just as well plow the seashore and sow seed in the sand[g] or try to fill a cask full of holes with water.[h] Those who have imbibed the Spirit who holds sway in our books have had a sufficient service from us already, and they can easily dispose of your performances; but as for those who read without the Spirit,[21] it is no wonder if they are shaken like a reed by every wind.[i] Why, even God could not say enough for such people, even if all God's creatures were turned into tongues. Hence I might well have decided to leave them alone, upset as they were by your book, along with those who are delighted with it and declare you the victor.

It was, then, neither pressure of work, nor the difficulty of the task, nor your great eloquence, nor any fear of you, but sheer dis-

---

g   Allusion to Ovid, *Heroides* 5, 115.
h   Allusion to Plautus, *Pseudolus* 269.
i   Cf. Matt. 11:7.

gust, anger, and contempt, or—to put it plainly—my considered judgment on your *Diatribe* that damped my eagerness to answer you. I need hardly mention here the good care you take, as you always do, to be everywhere evasive and equivocal;[22] you fancy yourself steering more cautiously than Ulysses between Scylla and Charybdis as you seek to assert nothing while appearing to assert something.[23] How, I ask you, is it possible to have any discussion or reach any understanding with such people unless one is clever enough to catch Proteus?[24] What I can do in this matter, and what you have gained by it, I will show you later, with Christ's help.

There have, then, to be special reasons for my answering you at this point. Faithful Christians are urging me to do so, and point out that everyone expects it, since the authority of Erasmus is not to be despised, and the truth of Christian doctrine is being imperiled in the hearts of many. Moreover, it has at length come home to me that my silence has not been entirely honorable, and that I have been deluded by my mundane prudence—or malice—into insufficient awareness of my duty, whereby I am under obligation both to the wise and to the foolish [Rom. 1:14], especially when I am called to it by the entreaties of so many Christians. For although the subject before us demands more than an external scholar, and besides him who plants and him who waters outwardly [1 Cor. 3:7], it requires also the Spirit of God to give the growth and to teach living things inwardly (a thought that has been much in my mind), yet since the Spirit is free, and blows not where we will but where he wills [John 3:8], we ought to have observed that rule of Paul, "Be urgent in season and out of season" [2 Tim. 4:2], for we do not know at what hour the Lord is coming [Matt. 24:42]. There may be, I grant, some who have not yet sensed the Spirit who informs my writings, and who have been bowled over by that *Diatribe* of yours; perhaps their hour has not yet come.[25]

And who knows but that God may even deign to visit you, excellent Erasmus, through such a wretched and frail little vessel[j] as myself, so that in a happy hour—and for this I earnestly beseech the Father of mercies[26] through Christ our Lord—I may come to you by means of this book, and win a very dear brother.

22. Equivocal terms in medieval theory of language meant terms with the same spelling and sound but different meanings.

23. Scylla and Charybdis were two monsters in antic tales, sitting opposite to one another in a strait, the first devouring human beings, the second dumping them in a swirl. Ulysses had to pass them and lost many of his companions.

24. Proteus was a sea goddess in antic tales, one able to transform himself into different shapes and so able to escape all who wanted to catch him.

25. Luther himself felt he was in the last days of the world, awaiting the imminent coming of the Lord.

26. *Pater misericordiae* (Lat.), "father of mercies"; this traditional expression could be translated as "parent of mercies" to express God's merciful relating to human beings in need of divine parental love.

j Cf. 2 Cor. 4:7.

For although you think and write wrongly about free choice,[k] yet I owe you no small thanks, for you have made me far more sure of my own position by letting me see the case for free choice put forward with all the energy of so distinguished and powerful a mind, but with no other effect than to make things worse than before. That is plain evidence that free choice is a pure fiction;[27] for, like the woman in the Gospel [Mark 5:25f.], the more it is treated by the doctors, the worse it gets. I shall therefore abundantly pay my debt of thanks to you, if through me you become better informed, as I through you have been more strongly confirmed. But both of these things are gifts of the Spirit, not our own achievement. Therefore, we must pray that God may open my mouth and your heart, and the hearts of all human beings, and that God may be present in our midst as the master who informs both our speaking and hearing.

But from you, my dear Erasmus, let me obtain this request, that just as I bear with your ignorance in these matters, so you in turn will bear with my lack of eloquence. God does not give all his gifts to one man, and "we cannot all do all things"; or, as Paul says: "There are varieties of gifts, but the same Spirit" [1 Cor. 12:4]. It remains, therefore, for us to render mutual service with our gifts, so that each with one's own gift bears the burden and need of the other. Thus we shall fulfill the law of Christ [Gal. 6:2].[28]

[Part I. Review of Erasmus's Preface]

[Christianity Involves Assertions; Christians Are No Skeptics]

I want to begin by referring to some passages in your Preface, in which you rather disparage our case and puff up your own. I note, first, that just as in other books you censure me for obstinate assertiveness, so in this book you say that you are so far from delighting in assertions that you would readily take refuge in the opinion of the Skeptics[29] wherever this is allowed by the

---

27. Luther had stated this as early as in his 1518 *Heidelberg Disputation* (WA 1:353–74; LW 31:[37–38] 39–70). Here he explains the free will to be just a word, not a real thing (*res de solo titulo*).

28. As evident with the biblical and traditional wording, Luther does not find the law just in the Old but also in the New Testament.

29. The Skeptics in antiquity denied the possibility of finding the absolute truth. Augustine (354–430), in his *Contra academicos*, gave severe criticism of skepticism.

---

k   In Latin, there is a difference between *voluntas*, which means "will" as a power in terms of psychology, and *arbitrium*, which stresses the ability to choose. Luther and Erasmus address mainly the latter.

inviolable authority of the Holy Scriptures and the decrees of the Church, to which you always willingly submit your personal feelings,[30] whether you grasp what it prescribes or not. This [you say] is the frame of mind that pleases you.

I take it (as it is only fair to do) that you say these things in a kindly and peace-loving mind. But if anyone else were to say them, I should probably go for that person in my usual manner; and I ought not to allow even you, excellent though your intentions are, to be led astray by this idea. For it is not the mark of a Christian mind to take no delight in assertions; on the contrary, a human being must delight in assertions to be a real Christian. And by assertion—in order that we may not be misled by words—I mean a constant adhering, affirming, confessing, maintaining, and an invincible persevering;[31] nor, I think, does the word mean anything else either as used by the Latins[32] or by us in our time.

I am speaking, moreover, about the assertion of those things that have been divinely transmitted to us in the sacred writings. Elsewhere we have no need either of Erasmus or any other instructor to teach us that in matters that are doubtful or useless and unnecessary, assertions, disputings, and quarreling are not only foolish but impious, and Paul condemns them in more than one place.[l] Nor are you, I think, speaking of such things in this place—unless, in the manner of some foolish orator, you have chosen to announce one topic and discuss another, like the man with the turbot,[33] or else, with the craziness of some ungodly writer, you are contending that the article about free choice is doubtful or unnecessary.

Let Skeptics and Academics[34] keep well away from us Christians, but let there be among us "assertors" twice as unyielding as the Stoics themselves.[35] How often, I ask you, does the apostle Paul demand that *plerophoria* (as he terms it)[m]—that most sure and unyielding assertion of conscience? In Romans 10[:10] he calls it "confession," saying, "with the mouth confession is made unto salvation." And Christ says, "Everyone who confesses me before people, I also will confess before my Father" [Matt. 10:32]. Peter bids us give a reason for the hope that is in us [1 Peter 3:15]. What need is there to dwell on this?

30. Indeed, Erasmus, in his *Diatribe*, had confessed his willingness to submit his sense to the Holy Scriptures and the decrees of the church.

31. These remarks, however, from the beginning on show the different approaches Luther and Erasmus had regarding the dispute: while Erasmus sees the question of free will as a matter of discussion, Luther is convinced that he has already found the unquestionable truth in in the Bible.

32. Luther refers to the Latin authors from antiquity as examples for modern humanists.

33. This figure of speech derives from Juvenal's fourth *Satire*, 65–150. Luther jokes about orators who do not see or understand the issue of their speech exactly.

34. The Academics were the followers of Plato in antiquity. Cicero had presented them as skeptics. From this stemmed Augustine's criticism against them.

35. The Stoics, the most important philosophical school in antiquity, maintained that the whole cosmos is dominated by the godly *logos* (reason/word).

l   Cf. 1 Tim. 1:6; 2 Tim. 2:23; Titus 1:10; 3:9.

m   Cf. 1 Thess. 1:5.

Nothing is better known or more common among Christians than assertion. Take away assertions and you take away Christianity. Why, the Holy Spirit is given them from heaven to glorify Christ [in them] and confess him even unto death—unless it is not asserting when one dies for one's confession and assertion. Moreover, the Spirit goes to such lengths in asserting that she takes the initiative and accuses the world of sin [John 16:8], as if she would provoke a fight; and Paul commands Timothy to "exhort" and "be urgent out of season" [2 Tim. 4:2]. But what a droll exhorter he would be, who himself neither firmly believed nor consistently asserted the thing he was exhorting about! Why, I would send him to Anticyra![36]

But it is I who am the biggest fool, for wasting words and time on something that is clearer than daylight. What Christian would agree that assertions are to be despised? That would be nothing but a denial of all religion and piety, or an assertion that neither religion, nor piety, nor any dogma is of the slightest importance. Why, then, do you too assert, "I take no delight in assertions," and that you prefer this frame of mind to its opposite?[37] [. . .]

[The Clarity of Scripture]

I come now to the second passage, which is of a piece with this. Here you distinguish between Christian dogmas, pretending that there are some which it is necessary to know, and some which it is not, and you say that some are [meant to be] obscure and others quite plain. You thus either play games with other human beings' words or else you are trying your hand at a rhetorical sally of your own. You adduce, however, in support of your views, Paul's saying in Romans 11[:33]: "Oh the depth of the riches and wisdom and knowledge of God," and also that of Isaiah 40[:13]: "Who has directed the Spirit of the Lord, or what counselor has provided instruction?"

It was easy for you to say these things, since you either knew you were not writing to Luther, but for the general public, or you did not reflect that it was Luther you were writing against, whom I hope you allow nonetheless to have some acquaintance with the Holy Scriptures and some judgment in respect of it. If you do not allow this, then I shall force you to it. The distinction I make—in order that I, too, may display a little rhetoric or

36. In Anticyra, hellebore was produced as a medicine against insanity (cf. Erasmus, *Adagia* 1,8,52). Luther means therefore that one should go to Anticyra to become cured from one's insanity.

37. With this rhetorical question, Luther suggests that Erasmus writes without any religious intention.

dialectic[38]—is this: God and the Scripture of God are two things, no less than the Creator and the creature are two things.

That in God there are many things hidden, of which we are ignorant, no one doubts—as the Lord himself says concerning the last day: "Of that day no one knows but the Father" [Mark 13:32], and in Acts 1[:7]: "It is not for you to know times and seasons"; and again: "I know whom I have chosen" [John 13:18], and Paul says: "The Lord knows those who are his" [2 Tim. 2:19], and so forth. But that in Scripture there are some things abstruse, and everything is not plain—this is an idea put about by the ungodly Sophists, with whose lips you also speak here, Erasmus; but they have never produced, nor can they produce, a single article to prove this mad notion of theirs. Yet with such a phantasmagoria[39] Satan has frightened people away from reading the sacred writings and has made Holy Scripture contemptible, in order to enable the plagues it has bred from philosophy to prevail in the Church.[40]

I admit, of course, that there are many texts in the Scriptures that are obscure and abstruse, not because of the majesty of their subject matter, but because of our ignorance of their vocabulary and grammar; but these texts in no way hinder a knowledge of all the subject matter of Scripture. For what still more sublime thing can remain hidden in the Scriptures, now that the seals have been broken, the stone rolled from the door of the sepulcher [Matt. 27:66; 28:2], and the supreme mystery brought to light, namely, that Christ the Son of God has been made man, that God is three and one,[41] that Christ has suffered for us and is to reign eternally? Are not these things known and sung even in the highways and byways? Take Christ out of the Scriptures, and what will you find left in them?[42]

The subject matter of the Scriptures, therefore, is all quite accessible, even though some texts are still obscure owing to our ignorance of their terms. Truly it is stupid and impious, when we know that the subject matter of Scripture has all been placed in the clearest light, to call it obscure on account of a few obscure words. If the words are obscure in one place, yet they are plain in another; and it is one and the same theme, published quite openly to the whole world, which in the Scriptures is sometimes expressed in plain words, and sometimes lies as yet hidden in obscure words. Now, when the item is in the light, it does not matter if this or that sign of it is in darkness,[43] since many other

38. Together with grammar, rhetoric and dialectics were parts of the studies of arts in the Middle Ages, together framing the so-called *Trivium*.

39. A delusion, a picture in a dream.

40. Luther's main argument against the Scholastics consists of criticism of their theology and philosophy. In general, Luther does not deny the means of philosophy but its use in theology. It is a kind of human wisdom, while theology has to deal with divine insights.

41. For Luther, the Trinity was clearly witnessed in the Holy Scriptures, which he read, in this regard, through the lenses of the ecumenical creeds' trinitarian formulation.

42. From his first lectures on the Bible (on Psalms and Romans) in the years 1513–1516, Luther was convinced about Christ being at the core of Scripture.

43. Luther here alludes to the famous distinction Augustine made between item/matter (*res*) and sign (*signum*) to interpret the sacraments, and widely used in the Middle Ages for that purpose.

signs of the same thing are meanwhile in the light. Who will say that a public fountain is not in the light because those who are in a narrow side street do not see it, whereas all who are in the marketplace do see it?

Your reference to the Corycian cave,[44] therefore, is irrelevant; that is not how things are in the Scriptures. Matters of the highest majesty and the profoundest mysteries are no longer hidden away, but have been brought out and are openly displayed before the very doors. For Christ has opened our minds so that we may understand the Scriptures [Luke 24:45], and the gospel is preached to the whole creation [Mark 16:15]; "Their voice has gone out to all the earth" [Rom. 10:18], and "Whatever was written was written for our instruction" [Rom. 15:4]; also: "All Scripture inspired by God is profitable for teaching" [1 Tim. 3:16]. See, then, whether you and all the Sophists[45] can produce any single mystery that is still abstruse in the Scriptures.

It is true that for many people much remains abstruse; but this is not due to the obscurity of Scripture, but to the blindness or indolence of those who will not take the trouble to look at the very clearest truth. [. . .]

To put it briefly, there are two kinds of clarity in Scripture, just as there are also two kinds of obscurity: one external and pertaining to the ministry of the Word,[46] the other located in the understanding of the heart. If you speak of the internal clarity, no human being perceives one iota of what is in the Scriptures unless he has the Spirit of God. All human beings have a darkened heart,[47] so that even if they can recite everything in Scripture, and know how to quote it, yet they apprehend and truly understand nothing of it. They neither believe in God, nor that they themselves are creatures of God, nor anything else, as Ps. 13[14:1] says: "The fool has said in his heart, 'There is no god.'"[48] For the Spirit is required for the understanding of Scripture, both as a whole and in any part of it.[49] If, on the other hand, you speak of the external clarity, nothing at all is left obscure or ambiguous, but everything there is in the Scriptures has been brought out by the Word into the most definite light and published to all the world.

44. Erasmus compared human knowledge of God with the antic knowledge of this cave near Tarsus with many hallways.

45. See n. 16, p. 159.

46. Referring to the public preaching.

47. Luther here describes the situation of human beings after the fall, stressing their loss of all good powers.

48. This verse was very famous in medieval theological literature: Anselm of Canterbury (1033–1109) used it to show the possibility of human beings denying God's existence. Against this attitude, he wrote his *Proslogion*, demonstrating God's existence.

[It Is Vital to Know the Truth about Free Choice]

But what is still more intolerable is that you count this subject of free choice among the things that are useless and unnecessary, and replace it for us with a list of the things you consider sufficient for the Christian devotion. It is such a list as any Jew or Gentile totally ignorant of Christ could certainly draw up with ease, for you make not the slightest mention of Christ, as if you think that Christian godliness can exist without Christ

Bust of Greek philosopher Epicurus.

so long as God is worshiped with all one's powers[50] as being by nature most merciful. What am I to say here, Erasmus? You reek of nothing but Lucian,[51] and you breathe out on me the vast drunken folly of Epicurus.[52] If you consider this subject unnecessary for Christians, then please quit the field; you and I have nothing in common, for I consider it vital. [. . .]

[It] is not irreverent, inquisitive, or superfluous, but essentially salutary and necessary for a Christian, to find out whether the will does anything or nothing in matters pertaining to eternal salvation. Indeed, as you should know, this is the core issue between us, the point on which everything in this controversy

49. With this, Luther does not plead for a fully spiritual basis of Christian understanding. This would be *schwärmerisch* ("fanatic") to him. What he wants to show is the indispensable connection of Spirit and Scripture.

50. Here, Luther saw a contradiction to the teaching of justification: to him, human powers were destroyed by the fall, and since then human beings were not able to worship God perfectly nor to follow God fully.

51. Lucian of Samosata (c. 125–180), a Greek writing satirist of the second century, had become famous through the translation of his works into Latin by Erasmus and Thomas Morus (1478–1535) (publication of all works in 1517).

52. Epicurus (341–270 BCE) was a Greek philosopher who taught that pleasure is the highest good (hedonism). He did not envision pleasure in the sense of gross indulgence; rather, he valued the contentment that results from giving up desires, fears, and ambitions. But many Greek and Roman Epicureans failed to make this distinction.

53. Deriving from this passage, many interpreters hold that Luther's position in *De servo arbitrio* is far different from philosophical determinism, because he is only engaged in the means of free will concerning matters of salvation. Here his clear answer is: the free will has nothing to do with salvation.

54. It is characteristic for Luther to understand "omnipotence" in the sense of God being active and efficient in all things.

55. Interestingly enough, Luther here picks up the argument of Rom. 1:20 that was central for medieval Scholastic theology for the possibility to demonstrate God's existence. As early as in the *Heidelberg Disputation* in 1518, Luther had proven himself quite skeptical against arguments like this, blaming them as a special type of "theology of glory."

56. Five years earlier, Luther identified his tract *On the Freedom of a Christian* (1520) as the sum of the Christian life.

57. This sentence that speaks of "anything" and "everything" clearly indicates a philosophical determinism, a position that all things happen by (divine) necessity.

turns.[53] For what we are doing is to inquire what free choice can do, what it has done to it, and what is its relation to the grace of God. If we do not know these things, we shall know nothing at all of things Christian, and shall be worse than any heathen. Anyone who does not feel this should confess to be no Christian. Anyone who even disparages or scorns it should know that he or she is the greatest enemy of Christians. For if I am ignorant of what, how far, and how much I can and may do in relation to God, it will be equally uncertain and unknown to me, what, how far, and how much God can and may do in me, although it is God who works everything in everyone [1 Cor. 12:6].[54] But when the works and power of God are unknown, I do not know God in Godself,[55] and when God is unknown, I cannot worship, praise, thank, and serve God, since I do not know how much I ought to attribute to myself and how much to God. It therefore behooves us to be very certain about the distinction between God's power and our own, God's work and our own, if we want to live a godly life.

So you see that this problem is one-half of the whole sum[56] of Christian issues, since on it both knowledge of oneself and the knowledge and glory of God quite vitally depend. That is why we cannot permit you, my dear Erasmus, to call such knowledge irreverent, inquisitive, and vain. We owe much to you, but godliness claims our all. Why, you yourself are aware that all the good in us is to be ascribed to God, and you assert this in your description of Christianity. But in asserting this, you are surely asserting also that the mercy of God alone does everything, and that our will does nothing, but rather is passive; otherwise, all is not ascribed to God. Yet a little later you say that it is not religious, pious, and salutary to assert or to know this. But a mind compelled to talk like that is inconsistent with itself, uncertain and inexpert in matters of religion.

[God's Foreknowledge; Contingency and Necessity]*n*

The other half of the Christian *summa* is concerned with knowing whether God foreknows anything contingently, and whether we do everything of necessity.[57] And this, too, you find irrever-

n   WA 18:614–20.

ent, inquisitive, and vain, just as all ungodly people do, or rather, as the demons and the damned[o] find it hateful and detestable. You are well advised to steer clear of such questions if you can, but you are a pretty poor rhetorician and theologian when you presume to discuss and expound free choice without the two subjects just mentioned. I will act as a whetstone and, although no rhetorician myself, will teach a distinguished rhetorician his business.

Suppose Quintilian, proposing to write about oratory, were to say: "In my judgment, that stupid and superfluous stuff about choice of subject, arrangement of material, style, memorization, delivery, ought to be omitted; suffice it to know that oratory is the art of speaking well"[p]—would you not ridicule such an exponent of the art? Yet you act no differently yourself. You propose to write about free choice, and you begin by rejecting and throwing away the whole substance and all the elements of the subject on which you are going to write. For you cannot possibly know what free choice is unless you know what the human will can do, and what God does, and whether he foreknows necessarily.

Do not even your rhetoricians teach you that when you are going to speak on any subject, you ought to say first whether it exists, then what it is, what its parts are, what things are contrary to it, akin to it, similar to it, etc.? But you deprive free choice (poor thing!) of all these advantages, and lay down no question concerning it, unless perhaps the first, namely, whether it exists; and you do this with arguments (as we shall see) of such a kind that, apart from the elegance of the language, I have never seen a feebler book on free choice. The very Sophists provide at least a better discussion on this subject, for while they have no idea of style, yet when they tackle free choice they do define all the questions connected with it—whether it exists, what it is, what it does, how it is related, etc.—though even they do not succeed in doing what they set out to do. In this book, therefore, I shall press you and all the Sophists hard until you define for me the strength and effectiveness of free choice; and I shall press you

---

o   *Daemones et damnati* is not just a linguistic game, but also refers to the center of the question under debate: the damned are those who are not predestinated "positively," that is, to the salvation.

p   Quintilian, *Insitutiones oratoriae* 2,15,38.

58. This argument obviously excludes all freedom from creatures. While with the divine prescience, some human freedom could prevail, God's purpose and acting by the divine immutable will makes all things completely dependent on God.

59. This argument shows that Luther, even when he speaks in terms of a general philosophical determination, starts with the question of grace and justification.

60. The question of predestination for Later Scholasticism was mainly a question of the logical possibility of God's immutable foreknowledge in a world of contingencies.

61. Luther interprets "contingency" as virtually equivalent to "chance." Luther's debate with Erasmus on "free will" relates to the centuries of debate regarding the meaning of the words *causality* and *necessity*. Aristotle was the first to argue for indeterminism identifying the prime mover and a chain of different causes (material, efficient, formal, and final). The medieval

(with Christ's aid) so hard that I hope I shall make you repent of ever having published your *Diatribe*.

Here, then, is something fundamentally necessary and salutary for a Christian, to know that God foreknows nothing contingently, but that God foresees and purposes and does[58] all things by God's own immutable, eternal, and infallible will. Here is a thunderbolt by which free choice is completely prostrated and shattered, so that those who want free choice asserted must either deny or explain away this thunderbolt, or get rid of it by some other means. However, before I establish this point by my own argument and the authority of Scripture, I will first deal with it in your words.

Was it not you, my dear Erasmus, who asserted a little earlier that God is by nature just, by nature most merciful? If this is true, does it not follow that God is immutably just and merciful—that as God's nature never changes, so neither does God's justice or mercy? But what is said of God's justice and mercy must also be said of God's knowledge, wisdom, goodness, will, and other divine attributes.[59] If, then, the assertion of these things concerning God is, as you state, religious, pious, and salutary, what has come over you that you now contradict yourself by asserting that it is irreverent, inquisitive, and vain to say that God foreknows necessarily? You declare that the will of God is to be understood as immutable, yet you forbid us to know that God's foreknowledge is immutable. Do you, then, believe that God foreknows without willing or wills without knowing? If God foreknows as God wills, then God's will is eternal and unchanging (because God's nature is so), and if God wills as God foreknows, then divine knowledge is eternal and unchanging (because God's nature is so).[60]

From this it follows irrefutably that everything we do, everything that happens, even if it seems to us to happen mutably and contingently,[61] happens in fact nonetheless necessarily and immutably, if you have regard to the will of God. For the will of God is effectual and cannot be hindered, since it is the power of the divine nature itself; moreover it is wise, so that it cannot be deceived. Now, if God's will is not hindered, there is nothing to prevent the work itself from being done, in the place, time, manner, and measure that God both foresees and wills. If the will of God were such that, when the work was completed, the work remained but the will ceased—like the will of human beings, which ceases to will when the house they want is built, just as it also comes to an end in death—then it could be truly said that things happen contingently and mutably. But here the opposite happens; the work comes to an end and the will remains, so remote is it from possibility that the work itself, during its production and completed existence, should exist or persist contingently. To happen contingently, however—in order that we may not misuse terms—means in Latin, not that the work itself is contingent, but that it is done by a contingent and mutable will, such as there is not in God. Moreover, a work can only be called contingent when it happens contingently to us and in the way of chance without our expecting it, because our will or hand seizes on it as something presented to us by chance, when we have thought or willed nothing about it previously.

[I could wish indeed that another and a better word had been introduced into our discussion than this usual one, "necessity," which is not rightly applied either to the divine or the human will. It has too harsh and incongruous a meaning for this purpose, for it suggests a kind of compulsion, and the very opposite of willingness, although the subject under discussion implies no such thing. For neither the divine nor the human will does what it does, whether good or evil, under any compulsion, but from sheer pleasure or desire, as with true freedom;[62] and yet the will of God is immutable and infallible, and it governs our mutable will, as Boethius (c. 480-524)[63] sings: "Remaining fixed, You make all things move";[q] and our will, especially when it is evil, cannot of itself do good. The reader's intelligence must therefore supply what the word *necessity* does not express, by understanding it to mean what you might call the immutability of the will of God and the impotence of our evil will, or what some have called the necessity of immutability, though this is not very good either grammatically or theologically.][r]

The Sophists have labored for years over this point, but in the end they have been beaten and forced to admit that everything happens necessarily, though by the necessity of consequence (as

Scholastics used reason as a way to explain the compatibility of divine foreknowledge and human freedom. Later the "empiricist philosophers" with natural sciences, rejected the idea of chance or indeterminism, or an "uncaused cause," and looked for evidence of strict causality and determinism as necessary for responsible actions. The prevailing options for different positions in the matter are basically three: (1) Determinists (with varying degrees) hold that there is a strict causality at play in reality, and that there is only one possible future; (2) Compatibilists consider free will—itself caused—as compatible with determinism and human character being determined; (3) Libertarians deny the compatibility of free will with any determinism (incompatibilists).

62. This means, a will, agreeing to what is necessary, is not under compulsion but has some freedom, not in the sense of having a free choice between alternatives, but in the sense of being in compliance with God.

63. Boethius was a Roman philosopher and learned man who eventually served as an adviser to Ostrogoth king Theordoric (451/456-526). His enemies accused him of being disloyal to Theodoric and plotting to restore "Roman liberty." Theodoric imprisioned him and eventually had him executed. In some places he is honored as a Christian martyr, but it is not clear whether he was a Christian.

---

q   In Boethius, *De consolatione philosophiae* 3, 9.

r   This passage in brackets is an addition to Luther's text in the first edition of Luther's complete works.

64. This distinction means that some things have to follow necessarily others (the necessity of consequence), even if they are contingent in themselves (lacking the necessity of the consequent).

65. What Luther summarizes here ironically means the distinction of the necessity of the consequence and of the consequent gave the Scholastics the possibility to state the full necessity of all actions, caused by God's immutable will, without making creatures necessary in themselves.

they say) and not by the necessity of the consequent.[64] They have thus eluded the full force of this question, or indeed it might rather be said they have deluded themselves. For how meaningless this is I shall have no difficulty in showing. What they call the necessity of consequence means broadly this: If God wills anything, it is necessary for that thing to come to pass, but it is not necessary that the thing which comes to pass should exist; for God alone exists necessarily, and it is possible for everything else not to exist if God so wills. So they say that an action of God is necessary if God wills it, but that the thing done is not itself necessary. But what do they achieve by this playing with words? This, of course, that the thing done is not necessary, in the sense that it has not a necessary existence. But this is no different from saying that the thing done is not of God. Nevertheless, it remains a fact that everything that comes into being does so necessarily, if the action of God is necessary, or if there is a necessity of consequence, however true it is that, when it has been brought into being, it does not exist necessarily, that is to say, it is not God and has not a necessary existence. For if I myself am brought into existence necessarily, it is of little concern to me that my being or becoming is mutable; for my contingent and mutable self, though not the necessary being that God is, is nonetheless brought into existence.

Hence their amusing idea, that everything happens by necessity of consequence but not by necessity of the consequent, amounts to no more than this: all things are indeed brought about necessarily, but when they have thus been brought about, they are not of God.[65] But what need was there to tell us this? As if there were any fear of our asserting that created things are God, or that they have a divine and necessary nature! Hence the proposition stands, and remains invincible, that all things happen by necessity. Nor is there here any obscurity or ambiguity. It says in Isaiah: "My counsel shall stand and my will shall be done" [Isa. 46:10]. What pupil does not know the meaning of these terms "counsel," "will," "shall be done," "shall stand"? [. . .]

[Should Divine Truth Be Kept from Common Ears?]

In the third chapter, you proceed to turn us into modest and peace-loving Epicureans, with a different sort of advice, though no sounder than the two already mentioned. That is to say, you tell us that some things are of such a kind that even if they were true and might be known, it would not be proper to divulge them before common ears.

Here again you confuse and mix everything up in your usual way, putting the sacred on a level with the profane and making no distinction between them at all, so that once again you have fallen into contempt and abuse of Scripture and of God. I said above that things that are either contained in or proved by the Holy Scriptures are not only plain, but also salutary, and can therefore safely be published, learned, and known, as indeed they ought to be. Hence your saying that they ought not to be divulged before common ears is false if you are speaking of the things that are in Scripture; and if you are speaking of other things, what you say does not interest us and is out of place, so that you are wasting your time and paper on it. Besides, you know that there is no subject on which I agree with the Sophists, so that you might well have spared me and not cast their misdoings in my teeth. For it was against me that you were to speak in that book of yours. I know where the Sophists go wrong without needing you to tell me, and they have had plenty of criticism from me. I should like this said once for all, and repeated every time you mix me up with the Sophists and make my case look as crazy as theirs, for you are being quite unfair, as you very well know.

Now, let us see the reasons for your advice. Even if it were true that "God, according to his own nature, is no less present in the hole of a beetle" or even in a sewer than in heaven (though you are too reverent to say this yourself, and blame the Sophists for blathering so), yet you think it would be unreasonable to discuss such a subject before the common herd.

First, let them blather who will; we are not here discussing what people do, but what is right and lawful, not how we live, but how we ought to live. Which of us always lives and acts rightly? But law and precept are not condemned on that account, but they rather condemn us.[66] Yet you go looking for irrelevancies like these, and rake a pile of them together from all sides, because this one point about the foreknowledge of God upsets you; and since you have no real argument with which to overcome it, you spend the time trying to tire out your reader with a lot of empty talk. But we will let that pass, and get back to the

66. This short remark relates to Luther's doctrine of the theological use of law that reveals sins.

subject. What, then, is the point of your contention that certain matters ought not to be discussed publicly? Do you count the subject of free choice among them? In that case, all I said above about the necessity of understanding free choice will round on you again. Moreover, why did you not follow your own advice and leave your *Diatribe* unwritten? If it is right for you to discuss free choice, why do you denounce such discussion? If it is wrong, why do you do it? On the other hand, if you do not count free choice among the prohibited subjects, you are again evading the real issue, dealing like a wordy rhetorician with topics that are irrelevant and out of place.

Even so, you are wrong in the use you make of this example, and in condemning as unprofitable the public discussion of the proposition that God is in the hole or the sewer. Your thoughts about God are all too human. There are, I admit, some shallow preachers who, from no motives of devotion or piety, but perhaps from a desire for popularity or a thirst for some novelty or a distaste for silence, prate and trifle in the shallowest way. But these please neither God nor people, even if they assert that God is in the heaven of heavens. But where there are serious and godly preachers who teach in modest, pure, and sound words, they speak on such a subject in public without risk, and indeed with great profit. Ought we not all to teach that the Son of God was in the womb of the Virgin and came forth from her belly? But how does a human belly differ from any other unclean place? Anyone could describe it in foul and shameless terms, but we rightly condemn those who do, seeing that there are plenty of pure words with which to speak of that necessary theme even with decency and grace. Again, the body of Christ himself was human as ours is, and what is fouler than that? Are we therefore not to say that God dwelt in it bodily, as Paul has said [Col. 2:9]?[67] What is fouler than death? What more horrifying than hell? Yet the prophet glories that God is present with him in death and hell [Ps. 139:8].

Therefore, a godly mind is not shocked to hear that God is present in death or hell, both of which are more horrible and foul than either a hole or a sewer. Indeed, since Scripture testifies that God is everywhere and fills all things [Jer. 23:24], a godly mind not only says that God is in those places, but must necessarily learn and know that God is there. Or are we to suppose that if I am captured by a tyrant and thrown into a prison or a

67. Luther is fighting here for a correct understanding of Christ's humanity; later on, in his struggle with Ulrich Zwingli (1484–1531), he had more opportunities to develop further his christological convictions, stressing the indivisible connection of both human and godly natures of Christ.

sewer—as has happened to many saints—I am not to be allowed to call upon God there or to believe that God is present with me, but must wait until I come into some finely furnished church?

If you teach us to talk such nonsense about God, and are so set against the locating of God's essence, you will end by not even allowing God to remain for us in heaven; for the heaven of heavens cannot contain God, nor is it worthy of God [1 Kings 8:27]. But as I have said, it is your habit to stab at us in this hateful way in order to disparage our case and make it odious, because you see that for you it is insuperable and invincible.

As for your second example, I admit that the idea that there are three Gods is a scandal if it is taught; but it is neither true, nor does Scripture teach it. The Sophists speak in this way with their newfound dialectic,[68] but what has that to do with us?[69] [...]

You, of course, always hold, or profess to hold, that human statutes can be observed without peril along with the Word of God. If they could, I should not hesitate to join you in the view you express here. So if you do not know it, I tell you again: human statutes cannot be observed together with the Word of God, because they bind consciences, while the Word sets them free. The two are as mutually incompatible as water and fire, unless the human statutes are kept freely, that is, as not being binding—a thing that the pope will not and cannot allow, unless he wants his kingdom ruined and brought to an end, since it is only maintained by the ensnaring and binding of consciences which the gospel asserts to be free. Therefore the authority of the Early Christian Teachers[s] is neither here nor there, and statutes wrongly enacted (as are all which are not in accordance with the Word of God) ought to be torn up and thrown away, for Christ ranks higher than the authority of these Teachers. In short, if this view of yours has reference to the Word of God, it is impious; if it refers to other things, your wordy argument in support of it is nothing to us, for we are arguing about the Word of God.

68. Dialectic was part of the seven liberal arts in medieval curriculum. It was mainly fulfilled by teaching of logic.

69. Roscelin of Compiègne (c. 1050-1125) in the eleventh century was accused of teaching about three godheads, but this seems to be a misunderstanding of his position.

s   Originally "Fathers."

[Should the Truth
of God's Necessitating Will Be Suppressed?]

In the last part of your Preface where you seriously try to dissuade me from my kind of doctrine, you think you have as good as won your point. What, you say, could be more useless than to publish this paradox to the world, that whatever is done by us is not done by free choice, but by sheer necessity? And Augustine's saying, that God works in us good and evil, and rewards God's own good works in us and punishes God's evil works in us[t]—what is the use of that? You are profuse in giving, or rather demanding, a reason here. What a window to impiety, you say, would the public avowal of this opinion open to finite human beings! What evildoer would correct his life? Who would believe he was loved by God? Who would war against one's own flesh? I am surprised that in your great vehemence and contentiousness you did not remember the point at issue and say: Where would free choice then remain?

My dear Erasmus, let me too say in turn: If you think these paradoxes are inventions of people, what are you contending about? Why are you so roused? Against whom are you speaking? Is there anyone in the world today who has more vigorously attacked the human dogmas than Luther? Therefore, your admonition has nothing to do with me. But if you think these paradoxes are words of God, how can you keep your countenance, where is your shame, where is—I will not say that well-known moderation of Erasmus, but the fear and reverence that are due to the true God, when you say that nothing more useless could be proclaimed than the Word of God? Naturally, your Creator must learn from you his creature what it is useful or useless to preach! That foolish, that thoughtless God did not previously know what ought to be taught until you, God's master, prescribed for God how to be wise and how to give commandments! As though God would not have known, if you had not been the teacher, that the consequences you mention would follow from this paradox! If, therefore, God has willed that such things should be openly spoken of and published abroad without regard to the consequences, who are you to forbid it?

---

t   Augustine, *De gratia Christi et de peccato originali* I, 17:18.

The apostle Paul, in his epistle to the Romans, discusses these same things, not in a corner, but publicly and before all the world, in the freest manner and in even harsher terms, when he says: "Whom he will he hardened," and, "God, willing to show God's wrath," etc. [Rom. 9:18, 22]. What could be harsher (to the unregenerate nature at least) than Christ's saying: "Many are called, but few chosen" [Matt. 22:14], or: "I know whom I have chosen" [John 13:18]? We have it, of course, on your authority that nothing more profitless could be said than things like these, because ungodly people are led by them to fall into desperation, hatred, and blasphemy.

Here, I see, you are of the opinion that the truth and usefulness of Scripture is to be measured and judged by the reactions of people, and the most ungodly people at that, so that only what has proved pleasing or seemed tolerable to them should be deemed true, divine, and salutary, while the opposite should forthwith be deemed useless, false, and pernicious. What are you aiming at with this advice, unless that the words of God should depend on, and stand or fall with, the choice and authority of human beings? Whereas Scripture says on the contrary that all things stand or fall by the choice and authority of God, and all the earth should keep silence before the Lord [Hab. 2:20]. To talk as you do, one must imagine the Living God to be nothing but a kind of shallow and ignorant ranter declaiming from some platform, whose words you can if you wish interpret in any direction you like, and accept or reject them accordingly as ungodly people are seen to be moved or affected by them. [. . .]

What then, you may ask, is the utility or necessity of publishing such things when so many evils appear to proceed from them? I answer: It would be enough to say that God has willed them to be published, and we must not ask the reason for the divine will, but simply adore it, giving God glory that, since God alone is just and wise, God does no wrong to anyone and can do nothing foolishly or rashly, though it may seem far otherwise to us. With this answer the godly are content. Still, out of our abundance we will do a work of supererogation and mention two considerations which demand that such things should be preached. The first is the humbling of our pride, and the knowledge of the grace of God; and the second is the nature of Christian faith itself.

70. This passage shows that it is not as easy to discern a theology of humility of Luther's younger years from his mature theology of justification, as some scholars (mainly Ernst Bizer) have suggested. See Ernst Bizer, *Fides ex auditu: eine Untersuchung über die Entdeckung der Gerechtigkeit Gottes durch Martin Luther* (Neukirchen: Verlag der Buchhandlung des Erziehungsvereins, 1958).

71. The concept of "desperation" in Luther's teaching is quite ambiguous: mostly he claims desperation to be the wrong way, while he stresses that human beings should respect their own inability (or disability) to "do the right" for salvation, without falling into desperation but instead finding the real ground for salvation in Jesus Christ.

First, God has assuredly promised grace to the humble [1 Peter 5:5], that is, to those who lament and despair of themselves.[70] But no human being can be thoroughly humbled until knowing that one's salvation is utterly beyond one's own powers, devices, endeavors, will, and works, and depends entirely on the choice, will, and work of another, namely, of God alone. For as long as one is persuaded that one can do even the least thing toward one's own salvation, the human being retains some self-confidence and does not altogether despair of oneself, and therefore is not humbled before God, but presumes that there is—or at least hopes or desires that there may be—some place, time, and work by which one may at length attain to salvation. But when one has no doubt that everything depends on the will of God, then one completely despairs[71] of oneself and chooses nothing for oneself, but waits for God to work; then this human being has come close to grace and can be saved.

It is thus for the sake of the elect that these things are published, in order that being humbled and brought back to nothingness by this means they may be saved. The rest resist this humiliation, indeed they condemn this teaching of self-despair, wishing for something, however little, to be left for them to do themselves; so they remain secretly proud and enemies of the grace of God. This, I say, is one reason, namely, that the godly, being humbled, may recognize, call upon, and receive the grace of God.

The second reason is that faith has to do with things not seen [Heb. 11:1]. Hence, in order that there may be room for faith, it is necessary that everything which is believed should be hidden. It cannot, however, be more deeply hidden than under an object, perception, or experience which is contrary to it. Thus, when God makes alive, God does it by killing; when God justifies, God does it by making human beings guilty; when God exalts to heaven by bringing down to hell, as Scripture says: "The LORD kills and brings to life; he brings down to Sheol and raises up" (1 Sam. 2[:6]). This is not the place to speak at length on this subject, but those who have read my books have had it quite plainly set forth for them.

Thus God hides divine eternal goodness and mercy under eternal wrath, God's righteousness under iniquity. This is the highest degree of faith, to believe God is merciful when saving so few and damning so many, and to believe God to be righteous when making us necessarily damnable, so that God seems, according to Erasmus, to delight in the torments of the wretched and to be worthy of hatred rather than of love. If, then, I could by any means comprehend how this God can be merciful and just who displays so much wrath and iniquity, there would be no need of faith. As it is, since that cannot be comprehended, there is room for the exercise of faith when such things are preached and published, just as when God kills, the faith of life is exercised in death. That is now enough by way of preface.

This way of dealing with people who argue about these paradoxes is better than yours. You advise silence and refusal to be drawn, with the idea of humoring their impiety; but you really achieve nothing by this. For if you either believe or suspect them to be true (since they are paradoxes of no small moment), such is the insatiable desire of mortals to probe into secret matters, especially when we most want them kept secret, that as a result of your publishing this warning everybody will now want to know all the more whether these paradoxes are true. They will have been aroused by your contention to such a degree that no one on our side will ever have provided such an opportunity for publicizing these paradoxes as you have done by this solemn and vehement warning. You would have been much wiser to say nothing at all about the need to beware of them if you wanted to see your desire fulfilled. The game is up when you do not directly deny that they are true; they cannot be kept dark, but the suspicion of their truth will prompt everybody to investigate them. Either, then, you must deny that they are true or set the example of silence if you want others to keep silence too.

[Divine Necessity and the Human Will]

As for the second paradox, that whatever is done by us is done not by free choice but of sheer necessity, let us look briefly at this and not permit it to be labeled most pernicious. What I say here is this: When it has been proved that salvation is beyond our own powers and devices, and depends on the work of God alone (as I hope to prove conclusively below in the main body of this disputation), does it not follow that when God is not present in us by God's own means of work,[72] everything we do is evil, and we necessarily do what is of no avail for salvation? For if it is not we, but only God, who works salvation in us, then before God

72. Here Luther still shows his early mystical conviction of God being present in the believer.

works we can do nothing of saving significance, whether we wish to or not.

Now, by "necessarily" I do not mean "compulsorily," but by the necessity of immutability (as they say) and not of compulsion. That is to say, when human beings are without the Spirit of God, they do not do evil against their own will, as if they were taken by the scruff of the neck and forced to it, like a thief or robber carried off against their own will to punishment, but they do it of their own accord and with a ready will. And this readiness or will to act they cannot by their own powers omit, restrain, or change, but they keep on willing and being ready; and even if the human beings are compelled by external force to do something different, yet the will within them remains averse and they resent whatever compels or resists it. These human beings would not be resentful, however, if it were changed and they willingly submitted to the compulsion. This is what we call the necessity of immutability: It means that the will cannot change itself and turn in a different direction, but is rather the more provoked into willing by being resisted, as its resentment shows. This would not happen if it were free or had free choice. Ask experience how impossible it is to persuade people who have set their heart on anything. If they yield, they yield to force or to the greater attraction of something else; they never yield freely. On the other hand, if they are not set on anything, they simply let things take their course.

By contrast, if God works in us, the will is changed, and being gently breathed upon by the Spirit of God, it again wills and acts from pure willingness and inclination and of its own accord, not from compulsion, so that it cannot be turned another way by any opposition, nor be overcome or compelled even by the gates of hell, but it goes on willing and delighting in and loving the good, just as before it willed and delighted in and loved evil. This again is proved by experience, which shows how invincible and steadfast holy people are, who when force is used to compel them to other things are thereby all the more spurred on to will the good, just as fire is fanned into flames rather than extinguished by the wind. So not even here is there any free choice, or freedom to turn oneself in another direction or will something different, so long as the Spirit and grace of God remain in a human being.

In short, if we are under the god of this world, away from the work and Spirit of the true God, we are held captive to God's will, as Paul says to Timothy [2 Tim. 2:26], so that we cannot will anything but what God wills. For God is that strong man armed, who guards his own palace in such a way that those whom he possesses are in peace [Luke 11:21], so as to prevent them from stirring up any thought or feeling against him; otherwise, the kingdom of Satan being divided against itself would not stand [Luke 11:18], whereas Christ affirms that it does stand. And this we do readily and willingly, according to the nature of the will, which would not be a will if it were compelled; for compulsion is rather (so to say) "unwill." But if a Stronger One comes who overcomes him and takes us as One's spoil, then through this Spirit we are again slaves and captives—though this is royal freedom—so that we readily will and do what he wills. Thus the human will is placed between the two like a beast of burden. If God rides it, it wills and goes where God wills, as the psalm says: "I am become as a beast [before you] and I am always with you" [Ps. 73:22f.]. If Satan rides it, it wills and goes where Satan wills; nor can it choose to run to either of the two riders or to seek him out, but the riders themselves contend for the possession and control of it.[73]

What if I can prove from the words you yourself use in asserting freedom of choice that there is no free choice? What if I convict you of unwittingly denying what you seek so carefully to affirm? Frankly, unless I do so, I swear to regard everything I write against you in the entire book as revoked, and everything your *Diatribe* either asserts or queries against me as confirmed.

You make the power of free choice very slight and of a kind that is entirely ineffective apart from the grace of God. Do you not agree? Now I ask you, if the grace of God is absent or separated from it, what can that very slight power do of itself? It is ineffective, you say, and does nothing good. Then it cannot do what God or God's grace wills, at any rate if we suppose the grace of God to be separated from it. But what the grace of God does not do is not good. Hence it follows that free choice without the grace of God is not free at all, but immutably the captive and slave of evil, since it cannot of itself turn to the good. If this is granted, I give you leave to make the power of free choice, instead of something very slight, something angelic, indeed if possible something

73. "The simile of the beast and its riders was not Luther's own invention. He appears to have derived it from the pseudo-Augustinian *Hypomenesticon III.* xi.20, where it is connected, as Luther connects it, with Ps. 73.22f. . . . Yet Luther does not use it quite in the traditional way, for he equates the beast simply with the will (instead of free will) and makes the riders God and Satan (instead of sin and grace), and gives the beast no option as to which rider it shall have" (LW 33:66 n. 71).

quite divine; yet if you add this mournful rider, that apart from the grace of God it is ineffective, you at once rob it of all its power. What is ineffective power but simply no power at all?

Therefore, to say that free choice exists and has indeed some power, but that it is an ineffective power, is what the Sophists call *oppositum in adiecto* ["a contradiction in terms"]. It is as if you said that there is a free choice which is not free, which is as sensible as calling fire cold and earth hot. For fire may have the power of heat, even infernal heat, but if it does not burn or scorch, but is cold and freezes, let no one tell me it is a fire at all, much less a hot one, unless you mean a painted or imaginary fire. But if the power of free choice were said to mean that by which a human is capable of being taken hold of by the Spirit and imbued with the grace of God, as a being created for eternal life or death, no objection could be taken. For this power or aptitude, or as the Sophists say, this disposing quality or passive aptitude, we also admit; and who does not know that it is not found in trees or animals? For heaven, as the saying is, was not made for geese.[74]

It is settled, then, even on your own testimony, that we do everything by necessity, and nothing by free choice, since the power of free choice is nothing and neither does nor can do good in the absence of grace—unless you wish to give "efficacy" a new meaning and understand it as "perfection," as if free choice might very well make a start and will something, though it could not carry it through. But that I do not believe, and will say more about it later. It follows now that free choice is plainly a divine term, and can be properly applied to none but the Divine Majesty alone; for God alone can do and does (as the psalmist says [Ps. 115:3]) whatever pleases the divine will in heaven and on earth.[75] If this is attributed to human beings, it is no more rightly attributed than if divinity itself also were attributed to them, which would be the greatest possible sacrilege. Theologians therefore ought to have avoided this term when they wished to speak of human ability, leaving it to be applied to God alone. They should, moreover, have removed it from the lips and language of people, treating it as a kind of sacred and venerable name for their God. And if they attributed any power at all to men, they should teach that it must be called by another name than free choice, especially as we know and clearly perceive that the common people are miserably deceived and led astray by

74. Luther addresses Erasmus's definition of free choice in part 3 of this treatise and sums up the definition by quoting Erasmus: "By free choice in this place we mean a power of the human will by which a [person] can apply oneself to the things which lead to eternal salvation, or turn away from them" (see p. 198).

75. Luther here connects the question of the human will with the traditional definition of God's omnipotence, as stressed mainly in the late medieval *Via moderna*. The distinction of God's absolute and ordained power was one of the main topics to reflect on God's possibilities: while God's ordained power was bound to God's good will, God would not do all that God could do by means of the divine absolute power.

that term, since they hear and understand it in a very different sense from that which the theologians mean and discuss.

For the expression "free choice" is too imposing, too wide and full, and the people think it signifies—as the force and nature of the term requires—a power that can turn itself freely in either direction, without being under anyone's influence or control. If they knew that it was not so, but that hardly the tiniest spark of power was meant by this term, and a spark completely ineffectual by itself as a captive and slave of the devil, it would be surprising if they did not stone us as mockers and deceivers who say one thing and mean something quite different, or rather who have not yet decided or agreed on what we do mean. For one who speaks sophistically is hateful, as the Wise Person says [Prov. 6:17], particularly if one does this in matters of piety, where eternal salvation is at stake.

Since, then, we have lost the meaning and content of such a vainglorious term, or rather have never possessed it (as the Pelagians[76] wanted us to, who like you were led astray by the term), why do we so stubbornly hold on to an empty term, deceptive and dangerous as it is for the rank and file of believers? It is as sensible as when kings and princes hold on to or claim for themselves and boast about empty titles of kingdoms and countries, when in fact they are practically paupers and anything but the possessors of those kingdoms and countries. That, however, can be tolerated, since they deceive or mislead no one by it, but simply feed themselves on vanity, quite fruitlessly. But in the present case, there is a danger to salvation and a thoroughly injurious illusion.

Who would not think it ridiculous, or rather very objectionable, if some untimely innovator in the use of words attempted to introduce, against all common usage, such a manner of speaking as to call a beggar rich, not because he possessed any riches, but because some king might perhaps give him his, especially if this were done in seeming seriousness and not in a figure of speech, such as antiphrasis or irony. In this way, one who was mortally ill could be said to be perfectly well because some other might give him his own health, and a thoroughly illiterate fellow could be called very learned because someone else might perhaps give him learning. That is just how it sounds here: Human beings have free choice—if, of course, God would hand over them God's own will! By this misuse of language, anyone might boast

76. Pelagius (354–420) was the main counterpart of Augustine who was blamed to stress human beings' liberty concerning salvation. For Luther, medieval theology was, for the most part, "Pelagian" in this sense.

Portrait of reformer
John Wycliffe
(1324–1384)

of anything, as for instance, that human beings are the lords of heaven and earth—if God would grant it to them. But that is not the way for theologians to talk, but for stage players and public informers. Our words ought to be precise, pure, and sober, and as Paul says, sound and beyond censure [Titus 2:8].

But if we are unwilling to let this term go altogether—though that would be the safest and most God-fearing thing to do—let us at least teach human beings to use it honestly, so that free choice is allowed to them only with respect to what is beneath them and not what is above them. That is to say, human beings should know that with regard to their faculties and possessions they have the right to use, to do, or to leave undone, according to their own free choice, though even this is controlled by the free choice of God alone, who acts in whatever way God pleases. On the other hand, in relation to God, or in matters pertaining to salvation or damnation, a human being has no free choice, but is a captive, subject and slave either of the will of God or the will of Satan. [. . .]

[Part II.
Comments on Erasmus's Introduction]

[The Evidence of Tradition
on Behalf of Free Choice]

In introducing the Disputation, then, you promise to abide by the canonical Scriptures, since Luther holds himself bound by the authority of no other writer.[77] Very well, I accept your promise, although you do not give it because you regard those other writers as useless for your purpose, but in order to spare yourself fruitless labor. For you do not really approve of my audacity, or whatever else this principle of mine should be called. You are not a little impressed by such a numerous body of most learned men, who have found approval in so many centuries, among whom were some most skilled in divine studies, some of most godly life, some of them martyrs, many renowned for miracles, besides more recent theologians and so many universities, councils, bishops, and popes. In short, on that side stand erudition, genius, multitude, magnitude, altitude, fortitude, sanctity, miracles—

77. This means, at least for the purpose of the argument, that Erasmus accepted the *Sola scriptura* principle as the basis of the dispute, even if he did not adopt it in his theology.

A seventeenth-century
copper engraving
of Lorenzo Valla
(c. 1407–1457).

78. In fact, John Wycliffe (1324–1384) in his earlier writings had fully denied human free will due to predestination, while later on he admitted a limited freedom to human beings (*Responsiones ad Strodum*). Erasmus, in his *De libero arbitrio*, referred to the earlier, strong position of the English reformer, who was declared heretical by the Council of Constance, 1415.

79. Lorenzo (Laurentius) Valla (c. 1407–1457) was a humanist thinker, famous mainly for his proof that the emperor Constantine (c. 272–337) never gave his big "donation" of countries and power to the popes, as it was held for centuries. For Luther and Erasmus, he was interesting because of his treatise *De libero arbitrio*. Herein Valla denies the free will of human beings in an argument deriving from the notion of godly foreknowledge and tries to harmonize this position with the concept of a benevolent God. For Luther, it was important to have a humanist witness, such as Valla's, for the bound will. Erasmus counted Valla among the defenders of a bound will but added that he was not well reputed among theologians. Besides, he mentioned the Manicheans as opponents of the free will. This group, founded by Mani (242–277), held a completely dualistic view of the world and for this reason was attacked by Augustine and many others.

80. Erasmus meant to agree with Augustine of Hippo.

everything one could wish. On my side, however, there is only Wycliffe[78] and one other, Lorenzo Valla (c. 1407–1457)[79] (though Augustine, whom you overlook, is entirely with me[80]), and these carry no weight in comparison with those; so there remains only Luther, a private individual and a mere upstart, with his friends, among whom there is no such erudition or genius, no multitude or magnitude, no sanctity, no miracles—for they could not even cure a lame horse. They make a parade of Scripture, yet they are as uncertain about it as the other side, and though they boast of the Spirit, they give no sign of possessing it; and there are other things "which at great length you could recount." So it is the same with us as the wolf said to the nightingale he had devoured, "You are a voice and nothing more." They talk, you say, and for this alone they want to be believed.

I confess, my dear Erasmus, that you have good reason to be moved by all these things. I myself was so impressed by them for

81. In his lecture on the *Sentences*, Luther, indeed, maintained the liberty of human will. He seems to think of his *Heidelberg Disputation* (1518) as the public expression of his critical position against it. Historically, one can describe a long development of this position with important steps taken in his lectures on the Romans (1515–1516).

82. The following is an example of Luther's approach to the theologians of the early church. Luther respected them seriously, but he was also convinced that their words had to be measured by the Holy Scripture.

more than ten years[81] that I think no one else has ever been so disturbed by them. I, too, found it incredible that this Troy of ours, which for so long a time and through so many wars had proved invincible, could ever be taken. And I call God to witness on my soul, I should have continued so, I should be just as moved today, but for the pressure of my conscience and the evidence of facts that compel me to a different view. You can well imagine that my heart is not of stone; and even if it were, it could well have melted in the great waves and storms with which it had to struggle and the buffeting it received when I dared to do what I saw would bring down all the authority of those whom you have listed like a flood upon my head.

But this is not the place to tell the story of my life or works, nor have we undertaken these things in order to commend ourselves, but in order to extol the grace of God. The sort of person I am, and the spirit and purpose with which I have been drawn into this affair, I leave to God, who knows that all these things have been effected by his free choice, not mine—though the whole world itself ought to have been long ago aware of this. You clearly put me into a very unpleasant position by this Introduction of yours, since I cannot easily get out of it without singing my own praises and censuring so many of the Teachers of the Early Church.[82] But I will be brief. In erudition, genius, the number of authorities supporting me, and everything else I am, as you rightly judge, inferior. But suppose I ask you what *is* a manifestation of the Spirit, what miracles are, what sanctity is; to these three questions, so far as I know you from your letters and books, you would seem to be too inexperienced and ignorant to give one syllable of an answer. Or if I should press you to say which human being, of all those you boast about, you can certainly show to have been or to be a saint, or to have had the Spirit, or to have performed real miracles, I think you would have to work very hard at it, and all to no purpose. You repeat many things that are commonly said and publicly preached, and you do not realize how much credibility and authority they lose when summoned to the bar of conscience. It is a true proverb that many pass for saints on earth whose souls are in hell.

But we will grant you, if you wish, that they all were saints, all had the Spirit, all performed miracles—though you do not ask for this. Tell me this: Was it in the name or by the power of free choice, or to confirm the dogma of free choice, that any of them became a saint, received the Spirit, and performed miracles? Far from it, you will say; it was in the name and by the power of Jesus Christ, and in support of the doctrine of Christ, that all these things were done. Why, then, do you adduce their sanctity, their possession of the Spirit, and their miracles in support of the dogma of free choice when these were not given or done for that purpose? Their miracles, their possession of the Spirit, and their sanctity, therefore, speak for us who preach Jesus Christ and not the powers or works of people. Now, how is it surprising if those individuals, holy, spiritual, and workers of miracles as they were, sometimes under the influence of the flesh spoke and acted according to the flesh, when this happened more than once even to the apostles in the time of Christ himself? For you yourself do not deny, but assert, that free choice is not a matter of the Spirit or of Christ, but a human affair, so that the Spirit, who was promised in order to glorify Christ [John 16:14] could in any case not preach free choice. If, therefore, the Teachers of the Early Church*u* have sometimes preached free choice, they have certainly spoken from carnal motives (since they were but human beings) and not by the Spirit of God, and much less have they performed miracles in support of free choice. So what you say about the sanctity, Spirit, and miracles of the Fathers is beside the point, since what is proved by them is not free choice but the dogma of Jesus Christ as opposed to the dogma of free choice. [. . .]

And what I have said about miracles, I say also about sanctity. If from such a series of ages, people, and everything else you have mentioned, you can show one work (if only the lifting of a straw from the ground), or one word (if only the syllable "my"), or one thought (if only the faintest sigh), arising from the power of free choice, by which they have applied themselves to grace or merited the Spirit or obtained pardon or done anything alongside God, however slight (I do not say by which they have been sanctified), then again you shall be the victors and we the vanquished—by the power, I say, and in the name of free choice. (For the things that are done in human beings by the power of divine creation have testimonies of Scripture in abundance.) And you certainly ought to give such a demonstration, unless you want

---

u   See n. 82, p. 186.

83. "The Stoics, from Zeno the founder of the school (at Athens, c. 308 BCE) to Seneca, Epictetus, and Marcus Aurelius, portrayed as ideal a [hu]man for whom virtue was the highest good, who was in strict control of one's passions, indifferent to pleasure or pain, and unmoved by such things as family affection, or any kind of calamity or misfortune" (LW 33:76 n. 8).

to look ridiculous as teachers by spreading dogmas through the world with such a superior air and such authority about a thing for which you produce no tangible evidence. Otherwise, they will be called dreams and of no consequence whatever, which is by far the most shameful thing that could happen to such great people of so many centuries with all their learning and sanctity and their power to work miracles. In that case we shall prefer the Stoics[83] to you, for although even they pictured such a wise individual as they never saw, yet they did endeavor to express some aspect of him in their lives. You people are not able to express anything at all, not even the shadow of your dogma.

I say the same with regard to the Spirit. If out of all the assertors of free choice you can show a single one who has had the strength of mind or feeling even in such small degree as to be able in the name and by the power of free choice to look beyond a single farthing, to forgo a single crumb, or to bear a single word or gesture of ill will (to say nothing of despising wealth, life, and reputation), then take the palm again, and we will willingly admit defeat. And this you really ought to demonstrate to us, after all your bragging words about the power of free choice, or again you will seem to be wrangling about goat's wool, like the man who watched the play in an empty theater. But I can easily show you, on the contrary, that holy people such as you boast about, whenever they come to pray or plead with God, approach God in utter forgetfulness of their own free choice, despairing of themselves and imploring nothing but pure grace alone, though they have merited something very different. This was often the case with Augustine, and it was so with Bernard when, at the point of death, he said, "I have lost my time, because I have lived like a lost soul."[v] I do not see that any power is claimed here which could apply itself to grace, but every power is accused of having done nothing but turn away from grace. It is true that these same saints sometimes in their disputations spoke differently about free choice, but that is just what I see happening to everybody; they are different when they are intent on words or arguments from what they are when they are concerned with feelings and actions. In the former case, they speak differently from what they previously felt, and in the latter, they feel differ-

---

v   Bernard of Clairvaux (1090–1153), *Sermo in Canticum Canticorum* 20,1. This sentence was quoted very often by Luther.

ently from what they previously said. But human beings are to be measured by their affections rather than their talk, whether they are godly or ungodly.

But we grant you still more. We do not demand miracles, the Spirit, sanctity; we return to the dogma itself. All we ask is that you should at least indicate to us what work or word or thought this power of free choice stirs up, attempts, or performs, in order to apply itself to grace. It is not enough to say, "There is a power, there is a power, there is a definite power of free choice," for what is easier to say than this? Nor is this worthy of those most learned and holy people who have found approval in so many centuries. The child must be named, as the German proverb says. We must have a definition of what that power is, what it does, what it suffers, what happens to it. For example, to put it very crudely, the question is whether this power has a duty, or makes an attempt, to pray, or fast, or labor, or discipline the body, or give alms, or anything else of this kind; for if it is a power, it must do some sort of work. But here you are dumber than Seriphian frogs and fishes.[84] And how could you give a definition, when on your own testimony you are still uncertain about the power itself, disagreeing with each other and inconsistent with yourselves? What is to be done about a definition when the thing defined does not itself remain constant? [. . .]

[The True Church, Which Does Not Err, Is Hidden from Human Sight]

This is my answer to your statement that it is incredible that God should have concealed an error in his Church for so many centuries, and should not have revealed to any of his saints what we claim to be the chief doctrine of the gospel. First, we do not say that this error has been tolerated by God in God's Church or in any of God's saints. For the Church is ruled by the Spirit of God and the saints are led by the Spirit of God (Rom. 8[:14]). And Christ remains with his Church even to the end of the world [Matt. 28:20]; and the Church of God is the pillar and ground of the truth [1 Tim. 3:15]. These things, I say, we know; for the creed that we all hold affirms, "I believe in the holy catholic church"; so that it is impossible for the Church to err, even in the smallest article. And even if we grant that some of the elect are bound in error all their lives, yet they must necessarily return to the right

84. The Seriphian frogs means dumb persons; cf. Erasmus, *Adagia* 1,5,31.

way before they die, since Christ says in John 10[:28]: "No one shall snatch them out of my hand."

But here is the task, here is the toil, to determine whether those whom you call the Church are the Church, or rather, whether after being in error all their lives they were at last brought back before they died. For it does not immediately follow that if God has permitted all those whom you quote, from as many centuries as you like and most learned though they were, to be in error, therefore God has permitted his Church to err.[85] Look at Israel, the people of God, where in so long a line of kings over so long a period of time not a single king is listed who did not err. And in the time of the prophet Elijah, everybody and everything in the public life of this people had so far fallen into idolatry that Elijah thought he alone was left [1 Kings 18:22]; and yet, although kings, princes, priests, prophets, and everything that could be called the People or Church of God was going to perdition, God had kept seven thousand [1 Kings 19:18]. But who saw them, or knew them to be the People of God? Who, then, even at the present time would venture to deny that, concealed under those outstanding figures—for you mention none but persons of public office and distinction—God has preserved for Godself a Church among the common people, and has permitted those others to perish as God did in the kingdom of Israel? For it is characteristic of God to lay low the picked people of Israel and slay their strong ones (Ps. 78[:31]), but to preserve the dregs and remnant of Israel, as Isaiah says [10:22].

What happened in Christ's own time, when all the apostles fell away [Matt. 26:31, 56] and he himself was denied and condemned by the whole people, and scarcely more than a Nicodemus, a Joseph, and the thief on the cross were saved? Were these then called the People of God? They were the remnant of the People, but they were not so called, and what was so called was not the People of God. Who knows but that the state of the Church of God throughout the whole course of the world from the beginning has always been such that some have been called the People and the saints of God who were not so, while others, a remnant in their midst, really were the People or the saints, but were never called so, as witness the stories of Cain and Abel, Ishmael and Isaac, Esau and Jacob? Look at the time of the Arians,[86] when scarcely five Catholic bishops were preserved in the whole world, and they were driven from their sees, while the Arians

85. The arguments Luther adopts here were used in late medieval ecclesiological debates, where authors showed that God's promises to the church that it would not err did not necessarily refer to ecclesiastical institutions but to the crowd of believers.

86. "The followers of Arius (c. 250–336), presbyter of Alexandria, were excommunicated in 318 for denying the divinity of Christ. His teaching, variously modified, won widespread acceptance and had the support of several emperors before the orthodox doctrine, formulated at the Council of Nicaea in 325, finally prevailed" (LW 33:86 n. 30).

reigned everywhere in the public name and office of the Church; nevertheless, Christ preserved his Church under these heretics, though in such a way that it was far from being recognized and regarded as the Church.

Under the reign of the pope, show me one bishop discharging his duty, show me one Council that has been concerned with matters of piety rather than robes, rank, revenues, and other profane trifles, which no one who was not insane could attribute to the Holy Spirit. Yet they are nonetheless called the Church, although all of them, at least while they live like this, are reprobates and anything but the Church. Yet even under them Christ has preserved his Church, but not so as to have it called the Church. How many saints do you suppose the minions of the Inquisition alone have burned and murdered during the last few centuries? I mean persons like John Hus, in whose time without doubt there lived many holy people in the same spirit.[87] [. . .]

But to return to the point. How is it surprising if God allows all the great ones of the Church to walk in their own ways, when God has thus allowed all the nations to walk in their own ways, as Paul says in Acts [14:16]? The Church of God is not as commonplace a thing, my dear Erasmus, as the phrase "the Church of God"; nor are the saints of God met with as universally as the phrase "the saints of God." They are a pearl and precious jewels, which the Spirit does not cast before swine [Matt. 7:6] but keeps hidden, as Scripture says [Matt. 11:25], lest the ungodly should see the glory of God. Otherwise, if they were plainly recognized by all, how could they possibly be as harassed and afflicted in the world as they are? As Paul says: "If they had known, they would not have crucified the Lord of glory" [1 Cor. 2:8]. [. . .]

[Scripture, with Its "Internal" and "External" Clarity, as the Test of Truth]

What, then, are we to do? The Church is hidden,[88] the saints are unknown. What and whom are we to believe? Or, as you very pointedly argue, who gives us certainty? How shall we prove the Spirit? If you look for learning, on both sides there are scholars; if for quality of life, on both sides are sinners; if for Scripture, both sides acknowledge it. But the dispute is not so much about Scripture which may not yet be sufficiently clear, as about

87. Jan Hus (c. 1369–1415), preacher for a pure church in Bohemia, was burned as a heretic at the Council of Constance in 1415.

88. This is a central conviction of Luther's ecclesiology, that only God sees the true members of the church.

the meaning of Scripture; and on both sides are men, of whom neither numbers nor learning nor dignity, much less fewness, ignorance, and humility, have anything to do with the case. The matter therefore remains in doubt and the case is still *sub judice*,[w] so that it looks as if we might be wise to adopt the position of the Skeptics, unless the line you take is best, when you express your uncertainty in such a way as to aver that you are seeking to learn the truth, though in the meantime you incline to the side that asserts free choice, until the truth becomes clear. [. . .]

What we say is this: The spirits are to be tested or proved by two sorts of judgment. One is internal, whereby through the Holy Spirit or a special gift of God, anyone who is enlightened concerning himself and his own salvation, judges and discerns with the greatest certainty the dogmas and opinions of all people. Of this it is said in 1 Cor. 1 [2:15]: "The spiritual person judges all things but is judged by no one." This belongs to faith and is necessary for every individual Christian. We have called it above "the internal clarity of Holy Scripture." Perhaps this was what those had in mind who gave you the reply that everything must be decided by the judgment of the Spirit. But this judgment helps no one else, and with it we are not here concerned, for no one, I think, doubts its reality.

There is therefore another, an external judgment, whereby with the greatest certainty we judge the spirits and dogmas of all men, not only for ourselves, but also for others and for their salvation. This judgment belongs to the public ministry of the Word and to the outward office, and is chiefly the concern of leaders and preachers of the Word. We make use of it when we seek to strengthen those who are weak in faith and confute opponents. This is what we earlier called "the external clarity of Holy Scripture."[89] Thus we say that all spirits are to be tested in the presence of the Church at the bar of Scripture. For it ought above all to be settled and established among Christians that the Holy Scriptures are a spiritual light far brighter than the sun itself, especially in things that are necessary to salvation. But because we have for so long been persuaded of the opposite by that pestilential saying of the Sophists that the Scriptures are obscure and ambiguous, we are obliged to begin by proving

89. For Luther the "clarity of Holy Scripture" meant that through the Bible, God's word is clear and accessible to those who hear it. Matters of doctrine and faith are made clear in Scripture, which then becomes the primary guide, especially in things necessary for salvation. This is in contrast to the church's teaching that Scripture is unclear without the explanation offered by the scholars or officials of the church. In Luther's contrasting view, because of Scripture's clarity, people do not need to to have it explained or interpreted by a pope or council in order for its meaning to be understood.

w   Latin for "under judgment."

even that first principle of ours by which everything else has to be proved—a procedure that among the philosophers would be regarded as absurd and impossible.[90] [. . .]

But here you will say, "All this is nothing to me; I do not say that the Scriptures are obscure in all parts (for who would be so crazy?), but only in this and similar parts." I reply: neither do I say these things in opposition to you only, but in opposition to all who think as you do;[91] moreover, in opposition to you I say with respect to the whole Scripture, I will not have any part of it called obscure. What we have cited from Peter holds well here, that the Word of God is for us "a lamp shining in a dark place" [2 Pet. 1:19]. But if part of this lamp does not shine, it will be a part of the dark place rather than of the lamp itself. Christ has not so enlightened us as deliberately to leave some part of his Word obscure while commanding us to give heed to it, for he commands us in vain to give heed if it does not give light.

Consequently, if the dogma of free choice is obscure or ambiguous, it does not belong to Christians or the Scriptures, and it should be abandoned and reckoned among those fables that Paul condemns Christians for wrangling about. If, however, it does belong to Christians and the Scriptures, it ought to be clear, open, and evident, exactly like all the other clear and evident articles of faith. For all the articles of faith held by Christians ought to be such that they are not only most certain to Christians themselves, but also fortified against the attacks of others by such manifest and clear Scriptures that they shut all men's mouths and prevent their saying anything against them; as Christ says in his promise to us: "I will give you a mouth and wisdom, which none of your adversaries will be able to withstand" [Luke 21:15]. If, therefore, our mouth is so weak at this point that our adversaries can withstand it, his saying that no adversary can withstand our mouth is false. Either, therefore, we shall have no adversaries while maintaining the dogma of free choice (which will be the case if free choice does not belong to us), or if it does belong to us, we shall have adversaries, it is true, but they will not be able to withstand us.

But this inability of the adversaries to withstand (since the point arises here) does not mean that they are compelled to abandon their own position, or are persuaded either to confess or keep silence. For who can compel people against their will

90. Luther thinks of the denial of circling arguments.

91. A remark like this shows Luther's awareness of the public debate among the learned readers potentially in all Europe.

to believe, to confess their error, or to be silent? "What is more loquacious than vanity?" as Augustine says.[x] But what is meant is that their mouth is so far stopped that they have nothing to say in reply and, although they say a great deal, yet in the judgment of common sense they say nothing. This is best shown by examples.

When Christ in Matthew 22[:23ff.] put the Sadducees to silence by quoting Scripture and proving the resurrection of the dead from the words of Moses in Exodus 3[:6]: "I am the God of Abraham," etc.; "This is not the God of the dead, but of the living," here they could not resist or say anything in reply. But did they therefore give up their own opinion? And how often did he confute the Pharisees by the plainest Scriptures and arguments, so that the people clearly saw them convicted, and even they themselves perceived it? Nevertheless, they continued to be his adversaries. Stephen in Acts 7 [6:10] spoke, according to Luke, in such a way that they could not withstand the wisdom and the Spirit with which he spoke. But what did they do? Did they give way? On the contrary, being ashamed to be beaten, and not being able to withstand, they went mad, and shutting their ears and eyes they set up false witnesses against him (Acts 8 [6:11–14]).

See how this man stands before the Council and confutes his adversaries! After enumerating the benefits which God had bestowed on that people from the beginning, and proving that God had never ordered a temple to be built for God (for this was the question at issue and the substance of the charge against him), he at length concedes that a temple was in fact built under Solomon, but then he qualifies it in this way: "Yet the Most High does not dwell in houses made with hands," and in proof of this he quotes Isaiah 66[:1]: "What house is this that you build for me?" Tell me, what could they say here against so plain a Scripture? Yet they were quite unmoved and remained set in their own opinion; which leads him to attack them directly, in the words: "Uncircumcised in heart and ears, you always withstand the Holy Spirit," etc. [Acts 7:51]. He says they withstand, although they were unable to withstand.

Let us come to our own times. When Jan Hus[y] argues as follows against the pope on the basis of Matthew 16[:18]: "The gates

---

x   Augustine, *De civitate Dei* 5:26.
y   Jan Hus, *De ecclesia*, ch. 7.

of hell do not prevail against my church" (is there any ambiguity or obscurity here?), "but against the pope and his followers the gates of hell do prevail, for they are notorious the world over for their open impiety and wickedness" (is this also obscure?), "therefore the pope and his followers are not the church of which Christ speaks"—what could they say in reply to this, or how could they withstand the mouth that Christ had given him? Yet they did withstand, and they persisted until they burned him, so far were they from altering their opinion. Nor does Christ overlook this when he says, "Your adversaries will not be able to withstand." They are adversaries, he says; therefore, they will withstand, for otherwise they would not be adversaries but friends; and yet they will not be able to withstand. What else does this mean but that in withstanding they will not be able to withstand?

If, accordingly, we are able so to confute free choice that our adversaries cannot withstand, even if they persist in their own opinion and withstand in spite of their conscience, we shall have done enough. For I have had enough experience to know that no one wants to be beaten and, as Quintilian says, there is no one who would not rather seem to know than to learn,[z] though it is a sort of proverb on everyone's lips nowadays (from use, or rather abuse, more than from conviction): "I wish to learn, I'm ready to be taught, and when shown a better way, to follow it; I'm only human, and I may be wrong." The fact is that under this mask, this fair show of humility, they find it possible quite confidently to say: "I'm not satisfied, I don't see it, he does violence to the Scriptures, he's an obstinate assertor"; because, of course, they are sure that no one will suspect such very humble souls of stubbornly resisting and even vigorously attacking recognized truth. So it is made to seem that their refusal to alter their opinion ought not to be set down to their own perverseness, but to the obscurity and ambiguity of the arguments. [...]

[Erasmus Is in a Dilemma]

Why do I go on? Why do we not end the case with this Introduction, and pronounce sentence on you from your own words, according to that saying of Christ: "By your words you will be justified, and by your words you will be condemned" [Matt. 12:37]?

---

z   Quintilian, *Institutiones* 3:1,6.

For you say that Scripture is not crystal clear on this point, and then you suspend judgment and discuss both sides of the question, asking what can be said for it and what against; and you do nothing else in the whole of this book, which for that reason you have chosen to call a diatribe rather than an apophasis[92] or anything else, because you write with the intention of collating everything and affirming nothing.

If, then, Scripture is not crystal clear, how is it that those of whom you boast are not only blind at this point, but rash and foolish enough to define and assert free choice on the basis of Scripture, as though it were quite positive and plain? I mean your numerous body of most learned individuals who have found approval in so many centuries down to our day, most of whom have godliness of life as well as a wonderful skill in divine studies to commend them, and some gave testimony with their blood to the doctrine of Christ that they had defended with their writings. If you say this sincerely, it is a settled point with you that free choice has assertors endowed with a wonderful skill in the Holy Scriptures, and that such individuals even bore witness to it with their blood. If that is true, they must have regarded Scripture as crystal clear; otherwise, what meaning would there be in that wonderful skill they had in the Holy Scriptures? Besides, what levity and temerity of mind it would argue to shed their blood for something uncertain and obscure! That is not the act of martyrs of Christ, but of demons!

Now, you also should "consider whether more weight ought not to be ascribed to the previous judgments of so many learned authors, so many orthodox, so many saints, so many martyrs, so many theologians old and new, so many universities, councils, bishops, and popes," who have found the Scriptures crystal clear and have confirmed this both by their writings and their blood, or to your own "private judgment" alone when you deny that the Scriptures are crystal clear, and when perhaps you have never shed a single tear or uttered one sigh on behalf of the doctrine of Christ. If you think those individuals were right, why do you not imitate them? If you do not think so, why do you rant and brag with such a spate of words, as if you wanted to overwhelm me with a sort of tempest and deluge of oratory—which nevertheless falls with the greater force on your own head, while my ark rides aloft in safety? For you attribute to all these great individuals the greatest folly and temerity when you describe them

92. A diatribe means "collation" or "discourse"; an *apophasis* refers to the raising of an issue by claiming not to mention it, or introducing a topic while denying that it should be brought up (e.g., "I will by no means speak of my opponent's faulty reasoning").

as so highly skilled in Scripture and as having asserted it by their pen, their life and their death, although you maintain that it is obscure and ambiguous. This is nothing else but to make them most inexpert in knowledge and most foolish in assertion. I should not have paid them such a compliment in my private contempt of them as you do in your public commendation of them.

I have you here, therefore, on the horns of a dilemma,[93] as they say. For one or the other of these two things must be false; either your saying that those individuals were admirable for their skill in the Holy Scriptures, their life, and their martyrdom or your saying that Scripture is not crystal clear. But since you are drawn rather to believing that the Scriptures are not crystal clear (for that is what you are driving at throughout your book), we can only conclude that you have described those individuals as experts in Scripture and martyrs for Christ either in fun or in flattery and in no way seriously, merely in order to throw dust into the eyes of the uneducated public and make difficulties for Luther by loading his cause with odium and contempt by means of empty words. I, however, say that neither statement is true, but both are false. I hold, first, that the Scriptures are entirely clear; secondly, that those individuals, insofar as they assert free choice, are most inexpert in the Holy Scriptures; and thirdly, that they made this assertion neither by their life nor their death, but only with their pen—and that while their wits were wandering.

I therefore conclude this little debate as follows. By means of Scripture, regarded as obscure, nothing definite has ever yet been settled or can be settled concerning free choice, on your own testimony. Moreover, by the lives of all human beings from the beginning of the world, nothing has been demonstrated in favor of free choice, as has been said above. Therefore, to teach something which is neither prescribed by a single word inside the Scriptures nor demonstrated by a single fact outside them is no part of Christian doctrine, but belongs to the *True History* of Lucian,[94] except that Lucian, by making sport with ludicrous subjects in deliberate jest, neither deceives nor harms anyone, whereas these friends of ours with their insane treatment of a serious subject, and one that concerns eternal salvation, lead innumerable souls to perdition.

In this way I also might have put an end to this whole question about free choice, seeing that even the testimony of my

93. In the Latin text, Luther here speaks of a syllogism. This means the most important logical technique, concluding one sentence from two others, e.g.: Socrates is a human being. All human beings are mortal. Thus, Socrates is mortal.

94. Lucian's *Vera historiae* was a parody about Homer and others.

adversaries favors my position and conflicts with theirs, and there can be no stronger proof than the personal confession and testimony of a defendant against oneself. But since Paul bids us silence empty talkers [Titus 1:10f.], let us go into the details of the case and deal with the subject in the order in which the *Diatribe* proceeds, first confuting the arguments adduced in favor of free choice, then defending arguments of our own that have been attacked, and lastly contending against free choice on behalf of the grace of God.

[Part III. Refutation of Arguments in Support of Free Choice]

[Erasmus's Definition of Free Choice]

Now first we will begin quite properly with the definition you give of free choice, where you say: "By free choice in this place we mean a power of the human will by which one can apply oneself to the things which lead to eternal salvation, or turn away from them." It is very prudent of you to give only a bare definition and not to explain (as others usually do) any part of it—perhaps because you were afraid you might be shipwrecked on more than one point. I am thus compelled to look at your definition in detail. What is defined, certainly if it is examined closely, is wider than the definition, which is of a kind that the Sophists would call "vicious," a term they apply whenever a definition does not exhaust the thing defined. For we have shown above that free choice properly belongs to no one but God alone. You might perhaps rightly attribute some measure of choice to human beings, but to attribute free choice to them in relation to divine things is too much; for the term "free choice," in the judgment of everyone's ears, means (strictly speaking) that which can do and does, in relation to God, whatever it pleases, uninhibited by any law or any sovereign authority. For you would not call a slave free, who acts under the sovereign authority of one's master; and still less rightly can we call a human being or angel free, when they live under the absolute sovereignty of God (not to mention sin and death) in such a way that they cannot subsist for a moment by their own strength.

Here, therefore, at the very outset, there is a conflict between the nominal definition of the real definition,[95] because the term signifies one thing and the real item is understood as another.[96] It would be more correct to speak of "vertible choice" or "mutable choice,"[97] in the way in which Augustine and the Sophists after him limit the glory and range of the word *free* by introducing the disparaging notion of what they call the vertibility of free choice. In such a way it would be fitting for us to speak, to avoid deceiving the hearts of human beings with inflated and high-sounding but empty words; just as Augustine also thinks we ought to make it a definite rule to speak only in sober and strictly appropriate words. For in teaching, simplicity and appropriateness of speech is required, not bombast and persuasive rhetorical images.[98] But in order not to appear to delight in quarreling about words, let us for the moment accept this misuse of terms, serious and dangerous though it is, and allow free choice to be the same as vertible choice. Let us also grant Erasmus his point when he makes free choice a power of the human will, as if angels did not have free choice, since in his book he has undertaken to deal only with the free choice of human beings; otherwise, in this respect too the definition would be narrower than the thing defined.

Let us come to those parts of the definition on which the whole matter hinges. Some of them are plain enough, but others shun the light as though guiltily aware that they have everything to fear; yet nothing ought to be more plainly and unhesitatingly expressed than a definition, since to define obscurely is the same as giving no definition at all. The plain parts are these: "a power of the human will," "by which a human being is able," and "to eternal salvation"; but the following are like blindfolded gladiators: "to apply," "to the things which lead," and "to turn away." How are we going to divine what this applying and turning away means? And what are the "things which lead to eternal salvation"? What is all this about? I am dealing, I see, with a real Scotus[99] or Heraclitus,[100] and am to be worn out by the double labor involved. For first I have to go groping nervously about amid pitfalls and darkness (which is a venturesome and risky thing to do) in quest of my adversary, and unless I find him I shall be tilting at ghosts and beating the air in the dark. Then if I do manage to drag him into the light, I shall have to come to grips with him on equal terms when I am already wearied with looking for him.

95. Luther here shows his good scholastic education: nominal definition and real definition were two different types of definition in late medieval logic, the first concerning the logical impact of the definition, the second including the reference to the real world outside the human mind.

96. The theory of signification also was one of the most discussed matters in late medieval philosophy. According to it, one's understanding of terms depends from the right signifying relation to the items meant by them.

97. E.g., Thomas of Aquinas, *Summa theologiae* II-II q. 24 a. 11 respondeo.

98. This is a clear adaption of the rules of late medieval *Via moderna* to avoid a plurality of words. One has to reduce the number of words, using just some words with clear signification.

99. Duns Scotus, the so called *Doctor subtilis*, was known for his intricate scholastic arguments.

100. Heraclitus, a Pre-Socratic philosopher well known for his sentence: "Everything flows." His work was regarded as quite obscure.

I take it, then, that what is meant by "a power of the human will" is a capacity or faculty or ability or aptitude for willing, unwilling, selecting, neglecting, approving, rejecting, and whatever other actions of the will there are. Now, what it means for that same power to "apply itself" and to "turn away" I do not see, unless it is precisely this willing and unwilling, selecting, neglecting, approving, rejecting, or in other words, precisely the action of the will. So that we must imagine this power to be something between the will itself and its action, as the means by which the will itself produces the action of willing and unwilling, and by which the action of willing and unwilling is itself produced. Anything else it is impossible either to imagine or conceive here. If I am mistaken, let the author be blamed who has given the definition, not I who am trying to understand it; for as the lawyers rightly say, if one speaks obscurely when one could speak more clearly, one's words are to be interpreted against oneself. And here for the moment I want to forget my Modernist friends[101] with their subtleties, since there is need of plain, blunt speaking for the sake of teaching and understanding.

Now, the things which lead to eternal salvation I take to be the words and works of God that are presented to the human will so that it may apply itself to them or turn away from them. By the words of God, moreover, I mean both the law and the gospel, the law requiring works and the gospel faith.[102] For there is nothing else that leads either to the grace of God or to eternal salvation except the word and work of God, since grace or the Spirit is life itself, to which we are led by God's word and work. [. . .]

On the authority of Erasmus, then, free choice is a power of the will that is able of itself to will and unwill (*nolle*)[a] the word and work of God, by which it is led to those things which exceed both its grasp and its perception. But if it can will and unwill, it can also love and hate, and if it can love and hate, it can also in some small degree do the works of the law and believe the gospel. For if you can will or unwill anything, you must to some extent be able to perform something by that will, even if someone else prevents your completing it. Now, in that case, since the works of God that lead to salvation include death, the cross, and all the

---

101. The "modernists" shaped the so-called *Via moderna* in the late Middle Ages as an alternative to the *Via antiquae*. While the latter one trusted in the reasonability of God and creation, the modernists stressed God's will and power. In their arguments, they made bright use of logical conclusions and critical analysis of language.

102. This is a central distinction in Luther's thoughts, which is not identical with the distinction of the Old and New Testaments. Law and gospel are two kinds of the word of God, spread out in both Testaments. The law in its theological use shows the sin of human beings; the gospel gives the promise that the sinner will be redeemed.

---

a   In Latin, *nolle*, meaning "to not want," "to not wish to pursue," etc., opposite to "want."

evils of the world, the human will must be able to will both death and its own perdition. Indeed, it can will everything when it can will the word and work of God; for how can there be anything anywhere that is below, above, within, or without the word and work of God, except God alone?[103] But what is left here to grace and the Holy Spirit? This plainly means attributing divinity to free choice, since to will the law and the gospel, to unwill sin and to will death, belongs to divine power alone, as Paul says in more than one place.

Clearly then, no one since the Pelagians[104] has written more correctly about free choice than Erasmus! For we have said above that free choice is a divine term and signifies a divine power, although no one has yet attributed this power to free choice except the Pelagians; for the Sophists, whatever they may think, certainly speak very differently. Erasmus, however, far outdoes even the Pelagians, for they attribute this divinity to the whole of free choice, but Erasmus only to half of it. They reckon with two parts of free choice—the power of discerning and the power of selecting—one of which they attach to reason, the other to the will, as the Sophists also do. But Erasmus neglects the power of discerning and extols only the power of selecting. So it is a crippled and only half-free choice that he deifies. What do you think he would have done if he had set about describing the whole of free choice?

But not content with this, he outdoes the philosophers too. For with them it is not yet finally settled whether anything can set itself in motion,[105] and on this point the Platonists and Peripatetics[106] disagree throughout the entire range of philosophy. But as Erasmus sees it, free choice not only moves itself by its own power, but also applies itself to things which are eternal, that is, incomprehensible to itself. Here is truly a novel and unprecedented definer of free choice, who leaves Pelagians, Sophists, and everyone else far behind! Nor is that enough for him; for he does not spare even himself, but is more at cross-purposes with himself than with all the rest. For he had previously said that the human will was completely ineffectual without grace (unless he said this in jest), but here where he is giving a serious definition, he says that the human will possesses this power by which it is capable of applying itself to the things that belong to eternal salvation, that is, to things that are incomparably beyond that power. So in this part Erasmus even surpasses himself as well.

---

103. Replacing *himself.*

104. "The followers of the British monk, Pelagius, who taught in Rome c. 400 CE and from 412/413 in Palestine. Pelagius denied original or inherited sin, and he held that humans have at all times the freedom to choose between good and evil; the only grace one needs is the knowledge of God's will and commandment. The Pelagian teaching was condemned as heretical at the Council of Ephesus in 431 CE. Luther is of course completely unjust in accusing Erasmus of this sort of heresy" (LW 33:107 n. 9).

105. Actually, in Aristotelian thinking, motion had to be caused by something extrinsic. This conviction was included in one of the main arguments of Thomas Aquinas (1225-1274) for the existence of God: going logically back in the line of moving things, Thomas pointed to the "unmoveable mover" as the origin.

106. The Aristotelians.

Do you see, my dear Erasmus, that with this definition you put yourself on record (unwittingly, I presume) as understanding nothing at all of these things, or as writing about them quite thoughtlessly and contemptuously, unaware of what you are saying or affirming? And as I said above, you say less and attribute more to free choice than all the others, in that you describe only part and not the whole of free choice and yet attribute everything to it. Far more tolerable is the teaching of the Sophists, or at least of their father, Peter Lombard,[107] when they say that free choice is the capacity for discerning and then also choosing the good if grace is present, but evil if grace is absent. Lombard clearly thinks with Augustine that free choice by its own power alone can do nothing but fall and is capable only of sinning, which is why Augustine, in his second book against Julian,[108] calls it an enslaved rather than a free choice.

You, however, make free choice equally potent in both directions, in that it is able by its own power, without grace, both to apply itself to the good and to turn away from the good. You do not realize how much you attribute to it by this pronoun "itself"—its very own self!—when you say it can "apply itself"; for this means that you completely exclude the Holy Spirit with all his power, as superfluous and unnecessary. Your definition is therefore to be condemned even by the standards of the Sophists, who if only they were not so enraged by blind envy of me, would be rampaging instead against your book. As it is, since it is Luther you are attacking, everything you say is holy and catholic, even if you contradict both yourself and them, so great is the endurance of saintly human beings.

I do not say this because I approve the view of the Sophists regarding free choice, but because I consider it more tolerable than that of Erasmus, since they come nearer the truth. For although they do not say, as I do, that free choice is nothing, yet when they (and particularly the Master of the Sentences[109]) say that it can do nothing without grace, they take sides against Erasmus. [. . .]

[Ecclesiasticus 15:14-17.
The Foolishness of Reason]

Now let us turn to the passage from Ecclesiasticus and compare with it, too, that first "probable" opinion. The opinion says that

---

107. Peter Lombard (c. 1096–1164) had collected and arranged the *Sentences* of the Teachers of the Church in the twelfth century. This book had become the common textbook for European theology, up to the early days of Luther, who commented on it in his Erfurt times.

108. Augustine, *Contra Iulianum*. Augustine's adversary here was Julian of Aeclanum (d. c. 455), holding a position similar to that of Pelagius.

109. Referring to Lombard.

free choice cannot will good, but the passage from Ecclesiasticus is cited to prove that free choice is something and can do something. The opinion that is to be confirmed by Ecclesiasticus, therefore, states one thing and Ecclesiasticus is cited in confirmation of another. It is as if someone set out to prove that Christ was the Messiah, and cited a passage that proved that Pilate was governor of Syria, or something else equally wide of the mark. That is just how free choice is proved here, not to mention what I pointed out above, that nothing is clearly and definitely said or proved as to what free choice is or can do. But it is worthwhile to examine this whole passage.

First it says, "God made human beings from the beginning." Here it speaks of the creation of man, and says nothing as yet either about free choice or about precepts. Then follows: "And left them in the hand of their own counsel." What have we here? Is free choice set up here? But not even here is there any mention of precepts, for which free choice is required, nor do we read anything on this subject in the account of the creation of man. If anything is meant, therefore, by "the hand of their own counsel," it is rather as we read in Genesis, chapters 1–2, that the human being was appointed lord of things, so as to exercise dominion over them freely, as Moses says: "Let us make a human being, and let them preside over the fish of the sea" [Gen. 1:26]. Nor can anything else be proved from those words. For in that state, human being was able to deal with things according to one's own choice, in that they were subject to him; and this is called a human counsel, as distinct from God's counsel. But then, after saying that human beings were thus made and left in the hand of their own counsel, it goes on. "God added God's commandments and precepts." What did God add them to? Surely the counsel and choice of human beings, and over and above the establishing of human beings' dominion over the rest of the creatures. And by these precepts God took away from human beings the dominion over one part of the creatures (for instance, over the tree of the knowledge of good and evil) and willed rather that they should not be free.

Then, however, when the precepts have been added, he comes to human being's choice in relation to God and the things of God: "If you want to observe the commandments, they shall preserve you," etc. It is therefore at this point, "If you want," that the question of free choice arises. We thus learn from Ecclesiasticus

110. The following shows Luther's attempt to avoid pure and total determinism.

that the human beings are divided between two kingdoms,[110] in one of which they are directed by their own choice and counsel, apart from any precepts and commandments of God, namely, in their dealings with the lower creatures. Here human beings reign and are the lord, as having been left in the hand of their own counsel. Not that God so leaves the human beings as not to cooperate with them in everything, but God has granted them the free use of things according to their own choice, and has not restricted them by any laws or injunctions. By way of comparison one might say that the gospel has left us in the hand of our own counsel, to have dominion over things and use them as we wish; but Moses and the pope have not left us to that counsel, but have coerced us with laws and have subjected us rather to their own choice.

In the other kingdom, however, human beings are not left in the hand of their own counsel, but are directed and led by the choice and counsel of God, so that just as in their own kingdom they are directed by their own counsel, without regard to the precepts of another, so in the kingdom of God they are directed by the precepts of another without regard to their own choice. And this is what Ecclesiasticus means by: "He added his precepts and commandments. If you will," etc.

If, then, these things are sufficiently clear, we have gained our point that this passage of Ecclesiasticus is evidence, not for, but against free choice, since by it human beings are subjected to the precepts and choice of God, and withdrawn from their own choice. If they are not sufficiently clear, at least we have made the point that this passage cannot be evidence in favor of free choice, since it can be understood in a different sense from theirs, namely in ours, which has just been stated, and which is not absurd but entirely sound and in harmony with the whole tenor of Scripture, whereas theirs is at variance with Scripture as a whole and is derived from this one passage alone, in contradiction to it. We stand, therefore, quite confidently by the good sense that the negative of free choice makes here, until they confirm their strained and forced affirmative.

When, therefore, Ecclesiasticus says: "If you will observe the commandments and keep acceptable fidelity, they shall preserve you," I do not see how free choice is proved by these words. For the verb is in the subjunctive mood ("If you will"), which asserts nothing. As the logicians say, a conditional asserts nothing indicatively: for example, "If the devil is God, it is right to worship God; if an ass flies, an ass has wings; if free choice exists, grace is nothing." Ecclesiasticus, however, should have spoken as follows, if he had wished to assert free choice: "Human beings can keep the commandments of God," or: "Human beings have the power to keep the commandments." [...]

[Erasmus's Failure to Distinguish between Law and Gospel]

In these passages our *Diatribe* makes no distinction whatever between expressions of the law and of the gospel; for she is so blind and ignorant that she does not know what law and gospel are.[111] For out of the whole of Isaiah, apart from that one verse, "If you are willing," she quotes not a single word of the law, all the rest being gospel passages, in which the brokenhearted and afflicted are called to take comfort from a word of proffered grace. But Diatribe turns them into words of law. Now, I ask you, what good will anyone do in a matter of theology or the Holy Scriptures, who has not yet got as far as knowing what the law and what the gospel is, or if one knows, nevertheless disdains to observe the distinction between them? Such a person is bound to confound everything—heaven and hell, life and death—and will take no pains to know anything at all about Christ. On this subject I will admonish, dear Diatribe, more fully below.

Look at those words from Jeremiah and Zechariah: "If you return, I will restore you" and "Return to me, and I will return to you." Does it follow from "Return" that you are therefore able to return? Does it follow from "Love the Lord your God with all your heart" that you will therefore be able to love him with all your heart? What, then, do arguments of this kind prove, unless that free choice does not need the grace of God but can do everything in its own strength? How much more correctly, therefore, are the words taken as they stand? "If you shall return, I also will restore you"; that is, if you leave off sinning, I also will leave off punishing you, and if after returning you live a good life, I also will do good to you by turning away your captivity and all your ills. But it does not follow from this that human beings return by their own power, nor do the words themselves say so, but they say simply: "If you return," by which human beings are told what they ought to do; and once God knew this and saw that they

111. Here Luther brings forth his fundamental distinction in the word of God: the law, expressing God's will, and the gospel, bringing God's promises even to the sinner.

could not do it, human beings would seek the means enabling them to do it, if Diatribe's leviathan (that is, her added comment and inference) did not intervene to say: "But it would be meaningless to say, 'Return,' if human beings could not return by their own power." What sort of notion that is, and what it implies, has already been sufficiently stated.

Only a human being in a stupor or a daze of some sort could suppose that the power of free choice is established by words such as "Return" and "If you return" without noticing that on the same principle it would also be established by the saying, "You shall love the Lord your God with all you heart," since the meaning of the one who commands and demands is the same in both cases. The love of God is certainly no less required than our conversion and the keeping of all the commandments, since the love of God is our true conversion. Yet no one tries to prove free choice from the commandment of love, though everyone argues for it from sayings such as "If you are willing"; "If you will hear"; "Return!" If, then, it does not follow from that saying ("Love the Lord thy God with all your heart") that free choice is anything or can do anything, it certainly does not follow from sayings such as "If you are willing"; "If you are obedient"; "Return!" which either demand less or demand it less imperiously than "Love God!"; "Love the Lord!"

Whatever, therefore, can be said against the use of the expression "Love God!" as an argument for free choice, the same can be said against the use of all other verbs of command or demand as arguments for free choice. And what can be said is that by the command to love we are shown the essential meaning of the law and what we ought to do, but not the power of the will or what we are able to do, but rather what we are not able to do; and the same is shown by all other expressions of demand. For it is well known that even the academics, with the exception of the Scotists[112] and the Moderns,[113] affirm that human beings cannot love God with all their heart[114]; and in that case, neither can they fulfill any of the other commandments, since all of them depend on this one, as Christ testifies [Matt. 22:40]. So the fact remains, even on the testimony of the Scholastic doctors, that the words of the law are no evidence for the power of free choice, but show what we ought to do and cannot do. [...]

See now how the *Diatribe* treats that famous verse of Ezekiel 18: "As I live, says the Lord, I desire not the death of a sinner, but

112. John Duns Scotus (c. 1266–1308), British philosopher and theologian of the Franciscan Order, taught in Oxford, Paris, and Cologne. He was known as *Doctor Subtilis,* "the subtle doctor."

113. For Modernists, see n. 101, p. 200.

114. In the tradition of the *Via moderna,* some thinkers, notably Gabriel Biel (c. 1420–1495), held that human beings could fulfill God's will in a purely natural "naked" state (*ex puris naturalibus*).

rather that the sinner should turn and live." First, Diatribe says: "In every case the words 'turns away . . . has done . . . has performed . . .' are repeated again and again, in the matter of doing good or evil, and where are those who deny that human beings can do anything?" Notice, please, the remarkable consequence. She was going to prove endeavor and desire on the part of free choice, and she proves a complete act, everything fully carried out by free choice. Where now, I ask you, are those who insist on grace and the Holy Spirit? For this is the subtle kind of way she argues: "Ezekiel says, 'If a wicked human being turns away from all sins and does what is lawful and right, that person shall live' [Ezek. 18:21]; therefore, the wicked human being forthwith does so and is able to do so." Ezekiel intimates what ought to be done, and Diatribe takes it that this is being and has been done, again trying to teach us by a new sort of grammar that to owe is the same as to have, to be required as to be provided, to demand as to pay.

Then she takes that word of sweetest gospel, "I desire not the death of a sinner," etc., and gives this twist to it: "Does the good Lord deplore the death of his people which he himself works in them? If he does not will our death and if we nonetheless perish, it is to be imputed to our own will. But what can you impute to a human being who can do nothing either good or ill?" This is just the song Pelagius sang when he attributed not merely desire or endeavor, but the complete power of fulfilling and doing everything, to free choice. For it is this power that these inferences prove if they prove anything, as we have said, so that they conflict just as violently and even more so with Diatribe herself, who denies that free choice has this power, and claims for it only an endeavor, as they conflict with us who deny free choice altogether. But not to dwell on her ignorance, we will confine ourselves to the point at issue.

It is an evangelical word and the sweetest comfort in every way for miserable sinners, where Ezekiel [Ezek. 18:23, 32] says: "I desire not the death of a sinner, but rather that the sinner may turn and live," like Psalm 28 [30:5]: "For God's anger is but for a moment, and God's favor is for a lifetime." Then there is Psalm 68 [109:21]: "How sweet is your mercy, O Lord" and "For I am merciful" [Jer. 3:12], and also Christ's saying in Matthew 11[:28]: "Come unto me, all you who labor, and I will give you rest," and that in Exodus 20[:6]: "I show mercy to many thousands, to those who love me." What, indeed, does almost more than half of Holy Scripture contain but sheer promises of grace, in which mercy, life, peace, and salvation are offered by God to human beings? And what else do words of promise have to say but this: "I desire not the death of a sinner"? Is it not the same thing to say, "I am merciful," as to say, "I am not angry, I do not want to punish, I do not want you to die, I want to pardon, I want to spare"? And if these divine promises were not there to raise up consciences afflicted with the sense of sin and terrified with the fear of death and judgment, what place would there be for pardon or hope? What sinner would not despair? But just as free choice is not proved by other words of mercy or promise or comfort, so neither is it proved by this one: "I desire not the death of a sinner," etc. [. . .]

For this also must be observed, that just as the voice of the law is not raised except over those who do not feel or acknowledge their sin, as Paul says in Romans 3[:20]: "Through the law comes knowledge of sin," so the word of grace does not come except to those who feel their sin and are troubled and tempted to despair. Thus in all expressions of the law you see that sin is revealed, inasmuch as we are shown what we ought to do, just as you see in all the words of promise, on the other hand, that the evil is indicated under which sinners, or those who are to be lifted up, are laboring. Here, for instance, "I desire not the death of a sinner" explicitly names death and the sinner, that is, the evil that is felt as well as the person who feels it. But in the words "Love God with all your heart," we are shown the good we ought to do, not the evil we feel, in order that we may recognize how unable we are to do that good.

Hence nothing could have been more inappropriately quoted in support of free choice than this passage of Ezekiel, which actually stands in the strongest opposition to free choice. For here we are shown what free choice is like, and what it can do about sin when sin is recognized, or about its own conversion to God; that is to say, nothing but fall into a worse state and add despair and impenitence to its sins, if God did not quickly come to its aid and call it back and raise it up by a word of promise. For God's solicitude in promising grace to recall and restore the sinner is a sufficiently strong and reliable argument that free choice by itself cannot but go from bad to worse and (as Scripture says) fall down into hell, unless you credit God with such levity as to pour out words of promise in profusion for the mere pleasure of talking, and not because they are in any way necessary for our salvation. So you can see that not only all the words of the law stand against free choice, but also all the words of promise utterly refute it; which means that Scripture in its entirety stands opposed to it.

[God Preached, God Hidden; God's Will Revealed, God's Will Secret]

This word, therefore, "I desire not the death of a sinner," has as you see no other object than the preaching and offering of divine mercy throughout the world, a mercy that only the afflicted and those tormented by the fear of death receive with joy and gratitude, because in them the law has already fulfilled its office and brought the knowledge of sin. Those, however, who have not yet experienced the office of the law, and neither recognize sin nor feel death, have no use for the mercy promised by that word. But why some are touched by the law and others are not, so that the former accept and the latter despise the offered grace, is another question and one not dealt with by Ezekiel in this passage. For he is here speaking of the preached and offered mercy of God, not of that hidden and awful will of God whereby God ordains by God's own counsel which and what sort of persons God wills to be recipients and partakers of the mercy of God preached and offered. This will is not to be inquired into, but reverently adored, as by far the most awe-inspiring secret of the Divine Majesty, reserved for God alone and forbidden to us much more religiously than any number of Corycian caverns.[b]

When now Diatribe pertly asks, "Does the good Lord deplore the death of his people, which he himself works in them?"—for this really does seem absurd—we reply, as we have already said, that we have to argue in one way about God or the will of God as preached, revealed, offered, and worshiped, and in another way about God as God is not preached, not revealed, not offered, not worshiped. To the extent, therefore, that God hides Godself and wills to be unknown to us, it is no business of ours. For here the saying truly applies, "Things above us are no business of ours."

---

b   See n. 44 above, p. 166.

And lest anyone should think this is a distinction of my own, I am following Paul, who writes to the Thessalonians concerning Antichrist that he will exalt himself above every God that is preached and worshiped [2 Thess. 2:4]. This plainly shows that someone can be exalted above God as God is preached and worshiped, that is, above the word and rite through which God is known to us and has dealings with us; but above God as God is not worshiped and not preached, but as God is in God's own nature and majesty, nothing can be exalted, but all things are under God's mighty hand.

God must therefore be left alone in this divine majesty, for in this regard we have nothing to do with God, nor has God willed that we should have anything to do with God. But we have something to do with God insofar as God is clothed and set forth in the Word, through which God is offered to us and which is the beauty and glory with which the psalmist celebrates God as being clothed. In this regard we say, the good God does not deplore the death of God's own people which God works in them, but rather deplores the death found in God's people and desires to remove from them. For it is this that God as God is preached is concerned with, namely, that sin and death should be taken away and we should be saved. For "God sent the word and healed them" [Ps. 107:20]. But God hidden in majesty neither deplores nor takes away death, but works life, death, and all in all. For there God has not bound Godself by this word, but has stayed free over all things.

Diatribe, however, deceives herself in her ignorance by not making any distinction between God preached and God hidden,[115] that is, between the word of God and God. God does many things that are not disclosed to us in the word; God also wills many things that God does not disclose as willing in the word. Thus God does not will the death of a sinner, according to God's word, but wills it according to God's inscrutable will. It is our business, however, to pay attention to the word and leave that inscrutable will alone, for we must be guided by the word and not by that inscrutable will. After all, who can direct oneself by a will completely inscrutable and unknowable? It is enough to know simply that there is a certain inscrutable will in God, and as to what, why, and how far it wills, that is something we have no right whatever to inquire into, hanker after, care about, or meddle with, but only to fear and adore.

115. This distinction of the preached or revealed and the hidden God (*Deus praedicatus/revelatus* or *Deus absonditus*) is one of the most widely debated questions in Luther research. While for some theologians, as Albrecht Ritschl, the *Deus absconditus* was the worst idea coming from Luther, others feel obliged to its theological depth. The theological roots seem to lie neither in the Platonic theology of Nicholas of Cusa (1401–1464), who wrote a treatise on *Deus absconditus* (*De deo abscondito*), nor in the *Via moderna*'s distinction of God's absolute and ordained power, but, rather, in the advice of Luther's confessor, Johan von Staupitz, who told Luther not to speculate about God's possibilities, but to trust in Jesus Christ alone. The function of the distinction is to direct faith immediately to the good will of God as shown in Christ and not to speculate about God's dark sides.

It is therefore right to say, "If God does not desire our death, the fact that we perish must be imputed to our own will." It is right, I mean, if you speak of God as preached; for God wills all human beings to be saved [1 Tim. 2:4], seeing God comes with the word of salvation to all, and the fault is in the will that does not admit God, as it says in Matthew 23[:37]: "How often did I want to gather your children, and you did not want!" But why that majesty of God does not remove or change this defect of our will in all human beings, since it is not in human beings' power to do so, or why God imputes this defect to human beings, when they cannot help having it, we have no right to inquire; and though you may do a lot of inquiring, you will never find out. It is as Paul says in Romans 11 [9:20]: "Who are you, to answer back to God?" Let these remarks suffice for that passage of Ezekiel, and let us go on to the rest.[116]

Diatribe next argues that all the exhortations in the Scriptures must be quite pointless, as must also the promises, threats, expostulations, reproaches, entreaties, blessings and curses, and all the swarms of precepts, if it is not in anyone's power to keep what is commanded. Diatribe is always forgetting the question at issue and doing something other than she set out to do, not realizing how it all militates more strongly against herself than against us. For on the basis of all these passages, by the force of the inference that she suggests from the words quoted, she proves a freedom and ability to keep everything, though what she wanted to prove was such a free choice as can will nothing good without grace, and a certain endeavor not ascribable to its own powers. I do not find that such an endeavor is proved by any of the passages quoted, but only that a demand is made regarding what ought to be done. This had already been said too often, were not such repetition necessary because Diatribe so often blunders on the same string, putting off her readers with a useless flow of words.

Almost the last passage she quotes from the Old Testament is that of Moses in Deuteronomy 30[:11ff.]: "This commandment which I command you this day is not above you, neither is it far off. It is not in heaven, that you should say, 'Who can go up for us to heaven, and bring it to us, that we may hear it and do it?' . . . But the word is very near you; it is in your mouth and in your heart, so that you might do it." Diatribe contends that by this passage it is declared not only that what is commanded

116. Regarding predestination, see n. 8, p. 157; n. 60, p. 170; and n. 142, p. 247.

is implanted in us, but also that it is like going downhill, i.e., is easy or at least not difficult. We are grateful for such erudition! If, then, Moses so distinctly announces that there is in us not only a faculty, but also a facility for keeping all the commandments, why are we sweating so much? Why did we not promptly produce this passage and assert free choice on a free field? What need is there now of Christ or of the Spirit? We have found a passage that shuts everyone's mouth, and not only distinctly asserts freedom of choice, but also distinctly teaches that the keeping of the commandments is easy. How foolish it was of Christ to purchase for us at the price of his shed blood the Spirit we did not need, in order that we might be given a facility in keeping the commandments, when we already have one by nature!

Nay, even Diatribe herself must recant her own words, in which she said that free choice could do nothing good without grace. Let her now say instead that free choice possesses such virtue that it not only wills good, but also finds it an easy task to keep the greatest and indeed all the commandments. Look, if you please, at what comes of having a mind out of sympathy with the subject, how it cannot help betraying itself! Is there still any need to confute Diatribe? Who could confute her more thoroughly than she confutes herself? She must be that beast they talk of which eats itself! How true it is that a liar ought to have a good memory!

We have spoken of this passage in our commentary on Deuteronomy,[c] so here we shall be brief; and we shall discuss it without reference to Paul, who has a powerful treatment of it in Romans 10[:6ff.]. You can see that nothing whatever is stated or even suggested by any syllable here about the ease or difficulty, power or impotence, of free choice or of human being in the matter of keeping or not keeping the commandments, except insofar as those who entangle the Scriptures in the net of their own inferences and fancies make them obscure and ambiguous for themselves so as to be able to make of them what they please. If you cannot use your eyes, at least use your ears or feel your way with your hands! Moses says it is "not above you, neither is it far off. It is not in heaven. . . . Neither is it beyond the sea." What is "above you"? What is "far off"? What is "in heaven"? What is

---

c Cf. WA 14:729–31. The commentary was published in the same year of 1525, when Luther wrote *De servo arbitrio*.

"beyond the sea"? Will they make even grammar and the commonest words obscure for us, till we are able to say nothing certain, just to gain their point that the Scriptures are obscure?

According to my grammar, it is not the quality or quantity of human powers but the distance of places that is signified by these terms. What is meant by "above you" is not a certain strength of will, but a place that is above us. Similarly, "far off," "beyond the sea," and "in heaven" say nothing about any power in human nature, but denote a place at a distance from us, upward, on the right, on the left, backward, or forward. I may be laughed at for making such an obvious point and treating such great individuals to an elementary explanation, as if they were little boys learning their alphabet and I were teaching them to put syllables together. But what am I to do when in so bright a light I see them looking for darkness and earnestly wishing to be blind as they reckon up for us such a succession of centuries, so many geniuses, so many saints, so many martyrs, so many doctors, and with such great authority produce and flaunt this passage of Moses, without ever condescending to examine the syllables of which it consists or to control their own flights of fancy so far as to give a moment's consideration to the passage they are shouting about? Let Diatribe now go on and tell us how it is possible for a single private individual to see what so many public figures, the leading lights of so many centuries, have not seen! For certainly this passage, as even a child could judge, proves them to have been not seldomly blind.

In this engraving from the 1523 publication of Luther's *Das Alte Testament deutsch*, which included the Pentateuch, Moses is depicted as kneeling before God, who appears in the clouds with decorative cherubim resting on columns.

What, then, does Moses mean by these very plain and open words, except that he himself has fulfilled his office as a faithful lawgiver excellently? For he has removed every obstacle to their knowing and keeping clearly before them all the commandments, and left them no room for the excuse that they were unaware of or did not possess the commandments, or had to seek them from elsewhere. Hence if they do not keep them, the fault will lie neither with the law nor with the lawgiver, but with themselves; for since the law is there, and the lawgiver has taught it, there remains no excuse on the grounds of ignorance, but only a charge of negligence and disobedience. It is not necessary, he says, to fetch laws from heaven or from places overseas or a long way off, nor can you pretend that you have not heard of them or do not possess them, for you have them close at hand. You have heard them by God's command through my lips, you have understood them in your heart and have received them as a subject of constant reading and oral exposition by the Levites in your midst, as this very word and book of mine bear witness. All that remains is for you to do them. I ask you, what is here attributed to free choice, beyond the fact that it is required to observe the laws given to it, and that any excuse of ignorance or absence of laws is taken away.

These are just about all the texts which Diatribe quotes from the Old Testament in support of free choice, and when these are dismissed, nothing remains that is not equally dismissed, whether she quotes any more or intends to quote more. For she can quote nothing but imperative or subjunctive or optative expressions, which signify, not what we do or can do (as we have so often told Diatribe in answer to her repeated assertions), but what we ought to do and what is demanded of us, in order that we may be made aware of our impotence and brought to the knowledge of sin. Otherwise, if by the addition of inferences and similes invented by human reason these texts prove anything, they prove this, that free choice consists not simply of some little bit of endeavor or desire, but of a full and free ability and power to do everything without the grace of God, without the Holy Spirit. Hence nothing is further from being proved by all that long, repetitive, and emphatic disputation than what had to be proved, namely, that "probable opinion" whereby free choice is defined as being so impotent that it can will nothing good without grace, but is forced to serve sin, though it possesses an endeavor that must not be ascribed to its own powers—a monstrosity[d] indeed that can do nothing by its own powers, yet has an endeavor among its powers, and consists in a quite obvious contradiction.

d   Lat., *monstrum.*

[New Testament Passages:
Matthew 23:37—Human Beings Must Not Pry
into the Secret Will of God]

We come now to the New Testament, where again a host of imperative verbs is mustered in support of that miserable bondage of free choice, and the aid of carnal Reason[117] with her inferences and similes is called in, just as in a picture or a dream you might see the king of the flies[118] with his lances of straw and shields of hay arrayed against a real and regular army of seasoned human troops. That is how the human dreams of Diatribe go to war with the battalions of divine words.

First, there steps forward as a sort of Achilles[119] of the flies that saying from Matthew 23[:37]: "Oh Jerusalem, Jerusalem, how often would I have gathered your children together, and you would not!" If all is determined by necessity, she says, could not Jerusalem rightly reply to the Lord: "Why do you torment yourself with vain tears? If you did not wish us to listen to the prophets, why did you send them? Why impute to us what has been done by your will and our necessity?" That is what Diatribe says. And here is our reply. Let us grant for the moment that this inference and proof of hers is right and good; what in fact is proved by it? The probable opinion which says that free choice cannot will the good? It instead proves that the will is free, sound, and capable of doing everything the prophets have said. But that is not what Diatribe set out to prove.

Indeed, let Diatribe herself reply to the following questions. If free choice cannot will good, why is it blamed for not having given heed to the prophets, to whom as teachers of good things it could not give heed by its own powers? Why does Christ weep vain tears, as if they could have willed what he certainly knows they cannot will? Let Diatribe, I say, acquit Christ of insanity in order to maintain that probable opinion of hers, and our opinion will soon be quit of that Achilles of the flies. This passage from Matthew, therefore, either proves total free choice or it militates just as strongly against Diatribe herself and strikes her down with her own weapon.

We say, as we have said before, that the secret will of the Divine Majesty is not a matter for debate, and the human temerity which with continual perversity is always neglecting necessary things in its eagerness to probe this one, must be called

117. This combination of words shows that, for Luther, "carnal" is more a theological qualification than a biological description.

118. Luther might not only have in mind the strange image of fighting flies, but it is noteworthy that "Baal Zebub" means "man of the flies," as Luther mentioned in his explanation of Rom. 11:4 in his early lecture on the Romans.

119. This Greek hero of the Trojan War was invulnerable except in his heel.

120. The *absconditia*, "hiddenness of God in light," is a popular idea in medieval mystical thinking.

off and restrained from busying itself with the investigation of these secrets of God's majesty, which it is impossible to penetrate because he dwells in light inaccessible,[120] as Paul testifies [1 Tim. 6:16]. Let it occupy itself instead with God incarnate, or as Paul puts it, with Jesus crucified, in whom are all the treasures of wisdom and knowledge, though in a hidden manner [Col. 2:3]; for through Christ it is furnished abundantly with what it ought to know and ought not to know. It is God incarnate, moreover, who is speaking here: "I would . . . you would not"—God incarnate, I say, who has been sent into the world for the very purpose of willing, speaking, doing, suffering, and offering to all human beings everything necessary for salvation. Yet Christ offends many, who being either abandoned or hardened by that secret will of the Divine Majesty do not receive him as he wills, speaks, does, suffers, and offers, as John says: "The light shines in the darkness, and the darkness does not comprehend it" [John 1:5]; and again: "He came to his own home, and his own people received him not" [John 1:11]. It is likewise the part of this incarnate God to weep, wail, and groan over the perdition of the ungodly, when the will of the Divine Majesty purposely abandons and reprobates some to perish. And it is not for us to ask why he does so, but to stand in awe of God who both can do and wills to do such things.

No one, I think, will wish to deny that this will concerning which it is said: "How often would I . . ." was disclosed to the Jews before God became incarnate, inasmuch as they are accused of having killed the prophets before Christ, and so of having resisted God's will. For it is well known among Christians that everything done by the prophets was done in the name of the Christ who was to come, concerning whom it had been promised that he should be God incarnate. Hence whatever has been offered to human beings from the beginning of the world through the ministers of the word is rightly called the will of Christ. [. . .]

[Part IV. Defense of Arguments against Free Choice]

Let the above suffice in answer to the first part of Diatribe, in which she has endeavored to establish free choice. Let us now look at the latter part, in which our arguments—i.e., those whereby free choice is abolished—are confuted. Here you will see what human-made smoke can do against the thunder and lightning of God!

First, after having marshaled innumerable passages of Scripture like a very formidable army in support of free choice (in order to inspire courage in the confessors and martyrs and all the saints of both sexes on the side of free choice, and fear and trembling in all those who deny and sin against free choice), she pretends there is only a contemptible little rabble against free choice, and actually allows only two passages, which are more conspicuous than the rest, to stand on this side, she being intent, of course, only on slaughtering them, and that without much trouble. One of these is Exodus 9[:12]: "The Lord hardened the heart of Pharaoh," and the other, Malachi 1[:2f.]: "Jacob I loved, but Esau I hated." Paul explains both of them at some length in the epistle to the Romans [9:11-21], but in Diatribe's judgment it is surprising that he should have engaged in such a distasteful and unprofitable discussion. Indeed, if the Holy Spirit did not know a little about rhetoric, there was a risk of his being shattered by such an artfully managed show of contempt, so that despairing altogether of the cause he would yield the palm to free choice before the bugle blew. But later on I as a mere reservist will with those two passages let our forces also be seen, although where the fortune of battle is such that one can put ten thousand to flight there is no need of any forces. For if any one text defeats free choice, its numberless forces will profit it nothing.

[Erasmus's Use of Tropes in Interpreting Scripture]

Here, then, Diatribe has discovered a new method of eluding the plainest texts by choosing to find a trope[121] in the simplest and clearest words. For just as previously, when she was pleading for free choice, she eluded all the imperative and subjunctive expressions of the law by tacking on inferences and similes, so now, when she is going to plead against us, she twists all the words of divine promise and affirmation in any way she pleases, by discovering a trope in them, so that on both hands she may be an uncatchable Proteus![e] Indeed, she demands in a very haughty

121. A trope is a rhetorical type of figurative speech.

e See n. 124, p. 161.

way that this should be allowed her by us, since we ourselves when we are hard pressed are in the habit of escaping by discovering tropes. For instance, with regard to the text, "Stretch out your hand to whatever you will" [Eccl. 15:16], we say this means "Grace will stretch out your hand to what it wills"; and with regard to, "Get yourselves a new heart" [Ezek. 18:31], we say, "That is, grace will make you a new heart"; and so forth. It seems most unfair, therefore, if it is permissible for Luther to impose such a forced and twisted interpretation that it should not be even more permissible to follow the interpretations of the most highly approved doctors.

You see, therefore, that the controversy here is not about the text itself, nor is it any longer about inferences and similes, but about tropes and interpretations. When, then, are we ever going to have a text pure and simple, without tropes and inferences, for free choice and against free choice? Has Scripture nowhere any such texts? And is the issue of free choice to be forever in doubt because it is not settled by any certain text, but is argued back and forth with inferences and tropes put forward by human beings at cross purposes with one another, like a reed shaken by the wind?[f]

Let us rather take the view that neither an inference nor a trope is admissible in any passage of Scripture unless it is forced on us by the evident nature of the context and the absurdity of the literal sense as conflicting with one or another of the articles of faith.[122] Instead, we must everywhere stick to the simple, pure, and natural sense of the words that accords with the rules of grammar and the normal use of language as God has created it in human beings. For if everybody is allowed to discover inferences and tropes in the Scriptures just as they please, what will Scripture as a whole be but a reed shaken by the wind or a sort of Vertumnus?[123] Then indeed there will be nothing certain either asserted or proved in connection with any article of faith which you will not be able to quibble away with some trope or other. We ought rather to shun as the deadliest poison every trope that Scripture itself does not force upon us.

Look what happened to that master of tropes, Origen, in his exposition of the Scriptures![124] What fitting objects of attack he

122. This hermeneutical principle Luther would maintain later on, when facing the Swiss reformer Ulrich Zwingli about the tropological interpretation of the words of institution in the Eucharist.

123. The mythological Roman god of seasons, change, and growing fruits and plants. He was able to use his power to change form at will.

124. Erasmus himself had introduced this ancient author into the discussion. Origen, in the third century (c. 185–c. 254), widely used the allegorical interpretation of the Scriptures to harmonize it with Neoplatonic theology. To find the philosophy in

f   Cf. Matt. 11:7.

provides for the calumnies of Porphyry,[125] so that even Jerome[126] thinks that the defenders of Origen have an impossible task. What happened to the Arians in that trope by which they made Christ into a merely nominal God? What has happened in our own time to these new prophets regarding the words of Christ, "This is my body," where one finds a trope in the pronoun "this," another in the verb "is," another in the noun "body"?[127]

What I have observed is this, that all heresies and errors in connection with the Scriptures have arisen, not from the simplicity of the words, as is almost universally stated, but from neglect of the simplicity of the words, and from tropes or inferences hatched out of men's own heads. [...]

the Bible, Origen used the so-called fourfold sense of Scripture. According to this theory, widely used in the Middle Ages, in each Bible passage one finds besides the literal or historical meaning a typological, moral, and eschatological one. The typological sense refers to the principles of faith, the moral one to the deeds of human beings, and the eschatological one to the future of the world in God.

125. Porphyry (234–305), with his *Isagoge* ("Introduction"), was one of the most influential philosophical writers of late antiquity in the Middle Ages. Though he was himself a Neoplatonist, nevertheless, he had attacked Origen because of his interpretation of Scripture.

126. Generally speaking, Jerome (c. 342–420) was quite skeptical toward Origen.

127. Here Luther starts the debate on the Eucharist: Andreas Bodenstein von Karlstadt (1486–1541) was the one who interpreted the word *this* in the sense that not the bread was meant with it, but the lively body of Christ; Zwingli interpreted *is* as "means," and Johannes Oecolampadius (1482–1531) interpreted the noun *body* as a metaphor.

Origen is depicted building a monastic cell with both tools and devotional items nearby. The artist responsible for the design was Maarten De Vos, but the engraving for the volume was done by Johannes Sadeler I (1550–1600) and Raphael Sadeler I, whose surname is at the lower right.

[Exodus 4:21—The Hardening of Pharaoh's Heart]

Here stands the Word of God: "I will harden Pharaoh's heart" [Exod. 4:21]. If you say this should or can be taken to mean "I will permit it to be hardened," I agree that it can be so taken, and that this trope is widely used in popular speech, as for instance: "I spoiled you, because I did not immediately correct you when you did wrong." But this is not the place for that kind of proof. The question is not whether that trope is in use, nor yet whether it is possible for anyone to make use of it in this passage of Paul, but the question is whether it is safe to use it and certain that it is rightly used in this passage, and whether Paul intended it to be so used. What is in question is not the use another person, the reader, may make of it, but the use the writer, Paul himself, makes of it.

What would you do with a conscience that questioned you like this: "Look, the Divine Author says, 'I will harden Pharaoh's heart,' and the meaning of the verb 'to harden' is plain and well known; but a human reader tells me that 'to harden' in this passage means 'to give an occasion of hardening,' inasmuch as the sinner is not immediately corrected. By what authority, for what reason, with what necessity is the natural meaning of the word thus twisted for me? What if the reader and interpreter should be wrong? What proof is there that this twisting of the word ought to take place in this passage? It is dangerous, and indeed impious, to twist the word of God without necessity and without authority." Will you proceed to help this troubled little soul by saying: "Origen thought so" or "Give up prying into such things, because they are curious and superfluous"? She will reply: "This warning ought to have been given to Moses and Paul before they wrote, and for that matter to God

In this etching published in 1530, Moses and Aaron appear before Pharaoh, but the result is harsher treatment for the Hebrew slaves.

also. What is the point of their worrying us with curious and superfluous sayings?"

This miserable refuge of tropes is thus of no help to Diatribe. Our Proteus must be held fast here until she makes us quite certain that there is a trope in this passage, either by the clearest Scripture proofs or by unmistakable miracles. To the fact that she thinks so, even though it is backed by the toilsome researches of all the centuries, we attach no importance whatever, but continue to insist that there can be no trope here, and that what God says must be taken quite simply at its face value. For it is not for us to decide to make and remake the words of God just as we please; otherwise, what remains in the entire Scripture that would not fit in with Anaxagoras's philosophy,[128] so that anything might be made of anything? I might say, for instance, "God created heaven and earth, i.e., set them in order, but did not make them out of nothing," or "God created heaven and earth, i.e., angels and demons, or the righteous and the ungodly." Who, I ask you, will not in that case become a theologian the moment the book is opened?

Let it be fixed and settled, then, that since Diatribe cannot prove that there is a trope inherent in these texts of ours, which she is trying to water down, she is bound to concede to us that the words must be taken as they stand, even though she might prove that the same trope is extremely common elsewhere, both in all parts of Scripture and in everyone's ordinary speech. On this principle, all the arguments of ours that Diatribe has sought to confute are defended at once, and her confutation is discovered to have absolutely no effect, no power, no reality.

When, therefore, she interprets that saying of Moses, "I will harden Pharaoh's heart," as meaning "My forbearance in tolerating a sinner brings some, it is true, to repentance, but it will make Pharaoh more obstinate in wrongdoing," this is prettily said, but there is no proof that it ought to be said; and we are not content with mere statement, but want proof. Similarly, Paul's saying, "God has mercy on whom God wills, and God hardens whom God wills" [Rom. 9:18], she plausibly interprets as "God hardens when God does not at once punish the sinner, and has mercy as soon as God invites repentance by means of afflictions." But what proof is there of this interpretation? Then there is Isaiah's saying: "You have made us err from your ways, you have hardened our heart, so that we fear you not" [Isa. 63:17].

128. According to Aristotle, Anaxagoras, one of the pre-Socratic thinkers, had taught that all things are made out of an innumerous crowd of components that can be combined in manifold different ways.

Granted that Jerome, following Origen, interprets it thus: "One is said to lead astray when one does not at once recall from error," but who can assure us that Jerome and Origen interpret it correctly? In any case, we have an agreement that we are willing to fight each other, not by appealing to the authority of any doctor, but by that of Scripture alone.

Who are these Origens and Jeromes, then, that Diatribe, forgetting our compact, throws at us? For hardly any of the ecclesiastic writers have handled the Divine Scriptures more ineptly and absurdly than Origen and Jerome. To put it in a word, this license of interpretation comes to this, that by a new and unprecedented use of grammar everything is jumbled up, so that when God says, "I will harden Pharaoh's heart," you change the person and take it to mean "Pharaoh hardens himself through my forbearance." "God hardens our hearts" means that we harden ourselves when God delays our punishment. "You, Lord, have made us err" means "We have made ourselves err because you have not punished us." So God's being merciful no longer means that God gives grace or shows compassion, remits sin, justifies, or delivers from evil, but on the contrary, it means that God inflicts evil and punishes!

With these tropes you will end up by saying that God had mercy on the children of Israel when deporting them to Assyria and Babylon, for there God punished sinners, there God invited repentance through afflictions. On the other hand, when bringing them back and liberating them, God did not have mercy on them but hardened them; that is, by God's forbearance and compassion God gave occasion for them to be hardened. In this way, his sending of Christ as Savior into the world will not be said to be an act of mercy on God's part, but an act of hardening, because by this mercy God has given human beings the occasion to harden themselves. On the other hand, by destroying Jerusalem and dispersing the Jews even down to the present day, God is having mercy on them because God is punishing them for their sins and inviting them to repent. When God takes the saints up to heaven on the Day of Judgment, this will not be an act of mercy, but of hardening, inasmuch as it will provide an opportunity for them to abuse God's goodness. But when thrusting the ungodly down into hell, God will be having mercy on them, because God is punishing sinners. I ask you, who ever heard of such acts of divine mercy and wrath as these? [. . .]

. . . God is said to harden when indulging sinners with God's forbearance, but to have mercy when God visits and afflicts them, inviting them to repentance by severity. What, I ask you, did God leave undone in the way of afflicting and punishing Pharaoh and calling him to repentance? Are there not ten plagues recorded? If your definition holds good, that having mercy means punishing and calling the sinner without delay, God certainly had mercy on Pharaoh. Why, then, does God not say, "I will have mercy on Pharaoh" instead of "I will harden Pharaoh's heart"? For in the very act of showing mercy to him, which as you put it means afflicting and punishing him, he says, "I will harden him," which as you put it means, "I will do good to him and bear with him." What more monstrous could be heard? What has now become of your tropes, your Origen, your Jerome? What of your most highly approved doctors whom a solitary individual like Luther is rash enough to contradict? But it is the foolishness of the flesh that compels you to speak like this, for it treats the words of God as a game, not believing them to be meant seriously.

The actual text of Moses, therefore, proves unquestionably that those tropes are worthless fictions in this passage, and that something far other and greater, above and beyond beneficence or affliction and punishment, is signified by the words "I will harden Pharaoh's heart," for we cannot deny that both of those methods were tried in Pharaoh's case with the utmost care and concern. For what wrath and chastisement could have been more prompt than when he was smitten with so many signs and plagues that even Moses himself testifies that there never were any to equal them? Why, Pharaoh himself is moved by them more than once and seems to be coming to his senses, though he is not moved deeply or with abiding results. What forbearance and beneficence, furthermore, could be more generous than when God so readily takes away the plagues and so often remits his sin, so often restores blessings and so often removes calamities? Yet neither is of any avail, and God still says, "I will harden Pharaoh's heart." You see, therefore, even if your ideas of hardening and mercy (that is, your glosses and tropes) are admitted to the fullest extent, as supported by custom and precedent, and such as one can see in the case of Pharaoh, there is still a hardening, and the hardening of which Moses speaks must be of a different sort from that of which you dream. [. . .]

[How God's Omnipotence
Can Be Said to Work Evil]

It may perhaps be asked how God can be said to work evils in us, such as hardening, giving human beings up to their lusts [Rom. 1:24], leading them astray, and so forth. We ought, of course, to be content with the words of God, and believe quite simply what they say, since the works of God are entirely beyond description. Yet in order to humor Reason, which is to say human stupidity, I am willing to be a silly stupid and see whether with a bit of babbling we can in any way move her.

To begin with, even Reason and Diatribe admit that God works all in all [1 Cor. 12:6] and that without God nothing is affected or effective; for God is omnipotent, and this belongs to God's omnipotence, as Paul says to the Ephesians. Now, Satan and human being, having fallen from God and been deserted by God, cannot will good, that is, things which please God or which God wills; but instead they are continually turned in the direction of their own desires, so that they are unable not to seek the things of self. This will and nature of theirs, therefore, which is thus averse from God, is not something nonexistent.[129] For Satan and ungodly human being are not nonexistent or possessed of no nature or will, although their nature is corrupt and averse from God. That remnant of nature, therefore, as we call it, in the ungodly human being and Satan, as being the creature and work of God, is no less subject to divine omnipotence and activity than all other creatures and works of God.

Since, then, God moves and actuates all in all, God necessarily moves and acts also in Satan and ungodly humans. But God acts in them as they are and as found by God; that is to say, since they are averse and evil, and caught up in the movement of this divine omnipotence, they do nothing but averse and evil things. It is like a horseman riding a horse that is lame in one or two of its feet; his riding corresponds to the condition of the horse, that is to say, the horse goes badly. But what is the horseman to do? If he rides such a horse alongside horses that are not lame, this will go badly while they go well, and it cannot be otherwise unless the horse is cured. Here you see that when God works in and through evil persons, evil things are done, and yet God cannot act maliciously although God does evil through evil human beings, because one who is good cannot act maliciously; yet God uses evil instruments that cannot escape the sway and motion of God's omnipotence.

It is the fault, therefore, of the instruments, which God does not allow to be idle, that evil things are done, with God setting them in motion. It is just as if a carpenter were cutting badly with a chipped and jagged ax. Hence it comes about that the ungodly human beings cannot but continually err and sin because they are caught up in the movement of divine power and not allowed to be idle, but will, desire, and act according to what kind of persons they are.

All this is settled and certain if we believe that God is omnipotent and also that the ungodly is a creature of God, although as one averse from God and left to God without the Spirit of God, this human being cannot will or do good. The omnipotence of God makes it impossible for the ungodly to evade the motion and action of God, for they are necessarily subject to it and obey it. But this corruption or aversion from God makes it impossible for the creature to be moved and carried along with good effect. God cannot lay aside his omnipotence on account of human beings' aversion, and ungodly human beings cannot alter their own aversion. It thus comes about that human beings perpetually and necessarily sin and err until they are put right by the Spirit of God.

Now in all this, Satan still reigns in peace; under this movement of divine omnipotence, the devil keeps its court undisturbed [Luke 11:21]. Next, however, follows the business of hardening, which can be illustrated thus: The ungodly, as we have said, are like Satan, the prince of the ungodly, in being wholly intent on their own interests; these human beings do not seek after God or care about the things that are God's, but they seek their own wealth, their own glories, works, wisdom, power, and in short their own kingdom, and these they wish to enjoy in peace. But if anyone resists or attempts to encroach upon any of these things, then by the same aversion from God that leads them to seek them, these ungodly human beings are moved to indignation and rage against their adversary and are as incapable of not being angry as of not desiring and seeking; and they are as incapable of not desiring as of not existing, for they are a creature of God, though a vitiated one.

This is the well-known fury of the world against the gospel of God. For by means of the gospel that Stronger One comes who is to overcome the peaceful keeper of the court,[g] and condemns those desires for glory, wealth, wisdom, and righteousness of one's own, and everything in which human beings trust. This provocation of the ungodly, when God says or does to them the opposite of what they wish, is itself their hardening or worsening. For not only are they in themselves averse through the very corruption of their nature, but they become all the more averse and are made much worse when their aversion is resisted or thwarted. So it was when God proposed to wrest ungodly Pharaoh's tyranny from him; God provoked him and increased the hardness and stubbornness of his heart by thrusting at him through the word of Moses, who threatened to take away his kingdom and withdraw the people from his tyranny, without giving him the Spirit inwardly but permitting his ungodly corrupt nature under the rule of Satan to catch fire, flare up, rage, and run riot with a kind of contemptuous self-confidence.

Let no one suppose, therefore, when God is said to harden or to work evil in us (for to harden is to make evil), that God does so by creating evil in us from scratch. [. . .] God works evil in us, i.e., by means of us, not through any fault of God, but owing to our faultiness, since we are by nature evil and he is good; but as God carries us along by God's own activity in accordance with the nature of God's omnipotence, good as God is in God's own being, God cannot help but do evil with an evil instrument, though God makes good use of this evil in accordance with God's wisdom for God's own glory and our salvation.

In this way God finds the will of Satan evil, not because God creates it so, but because it has become evil through God's deserting it and Satan's sinning;[130] and taking hold of it in the course of Satan's working, God moves it in whatever direction God pleases. [. . .]

It is thus that God hardens Pharaoh, when presenting to the ungodly and evil will a word and work which that will hates—owing of course to its inborn defect and natural corruption. And since God does not change it inwardly by the Spirit, but keeps on presenting and obtruding God's words and works from without, while Pharaoh keeps his eye on his own strength, wealth, and power, in which by the same natural defect he puts his

130. Here Luther explains the counterposition of God and Satan in a way that is not fully dualistic.

g　Cf. Luke 11:22.

trust, the result is that Pharaoh is puffed up and exalted by his own imagined greatness on the one hand, and moved to proud contempt on the other by the lowliness of Moses and the abject form in which the word of God comes, and is thus hardened and then more and more provoked and exasperated the more Moses presses and threatens him. Now, this evil will of his would not be set in motion or hardened if left to itself, but when the omnipotent Mover drives it along with inevitable motion like the rest of the creatures, it must of necessity will something. Then, as soon as God presents to it from without something that naturally provokes and offends it, it becomes as impossible for Pharaoh to avoid being hardened as it is for him to avoid either the action of divine omnipotence or the aversion or wickedness of his own will. The hardening of Pharaoh by God, therefore, takes place as follows: God confronts his wickedness outwardly with an object that the pharaoh naturally hates, without ceasing inwardly to move by omnipotent motion the evil will which is found there; and Pharaoh in accordance with the wickedness of his will cannot help hating what is opposed to him and trusting in his own strength, until he becomes so obstinate that he neither hears nor understands, but is possessed by Satan and carried away like a raving madman.

If we have carried conviction on this point, we have won our case, and having exploded the human tropes and glosses, we can take the words of God literally, with no necessity to make excuses for God or to accuse God of injustice.[131] [. . .]

[How God's Foreknowledge Imposes Necessity]

But let us look also at Paul, who takes up this passage from Moses in Romans 9[:15-18]. How miserably Diatribe is tormented here; to avoid losing free choice she twists herself into all sorts of shapes. At one moment she says that there is a necessity of consequence but not of the consequent; at another that there is an ordained will, or will signified, which can be resisted, and a will purposed, which cannot be resisted. At another the passages quoted from Paul are not opposed to free choice, for they are not speaking of a human being's salvation. At another the foreknowledge of God presupposes necessity, while at yet another it does not. At another grace preveniently moves the will to will, accompanies it on its way, and gives it a happy issue. At

131. Luther summarizes by saying, "God was quite certain, and announced with utmost certainty, that Pharaoh was to be hardened, because God was quite certain that Pharaoh's will could neither resist the notion of God's omnipotence nor lay outside its own badness nor welcome the introduction of its adversary, Moses" (LW 33:180).

another the First Cause does everything, and at yet another it acts through secondary causes while remaining itself at rest. In these and similar bits of juggling with words, [Diatribe's] only aim is to gain time by distracting our attention for a while from the main issue to something else. She credits us with being as stupid and senseless or as little concerned about the subject as she is herself. Or else, just as little children in fear or at play will put their hands over their eyes and then imagine that nobody sees them because they see nobody, so in all sorts of ways Diatribe, who cannot bear the rays, or rather lightning flashes, of the clearest possible words, pretends that she does not see the real truth of the matter, hoping to persuade us also to cover our eyes so that even we ourselves may not see.

But these are all signs of a mind under conviction and rashly struggling against invincible truth. That figment about the necessity of consequence and of the consequent has been refuted above. Diatribe may pretend and pretend again, quibble and quibble again, as much as she likes, but if God foreknew that Judas would be a traitor, Judas necessarily became a traitor, and it was not in the power of Judas or any creature to do differently or to change his will, though he did what he did willingly and not under compulsion, but that act of will was a work of God, set in motion by God's omnipotence, like everything else. For it is an irrefutable and self-evident proposition that God does not lie and is not deceived. There are no obscure or ambiguous words here, even if all the most learned human beings of all the centuries are so blind as to think and speak otherwise. And however much you are perplexed by it, your own and everyone else's conscience is convinced and compelled to say that if God is not deceived in what God foreknows, then the thing foreknown must of necessity take place; otherwise, who could believe God's promises, who would fear God's threats, if what God promises or threatens does not follow necessarily? Or how can God promise or threaten if God's foreknowledge is fallible or can be hindered by our mutability? Clearly this very great light of certain truth stops everyone's mouth, puts an end to all questions, ensures the victory over all evasive subtleties.

We know, of course, that human foreknowledge is fallible. We know that an eclipse does not occur because it is foreknown, but is foreknown because it is going to occur.[132] But what concern have we with that sort of knowledge? We are arguing about the

---

132. Indeed, the antic tradition and medieval astronomical tables enabled human beings in early modern times to predict eclipses quite exactly.

foreknowledge of God; and unless you allow this to carry with it the necessary occurrence of the thing foreknown, you take away faith and the fear of God, make havoc of all the divine promises and threatenings, and thus deny God's very divinity. But even Diatribe herself, after a long struggle in which she has tried every possible way out, is at length compelled by the force of truth to admit our view when she says: "The question of the will and the determination of God is more difficult. For God to will and foreknow are the same thing. And this is what Paul means by 'Who can resist God's will if God has mercy on whom God wills and hardens whom God wills?' Truly if there were a king who carried into effect whatever he willed, and nobody could resist him, he could be said to do whatever he willed. Thus the will of God, since it is the principal cause of all things that take place, seems to impose necessity on our will." So says she; and we can at last thank God for some sound sense in Diatribe. [...]

Granted foreknowledge and omnipotence, it follows naturally by an irrefutable logic that we have not been made by ourselves, nor do we live or perform any action by ourselves, but by God's omnipotence. And seeing that God knew in advance that we should be the sort of people we are, and now makes, moves, and governs us as such, what imaginable thing is there, I ask you, in us which is free to become in any way different from what God has foreknown or is now bringing about? Thus God's foreknowledge and omnipotence are diametrically opposed to our free choice, for either God can be mistaken in foreknowing and also err in action (which is impossible) or we must act and be acted upon in accordance with God's foreknowledge and activity. By the omnipotence of God, however, I do not mean the potentiality by which God could do many things which God does not,[133] but the active power by which God potently works all in all [cf. 1 Cor. 12:6], which is the sense in which Scripture calls God omnipotent. This omnipotence and the foreknowledge of God, I say, completely abolish the dogma of free choice. Nor can the obscurity of Scripture or the difficulty of the subject be made a pretext here; the words are quite clear and known even to schoolboys, and what they say is plain and easy and commends itself even to the natural judgment of common sense, so that it makes no difference hence how great a tally you have of centuries, times, and persons who write and teach differently.[134] [...]

133. This was the definition of the absolute power in the *Via moderna*. The Scholastic thinkers referred to it to show the wide range of possibilities God could have realized if God had wanted to do so.

134. Luther's argument here focuses on the relationship between God and God's creation: Omnipotence excludes any other power, for example, a human one. And God's foreknowledge in itself includes the knowledge of all future things, so that, in Luther's view, there cannot be any liberty for changing them.

[Jacob and Esau]

So much for the first passage, which has been about the hardening of Pharaoh, but which has in fact involved all the passages
and engaged a large part of our resources, invincible as they are.
Now let us look at the second, about Jacob and Esau, of whom
it was said before they were born: "The elder shall serve the
younger" [Gen. 25:23].[135] Diatribe gets round this passage by
saying that it "does not properly apply to the salvation of man.
For God can will that a human being, willy-nilly, be a slave or a
pauper, and yet not so as to be excluded from eternal salvation."
I beg you to notice how many sidetracks and bolt-holes a slippery
mind will seek out when it runs away from the truth; yet it does
not succeed in escaping. Suppose this passage does not apply to
the salvation of the human being (though more of this below).
Does this mean that Paul achieves nothing by quoting it [Rom.
9:12]? Are we to make out that Paul is ridiculous or inept in so
serious a discussion? That is the sort of thing that Jerome does,
who with a very superior air, but with sacrilege on his lips, dares
in more than one place to say that things have a polemic force
in Paul which in their proper contexts they do not have.[h] This
is as good as saying that when Paul is laying the foundations of
Christian dogma, he does nothing but corrupt the Divine Scriptures and deceive the souls of the faithful with a notion hatched
out of his own head and violently thrust upon the Scriptures.
That is the way to honor the Spirit in Paul, that saint and elect
instrument of God! And where Jerome ought to be read with
discrimination, and this statement ordered with a good many
other impious things which (owing to his halfhearted and dull-
witted way of understanding the Scriptures) that gentleman
writes, Diatribe drags him [Jerome] in quite uncritically, and
without deigning to make things easier by at least an explanatory comment, treats him as an infallible oracle by which she
both judges and modifies the Divine Scriptures. So it is that we
take the impious utterances of human beings as rules and norms
in interpreting Divine Scripture. And we are still surprised that
Scripture should be obscure and ambiguous, and that so many

135. The case of Jacob and Esau was
a main argument for the defenders
of predestination, because of the
use Paul made of it in Rom. 9:13. In
his first explanation of the question
of predestination, *Ad Simplicianum*,
Augustine refers to this extensively.

---

h   Cf. Jerome, Letter 48,13 *Ad Pammachium*. In his disputation against
      Scholastic theology, in September 1517, Luther had defended
      Augustine against the opinion that he would have spoken too harshly.

Teachers of the Early Church should be blind with regard to it when it is treated in this ungodly and sacrilegious manner!

Let therefore the person be anathema who says that things have a polemic force in Paul, which in their proper contexts are not in opposition. For this is only said, not proved, and it is said by those who understand neither Paul nor the passages cited by him, but are misled by taking the words in a sense of their own, that is, in an ungodly sense. For however truly this passage in Genesis 25[:21-23] might be understood of temporal bondage only (which is not the case), yet it is rightly and effectively quoted by Paul to prove that it was not through the merits of Jacob or Esau, but through *the one who calls* that Sarah[136] was told: "The elder will serve the younger" [Rom. 9:11f.]. Paul is discussing whether it was by the virtue or merits of free choice that these two attained to what is said of them, and he proves that it was not, but it was solely by the grace of "God who calls" that Jacob attained to what Esau did not. He proves this, however, by invincible words of Scripture, to the effect that they were not yet born and had done nothing either good or bad [Rom. 9:11]. And the whole weight of the matter lies in this proof; this is what our dispute is all about. [...]

136. Luther means Rebekah.

[The Potter and the Clay]

The third passage [Diatribe] takes up is from Isaiah 45[:9]: "Does the clay say to the one who fashions it, 'What are you making?'" and also Jeremiah 18[:6]: "Like the clay in the potter's hand, so are you in my hand." Again she says that these passages have more polemic force in Paul [Rom. 9:20ff.] than with the prophets from whom they are taken,

Esau (left), famished by a recent hunting expedition, agrees to sell his birthright to Jacob for a bowl of stew and some bread. Illustration by Pierre Eskrich (c. 1550–c. 1590).

since in the prophets they refer to temporal affliction, whereas Paul applies them to eternal salvation and reprobation; so that again she insinuates temerity or ignorance in Paul. But before we consider how she proves that neither of these texts excludes free choice, let me first say this, that Paul does not appear to have taken this passage out of the prophets, nor does Diatribe prove that he has. For Paul usually mentions the name of the writer or explicitly states that he is taking something from the Scriptures, and he does neither of these things here. So it is truer to say that Paul is taking this common simile, which others take for other purposes, and using it himself in his own spirit for a purpose of his own, just as he does with the saying, "A little leaven leavens the whole lump," which in 1 Cor. 5[:6] he applies to corrupt morals and elsewhere uses against those who corrupt the Word of God [Gal. 5:9], in the same way as Christ refers to the leaven of Herod and of the Pharisees [Mark 8:15].

No matter, then, how much the prophets may be speaking of temporal affliction (and I refrain from discussing that now, so as to avoid being so often taken up and sidetracked by irrelevant questions), Paul nevertheless uses it in his own spirit against free choice. But as for the idea that freedom of choice is not lost if we are as clay in God's hands when he afflicts us, I do not see the point of it or why Diatribe contends for it, since there is no doubt that afflictions come upon us from God against our will, and put us under the necessity of bearing them willy-nilly, nor is it in our power to avert them, although we are exhorted to bear them willingly. [. . .]

[Part V. Rebuttal of Erasmus's Critique of the Assertio]

[Genesis 6:3 and the Biblical Meaning of "Flesh"]

At length Diatribe comes to the passages cited by Luther against free choice, with the intention of confuting them too. The first of them is Genesis 6[:3]: "My spirit shall not abide in human being forever, for this is flesh." First, she argues that "flesh" here does not mean wicked desire, but weakness. Then she expands Moses' text, to the effect that "this saying does not apply to the whole human race, but only to the human beings of that day," and so it means "in these people." Moreover, it does not apply to all the human beings even of that age, since Noah is excepted. Finally, on the authority of Jerome,[i] she says that in Hebrew this saying gives a different impression, namely, of the clemency and not the severity of God—hoping perhaps to persuade us that since this saying does not apply to Noah but to the wicked, it is not the clemency but the severity of God that applies to Noah, while clemency and not severity applies to the wicked.

But let us leave these frivolities of Diatribe's, who never fails to make it clear that she regards the Scriptures as fables. With Jerome's trifling here we have no concern; it is certain he proves nothing, and we are not discussing Jerome's views but the meaning of Scripture. Let the perverter of Scripture pretend that the Spirit of God signifies indignation. We say he doubly lacks proof. First, he cannot produce a single passage of Scripture in which the Spirit of God stands for indignation, since, on the contrary, kindness and sweetness are everywhere attributed to the Spirit. Second, if he did chance to prove that the Spirit stands for indignation in some place, he still could not prove it to be a necessary consequence that Spirit should be so understood in this passage also. Similarly, he may pretend that flesh stands for weakness, yet he proves just as little. For when Paul calls the Corinthians carnal [1 Cor. 3:3], this certainly does not signify a weakness, but a fault, for he accuses them of forming sects and parties, which is not a matter of weakness or lack of capacity for more solid doctrine, but malice and the old leaven [1 Cor. 5:7f.], which he bids them cleanse out. Let us look at the Hebrew.

"My spirit shall not judge in human beings forever, for they are flesh"—that is what Moses literally says.[137] And if we would only get rid of our own dreams, the words as they stand are, I think, adequately plain and clear. That they are, moreover, spoken by God in wrath is sufficiently shown by what precedes and follows, together with the resultant flood. The reason for Moses' speaking them was that the children of human beings were marrying wives from the mere lust of the flesh, and then so filling the earth with violence that they compelled God in God's wrath to hasten the flood, and only delay for a hundred and twenty years [Gen. 6:3] what God would otherwise never have brought about at all. Read Moses attentively, and you will see plainly that this is what he means. But is there any wonder that the Scriptures are obscure, or that with them you can establish not only a

137. Here Luther assumes the traditional understanding of the time that Moses was author of the Pentateuch.

---

i Jerome, *Liber quaestionum hebraicorum in Genesim* 6:3.

free but even a divine choice, when you are allowed to play about with them as if you wanted to make a Virgilian patchwork out of them? That is what you call solving problems and removing difficulties by means of an "explanation." But it was Jerome and his master Origen who filled the world with such trifle, and set this pestilent example of not paying attention to the simplicity of the Scriptures.

For me it was enough to find proof in that passage that God called human beings flesh, and so far flesh that the Spirit of God could not abide among them but at an appointed time was to be withdrawn from them. For what God means by saying that the Spirit will not judge among human beings forever, God goes on to explain about setting a limit of a hundred and twenty years during which God will continue to judge. God contrasts "spirit" with "flesh," however, because human beings as being flesh give no admittance to the Spirit, while God being Spirit cannot approve of the flesh, and that is why the Spirit is to be withdrawn after a hundred and twenty years. So you may take Moses' text to mean: "My Spirit, which is in Noah and other holy men, accuses the ungodly by means of the preached word and the life of the godly—for to judge among human beings is to be active among them in the ministry of the word, convincing, rebuking, and exhorting, in season and out of season [2 Tim. 4:2]—but all in vain, because they are blinded and hardened by the flesh, and get worse the more they are judged, just as it always happens when the Word of God comes into the world, that human beings grow worse the more they are instructed. And this has the effect of hastening the wrath, just as the Flood was hastened then, for it not only means that sin is committed but also that grace is despised, and as Christ says: 'When the light comes, human beings hate the light'" [John 3:19].

Since, therefore, on the testimony of God himself, human beings are flesh and have a taste for nothing but the flesh, it follows that free choice avails for nothing but sinning.[138] [. . .] So a Christian should know that Origen and Jerome and all their tribe are perniciously wrong when they deny that flesh stands for ungodly desire in such passages. In 1 Cor. 3[:3], for example, "You are still of the flesh" refers to ungodliness. For Paul means that there are still some ungodly ones among them, and that even the godly, insofar as they have a taste for things carnal, are of the flesh, although they are justified through the Spirit.

138. In this passage, *flesh* is meant in a strictly theological sense, contrasted with the divine spirit, not with human mind.

In short, what you will find in the Scriptures is this: Wherever flesh is treated as in opposition to spirit, you can generally take flesh to mean everything that is contrary to the Spirit, as [in John 6:63]: "The flesh is of no avail."[139] But where flesh is treated on its own, you may take it that it signifies the bodily constitution and nature, as for example: "They shall be two in one flesh" [Matt. 19:5]; "My flesh is food indeed" [John 6:55]; or "The Word became flesh" [John 1:14]. In these passages you can drop the Hebraism and say "body" instead of "flesh," for the Hebrew language has only the one word "flesh" for what we express by the two words *flesh* and *body*, and I wish this distinction of terms had been observed in translation throughout the whole canon of Scripture. My passage from Genesis 6, will thus, I think, still stand firmly against free choice, when free choice is proved to be flesh, which Paul in Romans 8[:7] says cannot submit to God (as we shall see in that passage), and which Diatribe herself says can will nothing good. [...]

[The Whole Human Being— Body, Soul, and "Spirit"—Is "Flesh"]

[...] We call ungodly anyone who is without the Spirit of God, for Scripture says it is to justify the ungodly that the Spirit is given. But when Christ distinguishes the Spirit from the flesh by saying: "That which is born of the flesh is flesh," and adds that what is born of the flesh cannot see the kingdom of God [John 3:6, 3], it plainly follows that whatever is flesh is ungodly and under the wrath of God and a stranger to the kingdom of God. And if it is a stranger to the kingdom and Spirit of God, it necessarily follows that it is under the kingdom and spirit of Satan, since there is no middle kingdom between the kingdom of God and the kingdom of Satan, which are mutually and perpetually in conflict with each other. These are the facts that prove that the loftiest virtues of the heathen, the best things in the philosophers, the most excellent things in human beings, which in the eyes of the world certainly appear to be, as they are said to be, honorable and good, are nonetheless in the sight of God truly flesh and subservient to the kingdom of Satan; that is to say, they are impious and sacrilegious and on all counts bad. [...]

139. This biblical passage, a little later, would become central in the debate with Zwingli over the Last Supper. The Zurich reformer used it to deny the real presence of Christ's body in the Eucharist.

140. With this, Luther adopts the traditional Christian exegesis, interpreting Gen. 1:1 in the sense of a *creatio ex nihilo*.

[Divine Grace and Human Cooperation]

[. . .] We are not discussing what we can do through God's working, but what we can do of ourselves; that is to say, whether, created as we are out of nothing,[140] we do or attempt to do anything under the general motion of omnipotence to prepare ourselves for the new creation of the Spirit. Here an answer should have been given, instead of changing the subject. For the answer we give is this: [1] Before human beings are created and are human beings, they neither do nor attempt to do anything toward becoming a creature, and after human beings are created, they neither do nor attempt to do anything toward remaining a creature, but both of these things are done by the sole will of the omnipotent power and goodness of God, who creates and preserves us without our help; but God does not work in us without us, because it is for this God has created and preserved us, that God might work in us and we might cooperate with God, whether outside his kingdom through God's general omnipotence, or inside his kingdom by the special virtue of God's Spirit. [2] In just the same way (our answer continues), before human beings are changed into new creatures of the kingdom of the Spirit, they do nothing and attempt nothing to prepare them for this renewal and this kingdom, and when the human being has been recreated they do nothing and attempt nothing toward remaining in this kingdom, but the Spirit alone does both of these things in us, recreating us without us and preserving us without our help in our recreated state, as also James says: "Voluntarily did God bring us forth by the word of his power, that we might be a beginning of God's creature" [James 1:18]—speaking of the renewed creature. But God does not work without us, because it is for this very thing God has recreated and preserves us, that God might work in us and we might cooperate with God. Thus it is through us that God preaches, shows mercy to the poor, comforts the afflicted. But what is attributed to free choice in all this? Or rather, what is there left for it but nothing? And really nothing! [. . .]

[Erasmus's "Middle Way" Leads Nowhere]

Here we will bring to an end the defense of those arguments of ours which Diatribe has attacked, lest the book grow to an immoderate length. Any that remain, if they are worth noting, will be dealt with among the things we have to assert. For as to what Erasmus repeats in his Epilogue—that if our view stands, then all the precepts, all the threats, all the promises are in vain and there is no room left either for merits or demerits, rewards or punishments; and it is difficult to defend the mercy or even the justice of God if God damns those who cannot help sinning, besides other unfortunate consequences, which have so disturbed the greatest minds as to throw them quite off balance—with all these we have already dealt above. We neither accept nor approve that middle way which (in all sincerity, I believe) he recommends to us suggesting that we should concede "a tiny bit" to free choice, so that the contradictions of Scripture and the above-mentioned difficulties might be more easily removed; for by this middle way, not only is the issue not settled, but we are no further forward. For unless you attribute absolutely everything to free choice, as the Pelagians[j] do, the contradictions of Scripture remain, merit and reward are abolished, the mercy and justice of God are done away, and all the difficulties remain which we seek to avoid by means of a tiny, ineffectual power of free choice, as we have sufficiently shown above. We must therefore go all out and completely deny free choice, referring everything to God; then there will be no contradictions in Scripture, and the difficulties, if not cured, can be endured.

I beg of you, however, my dear Erasmus, not to believe that I am pursuing this case more out of passion than principle. I will not let myself be accused of such hypocrisy as to think one way and write another, and it is not true, as you suggest, that I have grown so heated in defense of my views as to be now for the first time denying free choice altogether, after having previously attributed something to it—you can show me no such thing in my books, I know. There are theses and treatises of mine in print, in which I have continually asserted, down to the present moment, that free choice is nothing; it is a reality—I used that word then—only in name.[141] It is under conviction of the truth, and as challenged and compelled by the debate, that I have thought and written as I have. As to my having gone about it with some vehemence, I acknowledge the fault, if fault it is; or rather, I greatly rejoice that this testimony is borne to me in the

141. Luther does so in his 1518 *Heidelberg Disputation*.

j   See n. 104, p. 201.

world in the cause of God. And may God confirm this testimony at the last day! For no one would be happier than Luther to be commended by the testimony of his time that he had been neither slack nor deceitful in maintaining the cause of truth, but had shown quite enough and even too much vehemence. I should then be blessedly out of reach of Jeremiah's word: "Cursed is that human being who does the work of the LORD with slackness" [Jer. 48:10]. [. . .]

[Part VI.
A Display of the Forces on Luther's Side]

We have come to the last part of this book, in which, as we promised, we must produce our forces against free choice. But we shall not produce all of them; for who could do that in one small book, when the whole of Scripture, every jot and tittle of it, is on our side? Nor is it necessary; on the one hand, because free choice is already vanquished and prostrate by a twofold conquest—once where we prove that everything Diatribe thought to be in its favor is actually against it, and again where we show that the arguments she sought to refute still stand invincible. On the other hand, even if free choice were not already vanquished, no more than a couple of missiles would be required to lay it low, and that would be enough. For what need is there, when an enemy has been killed by any one shot, to riddle his or her dead body with a lot more? Now, therefore, we shall be as brief as the subject will allow. And out of our numerous armies we will bring forward two high commanders with a few of their battalions, namely, Paul and John the Evangelist.

[St. Paul:
Universal Sinfulness Nullifies Free Choice]

This is how Paul, writing to the Romans, enters into an argument against free choice and for the grace of God: "The wrath of God is revealed from heaven against all ungodliness and wickedness of human beings who in wickedness hold back the truth of God" [Rom. 1:18]. Do you hear in this the general verdict on all human beings, that they are under the wrath of God? What else does this mean but that they are deserving of wrath and punishment? He gives as the reason for the wrath, the fact that they do nothing but what deserves wrath and punishment, because they are all ungodly and wicked, and in wickedness hold back the truth. Where now is the power of free choice to attempt anything good? Paul represents it as deserving the wrath of God, and pronounces it ungodly and wicked. And that which deserves wrath and is ungodly, strives and prevails against grace, not for grace. [. . .]

[. . .] Shortly before, Paul has said: "The gospel is the power of God for salvation to everyone who has faith, to the Jew first and also to the Greek" [Rom. 1:16]. Here are no obscure or ambiguous words; "to Jews and Greeks" means that to all human beings the gospel of the power of God is necessary in order that they may have faith and be saved from the wrath that is revealed. I ask you, when he declares that the Jews, rich as they are in righteousness, the law of God, and the power of free choice, are without distinction destitute and in need of the power of God to save them from the wrath that is revealed, and when God makes this power necessary for them, does God not deem them to be under wrath? What human beings will you pick out, then, as not liable to the wrath of God when you are obliged to believe that the finest human beings in the world, the Jews and the Greeks, were in that condition? Again, what exceptions will you make among the Jews and Greeks themselves when Paul without any distinction puts them all into one category and brings them all under the same judgment? Must we suppose that among these two most distinguished peoples there were not any who aspired to virtue? Did none of them strive with all the might of their free choice? But Paul pays no attention to this; he puts them all under wrath, declares them all ungodly and wicked. And must we not believe that in similar terms the rest of the apostles, each in his own sphere, consigned all the other nations also to this wrath?

This passage of Paul's, therefore, stands unyielding in its insistence that free choice, or the most excellent thing in human beings—even the most excellent human beings, who were possessed of the law, righteousness, wisdom, and all the virtues—is ungodly, wicked, and deserving of the wrath of God. Otherwise, Paul's whole argument is valueless; but if it is not, then the division he makes leaves no one on neutral ground, when he assigns salvation to those who believe the gospel, and wrath to all the rest, or takes believers as righteous and unbelievers as ungodly, wicked, and subject to wrath. For what he means is this: The righteousness of God is revealed in the gospel as being of faith, so it follows that all human beings are ungodly and wicked. For it would be foolish of God to reveal righteousness to human beings if they either knew it already or possessed the seeds of it. But seeing that God is not foolish and yet reveals to them the righteousness of salvation, it is evident that free choice, even in the highest type of persons, neither possesses nor is capable of anything, and does not even know what is righteous in the sight of God—unless perhaps the righteousness of God is not revealed to the highest type, but only to the lowest, despite Paul's boasting that he is under obligation both to Jews and Greeks, wise and foolish, barbarians and Greeks [Rom. 1:14].

Therefore, Paul in this passage lumps all human beings together in a single mass, and concludes that, so far from being able to will or do anything good, they are all ungodly, wicked, and ignorant of righteousness and faith. [. . .]

[Free Choice May Do the Works of the Law but Not Fulfill the Law]

In similarly grave terms, this also is said: "No human being will be justified in one's own sight by works of the law" [Rom. 3:20]. This is strong language—"by works of the law"—just as is also "the whole world" and "all the children of humanity." For it should be observed that Paul refrains from mentioning persons and speaks of pursuits, which means that he involves all persons and whatever is most excellent in them. For if he had said that the common people of the Jews, or the Pharisees, or certain ungodly people are not justified, it might have been thought that he had left out some who by the power of free choice and the help of the law were not altogether worthless. But when he condemns the works of the law themselves and makes them impious in the sight of God, it is clear that he is condemning all those whose strength lay in their zeal for the law and its works.

But it was only the best and noblest that were zealous for the law and its works, and that only with the best and noblest parts of themselves, namely, their reason and will. If, therefore, those who exerted themselves in respect of the law and works with the utmost zeal and endeavor both of reason and will—

in other words, with the whole power of free choice, and were assisted besides by the law itself as with divine aid, finding in it instruction and stimulation—if these, I say, are condemned for ungodliness and, instead of being justified, are declared to be flesh in the sight of God, what is there now left in the whole race of human beings that is not flesh and not ungodly? For all are alike condemned who rely on works of the law. For whether they have exercised themselves in the law with the utmost zeal or with only moderate zeal or with no zeal at all does not matter in the least. None of them could do anything but perform works of law, and works of law do not justify; and if they do not justify, they prove their doers ungodly and leave them in this condition; and the ungodly are guilty and deserving of the wrath of God. These things are so clear that no one can utter one syllable against them. [. . .]

But let us appeal to Paul himself as his own best interpreter, where he says in Gal. 3[:10]: "All who rely on works of the law are under a curse; for it is written, 'Cursed be everyone who does not abide by all things written in the Book of the Law, and do them.'" You see here, where Paul is making the same point in the same words as in the epistle to the Romans, that every time he mentions the works of the law he is speaking of all the laws written in the Book of the Law. [. . .]

From all this it is unmistakably plain that for Paul the Spirit is opposed to works of law in just the same way as he is to all other unspiritual things and to the whole gamut of powers and pretensions of the flesh. It is thus clear that Paul takes the same view as Christ, who in John 3[:6] says that everything not of the Spirit is of the flesh, no matter how splendid, holy, and exalted it may be, even including the very finest works of God's law, no matter with what powers they are performed. For there is need of the Spirit of Christ, without whom all our works are nothing else than damnable. It can be taken as settled, then, that by works of the law Paul means not simply ceremonial works, but all the works of the law in its entirety. With this it will also be settled that everything connected with the works of the law is condemned if it is without the Spirit. And one of the things without the Spirit is that very power of free choice—for this is the matter at issue—which is held to be the most outstanding thing a human being has. Now, nothing more excellent can be said of human beings than that they are engaged in works of the law; and Paul is speaking not of those who are engaged in sins and impiety contrary to the law but of these very ones who are engaged in works of the law, that is to say, the best of people, who are devoted to the law, and who, besides the power of free choice, have the help of the law itself to instruct and inspire them. If, therefore, free choice, assisted by the law and occupying all its powers with the law, is of no avail and does not justify, but remains in the ungodliness of the flesh, what may we suppose it is able to do by itself, without the law?

"Through the law," he says, "comes knowledge of sin" [Rom. 3:20]. He shows here how much and how far the law helps. In other words, he shows that free choice by itself is so blind that it is not even aware of sin, but has need of the law to teach it. But what effort to get rid of sin will anyone make who is ignorant of sin? Obviously, he will regard what is sin as no sin, and what is no sin as sin. Experience shows this plainly enough by the way in which the world, in the persons of those whom it regards as the best and most devoted to righteousness and godliness, hates and persecutes the righteousness of God proclaimed by the gospel, calling it heresy, error, and other abusive names, while advertising its own works and ways, which in truth are sin and error, as righteousness and wisdom. With this text, therefore, Paul stops the mouth of free choice when he teaches that through the law sin is revealed to it as to someone ignorant of one's own sin. That is how far he is from conceding to it any power of striving after the good.

Here we have also the answer to that question which Diatribe so often repeats throughout her book: "If we cannot do anything, what is the point of so many laws, so many precepts, so many threats and promises?" Paul here replies: "Through the law comes knowledge of sin." He replies to this question very differently from the way human beings or free choice thinks. He denies that free choice is proved by the law and cooperates with it to produce righteousness; for what comes through the law is not righteousness but knowledge of sin. It is the task, function, and effect of the law to be a light to the ignorant and blind, but such a light as reveals sickness, sin, evil, death, hell, the wrath of God, though it affords no help and brings no deliverance from these, but is content to have revealed them. Then, when human beings become aware of the disease of sin, they are troubled, distressed, even in despair. The law is no help, much less can these human beings help themselves. There is need of another light to reveal the remedy. This is the voice of the gospel, revealing Christ as the deliverer from all these things. [. . .]

[. . .] Paul's words here are absolute thunderbolts against free choice. First: "The righteousness of God is manifested apart from law." This distinguishes the righteousness of God from the righteousness of the law; for the righteousness of faith comes from grace apart from law. The phrase "apart from law" cannot mean anything else but that Christian righteousness exists apart from the works of the law, in the sense that works of law are utterly useless and ineffective for obtaining it, as he says immediately below: "We hold that human beings are justified by faith apart from works of law" [Rom. 3:28], and as he has said above: "No human being will be justified in God's sight by works of the law" [Rom. 3:20]. From all of which it is very clearly evident that all the devoted endeavors of free choice are worth absolutely nothing. For if the righteousness of God exists apart from law and the works of law, must it not much more exist apart from free choice? Especially as the highest aspiration of free choice is to practice moral righteousness, or the works of the law, with the help afforded by the law to its own blindness and ignorance. This expression "apart from" excludes morally good works; it excludes moral righteousness; it excludes preparations for grace. In a word, imagine whatever you may as being within the power of free choice, Paul will still persist in saying that the righteousness of God avails "apart from" that kind of thing. And suppose I allow that free choice can by its own endeavor achieve something—good works, let us say, or the righteousness of the civil or moral law—yet it does not attain to the righteousness of God, nor does God regard its efforts as in any way qualifying it for his righteousness, since he says that his righteousness functions apart from the law. But if it does not attain to the righteousness of God, what will it gain if by its own works and endeavors (if this were possible) it achieves the very sanctity of angels? The words are not, I think, obscure or ambiguous here, nor is there room for any kind of tropes. For Paul clearly distinguishes the two kinds of righteousness, attributing one to the law and the other to grace, maintaining that the latter is given without the former and apart from its works, while the former without the latter does not justify or count for anything. I should like to see, therefore, how free choice can stand up and defend itself against these things.

A second thunderbolt is his saying that the righteousness of God is revealed and avails for all and upon all who believe in Christ, and that there is no distinction [Rom. 3:21f.]. Once more in the plainest terms he divides the entire race of human beings into two, giving the righteousness of God to believers and denying it to unbelievers. Now, no one is crazy enough to doubt that the power or endeavor of free choice is something different from faith in Jesus Christ. But Paul denies that anything outside this faith is righteous in the sight of God; and if it is not righteous in the sight of God, it must necessarily be sin. For with God there is nothing intermediate between righteousness and sin, no neutral ground, so to speak, which is neither righteousness nor sin. Otherwise, Paul's whole argument would come to nothing, since it presupposes this division, namely, that whatever is done or devised among human beings is either righteousness or sin before God: righteousness if faith is present, sin if faith is absent. With men, of course, it is certainly a fact that there are middle and neutral cases, where human beings neither owe one another anything nor do anything for one another. But ungodly human beings sin against God whether eating or drinking or doing whatever, because they perpetually misuse God's creatures in their own impiety and ingratitude, and never for a moment give glory to God from the heart.

It is also no small thunderbolt when he says: "All have sinned and fall short of the glory of God" and "There is no distinction" [Rom. 3:23, 22]. I ask you, could he put it more plainly? Show me a worker of free choice and tell me whether in that enterprise he or she also sins. If there is no sin, why does not Paul make an exception here? Why does he include this worker "without distinction"? It is certain that one who says "all" eliminates no one in any place, at any time, in any work or endeavor. Hence if you exclude any human beings for any kind of effort or work, you make Paul a liar, because the subject of such work and endeavor of free choice is also included in "all" and Paul ought to have had enough respect for him not to place him so freely and without qualification among sinners.

Then there is the statement that they lack the glory of God. You can take "the glory of God" here in two senses, active and passive. This is an example of Paul's habit of using Hebraisms. Actively, the glory of God is that by which God glories in us; passively, it is that by which we glory in God. It seems to me, however, that it ought to be taken passively here—like "the faith of Christ," which suggests in Latin the faith that Christ has, but to the Hebrew mind means the faith we have in Christ. Similarly, "the righteousness of God" in Latin means the righteousness that God possesses, but a Hebrew would understand it as the righteousness that we have from God and in the sight of God. So we take "the glory of God" not in the Latin but in the Hebrew sense as that which we have in God and before God, and which might be called "glory in God." Now, human beings glory in God when they are certain that God is favorable to them and deigns to look kindly upon them, so that the things these human beings do are pleasing in God's sight, or if they are not, they are borne with and pardoned. If, then, the enterprise or endeavor of free choice is not sin, but good in God's sight, it can certainly glory and say with confidence as it glories: "This pleases God, God approves of this, God counts this worthy and accepts it, or at least bears with it and pardons it. For this is the glory of the faithful in God, and those who do not have it are rather put to shame before him." But Paul here denies this, saying that human beings are completely devoid of this glory. Experience proves that he is right; for ask all the exercisers of free choice to a human being, and if you are able to show me one who can sincerely and honestly say with regard to any effort or endeavor of his own, "I know that this pleases God," then I will admit defeat and yield you the palm. But I know there is not one to be found.

Now, if this glory is lacking, so that the conscience dare not say for certain or with confidence that "this pleases God," then it is certain it does not please God. For as human beings believe, so it is with them; and in this case the human beings do not believe with certainty that they please God, although it is necessary to do so, because the offense of unbelief lies precisely in having doubts about the favor of God, who wishes us to believe with the utmost possible certainty that God is favorable. We thus convict them on the evidence of their own conscience that free choice, when it is devoid of the glory of God, is perpetually guilty of the sin of unbelief, together with all its powers, efforts, and enterprises. [. . .]

[The Righteousness of Works and of Faith;
and a Summary of St. Paul's Testimony
Against Free Choice]

Let us take a look here at what Paul says later about the example of Abraham [Rom. 4:1-3]. "If Abraham," he says, "was justified by works, he has something to boast about, but not before God. For what does the Scripture say? 'Abraham believed God, and it was reckoned to him as righteousness.'" Please notice here too the distinction Paul makes by referring to a twofold righteousness of Abraham.

First, there is the righteousness of works, or moral and civil righteousness; but he denies that Abraham is justified in God's sight by this, even if he is righteous in the sight of human beings because of it. With this righteousness, he has indeed something to boast about before human beings, but like the rest he falls short of the glory of God. Nor can anyone say here that it is the works of the law, or ceremonial works, that are being condemned, seeing that Abraham lived so many years before the law was given. Paul is speaking simply about the works Abraham did, and the best ones he did. For it would be absurd to argue as to whether anyone is justified by bad works. If, therefore, Abraham is not righteous because of any works, and if both he himself and all his works remain in a state of ungodliness unless he is clothed with another righteousness, namely, that of faith, then it is plain that no human beings are brought any nearer to righteousness by their works; and what is more, that no works and no aspirations or endeavors of free choice count for anything in the sight of God, but are all adjudged to be ungodly, unrighteous, and evil. For if the human beings are not righteous, neither are their works or endeavors righteous; and if they are not righteous, they are damnable and deserving of wrath.

The other kind of righteousness is the righteousness of faith, which does not depend on any works, but on God's favorable regard and God's "reckoning" on the basis of grace. Notice how Paul dwells on the word "reckoned," how he stresses, repeats, and insists on it. "To one who works," he says, "that person's wages are not reckoned as a gift but as a due. And to one who does not work but has faith in him who justifies the ungodly, that person's faith is reckoned as righteousness, according to the plan of God's grace" [Rom. 4:4f.]. Then he quotes David as saying the same about the "reckoning" of grace: "Blessed are the human beings against whom the Lord will not reckon their sin," etc. [Rom. 4:6ff.]. He repeats the word *reckon* nearly ten times in this chapter. In short, Paul sets the one who works and the one who does not work alongside each other, leaving no room for anyone between them; and he asserts that righteousness is not reckoned to the former, but that it is reckoned to the latter provided he has faith. There is no way of escape for free choice here, no chance for it to get away with its endeavoring and striving. It must be classed either with the one who works or with the one who does not work. If it is classed with the former, so you are told here, it does not have any righteousness reckoned to it, whereas if it is classed with the latter—the one who does not work but has faith in God—then it does have righteousness reckoned to it. But in that case it will no longer be a case of free choice at work, but of a being created anew through faith.

Now, if righteousness is not reckoned to those who work, then clearly their works are nothing but sins, evils, and impieties in the sight of God. Nor can any impudent Sophist break in here with the objection that human beings' works need not be evil, even if they themselves are evil. For Paul purposely speaks, not simply of the human being as a human being, but of the person as a worker, in order to make it unmistakably plain that human works and endeavors themselves are condemned, no matter what their nature, name, or sign may be. It is, however, with good works that he is concerned, since he is arguing about justification and merit. Hence, although with the phrase "one who works" he refers quite generally to all workers and all their works, it is particularly of their good and virtuous works that he is speaking about. Otherwise, there would be no point in his distinction between the "one who works" and the "one who does not work."

I will not here elaborate the very strong arguments that can be drawn from the purpose of grace, the promise of God, the meaning of the law, original sin, or divine election, any one of which would be sufficient by itself to do away completely with free choice. For if grace comes from the purpose or predestination[142] of God, it comes by necessity and not by our effort or endeavor, as we have shown above. Moreover, if God promised

142. "Predestination" as a determination of human salvation or damnation has to be distinguished from "foreknowledge"/ "prescience," which just means that God knows everything even before determining or not.

grace before the law was given, as Paul argues here and in Galatians, then grace does not come from works or through the law; otherwise the promise means nothing. So also faith will mean nothing—although Abraham was justified by it before the law was given—if works count for anything. Again, since the law is the power of sin [1 Cor. 15:56] in that it serves only to reveal and not to remove sin, it makes the conscience guilty before God and threatens it with wrath. That is what Paul means when he says: "The law brings wrath" [Rom. 4:15]. How, then, could there be any possibility of attaining righteousness through the law? And if we receive no help from the law, what help can we expect from the power of choice alone?

Furthermore, seeing that through the one transgression of the one man, Adam, we are all under sin and damnation, how can we attempt anything that is not sinful and damnable? For when he says "all," he makes no exception either of the power of free choice or of any worker, but every human being, whether working or not, endeavoring or not, is necessarily included among the "all." Not that we should sin or be damned through that one transgression of Adam if it were not our own transgression. For who could be damned for another's transgression, especially before God? It does not, however, become ours by any imitative doing of it ourselves, for then it would not be the one transgression of Adam, since it would be we and not Adam who committed it; but it becomes ours the moment we are born—a subject we must deal with some other time. Original sin itself, therefore, leaves free choice with no capacity to do anything but sin and be damned. [. . .]

. . . In Romans 8[:5], where Paul divides the human race into two types, namely, flesh and spirit (just as Christ does in John 3[:6]), he says: "Those who live according to the flesh set their minds on the things of the flesh, but those who live according to the Spirit set their minds on the things of the Spirit." That Paul here calls carnal all who are not spiritual is evident both from this very partition and opposition between spirit and flesh, and from his own subsequent statement: "You are not in the flesh but in the Spirit if the Spirit of God really dwells in you. Anyone who does not have the Spirit of Christ does not belong to him" [Rom. 8:9]. What else is the meaning of "You are not in the flesh if the Spirit of God is in you" but that those who do not have the Spirit are necessarily in the flesh? And if anyone does not belong to Christ, to whom else does one belong but Satan? Clearly, then, those who lack the Spirit are in the flesh and subject to Satan.

Now let us see what he thinks of the endeavor and power of free choice in those he calls carnal. "Those who are in the flesh cannot please God" [Rom. 8:8]. And again: "The mind of the flesh is death" [v. 6]. And again: "The mind of the flesh is enmity toward God" [v. 7]. Also: "It does not submit to God's law, indeed it cannot" [v. 7]. Here let the advocate of free choice tell me this: how something that is death, displeasing to God, hostility toward God, disobedient to God, and incapable of obedience can possibly strive toward the good? For Paul did not choose to say simply that the mind of the flesh is "dead" or "hostile to God," but that it is death itself, hostility itself, which cannot possibly submit to God's law or please God, just as he had said a little before: "For what was impossible to the law, in that it was weak because of the flesh, God has done," etc. [v. 3].

I, too, am familiar with Origen's fable about the threefold disposition of flesh, soul, and spirit, with soul standing in the middle and being capable of turning either way, toward the flesh or toward the spirit.[143] But these are dreams of his own; he states but does not prove them. Paul here calls everything flesh that is without the Spirit, as we have shown. Hence the loftiest virtues of the best of human beings are in the flesh, that is to say, they are dead, hostile to God, not submissive to the law of God and not capable of submitting to it, and not pleasing to God. For Paul says not only that they do not submit, but that they cannot. So also Christ says in Matthew 7[:18]: "A bad tree cannot bear good fruit," and in Matthew 12[:34]: "How can you speak good when you are evil?" You see here not only that we speak evil, but that we cannot speak good. And although he says elsewhere that we who are evil know how to give good gifts to our children [Matt. 7:11], yet he denies that we do good even when we give good gifts, because although what we give is a good creation of God, we ourselves are not good, nor do we give these good things in a good way; and he is speaking to all people, including his disciples. Thus the twin statements of Paul are confirmed, that the righteous live by faith [Rom. 1:17], and that whatsoever is not of faith is sin [Rom. 14:23]. The latter follows from the former, for if there is nothing by which we are justified but faith, it is evident that those who are without faith are not yet justified; and those who are not justified are sinners; and sinners are

143. With this "tripartite" view of human nature, Origen drew from the Platonic anthropology, trying to combine it with Gal. 5:17. The tripartite view, on the basis of 1 Thess. 5:23; Heb. 4:12; and Gen. 2:7 was supported by, e.g., Irenaeus (c. 130–202), Justin Martyr (c. 100–165), Origen, Gregory of Nyssa (c. 335–394), and Basil of Caesarea (c. 330–379).

"bad trees" and cannot do anything but sin and "bear bad fruit." Hence, free choice is nothing but a slave of sin, death, and Satan, not doing and not capable of doing or attempting to do anything but evil.[144] [...]

[The Two Kingdoms, of Christ and of Satan. The Assurance of Faith]

For Christians know there are two kingdoms in the world, which are bitterly opposed to each other. In one of them Satan reigns, who is therefore called by Christ "the ruler of this world" [John 12:31] and by Paul "the god of this world" [2 Cor. 4:4]. It holds captive to its will all who are not snatched away from him by the Spirit of Christ, as the same Paul testifies, nor does he allow them to be snatched away by any powers other than the Spirit of God, as Christ testifies in the parable of the strong man guarding his palace in peace [Luke 11:21]. In the other kingdom, Christ reigns, and his kingdom ceaselessly resists and makes war on the kingdom of Satan. Into this kingdom we are transferred, not by our own power but by the grace of God, by which we are set free from the present evil age and delivered from the dominion of darkness.[145]

The knowledge and confession of these two kingdoms perpetually warring against each other with such might and main would alone be sufficient to confute the dogma of free choice, seeing that we are bound to serve in the kingdom of Satan unless we are delivered by the power of God. These things, I say, the common people know, and they confess them abundantly in their proverbs and prayers, their attitudes and their whole life. [...]

For my own part, I frankly confess that even if it were possible, I should not wish to have free choice given to me, or to have anything left in my own hands by which I might strive toward salvation. For, on the one hand, I should be unable to stand firm and keep hold of it amid so many adversities and perils and so many assaults of demons, seeing that even one demon is mightier than all men, and no human being at all could be saved; and on the other hand, even if there were no perils or adversities or demons, I should nevertheless have to labor under perpetual uncertainty and to fight as one beating the

144. See also *The Freedom of a Christian*, LW 31:327–378, and TAL, vol. 1, pp. 464–538.

145. The famous doctrine of the two kingdoms or of the two regiments was introduced by Luther in his tract about government (*Obrigkeitsschrift*) in 1523. The basic idea is that all human beings are divided up into the kingdom of Jesus Christ and the kingdom of the world or of Satan, as described above. To maintain order in the world and to bring about salvation, God has established two regiments: on the one hand, God reigns by means of the law in its political use, preventing human beings from sin. This regiment is mainly performed by the government. On the other hand, law in its theological use and gospel are preached in the church to redeem all those who come to faith.

air, since even if I lived and worked to eternity, my conscience would never be assured and certain how much it ought to do to satisfy God. For whatever work might be accomplished, there would always remain an anxious doubt whether it pleased God or whether God required something more, as the experience of all self-justifiers proves, and as I myself learned to my bitter cost through so many years.[146] But now, since God has taken my salvation out of my hands into God's hands, making it depend on God's choice and not mine, and has promised to save me, not by my own work or exertion but by God's grace and mercy, I am assured and certain both that God is faithful and will not lie to me, and also that God is too great and powerful for any demons or any adversities to be able to break God or to snatch me from God. "No one," Christ says, "shall snatch them out of my hand, because my Father who has given them to me is greater than all" [John 10:28f.]. So it comes about that, if not all, some and indeed many are saved, whereas by the power of free choice none at all would be saved, but all would perish together. Moreover, we are also certain and sure that we please God, not by the merit of our own working, but by the favor of God's mercy promised to us, and that if we do less than we should or do it badly, God does not hold this against us, but in a parental[k] way pardons and corrects us. Hence the glorying of all the saints in their God.

[The Mercy and Justice of God in the Light of Nature, Grace, and Glory]

Now, if you are disturbed by the thought that it is difficult to defend the mercy and justice of God who damns the undeserving, that is to say, ungodly human beings who are what they are because they were born in ungodliness and can in no way help being and remaining ungodly and damnable, but are compelled by a necessity of nature to sin and to perish (as Paul says: "We were all children of wrath like the rest" [Eph. 2:3], since they are created so by God from seed corrupted by the sin of the one man Adam)—rather must God be honored and revered as supremely merciful toward those whom God justifies and saves,

146. In a personal retrospect, written as a preface to the 1545 edition of his Latin works, Luther wrote of his agony and discovery: "Though I lived as a monk without reproach, I felt that I was a sinner before God with an extremely disturbed conscience. . . . I did not love, yes, I hated the righteous God who punishes sinners . . . I was angry with God. . . . I raged with a fierce and troubled conscience. . . . At last, by the mercy of God, meditating day and night I gave heed to the context of the words, namely, 'In it the righteousness of God is revealed,' as it is written, 'He who through faith is righteous shall live.' . . . There I began to understand that by which the righteous lives by a gift of God, namely, by faith. And this is the meaning: the righteousness of God is revealed by the gospel, namely, the passive righteousness with which merciful God justifies us by faith, as it is written, 'He who through faith is righteous shall live.' Here I felt that I was altogether born again and had entered paradise itself through open gates. There a totally other face of the entire Scripture showed itself to me" (LW 34:336-37).

---

k   The Latin text here has *Paterne*, which means "fatherly."

supremely unworthy as they are, and there must be at least some acknowledgment of God's divine wisdom so that God may be believed to be righteous where God seems to us to be unjust. For if God's righteousness were such that it could be judged to be righteous by human standards, it would clearly not be divine and would in no way differ from human righteousness. But since God is the one true God, and is wholly incomprehensible and inaccessible to human reason, it is proper and indeed necessary that God's righteousness also should be incomprehensible, as Paul also says where he exclaims: "Oh the depth of the riches of the wisdom and the knowledge of God! How incomprehensible are his judgments and how unsearchable his ways!" [Rom 11:33]. But they would not be incomprehensible if we were able in every instance to grasp how they are righteous. What is a human being compared with God? How much is there within our power compared with God's power? What is our strength in comparison with God's resources? What is our knowledge compared with God's wisdom? What is our substance over against God's substance? In a word, what is our all compared with God's?

If, therefore, we confess, as even nature teaches, that human power, strength, wisdom, substance, and everything we have is simply nothing at all in comparison with divine power, strength, wisdom, knowledge, and substance, what is this perversity that makes us attack God's righteousness and judgment only, and make such claims for our own judgment as to wish to comprehend, judge, and evaluate the divine judgment? Why do we

A statue of Pliny the Younger on the façade of the Cathedral of St. Maria Maggiore in Como.

not take a similar line here too, and say, "Our judgment is nothing in comparison with the divine judgment"? Ask Reason herself whether she is not convinced and compelled to confess that she is foolish and rash in not allowing the judgment of God to be incomprehensible when she admits that everything else divine is incomprehensible. In all other matters we grant God the divine majesty that belongs to God alone, and only in respect of God's judgment are we prepared to deny it. We cannot for a while believe that God is righteous, even though God has promised us that when God's glory is revealed, we shall all both see and feel that God has been and is righteous.

I will give an example to confirm this faith and console that evil eye which suspects God of injustice. As you can see, God so orders this corporal world in its external affairs that if you respect and follow the judgment of human reason, you are bound to say either that there is no God or that God is unjust. As the poet says: "Oft I am moved to think there are no gods!"¹ For look at the prosperity the wicked enjoy and the adversity the good endure, and note how both proverbs and that parent of proverbs, experience, testify that the bigger the scoundrel the greater his luck. "The tents of the ungodly are at peace," says Job [12:6], and Ps. 72 [73:12] complains that the sinners of the world increase in riches. Tell me, is it not in everyone's judgment most unjust that the wicked should prosper and the good suffer? But that is the way of the world. Here even the greatest minds have stumbled and fallen, denying the existence of God and imagining that all things are moved at random by blind Chance or Fortune. So, for example, did the Epicureans and Pliny;[147] while Aristotle, in order to preserve his Supreme Being from unhappiness, never lets this Being look at anything but itself, because he thinks it would be most unpleasant for it to see so much suffering and so many injustices. The prophets, however, who did believe in God, had more temptation to regard God as unjust—Jeremiah, for instance, and Job, David, Asaph, and others. What do you suppose Demosthenes and Cicero thought,[148] when after doing all they could they were rewarded with so tragic a death?

147. Pliny the Younger (61–c. 113) had presented his philosophical ideas in his letters, many of which still survive.

148. Demosthenes committed suicide; Cicero was murdered.

1 Ovidius, *Amores* 3,9,36.

Yet all this, which looks so very like injustice in God, and which has been represented as such with arguments that no human reason or light of nature can resist, is very easily dealt with in the light of the gospel and the knowledge of grace, by which we are taught that although the ungodly flourish in their bodies, they lose their souls. In fact, this whole insoluble problem finds a quick solution in one short sentence, namely, that there is a life after this life, and whatever has not been punished and rewarded here will be punished and rewarded there, since this life is nothing but an anticipation, or rather, the beginning of the life to come.

If, therefore, the light of the gospel, shining only through the Word and faith, is so effective that this question which has been discussed in all ages and never solved is so easily settled and put aside, what do you think it will be like when the light of the Word and of faith comes to an end, and reality itself and the Divine Majesty are revealed in their own light? Do you not think that the light of glory will then with the greatest of ease be able to solve the problem that is insoluble in the light of the Word or of grace, seeing that the light of grace has so easily solved the problem that was insoluble in the light of nature?

Let us take it that there are three lights—the light of nature, the light of grace, and the light of glory, to use the common and valid distinction. By the light of nature, it is an insoluble problem how it can be just that a good human being should suffer and a bad human being prosper; but this problem is solved by the light of grace. By the light of grace it is an insoluble problem how God can damn one who is unable by any power of his own to do anything but sin and be guilty. Here both the light of nature and the light of grace tell us that it is not the fault of the unhappy person, but of an unjust God; for they cannot judge otherwise of a God who crowns one ungodly human being freely and apart from merits, yet damns another who may well be less, or at least not more, ungodly. But the light of glory tells us differently, and it will show us hereafter that the God whose judgment here is one of incomprehensible righteousness is a God of most perfect and manifest righteousness. In the meantime, we can only *believe* this, being admonished and confirmed by the example of the light of grace, which performs a similar miracle in relation to the light of nature.

[Conclusion]

[That the Case against Free Choice Is Unanswerable
Let Erasmus Be Willing to Admit]

I will here bring this little book to an end, though I am prepared if need be to carry the debate further. However, I think
quite enough has been done here to satisfy the godly and anyone who is willing to admit the truth without being obstinate.
For if we believe it to be true that God foreknows and predes-
tines all things, that God can neither be mistaken in divine
foreknowledge nor hindered in God's predestation, and that
nothing takes place but as God wills it (as reason itself is forced
to admit), then on the testimony of reason itself there cannot be
any free choice in human being or angel or any creature.

Similarly, if we believe that Satan is the ruler of this world,
who is forever plotting and fighting against the kingdom of
Christ with all its powers, and that Satan will not let human
beings go who are its captives unless they are forced to do so by
the divine power of the Spirit, then again it is evident that there
can be no such thing as free choice.

Similarly, if we believe that original sin has so ruined us
that even in those who are led by the Spirit it causes a great deal
of trouble by struggling against the good, it is clear that in a
human being devoid of the Spirit there is nothing left that can
turn toward the good, but only toward evil.

Again, if the Jews, who pursued righteousness to the utmost
of their powers, rather ran headlong into unrighteousness, while
the Gentiles, who pursued ungodliness, attained righteousness
freely and unexpectedly, then it is also manifest from this very
fact and experience that human beings without grace can will
nothing but evil.

To sum up: If we believe that Christ has redeemed human
beings by his blood, we are bound to confess that the whole
human being was lost; otherwise, we should make Christ either
superfluous or the redeemer of only the lowest part of humanity,
which would be blasphemy and sacrilege.

My dear Erasmus, I beg you now for Christ's sake to do at
last as you promised; for you promised you would willingly yield
to anyone who taught you better. Have done with respecting of

persons! I recognize that you are a great man, richly endowed with the noblest gifts of God—with talent and learning, with eloquence bordering on the miraculous, to mention no others—while I have and am nothing, unless I may venture to boast that I am a Christian. Moreover, I praise and commend you highly for this also, that unlike all the rest, you alone have attacked the real issue, the essence of the matter in dispute, and have not wearied me with irrelevancies about the papacy, purgatory, indulgences, and such like trifles (for trifles they are rather than basic issues), with which almost everyone hitherto has gone hunting for me without success. You and you alone have seen the question on which everything hinges, and have aimed at the vital spot, for which I sincerely thank you, since I am only too glad to give as much attention to this subject as time and leisure permit. If those who have attacked me hitherto had done the same, and if those who now boast of new spirits and new revelations would still do it, we should have less of sedition and sects and more of peace and concord. But God has in this way through Satan punished our ingratitude.

Unless, however, you can conduct this case differently from the way you have in this diatribe, I could very much wish that you would be content with your own special gift, and would study, adorn, and promote languages and literature as you have hitherto done with great profit and distinction. I must confess that in this direction you have done no small service to me too, so that I am considerably indebted to you, and in this regard I certainly respect and admire you most sincerely. But God has not yet willed or granted that you should be equal to the matter at present at issue between us. I say this, as I beg you to believe, in no spirit of arrogance, but I pray that the Lord may very soon make you as much superior to me in this matter as you are in all others. There is no novelty in it if God instructs Moses through Jethro[m] and teaches Paul through Ananias.[n] For as to your saying that you have wandered very far from the mark if you are ignorant of Christ, I think you yourself see what it implies. For it does not follow that everybody will go astray if you or I do. God is preached as being marvelous in God's saints, so that we may

---

m   Exodus 18.
n   Acts 9:10-19.

regard as saints those who are very far from sanctity. And it is not difficult to suppose that you, since you are human, may not have rightly understood or observed with due care the Scriptures or the sayings of the Teachers of the Early Church under whose guidance you think you are attaining your goal; and of this there is more than a hint in your statement that you are asserting nothing, but have only "discoursed." No one writes like that who has a thorough insight into the subject and rightly understands it. I for my part in this book *have not discoursed, but have asserted and do assert*, and I am unwilling to submit the matter to anyone's judgment, but advise everyone to yield assent. But may the Lord, whose cause this is, enlighten you and make you a vessel for honor and glory.

Amen.

Vom abendmal
Christi/Bekendnis
Mart. Luther.

Wittemberg.

1 5 2 8.

M   L

Schlecht vnd recht behuete mich.
Psalm. 25.

In this title-page woodcut for Luther's confession
concerning the Lord's Supper of 1528, Luther's Rose
is held by two cherubs, flanked by Luther's initials.
The quotation near the bottom, from Ps. 25:21, says,
"May integrity and uprightness preserve me" (NRSV).

Confession of the Articles of Faith

against the Enemy of the Gospel and All Kinds of Heresies

1528

GORDON JENSEN

INTRODUCTION

Martin Luther's *Confession of Faith*[1] first appeared in the spring of 1528 as the third and final part of his treatise, *Confession Concerning Christ's Supper*. Luther had been involved in a very public debate on the Lord's Supper that had started four years earlier, and his *Confession Concerning Christ's Supper* was the last major treatise he wrote on the controversy over this sacrament.[2] However, the *Confession of Faith* (Part III) does not deal with the Lord's Supper controversy, except in passing. Instead, Luther reflects on his faith, using the Apostles' Creed as a framework.[3] Struggling with health, the threat of the plague,[4] and the price placed on his head by both the church and state,[5] Luther uses this apparent addendum to delineate his personal faith.

Shortly after the *Confession Concerning Christ's Supper* was printed in 1528, Luther's friend and former colleague Wenceslaus Linck (1482–1563), now a pastor in Nuremberg, asked Luther for permission to publish this creedal confession separately, along with a preface provided by Luther. Luther gave his permission in a letter dated 14 July 1528,[a] but did not provide a

1. "Confession of Faith" is the title given to this piece by the editors to the third part of the "Confessions Concerning Christ's Supper" of 1528; the longer title used here was given when it was first published as a stand-alone document by Linck later the same year (see footnote c below).

2. While Luther wrote a *Brief Confession Concerning the Holy Sacrament* in 1544 (LW 38:279–320) in response to Caspar Schwenkfeld's (1490–1561) attacks, his arguments repeat what he had written in the 1520s. His views on the Lord's Supper did not change or develop in any significant way after this 1528 treatise, as noted in Gordon A. Jensen, "Luther and the Lord's Supper," in Robert Kolb, Irene Dingel, and L'ubomir Batka, eds., *The Oxford Handbook of Martin Luther's*

---

a WA Br 4:494–99, no. 1294 (14 July 1528).

Theology (New York: Oxford University Press, 2014), 322–32.

3. By using the creeds as the framework for his confession of faith, there are, as a matter of course, many cases of Luther using the traditional male language for God, such as "Father" and "Son." While Luther uses this language, however, his focus is on the intra-Trinity relationships and God's relationship to humanity, rather than insisting on the maleness of God.

4. Luther had faced many health struggles in 1527, including an abscess on his lower leg, chest pain, dizziness, and buzzing in his ear. In midsummer, he became severely ill and felt he was going to die. His response to these health crises was to pray and seek absolution from his pastor and colleagues. The plague also broke out in 1527, forcing the university to relocate to Jena. However, Luther stayed in Wittenberg to help provide pastoral care for those afflicted. For more information about his health and the outbreak of the plague in the period leading up to his *Confession of Faith*, see Martin Brecht, *Martin Luther*, vol. 2: *Shaping and Defining the Reformation, 1521–1532*, trans. James L. Schaaf (Minneapolis: Fortress Press, 1990), 204–11.

5. Luther had been condemned by both the Roman Church and the Holy Roman Empire in 1521, and anyone who saw him was to arrest him and turn him over to the authorities. For a detailed description, see Martin Brecht, *Martin Luther*, vol. 1: *His Road to Reformation*, trans. James L. Schaaf (Philadelphia: Fortress Press, 1985), 389–470.

6. The *Schwabach Articles* were written by the Reformation scholars of Wittenberg in the late summer of 1529 in response

Wenceslaus Linck, the publisher of the *Confession of Faith*, had been an Augustinian monk and professor at Wittenberg along with Luther, and was a pastor in Nuremberg.

preface. Luther did ask, however, that Linck insert a paragraph on private confession, which had been inadvertently left out of the original publication.[b] Linck willingly did so, and published the document in Nuremberg later that year,[c] along with his own preface. Later editions were published in Wittenberg, and it was also translated into Latin in 1539 by Johannes Bugenhagen (1485–1558).[d] One of Luther's former professors from

b   WA Br 4:496 n.6.

c   Wenceslaus Linck published this confession under the title *Bekenntnis der Artikel des Glaubens wider die Feind des Evangelii und allerlei Ketzereien* (*Confession of the Articles of Faith against the Enemy of the Gospel and All Kinds of Heresies*), as noted in WA 26:250.

d   *Confessiones Fidei Duae altera D. Doctoris Martini Lutheri, altera D. Ioannis Bugenhagii Pomerani denuo recognitae, & singulari consilio iam primum latinæ editae.* Witebergae 1539 (WA 26:255).

Erfurt, Hieronymus Dungersheim (1465–1540), published a version of this *Confession* in Leipzig in 1530, with many hostile glosses inserted.[e]

Once published, the *Confession* had an impact in two directions. First, it formed a prototype for corporate, evangelical statements of faith by the Wittenberg theologians. Its influence can be seen in the *Schwabach Articles* of 1529,[6] which in turn shaped the *Augsburg Confession*. Luther's *Smalcald Articles* from 1537 also echo the *Confession*, since both use the Apostles' Creed as the basis for outlining Luther's theology, while also providing a critique of various current practices within the Roman Church. For example, Christian ethics and evangelical church practices are addressed within the second and third articles of this creedal structure. Yet even while addressing ethics and practice, Luther insists that salvation is by God's grace and action alone. In this *Confession*, he bluntly states, "To be holy and to be saved are two completely different things."[f] A person is made holy by living faithfully in the estates, or orders in the world, where God deliberately places them.[7]

Second, the *Confession* became a popular model for the "good confession" of the Evangelical faith for those facing illness or imminent death. Concerned that his opponents would misrepresent his faith after he died, this *Confession* provided an opportunity for Luther to make clear where he stood within the faith tradition. In this way, both the *Confession* and the *Smalcald Articles* reflect Luther's desire to provide people with a model for a deathbed testimony to their evangelical faith. It was a chance to state once again, "Here I stand, may God help me, Amen."[8] For example, when Dorothea Jörger (d. 1556) wrote to Luther for advice on writing her will in 1533,[9] Luther provided a template that included a short confession of faith similar to his own longer version of 1528.[g] While provision is made in her will for the disbursement of her worldly possessions, it comes only after she passes on her most important possession of all, her confession of faith. It was upon such confessions of faith, based on the

to the decisions made at the Diet of Speyer in April of that year, and also in preparation for the Marburg Colloquy held in early October. These articles laid out the "non-negotiable" teachings ascribed to by the Lutherans. The *Schwabach Articles* can be found in Robert Kolb and James A. Nestingen, eds., *Sources and Contexts of the Book of Concord* (Minneapolis: Fortress Press, 2001), 83–87.

7. Key Dates
    1527 Plague; Debates on the Lord's Supper
    1528 *Confession Concerning Christ's Supper*, including the *Confession of Faith*
    1528 Wenceslaus Linck publishes the *Confession of Faith* with his preface, Nuremberg
    1529 *Marburg Colloquy* and the resulting *Articles of Marburg* written to summarize its conclusions
    1529 *Schwabach Articles*, Luther's *Catechisms*
    1530 *Augsburg Confession*
    1539 Latin translation by Johannes Bugenhagen
    1537 *Smalcald Articles*
    1544 *Brief Confession Concerning the Holy Sacrament*

8. LW 32:112–13. This confession by Luther was made at the 1521 Diet of Worms, where Luther was subsequently declared a "notorious heretic" by Emperor Karl V (1550–1558) (LW 32:114 n. 9). Evidence suggests that in his closing speech, Luther said only, "May God help me," while the other words, "Here I stand," were added later. See LW 32:113 n. 8.

9. The widow Dorothea Jörger, whose husband had been an adviser to Emperor Maxmilian I (1459–1519), likely got the idea of such a confession

e   WA 26:254.

f   See p. 269 in this volume.

g   WA Br 6:406–409, no. 1988 (1 January 1533).

of faith within her will from none other than their mutual friend, Wenceslaus Linck of Nuremberg. Besides being an advocate of the Evangelical cause, she also provided student aid for students. In a letter of 7 March 1532, Luther thanks her for her desire to set up a student aid fund or bursary to help poor students at the University of Wittenberg (WA Br 6:273.7–15, no. 1910).

10. Luther addresses this many times, including his *Proceedings at Augsburg* in 1518 (LW 31:280–82), *The Papacy in Rome* in 1530 (LW 39:86–89; 92–101), and *Sermon Preached at Leipzig* in 1519 (LW 51:59–60). Philip Melanchthon (1497–1560) also pointedly addresses it in his *Treatise on the Power and Primacy of the Pope* found in the *Book of Concord* (BC).

11. The following translation of Part III, *Von Abendmahl Christi Bekenntnis*, is based on WA 26:499–509; LW 37:360–72; and it is assisted by the introductory comments by Karl Drescher, editor of this volume in WA 26:241–50.

12. The "sacramentarians" was a term often used by the Lutherans to designate those reformers (such as Andreas [Bodenstein] von Karlstadt [1486–1541] and Ulrich Zwingli [1484–1531]) who rejected the Lutheran teachings on the Lord's Supper in favor of a more "spiritual" view. Generally, this more spiritual view rejected the "real" bodily presence of Christ in the bread and wine of the Lord's Supper. The "rebaptizers" were those who rejected infant baptism (such as

gospel and God's word, that the faith community is built.[10] In this community, the word is active in revealing all attempts at self-justification through works, while also shaping and creating life and salvation. This evangelical proclamation is at the heart of Luther's *Confession of Faith*. This evangelical confession was especially important, given that he had been declared an outlaw by the state and a heretic by the church, and Luther and his followers did not yet have an official, approved common statement of their faith. The first such statement came two years later with the *Augsburg Confession*, while the first body of confessional statements was not compiled until after Luther's death. By his *Confession of Faith*, then, Luther was clearly stating what was at the heart of the Reformation movement for him. This is what he was willing to die for.

CONFESSION OF FAITH[11]

I SEE THAT SCHISMS AND ERRORS are increasing proportionately as time goes by, and that there is no end to the rage and fury of Satan. Therefore, in order that no one misuses my writings to confirm their error either during my lifetime or after my death, as the sacramentarians and rebaptizing fanatics[12] are already beginning to do, I desire with this treatise to confess my faith, point by point, before God and all the world. I am determined to abide by this faith until my death and (so help me God!) in this same faith depart from this world and appear before the judgment seat of our Lord Jesus Christ. Hence if anyone shall say after my death, "If Luther were living now, he would teach and hold this or that article of faith differently because he did not consider it sufficiently," and so forth, let me say once and for all that by the grace of God I have most diligently traced all these articles through the Scriptures, I have examined them again and again in the light of these Scriptures, and I have wanted to defend all of them as certainly as I have now defended the sacrament of the altar.[13] I am not drunk or irresponsible.[14] I know what I am saying, and I realize full well what this will mean for me before the Last Judgment at the coming of the Lord Jesus Christ.[15] Let no one make this out to be a joke or idle talk; I am dead serious, since by the grace of God I have learned a great deal about Satan. If Satan can twist and pervert the Word of God and the Scriptures, what will the deceiver[16] not be able to do with my or someone else's words?[h]

First, I wholeheartedly believe the sublime article of the majesty of God, that the Father, Son, and Holy Spirit,[i] three distinct persons, are by nature one true and genuine God, the creator of

Woodcut of Creation from Luther's
1528 sermons on Genesis.

the Anabaptists and Mennonites), arguing instead for a "believer's baptism." While the first generation of Anabaptists practiced rebaptism because they believed that baptism as an infant was not legitimate or biblically grounded, the term *Anabaptist* (literally, "rebaptizer") is not an accurate descriptor of their teachings, since they recognized only one baptism. This baptism was a confession of personal faith to the community when a person "came of age" and was able to understand what they were doing.

13. "Sacrament of the altar" refers to the Eucharist or the Lord's Supper. It provided a parallel to Luther's use of the phrase "sacrament of baptism."

14. Luther's former professor at Erfurt, Hieronymus Dungersheim, later accused Luther of these two things: an irresponsible drunkard. WA 26:500 n. 1.

15. As a declared heretic and outlaw since 1521—his life far from secure and settled—Luther was obviously concerned with the last judgment. To confess his faith (which was determined heretical) was a risky undertaking, especially when he contrasted it with what he saw were abusive, contrary practices in the Roman Church. In effect, he was throwing a match on the pile of wood meant to burn him as a heretic. This was definitely not a theoretical exercise!

16. Luther often refers to Satan as the one who is "always making an effort to deceive" (LW 26:194). The Gospel of John calls Satan the "father of lies" (John 8:44). It was not just Satan who got labeled as a deceiver by Luther, however. In his 1525 writing *Against the Heavenly Prophets*, Luther attacks Andreas von Karlstadt for perverting

h   This paragraph is quoted in the SD VII.29–31.

i   Luther naturally adheres to the ancient creedal wording which involves Father and Son, and even when desiring to use inclusive language, this formula and wording conveys what Luther wants to say about the Trinity in his historical context.

God's word in much the same way as did the devil (LW 40:100).

17. Luther uses the creeds of the church as an outline for his own confession of faith. This was a common practice, rooted in the baptismal liturgy, where the creed was recited by the one baptized to make a public statement of what they believed. By using the creed as a framework, Luther serves notice that his confession is not his own, but the confession of faith of the whole church. Luther's *Small Catechism* and *Large Catechism* express and expound this same "confession of faith."

18. Arius (c. 250–336) was condemned at the Council of Nicaea in 325 CE for teaching that Jesus was of a similar substance to God, rather than the same substance as God, thus questioning the true divinity of Christ. Macedonianism was named after the fourth-century archbishop of Constantinople who insisted that the Holy Spirit was not fully divine and thus not one of the divine persons. Macedonius's (d. c. 362) view was first condemned at a council at Alexandria in 362 CE. Sabellianism was a third-century form of modal monarchianism. It insisted that the Father, Son, and Holy Spirit were not distinct divine persons but simply different modes or even successive phases of the one God. At the Council of Nicaea, Sabellianism was declared a heresy. For a brief overview of heresies, see Mark J. Edwards, *Catholicity and Heresy in the Early Church* (Farnham, UK: Ashgate, 2009); or Alister E. McGrath, *Heresy: A History of Defending the Truth* (New York: HarperOne, 2009).

heaven and earth.[17] This is in complete opposition to the Arians, Macedonians, Sabellians,[18] and similar heretics, according to Genesis 1[:1]. Everything in this first article has been maintained up to this time both in the Roman Church and among Christian churches throughout the whole world.

Icon image of Mary and Jesus.

Second, I believe and know that Scripture teaches us that the second person in the Godhead, namely, the Son, alone became truly human, conceived by the Holy Spirit without the cooperation of a human male, and was born of the pure, holy Virgin Mary,[19] who was his real biological mother. St. Luke clearly describes this and the prophets foretold it; so that neither the Father nor the Holy Spirit became human, as certain heretics have taught.[20]

God the Son did not assume a body without a soul, as certain heretics have taught,[21] but he assumed both body and soul, that is, full, complete humanity, and he was born as the promised true seed or child of Abraham and David. He was born in a natural way, the son of Mary, in every way and from a true human being, in the same way that I myself and every other person is born, except that the Son alone was born without sin, by the Holy Spirit and through the Virgin Mary.

This human being Jesus was true God, one eternal and indivisible person, both God and human, and that the holy Virgin Mary was the real, true mother, not only of the human Christ, as the Nestorians teach,[22] but also of the Son of God, as Luke says [1:35], "The one to be born of you shall be called the Son of God," that is, my Lord and the Lord of all, Jesus Christ, is by nature the only, true Son of God and of Mary, true God and true human.

I further believe that our Lord Jesus Christ, the Son of God and the Son of Mary, suffered for us poor sinners, was crucified, died, and was buried, in order that he might redeem us from sin, death, and the eternal wrath of God by his innocent blood; and that on the third day he rose from the dead, ascended into heaven, and now sits at the right hand of God the Almighty,[j] Lord over all lords, the ruler over all rulers and all creatures in heaven, on earth, and under the earth, as well as the ruler over death and life, sin and righteousness.[k]

I also confess and can prove from Scripture that every human being descended from one person, Adam; and from this one person, through birth, everyone acquires and inherits the fall,

19. The Catholic Church's dogmas on Mary: (1) Mary is the Mother of God, *theotokos* (431); (2) Mary was a virgin (649); (3) Mary's immaculate conception (1854); (4) Mary's assumption to heaven (1950). See also Marina Warner, *Alone of All Her Sex: The Myth and the Cult of the Virgin Mary* (New York: Vintage, 1983); and Jaroslav Pelikan, *Mary through the Centuries: Her Place in the History of Culture* (New Haven: Yale University Press, 1998).

20. SA I.1, point 4, states, "That neither the Father nor the Holy Spirit, but the Son, became a human being." These heretics would include the second- and third-century Patripassians and Montanists. The Patripassians insisted that in Jesus, the Father suffered everything the Son suffered, including death on the cross. Montanus claimed that Jesus was an incarnation of the Holy Spirit.

21. Apollinaris of Laodicea, who lived in the fourth century, taught that the Divine Logos, or Word, replaced the human soul in Jesus. While Jesus appeared fully human, at least in the fleshly body, his soul was really divine; therefore, Jesus was not completely or fully human. His teachings were condemned at the Council of Chalcedon in 451 CE.

22. Nestorius, who lived in the fourth and fifth centuries CE, claimed that Mary was the mother or "bearer" of the *human* nature of Christ, but not the bearer of the *divine* nature of God (*theotokos*).

---

j   Luther gives a similar, condensed version of the second article of the Apostles' Creed in SA I.4.

k   *Gerechtigkeit.*

23. Luther here echoes Paul's arguments on the source of original sin in Rom. 5:12-21.

24. In 1525, Luther debated with Erasmus (1466–1536) on the bound or free will (LW 33). He had earlier expressed concerns about free will in his *Disputation against Scholastic Theology* of 1517 (LW 31:3–16), where the Scholasticism of John Duns Scotus (c. 1266–1308) and William of Occam (c. 1287–1347) are taken to task. See also Robert Kolb, *Bound Choice, Election, and Wittenberg Theological Method: From Martin Luther to the Formula of Concord* (Grand Rapids: Eerdmans, 2005); and Timothy J. Wengert, *Human Freedom, Christian Righteousness: Philip Melanchthon's Exegetical Dispute with Erasmus of Rotterdam*, Oxford Studies in Historical Theology, ed. David C. Steinmetz (New York: Oxford University Press, 1998).

25. The teachings of Pelagius (354–420) were condemned by the ecumenical councils of Ephesus in 431 and Orange in 529 CE. The *Augsburg Confession* also condemns these teachings in articles II and XVIII. Augustine of Hippo (354–430) had labeled Pelagius as a heretic who taught that a person's salvation could be obtained by exercising one's free will in choosing God's grace and mercy. This approach implied that original sin was a flaw that could be overcome with willpower, rather than something that destroys one's relationship with God. Lutherans argued that as a result of original sin, a person's free will to "choose" God no longer exists (CA XVIII.4–8). The idea that people can cooperate with God in obtaining their salvation is a legacy left to us by Pelagius.

guilt, and sin, which Adam, with Eve, committed in paradise[23] through the wickedness of the devil. Thus all people, along with Adam and Eve, are born, live, and die altogether in sin. As a consequence, everyone would be guilty of eternal death if Jesus Christ had not come to our aid and taken upon himself this guilt and sin as an innocent lamb and paid for us by his sufferings, and if Christ Jesus did not continue to intercede and plead for us as a faithful, merciful Mediator, Savior, and the only Priest and Bishop of our souls.

With this public confession of faith I therefore reject and condemn as absolute error all doctrines that glorify our free will,[24] since they are completely contrary to the help and grace of our Savior Jesus Christ. Outside of Christ, death and sin are our rulers and the devil is our god and the one whom we serve, and there is no power or ability, cleverness or reason by which we can make ourselves righteous and give ourselves life or even try to discover it. On the contrary, we can only be victims and captives of sin and the property of the devil, able to do and to think only what pleases sinful urges and the devil, even though it is contrary to God and God's commandments.[*] Thus I also condemn both the new and the old Pelagians[25] who will not admit that original sin is an actual sin, but interpret it instead as an infirmity or flaw. Since death has passed to all people, original sin is not merely an infirmity but is an enormous sin, as St. Paul says, "The payment for sin is death" [Rom. 6:23], and again, "Sin is a sting of death" [1 Cor. 15:56]. In the same way, David says in Ps. 51[:5], "Behold, I was conceived in sin, and my mother carried me in sin." Paul does not say, "My mother conceived me with sin," but, "I, I, I myself was conceived with my sins, and my mother has carried me with my sins, that is, I have grown from sinful seed in my mother's body,"[26] as the Hebrew text notes.

I also reject and condemn as absolute frauds and errors of the devil all monastic orders, rules, cloisters, religious foundations,[27] and all similar things devised and instituted by people

---

I   The paragraph to this point is quoted in SD II.43.

This woodcut by Eduard Schoen, c. 1535, depicts the devil playing a monk like a bagpipe, suggesting that monks were instruments of the devil. This image was used on broadsides along with anti-Catholic messages. Some have interpreted the monk in the image to be Luther, making it an anti-Luther image. However, no broadside featuring anti-Luther rhetoric on this image has been found.

26. Luther understands Paul to be saying that original sin does not come through the act of conception (embedded in the act of sex), as understood by many, but is in one's own body from the moment of conception. Thus, a person is accountable for one's own sin. It cannot be blamed on God, or even one's parents. This is clearly echoed in CA XIX and SA III.1.1–11.

27. Religious foundations were organizations established to support specific religious activities or charitable causes. They were often associated with cathedrals and private chapels owned by nobility. In some places they are also called "chapters," associations of secular priests. For example, the All Saints Foundation funded the priests in the Wittenberg castle church. Luther was critical of foundations that advocated "religiosity" at the expense of supporting those truly in need. In SA II.2.21, Luther wrote that such forms of religiosity "are not only purely human trifles, lacking God's word, completely unnecessary, and not commanded, but they are also contrary to the first article of redemption [that is, justification], and therefore they can in no way be tolerated."

28. Luther's *Address to the Christian Nobility of the German Nation Concerning the Reform of the Christian Estate* criticized some abbots, abbesses, and prelates for insisting that only they could grant absolution (LW 44:179–82). His treatise from the next year (1521), *The Judgment of Martin Luther on Monastic Vows*, extensively examined the abuses of vows in light of Scripture (LW 44:251–400).

beyond and apart from Scripture, and to which people have been bound by vows and obligations.[28] Although a great many saints have lived within these human institutions, the chosen of God have been misled by them even to this day. Nevertheless, by faith in Jesus Christ, they have been redeemed and have escaped from these frauds. Because these monastic orders, foundations, and factions have been maintained and perpetuated by the notion that by these practices and works people may seek and earn their salvation and escape from sin and death, they are nothing more than a disgraceful, nauseating blasphemy and denial of the unique help and grace of our only Savior and Mediator,

29. In the SA, Luther is insistent that redemption is through Christ alone, and that "God alone is righteous and justifies the one who has faith in Jesus." SA II.3–4.

30. Luther differentiates between God's word and Scripture, God's word, the life-giving proclamation of the gospel, is found in Scripture but is not restricted to it.

31. A year after writing this, Luther provided a "table of duties" for households in his *Small Catechism* (see BC, 365–67), that provided some guidelines for raising children. With little children now in his own household, it was no longer a theoretical issue for Luther.

32. Luther makes a distinction between "orders" (*Orden*) and "estates" (*Standen*).

33. In the *Large Catechism*, Luther names the three orders as "fathers by blood, fathers of a household, and fathers of the nation," thus replacing the "office of priest" with a familial category. LC, "Commandments," 4.158.

34. The "common chest" (*gemeinen Kasten*) was introduced early in the Reformation to provide financial resources to those in need. People could voluntarily contribute to this common chest, while the funds from the former practices of incomes, guilds, and endowments were also added. The distribution of funds was administered by representatives of different groups, each of whom had one of the keys needed to open the chest. For more details, see Luther's 1523 treatises, *Ordinance of a Common Chest* and *Fraternal Agreement on the Common Chest of the Entire Assembly at Leisnig*, in LW 45:159–94. See also Carter Lindberg,

Jesus Christ. [29] For "there is no other name given to us by which we must be saved than the one who is called Jesus Christ" [Acts 4:12]. It is impossible that there should be more saviors, ways, or means by which one can be saved other than through the one who is righteousness, namely, our Savior Jesus Christ, who has granted this righteousness to us and who is our only throne of grace[m] in God's presence, as stated in Romans 3:25.

It would be a good thing if monasteries and religious foundations were kept for the purpose of teaching young people God's Word, the Scriptures,[30] and Christian discipline, so that we might train and prepare fine, skilled people to become bishops, pastors, and other servants of the church, as well as competent, learned people for civil government, and fine, proficient, educated parents[n] capable of overseeing the household and raising children in a Christian manner.[31] But as a way of seeking salvation, these monasteries and religious foundations all stem from the devil's teaching and beliefs (1 Timothy 4, for example). However, the holy orders and true religious institutions established by God are these three:[32] the office of priest, the estate of marriage, and the worldly authorities.[33] All who are engaged in the pastoral office or in ministry of the Word are in a holy, proper, good, and God-pleasing order and estate, including those who preach, administer the sacraments, manage the common chest,[34] sacristans, messengers, or servants who assist them. Such works are altogether holy in God's sight. Consequently, those fathers and mothers who reign over their household wisely and draw their children into the service of God are engaged in pure holiness, in a holy work and a holy order. Similarly, a pure holiness is found whenever children and workers show obedience to their elders and those in authority: they are

---

m   The term "throne of grace" (*gnadenstuel*) is often translated as "mercy seat" (Lat.: *propitiatorium*). Luther's gloss on Rom. 3:25 in his *Commentary on Romans* (1515–1516) reveals the difficulty he had in translating this passage of Scripture (LW 25:32–33). This "throne of grace" or "mercy seat" language is also found in Heb. 9:5 and Exod. 25:17-22.

n   Literally, "wives" (*Weiber*). The main point is that those in the household be proficient, trained, and capable of running the Christian *Stand*, or "estate" of the household.

living saints on earth. Moreover, rulers or nobility, judges, civil officers, state and local officials,[o] and all who serve such persons, including their loyal staff—all these people are engaged in pure holiness and leading a holy life before God. For these three religious institutions or orders are dealt with in God's Word and command; and whatever is contained in God's Word must be holy, for God's Word is holy and sanctifies everything connected with it and involved in it.

Governing these three institutions and orders is the common order of Christian love, in which one does not only serve the three orders but every person in need with all kinds of compassionate activities, such as feeding the hungry, giving drink to the thirsty, forgiving enemies, praying for all people on earth, suffering all kinds of evil on earth, and so forth.[35] You see, all of these things are called good and holy works, but none of them are a way to earn salvation.[p] There remains only one way for salvation, and that is faith in Jesus Christ.

To be holy and to be saved are two completely different things.[36] We are saved through Christ alone; but we become holy both through this faith in Christ and through these divine institutions and orders. Even the godless may have many things about them that are holy, but that does not mean that they are saved. For God desires us to do such holy works to the praise and glory of God, and all who are saved in the faith of Christ do such works and maintain these orders.

What is said about the estate of marriage, however, should also be applied to widows and unmarried women, for they also belong to the household or domestic estate. Now if these orders and divine institutions do not save a person, what then can the devil's institutions and monasteries do, since they have arisen completely apart from God's Word, and strive and compete against the one and only way of faith?

Third, I believe in the Holy Spirit, who with the Father and the Son is truly one God, and who proceeds eternally from the Father and the Son,[37] yet is a distinct person in the one divine

Beyond Charity: Reformation Initiatives for the Poor (Minneapolis: Fortress Press, 1993); and Samuel Torvend, *Luther and the Hungry Poor: Gathered Fragments* (Minneapolis: Fortress Press, 2008).

35. These six actions (found in Matt. 25:31-46), along with the burying of the dead (Tob. 1:20-21; 2:1-2), were considered the "seven corporal works of mercy." Lindberg, *Beyond Charity*, 31. In the *Augsburg Confession*, these works are praised, while praying rosaries, practicing the cult of the saints, joining religious orders, taking pilgrimages, and keeping appointed fasts are called "childish, unnecessary works" (CA XX).

36. Luther plays on the similar sounding words here, "holy" (*heilig*) and "saved" (*selig*). While God alone saves a person and makes one holy, a person's holiness is a calling by God to live one's life as a "saved" person. A "saved" person lives in a "holy" way, but living in a holy way does not save a person. This is later clarified in SD III.25–40.

37. Luther uses the *filioque* ("and the Son") clause here, which was commonly used in the Nicene and Athanasian Creeds in Western Christianity but was rejected by the Eastern Orthodox churches. The Western, or Latin, church introduced this phrase in the early medieval period to try explain the interrelationships in the Trinity. It has often been blamed (somewhat unfairly) for the split between the Eastern (Orthodox) and Western (Roman) churches in 1054 CE. The *filioque* clause has generally been removed from the Nicene Creed today.

---

o   Luther here uses a series of technical titles (*Ampleute, Cantzler, Schreiber*) for various state, local, and civil officials.

p   The same point is made in CA X.9: "our works cannot reconcile us with God or obtain grace."

38. Luther is following the general wording of the Nicene and Athanasian Creeds at this point, emphasizing three distinct "personas" in the one "essence" of the Triune God. By these direct references to the creeds, Luther is reinforcing his claim that the faith to which he holds is not an innovation but the faith confessed by the traditional, ancient church.

39. Melanchthon argues in Ap IV.118 that by faith we can understand the work of Christ and receive the benefits of Christ; namely, the life-giving gospel.

40. The relationship between the gospel and the sacraments is later spelled out by Luther in his statement on the gospel in SA III.4. Further, the discussion on the sacraments here is echoed in Luther's later confessional documents, especially the *Large Catechism* and the *Smalcald Articles*.

41. In SC, "Baptism," 1–4, Luther makes it clear that this sacrament is commanded by Christ. Here, and elsewhere, Luther notes that there are three commonly used criteria required to qualify a rite as a sacrament: it must be instituted by a command from Christ; it must proclaim the promise (the gospel); and an earthly element (sign) is involved. Luther also describes these criteria in a general way in his 1520 treatise, *The Babylonian Captivity of the Church* (see esp. LW 36:36; 58–64; 124).

essence and nature.[38] Through this Holy Spirit, as a living, eternal, divine gift and legacy, all believers are clothed with faith and other spiritual gifts, raised from the dead, freed from sin, and made joyful and confident, free and certain in their conscience. For this is our comfort: if we feel this witness of the Spirit in our hearts, that God wills to be our Father,[q] forgive our sin, and bestow upon us life eternal.

These are the three persons and one God, who has totally and completely given all of God's own being to us, with everything that God is and has. As Father,[r] God's very being is given to us, along with heaven and earth and together with all creatures, in order that they serve and benefit us. But this gift became useless and was overshadowed through Eve and Adam's fall. Therefore the Son himself has subsequently given himself to us and has bestowed upon us all his works, sufferings, wisdom, and righteousness, and reconciled us to God in order that, returned to life and righteousness, we would also know and have God's own presence and gifts. But because this grace is useful to no one if it remains secretively hidden and could not come to us, the Holy Spirit comes and is given to us also, wholly and completely. This same Spirit teaches us to understand the benefits of Christ[39] which have been revealed to us, helps us receive and preserve these benefits which are useful for our needs, and distributes, increases, and extends them to others. The Spirit does this both inwardly and outwardly. Inwardly this happens by means of faith and other spiritual gifts. Outwardly, it happens through the gospel, baptism, and the sacrament of the altar,[s] through which as through three means or ways the Spirit comes to us and instills in us the sufferings of Christ for the sake of our salvation.

Consequently, I maintain and know that just as there is no more than one gospel and one Christ, so also there is no more than one baptism.[40] Baptism in itself is commanded by Christ,[41] as is the gospel of Christ. And in the same way that the gospel is

---

q   In using the term *Father*, Luther is using the traditional language of the creeds, rather than trying to make a provocative statement of the gender of God.

r   Literally, "the Father" (*Vater*). The point that Luther is making is that in Christ we are reconciled, not just to one "part" of the Trinity, but to God's whole, complete, Triune Being.

s   Luther presents a similar list concerning the gospel in SA III.4, describing the various ways in which God gives grace.

not false or unjust simply because some use or teach it dishonestly or do not believe it, so also baptism is not false or unjust even if some have received or administered it without faith or misused it in other ways. Accordingly, I completely reject and condemn the teaching of the Anabaptists and Donatists, and all those who rebaptize.[42]

Likewise, I also state and confess that in the sacrament of the altar the true body and blood of Christ are orally eaten and drunk in the bread and wine, even if the priest who distributes them or those who receive them do not believe or otherwise misuse the sacrament. The efficacy of the sacrament does not rest on a person's belief or unbelief but on the Word and God's ordinance—unless they first change God's Word and ordinance and misinterpret them, as the enemies of the sacrament do at the present time. Indeed, they have only bread and wine, for they do not also have the words and instituted ordinance of God; they have perverted and modified it according to their own imagination.[t]

Next, I believe that there is one holy Christian church on earth, that is, the community and number or gathering of all Christians in the whole world, the one bride of Christ. Christ is the only head of this spiritual body of Christ. Bishops or pastors are not the heads, rulers, or bridegrooms of this church, but servants, friends, and—as the word "bishop" indicates—overseers, guardians, or caretakers.[43] This Christian community[u] is found not only in the Roman Church or pope, but in all the world, as the prophets declared, saying that the gospel of Christ would spread into all the world, Ps. 2[:8], Ps. 19[:4]. Thus this Christian community is physically scattered among pope, Turks, Persians, and Tartars,[44] but spiritually gathered in one gospel

42. This is echoed in CA VIII. The Donatists arose in the fourth century in North Africa. Seeking to preserve the moral purity of the church, they taught that sacramental actions carried out by those who had been unfaithful under Roman persecution were no longer valid. Thus, the Donatists considered baptism administered by such priests— or ordained by such bishops—as invalid. To "correct" this, they rebaptized those who had been baptized by these unworthy priests. The church reacted by making rebaptism punishable by death, according to the Justinian Code. This code was used to "justify" the sixteenth-century persecution of Anabaptists by Catholics and Protestants alike.

43. Luther defines the word *bishop* in the 1521 treatise *Answer to Goat Emser* (LW 39:154–55). Melanchthon defines the responsibilities of a bishop in CA XXVIII.21–22.

44. Tartars are from northern Turkey or the Volga region of Russia. The Turks may refer to people from the Ottoman Empire or to Muslims, the main religious group of the Ottoman Empire.

---

t   This paragraph is quoted in the SD VII.32. See also CA VIII and X.

u   The German word used here is *Christenheit*. While German versions of the creed prior to Luther's time often used *Christenheit* to translate the Latin *ecclesia* (BC, 355 n.58), Luther uses the word to distinguish between this community of forgiven sinners or "holy ones" (Ger.: *Heiligen;* see SC II.6) and the institutional, or Roman Catholic, church (Ger.: *Kirche*). In the LC, II.48, Luther notes that church (*Kirche*) means nothing more than a public gathering. This "community of holy ones" is more than a public gathering—it is the community of those whom the Holy Spirit has created, thus allowing the gathered to encounter Christ. LC II.35–39.

45. Beginning in 1520, with his *Address to the Christian Nobility* (LW 44:133), Luther regularly identified the papacy with the Antichrist—someone who got in the way of Christ, or set themselves up over against Christ (SA II, 4.10–13). While Luther often referred to the pope and his advisers as the Antichrist, it was generally because he considered the pope led people away from Christ by providing alternate ways to justification and salvation, which could be accomplished by Christ alone. See also Luther's comments on 1 John 2:18, in LW 21:252.

46. Regarding Luther's view of the Turks, see *On War against the Turk* (LW 46:181, 196). In the 1541 treatise *Appeal for Prayer against the Turks*, Luther calls the papacy and the Turks the "last two plagues of the wrath of God" (LW 43:238).

47. Luther here plays with the Roman Church's understanding of Cyprian's (d. 258) famous dictum, "outside of the church there is no salvation" (*Epistles*, 73.21). Luther argues that there is no salvation outside the Christian community because outside of this community there is no forgiveness of sins. LC, "Creed," 3.56.

48. Novatians, a group from the third century, insisted that after baptism a person could no longer receive forgiveness for any serious sins. Luther comments on this in his 1530 treatise, *The Keys* (LW 40:374). Melanchthon also condemns Novatianism in CA XII.9.

49. Canon 21 of the Fourth Lateran Council of 1215 CE required everyone to come to confession at least once a year. Failure to do so would result in being barred from the church for life and make a person ineligible for a church funeral.

and faith, under one head, that is, Jesus Christ. For the papacy is definitely the true realm of Antichrist,[45] the real anti-Christian tyranny, who sits in the temple of God and rules with human commandments, as Christ declares in Matthew 24[:24] and Paul in II Thessalonians 2[:3-4]. However, the Turks and all heresies, wherever they may be, also belong to this abomination which has been prophesied to stand in the holy place, but they are not the same as the papacy.[46]

Wherever this Christian community is found, there is the forgiveness of sins, that is, a realm of grace and of true pardon. The gospel, baptism, and the sacrament of the altar are found in this community, for it is where the forgiveness of sins is offered, obtained, and received.[v] Moreover, Christ and the Spirit and God are there. Outside this Christian community there is no salvation[47] or forgiveness of sins: there is only everlasting death and damnation, even though there may be an impressive appearance of holiness and many good works. All of these things are useless. But this forgiveness of sins is not restricted to one time only, such as in baptism, as the Novatians[48] teach, but is given frequently and as often as a person needs it, until they die.

For this reason I have great regard for private confession, where God's word and absolution are spoken privately and specifically to each person for the forgiveness of their sins.[w] A person may have access to private confession as often as desired in order to receive this forgiveness, as well as for the comfort, counsel, and guidance which it gives. It is a precious, useful thing for souls, as long as no one is forced to go to private confession by means of laws and commandments.[49] Rather, sinners should be left free to make use of it, according to their own need, when and where they wish. In the same way, we are free to obtain advice and comfort,

---

v   Luther also talks about the various manifestations of the gospel in SA III.4.

w   The paragraph above (beginning with "For this reason") had inadvertently been left out of the *Confession Concerning Christ's Supper* by the printer, and when Linck asked to reprint the *Confession of Faith* as a separate document, Luther requested that it be added back into the text. The Lutherans held private confession in high esteem, even though they did not treat it as a sacrament. Luther had earlier advocated for private confession in the 1520 *Babylonian Captivity of the Church* (LW 36:86–89) and the 1526 treatise, *The Sacrament of the Body and Blood of Christ—Against the Fanatics* (LW 36:359–60).

Woodcut of a pastor listening to confession,
from a 1530 edition of the *Large Catechism* by Luther.

guidance and instruction when and where our needs or dispositions provoke us, as long as one is not forced to enumerate all their sins but only those sins which are most pressing upon them or which a person will name regardless, as I have described in my *Little Book on Prayer*.[50]

The indulgences and pardons which the papal church has and distributes are a malicious fraud, not only because they invent and devise a special forgiveness, beyond the general forgiveness[51] which is given through the gospel and the sacrament in the whole Christian community, and thus dishonor and nullify the general forgiveness, but also because they establish and base the satisfaction for sins upon human works and the merits of saints, even though only Christ can and has done enough for us to make satisfaction for us.[52]

50. While Luther does not specifically mention private confession in his 1522 *Little Book on Prayer*, which he refers to here, this little booklet was developed into the catechisms, where Luther reiterates many of the same things about private confession. Thus, in the *Small Catechism*, Luther provides a brief order for private confession (SC, "Baptism," 21–29), and in the *Large Catechism*, he explains its importance (LC, "Confession," 13–35). Melanchthon also makes it clear that Lutherans have not abolished private confession, although the emphasis is on God's proclamation of absolution rather than on the human actions of confessing (CA II.25).

51. General forgiveness was proclaimed to a gathered community, similar to "corporate" forgiveness at the beginning of a worship service today. In 1533, a debate arose in Nuremberg because their pastor, Andreas Osiander (1498–1552), had rejected this public, or general, forgiveness of sins and would only practice private confession. The Wittenberg theologians responded to the Nuremberg city council by supporting the practice of general forgiveness, even though they realized that some recipients of the declaration of forgiveness were not interested in being forgiven (LW 50:76–78).

52. While Lutherans were encouraged to remember the good examples of how the "saints" experienced grace in their own lives, in order to strengthen their own faith, the *Augsburg Confession* (CA XXI) made it clear that people could not earn or receive merit from them to aid in their own salvation.

53. Requiem Masses (*Seelenmessen*) were celebrated on the anniversary of a person's death, while a vigil was commemorated on the eve of the anniversary. Luther had already questioned the celebration of Masses for the dead in thesis 83 of the *95 Theses* in 1517 (LW 31:32). He also sharply criticized this practice in the 1520 treatise, *Address to the Christian Nobility* (LW 44:180–81).

54. Originally, Luther felt that purgatory was not so much a place as it was the fear and dread of punishment, or even a "bad conscience," and thus could be experienced even in this life. See here his *Explanations of the 95 Theses*, thesis 15 (LW 31:125–30), and the *Defense and Explanation of All the Articles*, especially articles 4 and 37 (LW 32:31–32, 95–97). By the time he wrote the *Smalcald Articles*, however, Luther considered it nothing but an "apparition of the devil" (SA II.212).

55. Luther provides a critique of the invocation of saints in thesis 58 of his *Explanations of the 95 Theses* (LW 31:212–18). He also criticizes many of the same practices noted here in SA II, 2.12–29. He asserts that these practices stem from a flawed understanding of the Mass. The invocation of saints is also critiqued in CA XXIV. While Luther insisted that the saints can provide an encouraging example of how people have lived faithful lives, they were not to replace Christ's role as the one, true intermediary between humans and God. To do so would be to make them "antichrists"—those who get in the way of Christ and bar access to Christ's benefits.

As for the dead,[x] since Scripture says nothing about it, I hold the position that it is not a sin to pray with a free expression of piety in this or some similar fashion: "Dear God, if this soul is in such a shape to be helped, be gracious to it." And when this has happened once or twice, that is enough. For vigils, requiem Masses, and yearly celebrations of such events[53] are of no use for the dead, and are the devil's annual fair.[y] Nor do we have anything in Scripture about purgatory. Indeed, it was created by noisy spirits.[z] Therefore, I maintain it is not necessary to believe in it, even though all things are possible for God, and God could very well allow souls to be tormented after they had left the body. But God has not allowed anything of this sort to be spoken about or written down; therefore God does not wish to have it believed. However, I know of a purgatory of another kind, but it would not be proper to teach anything about it in the community of faith nor deal with it through foundations or vigils.[54]

Others before me have attacked the invocation of saints, and this delights me. I also believe that Christ alone should be invoked as our Mediator. Scripture states this, and it is also certain that nothing is said about the invocation of saints in Scripture; therefore it is of necessity uncertain and is not to be believed.[55]

If unction[a] were employed in accordance with the gospel, Mark 6[:13] and James 5[:14], I would let it go. But to make a sacrament out of it is nonsense. In the same way, instead of vigils and Masses for the dead, it would be better to deliver a sermon on death and eternal life, and also pray during the funeral and meditate upon our own end, as it seems the elders did. It would also be good to visit the sick; and if anyone wished in addition to

---

x   That is, prayers for the dead.

y   The "devil's annual fair" (*des teuffels iarmarckt*) plays on the image of an excuse to celebrate an event, while forgetting the original purpose of the commemoration. WA 26:508b.5–6.

z   The German word is *Poltergeist*. These noisy spirits would prevent a person from hearing the gospel proclaimed, which would render purgatory pointless.

a   Supreme Unction or Last Rites. Luther also discusses unction, anointing with oil and prayer, in the 1520 treatise *Babylonian Captivity of the Church* (LW 36:118–23).

anoint them with oil, pray with and admonish them, they should be free to do so in the name of God.

There is also no need to make sacraments out of marriage and the office of the priesthood. These orders are holy enough in and of themselves.[56] So, too, penance is nothing other than the practice and the power of baptism.[57] Thus two sacraments remain: Baptism and the Lord's Supper; in them, along with the gospel, the Holy Spirit richly offers, grants, and accomplishes the forgiveness of sins.[58]

I consider the Mass the greatest of all abominations when it is preached or sold as a sacrifice or good work; which is the basis on which all religious foundations and monasteries now stand.[59]

In this painting (c. 1610) by Ludovico Carracci (1555–1619), an angel frees souls from purgatory.

56. In *The Babylonian Captivity of the Church*, Luther rejects marriage, confirmation, and ordination as sacraments (LW 36:92–117). On the other hand, Melanchthon was not opposed to treating ordination as a sacrament if it was correctly understood as a ministry of the word. See here, Ap XIII.11. But he was not as eager to call marriage a sacrament, since it was not a sign of the "New Testament and a testimony of grace and the forgiveness of sins" (Ap XIII.14–16).

57. Luther was ambiguous about whether penance (confession and absolution) was a sacrament. He notes its importance above (see the last paragraph on page 272, and note w on the same page). Luther often subsumed repentance under baptism, as noted in *The Babylonian Captivity of the Church* (LW 36:81–91; SC, "Baptism," 16–29; LC, "Baptism," 74–76), while Melanchthon considered it a sacrament in Ap XIII.3–4.

58. On the sacraments in the Catholic tradition, see *The Babylonian Captivity* (LW 36) and *The Annotated Luther*, vol. 3 (Minneapolis: Fortress Press, 2016).

59. Luther's criticisms of the Mass are found in *The Babylonian Captivity of the Church* (LW 36:35–36); SA II.2.1–11; and CA XXIV. His problem with the Roman practice of the Mass was because it "directly and violently opposes this chief article [justification]" (SA II.2.1). The Mass was also seen as a sacrifice offered up to God, thus focusing on human actions to please God, in order to obtain salvation, rather than on a Eucharist, in which God gives unmerited forgiveness to the gathered, receiving community. Thus, the Mass should not be confused with a service of Holy Communion.

But, God willing, they shall soon be left behind. Although I have been a great, grievous, shameful sinner and wasted my youth in an uncaring and damnable manner, yet my greatest sins were that I had been so holy a monk, and had angered, tortured, and plagued my dear Lord with countless Masses for more than fifteen years.[60] But praise and thanks be to God's unspeakable grace spoken into eternity, God led me out of this abomination, and still continues to preserve and strengthen me daily in the true faith, despite my great ingratitude.

Accordingly, I have advised and still advise people to abandon religious foundations and monasteries, together with their vows, and go out into the true Christian orders,[61] in order to escape these abominations of the Mass and this slanderous holiness such as "chastity, poverty, and obedience," by which people presume they are saved.[62] As appropriate as it was in the beginning of the Christian community to uphold virginity, now it is abominable when it is used to renounce the help and grace given through Christ. It is possible for a person to live in a state of virginity, widowhood, and chastity without these offensive abominations.[63] Furthermore, I regard images, bells, Eucharistic vestments, church ornaments, altar lights, and other such things as matters of indifference.[b] Anyone who wishes may omit them. Images or pictures taken from the Scriptures and from good histories, however, I consider very useful but indifferent and optional. I do not agree with the iconoclasts.[64]

Finally, I believe in the resurrection of all the dead, both the pious and the wicked, on the last day, that everyone may receive in their body just as they have deserved. Thus the pious will live eternally with Christ and the wicked will die eternally with the devil and his angels. I do not agree with those who teach that the devils also will at the end come to salvation.[65]

---

[b]   In SD X, these indifferent things are called *adiaphora*.

This is my faith, which all true Christians believe and which the Holy Scriptures also teach us. However, concerning those things about which I have said little, my other booklets give modest witness to them, especially those booklets of the last four or five years.[c] I ask that all pious hearts will bear witness to this, and pray that I may remain strong in this faith to the end of my life. As I have openly confessed, even if I should say something different—God forbid—in the midst of temptation or the pangs of death, it should be ignored because it would be incorrect and spoken under the devil's influence. Therefore, may my Lord and Savior Jesus Christ help me, who is blessed forever, Amen.

64. Luther's reactions to iconoclasts can be found in his *Eight Wittenberg Sermons*, preached when he returned from exile at the Wartburg (LW 51:81–86). He was strongly influenced by Lucas Cranach the Elder (1472-1553) on this matter, according to Steven E. Ozment, *The Serpent and the Lamb: Cranach, Luther, and the Making of the Reformation* (New Haven: Yale University Press, 2011).

65. Origen (c. 185-254) had taught, in *De Principiis*, I.6, 1-4 (*ANF* 4), that the devils would ultimately be converted. This view was condemned at Constantinople in 553 CE, but it became popular again in the sixteenth century. This heresy is condemned in CA XVII and in the *Schwabach Articles* (art. 13), as noted in Kolb and Nestingen, eds., *Sources and Contexts*, 87.

c   One can only guess what booklets Luther had in mind. Some of his most important writings of this period dealt with the Lord's Supper (*Sacrament of the Body and Blood of Christ—Against the Fanatics* [1526], LW 36:329-61; *That These Words of Christ, "This Is My Body," etc., Still Stand Firm against the Fanatics* [1527], LW 37:3-150); Baptism (*Order of Baptism, Newly Revised* [1526], LW 53:106-9; *Concerning Rebaptism* [1528], LW 40:225-62); *Bondage of the Will* (1525), which he considered one of his best writings (LW 33:3-295); various educational and social issues (*To the Councilmen of All Cities in Germany, That They Establish and Maintain Christian Schools* [1524], LW 45:339-78; *Parents Should Neither Compel or Hinder the Marriage of Their Children* [1524], LW 45:379-93; *Trade and Usury* [1524], LW 45:231-310; *Whether One May Flee from a Deadly Plague* [1527], LW 43:113-38); the development of worship materials (*German Mass and Order of Service* [1525], LW 53:51-90); and his countless biblical commentaries and published sermons. One can only speculate about whether Luther was also thinking of his writings against the peasants in 1525 (*Admonition to Peace: A Reply to the Twelve Articles of the Peasants*, LW 46:3-43; *Against the Robbing and Murdering Hordes of Peasants*, LW 46:45-55; and *Open Letter on the Harsh Book against the Peasants*, LW 46:57-85), which have caused controversy both then and now.

Title page of Luther's *Large Catechism.*
Deudsch Catechismus. Mart. Luther. Wittenberg:
Georgen Rhaw, MDXXIX. Aland 364;
Benzing 2548; WA 30,1.123–238.
Der Grosse Katechismus.

The Large Catechism of Dr. Martin Luther[a]

1529

KIRSI I. STJERNA

INTRODUCTION

In the *Large Catechism*, Martin Luther offers a radical reorientation[b] in the matters of theology and spirituality. After diagnosing what appeared to him as his church's failures to provide proper spiritual care, Luther set out to offer a new compass for religious life. The sweeping reforms he proposed took root primarily through preaching and education as people embraced the new vision and transmitted it to their children. He believed all Christian people—laity and priests—needed a guide to comprehend the basic biblical, creedal, and sacramental teachings.

---

a   Martin Luther, *The Large Catechism*, in the *Book of Concord*, ed. Timothy Wengert and Robert Kolb (Minneapolis: Fortress Press, 2000), [introduction, 377–79,] 379–480. *Der Große Katechismus*, in *Die Bekenntnisschriften der Evangelisch-Lutherischen Kirche*, 6. Auslage (Göttingen: Vanderhoeck & Ruprecht, 1967). See the new critical edition with parallel texts of the Early Modern High German and Latin, *Die Bekenntnisschriften der Evangelisch-Lutherischen Kirche* (Vollständige Neuedition), ed. Irene Dingel (Göttingen: Vandenhoeck & Ruprecht, 2014); and *Die Bekenntnisschriften der Evangelisch-Lutherischen Kirche: Quellen und Materialien* (Vollständige Neuedition), ed. Irene Dingel (Göttingen: Vandenhoeck & Ruprecht, 2014).

b   For interpretation of Luther's catechisms in English, see Timothy Wengert, *Martin Luther's Catechisms: Forming the Faith* (Minneapolis:

---

1. The 1530 *Augsburg Confession*, the first public Lutheran confession in twenty-eight articles, was presented at the long-awaited imperial Diet at Augsburg by Philip Melanchthon (1497–1560), Luther's closest colleague at Wittenberg. Melanchthon crafted the text on the basis of previous working documents prepared by a group of Wittenberg theologians, including Luther. The confession was presented in German (verbally) and Latin to Emperor Charles V, who immediately rejected it with Catholic theologians' *Confutatio*. Melanchthon's *Apology of the Augsburg Confession* (1531) is also included in the 1580 *Book of Concord*. See BC, 107–9. Also, Charles P. Arand, Robert Kolb, and James A. Nestingen, *The Lutheran Confessions: History and Theology of the Book of Concord* (Minneapolis: Fortress Press, 2012).

2. Philip Melanchthon, a humanist and a professor at the University of Wittenberg, was Luther's closest friend and an interpreter and systematizer of Luther's theology. A promoter of unity, he is known for writing the first Lutheran systematic theology, *Loci communes*. See also Timothy Wengert, *Philip Melanchthon, Speaker of the Reformation* (Farnham, UK: Ashgate Variorum, 2010).

3. *The Book of Concord*, from 1580, is the standard, official collection of Lutheran confessional texts. The book was facilitated by Martin Chemnitz and Jacob Andrae and their respective nobility from north and south concerned about the unity in the midst of increasing inner-Lutheran disputes. It includes the ecumenical Creeds, Luther's *Small Catechism* and *Large Catechism*, Melanchthon's *Augsburg Confession* and the *Apology of the Augsburg Confession*, Luther's *Smalcald Articles*,

Luther published two of the most popular catechisms of all time: the *Small Catechism*[c] for children and the less educated laity, and the *Large Catechism* for the clergy and more educated readers. While the *Small Catechism* utilizes the catechetical form of questions and answers, the *Large Catechism* does not. Both were adopted into use immediately in the new evangelical congregations. Along with the 1530 *Augsburg Confession*[1] by Philip Melanchthon,[2] Luther's catechisms stand apart as the most widely

Fortress Press, 2009); Charles P. Arand, *That I May Be His Own: An Overview of Luther's Catechisms* (St. Louis: Concordia, 2000); Robert Kolb, *Teaching God's Children His Teaching: A Guide for the Study of Luther's Catechism* (St. Louis: Concordia, 2012). The most comprehensive study is in the five volumes of Albrecht Peters, *Commentary on Luther's Catechisms* (Ten Commandments, Creed, Lord's Prayer, Baptism and Lord's Supper, Confession and Christian Life), trans. Thomas H. Trapp et al. (St. Louis: Concordia, 2009–2013).

c   See the *Small Catechism*, in TAL, vol. 4, forthcoming.

employed Lutheran confessional texts included in the 1580 compilation called the *Book of Concord*.[3]

According to his own recollection,[4] Luther already in 1516–17 was preaching[d] from the materials typically included in the medieval catholic catechisms:[e] the Ten Commandments, Apostles' Creed, Lord's Prayer, and the Ave Maria.[5] This was

Melanchthon's *Treatise on the Power and Primacy of the Pope*, and the *Formula of Concord* with its two parts: the Epitome and the Solid Declaration. See note a above for the newest critical edition of the confessions in the original languages.

4. Timeline

    1518 Sermons on catechesis materials

    1518 Exposition of the Lord's Prayer

    1521 Philip Melanchthon's *Loci Communes*

    1525 *Booklet for the Laity and Children*, Stephen Roth

    1522 *A Personal Prayer Book*

    1523 Reform of the Latin Mass

    1524 First evangelical hymns

    1526 German Mass

    1527 Summer: Visitations

    1527 November: Torgau meeting

    1528 Visitations articles

    1528 Ember sermons on catechesis

    1528 Catechisms by Johann Agricola

    1529 January: *Small Catechism*

    1529 April: *Large Catechism*

    1529 Latin translation [Revisions]

    1529 October: Marburg Colloquy, *Marburg Articles*

    1530 June: Diet of Augsburg, *Augsburg Confession*

    1538 Last edition of *Large Catechism* in Luther's lifetime

    1580 *Book of Concord*, includes catechisms

5. The word *catechism* comes from a Greek term, κατηχέω, meaning to "teach orally" (literally, "to echo back"). This method of utilizing "questions and answers" has long roots in Christian tradition. It has been employed since the second century to teach Christians the basics of Christian faith and for proper preparation for receiving the sacrament of the Lord's Supper. In

---

d   *Decem praecepta Wittenbergensi praedicata populo* (WA 1:394–521).

e   E.g., *An Exposition of the Lord's Prayer for Simple Laymen* (1519) (LW 42:15–81). Luther's *A Personal Prayer Book* (1522) included his 1519 preaching material on the Ten Commandments, the Apostles' Creed, and the Lord's Prayer (LW 43:5–45). See also TAL, vol. 4, forthcoming.

the early church, rigorous catechetic education of the adult converts took place for those desiring to be baptized, who then received the Creed, the Lord's Prayer, and permission to attend the eucharistic gathering.

6. In the Middle Ages, the catechetic tradition focused on the penitential practice. Manuals, after the model of Augustine of Hippo's fifth-century *Enchiridion* [*Handbook*] *on Faith, Hope, and Charity*, were designed to teach the meaning of the Creeds, the Commandments, and the Lord's Prayer in particular. One of the most popular of such medieval manuals, from a Franciscan preacher, Dietrich Kolde (1435–1515), *The Mirror of a Christian Man* (1470), gave instruction on what to believe, how to live, and how to die, with a premise that one could improve one's chances with right faith and action. The leading work in Luther's time came from the humanist Erasmus of Rotterdam (1466–1536), *The Handbook of the Christian Soldier* (1501). Catechetical methods of teaching have also been used in different religious and philosophical traditions (e.g., Socrates).

7. Catechetical preaching days coincided with so-called Ember Days: in the Western tradition, four times a year, sermons were offered in a set of three days in one week (often Wednesday, Friday, Saturday), with an invitation for Christians to pray and fast.

8. Johannes Bugenhagen (1485–1558) was Luther's friend, pastor, and colleague. Also a lecturer at the university, he was instrumental in organizing the evangelical churches and writing evangelical church orders in northern Germany and Denmark. See Kurt K. Hendel, ed., *Johannes Bugenhagen:*

not unusual in any way.[6] Regular "catechetical" preaching was normal and expected in certain areas in Germany already before the Reformation.[7] Often substituting as assistant pastor for his friend and colleague, the Wittenberg town pastor, Johannes Bugenhagen,[8] as was the case in 1528, Luther climbed the preaching pulpit at the Marienkirche (St. Mary's Church) in Wittenberg for three rounds of catechetical sermons. The listeners' notes from three sets of these sermons (18–30 May; 14–25 September; and 30 November–18 December 1528) give insights into Luther's singular method in both preaching and teaching, as evidenced in the printed catechisms.[f]

Education on the basic tenets of Christian faith and practices was essential for establishing the evangelical theology in praxis. While developing their distinctive Reformation Christian identity and faith language, Lutherans needed tools for interpretation and application. A flurry of new catechisms with evangelical theology flooded the busy market.[9]

The *Large Catechism* was published on the eve of the Marburg Colloquy of October 1529, which was convened by Philip of Hesse.[10] Here Luther would meet with his Swiss counterpart Ulrich Zwingli[11] to test the waters for unity that could potentially allow for a pan-Protestant alliance against the Catholic imperial powers. The major points of agreement resonate with the theology that was fleshed out in Luther's Catechism (which has potential as an ecumenical Christian source of devotion and

---

f   WA 30/1:2–122. The English translation of the third series is included in LW 51:135–93.

ethics). The central disagreement on the theology of the Lord's Supper, however, prevented unity between the Swiss and the German reformations.[12] Included in the *Large Catechism* is Luther's teaching on the Lord's Supper and explication of his emphasis on Christ's real presence in the sacrament offered to each recipient. This nonnegotiable point would remain one of the characteristic Lutheran teachings—closer to the Catholic teaching on the matter, actually, than any of the other Protestant explanations. This has not only been a sixteenth-century issue: efforts toward table fellowship among different Christian groups have kept the theology of the Lord's Supper at the center of ecumenical negotiations.

Reasons for Writing

The stimulus for Luther to write his very own catechisms came from at least three directions. In 1524, he had received an invitation to write a catechism for laypeople from Pastor Nicholas Hausmann (c. 1478-1538). He also wanted to address the theological controversy between Melanchthon and Johann Agricola[13] regarding the place of the law in Christian life. And finally, he was deeply disturbed by what he and others discovered in the Saxon Visitations of 1528, which continued in a first round until 1531.

Selected Writings, 2 vols. (Minneapolis: Fortress Press, 2015).

9. About thirty new catechisms were published just between 1522 and 1530. On the writing of evangelical catechisms, see Ferdinand Cohrs, *Die Evangelischen Katechismusversuche vor Luthers Enchiridion*, 4 vols. (Berlin, 1900-1902); and Johann Michael Reu, *Quellen zur Geschichte des kirchlichen Unterrichts in der evangelischen Kirche Deutschlands zwischen 1530 und 1600*, 9 vols. (Gutersloh, 1904-1935; Hildesheim and New York: Olms, 1976).

10. Philip of Hesse (1504-1567), "the Magnanimous," Landgrave of Hesse, was one of the primary princely leaders and supporters of the Reformation.

11. Ulrich Zwingli (1484-1531), a humanist and a chaplain, was the leader of the Reformation in Switzerland and Luther's most important "conversation partner" on the issue of Christ's presence in the Lord's Supper.

12. With hopes for a pan-Protestant unified front, Luther and Zwingli cordially met at the Marburg Castle and agreed on fourteen out of the fifteen articles of faith. The last one, on the Lord's Supper, presented a stumbling block, and the men left Marburg as sworn enemies. See the *Marburg Articles*, in English translation in *Sources and Contexts of the Book of Concord*, ed. Robert Kolb and James A. Nestingen (Minneapolis: Fortress Press, 2001), 88-92.

13. Johann Agricola (c. 1494-1566) was a former student of Luther and the head at the time of the Latin school in Eisleben. He was later a teacher in Wittenberg and, starting in the 1540s, a court preacher and a superintendent in Berlin. In the 1530s, he became a vocal proponent of an antinomian position, opposing Melanchthon and Luther. Agricola's criticism of the 1527 Latin version of the *Instructions* had irritated Melanchthon enough to launch him into writing his own catechism, a project he politely set aside as soon as Luther began to prepare his. See Timothy J. Wengert, *Law and Gospel: Philip Melanchthon's Debate with John Agricola of Eisleben over "Poenitentia"* (Grand Rapids: Baker, 1997).

14. For the translation, see LW 40:263–320. Luther, Melanchthon, and others led the early visitations that examined the health of the Saxon congregations, their finances, the quality of preaching and teaching, and the overall status of ministry. The written articles addressed a wide spectrum of doctrinal and practical concerns and served as the stepping-stone for catechisms and church orders that were to regulate life in evangelical communities. For an example of such articles, in English translation, see *The Saxon Visitation Articles* of 1592, in Kolb and Nestingen, eds., *Sources and Contexts*, 256–60.

Luther had made known his concerns about the sorry state of the churches in Saxony to Elector John Frederick 1 (1503–1554), who in 1527 issued a guide to be used by appointed visitors called *Instructions and Order for Dispatching Visitors.* Luther was not fully satisfied with the document, so Melanchthon created an alternate document in Latin called *The Articles of the Visitors,* which consisted of eighteen items, including the Ten Commandments, the sacraments, worship, theological issues such as Christian freedom, and societal topics, including the Turks and the office of superintendents of schools. The *Articles* were translated into German by Luther, Bugenhagen, and Melanchthon starting in September 1527. Then Luther himself wrote a preface to these instructions that appeared in print in early 1528 under the title *Instructions for the Visitors of Parish Pastors of Saxony.*[14]

Designated teams consisting of four persons—two from the elector's court, one from the school of law and one theologian (elected by the theology faculty)—all approved by the Saxon elector visited the regions and their churches for the purposes of examining the overall situation of congregations, including the teaching and preaching, the finances and the staffing. Luther himself briefly took part in the visitations in 1528. The teams returned with a sense of urgency to remedy the unacceptable ignorance and confusion even about the basics of the Christian faith, not to mention its evangelical orientation. In his preface to the *Small Catechism,* Luther reflected on the sad state of the churches uncovered through the visitation: "The deplorable, wretched deprivation that I recently encountered while I was a visitor has constrained and compelled me to prepare this catechism, or Christian instruction, in such a brief, plain, and simple version. . . . The ordinary person, especially in the villages knows nothing about the Christian faith, and unfortunately many pastors are completely unskilled and incompetent teachers."[g]

The ongoing debate with Agricola also fueled Luther's drive to write the catechism. With three catechisms of his own (1527–28), Agricola unambiguously taught Christian life on the basis of the promise of the gospel, diminishing any positive role for law and the fear of God's punishment in inducing necessary

g   BC, 347.

repentance. In Luther's—and Melanchthon's—opinion, omitting law meant watering down the gospel and led to illusions about human nature. Law and gospel together stimulated proper repentance that was to characterize the life of the baptized.[15]

A Theological Compass for Daily Life

The pedagogical format and the easy flow of the language Luther employs in the *Large Catechism* should not fool the reader to dismiss its theological ammunition. Its parts make up a spiritually oriented summation of Luther's doctrine. Luther masters the skill of theologizing in ways that make sense for a novice reader without compromising the complexity of issues at stake. Luther himself wrote: "I must still read and study the catechism daily, and yet I cannot master it as I wish, but must remain a child and pupil of the catechism—and I also do so gladly" (BC, 380:8).

The order with which Luther proceeds in the *Large Catechism* is deliberate, with a distinct theological rationale: the Commandments express God's expectations; the Creed proclaims God's promise; the Lord's Prayer translates law and gospel into a personal discourse with God; and the sacraments offer tangible expressions of God's grace and signs to lean on in faith. Through all these pieces, Luther follows the tracks of the Holy Spirit as the overarching enabler, to a degree that the *Large Catechism* could be named the "Book of the Spirit."

Beginning with the Ten Commandments, Luther demonstrates that the law has its place in Christian life—to judge, to illumine our sinful condition, and to guide. The constructive role of law becomes clear only in light of the gospel, and the old reality of sin is replaced by the new reality of forgiveness. Luther's explanation of the law is thus telling and expresses his confidence in God's promise of grace: the law maintains its positive function exactly because of the promise of grace expressed in the Creeds, and solely because of the merit of Jesus Christ and the ongoing work of the Holy Spirit in the word. With his positive teaching of the law, Luther emphasizes both the reality of sin in human life and points back to the redeeming work of Christ and God's grace.

According to Luther, the gospel is amply summarized in the Lord's Prayer, which serves as a compass for the Christian's daily

15. Luther, Bugenhagen, and Agricola met on 26–29 November 1527 in Torgau to address their different views on, e.g., law, repentance, and faith. These negotiations foreshadowed the direct conflict between Luther and Agricola in the so-called antinomian controversy of the late 1530s.

16. In Luther's vision, the daily Christian life entails a deeply mystical dimension on the basis of the real presence of Christ in faith, gratuitously affected by the word. The Finnish Luther scholar Tuomo Mannermaa introduced a hermeneutical shift in this regard with his ecumenically inspired rereading of Luther's doctrine of justification and the centrality of the effective righteousness, and the interconnectedness of faith and love in Luther's theology of salvation. See Mannermaa, *Christ Present in Faith: Luther's View of Justification* (Minneapolis: Fortress Press, 2005); and idem, *Two Kinds of Love: An Introduction to Luther's Religious World* (Minneapolis: Fortress Press, 2010).

17. Luther worked in particular on his third set of sermons from 1528, with extra attention to the revision of the second and third commandments, already printed; the added comments on these would be included in the end of the conclusions on the Commandments.

18. Luther was then focusing on the confession and the Eucharist. For an English translation, see *Martin Luther's Sermons from Holy Week and Easter, 1529*, Irving Sandberg, trans. (St. Louis: Concordia, 1999).

19. Comparing the different sermon and lecture notes, prints and texts, it is evident how instrumental preaching was for Luther's theological development and articulation. One example of this is the enhancement of the Lord's Prayer through the different versions available.

20. Lucas Cranach Sr. (1472–1555), a painter, printmaker, pharmacist, real estate mogul, and a dear friend of Luther offered multifaceted support for the Reformation, perhaps even shaping its direction. See Steven Ozment, *The*

life, in which we alone cannot live up to the demands of the law. We cannot fully realize the law's guidance on how to live to the benefit of our neighbor, nor are we able to love and respect God of our own accord. So we are encouraged to pray without ceasing and without doubting God's word.

In his *Large Catechism*, Luther states his unflappable trust in the powerful active presence of God in human life specifically through the word. He assures his fellow Christians of the certainty of God's promise to be present and active for those who engage God's word. He writes: "Nothing is so powerfully effective against the devil, the world, the flesh, and all evil thoughts as to occupy one's self with God's word, to speak about it and meditate upon it. . . . For this reason alone you should gladly read, recite, ponder, and practice the catechism" (BC, 381:9–11). "In such reading, conversation, and meditation the Holy Spirit is present" (BC, 381:9).

If one wants to talk about Luther's mysticism, the *Large Catechism* gives ample evidence of the experiential foundation of Luther's theological orientation and his personal religiosity. It seeks to lay the groundwork for the faithful to encounter God and to teach the many ways God's own word calls forth faith. In sum, Luther's *Large Catechism* is a book of faith and invites the reader to explore the many mysteries of God that intersect all dimensions of human life.[16]

The Printing and Publication

Luther started writing what became the *Large Catechism* in December 1528, beginning by revising his sermons from September.[17] In January 1529, he continued this work but, starting with the third commandment, especially used his December sermons as a basis for his work. When a period of illness forced Luther to stop working on this project, he picked it up again in March 1529; his Holy Week sermons (21–27 March 1529) greatly influenced his discussion of the Lord's Supper and (in the second edition) Confession.[18]

Luther's German Catechism, as the *Large Catechism* was first titled, came out in mid-April 1529, with immediate revisions to follow.[19] The printer, Georg Rhau (1488–1548), included an important pedagogical enhancement with woodcuts from Lucas

In this antique print, the Coburg Castle
stands on the hill overlooking the city of Coburg.

Cranach Sr.'s workshop.[20] The 1530 edition of the work included
Luther's longer preface, which he probably composed while at
Coburg Castle during the famous Diet of Augsburg in 1530,
which, as an outlawed, condemned heretic, he could not attend.[21]
The very last edition from Luther's lifetime comes from 1538,
and contains only minor corrections. While mostly known in
its German language, the *Large Catechism* was translated in 1529
into refined Latin (with classical citations) by Vincent Obsopoeus.[22] *The Book of Concord* from 1580 included Luther's catechisms
among the normative Lutheran confessions that have been in use

*Serpent and the Lamb: Cranach, Luther, and
the Making of the Reformation* (New Haven:
Yale University Press, 2012).

21. Since the 1521 Diet of Worms
and its edict that outlawed Luther, he
could not venture outside territories
friendly to the Reformation to attend
the Augsburg Diet, or any other similar
imperial gathering. He observed the
events from the Saxon elector's castle in
Coburg, where he was attended by the
later pastor in Nuremberg, Veit Dietrich,
and visited by his Bavarian friend Argula
von Grumbach (c. 1492–1568) on her
way to the Diet.

22. Vincent Obsopoeus [Vinzenz
Heidecker] (1485–1539), a humanist
and philologist, was a proponent of
Luther's works.

ever since. The catechisms were also employed with the church orders (*Kirchenordnung*) that effectively organized Lutheran religious life from the sixteenth century on.[23]

A Word about the Translation and Annotations

This translation is a revised version of James Schaaf's original work in *The Large Catechism of Dr. Martin Luther*.[24] Also consulted was *Der Große Katechismus*, in *Die Bekenntnisschriften der Evangelisch-Lutherischen Kirche*.[25] Schaaf's notes have been revised and incorporated in the new text provided here.

Most notably, the language of the translation has been thoroughly revised with the principle of inclusivity, with an eye toward Luther's theological and reasonable intent, and with appreciation of both the sixteenth-century linguistic traditions as well as the sensibilities of the contemporary global reader. Whereas a strictly literal translation would have in some places led to unintended exclusivity and distracted the larger theological point Luther is making, Luther's own principle of flexible translation in the service of the meaning and effective communication is applied in this editing process. Typically masculine words and male pronouns in reference to both humanity and divinity have been omitted or replaced with gender-inclusive or complementary expressions, except in places where the meaning of the sentence or a paragraph necessitates specifically either masculine or feminine wording. For instance, some of the traditional trinitarian "Father" language of the Creed has been preserved. Sometimes the change is simply a matter of replacing "he" with "one" or "person," or using a plural instead of a singular expression (e.g., "people" instead of "he" or "man"). The pronoun "himself" after the word "God" is systematically omitted.

This image from 1533 *Church Order*, published by Evangelisch-Lutherische Kirche in Ansbach, illustrates a violation of the third commandment: "You are to keep holy the day of rest." While the congregation is gathered for Sunday worship and instruction, a man is working outside.

23. The 1580 *Book of Concord* published in Leipzig used the so-called Jena edition of Luther's works, which has a reversed order of the prefaces and omitted the private confession. The 2000 Fortress Press edition, reflecting an edition of the Book of Concord printed in Magdeburg, follows the second,

The annotations and footnotes contextualize Luther's text broadly in Reformation history, provide references to relatively few and mostly recent studies, familiarize the reader with some of the key words in the original language(s), pinpoint central theological issues at stake, and offer leads for future study.

THE LARGE [GERMAN] CATECHISM OF DR. MARTIN LUTHER[h]

Martin Luther's Preface[26]

IT IS NOT FOR TRIVIAL REASONS that we constantly treat the catechism[27] and exhort and implore others to do the same, for we see that unfortunately many preachers and pastors[28] are very negligent in doing so and thus despise both their office[29] and this teaching. Some do it out of their great learnedness, while others do so out of pure laziness and concern for their bellies.[30] They approach the task as if they were pastors and preachers for their stomachs' sake and had nothing to do but live off the fat of the land, as they were used to doing under the papacy. Everything that they are to teach and preach is now so very clearly and easily presented in so many salutary books, which truly deliver what the other manuals promised in their titles: "Sermons That Preach Themselves," "Sleep Soundly," "Be Prepared," and "Thesaurus." Yet they are not upright and honest enough to buy such books, or, if they have them already, to consult or read them. Oh, these shameful gluttons and servants of their bellies[i] are better suited to be swineherds and keepers

revised and expanded edition of the *Large Catechism* of 1529.

24. BC, 377–480.

25. *Der Große Katechismus*, 545–733. The new critical edition with parallel texts of the Early Modern High German and Latin, cited above in n. a, p. 279, was not available at the time, but is highly recommended.

26. This 1530 longer preface, addressed to preachers and pastors, followed the 1529 shorter one, in accordance with the order of the 1556 Jena edition of Luther's works (the fourth German volume), and was printed in the 1580 *Book of Concord*. Luther may have written this longer preface in 1530 while in the nearby Coburg Castle during the Diet of Augsburg.

27. The word *Katechismus* (the noun from Augustine) describes originally an oral method of religious instruction. See the introduction, n. 5, p. 281.

28. *Prediger* ("preachers") were appointed to the preaching office only, whereas *Pfarrherren* (pastors) performed all the pastoral acts and duties entailed with the office, exclusive to men in Luther's world. Urgent needs for proper training for these offices warranted significant reforms in the sixteenth century.

29. With the word *Amt* ("office") Luther refers to the calling of those in ministry with specific duties.

30. With *Bauchsorge* ("belly worry") Luther chastises the priests and pastoral leaders for their selfish prioritizing on the opposite of what their duty called for. This is an expression of his overall criticism of the distorted focus in his church.

---

h   For the basis of the translation see the final section of the introduction, p. 288.

i   The German *Frecklinge und Bauchdiener* were pejorative terms, relating to Rom. 16:18, for gluttony.

31. Luther underscores the care of the soul as the primary calling of those in ministry, as opposed to the concerns of the belly.

32. Luther as a monk was familiar with the so-called seven canonical hours, or the Divine Office, as prescribed in the medieval breviary: in accordance with a monastic discipline established already during the first centuries of the Christian tradition and fixed in format by the ninth century, the daily intervals of prayer include matins/laudes, prime (6 AM), terce (9 AM), sext (noon), nones (3 PM), vespers (6 PM), and compline at the end of the day. The daily structured prayer originates from the Jewish prayer practice (Ps. 119:164—"Seven times a day I praise you for your righteous laws" [NIV]) and the hours come from the schedule of bells ringing for time in the forums of the Roman imperial cities.

33. Luther uses the words *Freiheit* (Ger.) and *Licentiam* (Lat.), "freedom" and "license," to refer to people taking the license to be lazy in their Christian calling, ignoring their duty.

34. Luther means people without preachers' or theologians' level of religious education.

35. Luther thinks of the times before reformation, when there was no Evangelical movement but all Christians belonged to the papal-led Catholic Church.

36. With adjectives such as *toll* (Ger.) and *insanes* (Lat.), Luther often disparages his fellow German-speaking Christians. There was, of course, no "Germany" or "German nation" as such yet, while the Reformation coincided with and strengthened the growing sense of national identities in European territory, including Luther's homeland.

of dogs than guardians of souls[31] and pastors. Now that they are free from the useless, bothersome babbling of the seven hours,[32] it would be much better if morning, noon, and night they would instead read a page or two from the catechism, the Prayer Book,*j* the New Testament, or some other passage from the Bible, and would pray the Lord's Prayer for themselves and their parishioners.*k* In this way they would once again show honor and respect to the gospel, through which they have been delivered from so many burdens and troubles, and they might feel a little shame that, like pigs and dogs, they are remembering no more of the gospel than this rotten, pernicious, shameful, carnal liberty.[33] As it is, the common people[34] take the gospel altogether too lightly, and we accomplish but little, despite all our hard work. What, then, can we expect if we are slothful and lazy, as we used to be under the papacy?[35]

Besides, along comes this horrible vice and secret, evil plague of security and boredom. Many regard the catechism as a simple, trifling teaching, which they can absorb and master at one reading and then toss the book into a corner as if they are ashamed to read it again. Indeed, among the nobility there are also some louts and skinflints who declare that they can do without pastors and preachers because we now have everything in books and can learn it all by ourselves. So they blithely let parishes fall into decay and brazenly allow both pastors and preachers to suffer distress and hunger. This is what one can expect of the crazy[36] Germans. We Germans have such disgraceful people among us and have to put up with[37] them.

But this I say for myself: I am also a doctor and a preacher, just as learned and experienced as all of them who are so high and mighty. Nevertheless, each morning, and whenever else I have time, I do as a child who is being taught the catechism and I read and recite word for word the Lord's Prayer, the Ten Commandments, the Creed, the Psalms, etc. I must still read and study the catechism daily, and yet I cannot master it as I wish,

j　Luther's *Personal Prayer Book, Betbüchlein,* from 1522, was an enhanced version of his *Brief Explanation of the Ten Commandments, the Creed, and the Lord's Prayer* (the *Kurze*/shorter form). See LW 43:3–45 and TAL, vol. 4, forthcoming.

k　*Pfarrkinder* ("parishioners") in its literal translation is "parish children."

but must remain a child and pupil of the catechism—and I also do so gladly.[38] These fussy, finicky folks would like quickly, with one reading, to be doctors above all doctors, to know it all and to need nothing more. Well this, too, is a sure sign that they despise both their office and the people's souls, yes, even God and God's own word. They do not need to fall, for they have already fallen all too horribly. What they need, however, is to become children and begin to learn the ABCs,[39] which they think they have long since outgrown.[/]

Therefore, I beg such lazy bellies and presumptuous saints,[40] for God's sake, to let themselves be convinced and believe that they are not really and truly such learned and exalted doctors

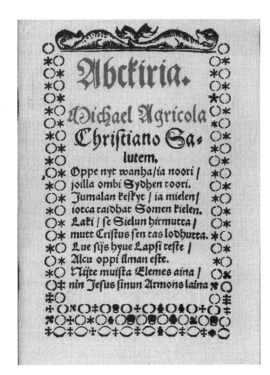

Finnish reformer Mikael Agricola's 1543 ABC book for the education of the Finns with the Reformation theology.

See the maps on pp. xiii–xiv in the front of this volume.

37. With the words *müssen leiden* (Ger.), Luther literally means "must suffer"; he expresses often his frustration with his compatriots.

38. Luther writes in his commentary on Psalm 117 (LW 14:8): "I confess this freely as an example to anyone; for here am I, an old doctor of theology and a preacher. . . . Yet even I must become a child; and early each day I recite aloud to myself the Lord's Prayer, the Ten Commandments, the Creed, and whatever lovely psalms and verses I may choose, just as we teach and train children to do. . . . I study them daily and remain a pupil of the Catechism."

39. One of the first and foremost steps of the reforms was the education of the common people, for which catechetical materials were provided. As a prime example, the Wittenberg-trained reformer Bishop Mikael Agricola (1510–1557) provided the first ABC book in the Finnish language to facilitate people's ability to read the Bible for themselves. Luther's emphasis on the education of every child is at the root of this vision of implementing theology in practice.

40. The word for the saints, the holy ones, *heiligen* (Ger.), shares the root with "to sanctify" and "to make holy" or "to hallow." Notice later, with the explanation of the Creed's third part, Luther's wording about the Holy Spirit's "sanctifying," "holy-making" work.

---

l A proverbial expression, "They have split their shoes."

41. The word for "present/presence" (Ger.: *Gegenwärtig*) is important here in Luther's argument about the tangible promises of God's presence in the intentional reflection of the word. The promise of studying the catechism is not only education but also evoking and realizing the manifold presence of God's Spirit.

42. Luther's word translates as "thinking," without necessarily implying a methodological contemplative prayer-reflection used in monastic life or specific spiritual practices. Here Luther presents an invitation for the ordinary Christian to learn a habit of prayer and in faith engage the word as the compass in one's life.

43. In Luther's medieval world, it was common to use "holy water," *das rechte Weihwasser* (Ger.), *aqua illa sancificat* (Lat.), or "sanctified water/water that sanctifies" in, e.g., exorcisms to drive away evil spirits.

44. Luther frequently cites the legend of Dietrich of Bern as an example of lies and fables. Dietrich of Bern was the name applied in medieval Teutonic legends to Theodoric the Great, king of the Ostrogoths.

45. Luther writes with the experience of medieval Christians in need of concrete sacramental measures in the ongoing warfare against the devil who, like death, was always lurking to take over. A unique perspective comes from Luther's rendition of the story of Mechtild of Hackeborn (Helfta, thirteenth century) beating the devil with her confession. See Carolyn Schneider, *I Am a Christian: The Nun, the Devil, and Martin Luther* (Minneapolis: Fortress Press, 2010).

as they think. I implore them not ever to imagine that they have learned these parts of the catechism perfectly, or that they know them sufficiently, even though they think they know them ever so well. Even if their knowledge of the catechism were perfect (although that is impossible in this life), it is still highly advantageous and fruitful to read it daily and practice it in reflection[m] and conversation. Namely, through such reading, discussion, and reflection, the Holy Spirit is present[41] and bestows ever new and greater light and devotion,[n] so that it tastes better and better and is digested, as Christ also promises in Matthew 18[:20], "Where two or three are gathered in my name, I am there among them."

Nothing is so powerfully effective against the devil, the world, the flesh, and all evil thoughts as to occupy one's self with God's word, to speak about it and meditate[42] on it, in the way that Psalm 1[:2] calls those blessed who "meditate on God's law day and night." Without doubt, you will offer up no more powerful incense or savor against the devil than to occupy yourself with God's commandments and words and to speak, sing, or think about them. Indeed, this is the true holy water and sign that scares the devil to run away.[43]

For this reason alone, you should gladly read, recite, ponder, and practice the catechism, even if the only advantage and benefit you obtain from it is to drive away the devil and evil thoughts; for it[o] cannot bear to hear God's word. And God's word is not like some idle tale, such as about Dietrich of Bern,[44] but, as St. Paul says in Romans 1[:16], it is "the power of God," indeed, the power of God that burns the devil's house down[p] and gives us immeasurable strength, comfort, and help.[45]

---

m   The words *Gedenken* (Ger.) and *meditatio* (Lat.) can be translated in different ways: the word *meditation*, used in the LW translation, associates with a specific prayer technique, whereas Luther's emphasis here is more generally on intentional reading and use of the words.

n   *Andacht* (Ger.), a term used for an attitude of devotion and reverence, but also for a prayer event; e.g., evening devotion.

o   Even if Luther typically addresses the devil in personal terms, his masculine pronoun *er* (Ger.), "he" in English, is translated here and throughout as "it."

p   "To cause damage to someone by means of arson," a typical expression with Luther.

Why should I waste words? If I were to tell all the benefits and advantages that God's word accomplishes, where would I find enough paper and time? The devil is called a master of a thousand arts. What then can we call God's word that routs and destroys such a master of a thousand arts along with all its cunning and power? Indeed, it must be master of more than a hundred thousand arts. Also, should we so flippantly despise such might, benefits, power, and fruit—especially we who want to be pastors and preachers? If so, we deserve not only to be given no food to eat, but also to have the dogs set upon us and to be pelted with horse manure. For not only do we daily need God's word just as we do our daily bread; we also must have it every day in order to stand against the daily and incessant attacks and ambushes of the devil with its thousand arts.

If this were not enough to admonish us to read the catechism daily, God's command should suffice to compel us. For God solemnly bids us in Deuteronomy 6[:7-8] that we should meditate on God's precepts while sitting, walking, standing, lying down, and rising, and we should keep them as an ever-present emblem and sign before our eyes and on our hands. God certainly does not require and command this so solemnly without reason. God knows our danger and need; God knows the constant and furious attacks and assaults of the devil. Therefore, God wishes to warn, equip, and protect us against them with good "armor" against their "flaming arrows,"[q] and with a good antidote against their evil infection and poison. Oh, what mad, senseless fools we are! We must ever live and dwell in the midst of such mighty enemies like the devils, and yet we would despise our weapons and armor, too lazy to examine them or give them a thought![46]

And what else are these bored, presumptuous saints doing—people who will not read and study the catechism daily and have no desire to—except thinking that they are more learned than even God[r] and all the holy angels, prophets, apostles, and all Christians? Even God is not ashamed to teach it daily; God knows of nothing better than to teach and always keeps on teaching this one thing without proposing anything new or different. And all the saints know of nothing better or different to

46. A similar concern was addressed with Europe's most celebrated educator and humanist Erasmus of Rotterdam's (1466–1536) "little dagger," *The Handbook of the Christian Soldier* from 1501. See *The Handbook of the Christian Soldier/ Enchiridion militis christiani*, ed. and trans. Charles Fantazzi, in *Collected Works of Erasmus: Spiritualia*, ed. John O'Malley, vol. 66 (Toronto: University of Toronto Press, 1988), 1–127.

q   Eph. 6:11, 16.
r   *Gott selbs* (Ger.) and *ipse Deus* (Lat.) are translated as "even God" here and following.

Enchiridion militis christiani, one of the best-selling pre-Reformation Christian manuals by Luther's rival Erasmus of Rotterdam. First published in 1501, this cover is from a 1528 version.

47. The German terms *Geistlich und weltlich Wesen* (Lat.: *civiles*) express the division of "spiritual" and "worldly/ temporal" realms of existence, each with different authority and appropriate "swords." Luther often addresses the tension and relation between the two realms, a distinction also pertinent to his doctrine of justification and the uses of the law in Christian life.

48. With *Stände* (Lat.: *status*; Ger.: *Stand*), "estates," "stations," or "walks of life," Luther refers to the way life was ordered in the medieval society. People belonged to different estates: the domestic (*oeconomia/Nährstad*), the political (*politia/Wehrstand*), and the ecclesiastical (*ecclesia/Lehrstand*), each with its own particular task and responsibility also before God. On this basis Luther teaches the different

learn, although they cannot learn it to perfection. Are we not the most marvelous fellows, therefore, who allow ourselves to imagine that, after reading and hearing it once, we know everything and need not read and study it anymore? We think we can learn in an hour what even God cannot finish teaching, even if God were to teach it from the beginning of the world until the end! All the prophets and all the saints have had to learn it, but they have always remained its pupils, and they must continue to be so.

Then this must be certain: those who know the Ten Commandments perfectly know the entire Scriptures and in all affairs and circumstances are able to counsel, help, comfort, judge, and make decisions in both spiritual and temporal matters.[47] They are qualified to be a judge over all doctrines, walks of life,[48] spirits, legal matters, and everything else in the world. Moreover, what is the whole Psalter but meditation and exercises based on the first commandment? Now, I know beyond a doubt that such lazy bellies and presumptuous spirits understand not even a single psalm, let alone the whole Scriptures, but they pretend they know and despise the catechism, which is a brief digest and summary of the entire Holy Scriptures.

Therefore, I appeal once more to all Christians, especially the pastors and preachers, that they not try to become doctors too soon and imagine that they know everything. (Vain imaginations, like new cloth, suffer shrinkage!)[s] Let all Christians drill themselves in the catechism daily, and constantly put it into practice, guarding themselves with the greatest care and diligence against the poisonous infection of such security or arrogance. Let them constantly read and teach, learn and meditate and ponder. Let them never stop until they have proved by experience and are certain that they have taught the devil to death and have become more learned than even God[t] and all of God's saints.

If they show such diligence, then I promise them—and their experience will bear me out—that they will gain much fruit and God will make excellent people out of them. Then in due time they will make the noble confession that the longer they work

s   A proverbial expression.

t   See n. 45 above, p. 292.

with the catechism, the less they know of it, and the more they have to learn. Only then, hungry and thirsty, will they for the first time truly taste what now they cannot bear to smell because they are so bloated and overindulged. To this end may God grant God's grace! Amen.

Preface[u]

This sermon has been designed and undertaken for the instruction of children and the uneducated. Hence from ancient times it has been called, in Greek, a "catechism"—that is, instruction for children.[49] It contains what every Christian should know. Anyone who does not know it should not be numbered among Christians nor admitted to any sacrament,[50] just as artisans who do not know the rules and practices of their craft are rejected and considered incompetent. For this reason, young people should be thoroughly taught the parts of the catechism (that is, instruction for children[51]) and diligently drilled in their practice.

Therefore, it is the duty of every head of a household[52] at least once a week to examine the children and servants one after the other and ascertain what they know or have learned of it, and, if they do not know it, to keep them faithfully at it. I well remember the time when we found ignorant, old, elderly people who knew nothing of these things—in fact, even now we find them daily—yet they still go to baptism and the Lord's Supper and exercise all the rights of Christians, although those who come to the sacrament certainly should know more and have a deeper understanding of all Christian teaching than children and beginners in school. As for the common people, however, we should be satisfied if they learn the three parts[53] that have been in Christendom from ancient days (although they were rarely taught and treated correctly), so that all who wish to be Christians for real as well as in name, both young and old, may be well trained in them and familiar with them. They are as follows:[v]

---

u This was the original brief preface of 1529, based on a sermon from 18 May 1528.

v This wording about the five parts does not agree with the text in Luther's *Small Catechism* and *Large Catechism*, or his translation of the Bible.

vocations (*officium/Amt*) with earthly and heavenly responsibilities.

49. *Kinderlehre* (Ger.), literally, "teaching or instruction of children." On catechisms as early Christian question-and-answer-type instruction on the basics of faith, see n. 5, p. 281.

50. A person could be excluded from the sacrament of the table as a punishment for serious transgressions. Also, in order to participate, one had to prepare with individual confession and be instructed in the catechesis. Exclusion from the Lord's Table meant excommunication from the Christian community, which, in Luther's world, was a scary scenario. Luther, in his catechisms, underscores both the importance of the sacraments and the sufficient understanding of the basic Christian teachings of faith, including the doctrine of the sacraments.

51. Ger.: *Kinderpredigt*. The words *preaching* and *instruction* are used synonymously about children's Christian education.

52. In Luther's patriarchal culture, fathers were considered the heads of the households (Ger.: *Hausvater*); the positions of authority belonged to men, and women and children were subjected to them both religiously and legally. In reality, however, women could find their own ways of influence, especially at households and through marriage. Luther's own wife, Katharina von Bora (1499–1552), is a stellar example of that.

53. Luther refers to the Ten Commandments, the Creed, and the Lord's Prayer. This basic catechetical instruction was expanded in 1525 Wittenberg to include also baptism and the Lord's Supper.

54. *Dega logoi*, "ten words," in Exod. 20:2-17; see Deut. 5:6-21. The commandments from the Hebrew Bible were employed by Christians in the Middle Ages in manuals for Christian living and for the practice of penance before attending the Mass. Protestants offered their own interpretation, with an addition of the doxology in the end, and with a different numbering of the commandments: in Luther's medieval Christian tradition, and reading of the standard Latin translation, the Vulgate (St. Jerome, fourth century), the first two commandments are joined, whereas the tenth commandment is split in two, thus preserving the number ten.

First: The Ten Commandments of God[54]

The first: You are to have no other gods besides me.[w]

The second: You are not to take the name of God in vain.

The third: You are to keep holy the day of rest.[x]

The fourth: You are to honor father and mother.

The fifth: You are not to kill.

The sixth: You are not to commit adultery.[y]

The seventh: You are not to steal.

The eighth: You are not to bear false witness against your neighbor.

The ninth: You are not to covet[z] your neighbor's house.

The tenth: You are not to covet your neighbor's spouse, male or female servants, cattle, or whatever is your neighbor's.[55]

This depiction of the Ten Commandments by Lucas Cranach the Elder (1472–1553) is in the town hall in Wittenberg.

Second: The Chief Articles of Our Faith[56]

I believe in God, the Father almighty,[57] creator of heaven and earth. And in Jesus Christ, God's[a] only Son, our Lord, who was conceived by the Holy Spirit, born of the Virgin Mary,[b] suffered under Pontius Pilate, was crucified, died, and was buried; he descended into hell. On the third day he rose again from the dead; he ascended into heaven, is seated at the right hand of God, the Father almighty, from where he will come to judge the living and the dead. I believe in the Holy Spirit, one holy Christian church,[58] the communion[c] of saints, the forgiveness of sins, the resurrection of the flesh, and a life everlasting. Amen.

w   Literally, *neben mir* (Ger.), "next to me," or *coram me* (Lat.), "in front of me."

x   *Den Feiertag heiligen* (Ger.), "day of celebration"; *sabbati sanctifices* (Lat.). The words used here imply "keeping holy," "sanctifying," or "hallowing."

y   The words *ehebrechen* (Ger.) and *moechabers* (Lat.) mean "to break a marriage."

z   The words for "covet" are the common synonyms for "desire" (Ger.: *begehren*; Lat.: *concupiscere*).

a   Here "his" is replaced with "God's."

b   The historically decisive words about Jesus' conception, *empfangen* (Ger.) and *conceptu* (Lat.), of Mary with the Holy Spirit, Luther takes for granted and discusses in detail in, e.g., *That Jesus Christ Was Born a Jew*, in LW 45:[195–98] 199–29, esp. 202–10; see also TAL, vol. 5, forthcoming.

c   For the *Gemeinschaft der Heiligen* (Ger.), *sanctorum communionem* (Lat.), both "communion" and "community" would be appropriate.

55. Luther follows the medieval tradition of numbering the commandments per the convention in the Vulgate, rather than the original order of the commandments in the Hebrew Bible. Also, here "his" and "wife" are replaced with "neighbor's" and "spouse."

56. The three-part statement of faith originates from the early church's liturgical formulation used in baptisms and worship. So-called *regula fidei* ("rules of faith") can be found in pieces in the New Testament and fragmented early Christian sources. The first ecumenical councils of Nicaea (325) and Constantinople (381) formulated the "orthodox" theological language of God's triune nature, the divinity-humanity of Christ, and the fundamental faith statements on the church and baptism, forgiveness and resurrection, and the promise of eternal life. In addition to the "Nicene-Constantinopolitan Creed," an early Roman baptismal formula from the second century evolved into the so-called Apostles' Creed, which has been the most frequently used creed in the West. The so-called Athanasian Creed, with an ambiguous history from the sixth-century Gaul, is falsely attributed to Athanasius of Alexandria (296–373). Luther focuses on the Apostles' Creed.

57. Luther uses the traditional wording of the Apostles' Creed when naming the first person of the Trinity as "father" (Ger.: *Vater*).

58. Luther follows the fifteenth-century German ecclesiastical language of translating the Latin *ecclesia catholica*, "church Catholic," by *christliche Kirche*, "Christian church."

59. *Oratio Dominica*, or *Pater Noster* (Lat.) is after the prayer Jesus taught his disciples, per the New Testament tradition, and it has been the central prayer in Christian worship. The wording comes in shorter (Luke 11:2-4) and longer (Matt. 6:9-13, the Sermon on the Mount) versions with seven petitions, which connect with the three parts of the Jewish prayers: praise, petition, and an expectation for the kingdom of God to come.

60. The word *kingdom* (Ger.: *Reich*; Lat.: *regnum*) is important for Luther's vision of the different dimensions of human existence in the worlds visible and (yet) invisible, and for the different realms of authority, worldly and spiritual.

61. Addressing the duties of the father as the head of the house (Ger.: *Hausvater*; Lat.: *patris familias*), Luther considers individuals in their specific calling in the hierarchy at home and in the society. This vision of vocations was imbedded into the *Haustafeln* ("Tables of Duties") that were widely used to structure the new Lutheran households' lives. See "The Household Chart of Some Bible Passages," in BC, 365–67.

62. Luther did not engage in refuting persistent, false legends about each of the apostles contributing to the wording of the Apostles' Creed.

Third: The Prayer, or Our Father, Which Christ Taught[59]

Our Father, you who are in heaven, may your name be hallowed.[d] May your kingdom[60] come. May your will come about also on earth as in heaven. Give us today our daily bread. And remit our debt, as we remit our debtors. And lead us not into temptation. But deliver us from evil. Amen.[e]

These are the most necessary parts that we must first learn to repeat word for word. The children should be taught the habit of reciting them daily, when they arise in the morning, when they go to their meals, and when they go to bed at night. Until they recite them, they should be given nothing to eat or drink. Every head of a household[61] is also obliged to do the same with the servants, male and female, and should dismiss them if they cannot or will not learn them. Under no circumstances should those people be tolerated who are so crude and unruly that they refuse to learn these things. For in these three parts, in short, plain, and simple terms, is understood everything we have in the Scriptures. Indeed, the dear Fathers or apostles (whoever they were) thus summed up the teaching, life, wisdom, and learning that constitute the Christian's conversation, conduct, and concern.[62]

When these three parts have been understood, it is appropriate that one ought also to know what to say about our sacraments, which Christ himself instituted, baptism and the holy body and blood of Christ, according to the texts in which Matthew and Mark describe at the end of their Gospels how Christ said farewell to his disciples and sent them forth.

Concerning Baptism

"Go and teach all nations, and baptize them in the name of the Father and of the Son and of the Holy Spirit." "The one who believes and is baptized will be saved; but the one who does not believe will be condemned."[f]

---

d   The words *geheiliget werde* (Ger.) and *sanctificatur* (Lat.) could be translated as "keep holy" or "sanctify."

e   Matt. 6:9-13; see Luke 11:2-4.

It is enough for an ordinary person to know this much about baptism from the Scriptures. The same applies to the other sacrament, mentioning a few, simple words according to the text of St. Paul.

Concerning the Sacrament

"Our Lord Jesus on the night when he was betrayed took the bread, gave thanks, broke it, gave it to his disciples, and said, 'Take and eat. This is my body that is given for you. Do this in remembrance[63] of me.' In the same way he took the cup also, after the supper, and said, 'This cup is a new covenant in my blood, which is shed for you for the forgiveness of sins. Do this, as often as you drink it, in remembrance of me.'"[g]

Thus we have, in all, five parts covering the whole of Christian teaching, which we should constantly teach and require recitation word for word. For you should not assume that the young people will learn and retain this teaching from sermons alone. When these parts have been well learned, one may assign them also some psalms or hymns,[64] based on these subjects, to supplement and confirm their knowledge. Thus young people will be led into the Scriptures and make progress every day.

It is not enough, however, for them simply to learn and repeat these parts verbatim. The young people should also attend sermons, especially during the ordered times of preaching[65] on the catechism, so that they may hear it explained and may learn the meaning of every part. Then they will also be able to repeat what they have heard and give a good, correct answer when they are questioned, so that the preaching will not be without benefit and fruit. The reason we take such care to preach on the catechism frequently is to impress it upon our young people, not in a lofty and learned manner but briefly and very simply, so that it may penetrate deeply into their minds and remain fixed in their memories. Therefore we shall now consider the above-mentioned parts one by one and in the plainest manner possible say about them as much as is necessary.

63. The words for "memory" and "remembrance" (Ger.: *Gedächtnis*; Lat.: *commemorationem*), have been interpreted in conflicting ways in the ongoing debates about the meaning of the Lord's Supper (Eucharist).

64. Psalms were often sung. Luther considered music as a powerful support to one's faith, having the power to drive the devil away. He wrote several hymns that are still in use, and also hymns based on the parts of the catechism. On the vital role of music in the Lutheran reformations, see LW 53; Christopher Boyd Brown, *Singing the Gospel: Lutheran Hymns and the Success of the Reformation* (Cambridge: Harvard University Press, 2005); and TAL, vol. 4, forthcoming.

65. In Wittenberg, preaching on the catechism was required by the Church Ordinance of 1533.

---

f   The words *verdampt/verdammt* (Ger.) and *judicatus* est (Lat.) mean "condemned" and "judged"; Matt. 28:19; Mark 16:16 (Luther's trans.).

g   1 Cor. 11:23-25 (Luther's trans.).

[The First Part: The Ten Commandments][h]

The First Commandment

"You are to have no other gods."[i]

That is, you are to regard me alone as your God.[j] What does this mean, and how is it to be understood? What does "to have a god" mean, or what is God?[66]

Answer: God is that in which we are to look for all good and in which we are to find refuge in all need. Therefore, to have a god is nothing else than to trust and believe in that one with your whole heart. As I have often said, it is the trust and faith of the heart alone that make both God and an idol. If your faith and trust are right, then your God is the true one. Conversely, where your trust is false and wrong, there you do not have the true God. For these two belong together, faith and God. Anything on which your heart relies and depends, I say, that is really your God.

The intention of this commandment, therefore, is to require true faith and confidence of the heart, which fly straight to the one true God and cling to God alone. What this means is: "See to it that you let me alone be your God, and never search for another." In other words: "Whatever good thing you lack, look to me for it and seek it from me, and whenever you suffer misfortune and distress, crawl to me and cling to me. I, I myself, will give you what you need and help you out of every danger. Only do not let your heart cling to or rest in anyone else."

So that it may be understood and remembered, I must explain this a little more plainly by citing some everyday examples of the opposite. There are some who think that they have God and everything they need when they have money and property; they

66. These questions are the foundation on which everything depends: proper reckoning of the one and only God, and unfolding the meaning of that relationship. Failing to keep this fountainhead command—since the "Garden of Eden" days—leads to sin and misery.

---

h This heading is missing from the 1580 *Book of Concord.* For a thorough treatment and commentary, see Albrecht Peters, *Ten Commandments,* in *Commentary on Luther's Catechisms,* trans. Holger K. Sonntag (St. Louis: Concordia, 2009).

i Literally, *neben mir* (Ger.), "next to me," or *coram me* (Lat.), "in front of me."

j With *Me solum pro Deo tuo habebis* (Lat.), *mich alleine für deinem Gott haben* (Ger.), Luther targets the meaning of "having" God, holding something in the status of God.

trust in them and boast in them so stubbornly and securely that they care for no one else. They, too, have a god—mammon[k] by name, that is, money and property—on which they set their whole heart. This is the most common idol on earth. Those who have money and property feel secure, happy, and fearless, as if they were sitting in the midst of paradise. On the other hand, those who have nothing doubt and despair as if they knew of no god at all. We will find very few who are cheerful, who do not fret and complain, if they do not have mammon. This desire for wealth clings and sticks to our nature all the way to the grave.

So, too, those who boast of great learning, wisdom, power, prestige, friendship,[l] and honor and who trust in them have a god also, but not the one, true God. Notice again, how presumptuous, secure, and proud people are when they have such possessions, and how despondent they are when they lack them or when they are taken away. Therefore, I repeat, the correct interpretation of this commandment is that to have a god is to have something in which the heart trusts completely.

Again, look at what we used to do in our blindness under the papacy. Anyone who had a toothache fasted and called on St. Apollonia; those who worried about their house burning down appealed to St. Laurence as their patron; if they were afraid of the plague, they made a vow to St. Sebastian or Roch.[67] There were countless other such abominations, and everyone selected their own saints and worshiped them and invoked their help in time of need. In this category also belong those who go so far as to make a pact with the devil so that it may give them plenty of money, help them in love affairs, protect

This woodcut, printed in 1520, depicts Christians worshiping the crucified Jesus while others break the first commandment by worshiping an idol.

---

k   Matt. 6:24.

l   *Freundschaft* (Ger.), *amicitia* (Lat.) is translated as "family" in the *Book of Concord*.

67. Apollonia was martyred on 9 February in 248 or 249, with her teeth being pulled out; she was called on for relief in toothache. Laurence, a Roman deacon, may have been roasted on a gridiron on 10 August in 258. Sebastian from Rome was reputedly executed by bow and arrow on 20 January in the early fourth century. A Franciscan monk called Roch (c. 1348–c. 1376/79) from Montpellier, who devoted himself to caring for victims of the plague in Italy, has his feast day on 16 August.

68. Ger.: *Abgötterei*, meaning "idolatry" or "idolization." While the term itself refers to extreme veneration and glorification of an object, in religious discourse, particularly biblically oriented, it denotes worship of an image or an object, something that is strictly forbidden in the Jewish law. Christians have experienced iconoclastic reactions in the course of a history as they negotiated the appropriateness of images and tangible symbols in Christian religious life. Most famous were the eighth- and ninth-century iconoclastic riots in Byzantium. Luther's concern is not the use of images or symbols for God but, more broadly, anything that one's heart clings to instead of God as the object of devotion.

69. Luther refers to Greco-Roman deities as examples of idolatry: the Romans venerated Hercules and Mercury as gods of wealth and prosperity; Venus, often identified with Aphrodite, gave success in love; Diana, identified with Artemis, was the Roman goddess of the moon; Lucina, the goddess of childbirth, was identified with Juno.

70. The definition of a "pagan" is practicing either no religion or one that is outside the main world religions. In Luther's case, pagans are every person who is not a Christian. The term *heiden* (Ger.), translated as "Gentile" or "pagan," in Luther's use, means typically *Nichtjuden*, "not-Jewish" (i.e., Gentile) if not used in a sense of *Nichtgläubige*, "nonbeliever" or "non-Christian."

their cattle, recover lost property, etc., as magicians and sorcerers do. All of them place their heart and trust elsewhere than in the true God, from whom they neither expect nor seek any good thing.

Thus you can easily understand what and how much this commandment requires, namely, that one's whole heart and confidence be placed in God alone, and in no one else. To have a God, as you can well imagine, does not mean to grasp God with your fingers, or to put God into a purse, or to shut God up in a box. Rather, you lay hold of God when your heart grasps and clings to God. Clinging with your heart is nothing else than entrusting yourself completely to God who wishes to turn us away from everything else apart from God and to draw us to God as the one, eternal good. It is as if God said: "What you formerly sought from the saints, or what you hoped to receive from mammon or from anything else, turn to me for all of this; look on me as the one who will help you and lavish all good things upon you richly."

Look, here you have the true honor and worship that please God, which God also commands under penalty of eternal wrath, namely, that the heart should know no other consolation or confidence than in God, nor let itself be torn from God, but risk everything for God's sake and disregard everything else on earth. On the other hand, you will easily see and judge how the world practices nothing but false worship and idolatry.[68] There has never been a nation so wicked that it did not establish and maintain some sort of worship. All people have set up their own god, to whom they looked for blessings, help, and comfort.

For example, the pagans, who put their trust in power and dominion, exalted Jupiter as their supreme god. Others, who strove for riches, happiness, pleasure, and the good life, venerated Hercules, Mercury, Venus, or others, while pregnant women worshiped Diana or Lucina, and so forth.[69] They all made a god out of what their heart most desired. Even in the mind of all the "pagans,"[70] therefore, to have a god means to trust and believe. The trouble is that their trust is false and wrong, for it is not placed in the one God, apart from whom there truly is no god in heaven or on earth. Accordingly the pagans actually fashion their own fancies and dreams about God into an idol and rely on an empty nothing. So it is with all idolatry. Idolatry does not consist merely of erecting an image and praying to it, but it is primarily a matter of the heart, which fixes its gaze upon other things and seeks help and consolation from creatures, saints, or devils. It neither cares for God nor expects good things from God sufficiently to trust that God wants to help, nor does it believe that whatever good it encounters comes from God.

There is, moreover, another false worship. This is the greatest idolatry that we have practiced up until now, and it is still rampant in the world. All the religious orders are founded upon it. This kind of worship involves only the kind of conscience that seeks help, comfort, and salvation in its own works and presumes to wrest heaven from God. Such worship keeps track of the endowments, fasts, and celebrations of the Mass, etc. It relies on such things and boasts of them, unwilling to receive anything as a gift of God, but desiring to earn everything by itself or to merit everything by works of supererogation,[71] just as if God were in our service or debt and we were God's liege lords.[72] What is this but to have made God into an idol—indeed, an "apple-god"[73]—and to have set ourselves up as God? But this reasoning is a little too subtle and is not suitable for young pupils.

This much, however, should be said to the common people,[74] so that they may mark well and remember the sense of this commandment: We are to trust in God alone, to look to God alone, and to expect God to give us only good things; for it is God who gives us body, life, food, drink, nourishment, health, protection, peace, and all necessary temporal and eternal blessings. In addition, God protects us from misfortune and rescues and delivers us when any evil befalls us. It is God alone (as I have repeated often enough) from whom we receive everything good and by whom we are delivered from all misfortune. This, I think, is why we Germans from ancient times have called God by a name more elegant and worthy than found in any other language, a name derived from the word "good,"[75] because God is an eternal fountain who overflows with pure goodness and from whom pours forth all that is truly good.

Although much that is good comes to us from human beings, nevertheless, anything received according to God's command and ordinance in fact comes from God. Our parents and all authorities—as well as everyone who is a neighbor—have received the command to do us all kinds of good. So we receive our blessings not from them, but from God through them. Creatures are only the hands, channels, and means through which

71. Supererogatory works (from Lat. *supererogare*, "pay too much") are "extra" good works performed beyond what God requires. In the teaching of the indulgences, these extra merits of the saints accumulate to form a special treasure that can benefit other, repenting Christians and decrease the time and amount otherwise required for acts of satisfaction. Luther voices questions on the system of forgiveness and retribution in his *95 Theses* of 1517 (LW 31:17–33), e.g., theses 56–58; see also TAL, vol. 1:41–42.

72. In the medieval feudal society, vassals were obligated to render allegiance and service to their lord and lady.

73. Ger.: *Apfelgott*. The word may possibly be a corruption of *Aftergott*, a "sham god." On 15 June 1539, Luther spoke of Holy Roman Emperor Ferdinand I (1503–1564) as an *Apfelkönig*, an "apple-king." In 1530 he wrote of *Apfelkönige oder gemalete Herrn*, "apple-kings or painted lords," the latter expression being a term of derision somewhat like "plaster saints."

74. Luther's choice of words to talk about "simple" people (Ger.: *Einfachen*; Lat.: *Simpliciorum*)—that is, uneducated people—would sound offensive today. The word "common" captures Luther's intent to talk about the "average Jim and Jane."

75. Ger.: *gut*, "good." This derivation is etymologically incorrect, as the words for "God" (*Gott*) and "good" (*gut*) are not related in either Gothic or in Middle High German. It is also noteworthy that the name of God and the word for "good" have many quite different renditions in European languages.

God bestows all blessings. For example, God gives to the mother breasts and milk for her infant or gives grain and all sorts of fruits from the earth for sustenance—things that no creature could produce by itself. No one, therefore, should presume to take or give anything unless God has commanded it. This forces us to recognize God's gifts and give God thanks, as this commandment requires. Therefore, we should not spurn even this way of receiving such things through God's creatures, nor are we through arrogance to seek other methods and ways than those God has commanded. For that would not be receiving them from God, but seeking them from ourselves.

Let each and everyone, then, see to it that you esteem this commandment above all things and not make light of it. Search and examine your own heart thoroughly, and you will discover whether or not it clings to God alone. If you have the sort of heart that expects from God nothing but good, especially in distress and need, and renounces and forsakes all that is not God, then you have the one, true God. On the contrary, if your heart clings to something else and expects to receive from it more good and help than from God and does not run to God but flees from God when things go wrong, then you have another god, an idol.

Consequently, in order to show that God will not have this commandment taken lightly but will strictly watch over it, God has attached to it, first, a terrible threat, and, then, a beautiful, comforting promise. Both of these should be thoroughly emphasized and impressed upon the young people so that they may take them to heart and remember them.[76] [. . .]

The Second Commandment

"You are not to take the name of God in vain."

Just as the first commandment instructs the heart and teaches faith, so this commandment leads us outward and directs the lips and tongue into a right relationship with God. For the first things that burst forth and emerge from the heart are words. As I have taught above how to answer the question of what it means to have a god,[m] so you must learn to understand simply the meaning of this and all the other commandments and apply it to yourself.

76. Luther believed that the Ten Commandments were arranged in the decreasing order of importance. Here the part "Explanation of the Appendix to the First Commandment" is left out, see BC, 390–92.

m See n. 68, p. 302.

If you are asked, "What does the second commandment mean?" or, "What does it mean to take the name of God in vain or to misuse it?" you should answer briefly: "It is a misuse of God's name if we call upon the Lord[77] God in any way whatsoever to support falsehood or wrong of any kind." What this commandment forbids, therefore, is appealing to God's name falsely or taking God's name upon our lips when our heart knows or should know that the facts are otherwise—for example, when taking oaths in court and one party lies about the other. God's name cannot be abused more flagrantly than when it is used to lie and deceive. Let this be the simplest and clearest explanation of this commandment.

From this all people can figure out for themselves when and in how many ways God's name is misused, although it is impossible to enumerate all its misuses. To discuss it briefly, however, misuse of the divine name occurs first of all in business affairs and in matters involving money, property, and honor, whether publicly in court or in the marketplace or wherever someone commits perjury and swears a false oath in God's name or by one's own soul. This is especially common in marriage matters when two people secretly betroth themselves to each other and afterward deny it with an oath.[78] The greatest abuse, however, is in spiritual matters, which affect the conscience, when false preachers arise and present their lying nonsense as God's word.

See, all of this is an attempt to deck yourself out with God's name or to put up a good front and justify yourself with God's name, whether in ordinary worldly affairs or in sophisticated and difficult matters of faith and doctrine. Also to be numbered among the liars are the blasphemers, not only the very cross ones who are known to everyone and disgrace God's name flagrantly—they should take lessons from the executioner, not from us—but also those who publicly slander the truth and God's word and consign it to the devil. There is no need to say anything more about this now.

77. Ger.: *Herrn; Herr,* literally "Lords," "Lord," or "Sir." This term encompasses the implications of Jesus' lordship over Christians' life and death. See, below, the explanation of the second part of the Creed, p. 356ff.

78. Marriage in Luther's time was formed with a promise and an intercourse between the two

This woodcut, printed in 1520, illustrates the violation of the second commandment, "You shall not misuse God's name" or "take God's name in vain." A gambler swears as Christ is crucified in the background.

parties, and at a time when parental involvement was considered instrumental in suitable marriage arrangements, the private promises of the "eloping" couples became a problem for Luther to address. Shortly after this, Luther addressed the subject of secret engagements in his *On Marriage Matters* (LW 46:259–320).

Let us learn and take to heart how much is at stake in this commandment and diligently guard against and avoid every misuse of the holy name as the greatest sin that can be committed outwardly. Lying and deceiving are themselves great sins, but they become much more serious when we try to justify and confirm them by invoking God's name and thus make it into a cloak to hide our shame. Thus one lie becomes two—indeed, a whole pack of lies.

Therefore God has added a solemn threat to this commandment: "For the Lord will not acquit anyone who misuses God's name."*n* This means that no one will be let off or go unpunished. As little as God will permit the heart that turns away from God to go unpunished, just as little will God permit God's name to be used to disguise a lie. Unfortunately, it is now a common affliction throughout the world that there are just as few who do not use God's name for lies and all kinds of wickedness as there are few who trust in God with their whole heart.

By nature we all have this lovely virtue that whenever we commit a wrong we like to cover it and gloss over our disgrace so that no one may see or know it. None of us is so audacious as to boast of the wickedness we have committed. We prefer to act in secret without anyone knowing about it. When we get caught, then God and God's name must be dragged into it, so that the dirty business may be made honorable and the disgrace noble. That is the common way things go in the world, and, like a great flood, it has inundated all lands. Therefore we get what we deserve: plague, war, famine, fire, flood, naughty spouses and children and servants, and troubles of every kind. Where else could so much misery come from? It is a great mercy that the earth keeps on supporting and feeding us. Above all else, therefore, our young people should be strictly required and trained to hold this as well as the other commandments in high regard. Whenever they violate them, we must be after them at once with the rod, confront them with the commandment, and continually impress it upon them, so that they may be brought up not merely with punishment but with reverence and fear of God.

Now you understand what it means to take God's name in vain. To repeat it briefly, it is either simply to lie and assert under

n　Exod. 20:7.

God's name something that is not true, or it is to curse, swear, practice magic,[79] and, in short, to do evil of any sort.

In addition, you must also know how to use the name of God properly. With the words "You are not to take the name of God in vain," God at the same time gives us to understand that we are to use God's name properly, for it has been revealed and given to us precisely for our use and benefit. Therefore, since we are forbidden here to use God's holy name in support of falsehood and wickedness, it follows, conversely, that we are commanded to use it in the service of truth and of all that is good—for example, when we swear properly where it is necessary and required, or also when we teach properly, or, again, when we call on God's name in time of need, or thank and praise God in time of prosperity, etc. All of this is summarized in the command in Psalm 50[:15]: "Call on me in the day of trouble; I will deliver you, and you shall glorify me." All of this is what it means to call on God's name to support the truth and to use it devoutly. In this way God's name is hallowed, as we pray in the Lord's Prayer.

Here you have the substance of the entire commandment explained. When it is understood in this way, you have easily solved the question that has troubled many teachers: why swearing is forbidden in the gospel, yet Christ, St. Paul, and other saints often took oaths.[80] The explanation is briefly this: We are not to swear in support of evil (that is, to a falsehood) or unnecessarily; but in support of the good and for the advantage of our neighbor we are to swear. This is a truly good work by which God is praised, truth and justice are confirmed, falsehood is refuted, people are reconciled, obedience is rendered, and quarrels are settled. For here God personally intervenes and separates right from wrong, good from evil. If one party swears falsely, there follows judgment: that person will not escape punishment. Although it may take a long time, nothing such people do will succeed in the end; everything gained by the false oath will slip through their fingers and will never be enjoyed. I have seen this in the case of many who broke their promise of marriage under oath; they never enjoyed a happy hour or a healthful day thereafter, and thus they came to a miserable end with their body, soul, and possessions.

Therefore I advise and urge, as I have done before, that by means of warning and threat, restraint and punishment, children be trained in due time to beware of lying and especially

79. Magic includes various techniques used with incantation to control or steer the forces of nature toward a desired outcome.

80. For example, Saints Augustine of Hippo (354–430) and Jerome (c. 347–420). The issue arose with particular urgency with the Anabaptists, who objected to taking oaths as unbiblical. This choice was considered by many to be an expression of civil disobedience and a danger to the public well-being. This objection to taking an oath or pledging allegiance led to their persecution by other Christians, Catholics and Protestants alike. See Matt. 5:33-37; 26:63-64; 2 Cor. 1:23; and Gal. 1:20. On taking oaths, see Luther's *Sermons on the Sermon on the Mount* (LW 21:99–104).

to avoid calling on God's name in support of it. Where they are allowed to act in this way, no good will come of it. It is evident that the world is more wicked than it has ever been. There is no government, no obedience, no fidelity, no faith—only perverse, unbridled people whom no teaching or punishment can help. All of this is God's wrath and punishment on such willful contempt of this commandment.

On the other hand, one must urge and encourage children again and again to honor God's name and to keep it constantly on their lips in all circumstances and experiences, for the proper way to honor God's name is to look to it for all consolation and therefore to call on it. Thus, as we have heard above, first the heart honors God by faith and then the lips by confession.

This is also a blessed and useful habit, and very effective against the devil, who is always around us, lying in wait to lure us into sin and shame, calamity and trouble. The devil hates to hear God's name and cannot long remain when it is uttered and invoked from the heart. Many a terrible and shocking calamity would befall us if God did not preserve us through our calling on God's name. I have tried it myself and have indeed experienced that often a sudden, great calamity was averted and vanished in the very moment I called on God.[81] To defy the devil, I say, we should always keep the holy name on our lips so that it may not be able to harm us as it would like to do.

For this purpose it also helps to form the habit of commending ourselves each day to God—our soul and body, spouse, children, servants, and all that we have—for God's protection against every conceivable need. This is why the *Benedicite*, the *Gratias*,[o] and other evening and morning blessings were also introduced and have continued among us. From the same source comes the custom learned in childhood of making the sign of the cross[82] when something dreadful or frightening is seen or heard, and saying, "Lord God, save me!" or, "Help, dear Lord Christ!" and the like. Likewise, if someone unexpectedly experiences good fortune— no matter how insignificant—one may say, "God be praised and

81. Luther recalls his encounter with the devil while hiding at the Wartburg Castle in 1521–22 and other times when he was aware of its presence. See Denis R. Janz, "Devil," in *The Westminster Handbook to Martin Luther* (Louisville: Westminster John Knox, 2010). Also, Volker Leppin, "Luther on Devil," *Seminary Ridge Review* 16, no. 2 (Spring 2014): 13–27. See n. 303, p. 414, on the devil.

82. The ritual of blessing by making the sign of the cross—forehead, lower chest or stomach, and both shoulders, with a trinitarian formula—has been in continuous use both in the East and the West since the second century (record from Tertullian; *De cor. Mil.*, iii).

o   Luther included in his *Small Catechism* the *Benedicite* (from Ps. 145:15-16) and the *Gratias* (from Ps. 106:1; 136:26; 147:9-11), from the medieval breviary, prayers for before and after the meals.

thanked!" "God has bestowed this on me!" etc.—just as children used to be taught to fast and pray to St. Nicholas and other saints.[83] But these practices would be more pleasing and acceptable to God than life in a monastery or Carthusian holiness.[84]

See, with simple and playful methods like this we should bring up young people in the fear and honor of God so that the first and second commandments may become familiar and constantly be practiced. Then some good may take root, spring up, and bear fruit, and people may grow to adulthood who may give joy and pleasure to an entire country. That would also be the right way to bring up children, while they may be trained with kind and agreeable methods.[p] For what a person enforces

83. The word *saint* refers to the persons revered as exceptionally holy and those recognized for their holiness by the church's official canonization. The saints would have their designated dates in the church calendar, and different saints were associated with particular causes and issues. For example, St. Nicholas Day on 6 December is a time for giving gifts. Saint Nicholas was a fourth-century bishop of Myra, in Lycia, a miracle worker and a secret gift giver, who in veneration became the patron saint of children.

84. The Carthusian Order, founded by St. Bruno (c. 1030–1101) at the Grande Chartreuse near Grenoble, France, in 1084, was frequently mentioned by Luther as an exceptional monastic order.

Saint Nicholas, fourth-century bishop of Myra,
is depicted in a twelfth-century Russian icon
of the Novgorod School in the
Holy Ghost Monastery Novgorod.

p   For more, see also the explanation of the fourth commandment.

85. The words *den Feiertag heiligen* (Ger.) and *sabbati sanctifices* (Lat.) refer to a day of special celebration, and could also be applied to church festivals, such as saints' days. In reference to the Sabbath observance, the translations "make holy" or "sanctify" can replace the traditional "hallow."

86. Together with circumcision and kosher laws, Sabbath observance was (and is) one of the three central characteristics of Jewish life and practice. Generally speaking, Luther continued to speak about Jewish observances as "laws" in a negative sense, associated with "works' righteousness" as opposed to "justification by faith." Luther judged Jewish law observance to be as harmful as the merit system he criticized in the medieval church.

87. In Luther's world, *Feierabend machen* was the eve of a celebration or a festival when working stopped; later, it came to mean simply "quitting time" on any day. Another expression Luther uses is *heiligen Abend geben*, literally, "to give a holy eve"—naming the practice of letting one's workers cease work the evening before the celebration. The Latin word *sanctificare* implies a more religious meaning and translates as "to sanctify" or "to keep holy."

by means of beatings and blows will come to no good end. At best, the children will remain good only as long as the rod is on their backs.

But this kind of training takes root in their hearts so that they fear God more than they do rods and clubs. This I say plainly for the sake of the young people, so that it may sink into their minds, for when we preach to children we must use baby talk. We have prevented the misuse of the divine name and taught its proper use, not only by how we speak but also by the way we act and live, so that everyone may know that God is well pleased with the right use of God's name and will just as richly reward it as God will terribly punish its misuse.

The Third Commandment

"You are to keep holy the day of rest."[85]

Our word "holy day" or "holiday" is so called from the Hebrew word "Sabbath,"[86] which properly means to rest, that is, to cease from work; hence our common expression for "stopping work"[q] literally means "taking a holiday."[87] In the Old Testament, God set apart the seventh day, appointed it for rest, and commanded it to be kept holy above all other days.[r] As far as outward observance is concerned, the commandment was given to the Jews alone.

They were to refrain from hard work and to rest, so that both human beings and animals might be refreshed and not be exhausted by constant labor. In time, however, the Jews interpreted this commandment too narrowly and grossly misused it. They slandered Christ and would not permit him to do the very same things they themselves did on that day, as we read in the gospel[s]—as if the commandment could be fulfilled by refraining from work of any kind. This was not its intention, but rather, as we shall hear, it meant that we should sanctify the holy day or day of rest.[t]

q   Ger.: *Feierabend machen. Feiern* means "to celebrate"; *Feiertag,* a "day of celebration," or "holiday."

r   Gen. 2:3.

s   Matt. 12:1-13; Mark 2:23-28; 3:2-4; Luke 6:1-10; 13:10-17; 14:1-6; John 5:9-18; 7:22-23; 9:14-16.

t   Ger.: *den Feier oder Ruhetag heiligten,* which means "to sanctify" or "to make holy" or "to keep holy" the day of celebration and rest.

Therefore, according to its outward meaning, this commandment does not concern us Christians. It is an entirely external matter, like the other regulations of the Old Testament associated with particular customs, persons, times, and places, from all of which we are now set free through Christ." But to give a Christian interpretation to the simple people of what God requires of us in this commandment, note that we do not observe holy days for the sake of intelligent and well-informed Christians, for they have no need of them. We observe them, first, because our bodies need them. Nature teaches and demands that the common people—menservants and maidservants who have gone about their work or trade all week long—should also retire for a day to rest and be refreshed. Second and most important, we observe them so that people will have time and opportunity on such days of rest (which otherwise would not be available) to attend worship services, that is, so that they may assemble to hear and discuss God's word and then offer praise, song, and prayer to God.[88]

But this, I say, is not restricted, as it was among the Jews, to a particular time so that it must be precisely this day or that, for in itself no one day is better than another.[89] Actually, worship ought to take place daily. However, because this is more than the common people can do, at least one day a week ought to be set apart for it. Because Sunday has been appointed for this purpose from ancient times, it should not be changed, so that things may be done in an orderly fashion and no one creates disorder by unnecessary innovation.[90]

This, then, is the simple meaning of this commandment: Because we observe holidays anyhow, we should use them to learn God's word. The real business of this day should be preaching for the benefit of young people and the poor common folk. However, the observance of rest should not be so restrictive as to forbid incidental and unavoidable work.

Accordingly, when you are asked what "You are to keep the day of rest" means, answer: "Keeping the day of rest means to keep it holy." What is meant by "keeping it holy"?" Nothing else than devoting it to holy words, holy works, and holy living. The day itself does not need to be made holy, for it was created holy.

88. Luther wrote in *Against the Heavenly Prophets in the Matter of Images and Sacraments* (1525): "It is not necessary to observe the Sabbath or Sunday because of Moses' commandment. Nature also shows and teaches that one must now and then rest a day, so that human beings and beasts may be refreshed. This natural reason Moses also recognized in his Sabbath law, for he places the Sabbath under human beings, as also Christ does (Matt. 12[:1ff.] and Mark 3[:2ff.]). For where [Sabbath] is kept for the sake of rest alone, it is clear that one who does not need rest may break the Sabbath and rest on some other day, as nature allows. The Sabbath is also to be kept for the purpose of preaching and hearing the word of God" (LW 40:98). See also the article on *Against the Heavenly Prophets* in this volume, pp. 38–125.

89. Luther often finds an occasion to criticize the Jewish traditions and rituals and following the Jewish laws, such as those ordering the celebration of the Sabbath and limiting activities.

90. Christians began gathering for worship on Sunday mornings already during the first century, also joined by Jewish Christians who observed Sabbath the day before. Emperor Constantine in the fourth century designated the "sun day" as a day of rest for all and a time for worship for Christians.

u   See Col. 2:16-17.

v   In this context, *den feiertag heiligen* (Ger.) means *als heilig halten*, that is, "to hold as holy" or "sanctify."

91. Young people's preparations for a dance.

92. Ger.: *Heiligtumb*; literally, "relic." Luther compares the word of God to a relic that is above all other "holy objects."

93. Relics were important in medieval Christian religious life as tangible insurances of protection or potentially beneficial closeness to holiness. Body parts or belongings of revered saints were collected in reliquaries for viewing (sometimes against a fee) for the sustenance of faith.

94. One of Luther's radical teachings on holiness and sainthood was that there was no such special status to be earned but that sinners were also saints, on account of Christ's grace. Losing the saints, given their important role in medieval religiosity, was difficult. This was the case also with Luther himself, who had grown up with the large family of saints from which to draw support. He had famously called upon St. Anna when caught by a thunderstorm. The saints never quite left Lutheran piety. Rather, Lutherans continued to respect the church's saints and began to honor with special veneration some among their own. See Robert Kolb, *For All the Saints: Changing Perceptions of Martyrdom and Sainthood in the Lutheran Reformation* (Macon, GA: Mercer University Press, 1987). See n. 83, p. 309.

But God wants it to be holy for you. So it becomes holy or unholy on your account, depending on whether you spend it doing something holy or unholy. How does such sanctifying[w] take place? Not when we sit behind the stove and refrain from hard work, or place a garland on our head and dress up in our best clothes,[91] but, as has been said, when we make use of God's word and exercise ourselves in it.

Truly, we Christians ought to make every day such a holy day and devote ourselves only to holy things, that is, to occupy ourselves daily with God's word and carry it in our hearts and on our lips. However, as we have said, because we all do not have the time and leisure, we must set aside several hours a week for the young people, or at least a day for the whole community, when we can concentrate only on these matters and deal especially with the Ten Commandments, the Creed, and the Lord's Prayer, and thus regulate our entire life and being in accordance with God's word. Whenever this practice is in force, a holy day is truly kept. When it is not, it ought not be called a Christian holy day. For non-Christians can spend a day in rest and idleness, too, and so can the whole swarm of clerics in our time who stand day after day in the church, singing and ringing bells, but without keeping a single day holy, because they neither preach nor practice God's word, but rather teach and live contrary to it.

For the word of God is the true holy object[92] above all holy objects.[93] Indeed, it is the only one we Christians know and have. Even if we had the bones of all the saints or all the holy and consecrated vestments gathered together in one pile, they would not help us in the least, for they are all dead things that cannot make anyone holy. But God's word is the treasure that makes everything holy. By it all the saints have themselves been made holy. At whatever time God's word is taught, preached, heard, read, or pondered, there the person, the day, and the work is hallowed, not on account of the external work but on account of the word that makes us all saints.[94] Accordingly, I constantly repeat that all our life and work must be based on God's word if they are to be God-pleasing or holy. Where that happens the commandment is in force and is fulfilled. Conversely, any conduct or work apart from God's word is unholy in the sight of God, no matter how

---

w   Ger.: *heiligen*.

splendid and brilliant it may appear, or even if it is altogether covered with holy relics, as are the so-called spiritual walks of life,[95] which do not know God's word but seek holiness in their own works.

Note, then, that the power and force of this commandment consists not in the resting but keeping the day holy, so that this day may have its special holy function. Other work and business are really not designated holy activities unless the person doing them is first holy. In this case, however, a work must take place through which a person becomes holy. This work, as we have heard, takes place through God's word. Places, times, persons, and the entire outward order of worship have therefore been instituted and appointed in order that God's word may exert its power publicly.

Because so much depends on God's word that no holy day is sanctified without it, we must realize that God wants this commandment to be kept strictly and will punish all who despise God's own word and refuse to hear and learn it, especially at the times appointed. Therefore this commandment is violated not only by those who grossly misuse and desecrate the holy day, like those who in their greed or frivolity neglect the hearing of God's word or lie around in taverns dead drunk like swine. It is also violated by that other crowd who listens to God's word as they would to any other entertainment, who only from force of habit go to hear the sermon and leave again with as little knowledge at the end of the year as at the beginning. It used to be thought that Sunday had been properly observed if one went to Mass or listened to the Gospel being read;[96] however, no one asked about God's word, and no one taught it either. Now that we have God's word, we still fail to eliminate this abuse, for we permit ourselves to be preached to and admonished, but we listen without serious concern.

Remember, then, that you must be concerned not only about hearing the word, but also about learning it and retaining it. Do not think that it is up to your discretion or that it is an unimportant matter. It is the commandment of God, who will require of you an accounting of how you have heard, learned, and honored the word.

In the same way those conceited spirits should also be punished who, after they have heard a sermon or two, become sick and tired of it and feel that they know it all and need no more

95. Luther refers to monks, nuns, priests, and bishops. See Luther's treatise *Against the Spiritual Estate of the Pope and the Bishops, Falsely So Called* (1522) (LW 39:239–99).

96. It was not uncommon for people to leave the Mass after the reading of the Gospel.

97. The term comes from Aristotle's *Ethics*, bk. IV. *Acedia* (or *acidia*) was one of the seven deadly sins: pride, envy, lust, gluttony, anger, greed, and sloth as the cardinal or capital sins since the early Christian centuries have expressed the different human tendencies to sin.

instructors. This is precisely the sin that used to be numbered among the mortal sins and was called acidia[97]—that is, laziness or weariness—a malignant, pernicious plague with which the devil bewitches and deceives many hearts so that it may take us by surprise and stealthily take the word of God away again.

Let me tell you this. Even though you know the word perfectly and have already mastered everything, you are daily under the dominion of the devil who does not rest day or night in seeking to take you unawares and to kindle in your heart unbelief and wicked thoughts against these three and all the other commandments. Therefore you must constantly keep God's word in your heart, on your lips, and in your ears. For where the heart stands idle and the word is not heard, the devil breaks in and does its damage before we realize it. On the other hand, when we seriously ponder the word, hear it, and put it to use, such is its power that it never departs without fruit. It always awakens new understanding, pleasure, and devotion, and it constantly creates clean hearts and minds. For this word is not idle or dead, but effective and living. Even if no other benefit or need drove us to the word, yet everyone should be motivated by the realization that through the word the devil is cast out and put to flight, this commandment is fulfilled, and God is more pleased than by any apparently brilliant hypocrisy.

The Fourth Commandment

So far we have learned the first three commandments, which are directed toward God. First, we are to trust, fear, and love God with our whole heart all our lives. Second, we should not misuse God's holy name to support lies or any evil purpose whatsoever, but use it for the praise of God and the benefit and salvation of our neighbor and ourselves. Third, on holy days or days of rest we should diligently devote ourselves to God's word so that all our conduct and life may be regulated by it. Now follow the other seven, which relate to our neighbor. Among these the first and greatest is: "You are to honor your father and mother."

God has given this walk of life, fatherhood and motherhood, a special position of honor, higher than that of any other walk of life under it. Not only has God commanded us to love parents but to honor them. In regard to brothers, sisters, and neighbors in general, God commands nothing higher than that we love them. But God distinguishes father and mother above all other persons on earth, and places them next to Divinity itself. For it is a much higher thing to honor than to love. Honor includes not only love, but also deference, humility, and modesty directed (so to speak) toward a majesty concealed within them. Honor requires us not only to address them lovingly[x] and with high esteem, but above all to show by our actions, both of heart and body, that we respect them very highly, and that next to God we give them the very highest place. For anyone whom we are wholeheartedly to honor, we must truly regard as high and great.[98]

It must therefore be impressed on young people that they revere their parents as God's representatives, and to remember that, however lowly, poor, feeble, and eccentric they may be, they are still their mother and father, given by God. They are not to be deprived of their honor because of their ways or failings. Therefore, we are not to think of their persons, whatever they may be, but of the will of God, who has created and ordained it so. We are indeed all equal in God's sight, but among ourselves it is impossible for there not to be this sort of inequality and proper distinction. Therefore God also commands that you are to obey me as your father and that I have authority over you.[99]

First, then, learn what this commandment requires concerning honor to parents. You are to esteem them above all things and to value them as the most precious treasure on earth. Second, in your words you are also to behave respectfully toward them and are not to speak discourteously to them, to criticize them, or to take them to task, but rather to submit to them and hold your tongue, even if they go too far. Third, you are also to honor them by your actions, that is, with your body and possessions, serving them, helping them, and caring for them when they are old, sick, feeble, or poor; all this you should do not only cheerfully, but also with humility and reverence, doing it as if for God. Those who know how they are to cherish their parents in their hearts will not let them endure want or hunger, but will place them above and beside themselves and share with them all they have to the best of their ability.

98. In Luther's medieval mind-set, the word *honor* implied proper relations and affection, including proper structures for authority and care. Feminist theologians, among others, have brought this concept under renewed scrutiny in light of the crimes that take place in hierarchical relationships, including parent-child relationships, where obedience expectation has enabled abuse.

99. Luther recognizes the holiness of normal human vocations, including and especially the parental calling. He writes, "A wife too should regard her duties in the same light, as she suckles the child, rocks and bathes it, and cares for it in other ways; and as she busies herself with other duties and renders help and obedience to her husband. These are truly golden and noble works" (*The Estate of Marriage* [1522]; LW 45:40). "Likewise, when a father washes diapers, he may be ridiculed by some as an effeminate fool, but "God, with all God's angels and creatures, is smiling—not because that father is washing diapers, but because he is doing so in Christian faith" (LW 45:40). See in the *Sermon on the Estate of Marriage* (1519) on good parenting benefiting the parents, the good of society, and the children as a gift from God (LW 44:12–14).

x   Lat.: *amantes.*

In the second place, notice what a great, good, and holy work is here assigned to children.[100] Unfortunately, it is entirely despised and brushed aside, and no one recognizes it as God's command or as a holy, divine word and teaching. For if we had regarded it in this way, it would have been apparent to everyone that those who live according to these words must also be holy people. Then no one would have needed to institute monasticism or spiritual walks of life.[101] Every child would have kept this commandment and all would have been able to set their consciences right before God and say: "If I am to do good and holy works, I know of none better than to give honor and obedience to my parents, for God has commanded it. What God commands must be much nobler than anything we ourselves may

Portraits of Luther's father, Hans,
and mother, Margaretha, painted by
Lucas Cranach the Elder in 1527.

devise. And because there is no greater or better teacher to be found than God, there will certainly be no better teaching than God personally gives. Now, God amply teaches what we should do if we want to do truly good works, and by commanding them God shows that they are amply God-pleasing. So, if it is God who commands this and knows nothing better to require, I will never be able to improve upon it."

100. Katharina and Martin had several children: Hans, Paul, Martin, Margaretha, and two other daughters who died young, Magdalena and Elisabeth, in addition to several foster children.

101. "Spiritual walk of life" or "estates" was a common term for priests and members of religious orders. Luther radically removes the gap between these and "ordinary" vocations.

In this way, you see, upright children would have been properly trained and reared in true blessedness. They would have remained at home in obedience and service to their parents, and everyone would have had an object lesson in goodness and happiness. However, no one has felt obligated to emphasize God's commandment. Instead, it has been ignored and skipped over, so that children could not take it to heart; they have simply gaped in astonishment at all the things we devised without ever asking God's approval.

For God's sake, therefore, let us finally learn that the young people should banish all other things from their sight and give first place to this commandment. If they wish to serve God with truly good works, they must do what is pleasing to their fathers and mothers, or to those to whom they are subject in their stead. For every child who knows and does this has, in the first place, the great comfort of being able joyfully to boast in defiance of all who are occupied with works of their own choice: "See, this work is well-pleasing to my God in heaven; this I know for certain." Let all of them come forward with their many, great, laborious, and difficult works and boast. Let us see whether they can produce a single work that is greater and nobler than obeying father and mother, which God has ordained and commanded next to obedience to God's own majesty. If God's word and will are placed first and are observed, nothing ought to be considered more important than the will and word of our parents, provided that these, too, are subordinated to God and are not set in opposition to the preceding commandments.[102]

For this reason you should rejoice from the bottom of your heart and give thanks to God who has chosen and made you worthy to perform works so precious and God-pleasing. You should regard it as great and precious—even though it may be looked at as the most trivial and contemptible thing—not because of our worthiness but because it has its place and setting within that jewel and holy shrine, the word and commandment of God. Oh, what a price would all the Carthusians,[103] both monks and nuns,[104] pay if in all their spiritual exercises they could present to God a single work done in accordance with God's commandment and could say with a joyful heart in God's presence: "Now I know that this work is well-pleasing to you." What will become of these poor wretched people when, standing in the presence of God and the whole world, they will blush with shame before a

102. Luther adds an important clause to the obedience expectation: there are situations when obedience is not warranted, when the gospel is in jeopardy and normal rules of obedience can be transgressed.

103. Vincent Obsopoeus, who translated the *Large Catechism* into Latin, substituted "Carmelites" for "Carthusians" here and in the following paragraph. (Only the second substitution was corrected in the printing of the Latin *Book of Concord* in 1584.) The Carmelite Order, founded c. 1154, originally practiced strict asceticism, but by the late Middle Ages it had been transformed into a mendicant order. Late in the sixteenth century it underwent a reform, led by the Spanish mystics St. Teresa of Ávila (1515–1582) and St. John of the Cross (1542–1591).

104. A Carthusian Order for women was founded in 1147.

little child who has lived according to this commandment and will confess that with their entire lives they are not worthy to offer that child a drink of water? That they must torture themselves in vain with their self-devised works[105] serves them right for their devilish perversity in trampling God's commandment under foot—for this they have only scorn and trouble for their reward.

Should not the heart leap and overflow with joy when it can go to work and do what is commanded of it, saying, "See, this is better than the holiness of all the Carthusians, even if they fast to death and never stop praying on their knees"? For here you have a sure text and a divine testimony that God has enjoined this but has not commanded a single word concerning those other works. But it is the plight and miserable blindness of the world that no one believes this—so thoroughly has the devil bewitched us with the false holiness and glamour of our own works.

Therefore, I repeat, I would be glad if people opened their eyes and ears and took this to heart so that we may not again be led astray from the pure word of God into the lying vanities of the devil. Then all would be well; parents would have more happiness, love, kindness, and harmony in their houses, and children would win their parents' hearts completely. On the other hand, where they are obstinate and never do what they are supposed to unless a rod is laid on their backs, they anger both God and their parents. Thus they deprive themselves of this treasure and joy of conscience and lay up for themselves nothing but misfortune. This is also the way things are now going in the world, as everyone complains. Both young and old are altogether wild and unruly; they have no sense of modesty or honor; they do nothing unless driven by blows; and they defame and disparage one another behind their backs in any way they can. Therefore God also punishes them so that they sink into all kinds of trouble and misery. Neither can parents, as a rule, do very much; one fool raises another,[y] and as they have lived, so live their children after them.

Religieuse Chartreuse
en habit de Choeur   *de Poilly f.*
56

A member of the Carthusian Order, or the Order of Saint Bruno, shown here in a choir robe. Engraved by François de Poilly (1623–1693).

y   A proverbial expression.

This, I say, should be the first and greatest reason for us to keep this commandment. If we had no father or mother, we should wish, on account of this commandment, that God would set up a block of wood or stone that we might call father or mother. How much more, since God has given us living parents, should we be happy to show them honor and obedience. For we know that it is highly pleasing to the divine Majesty and to all the angels, that it vexes all the devils, and, besides, that it is the greatest work that we can do, except for the sublime worship of God summarized in the previous commandments. Even alms-giving and all other works for our neighbor are not equal to this. For God has exalted this walk of life above all others; indeed, God has set it up in God's place on earth. This will and pleasure of God ought to provide us sufficient reason and incentive to do cheerfully and gladly whatever we can.

Besides this, it is our duty before the world to show gratitude for the kindness and for all the good things we have received from our parents. But here again the devil rules in the world; children forget their parents, as we all forget God. No one thinks about how God feeds, guards, and protects us and how many blessings of body and soul God gives us. Especially when an evil hour comes, we rage and grumble impatiently and forget all the blessings that we have received throughout our life. We do the very same thing with our parents, and there is no child who recognizes and considers this, unless led to it by the Holy Spirit.

God knows well this perversity of the world, and therefore, by means of the commandments, God reminds and impels all people to think of what their parents have done for them. Then they realize that they have received their bodies and lives from their parents and have been nourished and nurtured by their parents when otherwise they would have perished a hundred times in their own filth. Therefore the wise people of old rightly said, *Deo, parentibus et magistris non potest satis gratiae rependi*, that is, "God, parents, and teachers can never be sufficiently thanked or repaid."[106] Those who look at the matter in this way and think about it will, without compulsion, give all honor to their parents and esteem them as the ones through whom God has given them everything good.

Over and above all this, another strong incentive to attract us into keeping this commandment is that God has attached to it a lovely promise, "that you may have long life in the land

106. Luther writes in *A Sermon on Keeping Children in School* (1530): "I will simply say briefly that a diligent and upright schoolmaster or teacher, or anyone who faithfully trains and teaches boys, can never be adequately rewarded or repaid with any amount of money, as even the heathen Aristotle says" (LW 46:252–53). See also TAL, vol. 5, forthcoming. See Aristotle, *Nicomachean Ethics* 8, 16; and 9, 1.

where you dwell." Here you can see for yourself how important God considers this commandment. God declares not only that it is an object of pleasure and delight to God, but also that it is an instrument intended for our greatest welfare, to lead us to a quiet and pleasant life, filled with every blessing. Therefore St. Paul also highly exalts and praises this commandment, saying in Ephesians 6[:2-3]: "This is the first commandment with a promise: 'so that it may be well with you and you may live long on the earth.'" Although the other commandments also have their own promise implied, yet in none of them is it so plainly and explicitly stated.[z]

Here you have the fruit and the reward, that whoever keeps this commandment will enjoy good days, happiness, and prosperity. On the other hand, the penalty for those who disobey it is that they will die earlier and will not be happy in life. For, in the Scriptures, to have a long life means not merely to grow old, but to have everything that belongs to long life—for example, health, spouse and child, sustenance, peace, good government, etc.—without which this life cannot be enjoyed nor will it long endure. Now, if you are unwilling to answer to your father and mother or to take direction from them, then answer to the executioner; and if you will not answer to him, then answer to the grim reaper,[a] death! This, in short, is the way God will have it: render obedience, love, and service to God who will reward you abundantly with every blessing; on the other hand, if you anger God, upon you God will send both death and the executioner.

Why do we have so many scoundrels who must daily be hanged, beheaded, or broken on the wheel if not because of disobedience? They will not allow themselves to be brought up in kindness; consequently, because of God's punishment, they bring upon themselves the misfortune and grief that is seen in their lives. For it seldom happens that such wicked people die a natural and timely death.

The godly and obedient, however, receive this blessing in that they live long in peace and quietness. They see their children's

---

z   See a treatment on the interconnected topic of "Luther on Marriage, Sexuality, and the Family" by Jane E. Strohl, in *The Oxford Handbook of Martin Luther's Theology*, ed. Robert Kolb, Irene Dingel, and L'ubomír Batka (New York: Oxford University Press, 2015).

a   Ger.: *Streckebein*; literally, "stretch legs," which was a primarily Low German expression for death, used often by Luther.

children, as stated above, "to the third and fourth generation." Again, as we know from experience, where there are fine, old families who prosper and have many children, it is certainly because some of them were brought up well and honored their parents. On the other hand, it is written of the wicked in Psalm 109[:13]: "May their posterity be cut off; may their name be blotted out in a single generation." Therefore, let it be a warning to you how important obedience is to God who treasures it so highly, delights so greatly in it, rewards it so richly, and besides is so strict about punishing those who transgress it.

I say all this so that it may be thoroughly impressed upon the young people, for no one believes how necessary this commandment is, especially since up until now under the papacy it was neither heeded nor taught. These are plain and simple words, and everyone thinks that he or she already knows them well. So they pass over them lightly, fasten their attention on other things, and fail to perceive and believe how angry they make God when they neglect this commandment, and how precious and acceptable a work they perform when they observe it.

Furthermore, in connection with this commandment, we must mention the sort of obedience due to superiors, persons whose duty it is to command and to govern. For all other authority is derived and developed out of the authority of parents. Where a father is unable by himself to bring up his child, he calls on a schoolmaster to teach the child; if he is too weak, he seeks the help of his friends and neighbors; if he dies, he confers and delegates his responsibility and authority to others appointed for the purpose. In addition, he has to have servants—menservants and maidservants—under him in order to manage the household. Thus all who are called masters stand in the place of parents and must derive from them their power and authority to govern. They are all called fathers in the Scriptures because in their sphere of authority they have been commissioned as fathers and ought to have fatherly hearts toward their people. Thus from ancient times the Romans and peoples speaking other languages called the masters and mistresses of the household *patres et matres familias*, that is, housefathers and housemothers.[107] Again, their princes and overlords were called *patres patriae*,[108] that is, fathers of the whole country, to the great shame of us would-be Christians who do not speak of our rulers in the same way, or at least do not treat and honor them as such.

107. Regardless of the patriarchal culture, already in Luther's time, and before, women exercised significant power—if not in public then in the domestic scenes, regardless of the cultural regulations on their gender. For example, Elisabeth von Braunschweig (1510–1558) secured the acceptance of the *Augsburg Confession* in her land (Calenberg-Lüneburg), in addition to teaching her son (the heir to the throne) of the importance of obeying God, the emperor, and his mother. On this complex reality, see, e.g., Steven Ozment, *When Fathers Ruled: Family Life in Reformation Europe* (Cambridge: Harvard University Press, 1985); Kirsi Stjerna, *Women and the Reformation* (Hoboken, NJ: Wiley Blackwell, 2008).

108. Cicero received this title after exposing the conspiracy of Catiline; later it became a part of the Roman emperor's official title.

What a child owes to father and mother, all members of the household owe them as well. Therefore menservants and maidservants should take care not just to obey their masters and mistresses, but also to honor them as their own fathers and mothers and to do everything that they know is expected of them, not reluctantly, because they are compelled to do so, but gladly and cheerfully. They should do it for the reason mentioned above, that it is God's commandment and is more pleasing to God than all other works. They should even be willing to pay for the privilege of serving[109] and be glad to acquire masters and mistresses in order to have such joyful consciences and to know how to do truly golden works. In the past these works were neglected and despised; therefore everyone ran in the devil's name into monasteries, on pilgrimages, and after indulgences,[110] to their own harm and with a bad conscience.

If this could be impressed on the poor people, a servant girl would dance for joy and praise and thank God; and with her careful work, for which she receives sustenance and wages, she would obtain a treasure such as those who are regarded as the greatest saints do not have. Is it not a tremendous honor to know this and to say, "If you do your daily household chores, that is better than the holiness and austere life of all the monks"? Moreover, you have the promise that whatever you do will prosper and fare well. How could you be more blessed or lead a holier life, as far as works are concerned? In God's sight it is actually faith that makes a person holy;[111] it alone serves God, while our works serve people. Here you have every blessing, protection, and shelter under the Lord, and, what is more, a joyful conscience and a gracious God who will reward you a hundredfold. You are a truly noble person[b] if you are simply upright and obedient. If you are not, you will have nothing but God's wrath and displeasure; there will be no peace in your heart, and eventually you will have all sorts of trouble and misfortune.

If this will not convince you and make you upright, we commend you to the executioner and the grim reaper.[c] Therefore, all those willing to take advice should learn that God is not joking. God speaks to you and demands obedience. If you obey God, you

---

109. Such payments by apprentices were a normal part of the medieval guild system.

110. In medieval doctrine, indulgences granted remission of the temporal works of satisfaction for sins in this life or in purgatory. Administered by the pope, they relied on the treasury of "extra merits" accumulated by Christ, the Virgin Mary, and the saints. Popular opinion saw indulgences as providing remission of punishment for sin, and their sale flourished in the Middle Ages. Although contrition and confession were presupposed, in practice the indulgence certificates often were sold for a financial consideration, enabling people, in effect, to buy their way out of the purgatory. See *A Sermon on Indulgences and Grace by the Worthy Doctor Martin Luther, Augustinian Friar* (1517), WA 1:239–46; TAL, vol. 1:57–66.

111. Luther's reformation insight and main theological principle: it is faith that justifies and restores one's relationship with God.

---

b   Ger.: *Junker*, "a noble man."

c   Ger.: *Streckebein*, an expression.

will be God's dear child; but if you despise this commandment, you will also have shame, misery, and grief as your reward.

The same may be said of obedience to the civil authority,[112] which, as we have said, belongs in the category of "fatherhood" as a walk of life, and is the most comprehensive of all. For here one is the father not of an individual family, but of as many people as he has inhabitants, citizens, or subjects.[113] Through civil rulers, as through our own parents, God gives us food, house and home, protection and security, and God preserves us through them. Therefore, because they bear this name and title with all honor as their chief distinction, it is also our duty to honor and respect them as the most precious treasure and most priceless jewel on earth.

Those who are obedient, willing and eager to be of service, and cheerfully do everything that honor demands, know that they please God and receive joy and happiness as their reward. On the other hand, if they will not do so in love, but despise authority, rebel, or cause unrest, let them know that they will have no favor or blessing. Where they count on gaining a gulden,[114] they will lose ten times more elsewhere, or they will fall prey to the executioner, or perish through war, pestilence, or famine, or their children will turn out badly; servants, neighbors, or strangers and tyrants will inflict injury, injustice, and violence upon them until what we seek and earn will finally come home to roost and mete out payment.

112. With *weltlich Oberkeit* (Ger.), "worldly authority," Luther maintains the distinction between two reigns, spiritual and worldly.

113. Here Luther means fatherhood as only fathers were considered the legal heads and authorities in his society. A contemporary reader would want to understand Luther speaking of authority and responsibility in general terms and including women.

114. The word *gulden* refers to thick (typically) golden or, later, silver coins used in Germany, Austria, and Netherlands (the fifteenth-century origins of the word in Dutch).

In this woodcut by Lucas Cranach the Elder, the pope is pictured selling an indulgence.

If we were ever to let ourselves be persuaded that such works of obedience are so pleasing to God and have such a rich reward, we would be absolutely inundated with blessings and have whatever our hearts desire. But because people completely despise God's word and commandment, as if these things had come from some loudmouthed street vendor,[d] we shall see if you are the person who can defy God: how difficult will it be for that person to pay you back in kind? For this reason you will live much better with God's favor, peace, and blessing than you will with disfavor and misfortune. Why do you think the world is now so full of unfaithfulness, shame, misery, and murder? It is because all want to be their own lords, to be free of all authority,[e] to care nothing for anyone, and to do whatever they please. So God punishes one scoundrel by means of another,[f] so that when you defraud or despise your lord, another person comes along and treats you likewise. Indeed, in your own household you must suffer ten times as much wrong from your own wife, children, or servants.

We certainly feel our misfortune, and we grumble and complain about unfaithfulness, violence, and injustice. But we are unwilling to see that we ourselves are scoundrels who have rightly deserved punishment and are in no way better because of it. We spurn grace and blessing; therefore, it is only fair that we have nothing but misfortune without any mercy. Somewhere on earth there must still be some godly people, or else God would not grant us so many blessings! If it were up to us, we would not have a penny[115] in the house or a straw in the field. I have been obliged to use so many words to teach this in the hope that someone may take it to heart, so that we may be delivered from the blindness and misery in which we have sunk so deeply and may rightly understand the word and will of God and sincerely accept it. From God's word we could learn how to obtain an abundance of joy, happiness, and salvation, both here and in eternity.

So we have introduced three kinds of parents this commandment: parents by blood, parents of a household, and parents of the nation.[116] In addition, there are also spiritual parents—not like those in the papacy who have had themselves called "father"

115. *Heller* (Ger.), a small coin, an insignificant amount of money in popular expressions.

116. Luther speaks of fathers, not of mothers, in these positions of authority, on a par with how gender roles were understood at the time. See also n. 113 above.

d Ger.: *Holhipler*; literally, "waffle vendor."
e Ger.: *kaiserfrei*; literally, "free of the emperor."
f A proverbial expression.

but have not performed a fatherly function. For the name of spiritual father or mother belongs only to those who govern and guide us by the word of God. St. Paul boasts that he is such a father in 1 Corinthians 4[:15], where he says, "In Christ Jesus I became your father through the gospel." Because they are parents, they are entitled to honor, even above all others. But they very seldom receive it, for the world's way of honoring them is to chase them out of the country and to begrudge them even a piece of bread.[117] In short, as St. Paul says [1 Cor. 4:13], they must be "the rubbish of the world, the dregs of all things."

Yet it is necessary to impress upon the common people that they who would bear the name of Christian owe it to God to show "double honor"[g] to those who watch over their souls and to treat them well and make provision for them. If you do, God will also give you what you need and not let you suffer want. But here everyone resists and rebels; all are afraid that their bellies will suffer, and therefore they cannot now support one good preacher, although in the past they filled ten fat paunches.[118] For this we deserve to have God deprive us of God's word and blessing and once again allow preachers of lies[h] to arise who lead us to the devil—and wring sweat and blood out of us besides.

Those who keep God's will and commandment before their eyes, however, have the promise that they will be richly rewarded for all they contribute both to their natural and spiritual parents, and for the honor they render them. Not that they shall have bread, clothing, and money for a year or two, but long life, sustenance, and peace, and they will be rich and blessed eternally. Therefore, just do what you are supposed to do, and leave it to God how God will support you and provide for all your wants. As long as God has promised it and has never yet lied, then God will not lie to you either.

This ought to encourage us and so melt our hearts for joy and love toward those to whom we owe honor that we lift up our hands in joyful thanks to God for giving us such promises. We ought to be willing to run to the ends of the earth to obtain them. For the combined efforts of the whole world cannot add a single hour to our life or raise up from the earth a solitary grain

117. Luther reflects on the treatment of those who had preached social reforms, inspired by Luther's preaching, in the early years of the Reformation and in junction to the 1525 Peasants' Revolts. On Luther's hesitant involvement, see, e.g., *Admonition to Peace, A Reply to the Twelve Articles of the Peasants in Swabia* (LW 46:3–44); also TAL, vol. 5, forthcoming.

118. In the Middle Ages, the church positions had been typically paid with land and property endowments. With the reforms that took place, many of such endowments were expropriated by the civil authorities, leaving many an officeholder without a fixed income.

g   1 Tim. 5:17.
h   Ger.: *Lügenprediger*, "Preachers of lies" (see Mic. 2:11), a common sixteenth-century epithet.

of wheat for us. But God can and will give you everything abundantly, according to your heart's desire. Anyone who despises this and tosses it to the wind is unworthy to hear a single word of God.

More than enough has now been said to all those to whom this commandment applies. [. . .] But once again, the real trouble is that no one perceives or pays attention to this. Everyone acts as if God gave us children for our pleasure and amusement, gave us servants merely to put them to work like cows or donkeys, and gave us subjects to treat as we please, as if it were no concern of ours what they learn or how they live. No one is willing to see that this is the command of the divine Majesty, who will solemnly call us to account and punish us for its neglect. Nor is it recognized how very necessary it is to devote serious attention to the young. For if we want capable and qualified people for both the civil and the spiritual realms, we really must spare no effort, time, and expense in teaching and educating our children to serve God and the world. We must not think only of amassing money and property for them. God can provide for them and make them rich without our help, as indeed God does daily. But God has given us children and entrusted them to us precisely so that we may raise and govern them according to God's will; otherwise, God would have no need of fathers and mothers. Therefore let all people know that it is their chief duty—at the risk of losing divine grace—first to bring up their children in the fear and knowledge of God, and, then, if they are so gifted, also to have them engage in formal study and learn so that they may be of service wherever they are needed.[119]

If this were done, God would also bless us richly and give us grace so that people might be trained who would be a credit to the nation and its people. We would also have good, capable citizens, virtuous women, who, as good managers of the household [Titus 2:5], would faithfully raise upright children and servants. Think what deadly harm you do when you are negligent and fail to bring up your children to be useful and godly. You bring upon yourself sin and wrath, thus earning hell by the way you have reared your own children, no matter how holy and upright you may be otherwise. Because this commandment is neglected, God also terribly punishes the world; hence there is no longer any discipline, government, or peace. We all complain about this situation, but we fail to see that it is our own fault. We

119. Luther's interest in children and their well-being set new expectations for family relations and upbringing. On values and traditions regarding children and parenting in Luther's period, see Naomi J. Miller and Naomi Yavneh, eds., *Gender and Early Modern Constructions of Childhood* (Farnham, UK: Ashgate, 2011). See Jane Strohl, "The Child in Luther's Theology: 'For What Purpose Do We Older Folks Exist, Other Than to Care for the Young,'" in Marcia J. Bunge, ed., *The Child in Christian Thought* (Grand Rapids: Eerdmans, 2001), 134–59.

have unruly and disobedient subjects because of how we reign over them. This is enough to serve as a warning; a more extensive explanation will have to await another time.[120]

The Fifth Commandment

"You are not to kill."

We have now dealt with both the spiritual and the civil government, that is, divine and parental authority and obedience. However, here we leave our own house and go out among the neighbors in order to learn how we should live among them, how people should conduct themselves among their neighbors. Therefore neither God nor the government is included in this commandment, nor is their right to take human life abrogated. God has delegated authority to punish evildoers to the civil authorities in the parents' place; in former times, as we read in Moses [Deut. 21:18-20], parents had to judge their children themselves and sentence them to death. Therefore what is forbidden here applies to individuals, not to the governmental officials.

This commandment is easy enough to understand, and it has often been treated because we hear Matthew 5 every year in the Gospel lesson,[121] where Christ himself explains and summarizes it: We must not kill, either by hand, heart, or word, by signs or gestures, or by aiding and abetting. It forbids anger except, as we have said, to persons who function in God's stead, that is, parents and governing authorities. Anger, reproof, and punishment are the prerogatives of God and God's representatives and are to be meted out to those who transgress this and the other commandments.

120. Shortly after this came Luther's *A Sermon on Keeping Children in School* (1530), LW 46:207–58; see also TAL, vol. 5, forthcoming. The importance of Luther's labors in instituting mechanisms for public schools and in convincing the general population as well as those in charge of the vitality of children's education cannot be overemphasized. This is an area where the Reformation's impact was most widely felt.

121. Matthew 5:20-26 was the appointed Gospel for the sixth Sunday after Trinity (seventh Sunday after Pentecost). Sixteen of Luther's sermons on this text have been preserved.

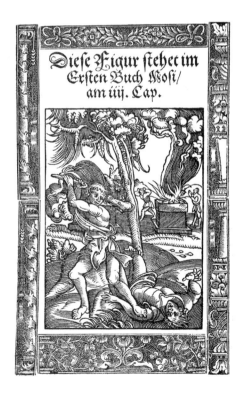

In this illustration of Genesis, chapter 4, Cain murders Abel after God favors Abel's sacrifice over his own as an illustration of the violation of the fifth commandment: "Thou shalt not kill." The artist of this engraving for the 1545 version of Luther's *Small Catechism* is the monogrammist HA.

But the occasion and need for this commandment is that, as God well knows, the world is evil and this life is full of misery.[i] Therefore God has erected this and the other commandments to separate good and evil. Just as there are many attacks against all the commandments, so here, too, we must live among many people who do us harm, and thus we have reason to be their enemy. For example, when your neighbors see that you have received from God a better house and property, or more possessions and good fortune than they, it irritates them and makes them envious of you so that they slander you.

Thus by the devil's prompting you acquire many enemies who begrudge you every blessing, whether physical or spiritual. When we see such people, our hearts turn in rage, and we are ready to shed blood and take revenge. Then follow cursing and blows, and eventually calamity and murder. Here God, like a kind father, steps in and intervenes to settle the quarrel before it turns into real trouble and one person kills the other. In short, God wants to have everyone defended, delivered, and protected from the wickedness and violence of others, and God has placed this commandment as a wall, fortress, and refuge around our neighbors, so that no one may do them bodily harm or injury.

The meaning of this commandment, then, is that no one should harm another person for any evil deed, no matter how much that person deserves it. For wherever murder is forbidden, there also is forbidden everything that may lead to murder. Many people, although they do not actually commit murder, nevertheless curse others and wish such frightful things on them that, if they were to come true, they would soon put an end to them. Everyone acts this way by nature, and it is common knowledge that no one willingly suffers injury from another. Therefore, God wishes to remove the root and source that embitters our heart toward our neighbor. God wants to train us to hold this commandment always before our eyes as a mirror in which to see ourselves, so that we may be attentive to God's will and, with heartfelt confidence and prayer in God's name, commit whatever wrong we suffer to God. Then we can let our enemies rave and rage and do their worst. Thus we may learn to calm our anger and have a patient, gentle heart, especially toward those who give us cause to be angry, namely, our enemies.[122]

122. Luther speaks against killing and harming one's neighbor, even enemies, with words or with deeds. At the same time, with appreciation of order and the system of "two kingdoms" and "two swords," that is, the distinction between organizing the affairs of the church and the society with different realms of authorities, he also reckons the necessity of using appropriately sanctioned violence for the benefit of the people—and ultimately of the gospel. See, e.g., his 1526 *Whether Soldiers, Too, Can Be Christians* (LW 46:87–137); TAL, vol. 5, forthcoming.

---

i   Ger.: *viel unglück hat*, "had much misfortune."

This, then, is the brief summary of this commandment (to impress it most clearly upon the common people what this commandment means by "not killing"). First, we should not harm anyone, either by hand or deed. Next, we should not use our tongue to advocate or advise harming anyone. Furthermore, we should neither use nor sanction any means or methods whereby anyone may be mistreated. Finally, our heart should harbor no hostility or malice against anyone in a spirit of anger and hatred. Thus you should be blameless in body and soul toward all people, but especially toward anyone who wishes or does you evil. For to do evil to someone who desires good for you and does you good is not human but devilish.

In the second place, this commandment is violated not only when we do evil, but also when we have the opportunity to do good to our neighbors and to prevent, protect, and save them from suffering bodily harm or injury but fail to do so. If you send a naked person away when you could clothe him, you have let him freeze to death. If you see anyone who is suffering from hunger and do not feed her, you have let her starve. Likewise, if you see anyone who is condemned[j] to death or in similar peril and do not save her although you have means and ways to do so, you have killed her. It will be of no help for you to use the excuse that you did not assist their deaths by word or deed, for you have withheld your love from them and robbed them of the kindness by means of which their lives might have been saved.[123]

Therefore God rightly calls all persons murderers who do not offer counsel or assistance to those in need and peril of body and life. God will pass a most terrible sentence upon them at the last day, as Christ himself declares. He will say: "I was hungry and you gave me no food, I was thirsty and you gave me nothing to drink, I was a stranger and you did not welcome me, naked and you did not give me clothing, sick and in prison and you did not visit me."[k] That is to say, "You would have permitted me and my family to die of hunger, thirst, and cold, to be torn to pieces by wild beasts, to rot in prison or perish from want."

123. Luther's emphasis on action on behalf of one's neighbor in need, and his vision for institutional ways to secure welfare of those in need, is well manifested in the catechisms and the Protestant church orders, but also already in his *95 Theses*; e.g., in theses 43 and 44 Luther argues for the importance of giving to the poor rather than buying indulgences. See Carter Lindberg, *Beyond Charity: Reformation Initiatives for the Poor* (Minneapolis: Fortress Press, 1993).

j The revised version of the *Large Catechism* published in Wittenberg in 1538, and the German *Book of Concord* (1580), has the variant reading: "innocently condemned."

k Matt. 25:42-43.

124. Luther's interpretation of violence involves acts and words of violence, as well as lack of actions and words that would prevent the suffering of a neighbor. Luther turns the commandment "Do not kill" to an exhortation to be proactive in doing good and preventing suffering and thus to support life.

125. Luther, an ex-monk himself, repeatedly condemns any illusions that such a lifestyle would make one a better person; rather, Luther came to underscore the holiness of all persons in all callings, which is one of the hallmarks of Luther's Reformation principles and Lutheran spirituality. This perspective is articulated throughout the Lutheran confessions, e.g., the *Augsburg Confession* (1530) statement in article XVI.

126. The Roman Catholic tradition distinguishes between divine "commands" (*praecepta*) that are obligatory to all and the "evangelical counsels" (*consilia evangelica*)—voluntary poverty, chastity, obedience—to be observed voluntarily only by those seeking special grace, such as those in a monastic calling. There was no sin in not observing the "counsels." The six duties of all Catholic Christians were (and are): to hear the Mass on Sunday and Holy Days; confess one's sins at least once a year; receive communion at least during the Easter season; observe fasting days; give to the church; and honor the church's marriage laws.

What else is this but to call these people murderous and bloodthirsty? For although you have not actually committed all these crimes, as far as you are concerned, you have nevertheless permitted your neighbors to languish and perish in their misfortune. It is just as if I saw someone who was struggling in deep water or someone who had fallen into a fire and I could stretch out my hand to pull him out and save him, and yet I did not do so. How would I appear before all the world except as a murderer and a scoundrel?

Therefore it is God's real intention that we should allow no one to suffer harm but show every kindness and love.[124] And this kindness, as I said, is directed especially toward our enemies. For doing good to our friends is nothing but an ordinary virtue of pagans, as Christ says in Matthew 5[:46-47].

Once again we have God's word by which God wants to encourage and urge us to true, noble, exalted deeds, such as gentleness, patience, and, in short, love and kindness toward our enemies. We are always reminded to recall the first commandment, that God is our God; that is, that God wishes to help, comfort, and protect us, so that God may restrain our desire for revenge.

If we could thoroughly impress this on people's minds, we would have our hands full of good works to do. But this would not be a preaching for the monastics.[125] It would too greatly undermine the "spiritual walk of life" and infringe on the holiness of the Carthusians.[/] It would be practically the same as forbidding their good works and emptying the monasteries. For in such a teaching the ordinary Christian life would be worth just as much, indeed much more. Everyone would see how the monks mock and mislead the world with a false, hypocritical show of holiness, because they have thrown this and the other commandments to the wind, regarding them as unnecessary, as if they were not commands but counsels.[126] Moreover, they have shamelessly boasted and bragged of their hypocritical calling and works as "the most perfect life," so that they might live a nice, soft life without the cross and suffering. This is why they fled into the monasteries, so that they might not have to suffer wrong from anyone or do anyone any good. Know, however, that

/ See above, n. 103, p. 317.

these works, commanded by God's word, are the true, holy, and divine works in which God rejoices with all the angels. In contrast to them, all human holiness is only stench and filth, and it merits nothing but wrath and damnation.

The Sixth Commandment

"You are not to commit adultery."[m]

The following commandments are easily understood from the preceding one, for they all teach us to guard against harming our neighbor in any way. They are admirably arranged. First, they deal with the person of our neighbors. Then they go on to speak of the person nearest to them, the most important thing to them after their own life, namely, their spouse, who is one flesh and blood with them.[n] With respect to no other blessing can one do them greater harm than here. Therefore, it is explicitly forbidden here to dishonor another's spouse.[o] Adultery is particularly mentioned, because among the Jewish people it was ordered and commanded that one marry. Young people were married at the earliest age possible, and the state of virginity[127] was not commended, nor were public prostitution[p] and lewdness tolerated as they are now. Accordingly, adultery was the most widespread form of unchastity among them.

But inasmuch as there is such a shameless mess and cesspool of all sorts of immorality and indecency among us, this commandment is also directed against every form of unchastity, no matter what it is called. Not only is the outward act forbidden, but also every kind of cause, provocation, and means, so that your heart, your lips, and your entire body may be chaste and afford no occasion, aid, or encour-

In this woodcut from a 1531 printing of Luther's *Large Catechism*, King David looks down from a palace balcony and sees Bathsheba bathing in a pool, accompanied by her attendants. It illustrates the commandment against committing adultery.

127. The German word for virginity, *Jungfrauenstand*, consists of the words "young" and "female." This is telling of the importance laid on women's status in this regard in both Jewish and Christian traditions. Sexual activity for women prior to marriage was not only frowned upon but had also possible legal consequences and could jeopardize already existing marriage arrangements. Virginity was expected

m   Ger.: *Ehebrechen*, literally "breaking the marriage."

n   Gen. 2:24.

o   Originally *Eheweibe* (Ger.) referred to a female spouse, wife.

p   The derogatory word *huren* (Ger.) is used for prostitution.

from women entering the marital contract. Similarly, it was required of women seeking spiritual perfection. The Latin word for virginity has its root in *vir*, "man"; and in medieval spirituality women could seek to "ascend" their female gender by becoming male-like through various spiritual feats, such as living "virginal-ly" in celibacy.

128. The institution of marriage was regarded as essential in protecting citizens against otherwise unavoidable moral chaos in sexual matters. Sex outside the marital union was not socially acceptable. Sexuality was legally, and theologically, tied to marriage. Marriage was understood to begin from the promise of faithfulness between the two parties and the act of intercourse to consummate the marriage.

129. Luther married his wife, an escaped Cistercian nun, Katharina von Bora, on 13 June 1525, and, by his own admission (via letters and Table Talks), the couple enjoyed a loving relationship and an equal partnership with distinct duties. In his testament, Luther even nominated his wife as the sole guardian of their children and possessions, a radical move that the Saxon lawyers immediately modified; Luther's colleague and family friend Philip Melanchthon was named as her guardian, which was a happy arrangement and allowed the widow the (semi-) autonomy Luther had intended. See Martin Treu, *Katherine von Bora: Luther's Wife*, English ed. (Wittenberg: Drei Kastanien Verlag, 2003).

agement to unchastity. Not only that, but you are to defend, protect, and rescue your neighbors whenever they are in danger or need, and, moreover, even aid and assist them so that they may retain their honor. Whenever you fail to do this (although you could prevent a wrong) or do not even lift a finger (as if it were none of your business), you are just as guilty as the culprit who commits the act. In short, all are required both to live chastely themselves and also to help their neighbors to do the same. Thus God wants to guard and protect every husband or wife through this commandment against anyone who would violate them. [128]

However, because this commandment is directed specifically toward marriage as a walk of life and gives occasion to speak of it, you should carefully note, first, how highly God honors and praises this walk of life, endorsing and protecting it by God's own commandment.[9] God endorsed it above in the fourth commandment, "You shall honor father and mother." But here, as I said, God has secured and protected it. For the following reasons, God also wishes us to honor, maintain, and cherish it as a divine and blessed walk of life. God has established it before all others as the first of all institutions, and God created man and woman differently (as is evident) not for indecency but to be true to each other, to be fruitful, to beget children, and to nurture and bring them up to the glory of God.[129] God has therefore blessed this walk of life most richly, above all others, and, in addition, has supplied and endowed it with everything in the world in order that this walk of life might be richly provided for. Married life is no matter for jest or idle curiosity, but it is a glorious institution and an object of God's serious concern. For it is of utmost importance to God that persons be brought up to serve the world, to promote knowledge of God, godly living, and all virtues, and to fight against wickedness and the devil.

Therefore I have always taught that we should not despise or disdain this walk of life, as the blind world and our false clergy do, but view it in the light of God's word, by which it is adorned

---

9   Luther wrote on marriage throughout his career, e.g., in *Sermon on the Estate of Marriage* (1519), LW 44:[3] 7–14; *The Estate of Marriage* (1522), LW 45:[13] 17–49; *On the Babylonian Captivity of the Church* (1520), LW 36:92–106; *A Marriage Booklet for Simple Pastors* (1529), in the *Small Catechism*, BC, 367–71, and LW 53:110–15; *On Marriage Matters* (1530), LW 46:[261] 265–320; *Judgment on Monastic Vows* (1521), LW 44:[243] 251–400.

and sanctified. Because of this word, it is not a walk of life to be placed on the same level with all the others, but it is before and above them all, whether those of emperor, princes, bishops, or any other. Important as the spiritual and civil walks of life are, these must humble themselves and allow all people to enter marriage as a walk of life, as we shall hear. It is not a restricted walk of life, but the most universal and noblest, pervading all Christendom and even extending throughout all the world.[130]

In the second place, you should also remember that it is not just an honorable walk of life but also a necessary one; it is solemnly commanded by God that in general both men and women

130. Luther's arguments about the nobility of the marital vocation, for women and men, were radical in a religious world where asexuality and celibacy were revered, and where women were not considered equal with men either in their creation or redemption. Luther's drastically egalitarian approach draws from his reading of Genesis and the creation of Eve as Adam's equal partner in grace and sin. See Luther's *Lectures on Genesis*, esp. 1:26–2:3; 2:21–25; 3:141–236; also TAL, vol. 6, forthcoming.

Portrait of Luther's wife, Katharina von Bora, painted by Lucas Cranach the Elder, c. 1530.

131. Luther considered marriage as fundamentally instituted by God who "brought husband and wife together, and ordained that they should beget children and care for them." For this reason, Luther interprets from Gen. 1:28 that "The estate of marriage and everything that goes with it in the way of conduct, works, and suffering is pleasing to God" (*The Estate of Marriage*, [1522], LW 45:38); see also TAL, vol. 5, forthcoming.

132. In his *Estate of Marriage* (1522) Luther imagined "eunuchs" (castrated men) as the "third category" for human beings, be they castrated from birth, made so by others, and self-inflicted. "Apart from these groups, let no one presume to be without a spouse" (LW 45:18–22).

133. Already in his foundational Reformation text, *On the Babylonian Captivity of the Church* (LW 36:92–106, esp. 92–96; see also TAL, vol. 3, forthcoming), Luther wrote against the several impediments the medieval Catholic Church had for marriage, including consanguinity, spiritual relationship, bad eyesight, vows, etc.

134. Luther wrote against clergy celibacy and monastic vows early on (preceded by his dean and colleague at first, and later a rival, Andreas Karlstadt von Bodenstein [1486–1541]), leading to arguments that led to instilling clergy marriage, pioneered by Luther's students in 1521 and Karlstadt in 1522. The Catholic Church would only reaffirm the celibacy rule at the Council of Trent (opened 1545 and closed

of all walks of life, who have been created for it, shall be found in this estate.[131] To be sure, there are some (albeit rare) exceptions whom God has especially exempted, in that some are unsuited for married life, or others God has released by a high, supernatural gift so that they can maintain chastity outside of marriage.[132] Where nature functions as God implanted it, however, it is not possible to remain chaste outside of marriage; for flesh and blood remain flesh and blood, and natural inclinations and stimulations proceed unrestrained and unimpeded, as everyone observes and experiences. Therefore, to make it easier for people to avoid unchastity in some measure, God has established marriage, so that all may have their allotted portion and be satisfied with it—although here, too, God's grace is still required to keep the heart pure.[133]

From this you see that our papal crowd—priests, monks, and nuns—resist God's ordinance and commandment when they despise and forbid marriage and boast and vow that they will maintain perpetual chastity while they deceive the common people with lying words and false impressions. For no one has so little love and inclination for chastity as those who under the guise of great sanctity avoid marriage and either indulge in open and shameless fornication[r] or secretly do even worse—things too evil to mention, as unfortunately has been experienced all too often. In short, even though they abstain from the act, yet their hearts remain so full of unchaste thoughts and evil desires that they suffer incessant ragings of secret passion, which can be avoided in married life. Therefore, all vows of chastity outside marriage are condemned and annulled by this commandment; indeed, all poor, captive consciences deceived by their monastic vows are even commanded to forsake their unchaste existence and enter the married life.[134] In this regard, even if the monastic life were godly, still it is not in their power to maintain chastity. If they remain in it, they will inevitably sin more and more against this commandment.

I say these things in order that our young people may be led to acquire a desire for married life and know that it is a blessed and God-pleasing walk of life. Thus it may in due time regain its proper honor, and there may be less of the filthy, dissolute, disorderly conduct that is now so rampant everywhere in public

---

r   Ger.: *hurerei*.

prostitution and other shameful vices resulting from contempt of married life.[135] Therefore parents and governmental authorities have the duty of so supervising the youth that they will be brought up with decency and respectability and, when they are grown, will be married honorably in the fear of God. Then God would add God's blessing and grace so that they might have joy and happiness in their married life.

Let it be said in conclusion that this commandment requires all people not only to live chastely in deed, word, and thought in their particular situation (that is, especially in marriage as a walk of life), but also to love and cherish the spouse whom God has given them. Wherever marital chastity is to be maintained, above all it is essential that husbands and wives live together in love and harmony, cherishing each other wholeheartedly and with perfect fidelity.[136] This is one of the chief ways to make chastity attractive and desirable. Under such conditions, chastity always follows spontaneously without any command. This is why St. Paul so urgently admonishes married couples to love and honor each other.[s] Here again you have a precious good work— indeed, many great works—in which you can happily boast over against all "spiritual walks of life" that are chosen without God's word and commandment.

The Seventh Commandment

"You are not to steal."

After your own person and your spouse, the next thing God wants to be protected is temporal property, and God has commanded us all not to rob or pilfer our neighbor's possessions. For to steal is nothing else than to acquire someone else's property by unjust means. These few words include taking advantage of our neighbors in any sort of dealings that result in loss to them. Stealing is a widespread, common vice, but people pay so little attention to it that the matter is entirely out of hand. As a result, if we were to hang every thief on the gallows, especially those who do not admit it, the world would soon be empty and there would be a shortage of both executioners and gallows. For, as I just said, stealing is not just robbing someone's safe or pocketbook but also taking advantage of someone in the market, in all

1563). Luther relentlessly ridiculed vows that he considered against human nature. E.g., "If you would like to take a wise vow, then vow not to bite off your own nose; you can keep that vow" (*Estate of Marriage* [1522], LW 45:27).

135. In an effort to regulate sexual behavior and direct gender relations into marriage, the Protestant cities tried to outlaw prostitution and close the brothels, with the result of the "sex workers" operating as freelancers or with pimps outside the city walls. On the topic, see, e.g., Lyndal Roper, *The Holy Household: Women and Morals in Reformation Augsburg* (New York: Oxford University Press, 1991). The problem was not unique to Protestant cities: see Tessa Storey, *Carnal Commerce in Counter-Reformation Rome* (Cambridge: Cambridge University Press, 2008).

136. Luther wrote, "Marriage is a covenant of fidelity" and "The estate of marriage consists essentially in consent having been freely and previously given to another" (*Sermon on the Estate of Marriage* [1519], LW 44:10–11). Today Luther's arguments about the spouses' mutual relationship can be applied to same-sex marriages, a practice not yet legally known in the sixteenth century, regardless of the reality of same-sex relations through human history.

---

s Eph. 5:22, 25; Col. 3:18-19.

stores, butcher shops, wine and beer cellars, workshops, and, in short, wherever business is transacted and money is exchanged for goods or services.

We shall make this a bit clearer to the common people, so that they may see how upright we are. Suppose, for example, that a manservant or a maidservant is unfaithful in his or her domestic duties and does damage or permits damage to be done when it could have been avoided. Or suppose that through laziness, carelessness, or malice a servant wastes things or is negligent with them in order to vex and annoy the master or mistress. When this is done deliberately—for I am not speaking about what happens accidentally or unintentionally—you can cheat your employer out of thirty or forty or more gulden[t] a year. If someone else had filched or stolen that much, that person would have been hung on the gallows,[137] but here you become defiant and insolent, and no one dare call you a thief!

I say the same thing about artisans, workers, and day laborers who act high-handedly and never know enough ways to overcharge people and yet are careless and unreliable in their work. These are all far worse than sneak thieves, against whom we can guard with lock and bolt. If we catch the sneak thieves, we can deal with them so that they will not do it anymore. But no one can guard against these others. No one even dares to give them a harsh look or accuse them of theft. People would ten times rather lose money from their purse. For these are my neighbors, my good friends, my own servants—from whom I expect good—who are the first to defraud me.

Furthermore, at the market and in everyday business the same fraud prevails in full power and force. One person openly cheats another with defective merchandise, false weights and measures, and counterfeit coins, and takes advantage of the other by deception and sharp practices and crafty dealings. Or again, one swindles another in a trade and deliberately fleeces, skins, and torments the person.

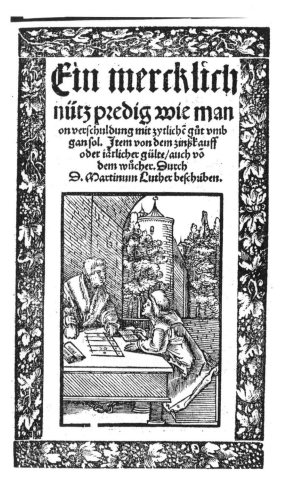

A historiated title-page border surrounds a central woodcut that illustrates a moneylender at work. This engraving adorns the title page of a sermon by Luther against usury. Woodcut by Hans Schäufelein (c. 1480–c. 1539).

---

t   See n. 114, p. 323.

Who can even describe or imagine it all? In short, thievery is the most common craft and the largest guild on earth. If we look at the whole world in all its situations, it is nothing but a big, wide stable full of great thieves. This is why these people are also called armchair bandits[138] and highway robbers. Far from being picklocks and sneak thieves who pilfer the cash box, they sit in their chairs and are known as great lords and honorable, upstanding citizens, while they rob and steal under the cloak of legality.[139]

Yes, we might well keep quiet here about individual petty thieves since we ought to be attacking the great, powerful arch-thieves *with whom lords and princes consort and*[u] who daily plunder not just a city or two, but all of Germany. Indeed, what would become of the head and chief protector of all thieves, the Holy See at Rome, and all its retinue, which has plundered and stolen the treasures of the whole world and holds them to this day?

In short, this is the way of the world. Those who can steal and rob openly are safe and free, unpunished by anyone, even desiring to be honored. Meanwhile, the petty sneak thieves who have committed one offense must bear disgrace and punishment to make the others look respectable and honorable. But they should know that God considers them the greatest thieves, and that God will punish them as they deserve.

This commandment is very far-reaching, as we have shown. Therefore, it is necessary to emphasize and explain it to the common people in order that they may be restrained in their wantonness and that the wrath of God always be kept before their eyes and impressed upon them. For we must preach this not to Christians but chiefly to knaves[140] and scoundrels, though it would certainly be more fitting if the judge, the jailer, or the executioner[141] did the preaching. Let all people know, then, that it is their duty, on pain of God's displeasure, not to harm their neighbors, to take advantage of them, or to defraud them by any faithless or underhanded business transaction. Much more than that, they are also obligated faithfully to protect their neighbors'

137. Death by hanging was often the penalty for theft.

138. *Stuhlräuber* (Ger.), a sixteenth-century expression for "usurers." Luther incorrectly derives the word from *Stuhl* ("chair") and *Räuber* ("robber"); the word actually comes from the Low German *Stôhl*, meaning capital that is loaned at interest.

139. Luther often wrote and preached against the so-called usury (Ger.: *Zinskauf*). The thirteenth- or fourteenth-century Latin term *usuria*, from *usus* or *uti*, the "use," refers to the practice of moneylending at interest. Luther criticized particularly the Jews for this practice, with no empathy for the fact that in the late medieval world, where most professions were prohibited from the Jews, moneylending business was one of the few permitted for the Jews (also by the Jews' own religious ethics), whose service in that role benefited the society at large in many significant ways. See *Trade and Usury* (1524), LW 45:[233–43] 245–310; TAL, vol. 5, forthcoming.

140. There is no good contemporary equivalent for "knave": a dishonest man, a scoundrel, or a "jack" in the deck of playing cards.

141. *Meister Hans* ("master Jack"), an expression Luther frequently used for the executioner.

u The words in italics were included in the first two editions of the *Large Catechism*, printed in Wittenberg and Erfurt in 1529. However, they were already removed while the first Wittenberg edition was in the press, probably by the printer. The passage was restored in the German *Book of Concord* (1580).

property and to promote and further their interests, especially when they get money, wages, and provisions for doing so.

Those who willfully disregard this commandment may indeed get by and avoid the executioner, but they will not escape God's wrath and punishment. Though they may pursue their defiant and arrogant course for a long time, they will still remain tramps and beggars and will suffer all kinds of troubles and misfortunes. Now, you ought to take care of your master's or mistress's[142] property, which enables you to stuff your craw and belly. But you take your pay like a thief and expect to be honored like a member of the nobility. Many of you are even insolent toward masters and mistresses and unwilling to do them the favor and service of protecting them from loss. Look at what you gain. When you acquire property yourself and sit in your own house—which God will help you acquire to your undoing—there will come a day of reckoning and retribution: thirty times over will you have to repay every penny of loss or harm you have caused.

The same thing will happen to artisans and day laborers, from whom one is now obliged to suffer such intolerable insolence. They act as if they were lords over other people's possessions and entitled to whatever they demand. Let them keep on fleecing others as long as they can. God will not forget God's commandment and will pay them what they deserve. God will hang them not on a green gallows but on a dry one.[143] They will neither prosper nor gain anything their whole life long. Of course, if there were a proper government in the country, one could soon put a stop to such insolence, as did the ancient Romans, who promptly took such people by the scruff of their neck so that others took warning.

The same fate will befall those who turn the free public market into nothing but a carrion pit and a robber's den. The poor are defrauded every day, and new burdens and higher prices are imposed. They all misuse the market in their own arbitrary, defiant, arrogant way, as if it were their privilege and right to sell their goods as high as they please without any criticism. We will stand by and let such people hustle, grab, and hoard. But we will trust God, who takes matters into God's own hands. After you have tightened your belt and saved for a long time, God will pronounce a blessing over you: May your grain spoil in the barn, your beer in the cellar, your cattle perish in the stall. Yes, where

142. The titles *Frauen und Herren* (Ger.) imply a position of authority; the contemporary English titles "Mrs. and Mr." would not mean quite the same.

143. Death on the gallows was considered a more ignominious punishment than death on a green tree ("green gallows").

you have cheated and defrauded anyone out of a gulden,[v] your entire hoard ought to be consumed by rust[w] so that you will never enjoy it.

Indeed, we have the evidence before our eyes every day that no stolen or wrongfully acquired possession thrives. How many people are there who scrape and scratch day and night and are not even a penny richer? Even though they amass a great amount, they have to suffer so many troubles and misfortunes that they can never enjoy it or pass it on to their children. But because everyone ignores this and acts as if it were none of our business, God must punish us and teach us morals[x] in a different way. God imposes one affliction after another on us, or God quarters a troop of soldiers among us; in one hour they clean out our safety boxes and purses down to the last penny, and then by way of thanks they burn and ravage house and home and assault and kill wife and children.

In short, no matter how much you steal, be certain that twice as much will be stolen from you. Anyone who robs and takes things by violence and dishonesty must put up with someone else who plays the same game. Because everyone robs and steals from everyone else, God has mastered the art of punishing one thief by means of another. Otherwise, where would we find enough gallows and ropes?

Anyone who is willing to learn should know that this is God's commandment and that God does not want it to be considered a joke. We will put up with those of you who despise, defraud, steal, and rob us. We will endure your arrogance and show forgiveness and mercy, as the Lord's Prayer teaches us. The upright, meanwhile, will have enough, and you will hurt yourself more than anyone else. But beware of how you deal with the poor—there are many of them now—who must live from hand to mouth.[144] If you act as if everyone has to live by your favor, if you skin and scrape them right down to the bone, if you arrogantly turn away those who need your aid, they will go away wretched and dejected, and, because they can complain to no one else, they will cry out to heaven. Beware of this, I repeat, as if it were the devil itself. Such

144. While many families and individuals suffered from extreme poverty in the Middle Ages and many supported themselves by begging, others opted for voluntary poverty and begging in their efforts for spiritual discipline and holiness—while those Christians offering them acts of charity would earn their own spiritual "benefit." Saints like Francis of Assisi (c. 1181–1226) and Clara (Chiara) of Assisi (1194–1253) modeled extreme poverty, and the Mendicant monastics traveled from town to town, relying on the charity Christians were obligated to offer. The reformers wished to eradicate poverty and begging, and Protestant theology did not allow for earning merits through any practice, such as voluntary poverty, begging or almsgiving. See Lindberg, *Beyond Charity*; and Samuel Torvend, *Luther and the Hungry Poor: Gathered Fragments* (Minneapolis: Fortress Press, 2008).

v   See above, n. 114, p. 323.

w   See Matt. 6:19-20; Luke 12:33.

x   The word *mores* (Lat.) refers to manners and moral attitudes.

sighs and cries are no laughing matter, but will have an effect too great for you and all the world to bear. For they will reach God, who watches over poor, troubled hearts, and God will not leave them unavenged. But if you despise and defy this, see whom you have brought upon yourself. If you succeed and prosper, however, you may call God and me liars before the whole world.*

We have now given warning and exhortation enough. Those who do not heed or believe this may go their own way until they learn it by experience. But it needs to be impressed upon the young people so that they may be on their guard and not go along with the old, wayward crowd but instead keep their eyes on God's commandment, lest God's wrath and punishment overtake even them. Our responsibility is only to instruct and to reprove with God's word. But it is the responsibility of the nobility and magistrates[145] to restrain open wantonness. They should be alert and courageous enough to establish and maintain order in all areas of trade and commerce in order that the poor may not be burdened and oppressed and in order that they themselves may not be responsible for other people's sins.

Enough has been said about what stealing is. It should not be narrowly restricted, but it should pertain to anything that has to do with our neighbor. We will sum it up, as we have done in the previous commandments: First, we are forbidden to do our neighbors any injury or wrong in any way imaginable, whether by damaging, withholding, or interfering with their possessions and property. We are not even to consent to or permit such a thing but are rather to avert and prevent it. In addition, we are commanded to promote and further our neighbors' interests, and when they suffer any want, we are to help, share, and lend to both friends and foes.

Anyone who seeks and desires good works will find here more than enough things to do that are heartily acceptable and pleasing to God. Moreover, God lavishes on them a wonderful blessing and generously rewards us for what we do to benefit and befriend our neighbor, as King Solomon also teaches in Proverbs 19[:17]: "Whoever is kind to the poor lends to the Lord, and will be repaid in full." Here you have a rich Lord, who is surely suf-

145. The words *fürsten und Oberkeit* (Ger.) refer to the different authorities, the landowning territorial nobility and the regional city governments and councils.

---

y   See Luther's 1523 *Ordinance of a Common Chest* and *Fraternal Agreement on the Common Chest of the Entire Assembly at Leisnig* (LW 45:159–94).

ficient for your needs and will let you lack or want for nothing. Thus with a happy conscience you can enjoy a hundred times more than you could scrape together by perfidy and injustice. Whoever does not desire this blessing will find wrath and misfortune enough.

The Eighth Commandment

"You are not to bear false witness against your neighbor."

Besides our own body, our spouse, and our temporal property,[146] we have one more treasure that is indispensable to us, namely, our honor and good reputation. For it is important that we not live among people in public disgrace and dishonor. Therefore God does not want our neighbors deprived of their reputation, honor, and character any more than of their money and possessions; God wants everyone to maintain self-respect before spouse, child, servant, and neighbor. In its first and simplest meaning, as the words stand ("You shall not bear false witness"), this commandment pertains to public courts of justice, where one may accuse and malign poor, innocent persons and crush them by means of false witnesses, so that consequently they may suffer punishment in body, property, or honor.

This appears to have little to do with us now, but among the Jews it was an extraordinarily common occurrence.[147] That nation had an excellent, orderly government, and even now, where there is such a government, this sin still has not diminished. The reason is this: Where judges, mayors, princes, or others in authority sit in judgment, it never fails to happen that, true to the usual course of the world, people are loath to offend anyone. Instead, they speak dishonestly with an eye to gaining favor, money, prospects, or friendship. Consequently, poor people are inevitably oppressed, lose their case, and suffer punishment.

And it is a common misfortune in the world that seldom do people of integrity[148] preside in courts of justice.[149] A judge must, above all, be a person of integrity, and not only that, but also wise and perceptive, in fact, a bold and fearless person.[150] Likewise, a witness must be fearless; more than that, someone who is a person of integrity. For those who are to administer justice equitably and to impose penalties will often offend good friends, relatives, neighbors, and the rich and powerful who could do much to harm or help them. Therefore they must be absolutely

146. The words *Zeitliches Gut* (Ger.) refer to the different "goods" one can own in this world.

147. Statements like this disclose Luther's ignorance of the Jewish ways and lives, on the one hand, and, on the other, the medieval Christians' prejudiced view of the Jewish people as being prone to conniving and deceit. In reality, it was often the fellow Christians' lies that cost Jews their livelihoods—and lives, even.

148. The words *frommer Mann* (Ger.) refer to upright and honest persons, without necessarily the connotation of religiously "pious."

149. As an example of such an upright, prudent, and wise jurist, Luther once named Gregory Brück (c. 1484–1557) the chancellor of Electoral Saxony (LW 54:150).

150. In Luther's time, only men could serve in the office of a judge or the equivalent.

151. The laws of the Holy Roman Empire included the civil law (*ius civile*) that applied to all citizens. Originating from Rome and the emperor Justinian's code in the sixth century, in the Middle Ages it served as a foundation for *Corpus iuris civilis*, which was adopted in different forms throughout Europe, also influencing the Catholic Church law, i.e., the canon law. Additionally, there were regional laws and special laws (e.g., the Jewish laws). See Albrecht Classen and Connie Scarborough, eds., *Crime and Punishment in the Middle Ages and Early Modern Age: Mental-Historical Investigations of Basic Human Problems and Social Responses* (Berlin: Walter de Gruyter, 2012); John Witte, *Law and Protestantism: The Legal Teachings of the Lutheran Reformation* (Cambridge: Cambridge University Press, 2002).

152. Luther condemns bearing false witness against one's neighbor and is in favor of "minding one's own business" in a climate of suspicion where the Inquisitional procedures could be easily launched by feeble witness accounts or suggestions of wrongdoing with no sustainable proofs. Most apparent victims of the distorted system were the Jews accused of heresy and violence against Christians, women (especially widows, midwives) suspected of witchcraft, and rebaptizers. Many innocent people were executed on false premises. Luther's admonition against harming one's neighbor with false words thus addresses a life-and-death issue. He knew how fatal the consequences of conniving words could be.

blind, closing their eyes and ears to everything but the evidence presented, and render judgment accordingly.

The first application of this commandment, then, is that all people should help their neighbors maintain their legal rights. One must not allow these rights to be thwarted or distorted but should promote and resolutely guard them, whether this person is judge or witness, no matter what the consequences may be. Here a special goal is set for our jurists: to take care that they deal fairly and honestly with cases, that they let right remain right, not perverting or concealing or suppressing anything on account of someone's money, property, honor, or power. This is one aspect of this commandment and its plainest meaning, applying to all that takes place in court.[151]

Next, it extends much further when it is applied to spiritual jurisdiction or administration. Here, too, all people bear false witness against their neighbors.[152] Wherever there are upright preachers and Christians, they must endure having the world

The burning of a sixteenth-century Dutch Anabaptist, Anneken Hendriks, charged by the Spanish Inquisition with heresy.

call them heretics, apostates,[z] even seditious and desperate scoundrels. Moreover, the word of God must undergo the most shameful and spiteful persecution and blasphemy; it is contradicted, perverted, misused, and misinterpreted. But let this pass; it is the blind world's nature to condemn and persecute the truth and the children of God and yet consider this no sin.[153]

The third aspect of this commandment, which applies to all of us, forbids all sins of the tongue by which we may injure or offend our neighbor. "Bearing false witness" is nothing but a work of the tongue. God wants to hold in check whatever is done with the tongue against a neighbor. This applies to false preachers with their blasphemous teaching, to false judges and witnesses with their rulings in court and their lying and malicious talk outside of court. It applies especially to the detestable, shameless vice of backbiting or slander by which the devil rides us.[a] Of this much could be said. It is a common, pernicious plague that everyone would rather hear evil than good about their neighbors. Even though we ourselves are evil, we cannot tolerate it when anyone speaks evil of us; instead, we want to hear the whole world say golden things of us. Yet we cannot bear it when someone says the best things about others.

To avoid this vice, therefore, we should note that none has the right to judge and reprove a neighbor publicly, even after having seen a sin committed, unless authorized to judge and reprove. There is a very great difference between judging sin and having knowledge of sin. You may certainly know about a sin, but you should not judge it. I may certainly see and hear that my neighbor sins, but I have no command to tell others about it. If I were to interfere and pass judgment on my neighbor, I would fall into a sin greater myself. When you become aware of a sin, however, do nothing but turn your ears into a tomb and bury it until you are appointed a judge and are authorized to administer punishment by virtue of your office.

Those who are not content just to know but rush ahead and judge are called backbiters. Learning a bit of gossip about someone else, they spread it into every corner, relishing and delighting in the chance to stir up someone else's dirt like pigs that roll in manure and root around in it with their snouts. This is nothing

153. The sin of blasphemy was deemed a grave offense. This was behind Luther's persistent criticism of the Jewish believers who, he feared (without due reason), put Christians' well-being in danger with their (in his assessment) blasphemy of not recognizing Jesus as the promised Messiah.

---

z   I.e., a deserter, traitor.

a   A proverbial expression.

else than usurping God's judgment and office and pronouncing the severest kind of verdict or sentence, for the harshest verdict a judge can pronounce is to declare someone a thief, a murderer, a traitor, etc. Therefore those who venture to accuse their neighbor of such guilt assume as much authority as the emperor and all rulers. For though you do not wield the sword, you use your venomous tongue to bring disgrace and harm to your neighbor.

Therefore God forbids you to speak evil about another, even though, to your certain knowledge, that person is guilty. Even less may you do so if you are not really sure and have it only from hearsay. But you say: "Why shouldn't I say it if it is the truth?" Answer: "Why don't you bring it before the proper judge?" "Oh, I can't prove it publicly; I might be called a liar and sent away in disgrace." Ah, my dear, now do you smell the roast?[b] If you do not trust yourself to stand before the persons appointed for such tasks and make your charges, then hold your tongue. If you know something, keep it to yourself and do not tell others. For when you repeat a story that you cannot prove, even though it is true, you appear as a liar. Besides, you act like a scoundrel, for no one should be deprived of one's honor and good name unless these have first been taken away from the person publicly.

Every report, then, that cannot be adequately proved is false witness.[154] Therefore, no one should publicly assert as truth what is not publicly substantiated. In short, what is secret should be left secret, or at any rate be reproved in secret, as we shall hear. Therefore, if you encounter someone with a worthless tongue who gossips and slanders someone else, rebuke such people straight to their faces and make them blush with shame. Then those who otherwise would bring some poor person into disgrace, from which one could scarcely clear one's self, will hold their tongues. For honor and good name are easily taken away but not easily restored.

So you see that we are absolutely forbidden to speak evil of our neighbor. Exception is made, however, of civil magistrates, preachers, and fathers and mothers in order that we may interpret this commandment in such a way that evil does not go unpunished. We have seen that the fifth commandment forbids us to injure anyone physically, and yet an exception is made of

154. This principle was often violated, e.g., with the Inquisition and in local court procedures, where false witness and lack of evidence could lead to torture and even execution of the individuals suspected of heresy or witchcraft. See n. 152 above.

b   A proverbial expression.

the executioner.[c] By virtue of that office, the executioner does not do the neighbor good but only harm and evil, yet the one in that office does not sin against God's commandment because God has instituted it, and, as the first commandment warns, God has reserved the right of punishment. Likewise, although no one personally has the right to judge and condemn anyone, yet if they are commanded to do so and fail to do it, they sin as much as those who take the law into their own hands apart from any office. In that case necessity requires one to report evil, to prefer charges, to give evidence, to examine witnesses, and to testify. It is no different than when a physician, in order to cure a patient, is sometimes compelled to examine and touch the patient's private parts. Just so, the authorities, fathers and mothers, and even brothers and sisters and other good friends are under a mutual obligation to reprove evil wherever it is necessary and helpful.

But the right way to deal with this matter would be to follow the rule laid down by the Gospel, Matthew 18,[d] where Christ says, "If your brother or sister sins against you, go and tell them their fault, between them and you alone."[e] Here you have a fine, precious precept for governing the tongue that ought to be noted carefully in order to avoid this detestable abuse. Let this be your rule, then, that you should not be quick to spread slander and gossip about your neighbors but admonish them privately so that they may improve. Likewise, do the same when others tell you what this or that person has done. Instruct them, if they saw the wrongdoing, to go and reprove the individual personally or otherwise to hold their tongue.

You can also learn this lesson from the day-to-day running of a household.[155] This is what the master of the house does: when he sees a servant not doing what he is supposed to do, he speaks to him personally. If he were so foolish as to let the servant sit at home while he went out into the streets to complain to his neighbors, he would no doubt be told: "You fool, it's none of our business! Why don't you tell him yourself?" See, that would be the proper, brotherly thing to do, for the evil would be corrected and

155. The word *Hausregiment* (Ger.) refers to the household as an operation in need of rules and order and division of duties. The medieval households were typically larger than modern, more private family structures. Luther's own house at the old Black Cloister had forty rooms and hosted a constant flow of guests in addition to the already large immediate family.

c   Ger.: *Meister Hans*, originally.

d   An incorrect reference to Matthew 19; corrected in later editions.

e   Matt. 18:15.

your neighbor's honor preserved. As Christ also says in the same passage: "If he listens to you, you have gained your brother."[f] There you will have done a great and excellent deed. For do you think that it is an insignificant thing to gain a brother? Let all the monastics and holy orders step forward with all their works piled together and see if they can boast of having gained one brother!

Christ teaches further: "But if you are not listened to, take one or two others along with you, so that every word may be confirmed by the evidence of two or three witnesses."[g] Thus the people involved are to be dealt with directly and not gossiped about behind their backs. If this does not help, bring the matter publicly before the community, either before the civil or the ecclesiastical court. Here you are not standing alone, but you have those witnesses with you through whom you can prove the accused's guilt and on whose testimony the judge can base the decision and pass sentence. This is the right and proper way of dealing with and improving a wicked[h] person. But if you gossip about someone in every corner and root around in the filth, no one will be improved. Moreover, when people are subsequently called upon to witness, they deny having said anything. It would serve such big mouths right to have their fun spoiled, as a warning to others. If you were acting to improve your neighbor or out of love for the truth, you would not sneak about in secret, shunning the light of day.

All of this refers to secret sins. But where the sin is so public that the judge and everyone else is aware of it, you can without sin shun and avoid those who have brought disgrace upon themselves, and you may also testify publicly against them. For when something is exposed to the light of day, there can be no question of slander or injustice or false witness. For example, we now censure the pope and his teaching, which is publicly set forth in books and shouted throughout the world. Where the sin is public, appropriate public punishment should follow so that everyone may know how to guard against it.

Now we have the summary and substance of this commandment: No one shall use the tongue to harm a neighbor, wheth-

---

f　Matt. 18:15.

g　Matt. 18:16.

h　Ger.: *Böse.*

er friend or foe. No one shall say anything evil of a neighbor, whether true or false, unless it is done with proper authority or for that person's improvement. Rather, we should use our tongue to speak only the best about all people, to cover the sins and infirmities of our neighbors, to justify their actions, and to cloak and veil them with our own honor. Our chief reason for doing this is the one that Christ has given in the gospel, and in which he means to encompass all the commandments concerning our neighbor, "In everything do to others as you would have them do to you."[i]

Nature, too, teaches us the same thing in our own bodies, as St. Paul says in 1 Corinthians 12[:22-23]: "The members of the body that seem to be weaker are indispensable, and those members of the body that we think less honorable we clothe with greater honor, and our less respectable members are treated with greater respect." No one covers their face, eyes, nose, and mouth; we do not need to, for they are the most honorable members we have. But the weakest members, of which we are ashamed, we carefully conceal. Our hands and eyes, even the whole body, must help to cover and veil them. Thus, in our relations with one another, all of us should veil whatever is dishonorable and weak in our neighbors, and do whatever we can to serve, assist, and promote their good name. On the other hand, we should prevent everything that may contribute to their disgrace. It is a particularly fine, noble virtue to put the best construction on all we may hear about our neighbors (as long as it is not an evil that is publicly known), and to defend them against the poisonous tongues of those who are busily trying to pry out and pounce on something to criticize in their neighbor, misconstruing and twisting things in the worst way. At present this is happening especially to the precious word of God and to its preachers.

This commandment, then, includes a great many good works that please God most highly and bestow abundant blessings, if only the blind world and false saints would recognize them. There is nothing around or in us that can do greater good or greater harm in temporal or spiritual matters than the tongue, although it is the smallest and weakest member.[j]

---

i   Matt. 7:12.
j   See James 3:5.

The Ninth and Tenth Commandments

"You are not to covet your neighbor's house."[k]

"You are not to covet his wife, manservant, maidservant, cattle, or whatever is your neighbor's."[l]

These two commandments, taken literally, were given exclusively to the Jews; nevertheless, in part they also apply to us. The Jews did not interpret them as referring to unchastity or theft, for these were sufficiently forbidden in the previous commandments. They also thought that they were keeping all the commandments when they outwardly did precisely the works commanded and did not do the ones forbidden. God therefore added these two so that people would also think that coveting a neighbor's spouse or property, or desiring them in any way, is sinful and forbidden. These commandments were especially needed because under the Jewish government menservants and maidservants were not free, as now, to earn a wage as long as they wanted. Rather, with their body and all they had they were their master's property, just the same as his cattle and other possessions. Moreover, every man had the power to put away his wife publicly by giving her a bill of divorce[m] and to take another wife. So there was a danger among them that if any man craved another's wife, he might find some sort of reason to put away his own wife and to alienate the other man's so that he might legally take her for himself. Among them this was no more a sin or disgrace than it is among us when a master dismisses his manservant or maidservant or entices someone else's servant away.

Therefore, I say, they interpreted these commandments correctly (even though they have a broader and higher application) to forbid anyone, even with an apparently good pretense and excuse, to harm a neighbor by intending or scheming to take away anything that belongs to this neighbor, such as spouse, servants, house and farm, fields, meadows, or cattle. Above, the seventh commandment prohibits seizing or withholding someone else's possessions to which you have no right. But here it is

---

k   The words for "covet" or "desire" are *begehren* (Ger.) and *concupiscere* (Lat.).

l   Here *begehren* (Ger.) is paralleled with *desirere* (Lat.), instead of the loaded *concupiscere*.

m   See Deut. 24:1.

also forbidden to entice anything away from your neighbor, even though in the eyes of the world you could do it honorably, without accusation or blame for fraudulent gain.

Such is nature that no one wants someone else to have as much as one has. Everyone tries to accumulate as much as one can and lets others look out for themselves. Yet we all consider ourselves persons of integrity[156] and put up a fine front to conceal our villainy. We hunt for and think up clever tricks and shrewd tactics—better and better ones are being devised daily—under the guise of justice. We brazenly dare to boast of it and defiantly insist that it should not be called rascality but shrewdness and foresight. In this we are abetted by jurists and lawyers who twist and stretch the law to suit their purpose, straining words and using them for pretexts, without regard for equity or for our neighbor's plight. In short, whoever is sharpest and shrewdest in such matters gets most advantage out of the law, for as the saying has it, "The law favors the vigilant."[n]

This last commandment, therefore, is not addressed to those whom the world considers wicked rogues, but precisely to the most upright—to people who wish to be commended as honest and virtuous because they have not offended against the preceding commandments. Especially the Jews saw themselves this way, as today the nobility, the lords and mistresses, and princes and princesses[o] do even more. The common masses belong much further back in the seventh commandment, however, for they are not much concerned about honor and right when acquiring possessions.

This occurs most often in lawsuits in which someone sets out to gain and squeeze something out of a neighbor. For example, when people wrangle and wrestle over a large inheritance, real estate, etc., they resort to anything that has the appearance of legality, so varnishing and garnishing it that the law must support them, and they gain such a title to the property that no one can raise an objection or initiate legal action. Similarly, if people covet a castle, city, county, or some other great thing, they practice bribery through friendly connections and any other means available to them, until the property is taken away from the

156. The words *wollen fromm sein* (Ger.) refer to the desire to be considered an upright person of integrity, that is, opposite to the scoundrels and the wicked.

---

n   A proverbial saying, given in Latin in the text: *Vigilantibus jura subveniunt.*

o   Here feminine counterparts added.

other person and legally awarded to them, complete with deed and official seal showing that they have lawfully obtained title from the prince.

The same thing also happens in ordinary business dealings, where people cunningly filch something out of another's hand so that the victim is helpless to prevent it. Or, seeing an opportunity for profit—perhaps where a person because of adversity or debt cannot hold on to property nor sell it without a loss—they hustle and harass the person until they get it for half price or less; and yet this is not to be considered as something acquired or obtained illegally, but rather as legitimately purchased. Hence the sayings, "First come, first served," and "Take care of yourself,"[p] and let the others take what they can. Who would be clever enough to make up all the ways by which people can acquire for themselves so much through such lovely pretexts, which the world does not consider wrong? The world does not want to see that the neighbor is being taken advantage of and is being forced to sacrifice what one cannot afford to lose. Who would want to experience this personally? From this it is clear that all these pretexts and shams are false.

This was also the case in ancient days in respect to wives. They knew tricks like these: If a man took a fancy to another woman, he managed, either personally or through others, by any number of ways to make her husband displeased with her, or she became so disobedient and hard to live with that her husband had to dismiss her and leave her to the other man. That sort of thing was undoubtedly quite prevalent in the time of the [Old Testament] law,[q] for we read even in the Gospel that King Herod took his brother's wife while the latter was still living, and yet posed as an honorable, upright man, as St. Mark testifies.[r] But such an example, I hope, will not be found among us, for in the New Testament married people are forbidden to be divorced.[s] Still in our day someone may trick another person out of a rich fiancée. Among us it is not uncommon for someone to entice or

---

p   Two proverbial expressions, literally, "The first is the best," and "Everyone is to look after one's own chances."

q   The Latin text includes "among the Jews."

r   Matt. 14:3-4; Mark 6:17-20.

s   Matt. 5:31-32; 19:3-9; Mark 10:2-12; Luke 16:18; 1 Cor. 7:10-11.

lure a person's manservant or maidservant away or otherwise estrange them with fine words.

However these things may happen, we must learn that God does not want you to deprive your neighbors of anything that is theirs, so that they suffer loss while you satisfy your greed, even though before the world you can retain the property with honor. To do so is underhanded and malicious wickedness, and, as we say, it is all done "under the table"[t] so as to escape detection. Although you may act as if you have wronged no one, you have certainly trespassed on your neighbors' rights. It might not be called stealing or cheating, but it is coveting—that is, having designs on your neighbors' property, luring it away from them against their will, and begrudging what God gave them. The judge and everyone else may have to let you keep the property, but God will not, for God sees your wicked heart and the deceitfulness of the world. Give the world an inch[u] and it will take a mile,[v] and open injustice and violence will result.

This, then, is the common meaning of this commandment. First, we are commanded not to desire to harm our neighbors, nor to assist in doing harm, nor to give occasion for it. Instead, we are gladly to let them have what is theirs and to promote and protect whatever may be profitable and serviceable to them, just as we wish others would do for us. So these commandments are aimed directly against envy and miserable covetousness, so that God may remove the root and cause from which arise all injuries to our neighbors. Therefore God sets it forth in plain words: "You shall not covet," etc. Above all, God wants the heart to be pure, even though, as long as we live here, we cannot accomplish that. So this commandment remains, like all the rest, one that constantly accuses us and shows just how upright we really are in God's sight.[w]

[. . .]

---

t   Literally, "under the hat," a proverbial expression derived from sorcery.

u   Literally, "finger," used as a measurement in German.

v   Ger.: *Elle*, a unit of measure, about fifteen to twenty inches.

w   Here the "Conclusions of the Ten Commandments" are omitted due to spatial limitations. See *The Large Catechism*, in BC, 428–31. The very length of Luther's treatment of the Ten Commandments establishes the point he wishes to make: the law belongs to the life of the baptized, and the preaching of the gospel needs to be paralleled with the word of the law.

Second Part: The Creed^x

Thus far we have heard the first part of Christian teaching, and in it we have seen all that God wishes us to do and not to do. The Creed properly follows, which sets forth all that we must expect and receive from God; in short, it teaches us to know God perfectly. It is given in order to help us do what the Ten Commandments require of us. For, as we said above, they are set so high that all human ability is far too puny and weak to keep them. Therefore it is just as necessary to learn this part as it is the other so that we may know where and how to obtain the power to do this. If we were able by our own strength to keep the Ten Commandments as they ought to be kept, we would need nothing else, neither the Creed nor the Lord's Prayer.[157] But before we explain the usefulness and necessity of the Creed, it is enough, as a first step, for very simple people to learn to grasp and understand the Creed itself.[158]

157. The law and gospel tension in Luther's theology is explicitly handled in the catechism and its deliberate order, starting with the law and centering on the Creed. Even without naming it always, Luther's judgments reflect his (not entirely accurate) understanding of the Jewish law in the Old Testamental sense vs. the Christian sense. See *How Christians Should Regard Moses*, LW 35:161–74; also in this volume, p. 127.

158. In addition to his catechisms, Luther offered other *summae* of his faith. See, e.g., Luther's *Confession of Faith* in this volume, p. 258, and LW 37:360–72; and the *Smalcald Articles*, p. 416, and BC, 295–328.

An image of the
Trinity c. 1501
by Albrecht Durer
(1478–1521).

—————

x   For a thorough treatment and commentary, see Albrecht Peters, *Creed*, in *Commentary on Luther's Catechisms*, trans. Thomas H. Trapp (St. Louis: Concordia, 2011).

In the first place, the Creed used to be divided into twelve articles.[159] Of course, if all the elements contained in Scripture and belonging to the Creed were gathered together, there would be many more articles, nor could they all be clearly expressed in so few words. But to make it most clear and simple for teaching to children, we shall briefly sum up the entire Creed in three main articles,[160] according to the three persons of the Godhead, to whom everything that we believe is related.*y* Thus the first article, concerning God, explains creation; the second, concerning the Son, redemption; the third, concerning the Holy Spirit, being made holy.[161] Hence the Creed could be briefly condensed to these few words: "I believe in God the Father, who created me; I believe in God the Son, who has redeemed me; I believe in the Holy Spirit, who makes me holy." One God and one faith, but three persons, and therefore also three articles or confessions. Let us comment briefly on these words.

The First Article*z*

"I believe in God, the Father almighty,*a* Creator of heaven and earth . . ."

This is the shortest possible way of describing and illustrating the nature, will, acts, and work of God the Creator.[162] Because the Ten Commandments have explained that we are to have no more than one God, so it may now be asked: "What kind of person is God? What does God do? How can we praise or portray or describe God in such a way so we may know God?" This is taught here and in the following articles. Thus the Creed is nothing else than a response and confession of Christians based on the

159. The ordering followed a fifth-century tradition that each of the twelve apostles contributed a phrase to the creed that became known as the Apostles' Creed.

160. Already in his 1522 *Personal Prayer Book* (LW 34:[5–10] 11–45) Luther had divided the Creed into "three chief parts, according to which the three persons of the holy, divine Trinity are to be related, corresponding first to the Father, second to the Son, and third to the Holy Spirit" (LW 43:24). See also TAL, vol. 4, forthcoming.

161. Luther follows the traditional creedal Father/Son/he language for the persons of Trinity. Here several of the "Father" references have been mostly preserved, whereas unnecessary "he" pronouns have been replaced to preserve Luther's theological emphasis: the early church's central decisions about the unity of the three persons of the triune God, the distinction between the persons, and the personal relationship through which Godhead interacts immanently and economically, that is, in God's own being, and in God's ways of relating to creation.

162. Here "Father" is replaced with "Creator," on a par with Luther's point about God's role and acts as the Creator.

---

y Ger.: *Gottheit, dahin alles, was wir gläuben, gerichtet ist;* "Godhead" could also be translated with "Divinity."

z See *Smalcald Articles* (BC, 300–301; pp. 427–28 in this volume) on the first article of faith. Luther has not much to add to the ecumenical creeds' statement about God the triune Creator.

a Ger.: *Vater allmächtigen.* In the following, much of the creedal Father language is retained, while occasionally replaced with "Creator" or "God." This statement relates to the first and second commandments, both confessing God's status as the only, omnipotent Deity to whom one is in an allegiance of obedience, love, and respect.

163. As above in n. 162.

Woodcut of the Creation (1527)
by Lucas Cranach the Elder, illustrating
a book on the apostles by Martin Luther.

first commandment. If you were to ask a young child, "My dear, what kind of God do you have? What do you know about God?" the child could say: "First, my God is the Creator,[163] who made heaven and earth. Aside from this one alone I regard nothing as God, for there is no one else who could create heaven and earth."

For the highly educated and those somewhat more well informed, however, all three articles can be treated more fully and divided into as many parts as there are words. But for the young pupils, it is now enough to indicate the most necessary points, namely, as we have said, that this article deals with creation. We should emphasize the words "creator of heaven and earth."

What is meant by these words or what do you mean when you say, "I believe in God, the Father almighty, creator," etc.? Answer: I hold and believe that I am God's creature, that is, that God has given me and constantly sustains my body, soul, and life, my members great and small, all my senses, my reason and understanding, and the like; my food and drink, clothing, nourishment, spouse and children, servants, house and farm, etc. Besides, God makes all creation help provide the benefits and necessities of life—sun, moon, and stars in the heavens; day and night; air, fire, water, the earth and all that it yields and brings forth; birds, fish, animals, grain, and all sorts of produce. Moreover, God gives all physical and temporal blessings—good government, peace, security. Thus we learn from this article that none of us has life—or anything else that has been mentioned here or can be mentioned—from ourselves, nor can we by ourselves preserve any of them, however small and unimportant. All this is comprehended in the word "Creator."

Moreover, we also confess that God the Father[b] has given us not only all that we have and what we see before our eyes, but also that God daily guards and defends us against every evil and misfortune, warding off all sorts of danger and disaster. All this God does out of pure love and goodness, without our merit, as a kind father[c] who cares for us so that no evil may befall us. But

b   Ger.: *Vater.* Luther uses the traditional "Father" language, whereas contemporary readers may refer to the first person of the Trinity as "Parent."

c   Ger.: *ein freundlicher Vater,* "a friendly/friendlier, kinder father. "

further discussion of this subject belongs in the other two parts of this article, where it says, "Father almighty."

Hence, because everything we possess, and everything in heaven and on earth besides, is daily given, sustained, and protected by God, it inevitably follows that we are in duty bound to love, praise, and thank God without ceasing, and, in short, to devote all these things to God's service, as God has required and enjoined in the Ten Commandments.

Here much could be said if we were to describe how few people believe this article. We all pass over it; we hear it and recite it, but we neither see nor think about what the words command us to do. For if we believed it with our whole heart, we would also act accordingly, and not swagger about and boast and brag as if we had life, riches, power, honor, and such things of ourselves, as if we ourselves were to be feared and served. This is the way the wretched, perverse world acts, drowned in its blindness, misusing all the blessings and gifts of God solely for its own pride, greed, pleasure, and enjoyment, and never once turning to God to thank God or acknowledge God as Lord or Creator. [164]

Therefore, if we believed it, this article should humble and terrify all of us. For we sin daily with eyes, ears, hands, body and soul, money and property, and with all that we have, especially those who even fight against the word of God. Yet Christians have this advantage, that they acknowledge that they owe it[d] to God to serve and obey God for all these things.

For this reason, we ought daily to practice this article, impress it upon our minds, and remember it in everything we see and in every blessing that comes our way.[165] Whenever we escape distress or danger, we should recognize how God gives and does all of this so that we may sense and see in them God's parental[e] heart and boundless love toward us. Thus our hearts will be warmed and kindled with gratitude to God and a desire to use all these blessings to God's glory and praise.

Such, very briefly, is the meaning of this article. It is all that ordinary people[166] need to learn at first, both about what we have and receive from God and about what we owe God in return. This is knowledge of great significance, but an even greater treasure.

164. Luther names sin as the reason why one cannot—on one's own—even believe what the Creed says about God and God's will toward human beings. Other sins follow. Saving faith has to be given by Jesus, as explained in the second article of faith. On sin as fundamental disobedience that leads to breaking of the Ten Commandments, see *Smalcald Articles*, BC, 310–11.

165. This article and the first commandment are the cornerstones, reminding the reader of the vital principal question on which everything depends: Who is your God? What does it mean to have a God? From the answers to these questions follows one's fundamental orientation in life.

166. The word *Einfältigen* (Ger.) refers to the "simple," uneducated people.

---

d   Ger.: *daß sie sich des schüldig erkennen*, "to know it is their responsibility."

e   Ger.: *Väterlich*, replaced here with "parental."

167. See *Smalcald Articles*, BC, 301–2, 325, on the second article of faith and justification by faith. This part about the redeeming work of Jesus gives the foundation for hope and faith that one "can" be redeemed, even in light of the onus of the law (commandments) one is unable to meet. Luther calls the statement about Jesus' redeeming work "the first and chief article": Christ taking away the sins of the human beings who are thereby justified by faith, apart from any merits. Nothing of the article of faith can be given up. "On this article stands all that we teach and practice." No doubts should be harbored about this.

168. Using the early church's christological logic, Luther teaches about the "happy exchange" (*fröhliche Wechsel*) when Christ takes all that human beings have, their sins, becoming even the greatest sinner, and in turn the human beings receive all that Christ has and is. This mystery is at the heart of justification and redemption in Christ, which brings one into a particular oneness with God in faith—all because of Christ. See *Two Kinds of Righteousness*, LW 31:297–306, esp. 298–30; and in this volume, pp. 8–24.

169. To "become Lord," *ein Herr werden* (Ger.), contains Luther's fundamental point in the Creed's second part: Christ becomes the Lord over human life by exercising control over sin and death, that is, freeing captive humanity from the control of sin and death. This freedom which only Christ can bring means salvation for human beings.

For here we see how we have received all of creation along with God's very being, so that we are abundantly provided for in this life, in addition also to showering us with inexpressible eternal blessings through the Son and the Holy Spirit, as we shall hear.

The Second Article[167]

"And [I believe] in Jesus Christ, God's only Son, our Lᴏʀᴅ. He was conceived by the Holy Spirit and born of Mary the virgin.[f] He suffered under Pontius Pilate, was crucified, died, and was buried. He descended into hell. On the third day he rose from the dead.[g] He ascended[h] into heaven and is seated at the right hand of God, the Father almighty. From there he will come again to judge the living and the dead."

Here we get to know the second person of the Godhead, and we see what we have from God over and above the temporal goods mentioned above, namely, how Christ has given himself completely to us, withholding nothing.[168] This article is very rich and far-reaching, but in order to treat it briefly for children, we shall take up one phrase and in it grasp the substance of the article so that everyone may learn from it, as we have said, how we are redeemed. We shall concentrate on these words, "in Jesus Christ, our Lᴏʀᴅ."

If anyone asks, "What do you believe in the second article about Jesus Christ?" answer as briefly as possible, "I believe that Jesus Christ, true Son of God, has become my Lord." What is it "to become a lord"?[169] It means that he has redeemed and released me from sin, from the devil, from death, and from all misfortune. Before this I had no lord or king but was captive under the power of the devil. I was condemned to death and entangled in sin and blindness.

---

f   Jesus' miraculous conception, *empfangen* (Ger.), *conceptu* (Lat.), as articulated in the ecumenical creeds, is fleshed in discussion on Mary's special nature in, e.g., *That Jesus Christ Was Born a Jew*, LW 45:[195–98] 199–229; also TAL, vol. 5, forthcoming. Luther makes the point that Jesus was conceived "by the Holy Spirit without male participation and was born of the pure, holy Virgin Mary" (*Smalcald Articles*, BC, 300).

g   Ger.: *auserstanden von den Toten*.

h   Ger.: *aufgefahren*.

For when we were created by God[i] from whom we received all kinds of good things, the devil came and led us into disobedience, sin, death, and all misfortune. As a result, we lay under God's wrath and displeasure,[j] sentenced to eternal damnation, as we had merited it and deserved it. There was no counsel, no help, no comfort for us until this only and eternal Son of God, in unfathomable goodness, had mercy on us because of our misery and distress and came from heaven to help us. Those tyrants and jailers have now been routed, and their place has been taken by Jesus Christ, the Lord of life, righteousness, and every good and blessing. Christ has snatched us, poor lost creatures,[k] from the jaws of hell, won us, made us free, and restored[l] us to God's[m] favor and grace. As God's own possession Christ has taken us under his protection and shelter, in order that he may rule us by divine righteousness, wisdom, power, life, and blessedness.[170]

Let this be the summary of this article, that the little word "LORD" simply means the same as Redeemer, that is, one who has brought us back from the devil to God, from death to life, from sin to righteousness, and keeps us there.[171] The remaining parts of this article simply serve to clarify and express how and by what means this redemption was accomplished—that is, how much it cost Christ and what he paid and risked in order to win us and bring us under his dominion. That is to say, Christ became a human being,[n] conceived and born without sin, of the Holy Spirit and the Virgin, so that he might become Lord over sin; moreover, he suffered, died, and was buried so that he might make satisfaction for me and pay what I owed, not with silver and gold but with his own precious blood. And he did all this

170. For more on Christians' passive (alien) righteousness received from Christ, which effects reconciliation and regeneration, followed by their active (proper) righteousness, in which Christ is the subject as well, see pp. 9–24 in this volume; also *Two Kinds of Righteousness*, LW 31:297–306.

171. Luther's Christocentric theology builds on the early church's ecumenical decision about Christ's two natures as human and divine, and his same substance (*homoousia*) within the Trinity and his ubiquitous presence as the ruler of life and death, that is, the lord over human existence. Luther's theology of justification depends on these basic christological convictions— and with that, his pneumatology and understanding of the workings of the word.

---

i   Here "Father" is replaced with "God" and the sentence modified accordingly.

j   Ger.: *in seinem Zorn und Ungnade lagen*; *Ungnade*, "un-grace," the opposite of grace.

k   Ger.: *uns arme, verlorne Menschen*, "us poor, forsaken people."

l   Ger.: *wiederbracht*, "brought back."

m   Here "Father" is translated "God."

n   Ger.: *er Mensch worden*, refers to Jesus becoming a human being (*Mensch*), not a man (*Mann*).

172. For Luther, the statement *daß er mein Herr würde* (Ger.), "that he became my Lord," crystallizes the Christian gospel and experience: that Jesus becomes the center and the foundation of one's personal life, and the shield and protector, and thus the ground of being.

173. Luther refers to the liturgical seasons of Christmas, Lent, Easter, Ascension, and the festivals in which the Gospel lessons, particularly, treat the life of Christ.

174. See the *Smalcald Articles* (BC, 301). This article focuses on the centrality of the Holy Spirit for human well-being in this life and beyond. The catechism demonstrates the connection of Luther's Pneumatology to his Christology: the impact and presence of Christ in Christian life and human communities becomes "real" through the person of the Holy Spirit. See Jeffrey G. Silcock, "Luther on the Holy Spirit and His Use of God's Word," in OHMLT, 294–309.

175. The first ecumenical councils' decisions on the Holy Spirit developed as the doctrines of Trinity and Christology were debated and clarified. In the eleventh century, the East and West split due to many reasons, one being the Western church's "unauthorized" addition of the word *filioque* in some creedal statements about the Holy Spirit. In the Nicene-Constantinopolitan Creed, this resulted in the wording of the Holy Spirit proceeding from the Father *and the Son*.

so that he might become my Lord.[172] For he did none of these things for himself, nor had he any need of them. Afterward he rose again from the dead, swallowed up[o] and devoured death, and finally ascended into heaven and assumed dominion at the right hand of the Father. The devil and all the devil's powers must be subject to Christ and lie beneath his feet until finally, at the Last Day, he will completely divide and separate us from the wicked world, the devil, death, sin, etc.

But the proper place to explain all these different points is not in the brief children's sermon, but rather the longer sermons throughout the whole year, especially at the times appointed[173] for dealing at length with such articles as Christ's birth, passion, resurrection, ascension, etc. Indeed, the entire gospel that we preach depends on the proper understanding of this article. Upon it all our salvation and blessedness are based, and it is so rich and broad that we can never learn it fully.[p]

The Third Article[174]

"I believe in the Holy Spirit,[175] one holy Christian church, the community[q] of saints, the forgiveness of sins, the resurrection of the flesh, and the life everlasting. Amen."[176]

To this article, as I have said, I cannot give a better title than "Being Made Holy."[177] In it are expressed and portrayed the Holy Spirit and her office, which is that the Spirit makes us holy.[r] Therefore, we must concentrate on the term "Holy Spirit," because it is so precise that we can find no substitute for it. Many other kinds of spirits are mentioned in Scripture, such as the human spirit,[s] heavenly spirits,[t] and the evil spirit.[u] But

---

o   See Isa. 25:7.

p   See Luther's *A Brief Instruction on What to Look for in the Gospels* (1522), LW 35:[115–16] 117–24; and in this volume, pp. 25–37.

q   Or "communion of saints," *Gemeinde der Heilige* (Ger.), *communio sanctorum* (Lat.).

r   Here the "Spirit" is referred to with a feminine pronoun, even if Luther does not do so.

s   Ger.: *Menschengeist*, e.g., 1 Cor. 2:11, "human spirit." Luther uses the same word *Geist* for human, divine, and evil spirits. See n. 47, p. 294.

t   Ger.: *himmlische Geister*, "heavenly spirits." Luther interpreted these as the good angels (e.g., 2 Macc. 11:6; 15:23).

u   Ger.: *böse Geist*, "wicked spirit" (e.g., 1 Sam. 16:14, 23; Tobit 3:8; Acts 19:12, 15).

God's Spirit alone is called a Holy Spirit, that is, the one who has made us holy and still makes us holy.[v] As the First Person of the Trinity[w] is called a Creator and the Son is called a Redeemer, so on account of her work the Holy Spirit must be called a Sanctifier, or one who makes us holy.[x] How does such sanctifying take

An illustration of the third section of the Apostles' Creed: at Pentecost the Holy Spirit descends on Jesus' disciples. From a 1545 printing of the *Small Catechism* with engraving by artist known as the monogrammist HA.

176. Elsewhere Luther explains the Spirit's work through the word of the gospel: "first, through the spoken word, in which the forgiveness of sins is preached to the whole world, which is the proper function of the gospel; secondly, through baptism; thirdly, through the holy Sacrament of the Altar; fourthly, through the power of the keys and also through the mutual conversation and consolation of brothers and sisters" (*Smalcald Articles*, p. 455 in this volume*).

177. The word *Heiligung* (Ger.) means *sanctification*, "being made holy." The English translation of this word has different options, some with a bearing not always intended. The word *sanctification* has been historically rejected in Lutheran language when associated with a spirituality that regards regeneration initiating a process toward holiness that involves individual's own choices and actions, and that results in distinctions between the degrees and status of sanctification to be made. Theologically, though, the word is not alien to Luther's arguments about the Holy Spirit's impact in cultivating the justifying faith: "sanctification" can be used to denote the presence and action of the Holy Spirit in one's life, as in the "effective" side of justification. It does not, ever, in Lutheran discourse imply a status or growth of holiness on one's own.

---

v The sentence *uns geheiligt hat und noch heiliget* (Ger.) has both the past tense and the present tense, implying active continuity of the Spirit's sanctifying work.

w Here "Father" is replaced with the language about the first person of the Trinity.

x Ger.: *Heiliger*, "sanctifier," and *Heiligmacher*, "one who makes holy" or "who sanctifies."

178. For Luther, the purpose of the church community is to proclaim the gospel of Christ in word and in the sacraments, and through care of one another in Christian love. Alternating with words *community* and *communion* (as noted below), Luther points to the reality of the church not as a building or an institution, essentially, but as action: where the word is proclaimed and where the word acts, there the Spirit works—and that is church.

place?[y] Answer: Just as the Son obtains dominion by purchasing us through his birth, death, and resurrection, etc., so the Holy Spirit effects our being made holy[z] through the following: the community[a] of saints or Christian church, the forgiveness of sins, the resurrection of the body, and the life everlasting. That is, the Spirit first leads us into the holy community, placing us in the church's lap, where the Spirit preaches to us and brings us to Christ.[178]

Neither you nor I could ever know anything about Christ, or believe in him and receive him as Lord, unless these were offered to us and bestowed on our hearts[b] through the preaching of the gospel by the Holy Spirit. The work is finished and completed; Christ has acquired and won the treasure for us by his sufferings, death, and resurrection, etc. But if the work remained hidden so that no one knew of it, it would have been all in vain, all lost. In order that this treasure might not remain buried but be put to use and enjoyed, God has caused the word to be published and proclaimed, in which God has given the Holy Spirit to offer and apply to us this treasure, this redemption. Therefore being made holy[c] is nothing else than bringing us to the Lord Christ to receive this blessing, to which we could not have come by ourselves.

Learn this article, then, as clearly as possible. If someone asks, "What do you mean by the words 'I believe in the Holy Spirit'?" you can answer, "I believe that the Holy Spirit makes me holy, as her[d] name states." How does she do this, or what are her ways and means? Answer: "Through the Christian church, the forgiveness of sins, the resurrection of the body, and the life everlasting." In the first place, she has a unique community[e] in the world, which is the mother that begets and bears every Christian through the word of God, which the Holy Spirit reveals and

---

y Ger.: *Wie gehet solch Heiligen zu?* In other words, "How does one become holy, how is one made holy or sanctified?"

z Ger.: *Die Heiligung*, "sanctification." See n. 177, p. 359.

a Ger.: *Gemeine*.

b Literally, "bosom," *Angetragen* (Ger.).

c Ger.: *Heiligung*, "sanctification."

d Here "her" instead of "his"; also "she" and "her" in the following sentence.

e Luther uses the word *Gemeine* (Ger.), and not *Gemeinschaft*.

proclaims, through which she[f] illuminates and inflames hearts so that they grasp and accept it, cling to it, and persevere in it.

Where the Holy Spirit does not cause it to be preached and does not awaken the understanding of it in the heart, all is lost, as happened under the papacy, where faith was swept completely under the rug and no one recognized Christ as the Lord or the Holy Spirit as the one who makes us holy. That is, no one believed that Christ is our Lord in the sense that he won such a treasure for us without our works and merits and made us acceptable to God.[g] What was lacking there? There was no Holy Spirit present to reveal this truth and have it preached. Rather, it was human beings and evil spirits who were there, who taught us to obtain grace and be saved by our works. Therefore there was no Christian church. For where Christ is not preached, there is no Holy Spirit to create, call, and gather the Christian church, apart from which no one can come to the Lord Christ. Let this be enough about the substance of this article. But because the parts enumerated in it are not quite clear to the common people, we shall run through them briefly.

The Creed calls the holy Christian church a *communio sanctorum,* "a communion[h] of saints." Both expressions have the same meaning. In earlier days the phrase was not included,[179] and it is odd and not understandable when put into German. If we were to render it clearly, we would have to speak quite differently in German. The word *ecclesia* properly means nothing but an assembly[i] in German. But we are accustomed to using the word *Kirche,* which the common people understand not as an assembled group of people, but as a consecrated house or building. But the house would not be called a church if it were not for the single reason that the group of people come together in it. For we who come together choose a special place and give the house its name because of this group.[180] Thus the word *church*[j] really

179. Already in 1519 Luther noted the expression *communio sanctorum* as a later addition to the Creed, meaning the "holy catholic church." The earliest extant version of the Creed that contains the phrase is attributed to Bishop Nicetas of Remesiana (c. 335–414).

180. Underscoring the importance of ongoing proclamation of the word and the work of the Spirit, Luther offers an alternate view to what the church is and why membership is important, not in a punitive sense but for sustenance in Christian community.

f   Here "she" instead of "he," as in Holy Spirit acting as mother.

g   Here "Father" replaced with "God."

h   Here Luther uses the word *Gemeinschaft* (Ger.), not *Gemeine.*

i   Ger.: *Versammlunge.* In Old High German, the Latin *ecclesia* was translated both with *Kirihha* and *Samanunga,* but in Middle High German only as *Kirche.*

j   Ger.: *Kirche,* the word for the church (also building).

181. Luther incorrectly associates the Latin word *curia* (which derives from *quiris*, a Roman citizen) with the Greek word *kuria*. However, in light of modern linguistic conclusions, the German word *Kirche* derives from the Greek *kuriakos* ("belonging to the Lord"). It is one of the earliest Christian words that has carried into other languages (even into non-Indo-European languages such as Finnish, *kirkko*), and physically transported by Arian missionaries from the kingdom of the Goths up the Danube River into Germany.

182. In his *Smalcald Articles* (BC, 295–328), Luther writes, "We do not concede to them that they are the church, and they are also not the church. We also do not want to hear what they command or forbid in the name of the church, because, God be praised, a seven-year-old child knows what the church is, namely, holy believers and 'the little sheep who hear the voice of their shepherd'" (p. 463 in this volume).

183. See 1 Cor. 1:9. In his translation of the Bible, Luther placed a marginal note at this passage: "That is, you are co-heirs and co-associates of all Christ's blessings."

means nothing else than a common assembly and is not of German but of Greek origin, like the word *ecclesia*. In that language the word is *kyria*, and in Latin *curia*.[181] Therefore, in our mother tongue and in good German it ought to be called "a Christian community or assembly,"[k] or best and most clearly of all, "a holy Christian people."[l]

Likewise, the word *communio*, which is attached to it, should not be translated "communion" but rather "community."[m] It is nothing but a comment or interpretation by which someone wished to explain what the Christian church is. But some among our people, who understand neither Latin nor German, have rendered it "communion of saints,"[n] although no German would talk that way or understand it. To speak proper German, we ought to say "a community of saints,"[o] that is, a community that is composed only of saints, or, still more clearly, "a holy community."[p] This I say in order that the word might be understood; it has become so established in usage that it cannot well be uprooted, and it would be next to heresy to alter a word.

This is the meaning and substance of this phrase: I believe that there is on earth a holy little flock and community of pure saints under one head, Christ. It is called together by the Holy Spirit in one faith, mind, and understanding. It possesses a variety of gifts and yet is united in love without sect or schism.[182] Of this community I also am a part and member, a participant and copartner[183] in all the blessings it possesses. I was brought into it by the Holy Spirit and incorporated into it through the fact that I have heard and still hear God's word, which is the beginning point for entering it. Before we had come into this

---

k   Ger.: *Gemeine*. In his Bible translation, Luther consistently uses *ecclesia* or *Gemeine*.

l   Ger.: *Ein heilige Christenheit*. In *On the Councils and the Church* (1539) (LW 41:143–44), Luther urged that *Christenheit*, "Christendom," or *christliches Volk*, "Christian people," was better than the non-German *Kirche*, which, in his opinion, was a meaningless word. See TAL, vol. 3, forthcoming.

m   Not *Gemeinschaft* (Ger.), "communion" or "company," but *Gemeine* (Ger.), "community." See David P. Daniel, "Luther on the Church" in OHMLT, 333–52.

n   Ger.: *Gemeinschaft der Heiligen*.

o   Ger.: *ein Gemeine der Heiligen*.

p   Ger.: *ein heilige Gemeine*.

community, we were entirely of the devil, knowing nothing of God and of Christ. The Holy Spirit will remain with the holy community[q] or Christian people until the last day. Through it the Spirit gathers us, using it to teach and preach the word. By it the Spirit creates and increases holiness, causing it daily to grow and become strong in the faith and in its fruits, which the Spirit produces. Further, we believe that in this Christian community we have the forgiveness of sins, which takes place through the holy sacraments and absolution as well as through all the comforting words of the entire gospel. This encompasses everything that is to be preached about the sacraments and, in short, the entire gospel and all the official responsibilities of the Christian community. Forgiveness is constantly needed, for although God's grace has been acquired by Christ, and holiness has been wrought by the Holy Spirit through God's word in the unity of the Christian church, yet we are never without sin because we carry our flesh around our neck.

Therefore everything in this Christian community is so ordered that everyone may daily obtain full forgiveness of sins through the word and signs appointed to comfort and encourage our consciences as long as we live on earth. Although we have sin, the Holy Spirit sees to it that it does not harm us, because we are a part of this Christian community. Here there is full forgiveness of sins, both in that God forgives us and that we forgive, bear with, and aid one another. Outside this Christian community, however, where there is no gospel, there is also no forgiveness, and hence there also can be no holiness.[184] Therefore, all who would seek to merit holiness through their works rather than through the gospel and the forgiveness of sin have expelled and separated themselves from this community.

Meanwhile, because holiness has begun and is growing daily, we await the time when our flesh will be put to death, will be buried with all its uncleanness, and will come forth gloriously and arise to complete and perfect holiness in a new, eternal life. Now, however, we remain only halfway pure and holy. The Holy Spirit must always work in us through the word, granting us daily forgiveness until we attain to that life where there will be no more forgiveness. In that life there will be only perfectly pure and holy people, full of integrity and righteousness, completely

184. With statements like this, Luther reiterates the medieval Christian view that there is no "salvation" outside the church, and underscores the main mission of the church. This position has been "confessed" with the Athanasian Creed that starts and ends with this exclusivist affirmation of membership (and good standing) in the church being a condition for salvation.

q   Ger.: *Gemeine.*

freed from sin, death, and all misfortune, living in new, immortal, and glorified bodies.[185]

All this, then, is the office and work of the Holy Spirit, to begin and daily increase holiness on earth through these two means, the Christian church and the forgiveness of sins.[186] Then, when we pass from this life, in the blink of an eye the Spirit will perfect our holiness and will eternally preserve us in it through the last two parts of this article.[187]

The phrase "resurrection of the flesh,"[r] however, is also not good German. For when we hear the word *Fleisch*,[s] we think no further than the butcher shop. In proper German we would say "resurrection of the body."[188] However, this is not of great importance, as long as the words are rightly understood.

This, then, is the article that must always remain in force.[t] For creation is now behind us, and redemption has also taken place, but the Holy Spirit continues her work without ceasing until the last day, and for this purpose she has appointed a community on earth, through which she speaks and does all her work. For the Spirit has not yet gathered together all of this Christian community, nor has she completed the granting of forgiveness. Therefore we believe in the Holy Spirit who daily brings us into this community through the word, and imparts, increases, and gives faith through the same word and the forgiveness of sins. Then when the Spirit's work has been finished and we abide in it, having died to the world and all misfortune, she will finally make us perfectly and eternally holy. Now we wait in faith for this to be accomplished through the word.

Here in the Creed you have the entire essence, will, and work of God exquisitely depicted in very brief but rich words. In them are comprehended all our wisdom, which surpasses all human wisdom, understanding, and reason. Although the whole world has sought painstakingly to learn what God might be and what God might think and do, yet it has never succeeded in the least. But here you have everything in richest measure. For in all three articles God has revealed and opened to us the most profound

---

185. In his catechism, in particular, Luther ties the working of the Holy Spirit to the word, and vice versa. The role of the Holy Spirit is essential for any speculation on Christ's continued presence in the Christian's life, and vice versa.

186. See also n. 174, p. 358 above.

187. Luther repeatedly underscores the integral influence of the Holy Spirit in the justification, granting faith, and in holding human being in God's holiness.

188. *Auferstehung des Leibs oder Leichnams*, literally, "resurrection of the body or the corpse." While the earliest Christians believed in the resurrection of the dead, some groups emerged that considered all material things (including the body) as evil, thus denying the salvation of both body and the soul. The creedal wording about the "resurrection of the flesh" directly opposed such views. See Luther on John 1:14 (LW 52:80–81): "'Flesh' here means total humanity, body and soul, according to the usage of Scripture which calls humans 'flesh,' . . . and in the Creed where we say: 'I believe in the resurrection of the flesh,' i.e., of all people." In English translations of the Creeds, the word "flesh" became replaced with "body."

---

r   Ger.: *Auferstehung des Fleisches*, "the resurrection of the flesh/body."

s   The German word *Fleisch* means both "flesh" and "meat."

t   Ger.: *im Werk*, "at work," that is, actively engaged, believed, and applied.

depths of the divine parental heart" and God's pure, unutterable love. For this very purpose God created us, so that God might redeem us and make us holy, and, moreover, having granted and bestowed upon us everything in heaven and on earth, God has also given us God's Son and his Holy Spirit, through whom God brings us to God personally. For, as explained above, we could never come to recognize God's favor and grace were it not for the Lord Christ, who is a mirror of God's heart." Apart from Christ we see nothing but an angry and terrible judge. But neither could we know anything of Christ, had it not been revealed by the Holy Spirit.

These three articles of the Creed, therefore, separate and distinguish us Christians from all other people on earth. All who are outside this Christian people, whether heathen," Turks,[189] Jews, or false Christians and hypocrites—even though they believe in and worship only the one, true God—nevertheless do not know what God's attitude is toward them. They cannot be confident of God's love and blessing, and therefore they remain in eternal wrath and condemnation. For they do not have the Lord Christ, and, besides, they are not illuminated and blessed by the gifts of the Holy Spirit.[190]

From this you see that the Creed is a very different teaching than the Ten Commandments. For the latter teach us what we ought to do, but the Creed tells us what God does for us and gives to us. The Ten Commandments, moreover, are written in the hearts of all people,[191] but no human wisdom is able to comprehend the Creed; it must be taught by the Holy Spirit alone. Therefore the Ten Commandments do not succeed in making us Christians, for God's wrath and displeasure still remain on us because we cannot fulfill what God demands of us. But the Creed brings pure grace and makes us righteous and acceptable to God. Through this knowledge we come to love and delight in all the commandments of God because we see here in the Creed how God gives Godself completely to us, with all God's gifts and power, to help us keep the Ten Commandments: the Father

189. Refers to members of several Turkic-speaking peoples that first appeared as nomadic tribes living in northeastern Mongolia. Unlike the Mongols, these peoples spoke a Turkic language. After various groups of these Turkic nomads became part of the armies of the Mongol conqueror Genghis Khan in the early thirteenth century, a fusion of Mongol and Turkic elements took place, and the Mongol invaders of Russia and Hungary became known to Europeans as Tatars (or Tartars).

190. With statements like this, Luther expresses the common conviction of medieval Christians that there is no salvation outside the parameters of a Christian church. Ironically, Luther himself as an excommunicated heretic was considered damned and outside the saving church. Luther's criteria for who is saved is twofold: one has to adhere to the doctrinal decisions of the ecumenical councils of the early church—particularly the Trinitarian doctrine—and one has to confess Christ as the only Lord and Savior. Thus any believer who denies the doctrine of Trinity or whose faith is not based on exclusively Christocentric principles is a heretic and self-condemned, in Luther's logic. This Christocentrism is one of the pillars of Luther's theology and a subject of critical reassessment in contemporary theological and interfaith conversation.

191. See Rom. 2:15. This reflects Luther's idea of the natural law and human beings' abilities with civil righteousness.

---

u Here "his Fatherly heart" replaced.

v Here the word "Father" replaced with "God."

w *Heiden* (Ger.), *Gentiles* (Lat.), see n. 70, p. 302 above.

192. The mystery of the gospel and the omnipresent role of the Holy Spirit revealing it to the unbelieving human being is most poignantly expressed in Luther's *Small Catechism* and the explanation of the third part of the Creed: "I believe that by my own understanding or strength I cannot believe in Jesus Christ my Lord or come to him, but instead the Holy Spirit has called me through the gospel, enlightened me with her gifts, made me holy and kept me in the true faith, just as she calls, gathers, enlightens, and makes holy the whole Christian church on earth and keeps it with Jesus Christ in the one common true faith. Daily in this Christian church the Holy Spirit abundantly forgives all sins—mine and those of all believers. On the Last Day the Holy Spirit will raise me and all the dead and will give to me and all believers in Christ eternal life. This is most certainly true" (*Small Catechism*, BC, 355–56).

193. The premise for Luther's teaching of the necessity and power of prayer is his radical notion of the devastating impact of the original sin. One of the central articles in Lutheran theology (e.g., the *Augsburg Confession*, Art. 2), Luther repeatedly elaborated the implications of the fall in human life and the human bondage to sin. For example, see in the *Heidelberg Disputation* (1518) in TAL, vol. 1, where Luther writes: "Free will, after [the fall into] sin, exists in name only, and when 'it does what is within it,' it commits a mortal sin. Free will, after [the fall into] sin, has the power to do good only passively but always has the power to do evil actively" (pp. 82–83). In *The Bondage of Will*, he states "Neither God nor Satan permits sheer unqualified

gives us all creation, Christ all his works, the Holy Spirit all her gifts.[192]

This is enough now concerning the Creed to lay a foundation for ordinary people without overburdening them. After they understand the substance of it, they may on their own initiative learn more, relating to these teachings all that they learn in the Scriptures, and thus continue to advance and grow in understanding. For as long as we live we shall have enough here in the Creed to preach and learn.

Third Part: The Lord's Prayer

We have now heard what we are to do and believe. The best and most blessed life consists of these things. Now follows the third part, how we are to pray.[x] We are in such a situation that no one can keep the Ten Commandments perfectly, even when one has begun to believe. Besides, the devil, along with the world and our flesh, resists them with all its power. Consequently, nothing is so necessary as to call on God incessantly and to drum into God's ears our prayer that God may give, preserve, and increase in us faith and the fulfillment of the Ten Commandments and remove all that stands in our way and hinders us in this regard.[193] That we may know what and how to pray, however, our Lord Christ himself has taught us both the way and the words, as we shall see.

But before we explain the Lord's Prayer part by part, the most necessary thing is to exhort and encourage people to pray, as Christ and the apostles also did.[y] The first thing to know is this: It is our duty to pray because of God's command.[194] For we heard in the second commandment, "You are not to take God's name in vain." Thereby we are required to praise the holy name and to pray or call upon it in every need. For calling upon it is nothing else than praying. Prayer, therefore, is as strictly and solemnly

---

x   For a thorough treatment and commentary, see Albrecht Peters, *Lord's Prayer*, in *Commentary on Luther's Catechisms*, trans. Daniel Thies (St. Louis: Concordia, 2011). See also Carter Lindberg, "Piety, Prayer, and Worship in Luther's View of Daily Life," in OHMLT, 414–26.

y   See, e.g., Matt. 7:7; Luke 18:1; 21:36; Rom. 12:12; Col. 4:2; 1 Thess. 5:17; 1 Tim. 2:1; James 1:6; 5:13; 1 Peter 4:8; Jude 20.

Woodcut by Hans Brosamer of Christ
teaching the disciples the Lord's Prayer
from the 1550 Frankfurt edition of the
Small Catechism of Martin Luther.

willing in us, but as you have rightly
said, having lost our liberty, we are
forced to serve sin, that is, we will sin
and evil, speak sin and evil, do sin and
evil" (LW 33:115).

194. With *wir ümb gottes Gebots willen
schüldig find zu beten* (Ger.), Luther
stresses the commandment of God
and the human beings "owing"
their prayer to God as a response to
God's command and will "of" them
and "for" them. In light of the first
commandment, prayer is the first and
foremost duty of the Christian who also
needs the prayer for herself, sinner as
she is.

commanded as all the other commandments (such as having
no other God, not killing, not stealing, etc.) lest anyone thinks
it makes no difference whether I pray or not, as vulgar people
do who say in their delusion: "Why should I pray? Who knows
whether God pays attention to my prayer or wants to hear it? If
I do not pray, someone else will." Thus they fall into the habit of
never praying, claiming that because we reject false and hypocritical prayers, we teach that there is no duty or need to pray.

It is quite true that the kind of babbling and bellowing that
used to pass for prayers in the church was not really prayer. Such
external repetition, when properly used, may serve as an exercise
for young children, pupils, and simple folk; while it may be useful in singing or reading, it is not actually prayer. To pray, as the
second commandment teaches, is to call on God in every need.
This God requires of us; it is not a matter of our choice. It is our
duty and obligation[195] to pray if we want to be Christians, just as
it is our duty and obligation to obey our fathers, mothers, and
the civil authorities. By invocation and prayer the name of God is
glorified and used to good purpose. This you should note above
all, so that you may silence and repel any thoughts that would

195. Literally, *sollen und müssen* (Ger.),
"need to and must." Prayer, for
Luther, is not a matter of choice but
existentially vital for the sinner in need
of grace and forgiveness, and tied to
the first commandment as the starting
point.

prevent or deter you from praying. Now, it would be improper for a son to say to his father: "What is the use of being obedient? I will go and do as I please; what difference does it make?" But there stands the commandment, "You shall and must obey!" Just so, it is not left to my choice here whether to pray or not, but it is my duty and obligation on pain of God's wrath and displeasure.*z*

This should be kept in mind above all things so that we may silence and repel thoughts that would prevent or deter us from praying, as though it made no great difference if we do not pray, or as though prayer were commanded for those who are holier and in better favor with God than we are. Indeed, the human heart is by nature so desperately wicked that it always flees from God, thinking that God neither wants nor cares for our prayers because we are sinners and have merited nothing but wrath.[196] Against such thoughts, I say, we should respect this commandment and turn to God so that we may not increase divine anger by such disobedience. By this commandment God makes it clear that we will not be cast out or driven away, even though we are sinners; God wishes rather to draw us to God so that we may humble ourselves before God, lament our misery and plight, and pray for grace and help. Therefore we read in the Scriptures that God is angry because those who were struck down for their sin did not return to God and assuage God's wrath and seek grace by their prayers.

From the fact that prayer is so urgently commanded, you ought to conclude that we should by no means despise our prayers, but rather prize them highly. Take an example from the other commandments. Children should never despise obedience to their father and mother, but should always think: "This act is an act of obedience, and what I do has no other purpose than that it befits obedience and the commandment of God. On this I can rely and depend, and I can revere it highly, not because of my worthiness, but because of the commandment." So, too, here. We should regard the words of our prayers and their purpose as something demanded by God and done in obedience to God. We should think, "On my account this prayer would not amount to

196. Luther goes so far as to name human beings as the enemy of God, by their own nature. The "alien" sin causes an alienation between the creature and the Creator, reconcilable only by the divine-human Christ—and with the ongoing involvement of the Holy Spirit.

---

z   The text in italics does not appear in the first edition of the *Large Catechism*, in the Jena edition of Luther's works, or in the German *Book of Concord* (1580). It is found in revised editions of the catechism (1529 and later), in the Latin translation (1544), and freshly translated in the Latin *Book of Concord* (1584).

anything; but it is important because God has commanded it." So, no matter what one has to pray for, everybody should always approach God in obedience to this commandment.[197]

We therefore urgently beg and exhort everyone to take these words to heart and in no case to despise prayer. Prayer used to be taught in the devil's name, in such a way that no one paid any attention to it, and people supposed it was enough if the act was performed, whether God heard it or not. But that is to stake prayer on luck and to mumble aimlessly. Such a prayer is worthless.

We allow ourselves to be impeded and deterred by such thoughts as these: "I am not holy enough or worthy enough; if I were as righteous and holy as St. Peter or St. Paul, then I would pray." Away with such thoughts! The very commandment that applied to St. Paul applies also to me. The second sommandment is given just as much on my account as on his. He can boast of no better or holier commandment than I.

Therefore you should say: "The prayer I offer is just as precious, holy, and pleasing to God as those of St. Paul and the holiest of saints. The reason is this: I freely admit that he is holier in respect to his person, but not on account of the commandment. For God does not regard prayer on account of the person, but on account of God's word and the obedience accorded it.[198] On this commandment, on which all the saints base their prayer, I, too, base mine. Moreover, I pray for the same thing for which they all pray, or ever have prayed."[a]

This is the first and most important point, that all our prayers must be based on obedience to God, regardless of our person, whether we are sinners or righteous people, worthy or unworthy. We must understand that God is not joking, but that God will be angry and punish us[199] if we do not pray, just as God punishes all other kinds of disobedience. Nor will God allow our prayers to be futile or lost, for if God did not intend to answer you, God would not have ordered you to pray and backed it up with such a strict commandment.

In the second place, what ought to impel and arouse us to pray all the more is the fact that God has made and affirmed a

197. Luther teaches the Lord's Prayer as a proper response to the first commandment in particular and as an expression of faith with the Creed.

198. Luther's fundamental doctrine of justification by faith through grace alone is applied here in his teaching of prayer and holiness: all praying Christians are on a par with saints like Paul, equal in their sin and equal recipients of grace. Likewise, Luther compares the efficacy of the prayer with the same principle that defines justification: it is *extra nos*, by the work of God's word alone.

199. Upon his rereading and study of Paul's letter to the Romans and the Psalms, Luther's personal fear of the righteous God who punishes human sins led him to his doctrine of grace and justification. See *Preface to Luther's Latin Writings*, LW 34:336–38; TAL, vol. 4, forthcoming. He holds in tension God's merciful and God's righteous side, and thus the necessity of both law and gospel in the life of a Christian who needs daily reminders in both regards. He approached this theological tension from different angles in the catechism.

---

a   The 1538 Wittenberg edition of the catechism and the German *Book of Concord* (1580) add: "and I need them just as much as and more than those great saints."

promise: that what we pray is a certain and sure thing. As God says in Psalm 50[:15], "Call on me in the day of trouble; I will deliver you," and Christ says in the Gospel in Matthew 7[:7-8], "Ask, and it will be given you," etc. . . . "For everyone who asks receives." Such promises certainly ought to awaken and kindle in our hearts a longing and love for prayer. For by God's word, God testifies that our prayer is heartily God-pleasing and will assuredly be heard and granted, so that we may not despise it, cast it to the winds, or pray uncertainly.

You can hold such promises up to God and say, "Here I come, dear God,[b] and pray not of my own accord nor because of my own worthiness, but at your commandment and promise, which cannot fail or deceive me." Those who do not believe such a promise should again realize that they are angering God, grossly dishonoring God, and accusing God of lying.

Furthermore, we should be encouraged and drawn to pray because, in addition to this commandment and promise, God takes the initiative and puts into our mouths the very words and approach we are to use.[200] In this way we see how deeply concerned God is about our needs, and we should never doubt that such prayer pleases God and will assuredly be heard. So this prayer is far superior to all others that we might devise ourselves. For in that case our conscience would always be in doubt, saying, "I have prayed, but who knows whether it pleases God or whether I have hit upon the right form and mode?" Thus there is no nobler prayer to be found on earth,[c] for it has the powerful testimony that God loves to hear it. This we should not trade for all the riches in the world.

It has been prescribed for this reason also, that we should reflect on our need, which ought to drive and compel us to pray without ceasing. A person who wants to make a request must present a petition, naming and describing something that he or she desires; otherwise it cannot be called a prayer.

Therefore we have rightly rejected the prayers of monks and priests, who howl and growl frightfully day and night, but not one of them thinks of asking for the least little thing.[201] If we gathered all the churches together, with all their clergy, they

200. In his *A Simple Way to Pray* (1535) (LW 43:187–212), Luther also teaches the method of praying with the Commandments, the Creed, and the Lord's Prayer, and promises that the Holy Spirit preaches through such prayer. See also in TAL, vol. 4, forthcoming.

201. Literally, "for a hair's breadth." Luther rarely misses a chance to ridicule the monastics, even though he continues to be influenced by his own monastic background. This shows especially clearly in his explanation of healthy prayer habits.

---

b   Here "Father" replaced with "God."

c   The 1538 Wittenberg edition of the catechism and the German *Book of Concord* (1580) add: "than the daily Lord's Prayer."

would have to confess that they have never prayed wholeheart-edly for so much as a drop of wine. For none of them has ever undertaken to pray out of obedience to God and faith in God's promise, or out of consideration for their own needs. They only thought, at best, of doing a good work as a payment to God, not willing to receive anything from God, but only to give God something.

But where there is to be true prayer, there must be utter ear-nestness. We must feel our need, the distress that drives and impels us to cry out. Then prayer will come spontaneously, as it should, and no one will need to be taught how to prepare for it or how to create the proper devotion. This need, however, that ought to concern us—ours and everyone else's—is something you will find richly enough in the Lord's Prayer. Therefore it may serve to remind us and impress upon our hearts that we not neglect to pray. For we are all lacking plenty of things: all that is missing is that we do not feel or see them. God therefore wants you to lament[202] and express your needs and concerns, not because God is unaware of them, but in order that you may kindle your heart to stronger and greater desires and open and spread your apron wide to receive many things.

Therefore from youth on we should form the habit of pray-ing daily for our needs, whenever we are aware of anything that affects us or other people around us, such as preachers, magis-trates, neighbors, and servants; and, as I have said, we should always remind God of God's own commandment and prom-ise, knowing that God does not want them despised. This I say because I would like to see people learn again to pray properly and not act so crudely and coldly that they daily become more inept in praying. This is just what the devil wants and works for with all its might, for the devil is well aware what damage and harm it suffers when prayer is used properly.

This we must know, that all our safety and protection con-sists in prayer alone.[203] For we are far too weak against the devil and all its might and forces arrayed against us, trying to trample us underfoot. Therefore we must keep this in mind and grasp the weapons with which Christians are to arm themselves for resisting the devil. What do you think has accomplished such great results in the past, parrying the counsels and plots of our enemies and checking their murderous and seditious designs by which the devil expected to crush us, and the gospel as well,

202. "Lamenting" has many examples in the Old Testament: the book of Lamentations, on the occasion of the destruction of Jerusalem, contains sorrowful poems expressing mourning and grief, and several poems of lament are found in the book of Psalms (e.g., Pss. 22, 74).

203. Luther's humanist rival Erasmus of Rotterdam also taught about the spiritual warfare in his "little dagger": "I hammered out an 'enchiridion,' that is, a sort of a dagger, which you should never put aside, not even at table or in bed, so that . . . you will not allow yourself to be overcome at any moment by that ambusher when you are totally unarmed." Erasmus admits that the book is small, "but if you know how to use it rightly together with the shield of faith, you will easily withstand the violent onslaught of the enemy and will not receive a mortal wound." In the end, one can expect to be transported by Christ to "everlasting peace and perfect tranquility. "In the meantime, however, all hope of salvation must be placed in this armor" (*Spirituality: Enchiridon / De contemptu mundi / De vidua christiana*, vol. 66 [University of Toronto Press, 1988], 38). Erasmus, *Handbook of the Christian Soldier,* 38.

204. Here *Vater* could be replaced with "God," but in keeping with the wording of the New Testament's prayer, Luther emphasizes with the word "Father" the familial, intimate relationship the praying person has with the Creator. In the following, many of the "Father" expressions are maintained for this reason, with the suggestion that the reader consider "Mother" an appropriate alternative.

except that the prayers of a few godly people intervened like an iron wall on our side? Otherwise they would have seen a far different drama: the devil would have destroyed all Germany in its own blood. Now they may confidently laugh and make their snide comments. But by prayer alone we shall be a match both for them and for the devil, if only we persevere and do not become weary. For whenever a good Christian prays, "Dear Father,[204] your will be done," God replies from above, "Yes, dear child, it shall be done indeed, in spite of the devil and all the world."

Let this be said as an admonition in order that we may learn above all to value prayer as a great and precious thing and may properly distinguish between vain babbling and asking for something. By no means do we reject prayer, but we do denounce the utterly useless howling and growling, as Christ himself rejects and forbids great wordiness.[d] Now we shall treat the Lord's Prayer very briefly and clearly. In seven successive articles or petitions are comprehended all the needs that continually beset us, each one so great that it should impel us to keep praying for it all our lives.

The First Petition

"May your name be hallowed."[205]

205. *Geheiliget werde* (Ger.), *sanctificetur* (Lat.), "be kept holy" or "sanctified," the same root for the language about "sanctification" and "being made holy." This speaks of the "holiness" connection between God and human. God "makes holy" and generates "holiness," whereas human beings can "be made holy" and, in turn, "keep holy" and "sanctify" what they can from their part, as with the name of God and the Sabbath. In all the uses, the word(s) lead to God as the origin and center of the holy; this is a reality Luther insists on in his catechetical teaching.

This is rather obscure and not in idiomatic German. In our mother tongue we would say, "Heavenly Father, grant that your name alone may be holy."[e] But what is it to pray that God's name may become holy? Is it not already holy? Answer: Yes, in its essence it is always holy, but our use of it is not holy. God's name

---

d Matt. 6:7; 23:14.

e For a contemporary reader, "Mother" could be a most appropriate alternative word for what the "Father" language, entails. There are theological reasons for the parental language, and the "Abba-cry" is not only modeled but made possible by Jesus himself. Albrecht Peters writes: "With the Lord's Prayer, one should not be concerned about 'an abstract holiness of God's name.'" Rather, "Trusting as children, those praying are given over into God's sovereign providence. . . . They stand instead in the nearness to God with the childlike certainty of those that are included in Jesus' Abba-cry. The address 'Unser Vater' governs each individual petition. . . . It makes it possible for the first time for children of men [*sic*] to plead so unconcerned for oneself for God's final appearance" (Peters, *The Lord's Prayer*, 40; see also 19–21, 39–43).

Woodcut panels depicting the petitions of the Lord's Prayer
by German artist Lucas Cranach the Elder, 1527.

was given to us when we became Christians and were baptized,
and so we are called children of God and have the sacraments,
through which God incorporates us into Godself with the result
that everything that is God's must serve for our use.

Thus it is a matter of grave necessity, about which we should
be most concerned that God's name receive due honor and be
kept holy and sacred as the greatest treasure and most sacred
thing that we have, and that, as good children, we pray that
God's name, which is in any case holy in heaven, may also be holy
and be kept holy on earth in our midst and in all the world.

How does it become holy among us? The plainest answer that
can be given is: when both our teaching and our life are godly
and Christian. Because in this prayer we call God our Father, it
is our duty in every way to behave as good children so that God
may receive from us not shame but honor and praise.

Now, the name of God is profaned by us either in words or
deeds. (For everything we do on earth may be classified as word
or deed, speech or act.) In the first place, then, it is profaned
when people preach, teach, and speak in the name of God anything that is false and deceptive, using God's name to dress up

their lies and make them acceptable; this is the worst desecration and dishonor of the divine name. Likewise, when people grossly misuse the divine name as a cover for their shame, by swearing, cursing, conjuring, etc. In the next place, it is also profaned by an openly evil life and wicked works, when those who are called Christians and God's people are adulterers, drunkards, gluttons, jealous persons, and slanderers. Here again God's name is necessarily being profaned and blasphemed because of us.

Just as it is a shame and a disgrace to an earthly father to have a bad, unruly child who antagonizes him in word and deed, with the result that on his account the father ends up suffering scorn and reproach, so God is dishonored if we who are called by God's name and enjoy God's manifold blessings fail to teach, speak, and live as upright and heavenly children, with the result that God must hear us called not children of God but children of the devil.

So you see that in this petition we pray for exactly the same thing that God demands in the second commandment: that God's name should not be taken in vain by swearing, cursing, deceiving, etc., but used rightly to the praise and glory of God. Whoever uses God's name for any sort of wrong, profanes and desecrates this holy name, as in the past a church was said to be desecrated when a murder or other crime had been committed in it, or when a monstrance[206] or relic was profaned, thus rendering unholy by misuse that which is holy in itself. This petition, then, is simple and clear if we only understand the language, namely, that to "hallow" means the same as in our idiom "to praise, extol, and honor" both in word and deed.

See, then, what a great need there is for this kind of prayer! Because we see that the world is full of sects and false teachers, all of whom wear the holy name as a cloak and warrant for their devilish doctrine, we ought constantly to shout and cry out against all who preach and believe falsely and against those who want to attack, persecute, and suppress our gospel and pure doctrine, as the bishops, tyrants, fanatics, and others do. Likewise, this petition is for ourselves who have the word of God but are ungrateful for it and fail to live according to it as we ought. If you ask for such things from your heart, you can be sure that God is pleased. For there is nothing that God would rather hear than to have God's glory and praise exalted above everything else and God's word taught in its purity, cherished and treasured.

206. A monstrance is a vessel in which the consecrated host is displayed for adoration—an important feature in Catholic piety where the priest performs the Mass for the congregation, and where the consecrated host is revered as the "true" body of Christ after the miracle of transubstantiation, by which the essence of the elements change.

The Second Petition

"May your kingdom[207] come."

In the first petition we prayed about God's name and honor, that God would prevent the world from using God's glory and name to dress up its lies and wickedness but would instead keep God's name sacred and holy in both teaching and life so that God may be praised and exalted in us. In the same way, in this petition we ask that God's kingdom may come. Just as God's name is holy in itself and yet we pray that it may be holy among us, so also God's kingdom comes of itself without our prayer, and yet we pray that it may come to us, that is, that it may prevail among us and with us, so that we may be a part of those among whom God's name is hallowed and God's kingdom flourishes.[208]

What is the kingdom of God? Answer: Simply what we heard above in the Creed, namely, that God sent the Son, Christ our Lord, into the world to redeem and deliver us from the power of the devil, to bring us to God, and to rule us as a king of righteousness, life, and salvation against sin, death, and an evil conscience. To this end God also gave the Holy Spirit to deliver this to us through God's own holy word and to enlighten and strengthen us in faith by God's own power.[209]

We ask here at the outset that all this may be realized in us and that God's name may be praised through God's holy word and Christian living. This we ask, both in order that we who have accepted it may remain faithful and grow daily in it and also in order that it may find approval and gain followers among other people and advance with power throughout the world. In this way many, led by the Holy Spirit, may come into the kingdom of grace and become partakers of redemption, so that we may all remain together eternally in this kingdom that has now begun.

"The coming of God's kingdom to us" takes place in two ways: first, it comes here, in time, through the word and faith, and second, in eternity, it comes through the final revelation.[210] Now, we ask for both of these things: that it may come to those who are not yet in it and that, by daily growth here and in eternal life hereafter, it may come to us who have attained it. All this is nothing more than to say: "Dear God, we ask you first to give us your word, so that the gospel may be properly preached throughout the world and then that it may also be received in faith and may work and dwell in us, so that your kingdom may pervade

207. *Reich* (Ger.), *regnum* (Lat.), terms for rule and territorial authority. Jesus' lordship requires his rule over the territory called human life.

208. This petition relates directly to the first commandment—know who your God is—and the second part of the Creed about Christ's lordship over human life and death and, thus, redemption from all that binds.

209. Luther repeatedly emphasizes the interrelatedness and the ongoing work of the word and the Holy Spirit in the birthing of the saving faith. Luther invites his readers to cultivate this faith and its impact in their lives with the word. For Luther's definition of faith and its origins in the Holy Spirit, see *Preface to Romans*, LW 35:[365–80].

210. The second coming of Christ (the *parousia*) was expected from the time of the first Jesus followers who interpreted the words of his "kingdom" to mean his imminent return to rule in the world known to them. Over the generations, and with the "delay" of the anticipated parousia, Christians began to reinterpret Jesus' words spiritually and with a broadened understanding of what the kingdom of God may entail in the temporal life and in the life after. The connector between the two is the Holy Spirit, through whom Christ's ubiquitous postresurrection presence is possible also in time.

among us through the word and the power of the Holy Spirit and the devil's kingdom may be destroyed so that it may have no right or power over us until finally its kingdom is utterly eradicated and sin, death, and hell wiped out, that we may live forever in perfect righteousness and blessedness."

From this you see that we are not asking here for crumbs[f] or for a temporal, perishable blessing, but for an eternal, priceless treasure and for everything that God alone possesses. It would be far too great for any human heart to dare to desire it if God had not commanded us to ask for it. But God is God who also claims the honor of giving far more abundantly and liberally than anyone can comprehend—like an eternal, inexhaustible fountain, which, the more it gushes forth and overflows, the more it continues to give. God desires nothing more from us than that we ask many and great things of God. And, on the contrary, God is angered if we do not ask and demand with confidence.

Imagine if the richest and most powerful emperor commanded a poor beggar to ask for whatever he might desire and was prepared to give lavish, royal gifts, and the fool asked only for a dish of beggar's broth. He would rightly be considered a rogue and a scoundrel, who had made a mockery of the imperial majesty's command and was unworthy to come into his presence. Just so, it is a great reproach and dishonor to God if we, to whom God offers and pledges so many inexpressible blessings, despise them or lack confidence that we shall receive them and scarcely venture to ask for a morsel of bread.

The fault lies wholly in that shameful unbelief that does not look to God even for enough to satisfy the belly, let alone expect, without doubting, eternal blessings from God. Therefore, we must strengthen ourselves against unbelief and let the kingdom of God be the first thing for which we pray. Then, surely, we shall have all the other things in abundance, as Christ teaches, "Strive first for the kingdom of God and God's righteousness, and all these things will be given to you as well."[g] For how could God allow us to suffer want in temporal things while promising eternal and imperishable things?[211]

---

211. This question begs discussion on the issue of theodicy and God's omnipotence, and, thus, predestination. Regardless of the certainty expressed in prayer, abundance of blessings in daily life is hardly universally experienced per human design. To this issue Luther gives no more satisfactory solution than any other theologian before or after him.

f   Ger.: *Parteken*; literally, "token alms."

g   Matt. 6:33; Luke 12:31.

The Third Petition

"May your will come[212] about also on earth as in heaven."

Thus far we have prayed that God's name may be hallowed by us and that God's kingdom may prevail among us. These two points embrace all that pertains to God's glory and to our salvation, in which we appropriate God with all God's treasures. But there is just as great need for us to keep firm hold on these two things and never to allow ourselves to be torn from them. In a good government there is need not only for good builders and rulers, but also for defenders, protectors, and vigilant guardians. So here also; although we have prayed for what is most necessary—for the gospel, for faith, and for the Holy Spirit, that she may govern us who have been redeemed from the power of the devil—we must also pray that God cause God's own will to be done. If we try to hold these treasures fast, we will have to suffer an astonishing number of attacks and assaults from all who venture to hinder and thwart the fulfillment of the first two petitions.

For no one can believe how the devil opposes and obstructs their fulfillment. It cannot bear to have anyone teach or believe rightly. It pains the devil beyond measure when its lies and abominations, honored under the most specious pretexts of God's name, are disclosed and exposed in all their shame, when they are driven out of people's hearts and a breach is made in its kingdom. Therefore, like a furious foe, the devil raves and rages with all its power and might, marshaling all its subjects and even enlisting the world and our own flesh as its allies. For our flesh is in itself vile and inclined to evil, even when we have accepted God's word and believe it. The world, too, is perverse and wicked.[213] Here the devil stirs things up, feeding and fanning the flames, in order to impede us, put us to flight, cut us down, and bring us once again under its power. This is the devil's only purpose, desire, and thought, and for this end it strives without rest day and night, using all the arts, tricks, methods, and approaches that it can devise.

Therefore we who would be Christians must surely expect to have the devil with all its angels[214] and the world as our enemies and must expect that they will inflict every possible misfortune and grief on us. For where God's word is preached, accepted, or believed, and bears fruit, there the holy and precious cross[215] will

212. *Dein Wille geschehe* (Ger.), *Fiat voluntas tua* (Lat.). This petition corresponds with the first and second commandments in particular and all the commandments in general. It also unfolds the meaning of the first part of the Creed and God's omnipotence on the one hand, and the reasons for endless gratitude of the creatures in their dependency on the Creator, on the other.

213. In Christian Scripture and discourse the terms *flesh*, *devil*, and *world* have been used almost synonymously for that which opposes God and thus presents a challenge to Christians' daily life. Here Luther uses the word *world* in a dualistic sense as opposite to the godly things.

214. On the devil's angels, see Matt. 25:41. Like the devil itself, its company was understood to consist of fallen spiritual beings, created by God but fallen out of their own volition. See n. 303, p. 413.

215. Luther's so-called theology of the cross has been much studied over the years. It seems to have its origin in his *Heidelberg Disputation*, prepared for his 1518 friendly hearing with his Augustinian fellow monks. In articles 20 and 21, Luther defines the true theologian as a theologian of the cross: "20. The person deserves to be called a theologian, however, who understands the visible and the 'backside' of God [Exod. 33:23] seen through suffering and the cross. 21. "A theologian of glory calls evil good and good evil. A theologian of the cross calls a thing what it actually is" (see TAL, vol. 1:84; also LW 31:37–38).

216. Luther's theology of the cross implies that a mark of a Christian life is suffering, in which God is present. Ultimately suffering is caused by human beings' inability to know God, who has reasons to work through (what seems to humans as God's) alien works and behind a mask. Unlike what much research on the topic suggests, ultimately Luther's theology of the cross addresses epistemological issues rather than theodicy: a theologian of the cross seeks to interpret life from God's (even paradoxical) self-revelations, in which the cross is central.

217. Among the several works published on the theology of the cross, see Gerhard Forde, *On Being a Theologian of the Cross: Reflections on Luther's Heidelberg Disputation, 1518* (Grand Rapids: Eerdmans, 1997); Deanna A. Thompson, *Crossing the Divide. Luther, Feminism, and the Cross* (Minneapolis: Fortress Press, 2004); Vitor Westhelle, *The Scandalous God: The Use and Abuse of the Cross* (Minneapolis: Fortress Press, 2007); Mannermaa, *Christ Present in Faith.*

218. The 1538 Wittenberg edition of the Catechism and the German *Book of Concord* (1580) add "pope." With the "bishops," here Luther means those consumed with power and self-gain who ignore their primary duties as spiritual leaders, and also the bishops who represent the papal church.

also not be far behind. And let no one think that we will have peace; rather, we must sacrifice all we have on earth—possessions, honor, house and farm, spouse and children, body and life. Now, this grieves our flesh and the old creature, for it means that we must remain steadfast, suffer patiently whatever befalls us, and let go whatever is taken from us.[216, 217]

Therefore, there is just as much need here as in every other case to ask without ceasing: "Dear Father,[h] your will be done and not the will of the devil or of our enemies, nor of those who would persecute and suppress your holy word or prevent your kingdom from coming; and grant that we may bear patiently and overcome whatever we must suffer on its account, so that our poor flesh may not yield or fall away through weakness or sloth."

Observe that in these three petitions we have needs that concern Godself in a very simple form, and yet everything has been for our sake. What we pray for concerns only ourselves in that, as mentioned above, we ask that what otherwise must be done without us may also be done in us. Just as God's name must be hallowed and God's kingdom must come even without our prayer, so must God's will be done and prevail even though the devil and all its host bluster, storm, and rage furiously against it in their attempt to exterminate the gospel utterly. But we must pray for our own sake so that God's will may be done also among us without hindrance, in spite of their fury, so that they may accomplish nothing and we may remain steadfast against all violence and persecution and submit to the will of God.

Such prayer must be our protection and defense now to repulse and vanquish all that the devil, bishops, tyrants, and heretics can do against our gospel.[218] Let them all rage and try their worst, let them plot and plan how to suppress and eliminate us so that their will and scheme may prevail. Against them a simple Christian or two, armed with this single petition, shall be our bulwark, against which they shall dash themselves to pieces. We have this comfort and boast: that the will and purpose of the devil and of all our enemies shall and must fail and come to naught, no matter how proud, secure, and powerful they think

h   Here "Father" could be replaced with "God," but the term is retained for the above mentioned reason and the reasonable alternative "Mother" in mind.

they are. For if their will were not broken and frustrated, the kingdom of God could not abide on earth nor God's name be hallowed.

The Fourth Petition

"Give us today our daily bread."[219]

Here we consider the poor breadbasket—the needs of our body and our life on earth. It is a brief and simple word, but very comprehensive. When you say and ask for "daily bread," you ask for everything that is necessary in order to have and enjoy daily bread and, on the contrary, against everything that interferes with enjoying it. You must therefore expand and extend your thoughts to include not just the oven or the flour bin, but also the broad fields and the whole land that produce and provide our daily bread and all kinds of sustenance for us. For if God did not cause grain to grow and did not bless it and preserve it in the field, we could never have a loaf of bread to take from the oven or to set on the table.[220]

To put it briefly, this petition includes everything that belongs to our entire life in this world, because it is only for its sake that we need daily bread. Now, our life requires not only food and clothing[i] and other necessities for our body, but also peace and concord in our daily activities, associations, and situations of every sort with the people among whom we live and with whom we interact—in short, in everything that pertains to the regulation of both our domestic and our civil or political affairs.[221] For where these two spheres are interfered with and prevented from functioning as they should, there the necessities of life are also interfered with, and life itself cannot be maintained for any length of time. Indeed, the greatest need of all is to pray for the civil authorities and the government, for it is chiefly through them that God provides us daily bread and all the comforts of this life. Although we have received from God all good things in abundance, we cannot retain any of them or enjoy them in security and happiness were God not to give us a stable, peaceful

219. Ger.: *Unser täglich Brot*, "our daily bread," refers to all the sustenance one needs in life, while bread and other foods made of grains were the staple of the medieval German diet, and especially so for the peasantry.

220. While expanding the reader's notion of what all the word *bread* entails, Luther offers a spiritual orientation to life that recognizes God's hand and presence in all aspects of human life, thereby bridging the traditionally conceived gap between spiritual and material. Like with the previous petitions, this one also invites the reader to consider the first two commandments, as well as the first part of the Creed and respectfully recognize who is one's God, and then give proper thanks.

221. Luther understands society consisting of the three estates (as in medieval social theory): the household, the civil government, and the church. All estates have their own role in the order of human life and in providing the "daily bread." On this basis, and with his doctrine of justification, Luther develops his inclusive and expansive notion of the holiness of all vocations.

---

i   See 1 Tim. 6:8: "But if we have food and clothing, we will be content." Until 1541 Luther rendered that passage as *Futter und Decke*, "feed and covering," and after 1541 as *Nahrung und Kleider*, "food and clothing."

222. A coat of arms is an arrangement, typically on a shield, of bearings, symbols, and figures to represent the distinctions of a family or person, or other entities and organizations.

223. In his sermon on the catechism on 15 December 1528 (LW 51:177), Luther preaches that the image of the emperor or prince be impressed on loaves of bread.

224. A black lion on gold is on the coat of arms of the March of Meissen, in the domains of ducal Saxony, ruled by Duke George of Saxony (1471–1539), a cousin of Elector John Frederick I (1503–1554), Luther's prince at this time; a red-and-white striped lion on blue decorates the coat of arms of the county of Thuringia (see p. 381), which lay in the domains of Elector John. Luther would design his own insignia, which came to be known as the Luther rose.

225. For example, on the coat of arms of Electoral Saxony. Rue is a woody or bushy herb native to Europe that was much used as a drug in medieval and later medicine.

226. Turkish armies were advancing into the Holy Roman Empire just as Luther was writing this text; in September 1529, they laid siege to Vienna. See Gregory Miller, "Luther's Views of the Jews and Turks," in OHMLT, 427–34.

227. The calamities Luther mentions here all relate to food: in time of war, pestilence, and catastrophe, hunger always follows.

government. For where dissension, strife, and war prevail, there daily bread is already taken away or at least reduced.

It would therefore be fitting if the coat of arms[222] of every upright prince were emblazoned with a loaf of bread[223] instead of a lion[224] or a wreath of rue,[225] or if a loaf of bread were stamped on coins,[j] in order to remind both the royalty and the subjects that it is through the rulers' office that we enjoy protection and peace and that without them we could neither eat nor preserve the precious gift of bread. Therefore, rulers are also worthy of all honor, and we are to render to them what we should and what we are able, as to those through whom we enjoy all our possessions in peace and quietness, because otherwise we could not keep a penny. Moreover, we should pray for them, that through them God may bestow on us still more blessings and good things.

Let us outline very briefly how comprehensively this petition covers all kinds of earthly matters. Out of it a person might make a long prayer, enumerating with many words all the things it includes. For example, we might ask God to give us food and drink, clothing, house and farm, and a healthy body. In addition, we might ask God to cause the grain and fruits of the field to grow and thrive abundantly. Then we might ask God to help us manage our household well by giving and preserving for us an upright spouse, children, and servants, causing our work, craft, or occupation, whatever it may be, to prosper and succeed, and granting us faithful neighbors, and good friends, etc. In addition, we may ask God both to endow with wisdom, strength, and prosperity the emperors, kings and queens, and all estates, especially the royal authorities of our land, all councilors, magistrates, and officials, so that they might govern well and be victorious over the Turks[226] and all our enemies, and to grant their subjects and the general populace to live together in obedience, peace, and concord. Moreover, we might ask that God would protect us from all kinds of harm to our body and to the things that sustain us—from storms, hail, fire, and flood; from poison, pestilence, and cattle plague; from war and bloodshed, famine, savage beasts, wicked people, etc. It is good to impress upon the common people that all these things come from God and that we must pray for them.[227]

---

j   The *Löwenpfenning*, "lion-penny," of Saxony and Brunswick shows a lion on the coat of arms.

But especially is this petition directed against our chief enemy, the devil,[228] whose whole purpose and desire it is to take away or interfere with all we have received from God. The devil is not satisfied to obstruct and overthrow the spiritual order by deceiving souls with its lies and bringing them under its power, but it also prevents and impedes the establishment of any kind of government or honorable and peaceful relations on earth. This is why the devil causes so much contention, murder, sedition, and war, why it sends storms and hail to destroy crops and cattle, why it poisons the air, etc. In short, it pains the devil that anyone should receive even a mouthful of bread from God and eat it in peace. If it were in the devil's power and our prayer to God did not restrain it, surely we would not have a straw in the field, a penny in the house, or even an hour more of life—especially those of us who have the word of God and would like to be Christians.

Thus, you see, God wishes to show us how God cares for us in all our needs and faithfully provides for our daily sustenance. Although God gives and provides these blessings bountifully, even to the godless and rogues, yet God wishes us to ask for them so that we may realize that we have received them from God's own hand and may recognize in them God's fatherly[k] goodness toward us. When God withdraws God's own hand,[l] nothing can prosper or last for any length of time, as indeed we see and experience every day. How much trouble there is now in the world simply on account of false coinage, yes, on account of daily exploitation and usury in public business, commerce, and labor on the part of those who wantonly oppress the poor and deprive them of their daily bread! This we must put up with, of course; but let those

228. See n. 303, p. 413.

In this painting from 1459 are depicted at top the coat of arms of Hesse and Thuringia, both of which featured a white lion with red stripes on a blue background.

---

k   The word *fatherly* could be replaced with *parental* or *motherly*, per Luther's intent.

l   A proverbial expression.

229. Intercessory prayer was, and is, a regular part of worship; as a proverbial expression, it means "lose public respect."

230. *Verlasse uns unser Schuld* (Ger.), *remitte debita* (Lat.); the wording refers to "guilt" rather than "acts" of wrong, akin to Luther's theological emphasis about sin. When simplifying or focusing the notion of sin, he underscores the orientation of "unfaith" as the root of the problem, rather than any particular sin, venial or mortal.

231. With therapeutically astute insights, Luther's diagnosis of sin as the root of unhappiness and suffering is complemented with his observation of the liberating power of forgiveness—the heart of the justification that promises transformation.

who do these things beware lest they lose the common intercession of the church,[229] and let them take care lest this petition of the Lord's Prayer be turned against them.

The Fifth Petition

"And remit our debt, as we remit what our debtors owe."[230]

This petition has to do with our poor, miserable life. Although we have God's word and believe, although we obey and submit to God's will and are nourished by God's gift and blessing, nevertheless we are not without sin. We still stumble daily and transgress because we live in the world among people who sorely vex us and give us occasion for impatience, anger, vengeance, etc. Besides, the devil is after us, besieging us on every side and, as we have heard, directing its attacks against all the previous petitions, so that it is not possible always to stand firm in this ceaseless conflict.

Here again there is great need to call on God and pray: "Dear Father,[m] forgive us our debts." Not that God does not forgive sins even apart from and before our praying; for before we prayed for it or even thought about it, God gave us the gospel, in which there is nothing but forgiveness. But the point here is for us to recognize and accept this forgiveness. For the flesh in which we daily live is of such a nature that it does not trust and believe God and is constantly aroused by evil desires and devices, so that we sin daily in word and deed, in acts of commission and omission. Thus our conscience becomes restless; it fears God's wrath and displeasure, and so it loses the comfort and confidence of the gospel. Therefore it is necessary constantly to run to this petition and get the comfort that will restore our conscience.[231]

This should serve God's purpose to break our pride and keep us humble. God has reserved this prerogative: those who boast of their goodness and despise others should examine themselves and put this petition uppermost in their mind. They will find that they are no more righteous than anyone else, that in the presence of God all people must fall on their knees and be glad that we can come to forgiveness. Let none think that they will

---

m   Here, "Dear God" or "Dear Mother" would be proper alternatives per Luther's intimate portrayal of God.

ever in this life reach the point where they do not need this forgiveness. In short, unless God constantly forgives, we are lost.

Thus this petition really means that God does not wish to regard our sins and punish us as we daily deserve but to deal graciously with us, to forgive according to God's own promise, and thus to grant us a joyful and cheerful conscience so that we may stand before God in prayer.[232] For where the heart is not right with God and cannot generate such confidence, it will never dare to pray. But such a confident and joyful heart can never come except when one knows that one's sins are forgiven.

There is, however, attached to this petition a necessary and even comforting addition, "as we forgive our debtors." God has promised us assurance that everything is forgiven and pardoned, yet on the condition that we also forgive our neighbor. For just as we sin greatly against God every day and yet God forgives it all through grace, so we also must always forgive our neighbor who does us harm, violence, and injustice, bears malice toward us, etc. If you do not forgive, do not think that God forgives you. But if you forgive, you have the comfort and assurance that you are forgiven in heaven—not on account of your forgiving (for God does it altogether freely, out of pure grace, because God has promised it, as the gospel teaches) but instead because God has set this up for our strengthening and assurance as a sign along with the promise that matches this petition in Luke 6[:37], "Forgive, and you will be forgiven." Therefore Christ repeats it immediately after the Lord's Prayer, saying in Matthew 6[:14], "If you forgive others their trespasses, your heavenly Father will also forgive you. . . ."[233]

Therefore, this sign[234] is attached to the petition so that when we pray we may recall the promise and think, "Dear God, I come to you and pray that you will forgive me for this reason: not because I can make satisfaction or deserve anything by my works, but because you have promised and have set this seal on it, making it as certain as if I had received an absolution pronounced by you yourself." For whatever baptism and the Lord's Supper, which are appointed to us as outward signs, can effect, this sign can as well, in order to strengthen and gladden our conscience. Moreover, above and beyond the other signs, it has been instituted precisely so that we can use and practice it every hour, keeping it with us at all times.

232. In light of the first commandment and human beings' failure to obey it, the gift of justification is expressed in the privilege of prayer, which in itself proclaims the gospel.

233. Forgiveness is the heart-matter of justification and reconciled relationship with God, and also the most powerful force in human interactions. Luther explicates the two dimensions of justification: alien and proper righteousness are lived out in the tension between being liberated by a word of forgiveness oneself while out of that liberation granting forgiveness for others from what binds them.

234. The word *Zeichen* (Ger.), or *signum* (Lat.), refers to the statement "as we forgive our debtors." Luther points to the presence of grace in one's life that allows one to extend grace to others as well.

The Sixth Petition

"And lead us not into temptation."[235]

We have now heard enough about the trouble and effort it takes to retain and persevere in all the gifts for which we pray. This, however, is not accomplished without failures and stumbling. Moreover, although we have acquired forgiveness and a good conscience and have been wholly absolved, yet such is life that one stands today and falls tomorrow. Therefore, even though at present we are upright and stand before God with a good conscience, we must ask once again that God will not allow us to fall and collapse under attacks and temptations.

Temptation (or, as our Saxons called it in former times, *Bekörunge*)[n] is of three kinds: of the flesh, the world, and the devil. For we live in the flesh and carry the old creature around our necks; it goes to work and lures us daily into unchastity, laziness, gluttony and drunkenness, greed and deceit, into acts of fraud and deception against our neighbor—in short, into all kinds of evil lusts that by nature cling to us and to which we are incited by the association and example of other people and by things we hear and see. All this often wounds and inflames even an innocent heart.[236]

Next comes the world, which assails us by word and deed and drives us to anger and impatience. In short, there is in it nothing but hatred and envy, enmity, violence and injustice, perfidy, vengeance, cursing, reviling, slander, arrogance, and pride, along with fondness for luxury, honor, fame, and power. For no one is willing to be the least, but everyone wants to sit on top and be seen by all.

Then comes the devil, who baits and badgers us on all sides, but especially exerts itself where the conscience and spiritual matters are concerned. The devil's purpose is to make us scorn and despise both the word and the works of God, to tear us away from faith, hope, and love, to draw us into unbelief, false security, and stubbornness, or, on the contrary, to drive us into

---

235. Lat.: *Et ne inducas nos in tentationem.* Temptation describes the conditions under which human beings are vulnerable to disorderly forces and desires that lead to disobedience of God and God's law. Because the inherent depraved condition, human beings are at constant risk of being tempted and falling. This reality does not change with justification. Regular nourishment of the sacraments, the word, and prayer are the most effective weapons in this spiritual warfare.

236. Luther's list of common sins echoes the so-called seven deadly sins or cardinal sins, which are wrath, greed, sloth, pride, lust, envy, and gluttony. However, Luther consistently identifies sin in its simplest and most devastating form as unfaith or unbelief that leads to all other forms of disobedience.

---

n   The word (*korunga* or *bikorunga*), common in Old High German translations of the Lord's Prayer, is still used today in Low German. Luther characterized the word as "very fine old German." By Saxony, Luther meant Lower Saxony; in the sixteenth century, *Plattdeutsch* (Low German) was spoken in Wittenberg.

despair, denial of God, blasphemy, and countless other abominable sins. These are snares and nets; indeed, they are the real "flaming darts"[o] that are venomously shot into our hearts, not by flesh and blood but by the devil.

Every Christian must endure such great, grievous perils and attacks—grievous enough even if they come one at a time. As long as we remain in this vile life, where we are attacked, hunted, and harried on all sides, we are constrained to cry out and pray every hour that God may not allow us to become faint and weary and to fall back into sin, shame, and unbelief. Otherwise it is impossible to overcome even the smallest attack.

This, then, is what "leading us not into temptation" means: when God gives us power and strength to resist, even though the attack is not removed or ended. For no one can escape temptations and allurements as long as we live in the flesh and have the devil prowling around us. We cannot help but suffer attacks, and even be mired in them, but we pray here that we may not fall into them and be drowned by them.

To experience attack, therefore, is quite a different thing from consenting to it or saying yes to it.[237] We must all experience it, though not to the same degree; some have more frequent and severe attacks than others. Young people, for example, are tempted chiefly by the flesh; adults and older people are tempted by the world. Others, who are concerned with spiritual matters (that is, strong Christians),[238] are tempted by the devil. But no one can be harmed by merely experiencing an attack, as long as it is contrary to our will and we would prefer to be rid of it. For if we did not experience it, it could not be called an attack. But to consent to it is to give it free rein and neither to resist it nor to pray for help against it.

Accordingly we Christians must be armed and expect every day to be under continuous attack. Then we will not go about securely and heedlessly as if the devil were far from us, but will at all times expect its blows and fend them off. Even if at present I am chaste, patient, kind, and firm in faith, the devil is likely at this very hour to send such an arrow into my heart that I can scarcely endure, for it is an enemy who never lets up or becomes weary; when one attack ceases, new ones always arise.

237. Luther writes in *An Exposition of the Lord's Prayer for Simple Lay People* (1519) (LW 42:73): "Thus we read in the book of hermits [i.e., Jerome's *Lives of the Hermits*] how a young brother longed to rid himself of his evil thoughts. The aged father said to him, 'Dear brother, you cannot prevent the birds from flying over your head, but you can certainly keep them from building a nest in your hair.'" Luther frequently uses this example in his writings.

238. Regardless of this off-hand statement, which appears to reinforce the medieval categorizing of people according to their spiritual aptitudes, the catechism validates all people as having equal status spiritually speaking. On Luther's rich writing on the matter, see Phil and Peter Krey, *Luther's Spirituality* (Mahwah, NJ: Paulist, 2007).

o Eph. 6:16.

At such times our only help and comfort is to run here and seize hold of the Lord's Prayer and to speak to God from our heart, "Dear God, you have commanded me to pray; let me not fall because of temptation." Then you will see that the temptation has to cease and eventually admit defeat. Otherwise, if you attempt to help yourself by your own thoughts and resources, you will only make the matter worse and give the devil a wider opening. For the devil has a serpent's head; if it finds an opening into which it can slither, the whole body will irresistibly follow.[239] But prayer can resist it and drive it back.

The Last Petition

"But deliver us from the evil.[p] Amen."

In the Greek[q] this petition reads, "Deliver or preserve us from the Evil One [or the Wicked One]." It seems to be speaking of the devil as the sum of all evil in order that the entire substance of our prayer may be directed against our archenemy. For it is the devil who obstructs everything for which we ask: God's name or honor, God's kingdom and will, our daily bread, a good and cheerful conscience, etc.

Therefore at the end we sum it up by saying, "Dear God, help us to get rid of all this misfortune." Nevertheless, this petition includes all the evil that may befall us under the devil's kingdom: poverty, disgrace, death, and, in short, all the tragic misery and heartache, of which there is so incalculably much on earth. For because the devil is not only a liar but a murderer as well,[r] it incessantly seeks our life and vents its anger by causing accidents and injury to our bodies. It crushes some and drives others to insanity; some it drowns in water, and many it hounds to suicide or other dreadful catastrophes. Therefore, there is nothing for us to do on earth but to pray without ceasing against this archenemy. For if God did not support us, we would not be safe from the devil for a single hour.

239. Luther observes the tradition of associating the devil with a snake, most prominently in his interpretation of Genesis 3 and the fall of Eve and Adam. See LW 1:141–54.

p   *Erlöse uns von dem Übel* (Ger.), *libera nos a malo* (Lat.), the words denoting "bad," "evil," or "wicked" one.

q   *The Large Catechism*'s first edition's erroneous translation "In the Hebrew" was corrected in later editions.

r   John 8:44.

Thus you see how God wants us to pray to God for everything that attacks even our bodily welfare so that we seek and expect help from no one or nothing else but God. But God has placed at the end this petition, for if we are to be protected and delivered from all evil, God's name must first be hallowed in us, God's kingdom come among us, and God's will be done. In the end God will preserve us from sin and disgrace and from everything else that harms or injures us.

Thus God has laid before us very briefly all the afflictions that may ever beset us in order that we may never have an excuse for failing to pray. But the efficacy of prayer consists in our learning also to say Amen to it—that is, not to doubt that our prayer is surely heard and will be answered. This word[240] is nothing else than an unquestioning word of faith on the part of the one who does not pray as a matter of luck but knows that God does not lie because God has promised to grant it. Where there is no faith like this, there also can be no true prayer.[241]

It is therefore a pernicious delusion when people pray in such a way that they dare not wholeheartedly add "Yes" and conclude with certainty that God hears their prayer. Instead, they remain in doubt, saying, "Why should I be so bold as to boast that God hears my prayer? I am only a poor sinner," etc. That means that they are looking not at God's promise but at their own works and worthiness, and thereby they despise God and accuse God of lying. Therefore they receive nothing, as St. James [1:6-7] says, "But ask in faith, never doubting, for the one who doubts is like a wave of the sea, driven and tossed by the wind; for the doubter . . . must not expect to receive anything from the Lord." Look! God has attached much importance to our being certain so that we do not pray in vain or despise our prayers in any way.

240. In *An Exposition of the Lord's Prayer for Simple Laymen* (1519) (LW 42:76), Luther astutely writes: "The little word 'Amen' is of Hebrew or Jewish origin. In German it means that something is most certainly true. It is good to remember that this word expresses the faith that we should have in praying every petition."

241. Praying, for Luther, is essential for living out the justifying faith, which enables one to be in a praying relationship with God in the first place.

Fourth Part: Concerning Baptism[s]

We have now finished with the three chief parts[t] of common Christian teaching. We must still say something about our two sacraments instituted by Christ.[242] For every Christian ought to have at least some brief, elementary instruction about them, because without them no one can be a Christian, although unfortunately nothing was taught about them in the past.[243] First, we shall take up baptism, through which we are initially received into the Christian community.[244] In order that it may be readily understood, we shall treat it in a systematic way and limit ourselves to that which is necessary for us to know.[245] How it is to be maintained and defended against heretics and sectarians[246] we shall leave to the scholars.

In the first place, we must above all be familiar with the words on which baptism is founded and to which everything is related that is to be said on the subject, namely, where the Lord Christ says in the last chapter of Matthew [28:19]: "Go into all the world, teach all the nonbelievers,[u] and baptize them in the name of the Father and of the Son and of the Holy Spirit."[v]

242. One of the most significant reforms Luther induced was the reduction of the number of sacraments from seven (baptism, Eucharist, confirmation, penance/reconciliation, last rites/anointing the sick, marriage, ordination/holy orders), a number that was settled by the Scholastic Peter Lombard (1095–1160), to two. Both rites he said were instituted by Jesus' own command in the New Testament. Each also made use of an earthly element (water, bread, wine) along with Jesus' words and the accompanying promise (the gospel). Luther adopted Augustine of Hippo's definition of a sacrament, while he launched his reforms with a massive criticism of the theological premises of the medieval practice of sacraments.

243. Luther criticizes the Catholic church for failing to educate the laity, and its clergy, even on the essentials. This urgency, which became evident during the so-called Visitations (see introduction, p. 284), prompted Luther to finally write his catechisms.

244. The practice of baptism is as old as Christianity. Originally an initiation practice with immersion of adults, a more uniform practice and a preference for infant baptism developed in the Middle Ages. Early Christians seem to have focused on the elaborate ritual aspect (for which there was considerable variety) and secured the indoctrination with a lengthy prebaptismal catechesis (up to three years), which culminated in receiving the Creed, baptism, and entrance to the Lord's Supper. Lutheran teaching of the sacrament has maintained the initiation idea while emphasizing the theological meaning of the rite.

---

s   On Luther's writings on sacraments, see *Babylonian Captivity of the Church*, LW 36:[5–10] 11–126 and in TAL, vol. 3, forthcoming; *Smalcald Articles* in BC, 295–328, and in this volume, p. 417. Also *The Holy and Blessed Sacrament of Baptism* (1519), *The Blessed Sacrament of the Holy and True Body of Christ* (omitting attack on brotherhoods) (1519), *The Sacrament of Penance* (1519), all in LW 35, and in TAL, vol. 1. For a thorough historical treatment and commentary, see Albrecht Peters, *Baptism and Lord's Supper*, in *Commentary on Luther's Catechisms*, trans. Thomas H. Trapp (St. Louis: Concordia, 2012). Also, interpreting Luther in ecumenical company, see Susan Wood, SCL, *One Baptism: Ecumenical Dimensions of the Doctrine of Baptism* (Collegeville, MN: Michael Glazier, 2009).

t   Luther uses the word *Hauptstück* (Ger.) in a twofold sense: for "major divisions" but also for "chief articles" or "the most essential." The present sense of "chief parts" of the catechism derives from the Nuremberg *Kinderbüchlein* (1531).

u   Ger.: *heiden*, translated as "Gentile" or "pagan," in Luther's use means typically *Nichtjuden*, "Gentile," "not-Jewish," if not used in a sense of *Nichtgläubige*, "nonbeliever" or "non-Christians."

v   Luther's own translation.

Likewise, in the last chapter of Mark [16:16]: "The one who believes and is baptized will be saved; but the one who does not believe will be condemned."

Observe, first, that these words contain God's commandment and institution, so that no one may doubt that baptism is of divine origin, not something devised or invented by human beings. As truly as I can say that the Ten Commandments, the Creed, and the Lord's Prayer were not spun out of anyone's imagination but are revealed and given by God, so I can boast that baptism is no human plaything but is instituted by God alone.[w] Moreover, it is solemnly and strictly commanded that we must be baptized or we shall not be saved,[x] so that we are not to regard it as an indifferent matter,[247] like putting on a new red coat.[248] It

Image of infant baptism in *Deudsch Catechismus* by Johannes Brenz, 1553.

245. Even if it is an often-repeated conclusion that Luther was not a "systematic theologian" in a contemporary sense of the word, he applied a method of systematizing, particularly when educating. Especially with the sacrament of baptism, Luther labored to synthesize his central convictions, pastoral message, and theological insights into a practical guidance for a general audience. In his treatment of baptism, Luther is at his most systematic mode. See Jonathan D. Trigg, *Baptism in the Theology of Martin Luther* (Leiden: Brill, 1997); and Eeva Martikainen, "Baptism," in Jukka-Pekka Vainio, ed., *Engaging Luther: A (New) Theological Assessment* (Eugene, OR: Wipf & Stock, 2010), 98–107.

246. With "sectarians" Luther refers mostly to those factions of Protestants who diverged from his teaching of the sacraments and his interpretation of Scripture, such as the Anabaptists. Ironically, a condemned heretic himself, Luther measures others' degree of heresy on the basis of their agreement with or deviation from his doctrinal convictions, most importantly about the sacraments.

247. Ger.: *leichtwertig Ding*, "not a light matter." While Luther is speaking theologically about baptism here, in practice, baptism could be a matter of life and death in a world where baptism was required by law.

248. A red coat was appropriate dress for a celebratory occasion.

w "God himself" translated with "God alone."

x Ger.: *sollen nich selig werden*, or "become blessed." In medieval Catholic imagination, a person without baptism belonged outside the Christian realm.

is of the greatest importance that we regard baptism as excellent, glorious, and exalted. It is the chief cause of our contentions and battles, because the world is now full of sects who scream that baptism is an external thing and that external things are of no use.[249] But no matter how external it may be, here stand God's word and command that have instituted, established, and confirmed baptism. What God institutes and commands cannot be useless. Rather, it is a most precious thing,[y] even though to all appearances it may not be worth a straw. If people used to consider it a great thing when the pope dispensed indulgences with his letters and bulls[250] and confirmed altars and churches solely by virtue of his letters and seals,[251] then we ought to regard baptism as much greater and more precious because God has commanded it. What is more, it is performed[z] in God's name. So the words read, "Go, baptize," not "in your name" but "in God's name."

To be baptized in God's name is to be baptized not by human beings but by God and God's own doing. Although it is performed by human hands, it is nevertheless truly God's own act. From this fact everyone can easily conclude that it is of much greater value than the work of any human being or saint. For what human work can possibly be greater than God's work?

But here the devil sets to work to blind us with false appearances and to lead us away from God's work to our own. It makes a much more splendid appearance when a Carthusian[252] does many great and difficult works, and we all attach greater importance to our own achievements and merits. But the Scriptures teach that if we piled together all the works of all the monks in a heap, no matter how precious and dazzling they might appear, they would still not be as noble and good as if God were to pick up a straw. Why? Because the person performing the act is nobler and better. Here one must evaluate not the person according to the works, but the works according to the person, from whom they must derive their worth. But mad reason rushes forth[a]

---

249. Ger.: "die Taufe sei ein äußerlich Ding, äußerlich Ding aber kein Nütz." This was an argument used by radical preachers in the sixteenth century, making the reception of the sacrament a matter of choice and distancing themselves from the Catholic teaching of the premise and effect of the sacrament.

250. A bull is the most formal type of papal decree. It takes its name from the capsule (Lat.: bulla) that contains the papal seal attached to the thick parchment of the document. Papal decrees of less universal significance are called "letters" or "briefs" and are written on thin parchment.

251. Certain altars and churches were "confirmed" by the pope as places to obtain the benefits of the indulgences.

252. See n. 103, p. 317.

---

y   With expressions like "ein eitel köstlich Ding" (Ger.), Luther underscored the preciousness of the sacrament as the medium for the unmerited gift of justification.

z   Ger.: geschicht.

a   The 1538 Wittenberg edition of the catechism and the German Book of Concord (1580): "But our mad reason will not consider this."

and, because baptism is not dazzling like the works that we do, regards it as worthless.

Now you can understand how to formulate a proper answer to the question, What is baptism? Namely, that it is not simply plain water, but water placed in the setting of God's word and commandment and made holy by them. It is nothing else than God's water, not that the water itself is nobler than other water but that God's word and commandment[253] are added to it.

Therefore it is sheer wickedness and devilish blasphemy that now, in order to blaspheme baptism, our new spirits[254] set aside God's word and ordinance, consider nothing but the water drawn from the well, and then babble, "How can a handful of water help the soul?" Yes, my friend! Who does not know that water is water, if it is considered separately? But how dare you tamper thus with God's ordinance and rip out God's most precious jewel, in which God's own ordinance is fastened and enclosed and from which God does not wish it to be separated? For the real significance of the water lies in God's word or commandment and God's name, and this treasure is greater and nobler than heaven and earth.

Note the distinction, then: Baptism is a very different thing from all other water, not by virtue of the natural substance but because here something nobler is added, for God stakes God's own honor, power, and might on it. Therefore it is not simply a natural water, but a divine, heavenly, holy, and blessed water—praise it in any other terms you can—all by virtue of the word, which is a heavenly, holy word that no one can sufficiently extol, for it contains and conveys all that is God's.[255,b] This, too, is where it derives its nature so that it is called a sacrament, as St. Augustine taught, "Accedat verbum ad elementum et fit sacramentum,"[c] which means that "when the word is added to the

253. With the reminder *Gottes Wort und gebot* (Ger.), Luther points to God's word and command as both the rationale and the cause of effectiveness with the sacrament.

254. Luther is referring to the Anabaptists, who denied the value of infant baptism and saw baptism as an act of witnessing one's faith.

255. Luther's notion of baptism is mystical in the sense of what it promises ontologically. When speaking of the effect of baptism, Luther draws from his notion of justification by faith and argues for the transformation or regeneration that ensues. The fullness of Luther's teaching of the sacrament's effect can best be appreciated with a due consideration to both dimensions of justification: being declared "not guilty" on the merit of Christ's favor "for us" (forensic righteousness) and being "made holy" and one with Christ, the gift who dwells "in us" (effective righteousness). The reality-changing impact of baptism depends on the ontological effect of justification, being made right and one with God.

---

b   On the differing interpretations on Luther's doctrine of justification, see, e.g., the forensic justification emphasized by Gerhard Forde, *Justification by Faith: A Matter of Death and Life* (repr., Eugene, OR: Wipf & Stock, 2012), and the unfolding of the meaning of the effective dimension with its implied faith-participation on Christ in Mannermaa, *Christ Present in Faith*. For a systematic treatment, see Veli-Matti Kärkkäinen, *One with God: Salvation as Deification and Justification* (Collegeville, MN: Liturgical, 2004).

c   Tractate 80, on John 15:3 (MPL 35:1840; NPNF, ser. 1, 7:344), reads *accredit*. Luther frequently quoted this passage.

element or the natural substance, it becomes a sacrament," that is, a holy, divine thing and sign.

Therefore, we constantly teach that we should see the sacraments and all external things ordained and instituted by God not according to the crude, external mask (as we see the shell of a nut) but as that in which God's word is enclosed. In the same way, we speak about fatherhood and motherhood and governmental authority. If we regard these people with reference to their noses, eyes, skin, and hair, flesh and bones, they look no different from Turks and heathen, and someone might come and ask, "Why should I think more of this person than of others?" But because the commandment is added, "You shall honor father and mother," I see another person, adorned and clothed with the majesty and glory of God. The commandment, I say, is the golden chain around the neck,[256] yes, the crown on the head, which shows me how and why I should honor this particular flesh and blood.

In the same manner, and to an even greater extent, you should give honor and glory to baptism on account of the word, for God has honored it by both words and deeds and has confirmed it by miracles from heaven. Do you think it was a joke that the heavens opened when Christ was baptized, that the Holy Spirit descended visibly,[d] and that the divine glory and majesty were manifested everywhere?

I therefore admonish you again that these two, the word and the water, must by no means be separated from each other. For where the word is separated from the water, the water is no different from the water that the maid uses for cooking and could indeed be called a bath-keeper's baptism.[e] But when the word is with it according to God's ordinance, baptism is a sacrament, and it is called Christ's baptism. This is the first point to be emphasized: the nature and dignity of the holy sacrament.

In the second place, because we now know what baptism is and how it is to be regarded, we must also learn why and for what purpose it has been instituted, that is, what benefits, gifts, and effects it brings. Nor can we better understand this than from the

256. An insignia of office.

d   Matt. 3:16.

e   See Luther's *Sermon on Baptism* (1534) (WA 37:642, 17–18): "A mere watery or earthly water, or (as the sectarians call it) a bathwater or dog's bath."

words of Christ quoted above, "The one who believes and is baptized will be saved."[f] This is the simplest way to put it: the power, effect, benefit, fruit, and purpose of baptism is that it saves. For no one is baptized in order to become royalty, but, as the words say, "to be saved." To be saved, as everyone well knows, is nothing else than to be delivered from sin, death, and the devil, to enter into Christ's kingdom, and to live with Christ forever.

Here again you see how baptism is to be regarded as precious and important, for in it we obtain such an inexpressible treasure. This indicates that it cannot be simple, ordinary water, for ordinary water could not have such an effect. But the word does it, and this shows also, as we said above, that God's name is in it. And where God's name is, there must also be life and salvation. Thus it is well described as a divine, blessed, fruitful, and gracious water, for it is through the word that it receives the power to become the "washing of regeneration,"[257] as St. Paul calls it in Titus 3[:5].

Our know-it-alls, the new spirits,[258] claim that faith alone saves and that works and external things add nothing to it. We answer: It is true, nothing that is in us does it but faith, as we shall hear later on. But these leaders of the blind are unwilling to see that faith must have something to believe—something to which it may cling and upon which it may stand. Thus faith clings to the water and believes it to be baptism, in which there is sheer salvation and life, not through the water, as we have sufficiently stated, but through its incorporation with God's word and ordinance and the joining of God's name to it.[259] When I believe this, what else is it but believing in God as the one who has bestowed and implanted God's word in baptism and has offered us this external thing within which we can grasp this treasure?[g]

Now, these people are so foolish as to separate faith from the object to which faith is attached and secured, all on the grounds that the object is something external. Yes, it must be external so that it can be perceived and grasped by the senses and thus brought into the heart, just as the entire gospel is an external,

257. The word *regeneration* in Luther's theology speaks of the person's purification of the sin-induced guilt and a renewal by the work of the Holy Spirit that each baptized person can receive in faith. That Lutheran language has different emphases on this is symptomatic of the tensions rooted in different interpretations of the nature of Christian life and the impact of both law and gospel. The emphasis on the word alone justifying with grace that comes from *extra nos* and not from oneself or by one's merit has had implications for how "sanctification" is used or understood. In the Lutheran tradition, drawing more from the Lutheran confessions rather than Luther, the concept of "regeneration" has remained in the background, and associated more with Luther's partners such as Andreas Karlstadt von Bodenstein. New research on the core of Luther's view of justification has provided rationale for reclaiming "regeneration," particularly in Lutheran baptismal language.

258. Luther refers to the followers of the Swiss reformer Ulrich Zwingli, or the Anabaptists.

259. Luther makes clear the essential connection between the word and faith, and points at God's work in justification and regeneration.

---

f Mark 16:16.

g In his *Prefaces to the New Testament*, Luther states: "Faith . . . is a divine work in us which changes us and makes us to be born again of God" (LW 35:370).

oral proclamation. In short, whatever God does and effects in us God desires to accomplish through such an external ordinance. No matter where God speaks—indeed, no matter for what purpose or through what means God speaks—there faith must look and to it faith must hold on. We have here the words, "The one who believes and is baptized will be saved." To what do they refer if not to baptism, that is, the water placed in the setting of God's ordinance? Hence it follows that whoever rejects baptism rejects God's word, faith, and Christ, who directs and binds us to baptism.

In the third place, having learned the great benefit and power of baptism, let us observe further who the person is who receives these gifts and benefits of baptism. This again is most beautifully and clearly expressed in these same words, "The one who believes and is baptized will be saved," that is, faith alone makes the person worthy to receive the saving, divine water profitably. Because such blessings are offered and promised in the words that accompany the water, they cannot be received unless we believe them from the heart. Without faith baptism is of no use, although in itself it is an infinite, divine treasure. So this single expression, "The one who believes," is so powerful that it excludes and drives out all works that we may do with the intention of gaining and meriting salvation through them. For it is certain that whatever is not faith contributes nothing toward salvation and receives nothing.[260]

But some are accustomed to ask, "If baptism is itself a work and you say that works are of no use for salvation, what place is there for faith?" Answer: Yes, it is true that our works are of no use for salvation. Baptism, however, is not our work, but God's work (for, as was said, you must distinguish Christ's baptism quite clearly from a bath-keeper's baptism). God's works are salutary and necessary for salvation, and they do not exclude but rather demand[h] faith, for without faith one cannot grasp them. Just by allowing the water to be poured over you, you do not receive or retain baptism in such a manner that it does you any good. But it becomes beneficial to you if you accept it as God's command and ordinance, so that, baptized in God's name, you may receive in

---

260. Luther's central teaching and emphasis is justification by faith. His theology of grace and salvation culminates in and opens up from the practice of baptism, which serves as the orientation for Lutheran spirituality. See Kirsi Stjerna, *No Greater Jewel: Thinking of Baptism with Luther* (Minneapolis: Augsburg Fortress, 2010).

---

h   Luther's word *fordern* may mean both "demand" (*forden*) and "further" (*fördern*).

the water the promised salvation. Neither the hand nor the body can do this, but rather the heart must believe it.

Thus you see plainly that baptism is not a work that we do but that it is a treasure that God gives us and faith grasps, just as the Lord Christ on the cross is not a work but a treasure placed in the setting of the word and offered to us in the word and received by faith. Therefore, those who cry out against us as if we were preaching against faith do commit violence against us. Actually, we insist on faith alone as so necessary that without it nothing can be received or enjoyed.

Thus we have considered the three things that must be known about this sacrament, especially that it is God's ordinance and is to be held in all honor. This alone would be enough, even if baptism were an entirely external thing. Similarly, the commandment "You shall honor father and mother" refers only to human flesh and blood, yet we look not at the flesh and blood but at God's commandment in which it is set and on account of which this flesh is called father and mother. In the same way, even if we had nothing more than these words, "Go and baptize," etc., we would still have to accept it as God's ordinance and perform it. But here we have not only God's commandment and injunction, but the promise as well. Therefore it is far more glorious than anything else God has commanded and ordained; in short, it is so full of comfort and grace that heaven and earth cannot comprehend it. However, a special knack belongs here: that each person believe it. For it is not the treasure that is lacking; rather, what is lacking is that it should be grasped and held firmly.[261]

In baptism, therefore, every Christian has enough to study and practice all his or her life.[262] Christians always have enough to do to believe firmly what baptism promises and brings—victory over death and the devil, forgiveness of sin, God's grace, the entire Christ, and the Holy Spirit with her gifts. In short, the blessings of baptism are so boundless that if our timid nature considers them, it may well doubt whether they could all be true. Suppose there were a physician who had so much skill that people would not die, or even though they died[i] would afterward live eternally. Just think how the world would snow and rain money on such a

261. Luther underscores the matter of obedience in regard to God's orders. His point about honoring one's parents implies also the fundamental expectation of obedience to God in all areas of life. In Luther's thinking, the church has made the commitment to continue the practice of baptism out of obedience to God, and individuals are released from deliberation on this regard. What they need to concern themselves with is the unfolding of the meaning of the gift for them personally.

262. Particularly in his teaching of the baptism, Luther reiterates the mystery of God's grace that goes beyond human comprehension and capacity to believe; he stresses the value of regular use of the Catechism in this regard.

---

i   The 1538 Wittenberg edition of the catechism and the German *Book of Concord* (1580) add: "would be restored to life and."

263. With his eschatological point about the resurrection, Luther makes an important anthropological statement about the body-spirit duality of human life. Building on the christological premise on Christ's two natures, Luther argues for the unity of the two dimensions that constitute human existence. In creation and in resurrection, human beings exist in body and spirit.

264. Luther's proof for the validity and rationale for infant baptism is somewhat anticlimactic. He draws evidence from history to argue that God must be pleased with the practice, to allow it to continue and that it leads to good lives. In addition, Luther gives a theological argument: infants have inherited original sin and are in need of purification and forgiveness; and grace is always given by God and received in the state of (infant-like) passivity.

265. Luther frequently mentioned Bernard of Clairvaux (1090–1153), a Cistercian abbott and a builder of Cistercian order as an example of piety.

266. Luther greatly respected Jean Gerson (1363–1429), a French scholar, educator, reformer, poet, and chancellor of the University of Paris, and a leader in the Conciliar movement.

267. The Bohemian reformer Jan Hus (c. 1369–1415) was condemned and executed by the Council of Constance (1414–1418) for his radical teachings akin to Luther's a century later: he underscored the authority of Scripture; preached the value of translating the Bible for people to read in their own vernacular languages; and criticized clergy corruption, abusive church practices, and the church's theology of the sacraments. He was lured

person! Because of the throng of rich people crowding around, no one else would be able to get near. Now, here in baptism there is brought, free of charge, to every person's door just such a treasure and medicine that swallows up death[j] and keeps all people alive.

Thus, we must regard baptism and put it to use in such a way that we may draw strength and comfort from it when our sins or conscience oppress us, and say: "But I am baptized! And if I have been baptized, I have the promise that I shall be saved and have eternal life, both in soul and body."[k] This is the reason why these two things are done in baptism; the body has water poured over it because all it can receive is the water, and in addition the word is spoken so that the soul may receive it. Because the water and the word together constitute one baptism, both body and soul shall be saved and live forever: the soul through the word in which it believes, the body because it is united with the soul and apprehends baptism in the only way it can.[263] No greater jewel, therefore, can adorn our body and soul than baptism, for through it we become completely holy and blessed, which no other kind of life and no work on earth can acquire. Let this suffice concerning the nature, benefits, and use of baptism as serves the present purpose.

[Infant Baptism][l]

At this point, we come to a question that the devil uses to confuse the world through its sects, namely, about infant baptism.[m] Do children believe, and is it right to baptize them? To this we reply briefly: Let the simple dismiss this question and leave it to the learned. But if you wish to answer, then reply in this way:

---

j   Isa. 25:7. This "swallowing" happens on account of Christ becoming the greatest sinner.

k   See esp. pp. 400–401 below.

l   This heading was not in the original printing. It was placed in the margin in the second edition (1529) and in the German editions of 1530 and 1538; for the first time it was inserted in the text in the German *Book of Concord* (1580).

m   The "sects" reference is to groups that challenges the practice of infant baptism. See *Concerning Rebaptism: A Letter of Martin Luther to Two Pastors* (1528) (LW 40:225–62); also TAL, vol. 3, forthcoming.

That the baptism of infants is pleasing to Christ is sufficiently proved from God's own work.[264] God has sanctified many who have been thus baptized and has given them the Holy Spirit. Even today there still are many whose teaching and lives attest that they have the Holy Spirit. Similarly by God's grace we have been given the power to interpret the Scriptures and to know Christ, which is impossible without the Holy Spirit. But if God did not accept the baptism of infants, God would not have given any of them the Holy Spirit—or any part of her. In short, all this time down to the present day there would have been no person on earth who could have been a Christian. Because God has confirmed baptism through the bestowal of the Holy Spirit, as we have perceived in some of the Fathers, such as St. Bernard,[265] Gerson,[266] John Hus,[267] and others,[n] and because the holy Christian church will not disappear until the end of the world, so they[268] must confess that it is pleasing to God. For God cannot contradict God's own self, support lies and wickedness, or give God's grace or Spirit for such ends. This is just about the best and strongest proof for the simple and unlearned. For no one can take from us or overthrow this article, "I believe in one holy Christian church, the communion of saints," etc.

Further, we say, we do not put the main emphasis on whether the person baptized believes or not, for in the latter case baptism does not become invalid. Everything depends on the word and commandment of God. This is a rather subtle point, perhaps, but it is based on what I have said, that baptism is simply water and God's word in and with each other; that is, when the word accompanies the water, baptism is valid, even though faith is lacking. For my faith does not make baptism; rather, it receives baptism. Baptism does not become invalid if it is not properly received or used, as I have said, for it is not bound to our faith but to the word.[269]

Even though a Jew should come today deceitfully and with an evil purpose, and we baptized him in good faith, we ought to say that his baptism was nonetheless valid.[270] For there would be water together with God's word, even though he failed to receive it properly. Similarly, those who partake unworthily of

to the Council of Constance with a safe passage but was killed there. Hus served as a warning example for what could have happened to Luther at the Diet of Worms (1521). More importantly, Luther publically associated with his predecessor at the Leipzig Debate of 1519 when his cardinal opponent, Johann Eck, accused Luther of "Hussite heresies."

268. Luther means those who oppose infant baptism, such as the Anabaptists, who practice believer's baptism.

269. In his arguments on the effectiveness of the sacraments, Luther remains anti-Donatist, standing with Augustine's definition: the effectiveness of the sacrament does not depend on the worth of the one who celebrates or the one who receives. Only God's word gives the means of grace their effectiveness.

270. Luther often uses the hypothetical "Jew/Jews" in his argumentation. With baptism, he wishes to point out the absolute, transformative effectiveness of the sacrament, regardless of the merits of the one baptized—or the one baptizing—and points to the power of God. He is exceptional in promoting full acceptance of a converted Jew, in a world where many conversions were forced and many a convert endured suspicion even after baptism. These positives do not, of course, redeem Luther's negative assessment of the Jewish faith per se. See Schramm and Stjerna, *Martin Luther, the Bible, and the Jewish People: A Reader* (Minneapolis: Fortress Press, 2012), 3–35.

---

n   The 1538 Wittenberg edition of the catechism and the German *Book of Concord* (1580) add: "who were baptized in infancy."

271. Luther's sacramental theology continues to echo with the principles behind the Catholic idea of *ex opere operato*: the sacraments's effectiveness does not depend on the recipient. In Catholic teaching, sacraments become valid and effective when performed "right" by the duly authorized clergy. While Luther's emphasis is that nothing makes a sacrament invalid per se while its validity depends on God whose work does not fail, at the same time he highlights the crucial part of the person participating in order to reap the benefits. These terms, *opus operantis* and *ex opere operatum*, important in the arguments against the Donatists, have remained decisive in Roman Catholic sacramental theology.

272. In his *Concerning Rebaptism* (1528) (LW 40:225–62), Luther speculates on the possibility of an infant's faith in making the argument for the infant baptism and for the reality of justification by faith through grace.

273. In the Holy Roman Empire, infant baptism was stipulated in the law, with severe penalties, even death, for rebaptizing. In these arguments, Luther both defends the traditional practice of infant baptism (as in, "if it is not broken, don't fix it") and stresses the necessary power of the sacrament in making one right with God—a gift one should not doubt. Doubting one's baptism would equal doubting God's saving grace and blaspheming Christ.

the sacrament receive the true sacrament even though they do not believe.[271]

Thus you see that the objection of the sectarians is absurd. As we said, even if infants did not believe—which, however, is not the case, as we have proved[272]—still the baptism would be valid and no one should rebaptize them. Similarly, the sacrament is not vitiated if someone approaches it with an evil purpose. Moreover, that same person would not be permitted on account of that abuse to take it again the very same hour, as if not having truly received the sacrament the first time. That would be to blaspheme and desecrate the sacrament in the worst way. How dare we think that God's word and ordinance should be wrong and invalid because we use it wrongly?[273]

Therefore, I say, if you did not believe before, then believe now and confess, "The baptism indeed was right, but unfortunately I did not receive it rightly." I myself, and all who are baptized, must say before God: "I come here in my faith and in the faith of others; nevertheless, I cannot build on the fact that I believe and many people are praying for me. Instead, I build on this, that it is your word and command." In the same way, I go to the Sacrament [of the Altar] not on the strength of my own faith, but on the strength of Christ's word. I may be strong or weak; I leave that for God to decide. This I know, however—that Christ has commanded me to go, eat, and drink, etc., and that Christ gives me his body and blood; he will not lie or deceive me.

Thus we do the same with infant baptism. We bring the child with the intent and hope that it may believe, and we pray God to grant it faith. But we do not baptize on this basis, but solely on the command of God. Why? Because we know that God does not lie. My neighbor and I—in short, all people—may deceive and mislead, but God's word cannot deceive.

Therefore only presumptuous and stupid spirits draw the conclusion that where there is no true faith, there also can be no true baptism. Likewise I might argue, "If I have no faith, then Christ is nothing." Or again, "If I am not obedient, then father, mother, and magistrates are nothing." Is it correct to conclude that when people do not do what they should, the thing they misuse has no existence or value? Friend, rather reverse the argument and conclude this: Baptism does have existence and value, precisely because it is wrongly received. For if it were not right in itself, no one could misuse it nor sin against it. The saying goes,

"Abusus non tollit, sed confirmat substantiam,"[274] that is, "Misuse does not destroy the substance, but confirms its existence." Gold remains no less gold if a harlot wears it in sin and shame.

Let the conclusion therefore be that baptism always remains valid and retains its complete substance, even if only one person had ever been baptized and that one person did not have true faith. For God's ordinance and word cannot be changed or altered by human beings. But these fanatics are so blinded that they do not see God's word and commandment, and they regard baptism as nothing but water in the creek or in the pot, and a magistrate as just another person. And because they see neither faith nor obedience, they believe that these things also have no validity. Here lurks a sneaky, seditious devil who would like to snatch the crown from the rulers and trample it underfoot and would, in addition, pervert and nullify all God's work and ordinances. Therefore we must be alert and well-armed and not allow ourselves to be turned aside from the word, by regarding baptism merely as an empty sign, as the fanatics dream.[275]

Finally,[o] we must also know what baptism signifies and why God ordained precisely this sign and external ceremony for the sacrament by which we are first received into the Christian community. This act or ceremony consists of being dipped into the water, which covers us completely,[276] and being drawn out again. These two parts, being dipped under the water and emerging from it, point to the power and effect of baptism, which is nothing else than the slaying of the old creature and the resurrection of the new creature, both of which must continue in us our whole lives long. Thus a Christian life is nothing else than a daily baptism, begun once and continuing ever after. For we must keep at it without ceasing, always purging whatever pertains to the old creature, so that whatever belongs to the new creature may come forth. What is the old creature? It is what is born in us from Adam and Eve,[p] irascible, spiteful, envious, unchaste, greedy, lazy, proud—yes—and unbelieving; it is beset with all vices and

---

o   Here, after the excursus on infant baptism, Luther resumes his general treatment of baptism with a fourth point. See par. 3, 23, and 32. Luther alternates with the terms "old Adam" (cf. Rom. 5:12–6:6) and "old creature" (*alter Mensch*). In translation, either "Eve" is added, or "the old Adam" is replaced with "the old creature."

p   Here "Eve" is added to better reflect what all the "old creature" means.

---

274. A legal maxim, cited also in *Concerning Rebaptism* (1528) (LW 40:248), where Luther adds: "Gold does not become straw because a thief steals and misuses it. Silver doesn't turn into paper if it is dishonestly obtained by a usurer."

275. In Luther's world, with the emergence of groups practicing believer's baptism, many practical concerns manifested. For example, what if one's gravely ill baby had been delivered by an Anabaptist midwife who had perhaps lied that she had performed an emergency baptism? Or in the cases of ambiguity, should the town priest repeat the act? In his advice on these matters, Luther remains quite flexible when speaking in a pastoral role or when addressing pastoral (care) situations. His main conviction remains that baptism is a gift surely given for the benefit of the human being and therefore should not be repeated; nothing would be gained by that.

276. It was still customary in the sixteenth century to immerse the child three times in the baptismal font (cf. LW 35:29; WA 2:727, 4–19). Another practice, which began in the fourteenth century, was that of infusion, pouring the baptismal water over the child three times.

by nature has nothing good in it. Now, when we enter Christ's kingdom, this corruption must daily decrease so that the longer we live the gentler and more patient and meek we become, and the more we break away from greed, hatred, envy, and pride.

This is the right use of baptism among Christians, signified by baptizing with water. Where this does not take place but rather the old creature is given free rein and continually grows stronger, baptism is not being used but resisted. Those who are outside of Christ can only grow worse day by day. It is as the proverb says, and it is the truth, "The longer evil lasts, the worse it becomes."[277] If a year ago someone was proud and greedy, this year such a person is much more so. Vice thus grows and increases in people from youth on. Young children[q] have no particular vices but become vicious and unchaste as they grow older. When they reach adulthood, the real vices become more and more potent day by day.

The old creature therefore follows unchecked the inclinations of its nature if not restrained and suppressed by the power of baptism. On the other hand, when we become Christians, the old creature daily decreases until finally destroyed. This is what it means truly to plunge into baptism and daily to come forth again. So the external sign has been appointed not only so that it may work powerfully on us but also so that it may point to something. Where faith is present with its fruits, there baptism is no empty symbol, but the effect accompanies it; but where faith is lacking, it remains a mere unfruitful sign. Here you see that baptism, both by its power and by its signification, comprehends also the third sacrament, formerly called penance,[278] which is really nothing else than baptism. What is repentance but an earnest attack on the old creature and an entering into a new life? If you live in repentance, therefore, you are walking in baptism, which not only announces this new life but also produces, begins, and exercises it. In baptism we are given the grace, Spirit, and strength to suppress the old creature so that the new may come forth and grow strong.

Therefore baptism remains forever. Even though someone falls from it and sins, we always have access to it so that we may again subdue the old creature. But we need not have the

277. Luther frequently cited this proverb, also in the form: "The older, the stingier; the longer it lasts, the worse it is." See WA 32:451, 33–34; LW 21:184.

278. In the Latin, *poenitentia* (Ger.: *Buße*) means either the sacrament (penance), or the act of satisfaction enjoined by the priest (penitence), or the inward attitude of repentance. As Luther moved away from teaching about the act of confessing and penance as the third sacrament, he shifted the focus to the sacrament of baptism involving life of repentance and confession, the latter practiced in multiple ways.

---

q   Here the singular for *das Kind*, "a child," is rendered in plural, "children."

water poured over us again. Even if we were immersed in water a hundred times, it would nevertheless not be more than one baptism, and the effect and significance would continue and remain. Repentance, therefore, is nothing else than a return and approach to baptism, to resume and practice what has earlier been begun but abandoned.[279]

I say this to correct the opinion, which has long prevailed among us, that baptism is something past that we can no longer use after falling back into sin. This idea comes from looking only at the act that took place a single time. Indeed, St. Jerome is responsible for this view, for he wrote, "Penance is the second plank[280] on which we must swim ashore after the ship founders," [the ship] in which we embarked when we entered the Christian community.[r] This takes away the value of baptism, making it of no further use to us. Therefore it is incorrect to say this.[s] The ship does not break up because, as we said, it is God's ordinance and not something that is ours. But it does happen that we slip and fall out of the ship. However, those who do fall out should immediately see to it that they swim to the ship and hold fast to it, until they can climb aboard again and sail on in it as before.

Thus we see what a great and excellent thing baptism is, which snatches us from the jaws[t] of the devil and makes us God's own, overcomes and takes away sin and daily strengthens the new person, and always endures and remains until we pass out of this misery into eternal glory.

Therefore let all Christians regard their baptism as the daily garment that they are to wear all the time. Every day they should be found in faith and with its fruits, suppressing the old creature and growing up in the new. If we want to be Christians, we must practice the work that makes us Christians and let those who fall away return to it. As Christ, the mercy seat,[281] does not withdraw from us or forbid us to return to him even though we sin, so all his treasures and gifts remain. As we have once obtained

279. After first considering confession and penance as a separate sacrament, per the teaching of the Catholic Church, Luther came to teach repentance as the nature of Christian life wherein one returns to the gift of baptism regularly, in remorse and confession. So, this sacrament of baptism includes both forgiveness in completion and the invitation to return to this gift regularly. Acts of confession are an extension of and return to baptism—and thus living out the justification in the paradoxical life of a saint-sinner. See Luther's *The Sacrament of Penance* (1519), LW 35:3–22, and TAL, vol. 1:181.

280. Baptism was regarded as the first plank.

281. See Rom. 3:25; Heb. 4:16. The expression "mercy seat" (Heb.: *kabboreth*) refers to the cover of the ark that contained the Ten Commandments (Exod. 25:17-22). Sharing the root with *atonement*, the word means "to cover, cleanse, appease." With the Greek word *hilasterion* in Rom. 3:25, Paul names Christ as the mercy seat or "propitiation."

---

r   Epistle 130.9 to Demetrias (MPL 22:1115; NPNF, ser. 2, 6:266). See also Epistle 122.4 to Rusticus (MPL 22:1046; NPNF, ser. 2, 6:229); Epistle 147.3 to Fallen Sabinianus (MPL 22:1197; NPNF, ser. 2, 6:291); and *Commentary on Isaiah*, chs. 3, 8–9 (MPL 24:65). Luther frequently quoted this statement from Jerome.

s   The 1538 Wittenberg edition of the Catechism and the German *Book of Concord* (1580) add: "or else it was never rightly understood."

t   Literally, "throat" or "gullet."

forgiveness of sins in baptism, so forgiveness remains day by day as long as we live, that is, as long as we carry the old creature around our necks.

[Fifth Part:] The Sacrament of the Altar[u]

As we heard about Holy Baptism, so we must speak about the second sacrament in the same way, under three headings, stating what it is, what its benefits are, and who is to receive it. All this is established from the words Christ used to institute it. So everyone who wishes to be a Christian and to go to the sacrament should know them.[282] For we do not intend to admit to the sacrament and administer it to those who do not know what they are seeking or why they come. The words are these:[v]

"Our Lord Jesus Christ, on the night when he was betrayed, took the bread, gave thanks, and broke it, and gave it to his disciples and said, 'Take, eat; this is my body, which is given for you. Do this in remembrance of me.'

"In the same way also he took the cup after supper, gave thanks, and gave it to them, and said, 'Take, drink of this, all of you. This cup is the New Testament in my blood, which is poured out for you for the forgiveness of sins. Do this, as often as you drink it, in remembrance of me.'"

Here, too, we do not want to quarrel and dispute with those who despise and desecrate this sacrament. Instead, as in the case of baptism, we shall first learn what is of greatest importance, namely, that the chief thing is God's word and ordinance or command. It was not dreamed up or invented by some mere human being but was instituted by Christ without anyone's counsel or deliberation. Therefore, just as the Ten Commandments, the Lord's Prayer, and the Creed retain their nature and value even

282. Proper education about and intentional use of the sacraments and their personal use was one of the main purposes of the catechisms. Baptism and the Lord's Supper were among the earliest Christian rituals and important signs of belonging to the Christian community and of connecting with the creedal faith. Over time the theologies regarding the meaning of the sacraments evolved, and more uniform practices were implemented in the medieval church. Globally, these rituals today are embraced with differing theological rationales and traditions regarding the practice. Still, the core remains the same: these symbols and acts are meant to unite, identify, and empower the followers of Christ, as they have throughout the centuries.

---

u See *The Sacrament of the Body and Blood of Christ—Against the Fanatics* (1526), LW 36:329–61; *That These Words of Christ, 'This Is My Body,' Etc., Still Stand Firm against the Fanatics* (1527), LW 37:99–150; *Confession Concerning Christ's Supper* (1528), LW 37:151–372. See treatments of this topic in TAL, vol. 1:225–55; and Jensen, "Luther and the Lord's Supper," in OHMLT, 322–32. For a most thorough treatment, see Peters, *Baptism and Lord's Supper.*

v Luther conflates the references to the institution of the Lord's Supper in 1 Cor. 11:23-25; Matt. 26:26-28; Mark 14:22-24; and Luke 22:19-20.

if you never keep, pray, or believe them, so also does this blessed sacrament remain unimpaired and inviolate even if we use and handle it unworthily. Do you think God cares so much about our faith and conduct that God would permit them to affect the godly ordinance? No, all temporal things remain as God has created and ordered them, regardless of how we treat them.[283] This must always be emphasized, for thus we can thoroughly refute all the babbling of the seditious spirits who, contrary to the word of God, regard the sacraments as something that we do.

Now, what is the Sacrament of the Altar? Answer: It is the true body and blood of the Lord Christ, in and under the bread and wine, which we Christians are commanded by Christ's word to eat and drink.[284] And just as we said of baptism that it is not mere water, so we say here, too, that the sacrament is bread and wine, but not mere bread and wine such as is served at the table.

283. With Augustine, Luther identifies the Lord's Supper as one of the central means of grace that Jesus himself commanded his followers to do, promising his continued presence for those who follow the model of the first followers of Christ and gather in his name in prayer and thanksgiving.

284. Luther began to address issues related to the practice and theology of the Lord's Supper early on in his role as a reformer, but it took him some years to formulate his own particular arguments that would be distinct from both the Catholic theology and other competing "reformed" views. His debates and the Marburg Colloquy (1529) with the Swiss reformer Ulrich Zwingli were decisive in this evolution. During the years 1526–1529 Luther wrote his foundational pieces on the Lord's Supper.

In this woodcut Lucas Cranach the Elder depicts in imaginary fashion reformers Martin Luther and Jan Hus (c. 1369–1415) serving both bread and wine at communion to the House of Saxony.

285. The earliest eucharistic gatherings included a meal with prayer and thanksgiving. As Christian communities grew in size, actual meals were substituted with a more symbolic meal, while the meaning given to the spiritual meal and its theological interpretation became enhanced.

286. Luther is adamantly anti-Donatist: he frequently and consistently stresses the validity of the sacraments regardless of the recipient's or administrator's goodness or shortcomings.

287. This "inclusivity" principle, based on Luther's notion of grace, was a central point to get across to the late medieval Christians who had grown up with a hierarchical view of holiness. The teachings of the day did little to empower an ordinary Christian to feel particularly holy in comparison to monastics or the celebrated saints of the church. One of the central discoveries of Luther's theology lies in his teaching of the democracy of grace: God's grace is for all and it is freely given, not earned. By the same token, holiness is of God and knows no human-made boundaries. In their sainthood, just as in their failings, human beings are equal. Philip Melanchthon articulates, succinctly, the foundational doctrine of justification by faith in Article 4 of the *Augsburg Confession*.

Rather, it is bread and wine set within God's word and bound to it.

It is the word, I say, that makes this a sacrament and distinguishes it from ordinary bread and wine, so that it is called and truly is Christ's body and blood.[285] For it is said, "Accedat verbum ad elementum et fit sacramentum," that is, "When the word is joined to the external element, it becomes a sacrament."[w] This saying of St. Augustine is so appropriate and well put that he could hardly have said anything better. The word must make the element a sacrament; otherwise, it remains an ordinary element. Now, this is not the word and ordinance of a prince or emperor, but of the divine Majesty at whose feet all creatures should kneel and confess that it is as is said, and they should accept it with all reverence, fear, and humility.

With this word you can strengthen your conscience and declare: "Let a hundred thousand devils, with all the fanatics, come forward and say, 'How can bread and wine be Christ's body and blood?' etc. Still I know that all the spirits and scholars put together have less wisdom than the divine Majesty has in the littlest finger. Here is Christ's word: 'Take, eat, this is my body.' 'Drink of this, all of you, this is the New Testament in my blood,' etc. Here we shall take our stand and see who dares to instruct Christ and alter what he has spoken. It is true, indeed, that if you take the word away from the elements or view them apart from the word, you have nothing but ordinary bread and wine. But if the words remain, as is right and necessary, then by virtue of them the elements are truly the body and blood of Christ. For as Christ's lips speak and say, so it is; Christ cannot lie or deceive."

Hence it is easy to answer all kinds of questions that now trouble people—for example, whether even a wicked priest can administer the sacrament, and similar questions. Our conclusion is: Even though a scoundrel receives or administers the sacrament, it is the true sacrament (that is, Christ's body and blood), just as truly as when one uses it most worthily.[286] For it is not founded on human holiness but on the word of God. As no saint on earth, yes, no angel in heaven can make bread and wine into Christ's body and blood, so likewise can no one change or alter the sacrament, even through misuse.[287] For the word by which

w   See p. 391.

it was constituted a sacrament is not rendered false because of an individual's unworthiness or unbelief. Christ does not say, "If you believe or if you are worthy, you have my body and blood," but rather, "Take, eat and drink, this is my body and blood." Likewise, when he says, "Do this" (namely, what I now do, what I institute, what I give you and bid you take), this is as much as to say, "No matter whether you are worthy or unworthy, you have here his body and blood by the power of these words that are connected to the bread and wine." Mark this and remember it well. For upon these words rests our whole argument, our protection and defense against all errors and deceptions that have ever arisen or may yet arise.

Thus we have briefly considered the first part, namely, the essence of this sacrament. Now we come also to its power and benefit, for which purpose the sacrament was really instituted.[288] For it is most necessary that we know what we should seek and obtain there. This is clear and easily understood from the words just quoted: "This is my body and blood, given and poured out for you for the forgiveness of sins." That is to say, in brief, that we go to the sacrament because there we receive a great treasure, through and in which we obtain the forgiveness of sins. Why? Because the words are there, and they impart it to us! For this reason Christ bids me eat and drink, that it may be mine and do me good as a sure pledge and sign[x]—indeed, as the very gift he has provided for me against my sins, death, and all evils.

Therefore, it is appropriately called food of the soul, for it nourishes and strengthens the new creature. For in the first instance, we are born anew through baptism. However, our human flesh and blood, as I have said, have not lost their old skin. There are so many hindrances and attacks of the devil and the world that we often grow weary and faint and at times even stumble. Therefore the Lord's Supper is given as a daily food and sustenance so that our faith may be refreshed and strengthened and that it may not succumb in the struggle but become stronger and stronger. For the new life should be one that continually develops and makes progress. But it has to suffer a great deal of

288. In his argumentation on the sacrament of the altar, Luther's main concern is that people actually use the sacrament and reap its benefits for their personal lives; that was far more important than futile attempts to define a formula of "how" the mystery happens.

---

x   Luther uses the word *Pfand und Zeichen* (Ger.) to indicate what the word truly imparts to the recipient in the sacrament. This is different from a Zwinglian language of a sign pointing to or symbolizing another reality.

opposition. The devil is a furious enemy; when it sees that we resist it and attack the old creature, and when the devil cannot rout us by force, it sneaks and skulks about at every turn, trying all kinds of tricks, and does not stop until it has finally worn us out so that we either renounce our faith or lose heart[y] and become indifferent or impatient. For times like these, when our heart feels too sorely pressed, this comfort of the Lord's Supper is given to bring us new strength and refreshment.

Here again our clever spirits contort themselves with their great learning and wisdom; they rant and rave, "How can bread and wine forgive sins or strengthen faith?" Yet they have heard and know that we do not claim this of bread and wine—for in itself bread is bread—but of that bread and wine that are Christ's body and blood and that are accompanied by the word.[289] These and no other, we say, are the treasure through which such forgiveness is obtained. This treasure is conveyed and communicated to us in no other way than through the words "given and shed for you." Here you have both—that it is Christ's body and blood and that they are yours as a treasure and gift. Christ's body cannot be an unfruitful, useless thing that does nothing and helps no one. Yet, however great the treasure may be in itself, it must be set within the word and offered to us through the word, otherwise we could never know of it or seek it.

Therefore it is absurd for them to say that Christ's body and blood are not given and poured out for us in the Lord's Supper and hence that we cannot have forgiveness of sins in the sacrament.[290] Although the work took place on the cross and forgiveness of sins has been acquired, yet it cannot come to us in any other way than through the word. How should we know that this took place or was to be given to us if it were not proclaimed by preaching, by the oral word? From what source do they know of forgiveness, and how can they grasp and appropriate it, except by steadfastly believing the Scriptures and the gospel? Now, the whole gospel and the article of the Creed, "I believe in one holy Christian church . . . the forgiveness of sins," are embodied in this sacrament and offered to us through the word. Why, then, should we allow such a treasure to be torn out of the sacrament?

289. In Luther's argumentation about Christ's presence in the Eucharist, the word *signum* equals *res*, that is, the sign is and contains what it points toward; this means Christ is present in the signs, in the matter, and in the receiving. Luther would not compromise this view but maintain his argument steadfastly, for example, with Zwingli in 1529 at the Marburg Colloquy. Though they agreed on fourteen out of the fifteen points of faith, he could not agree on the wording about the presence of Christ at the Lord's Supper. See the *Marburg Articles*, in English translation in Kolb and Nestingen, eds., *Sources and Contexts*, 88–92.

290. Luther stresses the gift of forgiveness given in the sacrament. He offers different logic regarding the Lord's Supper: unlike in the Christian practice where Christians were required first to partake of the sacrament of penance and only then approach the Lord's Table with a declaration of forgiveness from the priest (pending works of satisfaction toward the absolution), Luther invites Christians to run to the sacraments as sinners who need to receive forgiveness and receive it unconditionally.

---

y　A proverbial expression.

They[z] must still confess that these are the very words that we hear everywhere in the gospel. They can no more say that these words in the sacrament are of no value than they can dare to say that the whole gospel or word of God apart from the sacrament is of no value.

So far we have treated the whole sacrament from the standpoint both of what it is in itself and of what it brings and benefits. Now we must also consider who the person is who receives such power and benefit. Briefly, as we said above about baptism and in many other places, the answer is: It is the one who believes what the words say and what they give, for they are not spoken or preached to stone and wood but to those who hear them, those to whom he says, "Take and eat," etc. And because Christ offers and promises forgiveness of sins, it is part and parcel of the sacrament that it be received by faith. This faith Christ demands in the word when he says, "given for you" and "shed for you," as if he said, "This is why I give it and bid you eat and drink, that you may take it as your own and enjoy it." All those who let these words be addressed to them and believe that they are true have what the words declare. But those who do not believe have nothing, for they let this gracious blessing be offered to them in vain and refuse to enjoy it. The treasure is opened and placed at everyone's door, yes, on the table, but it is also your responsibility to take it and confidently believe that it is just as the words tell you.[a]

Now this is the sum total of a Christian's preparation to receive this sacrament worthily. Because this treasure is fully offered in the words, it can be grasped and appropriated only by the heart. Such a gift and eternal treasure cannot be seized with the hand. Fasting, prayer, and the like may have their place as an external preparation and children's exercise so that one's body may behave properly and reverently toward the body and blood of Christ. But the body cannot grasp and appropriate what is given in and with the sacrament. This is done by the faith of the heart that discerns and desires such a treasure.[291]

291. The practice of confession was still important as a personal preparation, but Luther shifted the focus from acts of penance (and fear) to the word of forgiveness (and security), received at the Lord's Supper. Luther often admits the impossibility of human reason to grasp the gift of grace and names the word and the Spirit as agents is making this kind of faith of the heart possible and actually receiving the gifts. For a pioneering study on this complex issue of knowing by heart, see Bengt R. Hoffmann, *Theology of the Heart: The Role of Mysticism in the Theology of Martin Luther*, trans. Pearl W. Hoffmann (Minneapolis: Kirkhouse, 2003).

---

[z]   Luther's opponents in the Sacramentarian controversy, the Zwinglians and Anabaptists. On the topic of "Luther and the Schwärmer," see Amy Nelson Burnett in OHMLT, 511–24.

[a]   See n. 269. p. 377, regarding the effectiveness of sacraments.

292. There should be no mistake of how crucial not only Luther but also his conversation partners considered the matter of being "right" about the sacrament: namely, the doctrine of God and salvation is at stake.

293. A central Reformation concern for Luther was to teach and encourage people to attend worship and partake in the sacraments, regularly and with intentionality and gratitude for the gift given "for them" personally. Instead of being satisfied with simply observing the priestly performance of the eucharistic Mass "for" them or even in their absence (such as performing the Mass in absentia of the worshiping community) or relying on the vicarious virtues of the saints and Jesus' mother, Mary, people were to boldly come to sacraments and trust the transformative grace promised and truly given "for them" personally. To teach this was one of the major reasons behind the catechism.

294. Words about "remembrance" and "remembering" have been at the heart of the eucharistic debates: Is the Lord's Supper a gathering of remembrance, in which his act of dying is remembered or memorialized? Or does the act of remembrance also express trust that Christ is truly present in the here and now? For Luther, only remembering was not enough, he labored to explain Christ's continued presence here and now in the sacrament and in the receiving of it.

This is enough on this sacrament, as far as is necessary for general teaching purposes. What else there is to say about it belongs at a different time.[b]

In conclusion, now that we have the right[292] interpretation and teaching concerning the sacrament, there is also great need to admonish and encourage us so that we do not let this great a treasure, which is daily administered and distributed among Christians, pass by to no purpose. What I mean is that those who want to be Christians should prepare themselves to receive this blessed sacrament frequently. For we see that people are becoming lax and lazy about its observance.[293] A great number of people who hear the gospel, now that the pope's nonsense has been abolished and we are freed from his compulsion and commands, let a year, or two, three, or more years go by without receiving the sacrament, as if they were such strong Christians that they have no need of it. Others let themselves be kept and deterred from it because we have taught that none should go unless they feel a hunger and thirst impelling them to it. Still others pretend that it is a matter of liberty, not of necessity, and that it is enough if they simply believe. Thus the great majority go so far that they become quite barbarous and ultimately despise both the sacrament and God's word.

Now it is true, as we have said, that no one under any circumstances should be forced or compelled, lest we institute a new slaughter of souls. Nevertheless, it must be understood that such people who abstain and absent themselves from the sacrament over a long period of time are not to be considered Christians. For Christ did not institute the sacrament for us to treat it as a spectacle, but he commanded his Christians to eat and drink it and thereby remember him.[294]

Indeed, true Christians who cherish and honor the sacrament should of their own accord urge and constrain themselves to go. However, in order that the simple people and the weak, who would also like to be Christians, may be induced to see the reason and the need for receiving the sacrament, we shall talk a little about this. As in other matters that have to do with faith, love, and patience, it is not enough just to teach and to instruct, but there must also be daily exhortation, so that on this subject

b   Shortly after this, Luther wrote *Admonition Concerning the Sacrament of the Body and Blood of Our Lord* (1530) (LW 38:91–137).

we must be persistent in preaching, lest people become indifferent and bored. For we know and feel how the devil always sets itself against this and every other Christian activity, hounding and driving people from it as much as it can.[295]

In the first place, we have a clear text in the very words of Christ, "Do this in remembrance of me." These are words that instruct and command us, urging all those who want to be Christians to partake of the sacrament. Therefore, whoever wants to be a disciple of Christ—it is those to whom he is speaking here—must faithfully hold to this sacrament, not from compulsion, forced by humans, but to obey and please the Lord Christ. However, you may say, "But the words are added, 'as often as you do it'; so he compels no one, but leaves it to our free choice." Answer: That is true, but it does not say that we should never partake of it. Indeed, precisely his words "as often as you do it" imply that we should do it frequently. And they are added because he wishes the sacrament to be free, not bound to a special time like the Passover, which the Jews were obligated to eat only once a year, precisely on the evening of the fourteenth day of the first full moon,[c] without variation of a single day. He means to say: "I am instituting a Passover or Supper for you, which you shall enjoy not just on this one evening of the year, but frequently, whenever and wherever you will, according to everyone's opportunity and need, being bound to no special place or time" (although the pope afterward perverted it and turned it back into a Jewish feast).[296]

Thus you see that we are not granted liberty to despise the sacrament. For I call it despising when people, with nothing to hinder them, let a long time elapse without ever desiring the sacrament. If you want such liberty, you may just as well take the further liberty not to be a Christian; then you need not believe or pray, for the one is just as much Christ's commandment as the other. But if you want to be a Christian, you must from time to time satisfy and obey this commandment. For such a commandment should always move you to examine yourself and think: "See, what sort of Christian am I? If I were one, I would surely have at least a little desire to do what my Lord has commanded me to do."

295. In his teaching about the Lord's Supper and introducing new ways for participation, Luther expressed remarkable pastoral sensitivity and patience. In his famous 1522 *Invocavit* (Lenten) sermons (LW 51:69–100), he admonished against the use of force in these matters and begged people to proceed with reforms in the spirit of love and compassion, which meant that nobody should be forced to receive the communion in both kinds before they were ready for this change. On these sermons, see TAL, vol. 4, forthcoming.

296. Passover is the major Jewish festival of seven days (from the fifteenth day of Nisan) each spring to commemorate the Hebrews' liberation from Egyptian slavery. Luther's knowledge of this celebration, or any Jewish traditions, came mostly from ethnographic sources written by converted Jews. He never participated in any Jewish celebration personally. On Luther and his relation to and knowledge of the Jewish tradition, see the introductions in Brooks Schramm and Kirsi Stjerna, *Martin Luther, the Bible, and the Jewish People* (Minneapolis: Fortress Press, 2012), 3–35.

c Lev. 23:5.

297. The Fourth Lateran Council (1215) decreed that Christians should "receive at least during Easter time the sacrament of the Eucharist." As a prerequisite, one was to go to confession with the priest at least once a year. In practice, people would not necessarily regularly attend the Mass, since their participation was not as central as the performance of the sacrament. The sacrament of penance, for the baptized, was the most regularly attended Christian ritual and most familiar to people in all walks of life.

298. See n. 287, p. 404, and n. 299 below.

299. Luther knew the angst of feeling unworthy in the face of the omnipotent God. His theology of grace and invitation to God's Table went hand in hand with his notion of the profundity of sin in human life and thus the need for means of grace, the sacraments. Convincing and educating people about their need and their worth with respect to grace was a major mission. Luther wanted everybody to participate regularly and joyfully.

Indeed, because we show such an aversion toward the sacrament, people can easily sense what sort of Christians we were under the papacy when we went to the sacrament purely from compulsion and fear of human commandments, without joy and love and even without regard for Christ's commandment.[297] But we neither force nor compel anyone, nor need anyone do so in order to serve or please us. What should move and induce you is that God desires it, and it pleases God. You should not let yourself be forced by human beings either to faith or to any good work. All we are doing is to urge you to do what you ought to do, not for our sake but for your own. Christ invites and incites you, and if you want to show contempt for his sacrament, you must answer for it yourself.

This is the first point, especially for the benefit of the cold and indifferent, that they may come to their senses and wake up. It is certainly true, as I have found in my own experience, and as everyone will find in one's own case, that if one stays away from the sacrament, day by day one will become more and more callous and cold and will eventually spurn it altogether. To avoid this, we must examine our heart and conscience and act like a person who really desires to be right with God. The more we do this, the more our heart will be warmed and kindled, and it will not grow entirely cold.

But suppose you say, "What if I feel that I am unfit?"[298] Answer: This is my struggle as well, especially inherited from the old order under the pope when we tortured ourselves to become so perfectly pure that God might not find the least blemish in us. Because of this we became so timid that everyone was thrown into consternation, saying, "Alas, you are not worthy!" Then nature and reason begin to contrast our unworthiness with this great and precious blessing, and it appears like a dark lantern in contrast to the bright sun, or as manure in contrast to jewels; then because they see this, such people will not go to the sacrament and wait until they are prepared, until one week passes into another and one half year into yet another. If you choose to fix your eye on how good and pure you are, to wait until nothing torments you, you will never go.[299]

For this reason we must make a distinction here among people. Those who are impudent and unruly ought to be told to stay away, for they are not ready to receive the forgiveness of sins because they do not desire it and do not want to be righteous. The others, however, who are not so callous and dissolute but would like to be good, should not absent themselves, even though in other respects they are weak and frail. As St. Hilary[300] has also said, "Unless people have committed such sins that they have to be expelled from the congregation and have forfeited the name of Christian, they should not exclude themselves from the sacrament," lest they deprive themselves of life. People never get to the point that they do not retain many common infirmities in their flesh and blood.

People with such misgivings must learn that it is the highest art to realize that this sacrament does not depend on our worthiness. For we are not baptized because we are worthy and holy, nor do we come to confession as if we were pure and without sin; on the contrary, we come as poor, miserable people, precisely because we are unworthy.[301] The only exception would be the person who desires no grace and absolution and has no intention of improving.

But those who earnestly desire grace and comfort should compel themselves to go and allow no one to deter them, saying, "I would really like to be worthy, but I come not on account of any worthiness of mine, but on account of your word, because you have commanded it and I want to be your disciple, regardless of my worthiness." This is difficult, however, for we always have this obstacle and hindrance to contend with, that we concentrate more on ourselves than on the words that come from Christ's lips. Nature would like to act in such a way that it may rest and rely firmly on itself; otherwise it refuses to take a step. Let this suffice for the first point.

In the second place, a promise is attached to the commandment, as we heard above, which should most powerfully draw and impel us. Here stand the gracious and lovely words, "This is my body, given for you," "This is my blood, shed for you for the forgiveness of sins." These words, as I have said, are not preached to wood or stone but to you and me; otherwise Christ might just as well have kept quiet and not instituted a sacrament. Ponder, then, and include yourself personally in the "you" so that he may not speak to you in vain.

For in this sacrament Christ offers us all the treasures he brought from heaven for us, to which he most graciously invites us in other places, as when he says in Matthew 11[:28]: "Come to me, all you that are weary and are carrying heavy burdens,

300. St. Hilary (300–368), bishop of Poitiers, a major character in defeating the Arians.

301. When speaking of the sacraments, Luther consistently makes a strong anti-Donatist point: sacraments' effectiveness does not depend on a human being's purity, but they function on the basis of God's promise and the work of the Holy Spirit through word. Human beings receive the grace, not earn it.

and I will give you rest." Surely it is a sin and a shame that when Christ so tenderly and faithfully summons and exhorts us for our highest and greatest good, we regard it with such disdain, neglecting it so long that we grow quite cold and callous and lose all desire and love for it. We must never regard the sacrament as a harmful thing from which we should flee, but as a pure, wholesome, soothing medicine that aids you and gives life in both soul and body. For where the soul is healed, the body is helped as well. Why, then, do we act as if the sacrament were a poison that would kill us if we ate of it?

Of course, it is true that those who despise the sacrament and lead unchristian lives receive it to their harm and damnation. To such people nothing can be good or wholesome, just as when a sick person willfully eats and drinks what is forbidden by the physician. But those who feel their weakness, who are anxious to be rid of it and desire help, should regard and use the sacrament as a precious antidote against the poison in their systems. For here in the sacrament you are to receive from Christ's lips the forgiveness of sins, which contains and brings with it God's grace and Spirit with all God's gifts, protection, defense, and power against death, the devil, and every trouble.

Thus you have on God's part both the commandment and the promise of the Lord Christ. Meanwhile, on your part, you ought to be induced by your own need, which hangs around your neck and which is the very reason for this command, invitation, and promise. For Christ himself says [Matt. 9:12], "Those who are well have no need of a physician, but those who are sick," that is, those who labor and are burdened with sin, fear of death, and the attacks of the flesh and the devil. If you are burdened and feel your weakness, go joyfully to the sacrament and let yourself be refreshed, comforted, and strengthened. For if you wait until you are rid of your burden in order to come to the sacrament purely and worthily, you will have to stay away from it forever. In such a case he pronounces the verdict, "If you are pure and upright, you have no need of me and I also have no need of you." Therefore the only ones who are unworthy are those who do not feel their burdens nor admit to being sinners.

Suppose you say, "What shall I do if I cannot feel this need or if I do not experience hunger and thirst for the sacrament?" Answer: For those in such a state of mind that they cannot feel it, I know no better advice than that they put their hands to their bosom to determine whether they are made of flesh and blood. If you find that you are, then for your own good turn to St. Paul's Epistle to the Galatians and hear what are the fruits of your flesh: "Now the works of the flesh (he says) are obvious: adultery, fornication, impurity, licentiousness, idolatry, sorcery, enmity, strife, jealousy, anger, quarrels, dissensions, factions, envy, murder, drunkenness, carousing, and things like these."[d]

For this reason, if you cannot feel the need, at least believe the Scriptures. They will not lie to you, since they know your flesh better than you yourself do. Yes, and St. Paul concludes in Romans 7[:18], "For I know that nothing good dwells within me, that is, in my flesh." If St. Paul speaks this way of his own flesh, let us not wish to be better or holier. But the fact that we do not feel it is all the worse, for it is a sign that ours is a leprous flesh, which feels nothing although it rages with disease and gnaws away at itself. As we have said, even if you are so utterly dead in sin, at least believe the Scriptures, which pronounce this judgment upon you. In short, the less you feel your sins and infirmities, the more reason you have to go to the sacrament and seek its help and remedy.[302]

Again, look around you and see whether you are also in the world. If you do not know, ask your neighbors about it. If you are in the world, do not think that there will be any lack of sins and needs. Just begin to act as if you want to become upright and cling to the gospel, and see whether you will not acquire enemies who harm, wrong, and injure you and give you cause to sin and do wrong. If you have not experienced this, then take it from the Scriptures, which everywhere give this testimony about the world.

Moreover, you will surely have the devil around you, too. You will not entirely trample the devil underfoot because our Lord Christ could not entirely avoid it. Now, what is the devil? Nothing else than what the Scriptures call the devil:[303] a liar and a

302. Luther writes about the origins of the sacrament to underscore to whom it is meant: "When they were thus full of sorrow and anxiety, disturbed by sorrow and the sin of betrayal, then they were worthy, and he gave them his holy body to strengthen them. By this he teaches us that this sacrament is strength and comfort for those who are troubled and distressed by sin and evil" (*The Blessed Sacrament of the Holy and True Body of Christ, and the Brotherhoods*," LW 35: p. 45; see also TAL, vol. 1:225).

303. As a medieval man, Luther was very familiar with the many manifestations of the fallen angel (LW 1:22). With his personal experiences of the devil's nuisance of a presence and on the basis of his biblical interpretation (e.g., in his Genesis lectures on the role of the devil and the snake in the fall), Luther portrays the culprit in leading unsuspicious people to temptations. On the basis of God's omnipotence and Christ's victory over evil, death, and the devil, Luther assures that the devil can do no real harm: "The only way to drive away the devil is through faith in Christ, by saying, 'I have been baptized, I am a Christian'" (WA Tr 6, nr. 6830, 217, 26–27).

---

d   Gal. 5:19-20. As with his translation of the Bible, Luther follows the reading that includes "murder" in the text, and translates *porneia* as "adultery, fornication."

murderer.*ᵉ* A liar who entices the heart away from God's word and blinds it, making you unable to feel your need or to come to Christ. A murderer who begrudges you every hour of your life. If you could see how many daggers, spears, and arrows are aimed at you every moment, you would be glad to come to the sacrament as often as you can. The only reason we go about so securely and heedlessly is that we neither imagine nor believe that we are in the flesh, in the wicked world, or under the kingdom of the devil.

Try this, therefore, and practice it well. Just examine yourself, or look around a little, and cling only to the Scriptures. If even then you still feel nothing, you have all the more need to lament both to God and to your brother or sister. Take the advice of others and ask them to pray for you: never give up until the stone is removed from your heart. Then your need will become apparent, and you will perceive that you have sunk twice as low as any other poor sinner and are desperately in need of the sacrament to combat your misery. This misery, unfortunately, you do not see, unless God grants grace so that you may become more sensitive to it and hungrier for the sacrament. This happens especially because the devil besieges you and continually lies in wait to trap and destroy you, soul and body, so that you cannot be safe from it for even one hour. How suddenly can the devil bring you into misery and distress when you least expect it!

Let this serve as an exhortation, then, not only for us who are old and advanced in years,[304] but also for the young people who must be brought up in Christian teaching and in a right understanding of it. With such training we may more easily instill the Ten Commandments, the Creed, and the Lord's Prayer into the young so that they will receive them with joy and earnestness, practice them from their youth, and become accustomed to them. For it is completely useless to try to change old people.[305] We cannot perpetuate these and other teachings unless we train the people who come after us and succeed us in our office and work, so that they in turn may bring up their children successfully. In this way God's word and a Christian community will be

---

304. Luther was forty-five years old when the *Large Catechism* was published. In the previous year, he had been afflicted with a series of serious illnesses and felt his age and finitude. The concept of aging and life expectancy in general was quite different in Luther's days when, with a high child mortality rate to begin with, one could hardly count on living past one's forties or fifties.

305. Who is old? Luther means people already established in their ways and underscores the importance of molding children who are more open to learning.

---

e   John 8:44.

preserved. Therefore let all heads of a household remember that it is their duty, by God's injunction and command, to teach their children or have them taught the things they ought to know.[306] Because they have been baptized and received into the people of Christ, they should also enjoy this fellowship of the sacrament so that they may serve us and be useful. For they must all help us to believe, to love, to pray, and to fight against the devil.[f]

306. Luther considered children a gift from God. "God makes children" not for our pleasure and enjoyment, but for our "salvation" and for the glory of God. See, e.g., *The Estate of Marriage*, LW 45:45–46. He persistently stressed, in print and proclamation, the priority of bringing up one's children well, for the benefit of God, Christendom, the world, and the church. See, e.g., *A Sermon on the Estate of Marriage*, LW 44:12. See Strohl, "The Child in Luther's Theology," in Bunge, *The Child in Christian Thought*, 134–59.

---

f   A section on confession was added first in the 1529 revised edition of the catechism. It was omitted in the Jena edition of Luther's works and in the German *Book of Concord* (1580), hence also in several later editions of the catechism. Here the section "Brief Exhortation to Confession" is left out and can be found in BC, 476–80. For discussion on Luther's notion of the confession, see *The Sacrament of Penance*, LW 35:[5–8] 9–22; TAL, vol. 1:181.

The image above depicts the title page of Luther's *Smalcald Articles*, writen for possible presentation to the Council of Mantua, which was called to explore potential reforms of the church. Jesus as the Good Shepherd and the arms of Martin Luther, Philipp Melanchthon, Justus Jonas, Johannes Bugenhagen, and Caspar Cruciger surround the title. Caspar Cruciger's signature is also added.

The Smalcald Articles

1538

KURT K. HENDEL

INTRODUCTION

Like most of Martin Luther's writings, the *Smalcald Articles* are an occasional document. The immediate impetus for the composition and publication of the *Articles* was the calling of the Council of Mantua by Pope Paul III.[1] The stated goal of the council was the eradication of heresy, and it was clear, both in Rome and in Wittenberg, that the Lutherans would be the primary focus of the council's deliberations.

Luther had called for a council since 1518, both because he realized that he would not receive a fair hearing before the papacy and because he hoped that a council would foster necessary reforms in the church.[a] However, the reformer and his supporters insisted that a council would have to be free of papal control, assemble outside Italy, invite representatives from the whole church, and make its decisions on the basis of Scripture.[b] The papacy was initially not inclined to summon a council, in

1. Paul III (1468–1549) served as bishop of Rome from 1534 until 1549. While he fostered the good fortunes of his Farnese family, including those of his own sons, he was also a patron of the arts, chose admirable men for the cardinalate, appointed Michelangelo to supervise the building of St. Peter's Basilica, and sought to protect the indigenous people of the Americas against enslavement. He also established a commission to study the conditions of the church and to propose necessary reforms. The Council of Mantua was called to continue such reform efforts, although the pope was not interested in negotiating with the Lutherans and other reform movements that had challenged papal authority. While the Council of Mantua never met,

---

a See WA 2:36–40; WA Br 1:224; LW 48:90; WA Br 2:217–18; LW 48:184. See also WA 7:75–82; 85–90.

b Charles P. Arand, Robert Kolb, and James A. Nestingen, *The Lutheran Confessions: History and Theology of the Book of Concord* (Minneapolis: Fortress Press, 2012), 143 (hereafter Arand et al.).

the Council of Trent, which was also summoned by Paul III, made crucial contributions to the theology and life of the Roman Church.

part because of these stipulations but also because both popes Leo X (1475–1521) and Clement VII (1478–1534) had other ecclesiastical and political priorities. Furthermore, the vivid memory of the conciliarist movement made them cautious. However, Paul III decided to change papal policy. He likely did so because of pressure from Holy Roman Emperor Charles V (1500–1558),[c] who had also urged the calling of a council, and because of his own interest in reforming the church.

When the council was announced, Elector John Frederick I (1503–1554), his political allies, and the Wittenberg theologians had to decide whether they would attend. The elector himself was not inclined to do so. Deeply committed to the Lutheran cause and theologically informed, he argued that attendance implied submission to papal power. The Lutherans should, therefore, inform the pope that they considered him to be their greatest enemy, that they were aware of his intention to judge the Lutherans and to suppress the gospel at the council, and that

Pope Paul III as painted
by Titian (1490–1576).

A portrait of
John Frederick I,
also called John the
Magnanimous,
the Elector of Saxony
(r. 1532–1547) and
Duke of Saxony
(r. 1547–1554).

c   Ibid., 144.

they would not attend. They should, however, express their willingness to participate in a free council where decisions are made solely on the basis of Scripture.[d] In spite of his clear convictions, John Frederick knew that he would not be able to make a unilateral decision. Both the theologians and the other members of the Smalcaldic League would need to be consulted. He first invited the opinion of the Wittenberg theologians.

Philip Melanchthon (1497–1560) formulated their counsel in August 1536. He and his colleagues cautioned that if the Lutherans did not attend they would simply be condemned without a hearing or they would be accused of preventing the council by their refusal to participate. Acknowledging the pope's authority to call a council would not be an affirmation that he was superior to the council. They had to insist, therefore, that their teachings be judged by the council, which was the supreme ecclesiastical authority, not by the pope. Attendance was advisable, however.[e]

John Frederick was not convinced. Therefore, he considered the possibility of calling a council himself that would meet the Lutheran criteria.[f] On 1 December 1536, he requested the opinion of the theologians regarding this proposal. In their prompt response of 6 December, the theologians advised that the emperor be petitioned to provide assurances that the council would promote the unity of the church, urged that a countercouncil not be called, since that would be viewed as a schismatic act, and recommended that the princes agree to

EFFIGIES PHIL MELANCHTHONIS ANN AET XXX CZ LVCA CRONACHIO PICTORE M D XXXVII

A portrait of Philip Melanchthon
by Lucas Cranach
the Elder (1472–1553).

---

d   F. Bente, *Historical Introductions to the Book of Concord* (St. Louis: Concordia, 1965), 48 (hereafter Bente).

e   Ibid., 49.

f   BSLK, XXIV.

defend their people if force was used to compel the Lutherans to submit to the authority of the pope.[g]

Even as he considered calling a free council, John Frederick also decided to prepare for possible attendance at Mantua. He, therefore, asked Luther to prepare a document that would serve both as the reformer's own confession of faith and as the confession of the Lutheran community. The document was to clarify essential theological points that could not be compromised as well as those points that were open for discussion and potential negotiation.

While Luther was also skeptical that the council would address the religious conflicts in a positive manner and foster reform, he assured the papal legate, Cardinal Peter Paul Vergerio (c. 1498–1565), who had traveled to Wittenberg in order to extend the official invitation to the council, that he was willing to attend.[h] He was also eager to prepare another personal confession of faith that would serve as an addendum to his 1528 confession[i] and clarify theological issues not addressed in the *Augsburg Confession*. Persistent health issues enhanced his eagerness. The elector's request was addressed to Luther in August 1536 and repeated on 1 December 1536.[j] Luther composed the *Articles* in December, although his work was slowed down by an apparent heart ailment on December 18. The original manuscript was written in Luther's hand until that date. Thereafter, Caspar Cruciger Sr. (1504–1548) and an unknown scribe recorded Luther's dictations. The *Articles* were reviewed on 28 December by Johann Agricola (c. 1494–1566), Nicholas von Amsdorf (1483–1565), Georg Spalatin (1484–1545), Philip Melanchthon, Johannes Bugenhagen (1485–1558), Justus Jonas (1493–1555), and Caspar Cruciger. A paragraph on the invocation of the saints was added as a result of this conversation, and the *Articles* were affirmed and signed, although Melanchthon raised concerns regarding the statement on the papacy. Spalatin also made a copy of the *Articles*.[k]

---

g   Bente, 51.

h   Arand et al., 143.

i   See Luther's *Confession Concerning Christ's Supper,* LW 37:151–372, esp. 360–72. See also WA 26:261–509, esp. 499–509.

j   Bente, 51–52.

k   The Spalatin copy is available in the main archive of Thuringia in Weimar.

In February 1537, representatives of the Smalcaldic League and theologians from various parts of Germany met in Smalcald ("Schmalkalden" on map, p. xiv) to discuss the *Articles* and to consider the question of conciliar attendance. Luther was initially present at the meeting; however, a severe attack of kidney stones and the resulting uremic poisoning made it impossible for him to participate in the discussions and compelled him to leave the meeting early. The elector expected that the *Articles* would be adopted as an official Lutheran confessional statement. However, substantial disagreement emerged among the gathered representatives. Philip of Hesse (1504–1567), the other chief political leader of the Smalcaldic League, was concerned that the content of the *Articles* would prevent the expansion of the League. Melanchthon shared Philip's concern because the south German theologians were clearly troubled by Luther's eucharistic theology. Melanchthon also worried that Luther's statement regarding the papacy assured that there would be no progress in healing the theological conflicts with Rome at the council. He argued further that the *Augsburg Confession* and the *Apology of the Augsburg Confession* already served as Lutheran confessional documents. Another statement was, therefore, not necessary. The gathered assembly empathized with these concerns and declined to adopt the *Articles*. However, many theologians chose to sign them after Bugenhagen suggested that they do so voluntarily.[l]

While they neither adopted nor rejected the *Articles*, the representatives at Smalcalden did agree that a clear statement regarding the papacy was necessary. Melanchthon therefore composed the *Treatise on the Primacy and Power of the Pope*.[m] The representatives also agreed that attendance at the Council of Mantua

An etching of Philip I of Hesse
by Matthäus Merian (1593–1650).

---

l   Bente, 57.

m   See *Treatise on the Primacy and Power of the Pope*, in Robert Kolb and
    Timothy J. Wengert, *The Book of Concord* (Minneapolis: Fortress Press,
    2000), 329–44 (hereafter BC, Tr).

was not possible since the council did not meet the criteria the Lutherans had outlined.[n]

Luther prepared his *Articles* for publication in 1538. He added a preface to the original text, in which he mistakenly claimed that the *Articles* had been adopted officially at Smalcalden, and expanded the sections dealing with the Mass, purgatory, the invocation of the saints, repentance, confession, and absolution.[o] Two Latin translations of the *Smalcald Articles* were prepared during the sixteenth century, one by the Dane Petrus Generanus (1520–1584) in 1541 and the other for the Latin edition of the *Book of Concord* by Nicholas Selnecker (1530–1592).[p]

The respect that Luther enjoyed among the Lutherans and the continuing support of the *Articles* by Elector John Frederick contributed to their eventual acceptance as an authoritative statement of essential Lutheran doctrines. Together with the *Augsburg Confession*, they were cited as normative expressions of the evangelical heritage during the diverse conflicts that divided the Lutheran community after 1546. They were also included in various Lutheran *corpora doctrinae* and officially adopted in places like Hesse, Lübeck, Hamburg, Lüneburg, and Schleswig-Holstein.[q] In 1580 they were also included in the *Book of Concord*. While the *Smalcald Articles* were never presented at the Council of Mantua, they did ultimately serve the purpose originally envisioned by Elector John Frederick and by Luther, namely, to be a clear and bold statement of chief aspects of the faith, as it was confessed by the Evangelicals. Luther divided the *Articles* into three sections, thereby responding to the Elector's directive. The first was a creedal statement confessing the Triune God. The second focused on the doctrine of justification and its implications. Nothing in this section could be compromised. The third identified articles open for discussion, although Luther again formulated the specific topics in light of his understanding of the gospel and thereby emphasized their importance for the life of the church.

The polemical tone of the *Smalcald Articles* may well be jarring to the dialogical sensitivities and ecumenical commitments

---

n   Arand et al., 152.

o   Ibid., 157.

p   BSLK, XXVI.

q   Bente, 58.

of contemporary Christians. Nevertheless, Luther's passion for the gospel—so strikingly evident in this confession of his faith—and his insistence that the church's proclamation, theology, and piety must be shaped, evaluated, affirmed, and rejected in light of that gospel remain relevant and precious gifts to the diverse Lutheran communities of faith in different places and times. The *Smalcald Articles* are, therefore, rightly included among Luther's essential writings.

THE SMALCALD ARTICLES[2]

ARTICLES OF CHRISTIAN DOCTRINE,

which were to have been presented by our side at the council in Mantua,[3] or wherever else it was to have met, and which were to indicate what we could or could not accept or give up, etc. Written by Doctor Martin Luther in the year 1537.[r]

The Articles 1537

There is sufficient teaching for the life of the church in these Articles. Otherwise, in political and economic matters, there is sufficient law to which we are bound so that beyond these burdens there is no need to devise others. For we are warned: "Today's trouble is sufficient for today." [Matt. 6:34][s]

2. The following translation is a revision of the *Smalcald Articles* (BC, 297–328), which was based on the text *Artikel christlicher Lehre* in *Die Bekenntnisschriften der evangelisch-lutherischen Kirche* (Göttingen: Vandenhoeck & Ruprecht, 1963).

3. Mantua is a city in northern Italy in the region of Lombardy.

r   This introduction is included in the German edition of the 1580 *Book of Concord* but not in the 1538 or the 1543 editions of the *Smalcald Articles.*

s   Luther added this paragraph in his handwritten manuscript of the *Smalcald Articles.* The manuscript is available in the Heidelberg University library (cod. Pal. Germ. 423, 4). The paragraph is not included in Spalatin's copy or in any printed editions of the *Smalcald Articles.* The precise quotation is difficult to decipher because of

The Preface of Doctor Martin Luther[t]

Pope Paul III called a council to meet at Mantua last year around Pentecost.[4] Afterward he moved it from Mantua, so that it is still not known where he intends to hold it, or whether he can hold it.[5] We on our part had to prepare for the eventuality that, whether summoned to the council or not, we would be condemned. I was therefore commanded[6] to compose and gather together articles of our teaching in case it came to negotiations about what and how extensively we would or could yield to the papists, and in which things we definitely intended to persist and remain firm.

Therefore, I gathered together these articles and submitted them to our side.[u] They were also accepted[7] and unanimously confessed by us, and it was resolved that they should be publicly submitted and presented as the confession of our faith (should the pope and his adherents ever become so bold as to convene a truly free council[8] in a serious and genuine spirit, without deception and treachery,[v] as he would surely be obliged to do). However, the Roman court is so dreadfully afraid of a free council and so shamefully flees from the light that it has also deprived those who are on the pope's side of the hope that he will ever tolerate a free council, much less actually convene one himself. They are rightly greatly offended and are quite troubled when they perceive thereby that the pope would rather see all of Christendom lost and every soul damned than to allow himself or his followers to be reformed even a little and to permit limits on his tyranny.

Therefore I meanwhile wanted to publicize these articles through the public press, in case (as I fully expect and hope) I should die before a council could take place, for the scoundrels, who flee from the light and avoid the day, are taking such great pains to postpone and hinder the council. I wanted to do this so that those who live and remain after me will have my

---

4. Paul III published the council bull, *Ad dominici gregis curam*, on 2 June 1536. Pentecost in 1537 fell on 20 May.

5. In 1538, when Luther wrote the preface and published the *Smalcald Articles*, the council had already been postponed twice, and it did not meet until December 1545 at Trent.

6. John Frederick gave Luther this assignment on 11 December 1536. (See John Frederick's letter to the theologians at Wittenberg, WA Br 7:613–14.) The bulk of the *Smalcald Articles* was written during the next two weeks.

7. The *Smalcald Articles* were never officially accepted by the Evangelicals during their meeting in Smalcalden in February of 1537, nor was the decision made to submit them publicly as a confessional statement of the Lutherans at the anticipated council.

8. When Luther and the Evangelicals spoke of a free council they envisioned it to be free of papal control and ecumenical. They also insisted that it must meet on German soil and that its decisions must be based on Scripture.

---

    the condition of the ink in the original. The reconstruction here is based on *Die schmalkaldischen Artikel*, ed. Helmar Junghans, in *Martin Luther: Studienausgabe*, ed. Hans-Ulrich Delius (Berlin: Evangelische Verlagsanstalt, 1992), 5:350, except reading *nexemur* ("we are warned") for *nixemur* ("we rely upon").

t   The following preface was added to the printed version in 1538 and hence is italicized.

u   See BC, *Formula of Concord* (hereafter FC), "The Epitome," 486–87 . It is not clear whether Luther here refers to a December 1536 gathering of select theologians at Wittenberg or to the provincial diet at Smalcalden in February 1537.

v   BC, *Augsburg Confession*, Preface, 21, 34 (hereafter BC, CA). See also n. a above.

testimony and confession[9] to present, in addition to the confession that I have already published.[w] I have also endured in this confession until now, and I will continue to endure in it by God's grace. What should I say? How can I complain? I am still alive, and every day I write, preach, and lecture. Yet there are such poisonous people, not only among our adversaries, but also unfaithful associates,[x] who want to be on our side and who dare to use my writing and teaching directly against me. They let me look on and listen, even though they surely know that I teach otherwise. They want to adorn their poison with my work and mislead the poor people by using my name. What will happen in the future after my death?[y]

Indeed, should I respond to everything while I am still living? Of course, on the other hand, how can I alone stop all the mouths of the devil, especially those (although they are all poisoned) who do not want to listen or pay attention to what we write? Instead, they devote all their energy to one thing: how they might most shamefully pervert and corrupt our words down to the very letters. I let the devil answer such people or ultimately God's wrath, as they deserve. I often think of the good Gerson,[10] who questions whether one should be writing something good publicly. If one does not, then many souls that could have been saved are neglected. However, if one does, then the devil is there with innumerable pernicious, evil mouths that poison and distort everything so that it, nevertheless, bears no fruit. Still, what they gain thereby is seen clearly. For although they so shamelessly slandered us and wanted to keep the people on their side with their lies, God has perpetually furthered his work, has made their number continually less and ours continually larger, and has allowed and continues to allow them and their lies to come to naught.

I must tell a story. A doctor[11] sent from France was here in Wittenberg. He stated publicly in our presence that his king[12] was persuaded beyond the shadow of a doubt that there was no church, no government, and no marriage among us, but rather that everyone carried on with each other like cattle, and all did what they wanted. Now imagine, how will those people, who in their writings have represented as pure truth such gross lies to the king and to other countries, face us on that day before the judgment seat of Christ? Christ, the Lord and Judge of us all, surely knows

9. Luther considered these *Articles* to be his confession or testament, and Chancellor Gregory Brück (c. 1484–1557) spoke of Luther's "Testament" already on 3 September 1536. See *CR* III, 140, 147.

10. John Gerson (1363–1429) was a French scholar, writer, and reformer who served as chancellor of the University of Paris and was a defender of conciliarism, the reform movement that insisted that a council, not the pope, is the ultimate authority in the church. He also labored diligently to resolve the Great Schism and supported the decisions of the Council of Constance, both in calling for the resignation of the Pisan pope, John XXIII (c. 1370–1419), and in condemning the Bohemian reformer, Jan Hus (c. 1369–1415). See his *De laude scriptorium ad Carthusiensis et Coelestinos* (Cologne: Printer of Augustinus "de fide," c. 1473), consid. XI.

11. Gervasius Waim, (c. 1491–1554), who was trained under Johann Eck (1486–1543) and was a legate for Francis I of France, came to Saxony in 1531. See Luther's letter to Elector John Frederick, dated around 9 February 1537 (WA Br 8:36; LW 50:160).

12. The king of France at this time was Francis I (1494–1557), who ruled his realm from 1515 until 1547. His older sister Marguerite de Navarre (1492–1549) was a supporter of the humanists and reformers of the time.

---

w   See WA 26:499–509; LW 37:360–72; WA 50:262–83.

x   Literally, "false brothers" (cf. Gal. 2:4). Luther may be thinking of John Agricola, with whom he debated the role of the law in the Christian's life.

y   BC, *Smalcald Articles* III, 15, 3, 326 (hereafter BC, SA when specific paragraphs are cited). See also WA 26:500–502; LW 37:361–62.

that they lie and have lied. They will have to hear his judgment again; that I know for sure. May God bring to repentance those who can be converted. For the rest, there will be eternal suffering and woe.

So that I return to the subject, I would indeed very much like to see a true council whereby a variety of matters and many people would surely be aided. Not that we need it, for through God's grace our churches are now enlightened and provided with the pure Word and right use of the sacraments, a proper understanding of the various walks of life, and true works. Therefore we do not ask for a council for our sakes, and we cannot hope for or expect any improvement from the council in such matters. Rather, we see in bishoprics everywhere so many parishes empty and deserted[13] *that our hearts are ready to break. And yet, neither bishops nor cathedral canons ask how the poor people live or die—people for whom Christ surely died. And should not these people hear this same Christ speak to them as the true shepherd with his sheep?*[z] *It horrifies and frightens me that Christ might cause a council of angels to descend on Germany which will totally destroy us all, like Sodom and Gomorrah, because we mock him so blasphemously with the council.*[a]

In addition to such necessary concerns of the church, there are also countless important matters in worldly affairs that need improvement. There is disunity among the princes and the estates. Greed and usury have burst in like a great flood and have attained a semblance of legality.[b] *Caprice; lewdness; wantonness in dress; gluttony; gambling; extravagance with all kinds of vice and wickedness; disobedience of subjects, servants, and laborers; extortion by all the artisans and the peasants*[c] *(who can list everything?) have so gained the upper hand that it is impossible to set things right again with ten councils and twenty imperial diets.*[14] *If participants in the council were to deal with the chief concerns in the spiritual and secular estates that are opposed to God, then they would surely be so busy that they would forget all about the child's play and the foolishness of long robes,*[15] *great tonsures,*[16] *broad cinctures, bishop's and cardinal's hats, crosiers, and similar tomfoolery. If we had already fulfilled God's command and precept in the spiritual and secular estates, then we would have had enough time to reform food, vestments, tonsures, and chasubles.*

13. In 1538 it was reported in Wittenberg that there were some six hundred vacant parishes in the bishopric of Würzburg (WA TR 4, no. 4002; LW 54:308).

14. Imperial diets were assemblies of the political representatives of the Holy Roman Empire and were called by the Holy Roman Emperor. They met periodically in various places throughout the empire.

15. Luther is referring to albs.

16. The tonsure was the distinctive haircut worn by medieval monks.

---

z   John 10:3. BC, SA III, 12, 2, 324–25.

a   The Latin translation: "pretext of a council." For the story of Sodom and Gomorrah, see Genesis 19.

b   See WA 15:293–313, 321–22; 6:36–60; LW 45:231–310.

c   BC, *The Large Catechism*, "Ten Commandments," 6, par. 226, 416 and par. 235, 418 (hereafter BC, LC).

But if we swallow such camels and strain out gnats or let logs stand and dispute about specks,[17] then we might, indeed, also be satisfied with such a council.

I, therefore, have provided only a few articles, because in any case we already have received from God so many mandates to carry out in the church, in the government, and in the home[18] that we can never fulfill them. What is the point or what is the use of making so many additional decretals and regulations in the council, especially if no one honors or observes these chief things commanded by God? It is as if God had to honor our buffoonery because we trample God's solemn commands underfoot. In fact, our sins burden us and prevent God from being gracious to us, because we also do not repent and moreover want to defend every abomination.

Oh dear Lord Jesus Christ, hold a council of your own and redeem your people through your glorious return! The pope and his people are lost. They do not want you. Thus help us poor and miserable ones, who sigh to you and earnestly seek you, according to the grace you have given us through your Holy Spirit, who with you and the Father lives and reigns, forever praised. Amen.

1537

17. Matt. 23:24 and 7:3-5.

18. Luther is identifying the three "orders of creation."

A bishop blesses the priestly vestments and sprinkles them with holy water.

[I.]

The First Part of the Articles deals with the lofty articles of the divine Majesty, namely:

1. That Father, Son, and Holy Spirit, three distinct persons in one divine essence and nature, is one God, who created heaven and earth, etc.[19]

2. That the Father was begotten by no one, the Son was begotten by the Father, and the Holy Spirit proceeds from the Father and the Son.[d]

3. That neither the Father nor the Holy Spirit, but the Son, became a human being.

19. Luther is paraphrasing the Nicene Creed. He uses traditional creedal language as he confesses the doctrine of the Trinity. Neither the doctrine of the Trinity nor trinitarian terminology were points of disagreement between Luther and his Roman opponents, and both Roman and Lutheran communities continued to use the creedal terminology in their liturgical practices

---

d Cf. the Athanasian Creed.

and theological writings. However, the discussion of God language is a vibrant one within the contemporary Christian community. A commitment to the use of inclusive language and the recognition that patriarchy has significantly shaped theological constructs and negatively impacted the faith and piety of both women and men have inspired creative conversations. Contemporary theological perspectives range from the conviction that "Father, Son, and Holy Spirit" is the name of God to an insistence that more inclusive language must be used by the church whenever it references God and, particularly, when it makes its trinitarian confession.

In this image of the Trinity from a 1527 New Testament publication, God holds the dead body of Christ with the Holy Spirit as dove overhead.

20. Luther is using the word *teach* to refer to basic Christian instruction: the Ten Commandments, the Apostles' Creed, and the Lord's Prayer. See his comments on this material in BC, *The Small Catechism*, "Creed," 2, 3–4, 355 (hereafter BC, SC). See also BC, LC, "Creed," 2, 25–33, 434–35.

21. Luther initially wrote "believe and confess" but later deleted "believe and." The deletion may suggest that he was uncertain about the faith of his opponents. See, e.g., WA 50:269; LW 34:210–11.

4. That the Son became a human being in this way: he was conceived by the Holy Spirit without male participation and was born of the pure, holy Virgin Mary.[e] After that, he suffered, died, was buried, descended into hell, rose from the dead, ascended into heaven, is seated at the right hand of God. In the future he will come to judge the living and the dead, etc., as the Apostles' and the Athanasian Creeds and the common children's catechism teach.[20]

These articles are not matters of dispute or conflict, for both sides confess them.[21] Therefore it is not necessary to deal with them at greater length now.

e   The Latin translation reads *semper virgine*, "always virgin."

[II.]

The Second Part is about the articles that pertain to the office and work of Jesus Christ, or to our redemption.

The First Article

Here is the first and chief article:

That Jesus Christ, our God and Lord, "died for our trespasses and was raised for our justification" (Rom. 4[:25])[f]; and he alone is "the Lamb of God, who bears the sin of the world" (John 1[:29]); and "God has laid all of our sin on him" (Isa. 53[:6]); furthermore, "They are all chiefly sinners and are justified without merit out of his grace through the redemption of Jesus Christ in his blood" (Rom. 3[:23-25]).

Now because this must be believed and may not be obtained or grasped otherwise with any work, law, or merit, it is clear and certain that such faith alone justifies us,[22] as St. Paul says in Rom. 3[:28, 26]: "For we hold that a person is justified by faith without the works of the law"; and furthermore, "that he alone is righteous and justifies the one who has faith in Jesus."

Nothing in this article can be conceded or given up[g] even if heaven and earth or whatever is transitory passes away, for St. Peter says in Acts 4[:12]: "There is no other name given to human beings by which we must be saved." "And by his wounds we are healed" (Isa. 53[:5]).

On this article stands all that we teach and practice against the pope, the devil, and the world. Therefore we must be quite certain and have no doubt about it. Otherwise everything is lost, and the pope, and the devil, and whatever opposes us gains victory and is proven right.[23]

22. See BC, SA III, 13. See also WA 30/2:632-33, 636-37, 639-43; LW 35:181-83, 187-89, 193-98. The original reads *daß allein solcher Glaube uns gerecht mache*. Luther's consistent emphasis on justification by grace through faith throughout his writings reflects his reading of Paul. It is also informed by his spiritual quest for a gracious God. The radical good news that faith alone justifies embodied the gospel for Luther and brought peace and comfort to his troubled soul, particularly during his persistent *Anfechtungen*, or spiritual struggles. The doctrine of justification was never simply a theological construct for the reformer. It was God's ultimate message of grace addressed to all of humanity. It is for this reason that Luther insisted that on "this article stands all that we teach and practice."

23. This emphasis of Luther is noteworthy. He refuses to compromise the doctrine of justification in any ecclesiastical or political negotiations since he is convinced that it is a faithful exposition of the gospel, since it constitutes the core of his theology, and since it is essential good news for his own faith journey. See n. 22.

---

f   Luther's rendering of scriptural quotations is translated throughout the document.

g   The Latin translation adds: *aliquid contra illum . . . permittere nemo piorum potest,* "no believer can . . . permit anything contrary to it."

24. According to Luther's understanding, what follows (BC, SA II, 2–4) is connected directly to the office and work of Christ because it detracts from or replaces the biblical soteriology he outlined in SA II, 1, and because, as in the early church, teaching a doctrine correctly always entails condemnation of false doctrines that oppose it.

25. Here Luther is not referring to the Lord's Supper but to the sacrifice of the Mass and the liturgy and practices that had grown up around it.

26. The significance of the second article is indicated by its placement. Luther clearly considers the sacrificial understanding of the Roman Mass to be a contradiction of the doctrine of justification and, therefore, of the gospel. See Luther's discussion of the Mass in WA 2:742–58; LW 35:45–73; WA 6:353–78; LW 35:75–111; WA 6:502–26; LW 36:19–57; WA 8:411–76; 482–563; LW 36:127–228; WA 10/2:11–41; LW 36:237–65; WA 30/2:595–626; LW 38:91–137; WA 38:195–256; LW 38:139–214.

27. Luther is not suggesting that the validity of the sacrament depends on the character of the priest. Rather, he is rejecting the church's sacrificial understanding of the Mass. See further in WA Br 5:431; WA 6:371–72; LW 35:102–3; WA 6:525–26; LW 36:55–57. See also the position of Thomas Aquinas (1225–1274) in the *Summa theologica*, pt. III, q. 64, art. 5 and 9, concerning the worthiness and unworthiness of the priest (hereafter *STh*).

The Second Article[24]

That the Mass under the papacy[25] has to be the greatest and most horrible abomination, as it directly and violently opposes this chief article.[26] In spite of this, it has been the supreme and most precious of all the various papal idolatries, transcending all the others. For it is held that this sacrifice or work of the Mass (even when performed by a rotten scoundrel[27]) delivers people from sin, both here in this life and beyond in purgatory, even though the Lamb of God alone should and must do this, as mentioned above. Nothing is to be conceded or compromised in this article either, because the first article does not allow it.

And wherever there might be reasonable papists, one might wish to speak with them in a friendly manner about why they cling so tenaciously to the Mass.[28]

1. After all, it is nothing but a mere human invention, not commanded by God, and we may discard all human inventions, as Christ says in Matt. 15[:9]: "They serve me in vain with human precepts."[h]

2. It is an unnecessary thing that can surely be omitted without sin or danger.

3. The sacrament can be received in a much better and more blessed way (indeed, it is the only blessed way), when it is received according to Christ's institution. Why should one want to force the world into misery and destitution for the sake of unnecessary fabrications, especially when the sacrament can be received in a better and more blessed way?

Let it be publicly preached to the people that the Mass, as a human trifle, may be discontinued without sin and that no one will be condemned who does not observe it but may in fact be saved in a better way without the Mass. What do you want to bet that the Mass falls of its own accord, not only among the mad mob but also among all devout, Christian, reasonable, and God-fearing hearts? How much more would this be the case were they to hear that the Mass is a dangerous thing, fabricated and invented without God's Word and will?[i]

4. Because such innumerable, unspeakable abuses have arisen throughout the whole world with the buying and selling

---

h   The NRSV reads "teaching human precepts."

i   This paragraph was added to the printed version of 1538.

Roman Catholic observance of the Mass.

28. What follows reflects Luther's argument in this imaginary conversation.

of Masses, they should properly be abandoned, if only to curb such abuses, even if in and of themselves Masses did contain something useful and good. How much more they should be abandoned in order to guard forever against such abuses, since the Masses are completely unnecessary, useless, and dangerous, and everything can be received in a more necessary, useful, and certain manner without the Mass.

5. (As the canon of the Mass and all the handbooks say,)[29] the Mass is and can be nothing but a human work (even a work of rotten scoundrels), performed in order that individuals might reconcile themselves and others to God and acquire and merit the forgiveness of sins and grace. (When the Mass is observed in the very best possible way, it is observed with these intentions. What purpose would it otherwise have?) Thus the Mass should and must be condemned and repudiated, because this is directly

29. For example, William Durandus (c. 1237–1296), in his *Rationale divinorum officiorum* IV, 35, 12, states, "It has been passed down that Pope Gelasius, the fiftieth Primate since Saint Peter, first ordained in the canon. . . ." For Luther's comments on the canon of the Mass, see *The Abomination of the Secret Mass* (1525) (WA 18:22–36; LW 36:311–28).

contrary to the chief article, which says that it is not an evil or devout servant of the Mass with his work but rather the Lamb of God and the Son of God who takes away[j] our sin [John 1:29].

If some want to justify their position by saying that they want to commune themselves for the sake of their own edification,[k] they cannot be taken seriously.[30] For if they seriously desire to commune, then they do so with certainty and in the best manner by receiving the sacrament administered according to Christ's institution. However, to commune oneself is a human notion, uncertain, unnecessary, and even forbidden. Such people also do not know what they are doing, because they are following a false human notion and innovation without God's Word. Thus it is also not right (even if everything else were otherwise in order) to use the common sacrament of the church for one's own edification and to play with it according to one's own pleasure apart from God's Word and outside the church community.

This article on the Mass will be the decisive issue in the council because, were it possible for them to give in to us on all other articles, they surely cannot give in on this article. As Campeggio[31] said at Augsburg, he would sooner allow himself to be torn to pieces before he would abandon the Mass.[l] In the same way I, too, with God's help, will rather allow myself to be burned to ashes before I will allow a servant of the Mass, whether good or evil, and his work to be equal to or greater than my Lord and Savior Jesus Christ. Thus we are and remain eternally divided and opposed to one another. They are certainly aware that if the Mass falls, the papacy falls. Before they allow this to happen, they will kill us all, if they can do it.

30. Luther counsels against the common practice of priests communing themselves. See WA Br 5:504–5; WA 8:437–39; 513–15; LW 36:170–72.

31. Lorenzo Campeggio (1474–1539) was elevated to the cardinalate in 1517 and served the church as a papal legate. In that role he opposed Henry VIII's (1491–1547) attempts to annul his marriage to Catherine of Aragon (1485–1536) and also became involved in negotiations with the Lutherans, particularly at the Diet of Augsburg, which he attended.

---

j   The original reads *trägt*, that is, "carries."

k   The original reads *Andacht*, which the BSLK interprets to mean *Erbauung*. The translation reflects that interpretation.

l   Luther mentions this event a number of times, e.g., in WA 30/3:311; LW 47:45; WA 30/3:352–53, 362; in a Table Talk, recorded 12 December 1536, while he was working on the *Smalcald Articles*, WA TR 3:361–62, no. 3502; LW 54:215–16, no. 3502; and in WA TR 3:577–78, no. 3732.

Besides all this, this dragon's tail,*m* the Mass, has produced much vermin and excrement of various idolatries:

First, purgatory.*n* Here they rushed into purgatory headlong with requiem Masses; vigils celebrated after seven days, thirty days, and a year;[32] and, finally, with the Common Week,[33] All Souls' Day,[34] and the Soul Bath,[35] so that the Mass is only used on behalf of the dead, although Christ, nevertheless, instituted the sacrament only for the living. Purgatory, therefore, with all its pomp, worship services, and transactions, is to be regarded as a clear apparition of the devil, for it, too, is against the chief article that Christ alone, and not human works, is to help souls. Besides, concerning the dead we have received neither command nor instruction.*o* [For this reason, it may, indeed, be abandoned, even if it were neither error nor idolatry.]*p*

*The papists cite Augustine*q *and some of the Fathers who have supposedly written about purgatory regarding this matter. They believe that we do not see for what purpose and for which reason they use such passages. St. Augustine does not write that there is a purgatory and cites no passage of Scripture that persuades him to adopt such a position. Instead, he leaves it undecided whether there is a purgatory or not and says that his mother asked to be remembered at the altar or sacrament.*r *Now all of this is nothing but the human opinion of a few individuals, who establish no article of faith (which only God can do). However, our papists employ such human words in order that people might believe in their shameful, blasphemous, accursed fairs of requiem Masses offered up into purgatory, etc. They will never prove such a thing from Augustine. Now when they have given up*

32. The celebration of the Mass on the eve of the anniversary of the deceased is mentioned as early as Tertullian (c. 160–c. 225) in *The Chaplet, or De Corona* 3 (MPL 2:79; *ANF* 3:94), and celebrations on the week or month following death are mentioned by Ambrose (c. 340–397) in "On the Death of Theodosius," 3 (MPL 16:1386; *Funeral Orations by Saint Gregory Nazianzen and Saint Ambrose*, trans. Leo P. McCauley et al., The Fathers of the Church 22 [New York: Fathers of the Church, 1953], 308).

33. The week following St. Michael's Day (29 September), when many Masses were offered for the dead.

34. 2 November, when all the souls of the departed (as opposed to all the [unknown] saints, who were prayed for on November 1) were commemorated.

35. Free baths endowed for the poor in the hope that they would pray for the salvation of the donors.

---

m Rev. 12:3; 20:2. Cf. WA 30/2:506; LW 40:376.

n For Luther's position on purgatory, see WA 1:555–58; 2:322–44; 8:452–57; 531–37; LW 36:190–98; WA 11:451; LW 36:299; WA 26:508; LW 37:369; WA 30/2:369–90; 30/3:309–10; LW 47:42–43.

o See WA 26:508; LW 37:369.

p The original places this sentence in brackets.

q Augustine (354–430), *City of God* XXI, 24 (MPL 41:738; CSEL 40/2:559; NPNF, ser. 1, 2:470); and idem, *Enchiridion* 67–69 (MPL 40:263–65; NPNF, ser. 1, 3:260).

r Augustine, *Confessions* IX, 11, 27, and IX, 13, 36 (MPL 32:775, 778–80; CSEL 33:219, 223, 225; NPNF, ser. 1, 1:138, 141).

their purgatorial Mass fairs, of which Augustine never dreamed, then we will discuss with them whether St. Augustine's word, lacking support from Scripture, may be tolerated and whether the dead may be commemorated at the sacrament. It is of no value to formulate articles of faith on the basis of the works or words of the holy Fathers. Otherwise, their food, clothes, houses, etc., would also have to become articles of faith, as has been done with relics. This means that[s] the Word of God, and no one else, not even an angel, should establish articles of faith.[t]

Second, as a result of their teaching regarding the Mass, evil spirits have caused much rascality, and, appearing as souls of the departed,[u] they have demanded Masses, vigils, pilgrimages, and other alms with unspeakable lies and cunning. We all had to hold these matters as articles of faith and live according to them. The pope confirms this along with the Mass and all the other horrors. Here, too, there is no room for compromise or concession.

Third, pilgrimages.[36] Masses, the forgiveness of sins, and God's grace were also sought here, for the Mass ruled everything. Now, it is indeed certain that, lacking God's Word, such pilgrimages are neither commanded nor necessary. For we can have forgiveness and grace in a much better way and can omit pilgrimages without any sin or danger. Why would one neglect one's own parish, God's Word, spouse and child, etc., which are necessary and commanded, and run after unnecessary, uncertain, harm-

---

36. Luther was concerned about the negative spiritual impact of much of medieval piety, including pilgrimages, which encouraged people to rely on their own works in order to merit God's gifts of grace. He also recognized the negative social and economic effects of pilgrimages. Because of the fiscal costs involved, they resulted in hardships, particularly among families with limited resources, while the institutional church benefited economically. The reformer notes these concerns in this section of the SA. For other examples of the Luther's critique of pilgrimages, see WA 6:437–38, 447–51; LW 44:169–72, 185–89; WA 30/2:296–97; LW 34:25; WA 51:489; LW 41:200; WA 10/3:344; LW 51:107.

---

s   The Latin translation reads: "We have a different rule, namely, that. . . ."

t   Gal. 1:8. See also WA 2:427–28; 7:131–33, 423–26. BC, SA II, 2, 13–15 was not a part of Luther's original manuscript or of the copy made by Spalatin and subscribed to at Smalcald in 1537. Luther inserted this paragraph into the text for the SA's publication in 1538.

u   Luther apparently refers here to the reports of apparitions mentioned by Gregory I the Great (c. 540–604), *Dialogues* IV, 40 (in *Saint Gregory the Great: Dialogues*, The Fathers of the Church 40 [Washington, DC: Catholic University of America, 1959]); and Peter Damian (c. 1007–1072/73), *Opusculum* 34, 5 (MPL 145:578–79).

ful, demonic apparitions?[v] Only because the devil has driven the pope into praising and confirming such practices, so that the people routinely deserted Christ for their own works and became idolatrous. That is the worst of all! Apart from the fact that they are unnecessary, not commanded, unwise, uncertain, and even harmful. Therefore here, too, there is nothing to concede or give up, etc. Let it be preached that they are unnecessary as well as dangerous, and then see where pilgrimages stand.[w]

Fourth, fraternities.[37] The monasteries, foundations, and lower clergy have assigned and passed on to themselves (by lawful and open sale) all Masses, good works, etc., for both the living and the dead. They are not only purely human trifles, lacking God's Word, completely unnecessary, and not commanded, but they are also contrary to the first article of redemption, and therefore they can in no way be tolerated.

Fifth, relics. Here so many open lies and foolishness are invented concerning the bones of dogs and horses.[38] Because of such tomfoolery, at which even the devil laughs, they should have been condemned long ago, even if there were something good in them. In addition, they are neither commanded nor commended without God's Word and are a completely unnecessary and useless thing. The worst part is that relics, like the Mass, etc., were also to have produced an indulgence and the forgiveness of sin as a good work and act of worship.

Sixth, those precious indulgences[39] belong here, which are given (for money, of course,) to both the living and the dead. The accursed Judas, or pope, sells the merits of Christ together with the superabundant merits of all the saints and the entire church, etc. All of this is not to be tolerated, not only because it is not necessary without God's Word and not commanded, but because it is contrary to the first article. Christ's merit is not acquired

37. Since the eighth century, members of certain monasteries obligated themselves to offer prayers and perform works of piety for their deceased brothers. In the late Middle Ages, similar obligations were assumed by groups called *fraternities,* comprised of members of the clergy and/or the laity. See WA 2:754–57; LW 35:67–72.

38. See WA 51:135–38 and especially Luther's 1539 treatise *On the Councils and the Church*, where Luther describes the true "holy possessions" of the church, WA 50:628–43 and LW 41:148–67. Relics were a popular aspect of medieval piety, and their use was intimately related to the church's emphasis on the commemoration and veneration of the saints. Relics also served as tangible, visible connections with the spiritual realm and even with the divine for faithful medieval Christians. Furthermore, whenever they venerated the relics and made their monetary contributions to the church's treasury, indulgence could be earned by the pious. Not surprisingly, Luther opposed relics for spiritual, theological, and economic reasons, and he voiced his opposition already early in his reforming career, especially since a significant relic collection was housed in the castle church in Wittenberg. See the discussion of the Wittenberg relic collection in Martin Brecht, *Martin Luther*, vol. 1: *His Road to Reformation 1483–1521*, trans. James L. Schaaf (Philadelphia: Fortress Press, 1985), 115–18.

39. The sale of indulgences was one aspect of the extensive penitential system implemented during the Middle Ages. For the payment of a specific amount of money, an indulgence was granted which fulfilled the penitential obligations assigned by confessors.

---

v   The original reads *Teufelsirrwischen.*
w   The Latin translation adds: "For in this way they will spontaneously perish."

Indulgences could also be purchased to address the incompleted penance of souls languishing in purgatory. Some exuberant indulgence preachers convinced people that indulgences assured their salvation. Luther was deeply concerned about the detrimental spiritual effects of the penitential system, including indulgences. He therefore addressed indulgences throughout his reforming career, although his comments were most persistent during the early years of the Reformation. See, e.g., WA 1:233–38; LW 31:17–33; WA 1:525–628; LW 31:77–252; WA 2:6–26; LW 31:253–92; WA 2:344–58; 7:399–405; 18:255–69; 26:507; LW 37:369; WA 30/2:281–86; LW 34:16–18; WA 51:488; LW 41:200.

40. It is important to note that Luther criticizes the church's sacramental theology and piety in light of the gospel. His chief concern is, therefore, that a theology of works and merit is promoted by Rome. It is for this particular reason that he rejects the various practices and institutions discussed under the previous six points.

41. While Luther affirmed the intercession of angels, fellow believers, and, possibly, the saints in heaven, he was opposed to the invocation of the saints and the related piety that was popular during the Middle Ages. Luther's position, which was shared by the theologians who had gathered in Wittenberg to review the draft of the *Smalcald Articles*, is articulated in this section of the document. Luther and his colleagues were concerned to avoid idolatry and insisted that prayers should be addressed to God alone.

through our work or penny, but through faith by grace, without any money and merit. It is offered not by the pope's authority but by preaching a sermon or God's word.[40]

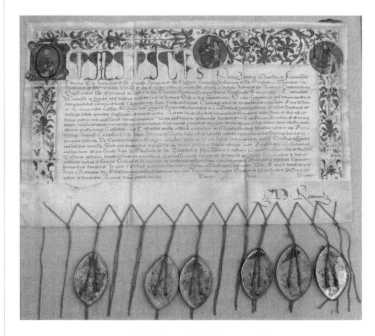

A 1516 papal indulgence.

Concerning the Invocation of Saints[41]

The invocation of saints is also one of the abuses of the Antichrist that is in conflict with the first, chief article and that destroys the knowledge of Christ. It is also neither commanded nor recommended, has no precedent in the Scripture, and, even if it were a precious possession, which it is not, we have everything a thousand times better in Christ.

Although the angels in heaven pray for us (as Christ himself also does), and in the same way also the saints on earth and perhaps those in heaven, it does not follow from this that we ought to invoke angels and saints; pray to them; keep fasts and hold festivals for them; celebrate Masses; make sacrifices; establish churches, altars, or worship services for them; serve them in still other ways; and consider them as helpers in time of need; attribute all kinds of assistance to them; and claim a specific function for each saint, as the papists teach and do. This is idolatry. Such honor belongs to God alone. As a Christian and saint on earth, you can pray for me, not only in one but in every need. However, I ought not pray to you, invoke you, hold a festival, keep a fast, make a sacrifice, celebrate a Mass in your honor, and put my faith in you for salvation for that reason. I can honor, love, and thank you in Christ in other ways. Now when such idolatrous honor is taken away from the angels and dead saints, then the honor that remains will do no harm and will indeed soon be forgotten. When physical and spiritual benefit and help are no longer to be expected, then people will, no doubt, leave the saints in peace, both in the grave and in heaven. For no one will remember, esteem, or honor them much out of love, with no hope of reward.

In summary, we cannot tolerate and must condemn what the Mass is, what has resulted from it, and what is connected to it, so that we may retain the holy sacrament in purity and with certainty because it is used and received with faith according to the institution of Christ.[42]

The Third Article

That foundations[43] and monasteries, established in former times with good intentions for the education of learned people and decent women, should again be regulated for such use so that one may have pastors, preachers, and other servants of the church, as well as other people necessary for earthly government in cities and states, and also well-trained young women to head households and manage them.

Where they are not willing to serve in this way, it is better if they were abandoned or torn down than that they, with their blasphemous worship devised by human beings, should be regarded as something better than everyday Christian walks of life and the offices and orders established by God.[44] For all of this, too, is contrary to the first and chief article concerning redemption in Jesus Christ. Furthermore, they (like all other human inventions) are also not commanded, not necessary, not useful—while

A careful distinction was, therefore, made between praying for someone and praying to someone. The Lutherans argued that the latter was reserved for God. See WA 1:411–26; 2:69–70; 10/1/2:82–84; 10/2:164–68; 15:192–98; 30/2:643–45; LW 35:198–200.

42. The previous three paragraphs were composed by the theologians who were invited to review the *Articles* prepared by Luther and who had gathered in Wittenberg at the end of December 1536.

43. The foundations, also named chapters, were associations of secular priests, called canons, especially in cathedral churches. For example, prior to 1527 some members of the University of Wittenberg faculty were members of the All Saints' Foundation. *Kanonissenstifter* were related institutions. They were associations of women called *canonicae*. These women were not nuns, however, since they did not make vows and retained their property. See WA 6:439–40, 452–53, 461; LW 44:174–75, 192–93, 205–6; WA 15:27–53; LW 45:339–78; WA 30/2:315–19; LW 34:36–38; WA 50:617, 651–52; LW 41:134–35, 176–77.

44. With his doctrines of the priesthood of the baptized and of vocation, Luther emphasized that all callings that Christians pursue in their lives are gifts of God in which they are able to express their faith in loving service of God and of other human beings. There should be no hierarchy of spiritual and temporal offices. The reformer and his Wittenberg colleagues, particularly Philip Melanchthon and Johannes Bugenhagen, also stressed that education was essential if people were to serve church and society in the most effective ways, and they counseled that ecclesiastical property should be used to support education. Luther was an advocate and publicist for educational efforts, and Melanchthon focused on the reform of university education. However, Bugenhagen was eager to promote education from the primary to the university level. He included a section on education in the church orders that he produced for cities and territories throughout northern Germany and for Denmark and provided detailed instructions regarding the establishment of schools and the curricula.

45. The institution of the papacy and its power is addressed repeatedly in Luther's writings. See, e.g., WA 2:19–20; LW 31:280–82; WA 2:183–240; 254–322; 628–42; 6:285–324; LW 39:49–135; WA 6:415–16; LW 44:139–40; WA 7:409–19; LW 32:67–74; WA 7:705–78; 26:152–53; LW 40:237–39; WA 30/2:487–90; LW 40:353–56; WA 54:206–99; LW 41:257–376.

46. For example, the Councils of Nicea (325), Constantinople (381), Ephesus (431), and Chalcedon (451). Canon IV of the Council of Nicea stipulates that bishops should be elected by their own churches in the presence of one or more neighboring bishops.

causing dangerous and futile effort besides. The prophets call such worship *aven*, which means "wasted effort."[x]

The Fourth Article[45]

That the pope is not the head of all Christendom "by divine right"[y] or on the basis of God's Word[z] (because that belongs only to the one who is called Jesus Christ).[a] Instead, the pope is only bishop, or pastor,[b] of the church in Rome and of those who willingly or through a human institution (that is, through temporal authority)[c] have joined themselves to him in order to be Christians alongside him as a brother and companion but not under him as a lord, as the ancient councils[46] and the time of St. Cyprian (c. 200–258)[d] demonstrate. However, now no bishop dares to call the pope "brother," as at that time, but instead must address him as his "most gracious lord," as if he were a king or emperor. We do not wish to impose this upon our consciences and also should not and cannot do so. Whoever wishes to do so, however, should do it without us.

It follows from this that everything the pope has done and undertaken on the basis of such false, wanton, blasphemous, adapted power was and still is a purely diabolical affair and business, which corrupts the entire holy Christian church (however much it depends on him) and troubles the first, chief article on redemption by Jesus Christ. (The only exception concerns the

---

x   The Hebrew word *aven* literally means "wickedness," "emptiness," "vanity," "futility." Luther translated it *Mühe*, which properly means "effort," "trouble," "labor," "pain." In a marginal note on Isa. 29:20 in the German Bible, he connected *Mühe* with the prophet's denunciation of "false teaching and works." See also WA 13:444; LW 19:140; WA 31/2:181; LW 16:249.

y   Luther uses the technical term *iure divino*.

z   See also BC, Tr, par. 12, 332.

a   Eph. 1:22; 4:15; 5:23; Col. 1:18. See also WA 2:257.

b   See WA 7:628–32.

c   For a concise explication of Luther's point, see WA 12:328.

d   See BC, Tr, par. 14, 332. Cyprian, as bishop of Carthage, addressed Pope Cornelius (c. 190–253) as his "very dear brother." See, e.g., his *Epistles*, XL–XLII, XLIV, XLVI, XLVIII, LIII, LIV, LVI (MPL 3:700, 703, 708, 710, 725, 731, 796, 830; CSEL 3/2: 597, 599, 605, 606, 614, 616, 666, 691; *ANF* 5:319–22, 324–25, 336, 338, 351).

Cardinals and bishops
observe the coronation of a pope.

area of political government, where God surely also allows much good to come to a people through a tyrant or scoundrel.)

All his bulls and books are available, in which he roars like a lion (as the angel of Rev. [10:3] indicates) that Christians cannot be saved unless they are obedient and submit to him in all things—what he wills, what he says, what he does.[47] This is essentially to say: "Even if you believe in Christ and have everything that is necessary for salvation in him, nevertheless, it is nothing and all in vain unless you consider me your god and are subject and obedient to me." Yet it is obvious that the holy church was without a pope for over five hundred years at least,[48] and even today the Greek church and many churches that use other languages have never been under the pope and still are not.[49] Thus, as has often been said, it is a human fiction. It is not commanded. There is no need for it, and it is useless. The holy Christian church can surely survive without such a head. It would, no doubt, have been much better off if such a head had not been raised up by the devil. The papacy also does not benefit the church, because it exercises no Christian office, and thus the church must continue and endure without the pope.

47. Pope Boniface VIII (c. 1235–1303) expressed an exulted claim of papal authority in the 1302 bull, *Unam Sanctam*: "We declare, say, define, and pronounce that it is altogether necessary to salvation for every human creature to be subject to the Roman pontiff."

48. Luther considered Gregory I to be the last bishop of Rome prior to the rise of the papacy per se. See BC, Tr , par. 19, 333 and WA 54:229–30.

49. Luther noted repeatedly that the pope's authority was not recognized throughout Christendom. See, e.g., WA 2:225, 236; 6:286–87; 7:127–31; 411; 50:84; 54:235, 243. While Luther challenged papal authority throughout his reforming career, his critique of the papacy became increasingly polemical as the years passed.

50. John XXIII (c. 1370–1419) was deposed at Constance on 29 May 1415. Gregory XII (c. 1326–1417) abdicated on 4 July 1415. Benedict XIII (1328–1423) was deposed on 26 July 1417. Martin V (1368–1431) was elected pope on 11 November 1417.

51. While Luther does not specifically endorse a conciliarist understanding of ecclesial government and of papal elections here and warned about its potential harmful effects, he nevertheless chooses to mention the conciliarist perspective as a potential alternative for canonical papal elections. The reference to the conciliar movement and to the Council of Constance sharpened his critique of papal authority and served as an irritant to the papacy. The memory of conciliarism and of Constance was a major reason why the papacy was reluctant to call a council when Luther, his supporters, and even Emperor Charles V urged the convening of such an ecclesiastical assembly. As Luther indicates at the conclusion of the paragraph, the papacy was fully aware that conciliarism was radically opposed to papal claims of authority.

52. The papal residence had been at Avignon, France, from 1309 to 1377.

Suppose, for the sake of argument, that the pope wanted to renounce his claim that he is the supreme head of the church "by divine right" or by God's command. Suppose instead, in order that the unity of Christendom might be much better preserved against sects and heresy, that there must be a head to whom all others adhere. Now such a head would be elected by the people, and it would remain incumbent upon their choice and power whether to change or depose this head. This is virtually the way the council at Constance dealt with the popes, deposing three[50] and electing the fourth. Now just suppose, (I say), that the pope and the see of Rome relinquished their authority and accepted this view, which, of course, is impossible because the pope would have to allow the overthrow and destruction of his entire government and position with all his laws and books; in short, he cannot do it.[51]

Even if he could, Christianity would not be helped in any way, and there would be even more sects than before. Because one would not have to submit to such a head on the basis of God's command but rather as a matter of human goodwill, he would rather easily and quickly be despised, until finally he would not have even one adherent. He would also no longer have to reside in Rome or at some other set place,[52] but wherever and in whatever church God provided a man suitable for the position. Oh, that would become a complicated and disorganized state of affairs!

Therefore the church cannot be better ruled and preserved than if we all live under one head, Christ, and all the bishops, equal according to the office (although they may be unequal in their gifts),[e] keep diligently together in unity of teaching, faith, sacraments, prayers, and works of love, etc. So St. Jerome (c. 342–420) writes that the priests at Alexandria ruled the churches together in common, as the apostles also did and afterward all bishops throughout Christendom,[53] until the pope elevated himself over them all.

This matter shows irrefutably that he is the true end-times Antichrist,[f] who has raised himself over and set himself against Christ, because the pope does not allow Christians to be saved

---

e   1 Cor. 12:4, 8-10; Rom. 12:6-8.

f   Luther uses two terms here, *Endchrist* (the "Christ" who comes in the end times) and *Widerchrist* (the Antichrist).

Image of Avignon, France, in the early fifteenth century
by Boucicaut Master, an anonymous French
or Flemish miniaturist and illuminator.

53. Luther refers from memory to two passages from Jerome, which he joins and employs in other contexts as well, e.g., in WA 2:228–29; 259; 38:237; LW 38:196–97. The citations are from Jerome's *Commentary on the Epistle to Titus* 1:5, 6 (MPL 26:562), where Alexandria is, however, not mentioned, and from Epistle 146, to Euangelus the Presbyter (MPL 22:1194; CSEL 66:310; NPNF, ser. 2, 6:288–89).

54. 2 Thess. 2:4. Luther uses this passage most frequently in support of his contention that the pope is the Antichrist.

without his authority, which, nevertheless, amounts to nothing and is not ordered or commanded by God. This truly means "setting oneself over God and against God," as St. Paul says.[54] However, neither the Turks nor the Tartars, despite being great enemies of the Christians, do any such thing. Rather, they allow whoever desires it to have faith in Christ, and they receive physical tribute and obedience from the Christians.[g]

Anticristi / Anno rri.

A king bows to kiss
the feet of a pope.

The pope, however, will not allow faith, but asserts that one should be obedient to him. This is how one will be saved. We are unwilling to do this, even if we have to die in God's name on account of it. All of this stems from his claim to be head of the Christian church "by divine right."[h] Therefore he had to set himself up as equal to and even greater than Christ and let himself be praised first as the head of the church, then as its lord, and finally as lord of the entire world and nothing short of an earthly god until he even dared to command the angels in heaven.[55]

When the pope's teaching is distinguished from that of Holy Scripture or when it is compared to and held over against it, it is discovered that the pope's teaching, at its very best, is taken from the imperial, pagan law[56] and teaches about temporal dealings and judgments, as his *Decretals*[57] show. Accordingly, it gives instruction about ceremonies involving churches, vestments, foods, personnel, along with child's play, imaginary work, and fool's work without limit. However, in all these things, there is absolutely nothing about Christ, faith, and God's commandments.

---

g   See WA 30/2:195.

h   Gratian (d. c. 1159), *Decretum* I, dist. 21, ch. 3, and dist. 22, chs. 1–2.

Finally, this is nothing but the devil through and through, since the pope promotes his lies about Masses, purgatory, monastic life, one's own works and worship (which are the essence of the papacy) above and against God. The devil damns, slays, and plagues all Christians who do not exalt and honor his abominations above all things. Therefore, as little as we can worship the devil himself as a lord or god, so little can we tolerate his apostle, the pope or Antichrist, as head or lord in its government. The devil's papal government is really lying and murder and the eternal ruin of body and soul, as I have proven in many books.[i]

These four articles will furnish them with enough to condemn at the council. They neither can nor will concede to us the tiniest fraction of even one of these articles.[58] Of this we must be certain, and we must rely on the hope that Christ our Lord has attacked his enemy and will carry the day, both by his Spirit and at his return.[j] Amen.

At the council, we will not stand (as at Augsburg)[59] before the emperor or the secular authority, which issued a most gracious summons[60] and allowed the matters to be heard in a gracious manner. Rather, we will stand before the pope and the devil itself, who do[k] not intend to listen but simply to damn us, to murder us, and to force us into idolatry. Therefore we must not kiss his feet[61] here or say, "You are my gracious lord." Rather, we ought to speak as the angel[62] spoke to the devil in Zech. [3:2], "The Lord rebuke you, O Satan!"

[III.] The Third Part of the Articles

We may discuss the following matters or articles with learned, reasonable people or among ourselves. The pope and his kingdom do not value these matters very much, because the conscience[l] means nothing to them; money, honor, and power mean everything.

55. Luther is referring to what is now generally held to be a spurious bull, *Ad memoriam reducendo*, dated 27 June 1346 and ascribed to Pope Clement VI (1291–1352), which commanded the angels "to lead to heaven the souls of the pilgrims who might die on their way to Rome" during the jubilee year of 1350.

56. The reference is to Roman law.

57. Decretals are encyclical pronouncements of the popes.

58. Luther had little hope that there would be productive theological discussion at the proposed council that would lead to a resolution of the diverse issues that divided the Roman and Lutheran theologians and their allies. The *Smalcald Articles* are a clear indication that Luther was not inclined to negotiate. They also confirm that he did not expect his Roman opponents to compromise with regard to chief issues that divided the two parties.

59. Luther is recalling the imperial diet held at Augsburg in the summer of 1530 when the *Augsburg Confession* was presented to Emperor Charles V.

60. Charles V's proclamation of the Diet of Augsburg, dated 21 January 1530, included these words: ". . . to listen to, understand, and consider each belief, opinion, and viewpoint between us in love and kindness, so that we might come to Christian truth." See WA 30/3:287; 291–92; LW 47:24–25, 30–31.

61. This was a required act of homage (*adoratio*) to the pope in the Middle Ages. See WA 6:435–36; LW 44:168.

62. The Lord spoke according to the book of Zechariah.

---

i   See n. 45 above.

j   2 Thess. 2:8.

k   The pronoun and the verb in the original are singular.

l   Luther uses a Latin word, *conscientia*.

A depiction of God expelling Adam and Eve from the Garden of Eden after the fall, from a 1545 printing of Luther's *Small Catechism*.

[1:]*m* Concerning Sin*n*

Here we must confess, as St. Paul says in Rom. 5[:12], that sin has originated from that one human being, Adam, through whose disobedience all people became sinners and subject to death and the devil. This is called the original sin*o* or the chief sin.

The fruits of this sin are the subsequent evil works, which are forbidden in the Ten Commandments, such as unbelief, false belief, idolatry, being without the fear of God, presumptuousness, despairing, blindness, and, in summary, not knowing or honoring God. Beyond that, there is lying, swearing [falsely] by God's name,*p* not praying or calling on God's name, neglecting God's Word, being disobedient to parents, murdering, unchastity, stealing, deceiving, etc.

Such inherited sin is such a deep, evil corruption of nature that reason does not comprehend it; rather, it must be believed on the basis of scriptural revelation in Ps. 51[:5]*q* and Rom. 5[:12]; Exod. 33[:20]; Gen. 3[:6ff.]. Therefore, the scholastic theologians have taught pure error and blindness against this article:

1. Namely, that after the fall of Adam the natural powers of the human being have remained whole and uncorrupted and that each human being possesses by nature sound reason and a good will, as the philosophers teach.

2. Furthermore, that the human being has a free will, either to do good and reject evil or, on the other hand, to reject good and do evil.*r*

3. Furthermore, that the human being is able to keep and carry out every command of God by using natural powers.

---

m　The 1580 *Book of Concord* supplies numbers for the articles in Part III.

n　For extensive explorations of Luther's anthropology and understanding of sin, see, e.g., WA 8:43–128; LW 32:133–260; WA 18:600–787; LW 33; WA 56; LW 25.

o　The original reads *Erbsunde,* inherited sin.

p　See BC, SC, "The Ten Commandments," 2, 4, 352 n.32. See also BC, LC, "The Ten Commandments," 2, 65–68, 394–95.

q　The original reads Psalm 50, according to the numbering of the Vulgate.

r　See WA 2:246–48; 424–26; 7:142–49; 445–50; 18:600–787; LW 33; WA 26:502–503; 30/3:359–64.

4. Furthermore, that human beings are able, using natural powers, to love God above all things and their neighbor as themselves.[s]

5. Furthermore, that if human beings do as much as is in their power, then God will certainly give grace to them.[t]

6. Furthermore, that if someone wants to go to the sacrament, it is not necessary to have a proper intention to do good, but it is enough for that person not to have an evil intention to commit sin,[63] because human nature is so completely good and the sacrament is so powerful.

7. That there is no basis in Scripture that the Holy Spirit with his grace is necessary for performing a good work.

Such and many similar things have arisen from a lack of understanding and ignorance about both sin and Christ our Savior. This is purely pagan teaching which we cannot tolerate, because, if this teaching were right, then Christ has died in vain.[u] For there would be no defect or sin in humankind for which he had to die, or else he would have died only for the body and not for the soul, because the soul would be healthy and only the body would be subject to death.

[2:] Concerning the Law[64]

Here we maintain that the law is given by God, in the first place, to curb sin by means of the threat and terror of punishment and by means of the promise and offer of grace and favor. However, all of this failed because of the evil that sin worked in humankind. Some, who are enemies of the law because it prohibits what they want to do and commands what they do not want to do, became worse because of it. On account of this, insofar as they are not restrained by punishment, they act against the law even more than before. These are the coarse, evil people who do evil whenever they have an opportunity.

63. In the 1520 papal bull *Exsurge Domine*, Luther was threatened with excommunciation by Pope Leo X for rejecting this assertion. See WA 7:316–29; LW 32:12–19; WA 1:324; 6:608, 622; 17/2:80.

64. Luther describes two functions or uses of the law in this article. The *Formula of Concord* also affirms that the law functions to curb the effects of sin and to reveal sin to human beings. However, it also adds a third function, namely, to serve as a guide for faithful living. See BC, FC, Ep VI, 502–503; BC, FC, SD VI, 587–91. See also WA 7:23–24; LW 31:348–49; WA 10/1/1:449–70; 18:65–66; LW 40:82–83; WA 39/1:359–584; 50:468–77; LW 47:98–118.

s   E.g., John Duns Scotus (c. 1266–1308), *Commentary on the Sentences* III, d. 27, q. 1, and Gabriel Biel (c. 1420–1495), *Collectorium* III, d. 27, q. 1, a. 3, dub. 2.

t   E.g., Gabriel Biel, *Collectorium* III, d. 27, q. 1, a. 3, dub. 2. Here Luther paraphrases the medieval principle, *facere quod in se est* ("to do what is in one or to do what one is able").

u   Gal. 2:21.

Others become blind and presumptuous, imagining that they can and do keep the law by their own powers, as has just been said above about the scholastic theologians.[65] This attitude produces hypocrites and false saints.

However, the foremost office or power of the law is that it reveals inherited sin and all of its fruits. It shows human beings into what utter depths their nature has fallen and how completely corrupt it is.[v] The law must say to them that they neither have nor respect any god or that they worship foreign gods. This is something that they would not have believed before and without the law. Thus they are terrified, humbled, despondent, and despairing. They anxiously desire help but do not know where to find it; they start to become enemies of God and to murmur,[w] etc. This is what is meant by Rom. [4:15]: "The law incites wrath,"[x] and Rom. 5[:20], "Sin becomes greater through the law."

[3:] Concerning Repentance[66]

The New Testament retains this office of the law and also teaches it, as Paul does and says in Rom. 1[:18]: "The wrath of God is revealed from heaven against all people." Furthermore, Rom. 3[:19-20]: "The whole world is guilty before God, and no human being is justified before him"; and Christ says in John 16[:8]: the Holy Spirit "will punish the world because of sin."[y]

Now this is the thunderbolt of God, by means of which he destroys both the open sinner and the false saint[z] and allows no one to be right but drives the whole lot of them into terror and despair. This is the hammer (as Jeremiah says): "My word is a hammer that breaks the rocks in pieces" [Jer. 23:29]. This is not "active contrition,"[a] a contrived remorse, but "passive contrition,"[b] true affliction of the heart, suffering, and the perception of death.

---

65. BC, SA III, 1.

66. The German phrase *Buße tun* (Lat.: *poenitentiam agere*) may be translated "do penance," "repent," or "be penitent," depending on the context. In this paragraph and throughout this article, Luther is playing on these various meanings. See WA 1:98–99; 233; 243–46; 319–24; 529–33; LW 31:83–88; WA 1:648–57; WA 2:359–83; 713–23; WA 6:543–49; LW 36:81–90; WA 18:65; LW 40:82; WA 30/2:288–92; LW 34:19–21; WA 39/1:342–50. The title of the article in the original reads *Von der Buße*.

---

v   Rom. 3:20; 7:7.

w Rom. 5:10; Exod. 16:8; Luke 15:2; 19:7.

x   Luther mistakenly refers to Romans 3.

y   This is the alternate reading in the NRSV.

z   See BC, SA III, 2.

a   Luther uses a Latin phrase, *activa contritio*.

b   Luther uses a Latin phrase, *passiva contritio*.

This is really what it means to begin true repentance. Here a person must listen to a judgment such as this: "You are all of no account, whether you are manifest sinners or saints.ᶜ You must all become something different from what you are now and act in a different way than you do now, no matter who you are now and what you do. You may be as important and great, wise, powerful, and holy as you wish, but no one is righteous here, etc."ᵈ

However, to this office of the law the New Testament immediately adds the consoling promise of grace through the gospel, which we should believe. As Christ says in Mark 1[:15]: "Repent and believe in the good news," that is, "Become someone else and act differently and believe my promise." Even before Jesus, John the Baptizer is called a preacher of repentance, but for the purpose of the forgiveness of sins. That is, John was to rebuke them all and turn them into sinners, so that they would know who they were before God and would recognize themselves as lost people. In this way they were to be prepared for the Lordᵉ to receive grace and to await and receive from God forgiveness of sins. Jesus himself says in Luke 24[:47]: "Repentance and forgiveness must be preached in my name throughout the world."ᶠ

However, where the law exercises its office alone, without the addition of the gospel, there areᵍ death and hell, and the human being must despair, like Saul and Judas. As St. Paul says: "The law kills through sin."ʰ Moreover, the gospel does not give consolation and forgiveness in only one way, but through the Word, sacrament, and the like, as we shall hear,ⁱ so that with God there is certainly abundant redemption from the great prison of sin (as Ps. 130[:7-8] says).

However, now we must compare the false penance of the sophists[67] with true repentance, in order that they both might be better understood.

67. Luther uses this term to refer to the Scholastic theologians.

---

c The Latin translation adds: "in your own opinion."

d Rom. 3:10-12. See also BC, SA III, 3.

e Cf. Mark 1:3.

f Luther paraphrases the biblical text.

g The Latin translation: "nothing else but."

h See Rom. 7:10; for Saul, see 1 Sam. 28:20 and 31:4; for Judas, see Matt. 27:3-5. See BC, the *Apology of the Augsburg Confession* XII, 8, 189 (hereafter referred to as BC, Ap.).

i BC, SA III, 4.

68. Luther is rejecting late medieval Nominalist anthropology, specifically, the notion of *facere quod in se est*, which asserts that human beings retain their free will and, therefore, an inherent, although a curtailed, ability to do God's will, in spite of original sin.

69. The medieval church did not consider concupiscence, or the inclination to sin, to be actual sin, while Luther argues that even this inclination is sinful since it is a manifestation of the effects of original sin on human nature. Contemporary Roman Catholics and Lutherans continue to differ in their understanding of concupiscence. See the "Joint Declaration on the Doctrine of Justification," sec. 4.4.

70. This division of the sacrament of penance is found already in Peter Lombard (c. 1100–c. 1160), *Sentences* IV, d. 16, c. 1. Luther discusses these three parts of penance in what follows. See also WA 1:98–99; 319–24; 6:610; 624–25; 7:112–13; 351–55; 34/1:301–10.

71. This phrase, or its equivalent, dates back to at least the tenth century and was spoken by the priest, in behalf of the congregation, at the conclusion of the sermon.

72. In Constitution 21 of the Fourth Lateran Council (1215) it was stipulated that all who had reached the age of discretion (seven years) must confess their sins to a priest at least once a year. See *Decretalium D. Gregorii Papae IX*, liber V, tit. XXXVIII, cap. 12.

Concerning the False Penance of the Papists[j]

It was impossible for them to teach correctly about penance because they did not recognize what sin really is. (As mentioned above),[k] they do not hold the correct position about original sin. Instead, they say that the natural powers of humankind have remained whole and uncorrupted; that reason can teach correctly and the will can act properly according to it; that God surely gives God's grace if human beings do as much as is in their power,[68] according to human free will.

From this it had to follow that they only did penance for actual sins, such as evil thoughts to which they consent (because an evil impulse, desire, and attraction were not sin);[69] evil words; and evil works, which the free will could well have avoided.

They divide such penance into three parts,[70] contrition, confession, and satisfaction, with this comfort and pledge: when people are truly contrite, go to confession, and make satisfaction, they merit forgiveness thereby and have paid for sin before God. In this way, they directed the people to place confidence in their own works in penance. From this came the phrase that was spoken from the pulpit when the general confession was recited on behalf of the people: "Spare my life, Lord God, until I do penance for my sin and improve my life."[71]

There was no Christ here, and nothing was mentioned about faith. Instead, people hoped to overcome and blot out sin before God with their own works. We also became priests and monks with this intention, namely, to set ourselves against sin.

Contrition was handled in this way: Because no one could recall every sin (particularly those committed during an entire year),[72] they resorted to the following loophole.[l] If unknown sins were remembered later, then a person was also to be contrite for them and confess them, etc. Meanwhile, they were commended to God's grace.

---

j   See BC, Ap XII, 203–18.

k   This paragraph summarizes the numbered section of BC, SA III, 1.

l   Luther uses an idiom, which, translated literally, is, "they mended the coat" or "patched the hide" (*flickten sie den Pelz*).

Moreover, since no one knew how great the contrition should be so that it would surely suffice before God, they offered such consolation: Whoever could not have *contritio*, that is, contrition, should have *attritio*, what I might call a halfway or beginning contrition.[73] For they themselves have not understood either word, and they still know as little about what they mean as I do. Such *attritio* was then counted as *contritio* when one went to confession.

And if it happened that some said they could not repent or be sorrowful for their sins, as might happen in fornication or revenge, etc., they were asked whether they at least wished or really desired to have contrition. If they said yes (because who would say no, except the devil himself?), it was considered to be contrition, and their sins were forgiven on the basis of their good work. Here they pointed to the example of St. Bernard.[m]

Here it is apparent how blind reason gropes around in the things of God and seeks comfort in its own works, according to its own darkened opinion. It cannot consider Christ or faith. Now, if this is considered in the light, then such contrition is a contrived and imaginary idea that comes from one's own powers, without faith, without knowledge of Christ. In this state, a poor sinner who reflected on this lust or revenge would at times have more likely laughed than cried, except for those who were truly struck down by the law or plagued by the devil uselessly with a sorrowful spirit. Otherwise, such contrition was certainly pure hypocrisy and did not kill the desire to sin. They had to be contrite but would rather have sinned more had it been without consequences.

Confession worked like this: Each person had to enumerate all of his or her sins (which is impossible). This was a great torment. However, whatever the person had forgotten was forgiven on the condition that when it was remembered it still had to be confessed.

Under these circumstances people could never know whether they had confessed genuinely enough or whether the confessing would ever end. At the same time, people were directed to their works and told that the more genuinely they confessed, the more

73. Medieval theologians often defined contrition as sorrow for sin inspired by love of God and attrition as sorrow for sin inspired by fear of punishment.

---

m   Bernard of Clairvaux (1090–1153), *Treatise on Grace and Free Will* IV, 10 (MPL 182:1007).

ashamed they were, and the more they degraded themselves before the priest, the sooner and better they would make satisfaction for their sin. For such humility would certainly earn the grace of God."

Here, too, there was neither faith nor Christ, and the power of the absolution was not explained to them. Rather, their comfort was based on the enumeration of sins and humiliation. However, it is not possible to recount what torment, rascality, and idolatry such confession has produced.°

Satisfaction[p] is truly the most far-reaching of the three because no one could know how much should be done for a single sin, to say nothing for all sins. Now, here they found a solution, namely, they imposed minimal satisfaction that a person could surely fulfill, such as saying the Lord's Prayer five times, fasting for a day, etc. For the penance that remained, people were directed to purgatory.

Now here, as well, there was only pure misery and destitution. Some thought that they would never get out of purgatory because, according to the ancient canons, each mortal sin carried with it seven years of penance.[74] Still, confidence was also placed in our work of satisfaction, and if the satisfaction could have been perfect, confidence would have been placed totally in it, and neither faith nor Christ would have been of any use. However, such confidence[q] was impossible. Now, if they had done penance for a hundred years in this manner, they would still not have known whether they had been penitent enough. This means always doing penance but never arriving at repentance.

Now, at this point, the Holy See of Rome came to the rescue of the poor church and invented indulgences. With these the

74. Luther is making reference to the *47 canones poenitentiales,* a collection of rules for the penitential drawn from canon law and used widely in the Middle Ages.

---

n See Peter Abelard, *Ethica seu scito te ipsum,* ch. 24 (MPL 178:668), translated in *Peter Abelard's Ethics,* trans. D. E. Luscombe (Oxford: Clarendon Press, 1971), 98–101.

o The Latin translation inserts a reference to John Chrysostom's (c. 347–407) "Sermon on Penance" [MPG 49:285–87]; and idem, "Concerning St. Philogonius," Homily 6 (MPG 48:754).

p See WA 1:65–69; 98; 243–46; 319–24; 383–87; 6:548–49; LW 36:90–91; WA 6:610; 624–25; 51:487–88; LW 41:199–200.

q Luther uses the pronoun *sie* here, not a noun. The pronoun could also refer to *Genugtuung.* Hence, this sentence could also be interpreted to read: "However, the satisfaction was impossible." It is unclear to which noun Luther is referring with the pronoun, although "confidence" is the likely choice since it is the closest antecedent.

pope forgave and remitted the satisfaction, first for seven years in a particular case, and then for a hundred years, etc. He also distributed indulgences among the cardinals and bishops, so that one could grant a hundred years and another hundred days of indulgence. However, the pope reserved for himself alone the right to remit the entire satisfaction.[75]

Now since this practice began to bring in money and the market in bulls was lucrative, the pope devised the jubilee year, which offered the forgiveness for all penalties and guilt,[76] and attached it to Rome. Then the people came running, because everyone wanted to be set free from this heavy, unbearable burden. This was called "finding and digging up the treasures of the earth."[77] The pope immediately proceeded with alacrity and declared many jubilee years, one after another. However, the more money he swallowed, the wider his gullet became. Therefore, through his legates he dispatched his jubilee years across the lands, until all the churches and every home was overflowing with them.[78] Finally, he stormed into purgatory among the dead, first with Masses and the establishment of vigils, and after that, with indulgences and the jubilee year. In the end, souls became so cheap that he sprung one for a nickel.[79]

Even all of this did not help. For although the pope taught the people to rely on and trust in such indulgences, he himself once again made the process uncertain when he asserted in his bulls, "Whoever desires to partake of the indulgence or the jubilee year should be contrite, go to confession, and give money."[80] Now we have heard above that such contrition and confession are uncertain and hypocritical among them.[r] Similarly, no one knew which soul was in purgatory, and, if some were there, no one knew which had been truly contrite and had confessed. Thus, the pope took the money, comforted people with his authority and indulgence, and nevertheless directed them once again to their uncertain work.

Now, there were a few who did not consider themselves guilty of any actual sins of thought, word, and deeds, such as I and others like me, who wanted to be monks and priests in monasteries and foundations. We resisted evil thoughts with fasting, keeping vigils, praying, celebrating Masses, using rough clothing

75. Plenary, or full, indulgences were instituted in 1095 by Pope Urban II (c. 1035–1099) in connection with the first crusade.

76. Luther refers here in German to the Latin expression *remissio poenae et culpae*, which was definitely used by the mid-thirteenth century but which disappears from official papal documents after the Council of Constance (1414–17). The phrase Luther uses for "jubilee year" is *Guldenjahr* ("golden year"), which the Latin renders *auriferum annum* ("gold-producing year").

77. Cf. Dan. 11:43. In the Middle Ages, Christians used this passage to express their conviction that the devil would show the antichrist where the concealed riches of the earth were hidden so that the devil might thereby lead people astray.

78. For example, Nicholas of Cusa (1401–1464) proclaimed the jubilee of 1450 in Germany. The jubilee years were held in 1300, 1390, 1425, 1450, 1475, 1500, and 1525.

79. For vigils, see BC, SA II, 2, 12, 303. The first indulgences for the dead seem to have been offered in 1476 or 1500. Luther may be referring to the infamous verse of the indulgence preachers: "When the coin in the coffer rings, the soul from purgatory springs!"

80. By the middle of the thirteenth century, contrition and confession were regularly connected with indulgences.

r   BC, SA III, 3.

and beds, etc. With earnestness and intensity we desired to be holy. Still, while we slept, the hereditary, inborn evil was at work according to its nature (as St. Augustine[s] and St. Jerome,[t] along with others, confess). However, each one held that some of the others were so holy, as we taught, that they were without sin and full of good works. On this basis, we transferred and sold our good works, which were deemed to exceed what we needed to enter heaven, to others.[81] This really is true, and there are seals, letters, and copies available to prove it.

Such people did not need repentance, because for what did they need to be contrite, since they had not consented to evil thoughts? What did they need to confess, since they avoided evil words? For what did they need to make satisfaction, since they were, in fact, guiltless so that they could also sell their excess righteousness to other poor sinners? At the time of Christ, the Pharisees and scribes were such saints, too.[u]

At this point, the fiery angel St. John, the preacher of true repentance, comes and destroys both sides with a single thunderclap, saying, "Repent!"[v] The one side thinks: "But we have already done penance." The other thinks: "We do not need repentance." John says, "Both of you repent, for you are false penitents, and those, on the other hand, are false saints. You both need the forgiveness of sins because both of you still do not know what true sin is, not to mention that you ought to repent of it or avoid it. Not one of you is good. You are full of unbelief, stupidity, and ignorance regarding God and his will. For God is present there, in the One from whose fullness we all must receive grace upon grace and without whom no human being can be justified before God.[w] Therefore, if you want to repent, then repent in the right way. Your penance does not do it. And you hypocrites, who

81. This is a reference to works of supererogation, good deeds above and beyond those necessary for a person's salvation, especially the monastic vows of poverty, chastity, and obedience, the merits of which could be assigned to others.

---

s   See St. Augustine's *Confessions* II, 2, and X, 30 (MPL 32:674–77, 796f.; CSEL 33:29–32, 257f.; NPNF, ser. 1, 1:55f. and 153f.).

t   Jerome, Epistle 22 (to Julia Eustochium), 7 (MPL 22:398; NPNF, ser. 2, 6:25).

u   The Latin translation adds: "and hypocrites."

v   Matt. 3:2. Regarding the fiery angel, see Mal. 3:1 and Matt. 11:10.

w   John 1:16 (which Luther reads as John the Baptizer's statement; cf. John 1:29) and Gal. 2:16.

think you do not need repentance, you brood of vipers, who has assured you that you will escape the wrath to come, etc.?"[x]

St. Paul also preaches this way in Rom. 3[:10-12] and says, "No one has understanding; no one is righteous; no one heeds God; no one acts charitably, not even one; they are altogether unfit and rebellious." And in Acts 17[:30]: "However, now God commands all people everywhere to repent." (He says), "all people"—no single human being is exempted. This repentance teaches us to recognize sin, namely, that we are all lost, that nothing about us is good, and we must become absolutely new and different people.

This repentance is not fragmentary or paltry, like the kind that does penance for actual sins, nor is it uncertain like that kind. It does not debate over what is a sin or what is not a sin. Instead, it simply lumps everything together and says, "Everything is pure sin with us. What do we want to spend so much time investigating, dissecting, or distinguishing?" Therefore, contrition is also not uncertain here, because there remains nothing that we might consider a "good" with which to pay for sin. Rather, there is pure, certain despair concerning all that we are, think, say, or do, etc.

Similarly, confession also cannot be false, uncertain, or fragmentary. All who confess that everything is pure sin with them encompass all sins, omit none, and also do not forget a single one. Thus, satisfaction cannot be uncertain either, for it is not our uncertain, sinful works but rather the suffering and blood of the innocent "little Lamb of God, who bears the sin of the world" [John 1:29].[y]

John preached about this repentance and, after him, Christ in the gospel, and we, too. With this repentance, we topple the pope and everything that is built upon our good works, because it is all built upon a rotten, flimsy foundation, which is called good works or law. In fact, there is no good work there but exclusively evil works, and no one keeps the law (as Christ says in John 7[:19]), but all transgress it. Therefore the whole edifice is nothing but deceitful lies and hypocrisy, especially where it is at its holiest and most beautiful.

---

x   Matt. 3:7.
y   See also BC, SA II, 1.

This repentance endures among Christians until death because it struggles with the sin that remains in the flesh throughout life, as St. Paul bears witness in Rom. 7[:23] that he wars with the law in his members, etc., not by using his own powers but with the gift of the Holy Spirit which follows from the forgiveness of sins.[z] This same gift daily cleanses and sweeps away the sins that remain and works to make people truly pure and holy.[a]

The pope, theologians, lawyers, and all human beings know nothing about this. Rather, it is a teaching from heaven, revealed through the gospel, which must be called heresy among the godless saints.

Then again, some fanatical spirits might arise—perhaps some already are present, just as I saw for myself at the time of the revolt [82]—who maintain that all who once have received the Spirit or the forgiveness of sin or have become believers, should they sin after that, would still remain in the faith, and such sin would not harm them. They shout this: "Do what you will! If you believe, then nothing else matters. Faith blots out all sin," etc. They say, in addition, that if someone sins after receiving faith and the Spirit, then that person never really had the Spirit and faith. I have encountered many such foolish people, and I am concerned that such a devil is still present in some.

Therefore it is necessary to know and teach that when holy people—aside from the fact that they still have and feel original sin and also daily repent of it and struggle against it—somehow fall into a public sin, such as David, who fell into adultery, murder, and blasphemy against God,[b] at that point faith and the Spirit had departed. The Holy Spirit does not allow sin to rule and gain the upper hand so that it is brought to completion, but the Spirit checks and resists so that sin is not able to do whatever it wants. However, when sin does whatever it wants, then the Holy Spirit and faith are not present. As St. John says [1 John 3:9]: "Those who have been born of God do not sin and cannot sin." Nevertheless, this is also the truth (as the same St. John writes [1 John 1:8]): "If we say that we have no sin, we lie, and the truth of God[c] is not in us." [83]

This woodcut of the crucifixion of Jesus, with the Apostle John and Mary the mother of Jesus standing nearby, was included in a 1519 treatise by Luther on the worthy reception of the Eucharist.

82. Luther is recalling the Peasants' War of 1525. He often linked "fanatical spirits" to his encounters with the likes of Thomas Müntzer (c. 1489–1525) and other leaders of the rebellion.

83. BC, SA III, 3, 42–45 was added to the text by Luther as he prepared the document for publication in 1538. The emphasis here would seem to be directed against Johann Agricola (1494–1566) and the "antinomians," who taught that the law did not apply to Christians. There was a heated

---

z   Rom. 8:2.

a   See BC, SC, "The Sacrament of Baptism," 12, 360.

b   2 Samuel 11.

c   Luther adds the words "of God."

[4:] Concerning the Gospel[84]

We now want to return to the gospel[d] again, which gives counsel and help against sin in more than one way,[85] because God is extravagantly rich in his grace: first, through the spoken word, in which the forgiveness of sins is preached to the whole world, which is the proper function of the gospel; secondly, through baptism; thirdly, through the holy Sacrament of the Altar; fourthly, through the power of the keys and also through the mutual conversation and consolation of brothers and sisters.[e] Matt. 18[:20]: "where two are gathered."[86]

[5:] Concerning Baptism[87]

Baptism is nothing other than God's word in the water, commanded by God's institution, or, as Paul says, "washing by the word."[f] Moreover, Augustine says: "Let the word be added to the element, and it becomes a sacrament."[g] Therefore we do not agree with Thomas and the Dominicans who forget the word (God's institution) and say that God has placed a spiritual power in the water which washes away sin through the water. We also disagree with Scotus and the Franciscans,[88] who teach that baptism washes away sin through the assistance of the divine will, that is, that this washing takes place only through God's will and not at all through the word and the water.

---

d   WA 1:104–6; 616–17; 7:720–22; 10/1/1:668–73; 10/1/2:158–63; 12:259–60; 15:228; 18:65; LW 40:82.

e   Luther uses a Latin phrase (*per mutuum colloquium et consolationem fratrum*), which may have originated in the monastic practice of mutual confession as a way of referring to absolution by a neighbor or friend. See WA 47:297–305; 6:545–47; LW 36:85–88.

f   Eph. 5:26 is quoted according to the Latin Vulgate.

g   Luther cites from memory the Latin of Augustine's *Tractates on the Gospel of St. John* 80, 3, on John 15:3 (MPL 35:1840; NPNF, ser. 1, 7:344). Augustine's actual words were, "The Word is added to the element, and a sacrament results." The reformer refers to this statement in other contexts: BC, LC, "Concerning Baptism," 18, 458; and BC, LC, "The Sacrament of the Altar," 10, 468.

controversy over this issue among the Wittenberg theologians in the middle and late 1530s. These paragraphs were not part of the document to which Agricola subscribed in December 1536.

84. From this point forward, Luther was forced to dictate the rest of the *Smalcald Articles* because of an apparent heart attack. Caspar Cruciger Sr. recorded BC, SA III, 4–9, 319–23, and BC, SA III, 13–15, 325–26; and another, unknown secretary recorded BC, SA III, 10–12, 323–25.

85. Luther explicates three of these ways, namely, baptism, the sacrament of the altar, and the keys, in the following articles 5–9.

86. Luther cites the text in Latin as "Where two are gathered . . . ," conflating this text with Matt. 18:19.

87. The reformer explores the sacrament of baptism in various writings, including catechetical sermons. See, e.g., WA 2:727–37; LW 35:23–43; WA 6:526–43; LW 36:57–81; WA 12:38–48; LW 53:95–103; WA 37:627–72; LW 40:225–62; BC, SC, "The Sacrament of Holy Baptism," 359–62; "The Baptismal Booklet: Translated into German and Newly Revised," 371–75; BC, LC, "Concerning Baptism," 456–67.

88. John Duns Scotus, *Commentary on the Sentences* IV, d. 1, q. 2. He was followed by Franciscans like William of Occam (c. 1287–1347), *Sentences* IV, q. 1.

Concerning Infant Baptism

We maintain that we should baptize children because they also belong to the promised redemption that was brought about by Christ.[h] The church ought to extend it[i] to them.

89. The sacrament of the altar was a highly controversial issue during the sixteenth century. Luther challenged not only the Roman Church's eucharistic theology, but he also opposed Ulrich Zwingli (1484–1531) and his followers, as well as representatives of the Radical Reformation. Luther, therefore, addressed his diverse adversaries and explored this sacrament in a variety of writings. See, e.g., WA 6:353–78; LW 35:75–111; WA 6:502–26; LW 36:19–57; WA 8:482–563; LW 36:127–230; WA 10/2:11–41; LW 36:231–67; WA 18:37–214; LW 40:73–223; WA 23:64–320; LW 37:3–150; WA 26:261–509; LW 37:151–372; WA 30/2:595–626; LW 38:91–137; WA 30/3:92–171; LW 38:3–89; WA 30/3:558–65; 39/2:3–33; LW 38:235–77.

90. In Luther's rough draft of his original manuscript, he had first written "under the bread and the wine." The *Wittenberg Concord*, an agreement between the South German Protestants, especially Martin Bucer (1491–1551) and other Strasburg preachers, and the Wittenberg theologians, signed in 1536, reads, "With the bread and wine the body and blood of Christ are truly and substantially present, exhibited and received." See BC, CA X, 1, 44.

This image illustrates a Lutheran church service, in which the preacher addresses his congregation. An infant is being baptized in a font on one side and the Eucharist is being distributed on the other.

---

h   Matt. 19:14.

i   The Latin translation of the *Smalcald Articles* refers this ambiguous pronoun to both baptism and redemption.

[6:] Concerning the Sacrament of the Altar[89]

We maintain that the bread and the wine in the Supper are the true body and blood of Christ[90] and that they are not only offered to and received by upright Christians but also by evil ones.[91]

This engraving of communion being served to a communicant in both kinds illustrates a sermon by Luther on the Eucharist.

91. The *Wittenberg Concord* reads, "As Paul says that the unworthy also eat, so they [the signers] hold that, where the words and institution of Christ are retained, the body and blood of the Lord are truly offered also to the unworthy, and that the unworthy receive."

92. The 15 June 1415 decree of the Council of Constance states that "the entire body and blood of Christ is in truth contained both under the form of the bread and under the form of the wine." For Luther's analysis of the decision of the council, see WA 39/1:13–38. The doctrine of concomitance served as the Roman Church's theological justification for distributing only one of the sacramental elements to the laity. In this article Luther rejects the doctrine of concomitance and insists that Christ's institution and command must be obeyed. The laity, as well as the clergy, should, therefore, receive both sacramental elements. Other Lutheran confessional writings also insist that the sacrament be celebrated in accordance with Christ's institution. See, e.g., BC, CA, XXII, 62–64; BC, Ap, XXII, 245–47; BC, FC, Ep VII, 507; BC, FC, SD, VII, 612. The doctrine of concomitance has not been revoked by the Roman Catholic Church, although priests are permitted to serve both elements to the laity since Vatican II. See Second Vatican Council, *Sacrosanctum Concilium*. Lutherans have never adopted the doctrine of concomitance, and both elements continued to be offered during the distribution of the sacrament.

And we maintain that only one kind in the sacrament should not be distributed. Nor do we need the lofty learning which teaches us that there is as much under one kind as under both, as the sophists and the Council of Constance teach.[92] Even if it were true that there is as much under one kind as under both, one kind is still not the complete order and institution as established and commanded by Christ. We especially condemn and curse in God's name those who not only do not distribute both kinds but also tyrannically prohibit, condemn, and slander the distribution of both kinds as heresy. Thereby they set themselves against and above Christ, our Lord and God, etc.

Concerning transubstantiation, we have absolutely no regard for the subtle sophistry[93] whereby they teach that bread and wine surrender or lose their natural substance and that only the form and color of the bread remain and not real bread. For it is in closest agreement with Scripture that bread is and remains there, as St. Paul himself indicates [1 Cor. 10:16; 11:28]: "The bread that we break . . ." and, furthermore, "Eat of the bread this way . . ."

[7:] Concerning the Keys[j]

The keys are an office and authority given to the church by Christ[k] to bind and loose sins, not only the coarse and public sins but also the subtle, secret ones that only God knows, as it is written [Ps. 19:12], "But who can detect how much they err?" And Paul himself complains in Rom. 7[:23] that with his flesh he serves the "law of sin." For it is not in our power but in God's alone to judge which, how great, and how many sins there are. As it is written [Ps. 143:2]: "Do not enter into judgment with your servant, for no one living is righteous before you." And Paul also says in 1 Cor. 4[:4]: "I am not aware of anything, but I am not acquitted on that account."

[8:] Concerning Confession[94]

Because absolution or the power of the keys is also a comfort and help against sin and a bad conscience and was instituted by Christ in the gospel,[l] confession, or absolution, should by no means be allowed to fall into disuse in the church, especially for the sake of weak consciences and the wild young people, so that they may be examined and instructed in Christian teaching.

93. In *To the Christian Nobility of the German Nation Concerning the Reform of the Christian Estate* (1520) (WA 6:456; LW 44:199), Luther called transubstantiation a "delusion" [Ger.: *Wahn;* cf. LW: "opinion"] of St. Thomas and the pope. See also WA 6:508–12; LW 36:28–34; WA 10/2:202–208; 245–49; 11:441; LW 36:287–88; WA 26:437–45; LW 37:294–303 for further comments by Luther regarding transubstantiation.

94. Luther became well acquainted with the sacrament of penance and the common practice of private confession during his monastic years. He discovered, however, that the insistence on the enumeration of sins, the practice of assigning penance, and the focus on confessing rather than on the radical good news of forgiveness did not address his *Anfechtungen,* or spiritual struggles, and brought him little comfort and peace. Luther did not reject the office of the keys but encouraged confessing believers to

j   See WA 1:593–96; 2:187–94; 248–49; 714–23; LW 35:3–22; WA 6:309–12; 12:183–85; LW 40:25–28; WA 30/2:435–507; LW 40:321–77; WA 47:285–97; 50:631–32; LW 41:153–54; WA 54:249–52; LW 41:315–18.

k   Matt. 16:19; 18:18; and John 20:23.

l   See above, n. k .

In this painting by Lucas Cranach the Elder, Johannes Bugenhagen, Luther's friend, confessor, and pastor in Wittenberg, is pictured holding the keys of the kingdom.

focus on God's word of forgiveness rather than on their own confessing or on the penitential practices prescribed by the church. God's work and the radical good news of the gospel should be emphasized, not human works; then people of faith would experience comfort and peace rather than anxiety and uncertainty. See WA 6:157–69; LW 39:23–47; 6:543–49: LW 36:81–91; WA 7:351–89; LW 32:32–55; WA 8:138–85; 10/2:32–33; LW 36:258; WA 10/3:58–64; 15:481–89; 19:513–23; WA 26:507; LW 37:368; 29:136–46; 30/2:287–88; WA 30/3:166–67; LW 38:87; WA 30/3:565–70.

However, the enumeration of sins ought to be a matter of choice for each individual. Each person should be able to determine what and what not to enumerate. As long as we are in the flesh, we will not lie when we say, "I am a poor person, full of sin."[m] Rom. 7[:23] states: "I experience another law in my members, etc." Because private absolution[n] is derived from the office of the keys, it should not be despised but valued highly, just as all the other offices of the Christian church.

---

[m] 2 Esd. 7:68. This is a reference to the general confession. See BC, SC, "Baptism," 22.

[n] Luther uses a Latin phrase, *absolutio privata* (private absolution), rather than the customary *confessio privata* (private confession). See BC, LC, "A Brief Exhortation to Confession," pars. 15–17, 478.

95. As was his custom, Luther uses the German form of a technical Greek and Latin term for a person in whom the god dwells (*en-theou*), that is, a "spiritist" or spiritualist. It also became a general epithet for a heretic. In other writings, he uses the German word *Schwärmer*, that is, a fanatic or enthusiast, one who raves (cf. the English cognate, "swarm").

96. Thomas Müntzer was an early proponent of the Radical Reformation who encouraged the peasants in their uprising against the princes. He emphasized the continuing, direct revelation of the Holy Spirit and claimed the right to interpret Scripture in light of that revelation.

97. Early in his reforming career, Luther rejected various aspects of the antisemitism that characterized medieval European society (see his *That Jesus Christ Was Born a Jew* [1523], LW 45:195–229). The reformer always sought the conversion of the Jews, however, and became increasingly critical of the Jewish community when that community continued to affirm their religious heritage in spite of the proclamation of the gospel by the Evangelicals. Luther's attitude was informed by his christological interpretation of the Scriptures and his conviction that also the Hebrew Scriptures clearly point to Christ. The reformer's understanding of the First Testament is evident in his *On the Jews and Their Lies* (1543), LW 47:121–306. While they were informed by his concern about blasphemy, his recommendations contradict Luther's own convictions regarding the use of

In these matters, which concern the spoken, external word, it must be firmly maintained that God gives God's Spirit or grace to nobody except through or with the external word which goes before. We say this to protect ourselves from the Enthusiasts,[95] that is, the "spirits," who boast that they have the Spirit apart from and before contact with the word. Thereafter, they judge, interpret, and twist Scripture or the oral word according to their pleasure. Müntzer[96] did this, and there are still many doing this today, who wish to be shrewd judges between the spirit and the letter without knowing what they say or teach.[o] The papacy is also purely enthusiasm[p] in which the pope boasts that "all laws are in the shrine of his heart"[q] and what he decides and commands in his churches is supposed to be spirit and law, even when it is above or contrary to Scripture or the spoken word.[r] This is all the old devil and old snake, who also turned Adam and Eve into enthusiasts and led them from the external word of God to enthusiasm and their own presumption, and who, indeed, also accomplished this by means of other, external words. In the same way, our Enthusiasts also condemn the external word, and yet they themselves do not keep silent. Instead, they fill the world with their chattering and scribbling, as if the Spirit could not come through Scripture or the spoken word of the apostles, but the Spirit must come through their own writing and word. Why do they not also discontinue their preaching and writing until the Spirit comes into the people without and in advance of their writing? After all, they boast that the Spirit has come into them without the preaching of Scripture. There is no time here to debate these matters more extensively. We have dealt with this matter sufficiently elsewhere.[s]

For both those who believe prior to baptism and those who become believers in baptism have everything through the external word that comes first. For example, adults who have reached the age of reason must have heard previously, "The one who believes and is baptized is saved" [Mark

---

o   See BC, CA V, 4, 41, as well as WA 18:136–39; LW 40:146–49; WA 21:468–69; 36:499–506; 50:646–48; LW 41:169–72; WA 54:172–73. Cf. 2 Cor. 3:6.

p   Ger.: *Enthusiasmus,* a Greek loan word meaning possessed by the god within oneself.

q   *Corpus juris canonici, Liber Sextus* I, 2, c. 1. See also WA 6:459; LW 44:202.

r   See BC, Tr 6, 330–31.

s   See, e.g., WA 18:136–39; LW 40:146–49; WA 36:491, 497–507; LW 28:67–68, 73–82.

16:16], even though, having been without faith initially, they received the Spirit and baptism only after ten years. In Acts 10 Cornelius had for a long time heard among the Jews about a future Messiah, through whom he would be justified before God. His prayers and alms were acceptable in such faith (so Luke calls him "righteous and God-fearing" [Acts 10:2, 22]). Without such a preceding word or hearing, he could neither believe nor be righteous. However, St. Peter had to reveal to him that the Messiah (in whom he had until that time believed as the one who was to come) had now come and that his faith in the future Messiah did not hold him captive along with the hardened, unbelieving Jews. Rather, he knew that now he had to be saved by the present Messiah and not, in consort with the Jews, deny or persecute him.[97]

In short, enthusiasm clings to Adam and his children from the beginning to the end of the world, imparted to and injected int them as poison by the old dragon. It is the source, power, and might of all the heresies, including that of the papacy and Muhammad.[98] Therefore we should and must insist that God does not want to deal with us human beings, except by means of his external word and sacrament.[99] However, everything that is boasted about the Spirit apart from such a word and sacrament is of the devil. For God even desired to appear to Moses first in the burning bush and by means of the spoken word,u and no prophet, not even Elijah or Elisha, received the Spirit outside of or without the Ten Commandments. John the Baptist was not conceived without Gabriel's preceding word,v nor did he leap in his mother's womb without Mary's voice.w And St. Peter says that the prophets did not prophesy "by human will" but "by the Holy Spirit," yet, as "holy people of God."x However, without the external word they were not holy, much less would the Holy Spirit have moved them to speak while they were still unholy. Peter says they were holy because the Holy Spirit speaks through them.[100]

force in matters of faith and conscience and have rightfully been renounced by the reformer's theological heirs. Christian perspectives regarding the conversion of Jews have also changed significantly in light of contemporary understandings of Romans 9–11. This treatise also includes a series of recommendations to temporal and spiritual authorities regarding the treatment of the Jews. See Brooks Schramm and Kirsi Stjerna, eds., *Martin Luther, the Bible, and the Jewish People* (Minneapolis: Fortress Press, 2012).

98. Luther, like most Christians of his day, viewed Muhammad as guilty of a christological heresy.

99. This persistent emphasis of Luther does not only reflect his concern with enthusiasm and the related claim of the direct inspiration of the Holy Spirit, a concern heightened particularly by his experiences with representatives of the Radical Reformation, but it is also indicative of his insistence that the Holy Spirit works through means, particularly the means of grace, namely, the word and the sacraments.

100. The previous italicized section is only included in the printed versions of the *Smalcald Articles* but do not appear in Luther's handwritten notes.

---

t   Ger.: *gestiftet und gegiftet.*

u   Exod. 3:2-6.

v   Luke 1:13-20.

w   Luke 1:41-44.

x   2 Pet. 1:21 according to the alternate reading in the NRSV.

[9:] Concerning Excommunication[y]

We maintain that the "great" excommunication, as the pope calls it, is a purely secular penalty and does not concern us who serve the church. However, the "small," that is, the truly Christian excommunication, is that public, obstinate sinners should not be admitted to the sacrament or other fellowship in the church until they improve their behavior and avoid sin. The preachers should not mix civil punishment together with this spiritual penalty or excommunication.[101]

[10:] Concerning Ordination and Vocation[102]

If the bishops desired to be true bishops and to attend to the church and the gospel, then one might, for the sake of love and unity but not out of necessity, give them leave to ordain and confirm us and our preachers, provided all the pretense and fraud of unchristian ceremony and pomp were set aside. However, they are not now and do not want to be true bishops. Rather, they are political lords and princes who do not want to preach, teach, baptize, commune, or perform any work or office of the church. In addition, they persecute and condemn those who, being called, exercise such an office. Despite this, the church must not remain without servants on their account.

Therefore, as the ancient examples of the church and the theologians[103] teach us, we intend and should ordain suitable persons to this office ourselves.[104] They may not forbid this or prevent us to do so, even according to their own law, because their laws say that those who are also ordained by heretics should be regarded as ordained and remain ordained.[z] Similarly, St. Jerome writes about the church at Alexandria that it had originally been ruled by the priests and preachers together, without bishops.[a]

101. The *excommunicatio major* excluded a person from both the church and political communities, while the *excommunicatio minor* only prevented a person from receiving the sacrament.

102. Luther uses a latinized German word, *Vokation,* which refers to an ecclesiastical vocation or call. For further discussion of ordination see, e.g., WA 6:56–67; LW 36:106–17; WA 10/2:220–21; 12:169–96; LW 40:3–44; WA 38:236–56; LW 38:194–214; WA 50:632–41; LW 41:154–64.

103. Luther uses the term *Väter,* or *fathers,* which is the traditional term used to refer to the chief theologians of the early church.

104. The first ordination conducted by the Wittenberg reformers in Wittenberg took place on 20 October 1535. Luther essentially viewed ordination as the public confirmation of the call. See WA 38:238; LW 38:197.

---

y   See also WA 1:638–43; 6:63–75; LW 39:3–22; WA 6:445; LW 44:181–82; WA 7:126–27; 404–22; LW 32:66–76; WA 26:233–35; LW 40:311–13; WA 30/2:250; 309–19; LW 34:32–38; WA 30/2:501–7; LW 40:369–77; WA 47:279–97.

z   Gratian, *Decretum* I, dist. 68, ch. 1; III, dist. 4, ch. 107.

a   See n. 53, p. 441 for the references.

[11:] Concerning the Marriage of Priests[105]

They have had neither the authority nor the right to forbid marriage and burden the divine estate of priests with perpetual celibacy. Instead, they have acted like anti-Christian, tyrannical, wicked scoundrels and thereby have given occasion for all kinds of horrible, abominable, and countless sins of unchastity, in which they are still mired. Now, as little as the power has been given to us or to them to make a female out of a male or a male out of a female[b] or to abolish gender distinctions altogether, so little did they have the power to separate such creatures of God or to forbid them from living together honorably in marriage. Therefore we are unwilling to consent to their miserable celibacy, nor will we tolerate it. Rather, we want marriage to be free, as God ordered and instituted it. We do not want to tear apart or inhibit God's work, for St. Paul says that would be "a demonic teaching."[c]

[12:] Concerning the Church[106]

We do not concede to them that they are the church, and they are also not the church. We also do not want to hear what they command or forbid in the name of the church, because, God be praised, a seven-year-old child[107] knows what the church is, namely, holy believers and "the little sheep who hear the voice of their shepherd,"[d] for children pray in this way: "I believe in one holy Christian church."[108] This holiness does not consist of surplices, tonsures, long albs, or other ceremonies of theirs that they have invented over and above the Holy Scriptures. Its holiness exists in the word of God and true faith.

105. For further discussion of clerical marriage see, e.g., WA 6:440–43; LW 44:175–79; WA 7:674–78; LW 39:206–15; WA 10/2:126–31, 149–53, 156–57; LW 39:266–68, 289–94, 296–98; WA 12:92–142; 30/2:323–40; LW 34:40–49; WA 50:634–41; LW 41:156–64.

106. For additional insights into Luther's doctrine of the church, see WA 6:292–301; LW 39:64–75; WA 18:649–51; LW 33:85–88; WA 47:772–79; LW 51:301–12; WA 50:624–53: LW 41:143–78; WA 51:469–572: LW 41:179–256.

107. This was the age by which a child had learned the Apostles' Creed, which Luther sometimes called the Children's Creed (see WA 50:624; LW 41:143). It was also traditionally considered to be the age of discernment or of reason.

108. Luther quotes from a German translation of the Creed that had been in use in Germany since the fifteenth century. See also BC, SC, "The Creed," 3, 355; and BC, LC, "The Creed," 3, 435.

---

b   Luther uses the diminuatives *Männlin* and *Fräulin*.

c   1 Tim. 4:1.

d   Cf. John 10:3.

[13:] How a Person Is Justified and Concerning Good Works[e]

I cannot change at all what I have consistently taught about this until now, namely, that "through faith" (as St. Peter says)[f] we receive a different, new, clean heart and that, for the sake of Christ our mediator, God desires to regard us and does regard us as completely righteous and holy. Although sin in the flesh is still not completely gone or dead, God will nevertheless not count it or consider it.

Good works follow such faith, renewal, and forgiveness of sin, and whatever in these works is still sinful or deficient should not even be counted as sin or deficiency, precisely for the sake of this same Christ. Instead, the human being should be called and should be completely righteous and holy both according to the person and his or her works, by the pure grace and mercy that have been poured and spread over us in Christ. Therefore we cannot boast about the great merit of our works, when they are viewed apart from grace and mercy. Rather, as it is written, "Let the one who boasts, boast in the Lord" [1 Cor. 1:31; 2 Cor. 10:17], that is, if one has a gracious God, then everything is good. Furthermore, we also say that when good works do not follow, then faith is false and not true.

This engraving illustrates the blessing of a new bell for a church. The bishop makes seven crosses with his right hand on the outside of the bell using holy oil.

---

e   See particularly Luther's lectures on Romans and Galatians, WA 2:443–618; WA 40/1:33–40/2:184; LW 26 and 27; WA 56:1–528; LW 25. See also WA 2:145–52; LW 31:293–306; WA 6:202–76; LW 44:15–114; WA 7:20–73; LW 31:327–77; WA 39/1:82–126; LW 34:145–96.

f   See Acts 15:9.

[14:] Concerning Monastic Vows[g]

Because monastic vows are in direct conflict with the first and chief article,[h] they should simply be done away with. It is about these that Christ speaks in Matt. 24[:5]: "I am Christ ... ,"[i] for those who vow to live a monastic life believe that they lead a better life than the ordinary Christian, and through their works they intend to help not only themselves but others get to heaven. This is to deny Christ, etc. They boast, on the basis of their St. Thomas, that monastic vows are equal to baptism.[109] This is blasphemy against God.[110]

[15:] Concerning Human Regulations[j]

That the papists say human regulations help attain the forgiveness of sins or merit salvation is unchristian and damnable. As Christ says [Matt. 15:9], "In vain do they worship me, because they teach such doctrines that are nothing but human precepts." Furthermore, the letter to Titus [1:14] mentions "those who reject the truth." Furthermore, it is also not right when they say that it is a mortal sin to break such regulations.

These are the articles on which I must stand and on which I intend to stand, God willing, until my death. I can neither change nor concede anything in them. If anyone desires to do so, it is on that person's conscience.

Finally, there still remains the papal bag of tricks, filled with foolish, childish articles such as the consecration of churches, baptizing bells, baptizing altar stones, and inviting to the rites the "godparents" who give money for these things. This baptizing is a mockery and ridicule of Holy Baptism and ought not be tolerated.[111]

109. Thomas Aquinas, *STh* II, 2, q. 189, a. 3, ad. 3, and BC, CA XXVI, 49–50. See also WA 38:148–58.

110. The last sentence of BC, SA III, 14 was written into the text of the original manuscript by Luther himself.

111. Bishops or suffragan bishops consecrated churches, bells, and altars. When bells were "baptized," they were typically assigned the name of a saint, and the witnesses, who were often numerous and considered to be sponsors, were expected to give baptismal gifts to the church and its priests. See WA 30/2:254–55, 347–48; LW 34:54.

g   For additional discussions of monastic vows, see, e.g., WA 2:735–36; LW 35:40–42; WA 6:440–43; LW 44:175–79; WA 6:538–43; LW 36:74–81; WA 8:323–35; 573–669; LW 44:243–400; WA 10/1/1:481–99; 681–709; 19:287–93.

h   BC, SA II, 1.

i   This is an alternate reading in NRSV.

j   See also WA 30/3:91, 168; LW 38:88.

112. On Holy Saturday the "old fire" was extinguished in the church by the priest, and the "new fire" was lit and sprinkled with holy water. At the Easter Vigil the Easter candle was consecrated and lit from this "new fire." On Candlemas (2 February), candles were consecrated. On Palm Sunday, palms were consecrated. On the Assumption of Mary (15 August), herbs, flowers, ears of corn, honey, grapevines, etc., were consecrated. On St. Stephen's Day (26 December), oats were consecrated. On Easter Sunday, unleavened Easter cakes were consecrated.

113. The three last paragraphs of the *Smalcald Articles* form a conclusion of sorts to the entire document. Both the original publication of 1538 and the *Book of Concord* begin this section with a separate ornamental initial.

114. Philip Melanchthon began to spell his name "Melanthon" in 1531.

115. These first eight subscriptions to SA were obtained during a gathering of theologians at Wittenberg in December 1536.

Moreover, there is the consecration of candles, palms, spices, oats, flat cakes, etc.,[112] which surely cannot be called consecration, nor is it. Rather, they are pure mockery and deception. As far as these innumerable magic tricks go, which we entrust to their god and to them for adoration until they become tired of them, we do not wish to be bothered with these things.[113]

Subscriptions to the Smalcald Articles

Dr. Martin Luther subscribes

Dr. Justus Jonas, rector, subscribes with his own hand

Dr. Johannes Bugenhagen of Pomerania subscribes

Dr. Caspar Cruciger subscribes

Nicholas Amsdorf of Magdeburg subscribes

Georg Spalatin of Altenburg subscribes

I, Philip [Philippus] Melanthon,[114] also regard the above articles as true and Christian. However, concerning the pope I maintain that if he would allow the gospel, we, too, may, for the sake of peace and general unity among those Christians who are now under him and might be in the future, grant to him his superiority over the bishops which he has "by human right."[k]

Johann Agricola of Eisleben subscribes[115]

Gabriel Zwilling subscribes

I, Dr. Urban Rhegius, superintendent of the churches in the duchy of Lüneburg, subscribe for myself and in the name of my brothers and in the name of the church of Hanover

I, Stephan Agricola, as minister in Hof, subscribe

And I, Joannes Draconites, professor and minister of Marburg, subscribe

I, Conrad Figenbotz, subscribe to the glory of God that I have believed and now preach and believe firmly as above

I, Andreas Osiander, minister of Nuremberg, subscribe

Master Veit Dietrich, minister of Nuremberg

I, Erhard Schnepf, preacher of Stuttgart, subscribe

Conrad Oettinger of Pforzheim, preacher of Duke Ulrich [of Württemberg]

---

k The phrase "by human right" is rendered in Latin (*iure humano*). See BC, CA XXVIII, 29, 94.

Simon Schneeweiss, pastor of the church in Crailsheim

I, Johannes Schlaginhaufen, pastor of the church of Köthen, subscribe

Master George Helt of Forchheim

Master Adam [Krafft] of Fulda, preacher of Hesse

Master Anton Corvinus

I, Johannes Bugenhagen, subscribe again in the name of Master Johannes Brenz, who, when leaving Smalcald, directed me both orally and in a letter,[116] which was shown to these brothers, who have subscribed, to do so

I, Dennis Melander, subscribe to the Augsburg Confession, the Apology, and the Wittenberg Concord on the subject of the Eucharist

Paul von Rhode, superintendent of Stettin

Gerhard Oemcken, superintendent of the church of Minden

I, Brixius Northanus, minister of the church of Christ in Soest, subscribe to the articles of the Reverend Father Martin Luther and confess that until now I have believed and taught this and, by the Spirit of Christ, will in like manner believe and teach

Michael Coelius, preacher of Mansfeld, subscribes

Master Peter Geltner, preacher in Frankfurt [am Main], subscribes

Wendell Faber, pastor of Seeburg in Mansfeld

I, Johannes Aepinus, subscribe

Likewise, I, Johannes [Timann] from Amsterdam of Bremen

I, Fredrich Myconius, pastor of the church of Gotha in Thuringia, subscribe for myself and in the name of Justus Menius of Eisenach

I, Johannes Lang, doctor and preacher of the church in Erfurt, in my name and on behalf of my coworkers in the gospel, namely,[117]

The Rev. Licentiate Louis Platz of Melsungen

The Rev. Master Sigmund Kirchner

The Rev. Wolfgang Kiswetter

The Rev. Melchior Weittmann

The Rev. Johannes Thall

The Rev. Johannes Kilian

The Rev. Nicholas Faber

I, The Rev. Andreas Menser, subscribe in my own hand

And I, Egidius Melcher, have subscribed with my own hand

116. Brenz's note to Bugenhagen, dated 23 February 1537, reads in part: "I have read and reread again and again the Confession and Apology presented at Augsburg . . . the Formula of Concord concerning the sacrament, made at Wittenberg with Dr. Bucer and others . . . the *Articles* written at the Assembly at Smalcald in the German language by Dr. Martin Luther . . . and the tract concerning the Papacy and the Power and Jurisdiction of Bishops. . . . I judge that all these agree with Holy Scripture, and with the belief of the true and pure catholic church. . . . I ask you . . . Dr. Johannes Bugenhagen . . . that your excellency add my name, if it be necessary, to all the others. . . ."

117. The final ten subscriptions were obtained in March 1537, when Luther and his entourage stopped in Erfurt on their way back to Wittenberg from Smalcald.

Excursus: Subscribers to the Smalcald Articles

Martin Luther (1483–1546)

Justus Jonas (1493–1555) earned doctorates in canon law (1518) and theology (1521) and taught both disciplines at the University of Wittenberg. He became a close colleague and supporter of Luther and made important contributions to the Reformation movement, particularly as a translator of Luther's and Melanchthon's works; as a theological adviser at imperial diets, including the Diet of Augsburg; as a participant in church visitations; and as a writer of church orders and theological works. He also served as superintendent in Halle, where he played a crucial role in the organization of the Reformation.

Johannes Bugenhagen (1485–1558) joined the Reformation movement in 1521 and became Luther's pastor, colleague, and supporter. He was called as pastor of St. Mary's congregation in Wittenberg in 1523, after his marriage to Walpurga, whose family name may have been Rörer, in 1522. He served this congregation for the remainder of his life, lectured at the university, and joined the theological faculty officially after he was awarded the doctorate in 1533. He is particularly known as the organizer of the Evangelical churches in northern Germany and Denmark, providing crucial leadership in a variety of cities and territories and preparing church orders. He also published numerous biblical commentaries and theological treatises in which he focused particularly on the doctrine of justification, the relationship of faith and works, and sacramental theology.

Caspar Cruciger (1504–1548) studied at the Universities of Leipzig and Wittenberg. He became a professor at the latter, teaching philosophy. After earning his doctorate in 1533, he also lectured in theology. In addition to assisting in the translation of the Bible, he also recorded and published many of Luther's sermons, and, together with Georg Rörer (1492–1557), helped prepare the Wittenberg edition of Luther's works. He also served as preacher of the castle church in Wittenberg, participated in theological convocations, and contributed to the establishment of the Reformation in Leipzig.

Nicholas von Amsdorf (1483–1565) studied at the University of Wittenberg; served as a canon and professor in Wittenberg; and became an early supporter of Luther, whom he accompanied to the Diet of Worms. He was pastor and superintendent of Magdeburg from 1524 to 1541 and contributed significantly to the success of the Reformation in this episcopal city. In 1542 Elector John Frederick (1503–1554) appointed him bishop of Naumburg-Zeitz. After losing his episcopal see as a result of the Smalcaldic War, he became a leader of the Gnesio-Lutherans and participated in various intra-Lutheran controversies as an ardent defender of what he considered to be faithful Lutheranism. In this role, he also encouraged the estab-

lishment of the University of Jena and supported the publication of the Jena edition of Luther's works.

Georg (Burkhardt) Spalatin (1484–1545) changed his name to reflect his birthplace, Spalt, near Nürnberg. Educated at Erfurt and Wittenberg, he earned the M.A. at the latter institution in 1503. He was ordained in 1508 but was appointed as tutor of the children of Elector Frederick of Saxony (1463–1525). His responsibilities were quickly expanded, and he served the elector both in a pastoral and secretarial role. He also befriended Martin Luther and became the primary intermediary between the reformer and his prince, providing helpful advice to both men, fostering the Reformation cause, and encouraging the Elector to support Luther. He continued to serve the electors of Saxony, even after leaving Wittenberg and becoming superintendent of Altenburg. His diplomatic skill, legal expertise, and theological commitments enabled him to make valuable contributions to the Reformation as a participant in various imperial diets and meetings of the Smalcaldic League.

Philip Melanchthon (1497–1560), who began spelling his name "Melanthon" in 1531, was Luther's most important and influential Wittenberg colleague. Trained as a humanist scholar of Greek at the universities of Heidelberg and Tübingen, he was appointed to the Wittenberg faculty in 1518 and quickly emerged as an incisive theologian and brilliant ally of Luther. He was the systematizer of Luther's thought, particularly in his *Loci communes*; an able, though reluctant, theological diplomat; a writer of confessional documents; a creative and independent evangelical theologian; and a reformer of university education. He was also an irenic personality, eager to promote unity within the church and to resolve the theological conflicts that divided Western Christianity during the sixteenth century. Hence, he sought to distinguish what is of the essence and what are adiaphora, to promote diligent theological negotiation, and to manifest a spirit of compromise. During the last decades of his life, in particular, he was accused of betraying Luther's heritage, especially with regard to the doctrine of justification and the sacramental presence of Christ.

Johann Agricola (1494–1566) studied in Wittenberg, was befriended by Luther, and taught at the university from 1519 to 1525 and again from 1536 to 1540. After a short ministry in Frankfurt, he served as teacher and preacher in his home town of Eisleben. During the 1520s and 1530s Agricola came into conflict with both Luther and Melanchthon because of his antinomian stance. He,

therefore, eventually moved to Berlin where he was appointed court preacher and general superintendent. Both his antinomianism and his contributions to the writing of the Augsburg Interim in 1548 alienated him from most fellow Lutherans.

Gabriel Zwilling (c. 1487–1558), who signed the SA as Gabriel Didymus in January 1537, was Luther's former Augustinian brother in the Wittenberg monastery. During Luther's stay at the Wartburg after his condemnation at the Diet of Worms, Zwilling was one of the first friars to leave the monastery and emerged as one of the promoters of the radical reforms that inspired Luther to return to Wittenberg in March 1522. Influenced by Luther, Zwilling regretted his radicalism and reconciled with the reformer. He served most of his ministry as preacher, pastor, and eventually as superintendent in Torgau, where he ministered from 1523 until 1549. He was removed from his office in the latter year by Elector Maurice of Saxony (1521–1553) because of his opposition to the Leipzig Interim.[1] During his years of service, Zwilling gained a particular reputation as a fine preacher.

---

1 After the Lutherans lost the Schmalkaldic War to Emperor Charles V, he issued the Augsburg Interim, which was to settle the religious conflict until the Council of Trent decided all pertinent theological debates. The Augsburg Interim insisted that the Lutheran communities submit to the Bishop of Rome and accept the theology of the church. The Lutherans were given only a few concessions. The new Elector of Saxony, Maurice, realized that the Augsburg Interim could never be enforced in Elector Saxony. He, therefore, requested that Philip Melanchthon produce an alternative interim agreement. This is known as the Leipzig Interim. Melanchthon believed that he conceded to the Emperor and the Church of Rome what he considered to be adiaphora while preserving the essentials of the evangelical tradition, particularly the doctrine of justification. A controversy broke out among the Lutherans regarding the compromises contained in the Leipzig Interim.

Urbanus Rhegius (1489–1541) studied at the universities of Freiburg, Ingolstadt, and Baselm, earning the doctorate at the latter in 1520. Ordained as priest in 1519, he became cathedral preacher in Augsburg in 1520. While he initially read Luther with the intention of opposing his theological perspectives, his study of the reformer's writings inspired him to become an advocate of evangelical reform in Augsburg. His writing and preaching resulted in his expulsion from the city in 1521, but he returned in 1524, married Anna Weisbrucker (dates unknown) in 1525, and served in Augsburg until 1530. During his time in Augsburg, he provided consistent leadership to the reform movement, even as he opposed more radical expressions of reform, especially during the Peasants' War. During the Diet of Augsburg, Rhegius participated in the theological discussions among the Lutherans that led to the formulation of the *Augsburg Confession*. Shortly after the diet, he accepted the invitation of Duke Ernst of Braunschweig-Lüneburg (1497–1546) to become pastor in Celle, where he began his ministry in September 1530, and was appointed superintendent of the duchy in 1531. In the following years, he was the primary organizer and leader of the Reformation in Celle and in the territory of Lüneburg. He also served as adviser and proponent of the reform movement in various other parts of northern Germany.

Stephen Agricola (1494–1547), also known as Stephan Castenpauer, was an Augustinian friar who allied himself with Luther by 1522 and served as a preacher in Augsburg. He participated in the Marburg Colloquy in 1529 and signed the *Marburg Articles*. After returning to Augsburg, he ardently opposed Zwinglian influences in the city. In 1531 he was appointed pastor in Hof and thereafter in Sulzbach (1542) and Eisleben (1546).

Johannes Draconites (1494–1566), or Johannes Drach, received a humanistic training at the University of Erfurt, where he earned the M.A. degree in 1514. Attracted by Luther's reforms, he was awarded a doctorate at Wittenberg in 1523 with an emphasis on Hebrew studies, served in several parishes, and then became professor and pastor in Marburg in 1534. After four years in Lübeck, he was appointed professor at the University of Rostock in 1551 and also assumed the responsibilities of superintendent in 1557. Three years later he became president of the Prussian bishopric of Pomesanien but was removed from this office in 1564 because of prolonged absences in Wittenberg, where he worked on an Old Testament polyglot.

Conrad Fiegenbotz, whose dates are unknown, served as pastor in the north German cities of Halberstadt, Goslar, and Zerbst, and was apparently the representative of the pastors in Zerbst at the meeting during which the *Smalcald Articles* were discussed.

Andreas Osiander (1498–1552) was a leader of the Reformation in Nürnberg, where he served the St. Lawrence church from 1522 to 1548. He was present at the Marburg Colloquy and at the Diet of Augsburg and emerged as a creative Evangelical theologian. He particularly challenged the forensic understanding of justification, especially while he served as professor at the University of Königsberg from 1549 to 1552. As a result, he inspired an intense theological conflict in the city and the university and was also opposed by the Wittenberg theologians, especially Melanchthon and Bugenhagen. The Osiandrian controversy is addressed in the *Book of Concord*, FC, Ep 3 and FC, SD 3.

Veit Dietrich (1506–1549) was a native of Nürnberg who studied at the University of Wittenberg, where he earned the M.A. degree in 1529. He was befriended by Luther, whom he accompanied to the Marburg Colloquy and to Coburg, where Luther resided during the Diet of Augsburg. Dietrich recorded many of Luther's table talks and published his notes of Luther's lectures, sometimes without the reformer's permission. He is also responsible for the publication of Luther's *Hauspostille* or "house postil" of 1530–34. Dietrich returned to Nürnberg in 1535 as preacher at St. Sebald parish and served as a leader of the Lutheran movement in the city. As such, he also promoted the Reformation in other parts of south Germany and ardently opposed the Augsburg and Leipzig Interims.

Erhard Schnepf (1495–1558) was a persistent proponent of the Lutheran Reformation in southwestern Germany, particularly in Württemberg while he

served as pastor in Stuttgart from 1534 to 1544 and as professor at the University of Tübingen from 1544 to 1548. Prior to earning his doctorate at Tübingen in 1544, he had received the M.A. degree in 1513 and the bachelor's degree in theology in 1518 from the University of Heidelberg. He also taught at Marburg from 1527 to 1534 and at Jena from 1549 to 1558. As professor and as superintendent in Jena, he joined the Gnesio-Lutheran party and opposed Philip Melanchthon and the Philippists during the intra-Lutheran theological conflicts of the mid-sixteenth century.

Conrad Oettinger, dates unknown, served as court preacher of Margrave Philip of Hesse (1504–1567) and of Duke **Ulrich of Württemberg** (1487–1550).

Simon Schneeweiss, dates unknown, was court preacher of Margrave George of Brandenburg (1484–1543) and, after 1534, pastor in Crailsheim in Württemberg.

Johannes Schlaginhaufen, dates unknown, was pastor and eventually superintendent in Köthen, a town near Halle.

George Helt, dates unknown, earned the M.A. at the University of Leipzig in 1505 and served as an educator in the territory of Anhalt as well as counselor of Prince George III (1507–1553) of Anhalt.

Adam Krafft (1493–1558) studied at Erfurt, where he was trained as a humanist and earned the M.A. degree in

1519. After becoming acquainted with Luther's theology and joining the reform movement, he served as preacher in Fulda from 1521 to 1525, as court preacher of Margrave Philip of Hesse in 1525, and as superintendent in Marburg beginning in 1526. In those positions he worked diligently to implement the Reformation throughout Hesse. While he functioned as superintendent and general visitor in Hesse, he also assumed a professorship at the newly established University of Marburg in 1527 and taught until 1558.

Anton Corvinus (1501–1553), also known as Anton Rabe, joined the Cistercian Order in 1519 but was attracted to the Reformation through the writings of Luther and was expelled from his monastery in Riddagshausen in 1523. After serving in two parishes, he earned the M.A. degree at Marburg in 1536 and subsequently fostered the implementation of evangelical reforms in various areas of northern Germany, including Braunschweig and Hildesheim, where he assisted Bugenhagen. He is particularly known as the reformer of the duchy of Calenberg-Göttingen and served as superintendent, supervised a visitation, and produced a church order in this region. Because of his opposition to the Augsburg Interim he was imprisoned for almost three years.

Johannes Brenz (1499–1570) was the most influential Lutheran reformer of Württemberg and a persistent opponent of Zwinglian and Calvinist influences in southwestern Germany. Having studied

at Heidelberg, he became a follower of Luther after attending the Heidelberg Disputation in April 1518. As pastor in Schwäbisch Hall, beginning in 1522, he introduced the Reformation in this city. Duke Ulrich (1487–1550) and his successor, Duke Christoph (1515–1568), encouraged him to carry out the reform of the duchy of Württemberg, and he did so ably and successfully after 1534. Brenz was also an important Lutheran theologian who was an able defender of Lutheran eucharistic theology, an author of biblical commentaries, and a writer of confessional documents.

Dennis Melander (c. 1486–1561) joined the Dominican Order in 1505 and spent his first years of ministry as an itinerant preacher in southwestern Germany. The impetus that inspired Melander to join the Reformation did not come from Luther but from Ulrich Zwingli (1484–1531), Johannes Oecolampadius (1482–1531), Martin Bucer (1491–1551), and Wolfgang Capito (1478–1541). Nevertheless, his ministry was carried out among Lutherans. His first position was in Frankfurt, where he served as pastor from 1525 to 1535. During that time, he opposed the Roman clergy, abolished the Mass, and also supported the destruction of images. Although he was criticized for a lack of learning and because of his support of iconoclasm, he was, nevertheless, appointed as court preacher and as a pastor in Cassel by Margrave Philip of Hesse, who appreciated his abilities as a preacher. In signing the *Smalcald Articles*, Melander specifically confirmed his agreement with the sacramental teachings of the *Augsburg Confession*, the *Apology*, and the *Wittenberg Concord*.

Paul von Rhode (1489–1563) earned the M.A. degree at the University of Wittenberg in 1520. With Luther's commendation, he was called as pastor to Stettin, possibly in 1523. He preached wherever he could and promoted the Reformation movement, although political realities and the opposition of the supporters of Rome prevented a specific ecclesiastical appointment until 1535, when he officially became pastor of St. Jacob congregation and, at the suggestion of Bugenhagen, one of three superintendents appointed for Pomerania. In this supervisory role, von Rhode provided leadership in the revision of the liturgy, the visitation of the churches, the appointment of pastors, and the resolution of theological conflicts. His contributions to the introduction and establishment of the Lutheran church in Pomerania were, therefore, diverse and formative.

Gerhard Oemcken (c. 1485–1562) served parishes in Lemgo and Soest and as superintendent in Minden and Güstrow in northwestern and northern Germany.

Brixius Northanus (?–1557), or Brixius thon Norde, served a number of parishes as a Lutheran pastor for short periods of time, but was compelled to move consistently because of his opposition to Rome and to the Radical Reformers. His ministry in Soest, where he was pastor

and superintendent from 1534 to 1548, was a lengthy one, however. He was also a pastor in Lübeck.

Michael Coelius (1492–1559) studied in Leipzig and was active in a variety of contexts, both as a teacher and pastor. After the Leipzig Debate, where he was present, he became interested in Luther and spent time in Wittenberg. Luther recommended him as court preacher to Count Albert of Mansfeld (1480–1560), and he served in that capacity after 1525. In 1548 he also became city pastor of Mansfeld. He remained a steadfast defender of Luther's theology in the reformer's home region, opposed both the Augsburg and Leipzig Interims, and tended in the direction of Gnesio-Lutheranism.

Peter Geltner (?–1572) was a pastor in Erfurt and Frankfurt.

Wendell Faber, dates unknown, was a teacher in Eisleben and then served as court preacher of Count Gebhard of Mansfeld (1478–1558) in Seeburg. He was also an opponent of Johann Agricola during the antinomian controversy.

Johannes Aepinus (1499–1553), also known as John Hoeck, became a follower of Luther during his student days at Wittenberg. He served as rector of a school in Stralsund, Pomerania, where he also produced a church order for the city. In 1529 he became pastor of St. Peter in Hamburg, and in 1532 he assumed the responsibilities of superintendent as well as pastor of the cathedral. A year later he was awarded the doctorate at the University of Wittenberg. In 1534 he traveled to England in order to support the reform movement and advised King Henry VIII (1491-1547) regarding the annulment of his marriage to Catherine of Aragon (1485-1536). He returned to Hamburg and initiated a theological conflict regarding Christ's descent into hell, which Aepinus interpreted as part of Christ's passion. The conflict was addressed in the *Book of Concord*, FC, Ep IX and FC, SD IX. Aepinus had originally subscribed to the SA thusly: "John Aepinus of Hamburg subscribes; concerning the superiority of the pontiff, he agrees, with all the representatives from Hamburg, to the opinions of Reverend Philip, which were added at the end." He then crossed this out and signed without reservation.

Johannes Timann (?-1557), who signed the *Smalcald Articles* as Ionnes Amsterdamus, hailed from Amsterdam and was a leading reformer of Bremen. He left his home after Emperor Karl V (1500-1558) permitted the persecution of reform-minded people in the Netherlands and spent time in Wittenberg. In 1524 he began a long ministry in Bremen as pastor of St. Martin and as a leader of the Reformation in the city. Among his diverse accomplishments is the production of a church order in 1534, which he modeled after Bugenhagen's church orders. He also represented Bremen in various convocations, including the meeting at Smalcald when he signed the *Smalcald Articles*. He remained an ardent Lutheran throughout his ministry, opposing the Augsburg Interim and defending the real presence and the doctrine of ubiquity against the challenges of theologians impacted by Swiss sacramental theology.

Frederick Myconius (1490-1546), or Mecum, became a Franciscan friar in 1510 and was ordained in 1516. He was attracted by the emerging reform movement and became a good friend of Luther. As pastor in Gotha, where he began his ministry in 1524, he married Margaret Jäcken (dates unkown) and introduced the Reformation. From his base in Gotha, where he was also appointed superintendent, he assisted in the reform of churches and educational institutions throughout Thuringia and was also part of a Lutheran delegation to England in 1538 that hoped to convince Henry VIII to accept the *Augsburg Confession*. His *Historia reformationis* included many of his own experiences during the initial decades of the Reformation.

Justus Menius (1499-1558) studied at Erfurt, where he earned the M.A. in 1516, and at Wittenberg. He began his ministry at St. Thomas church in Erfurt in 1525 and participated in the Saxon visitation of 1528-29. In 1529 he was appointed pastor and superintendent in Eisenach and worked to establish the reform movement in various parts of Saxony. He was a persistent opponent of the Radical Reformers, whom he also addressed in writings. In 1546 he also became superintendent of Gotha. He rejected both the Augsburg and Leipzig Interims but remained an ally of Melanchthon in the conflicts between the Philippists and the Gnesio-Lutherans.

As a result of those conflicts, he left Eisenach in 1552 and Gotha in 1556 and spent his last years as pastor of the St. Thomas church in Leipzig. During this time he also carried out a literary dispute with Matthias Flacius Illyricus (1520–1575), the chief spokesperson of the Gnesio-Lutherans. Menius was present in Smalcald, but he could not sign the *Smalcald Articles* personally because he had to leave the meeting before the signatures were appended.

Johannes Lang (c. 1487–1548) was a close friend of Luther with whom he became acquainted as a fellow Augustinian friar in Erfurt and Wittenberg. He studied in Erfurt but went to Wittenberg with Luther and began to teach at the university in 1512. After returning to Erfurt in 1516, he earned the doctorate there in 1519. Although he was promoted to leadership positions within his Augustinian Order, he decided to leave the community and marry in 1522. As he labored on behalf of the Reformation in Erfurt and continued to face the opposition of those loyal to Rome, he also opposed more radical expressions of reform. Except for his publications, his sphere of activity was limited to Erfurt, and he deserves to be recognized as the leading reformer of the city.

Ludwig Platz (?–1547), also known as Placenta, earned the M.A. degree at Erfurt in 1504 and taught there until 1536, serving both as rector and as dean of the philosophical faculty. He did not join the Reformation movement until about 1530 and then decided to serve as preacher in Walschleben, near Erfurt, beginning in 1536.

Sigmund Kirchner (1480–1561) studied at Erfurt and then served as pastor of the St. Thomas and the Merchants' congregations in the city after 1528.

Wolfgang Kiswetter, dates unknown, studied in Leipzig and Erfurt and was a pastor in the latter.

Melchior Weittmann, dates unknown, was an Augustinian friar in Erfurt. After leaving monastic life, he served as the first Lutheran pastor of St. Andrew in Erfurt, beginning in 1525.

Johannis Thall (?–1550) was pastor of the Merchants' church in Erfurt from 1536 to 1550.

Johannes Kilian, dates unknown, was connected with the University of Erfurt as a canon beginning in 1508 and served as pastor of the Regler church in the city.

Nicholas Faber, dates unknown, was pastor of St. George and then of the Augustinian church in Erfurt.

Andrew Menser (?–1556) served as curate of St. Michael's congregation in Erfurt from 1536 to 1549.

Egidius Melcher (?–1547) was a Franciscan friar until 1521 and then functioned as preacher of St. Bartholomew and of the Franciscan congregation in Erfurt.

Image Credits

xiii, xiv (maps): Map © 2006 Lucidity Information Design, LLC.
Used by permission.

5, 35, 38, 278: Courtesy of the Rare Books Collection of the Lutheran School
of Theology at Chicago.

8, 90, 138, 150, 159, 213, 220, 258, 263, 273, 288, 301, 305, 327, 331, 336, 359, 389, 416,
418 (right), 427, 428, 431, 439, 442, 444, 454, 456, 457: Courtesy of the Richard C. Kessler
Reformation Collection, Pitts Theology Library, Candler School of Theology, Emory
University.

10 (top), 71 (right), 129, 185, 309, 403: The Granger Collection / New York.

10 (bottom), 12, 19, 219, 231, 318, 464: Courtesy of the Pitts Theology Library,
Candler School of Theology, Emory University.

132: Photo: Magnus Manske / CC-by-2.0 license.

137: Gianni Dagli Orti / The Art Archive at Art Resource, NY.

167, 184: Photos.com/Thinkstock.

252: Wolfgang Sauber / Wikimedia Commons GNU Free Documentation License.

264: iStock/Thinkstock.

436: © Evangelical Lutheran Church in America. All rights reserved.

Index of Scriptural References

Index of Names

Index of Works
by Martin Luther

Index of Subjects